The Lessons of Modern War

Volume III:
The Afghan and Falklands Conflicts

Anthony H. Cordesman
and Abraham R. Wagner

Westview Press
BOULDER AND SAN FRANCISCO

Much of the research presented in this volume was supported by the Defense Advanced Research Projects Agency (DARPA). The views expressed are, of course, those of the authors and are not intended to reflect any position of DARPA or the U.S. Department of Defense. The authors are deeply indebted to Dr. Craig Fields and Dr. Anthony Tether of DARPA for their continued support and insight.

Published in 1990 in the United States of America by Westview Press, Inc., 5500 Central Avenue, Boulder, Colorado 80301, and in the United Kingdom by Westview Press, 36 Lonsdale Road, Summertown, Oxford OX2 7EW

Reprinted in March 1991

Library of Congress Cataloging-in-Publication Data
Cordesman, Anthony H.
   The lessons of modern war.
   Includes bibliographical references.
   Contents: v. 1. The Arab-Israeli conflicts,
1973–1989—   —v. 3. The Afghan and Falklands
conflicts.
   1. Military art and science—History—20th century.
2. Military history, Modern—20th century.
3. Middle East—History, Military.   I. Wagner, Abraham R.
II. Title.
U42.C59 1990   355.4′8   89-16631
Vol. I: ISBN 0-8133-0954-9—ISBN 0-8133-1329-5 (pbk.)
Vol II: ISBN 0-8133-0955-7—ISBN 0-8133-1330-9 (pbk.)
Vol III: ISBN 0-8133-0956-5—ISBN 0-8133-1331-7 (pbk.)

Printed and bound in the United States of America

The paper used in this publication meets the requirements
of the American National Standard for Permanence of Paper
for Printed Library Materials Z39.48-1984.

10   9   8   7   6   5   4   3

*To David Boulton and Fred Praeger
for their patient efforts and support*

CONTENTS

List of Tables and Figures   xi
Preface   xiii
List of Acronyms   xv

1 INTRODUCTION   1

2 THE SOVIET INVASION OF AFGHANISTAN   3

The Combatants, 3
Selected Chronology of the Afghan War, 22
The Terrain, 99
Threat Assessment Technologies, 104
Effective and Secure C³, 112
Combined Arms, 123
Infantry, 135
Tanks and Armored Vehicles, 148
Precision-Guided and Specialized Land Munitions, 154
Tube Artillery, Multiple Rocket Launchers,
    and Mortars, 156
Surface-to-Surface Rockets and Missiles, 162
Mines and Barriers, 164
All-Weather and Night Target Acquisition Systems, 168
Anti-Aircraft Artillery, 169
Surface-to-Air Missiles, 171
The Soviet Air Buildup in Afghanistan, 178
Fixed-Wing Close Air Support, 180
Interdiction and Long-Range Air Attack, 187
Air Reconnaissance, C³I, IFF, and AC&W, 191
Helicopters, 192
Combined Operations, 206
Logistics and Support, 208
Chemical/Biological Weapons and Defensive Systems, 214
Nuclear Weapons, 218
Conclusions, 219
Notes, 219

3 THE FALKLANDS WAR 238

The Combatants, 238
The Falklands War: Chronology of Key Events, 239
The Forces Engaged, 260
The Terrain, 266
Threat Assessment Technologies, 269
Effective and Secure C³I, 280
Combined Arms, 282
Infantry, 283
Tanks and Armored Vehicles, 287
Precision-Guided and Specialized Land Munitions, 288
Tube Artillery, 289
Surface-to-Surface Rockets and Missiles, 291
Mines and Barriers, 291
All-Weather and Night Target Acquisition Systems, 293
Anti-Aircraft Artillery, 294
Surface-to-Air Missiles, 295
Ground Attack and Close Air Support, 300
Air Reconnaissance, C³I, IFF, and AC&W, 323
Helicopters, 325
Combined Operations, 327
Logistics and Support, 330
Naval Systems, 334
Chemical/Biological Weapons, 350
Nuclear Weapons, 350
The Key Lessons of the Falklands, 350
Notes, 353

4 ANALYSIS OF THE LESSONS OF LIMITED
ARMED CONFLICTS 362

Threat Assessment Technologies, 363
Secure and Effective C³I, 368
Combined Arms, 370
Infantry, 373
Tanks, 374
Other Armored Vehicles, 377
Anti-Armor and Surface-to-Surface PGMs, 379
Tube Artillery and Multiple Rocket Launchers, 381
Surface-to-Surface Rockets and Missiles, 382
Mines and Barriers, 382
All-Weather and Night Target Acquisition Systems, 383
Anti-Aircraft Artillery, 384

Surface-to-Air Missiles, 385
Suppression of Ground- and Sea-Based Air Defenses, 386
Air-to-Air Combat, 387
Close Air Support, 388
Interdiction and Long-Range Air Attack, 389
Air Reconnaissance, C^3, IFF, and AC&W, 390
Helicopters, 391
Combined Operations, 393
Logistical Systems, 395
Naval Systems, 398
Chemical and Biological Weapons, 398
Nuclear Weapons, 399
Notes, 401

5 A STRATEGIC TECHNOLOGY STRATEGY FOR
   LIMITED FORCE ENGAGEMENTS   402

Force Structure and Contingency Requirements, 402
Technology Requirements and Thrusts, 412
The High-Technology Content of Low-Level Wars, 425
Restructuring Technological Priorities
    to Minimize Casualties and Collateral Damage, 431
Notes, 433

Sources and Methods   434
Bibliography   437
Index   452

TABLES AND FIGURES

Tables

2.1	Increase in Forces in Afghanistan: 1980–1984	5
2.2	Forces in Afghanistan at the Peak of the Fighting, 1986	7
2.3	Afghan War: Casualties and Losses 1979–1988	10
2.4	Casualties Due to Border Violations by Soviet/DRA Forces and Terrorist Attacks in Pakistan: 1980–October 1987	71
2.5	Key Lines of Communication in the Afghan Conflict	106
2.6	Typical Soviet Army Tactical Field Communications Equipment Early in the War	115
2.7	Characteristics of Crew-Served AGS-17 Automatic Grenade Launchers	127
2.8	Soviet Rocket-Propelled Grenade Launchers	156
2.9	Characteristics of the Soviet 76-mm Mountain Gun (M-1966)	159
2.10	Major Shoulder-Fired Surface-to-Air Missiles that Impacted on the Fighting in Afghanistan	173
2.11	The Tu-16 Badger	188
2.12	The Tu-22 Blinder D	189
2.13	The Su-24 Fencer	190
2.14	Specifications of Soviet Military Helicopters	198
2.15	Soviet Gas Warfare Attacks in 1982	217
3.1	Composition of British Task Force: 1982	244
3.2	Additional Ships for the Falkland Islands Task Force	252
3.3	Falklands War: Forces and Force Ratios	261
3.4	Material Supplied to Britain by the United States During the Falklands War	263
3.5	Argentine Military Buildup	265
3.6	Falklands War: Casualties and Losses	267
3.7	British Land-Based Armor in the Falklands	288
3.8	The Artillery of the Falklands War	290
3.9	British Air Base and Air Defense Facilities in the Falklands	301
3.10	British Helicopter Sorties and Flying Time	301
3.11	Argentine Aircraft Losses by Type/Cause	304

3.12   British Aircraft Losses by Type/Cause   305
3.13   British Naval Logistics Effort in the Falklands Conflict   332
3.14   Argentine Ships Lost or Damaged in the Falklands War   336
3.15   British Ships Damaged in the Falklands War   337
3.16   British Ships Lost in the Falklands War   338
3.17   Differences in Submarine Technology   344
3.18   Sea-Based Missiles and Guns   346

4.1   Marginal Utility of Expensive and Complex
       Military Systems   363

5.1   USCENTCOM Forces in 1988   403
5.2   U.S. Military Contingency Facilities in the Near East   405
5.3   Maximum Probable European Amphibious and Ground
       Forces for Low- to Medium-Level Contingencies in
       Southwest Asia and Africa   408
5.4   The Political/Terrain/Weather Challenge   410
5.5   The Critical Impact of Indigenous Gulf Forces on
       Western Operations   426
5.6   Probable Shifts in Force Quality in the Near East
       by 1990–1995   427
5.7   Progress in Creating an Effective Air Defense System
       in the Southern Gulf States   429

Figures

2.1   Afghanistan: A Soviet Vietnam?   96
2.2   The Terrain of Combat in Afghanistan   100
2.3   Afghanistan: Major Cities and Lines of Communication   102
2.4   Afghanistan: Kabul and the Surrounding Provinces   103
2.5   Afghanistan: Military Areas in the Northeast   104
2.6   Afghanistan: Soviet Major Combat Unit Deployments
       in December 1987   105
2.7   The Soviet Communication System in Afghanistan
       in 1983–1984   113
2.8   The Soviet Chain of Command in Afghanistan   114
2.9   The Soviet Air Buildup in Afghanistan   179

3.1   Map of the Falkland Islands   268
3.2   Coverage by U.S. and Soviet Photographic
       Reconnaissance Satellites During 1982   271
3.3   Ground Tracks over Argentina and the Falklands   272
3.4   Ground Tracks over the U.K. of the Soviet
       Satellite *Cosmos*   273

PREFACE

This is the final volume in a series of three volumes that the authors have written with the assistance of Raymond J. Picquet, W. Andrew Terril, and Carol K. Wagner and with the support of the Royal United Services Institute. These volumes cover five major wars: the Arab-Israeli conflict of October 1973, the Israeli invasion of Lebanon in 1982, the Iran-Iraq War, the Soviet invasion of Afghanistan, and the Falklands conflict with Argentina. Volume I covers the lessons of the Arab-Israeli arms race between 1973 and 1989 and of the Arab-Israeli conflicts of 1973 and 1982. Volume II in this series covers the Iran-Iraq War. Volume III covers the Falklands and Afghan conflicts and provides the general conclusions of the study.

Each of the three volumes is written as an independent work, but the analysis of the wars in question is standardized as much as possible. The analysis of major conflicts is divided into sections that analyze the forces involved, the history of the conflict, key aspects of the operational art of war, and the impact of major types of forces and weapons. Where the source data permit, these sections are as comparable as possible.

The analysis in each volume focuses on military events and lessons and treats the politics of each conflict only to the extent necessary to understand military events. Only summary histories are provided of given battles, except where a description of military action will help the reader understand the broader lessons involved. Where possible, key events and data are described in a way that will allow the reader to draw his or her own conclusions. A deliberate effort has been made to avoid oversimplifying the complex nature of modern war.

The sources and methods used in each volume are described at its end, and a research bibliography is provided for each conflict. Frequent use is made of tables and charts to allow comparisons of forces, portray force shifts over time, and show the key performance features of major weapons. In most cases, the data are shown as provided in the original source rather than standardized or altered to eliminate minor conflicts. This is done to allow the reader to see the original data on which the analyses are based.

Anthony H. Cordesman

ACRONYMS

AC&W	air control and warning
AES	Aviation Engineering Service
AEW	airborne early warning
AFV	armored fighting vehicle
APC	armored personnel carrier
ASM	air-to-ship missile
ASW	anti-submarine warfare
ATGM	anti-tank guided missile
AWACS	airborne warning and air control system
BVR	beyond visual range
C^3/BM	command, control, communications/battle management
C^3I	command, control, communications, and intelligence
CARB	combined arms reinforced battalion
CAS	close air support
CBW	chemical/biological warfare
COMINT	communications intelligence
CW	chemical warfare
DRA	Democratic Republic of Afghanistan
DShB	(*desantno-shturmovyata brigade*) landing assault brigade
ECCM	electronic counter-countermeasures
ECM	electronic countermeasures
ELINT	electronic intelligence
EOB	electronic order of battle
ESM	electronic support measures
ESSM	electronic systems support measures
EW	early warning
FAC	forward air controller
FLIR	forward-looking infrared
GSR	ground surveillance radar
GTVD	Soviet front high command
HEAT	high-explosive anti-tank
HUMINT	human intelligence
I&W	indications and warning

IFF	identification of friend and foe
IFV	infantry fighting vehicle
IISS	International Institute for Strategic Studies
KAM	Afghan secret police
KGB	Soviet secret police
KHAD	(Khedemati-e-Dolati) Afghan Ministry of State Security
LAV	light armored vehicle
LCSFA	Limited Contingent of Soviet Forces in Afghanistan
LOC	lines of communication
MD	military district
MRL	multiple rocket launcher
MVD	Soviet Ministry of Internal Affairs
NCOs	noncommissioned officers
O&M	operations and maintenance
PDPA	People's Democratic Party of Afghanistan
PGM	precision-guided munition
PHOTINT	photo intelligence
RPG	rocket-propelled grenade
RPV	remotely piloted vehicle
SAM	surface-to-air missile
SAR	synthetic aperture radar
SAS	Special Air Service
SBS	Special Boat Squadron
SHORADS	short-range air defense systems
SIGINT	signals intelligence
SLAR	side-looking airborne radar
TVD	Soviet theater or front
USCENTCOM	U.S. Central Command
VDV	(*vozdushno-desantnaya-voiska*) air assault forces
VSTOL	vertical and short take-off and landing

1

INTRODUCTION

The two wars analyzed in this volume involve very different types of conflict. In fact, in some ways they span the range of what has come to be called "low-intensity conflict"—although this is a term that would be hard to explain to the Afghan people, who have suffered through nine years of brutal and nationwide war.

The Falklands conflict was an exercise in power projection involving land, air, and naval forces. It involved a conflict between modern forces which were not designed to fight under the conditions they were forced to and whose power projection capabilities were strained to their limits. Although the Falklands conflict involved extensive fighting on the land, its outcome was decided by a duel between the Argentine Air Force and the British Royal Navy. The Falklands conflict was relatively brief, had little impact on the civil population of the nations involved, and had very limited casualties.

The Afghan conflict began with a Soviet military coup d'etat of an unstable but strongly pro-Soviet and pro-Marxist regime. The USSR, however, failed to create a stable replacement for the government it overthrew and soon found its intervention to be perceived as an invasion of conquest. The result was nearly a decade of struggle which became as brutal as the U.S. intervention in Vietnam and which produced hundreds of thousands of casualties and millions of refugees. It was a war that pitted Soviet regular forces and Soviet advanced technology, backed by the forces of the Soviet puppet regime, against small, divided bands of poorly armed guerrillas. Nevertheless, it was a war that the Soviet Union lost.

The contrast between these two wars provides a broad picture of the many different ways in which the tactics and technology of armed forces can be be used in combat. It also shows how easily a war can start and escalate to involve millions of lives.

In the case of the Falklands, the fight for control of the islands was largely a matter of principal and politics; the area was not of vital strategic interest to either side. Both Britain and Argentina fought deliberately limited conflicts between regular armed forces and kept casualties to a minimum. Partly by choice and partly because of the basic geography of the conflict, escalation was limited to a small group of islands and to attacks on naval forces.

It is not clear that the USSR had any more strategic reason to launch an invasion of Afghanistan to change its government than Argentina had to invade the Falklands. The Soviets, once they agreed to leave Afghanistan, described their intervention as a major strategic miscalculation. It is clear that the Soviets did not originally plan to fight the large-scale war they did; nor did they have any idea that the situation could escalate so rapidly into a nationwide guerrilla war.

Like the U.S. intervention in Vietnam, the Afghan conflict's perceived strategic value expanded with—but was not driven by—its intensity and the degree of involvement. In retrospect, the complex geostrategic rationales the USSR used to justify its actions in Afghanistan made no more real sense than the variants of the domino theory the U.S. used more than a decade earlier in Vietnam.

Both the Falklands and the Afghan conflicts illustrate the fact that low-intensity conflict can rapidly become isolated from grand strategy. The Soviet Union, Argentina, and the United Kingdom all shared one thing in common: They became involved in wars that had no real grand strategic purpose, and they became involved almost without regard for what they predicted the outcomes of the wars to be. It was possible for all three nations to win or lose the fighting, but it was not possible for any of them to win anything worth the cost of the fighting. In effect, politics became the extension of war by other means.

Only the people of the Falklands, who did not suffer severely from the conflict, and the Afghan people, who suffered to the point of near-genocide, had clear strategic objectives. Their objectives, however, were to survive and recover control of their own destinies. The people of the Falklands were lucky enough to succeed in their objective. The future of the people of Afghanistan remains unclear.

2

THE SOVIET INVASION
OF AFGHANISTAN

The Combatants

The war in Afghanistan between the Muslim freedom fighters, or Mujahideen, and the Soviet Union and the Marxist Democratic Republic of Afghanistan began in December 1979. It reached a kind of ending with Soviet withdrawal on 15 February 1988. It is far from clear at this writing, however, how the fighting between the Soviet-backed Republic of Afghanistan and the various factions of Mujahideen will end and what kind of state will emerge.

The war has been a major conflict. More than nine years elapsed between the Soviet invasion and Soviet withdrawal, and the war has created millions of refugees and has left hundreds of thousands dead. The war has pitted a poorly armed people against a superpower with access to the latest military technology. At the same time, virtually an entire nation has struggled against an occupation force and narrowly based puppet regime which achieved power only as the result of the Soviet invasion.

The war has also been a war of innovation and change. The Soviet forces that initially invaded Afghanistan were poorly trained and equipped for the kind of guerrilla war they were forced to fight. From 1979 to 1984, however, the Soviet and Afghan government forces gradually evolved a far more effective mix of small unit tactics, helicopter assault capabilities, and strategic bombing. These changes were so successful that they threatened to suppress the Mujahideen during 1985 and 1986.

Yet, the Mujahideen also changed with time and were able to acquire more sophisticated weapons. Some of the most critical of these weapons were improved manportable surface-to-air missiles, which allowed the Mujahideen to counter the Soviet advantage in helicopters. The Mujahideen also learned how to use improved artillery, mines, and small arms. While the Mujahideen never succeeded in capturing a major city or base held by Soviet troops, they did succeed in raising the cost of the war to levels that the USSR found unacceptable.

Like the U.S. in Vietnam, the USSR could win virtually every major battle, but it could not win the war. It could not sustain the economic, political, and military costs of attempting to support a government that could not win the hearts and minds of its own people. As a result, the USSR was eventually confronted with the fact that the cost in lives and resources was simply not worth the effort.

Changes in Soviet Forces

Table 2.1 shows the increase in Soviet forces from the start of the Soviet invasion to the point when the Soviet Union changed its forces to suit the conditions of warfare in Afghanistan. Table 2.2 shows the forces on both sides in 1986, at the peak of the fighting. The USSR changed its formations to add some 20,000 to 30,000 special counterinsurgency troops between 1984 and 1988, but an accurate unclassified count of the post-1984 shifts in Soviet formations is not available.

Useful data are available, however, on the overall strength of Soviet forces at the beginning and end of the war. The initial level of Soviet troops in Afghanistan was roughly 85,000 men. This included a force under the 40th Army, which was headquartered in the Soviet border town of Termez. The forces deployed in Afghanistan under the command of the 40th Army as part of the first wave of the invasion included the 105th Guards Air Assault Division (Bagram and Kabul), one paratroop regiment of the 103rd Guards Air Assault Division (Pol-e-Khumri), one paratroop regiment of the 104th Guards Air Assault Division, the 66th and 357th motorized rifle divisions (Herat), and the 360th Motorized Rifle Division (Kabul). These units were reinforced early in 1980 by the 201st Motorized Rifle Division (Jalalabad), the 5th Guards Motorized Rifle Division (Farah), and the 54th Motorized Rifle Division (Herat). There also was an independent artillery brigade and an SA-4 surface-to-air missile brigade, plus support units and chemical decontamination units.[1]

These Soviet forces were radically restructured beginning in June 1980. Many of the Soviet units in the initial invasion force had no rationale for being deployed other than the fact that they had been mobilized with their parent units, and many of these units and their materiel were withdrawn. The Soviets also withdrew tanks as well as a number of anti-aircraft, anti-tank, ECM, and FROG

TABLE 2.1 Increase in Forces in Afghanistan: 1980–1984

I. TOTAL SOVIET FORCES IN AFGHANISTAN

SOVIET FORCES	1984	1983	1982	1981	1980
COMBINED ARMS ARMY	1	1	1	1	1
MOTORIZED RIFLE DIVISIONS	3	3	3(Isby:8)	3	3
AIRBORNE DIVISIONS	1	1	1	1	1
MOTORIZED RIFLE BDE/REGTS	4/3	4/2	4	2 to 3	2
AIR ASSAULT BDE/REGTS	1	1	1(Isby:5)	1	–
AIRBORNE/AIRMOBILE BDE	1	1	(Poss 1)	–	–
MULTIPLE ROCKET LAUNCHER REGTS	1	1	1	–	–
ATTACK HELICOPTER REGTS	2	2	2	1	–
PERSONNEL (TOTAL)	80,000 (Isby: 105,000)	75,000–80,000 (Isby: 152,000)	70,000 (Isby: 85,000)		

(continues)

TABLE 2.1 (continued)

II. SOVIET LAND UNITS IN AFGHANISTAN

UNIT	HOME/LOCATION MILITARY DISTRICT (VO)	INVASION	1980	1981	1982	1983	1984	CURRENT LOCATION
105th ABN GDS	FERGANA/TURKESTAN	X	X	–	–	–	–	
104th ABN GDS	KIROVABAD/TRANSCAUCASUS	X	X	–	–	–	–	
103rd ABN GDS	VITEBSK/BELORUSSIAN	X	X	X	X	X	X	KABUL
360th MRD*	TERMEZ/TURKESTAN	X	X	(SEE 108th)	–	–	–	
357th MRD	KUSHKA/TURKESTAN	X	–	–	–	–	–	
201st MRD	DUSHANBE/CENTRAL ASIAN	X	X	X	X	X	X	QINDUZ
54th GDS MRD	KIZYL ARVAT/TURKESTAN	X	–	–	!	–	–	
5th GDS MRD	KUSHKA/TURKESTAN	X	X	X	X	X	X	SHINDAND
108th MRD	TERMEZ/TURKESTAN	–	–	X	X	X	X	BAGRAM/KABUL
16th MRD (ELEMENTS OF)		X	X	–	–	–	–	
66th MRD	ASHKHADAD/TURKESTAN	X	X	–	–	–	–	
U/I AIR ASSAULT BDE		–	(?)	X	X	X	X	BAGRAM
70th MR BDE		–	–	X	(OR X)	X	X	QANDAHAR
66th MR BDE		–	–	X	(OR X)	X	X	JALALABAD
U/I MR BDE		–	–	X	X	X	X	QONDUZ
U/I ATTACK HELICOPTER REGT		–	–	X	X	X	X	SHINDAND
U/I ATTACK HELICOPTER REGT		–	–	–	X	X	X	QONDUZ
860th MR REGT		–				X	X	FAIZABAD
187th MR REGT		–	–	–	–	X	X	MAZAR-I-SHARIF
191st MR REGT		–					X	GHAZNI
U/I ROCKET LAUNCHER REGT		–	–	–	–	X	X	SHINDAND
U/I TRANSPORT HELICOPTER REGT		–	–	X	X	X	X	SHINDAND
U/I TRANSPORT HELICOPTER REGT		–	–		X	X	X	KANDAHAR

*Renumbered 108th MRD in 1980 after initial stationing in Afghanistan.
Key: ABN GDS = Airborne Guards; MRD = Motorized Rifle Division.

SOURCE: Adapted from G. Jacobs, "Afghanistan Forces: How Many Soviets Are There?" Jane's Defence Weekly, June 22, 1985, pp. 1228–1233.

TABLE 2.2 Forces in Afghanistan at the Peak of the Fighting, 1986

SOVIET FORCES	
Total Armed Forces	115,000 (some 10,000 MVD, KGB)
Armed Forces	1 HQ, 3 mortar rifle, 1 AB divs.: 1 air assault bde.
Air Force	Equivalent possibly 2 air divs.: (4 AC, 6 hel. regts.: 180 AC, 270 hel.); VTA and Aeroflot tpt. AC from USSR in spt.

AFGHAN GOVERNMENT FORCES	
Total Armed Forces	46,000
Armed Forces	40,000 (mostly conscripts). 3 corps Hq., 11 inf. divs. (under strength bdes.), 3 armed divs. (under strength bdes.), 1 mech. inf. bde., 2 mountain inf. regts., 1 arty. bde. w/3 arty. regts., 3 cdo. regts., 50 T-34, 300 T-54/-55, 100 T-62 MBT; 60 PT-76 lt. tks.; 40 BMP-1 MICV; 400 BTR-40/-50/-60/-152 APC; 900 76mm, M-1944 100mm guns and M-30 122mm, D-1 152 how.; 82mm, 100 120mm, 160mm mor.; 50 BM-13-16; 132mm MRL; SPG-9 73mm, 82mm RCL; 76mm, 100mm ATK guns; 350 23mm, 37mm, 57mm, 85mm, and 100mm towed, 20 ZSU-23-4 SP AA guns.
Reserve Forces	No formal reserve force identified; call-up from ex-servicemen, Youth League, and regional tribes from age 20 to age 40.
Air Force	6,000 (incl. Air Defense Comd.); perhaps 150 combat AC, some 20 armed hel. 1 lt. bbr. sqn. with some 15 Il-28 (status unclear), 12 FGA sqns.: 4 w/some 40 MiG-17, 3 with 35 MiG-21 Fishbed, 4 w/48 Su-7B Fitter A, 1 with 12 Su-17 Fitter C, 1 OCU w/MiG-15/-17/-19/-21/-23UTI/U, Il-18U, 2 attack hel. sqns. w/some 20 Mi-24, 4 tpt. sqns.; 1 VIP w/2 Il-18D, 4 An-24 Coke; 3 w/some 10 An-2, 10-15 An-26, 1 tpt. hel. regt. (4 sqns.) w/some 12 Mi-4, up to 40 Mi-8, 1 flying school w/Yak-18, L-39C, 1 AD div.; 2 SAM bdes. (each 3 bns.) w/120 SA-2, 115 SA-3; 1 AA bde. (2 bns.) w/37mm, 85mm, 100mm guns, 1 radar bde. (3 bns.).
Paramilitary Forces	Gendarmerie 30,000. Border Force. Ministry of Interior: Khad (secret police); Sarandoy "Defense of the Revolution" forces, largely ex-military to age 55 org. in provincial regts. Regional militias incl. "Revolution Defense Groups" (Civil Defense), Pioneers, Afghan Communist Party Guards, Khalqi Youth, tribal.

(continues)

TABLE 2.2 *(continued)*

OPPOSITION FORCES	Perhaps 90,000 guerrillas (possibly 20,000 intermittently active) supported by some 15 exile political groups (6 active). Eqpt: small arms, T-55 MBT; BMP MICV, BTR-60 APC; D-30 122mm how.; AGS-17 30mm grenade launchers; 2-in. (51mm), 60mm, M-41 82mm mor.; RPG-7 RL; SPG-9, 3 75mm, 82mm RCL; 12.7mm, 14.5mm AA machine guns, ATK mines; some SA-7 SAM.

SOURCES: Adapted from the IISS *Military Balance, 1984/85* (London: International Institute for Strategic Studies), and from James B. Curren and Phillip A. Karber, "Afghanistan's Ordeal," *Armed Forces Journal*, March 1985, p. 78.

surface-to-surface rocket units.[2] Roughly 5,000 to 10,000 troops associated with such weapons systems left Afghanistan. They were replaced by "new and more useful units."[3]

By mid-1981, the Soviet forces in Afghanistan had been converted from a force of seven understrength and under-equipped regular motorized rifle divisions to a force of three motorized rifle divisions, two independent motorized rifle brigades, and two motorized rifle brigades. The force of one air assault division and two independent air assault regiments was converted to a force of one expanded air assault division.[4] Soviet forces then underwent a process of continuous change and expansion until the Soviet decision to withdraw in 1988. Total manning rose to around 115,000 men by 1984 and 120,000 men by the spring of 1987, in spite of reports of troop "withdrawals" in 1986. In 1987, approximately 20,000 more troops were deployed across the border in the USSR to play various support roles.[5]

Soviet force levels peaked in early 1988. The total number of Soviet forces assigned to full-time missions in support of the Soviet invasion of Afghanistan included 156,000 men in the Southern Strategic Theater (GTVD). There were with 118,000 regular troops and 10,000 Ministry of the Interior (MVD) troops in Afghanistan and 30,000 more regular troops across the border in support roles.

The major Soviet combat formations in Afghanistan in early 1988 were placed under the 40th Army, with its main headquarters at Termez in the USSR and a forward headquarters in Kabul. They included an army headquarters at Kabul, five motorized rifle divisions, the 103rd Guards airborne division, two motorized rifle brigades, one to three reconnaissance (Spetsnaz?) brigades, one air assault brigade, two motorized rifle regiments, one airborne regiment, and a number of support formations.[6] These Soviet forces were nearly all Category I (combat-ready) forces, although the formations involved had been adapted to the war and lacked some surface-to-surface missile, air defense, and support formations in regular Soviet units.

The nature of the Soviet manpower deployed to Afghanistan also changed over time. The largely Asiatic forces that the USSR initially deployed to Afghanistan were not high-grade Soviet forces and were poorly trained for their mission. They did not adapt to, or fight well in, what rapidly became a brutal counterinsurgency campaign fought under some of the worst possible terrain conditions.[7] The USSR first attempted to change this situation by deploying largely White Russian troops and then systematically changed its training and command methods to develop manpower of higher quality and readiness.

Although some Soviet combat troops were well trained and equipped, particularly later in the war, many troops were not. Major problems existed in the garrison and conscript forces throughout the war, and the USSR did not provide the degree of services and support that are common in most Western armies. Some reports indicate that only about 20 percent of the Soviet troops were permanently housed after more than seven years of war. Virtually all sources indicate that routine medical services and hygiene were poor and that drug and alcohol abuse were common.[8] In addition, some troops were shot for desertion and mutiny.[9] As Table 2.3 shows, there were also serious cumulative Soviet losses.

Like the organization and manpower of Soviet forces, Soviet equipment holdings changed with time, and accurate estimates are difficult or impossible to make. The first wave of Soviet forces seems to have had about 1,200 main battle tanks, 45–60 helicopters, and around 100 combat aircraft on Afghan soil in December 1979. This rapidly built up to a total Soviet force on both Afghan and Soviet soil of 1,750 tanks, 2,100 APCs, 500 combat aircraft, and 200 helicopters. These equipment totals included the holdings of some elite airborne elements, but most consisted of the equipment holdings of relatively low-grade motorized rifle divisions which were designed mainly for warfare against NATO or conventional PRC army forces.[10] The equipment mix in these forces was so inappropriate to the kind of war being fought that a major portion of the forces had to be withdrawn and the Soviet force posture in Afghanistan had to be completely reorganized.

As the following historical discussion shows, the USSR radically reorganized this equipment mix in mid-1980 and continued to change its equipment mix throughout the war. In early 1988, before Soviet withdrawals began, the USSR had about 320–460 main battle tanks,

TABLE 2.3 Afghan War: Casualties and Losses 1979–1988

SOVIET AND AFGHAN GOVERNMENT LOSSES

13,310–15,000	Soviet military personnel killed[a]
35,478–37,000	Soviet military personnel wounded[b]
312	Soviet missing in action
34,000–42,000	Soviet-controlled Afghan army killed or wounded
52,000–60,000	Soviet-controlled Afghan army desertions

SOVIET AND AFGHAN GOVERNMENT EQUIPMENT LOSSES

700–750	aircraft (includes helicopters)
504–600	tanks
740–850	armored personnel carriers
720–950	artillery pieces and mortars
5,400–6,000	vehicles

AFGHAN LOSSES

140,000–200,000	full-time Mujahideen killed or wounded[b]
40,000–90,000	civilians or part-time Mujahideen killed or critically wounded
1,500,000	civilians living under direct threat in areas of combat (many have suffered at least minor wounds)
6,000,000	refugees, 2,900,000 in Pakistan, 1,900,000 in Iran, and 1,200,000 internal

---

[a]Data based on report by General Alexei Lizichev, Chief of the Soviet Armed Forces Political Directorate, May 25, 1988, and *Litteraturnaya Gazeta*, February 6, 1989. Other Soviet sources indicate some 50,000 more serious medical cases due to "disease" and up to 25,000 killed due to "disease." These figures compare with a U.S. casualty total in Vietnam of 58,135 dead and 153,303 wounded. The percentage of casualties relative to those engaged is somewhat similar, however, since the U.S. had a peak manpower deployed of 543,400 in 1969 versus a peak Soviet presence of 115,000–130,000.

[b]Some estimates of total Afghan Mujahideen killed go as high as 500,000. One French study indicates that 9 percent of the total population has died as the result of the direct and indirect costs of the war.

SOURCES: This assessment draws on inputs from high-ranking Pakistani sources. Also see Avigdor Haselkorn, *Analyses of Soviet Military Casualties in Afghanistan: Knowns and Unknowns* (Marina del Rey, Calif: Analytical Assessments Corporation, April 1980), p. 1-5; and Craig Karp, "Afghanistan: Eight Years of Soviet Occupation," *Department of State Bulletin*, Vol. 88, No. 2132, pp. 1–24, March, 1988.

1,500 other armored fighting vehicles, 1,500 armored personnel carriers, 550–600 major artillery weapons, and 12 surface-to-surface missile launchers.

These equipment holdings reflected the fact that in early 1988 the Soviet forces in Afghanistan were a mix of specially tailored units designed for warfare in that country. The army units in Afghanistan had an exceptionally large helicopter force of 270 combat helicopters. These included 140 Mi-24 Hind attack helicopters, 130 Mi-8 Hip assault and transport helicopters, and Mi-2 Hoplite and Mi-6 Hook transport helicopters.

By early 1988, there also was a Soviet Air Army at Bagram near Kabul with at least 145 combat aircraft. These included 90 Su-25 Frogfoot attack fighters, 45 MiG-23B/G Flogger fighters, and 10 Su-17 reconnaissance fighters. There also were a substantial number of MiG-21s. This air army was supported by heavy and medium bomber forces in the USSR and by Su-24 long-range strike fighters and a number of other combat aircraft in the Southern Strategic Theater (GTVD) of the USSR. It also had extensive air transport resources and a large number of heavy lift helicopters in support near the border.[11]

The Regular Forces of the
Democratic Republic of Afghanistan (DRA)

The forces of the the Democratic Republic of Afghanistan, or DRA, had built up steadily during the mid-1970s from about 130,000 men in 1975 to 143,000 men in 1977.[12] These forces had increasingly politicized leadership, and their leaders often belonged to different factions. From April 1978 onward, growing internal political conflicts began to divide the leadership of the Afghan military forces; the result was to sharply reduce the total size of DRA forces.

Estimates of the size of DRA regular military forces vary widely. U.S. government estimates indicate that DRA active military manpower was 143,000 in 1977, 110,000 in 1978, 89,000 in 1979, 43,000 in 1980, 45,000 in 1981, 55,000 in 1982, 75,000 in 1983, 60,000 in 1984, and 55,000 in 1985.[13] The International Institute for Strategic Studies (IISS) estimates indicate that DRA active regular military manpower was 110,000 in 1977, 100,000 in 1978, 90,000 in 1979, 40,000 in 1980, 43,000 in 1981, 46,000 in 1982, 47,000 in 1983, 46,000 in 1984, 47,000 in 1985, 60,000 in 1984, 55,000 in 1985, 50,000 in 1986, 50,000 in 1987, and 55,000 in 1988.[14] The differences in these estimates result at least in part from the inability to count the number of paramilitary forces, which took over an increasingly important role with time.

The DRA forces presented continuing problems to both the DRA government and the USSR throughout the war. The DRA Air Force was generally more loyal to the government than to the Army, as was the KHAD (Ministry of State Security). The DRA Army did, however, have some elite units that often fought well. These units included the 37th Commando Brigade, 38th Commando Brigade, 466th Commando Battalion, and the armored brigades of the 7th and 8th Divisions.[15]

The bulk of the units in the DRA forces were often unwilling to engage in intense combat for the sake of the Marxist regime in Kabul, and the tradition of blood feuds in Afghanistan created a situation in which Afghan troops feared the possible future consequences of killing members of the Mujahideen in combat.[16] In spite of constant Soviet efforts to improve the situation, Afghan troops still lacked motivation and were still unreliable at the time Soviet withdrawals were completed in February 1989. There was a consistently high incidence of desertions. Many deserters, including several generals, joined the Mujahideen, although military analysts differ sharply over the percentages of those who actively defected to fight against the DRA and those who simply returned to their homes.[17]

The DRA Army also continued to suffer from the internal divisions and fighting within the DRA government. The Afghan forces were subjected to heavy purging during 1978 and 1979. This purging was originally initiated to insure the political loyalty of Afghan officers to the government and to the Khalq faction of the Afghan communist party to which both Presidents Taraki and Amin belonged.[18] The Khalq faction was especially adept at placing its members within the armed forces and internal security organs, and its members were well entrenched in these organizations when the Soviets invaded Afghanistan in 1979.[19]

A Soviet-backed coup brought a rival Marxist faction to power at the start of the Soviet invasion. The new Soviet-backed president, Babrak Karmal, was the leader of the rival Parcham faction of the Afghan communist party. The Khalqis, who had largely backed the murdered President Amin, had no reason to be loyal to the new Afghan regime. This led many to flee the country and others to join the Mujahideen. Karmal found himself embroiled in a major conflict with a decimated and potentially disloyal officer corps. The fear of alienating the remaining Khalqi officers limited Karmal's ability to carry out additional large-scale purges. Even so, full-time, active Afghan forces may have been as low as 35,000 during some of the worst periods in 1980.[20]

The IISS estimated the total size of DRA forces in 1980 as 40,000 regulars. The army had 32,000 men with three corps headquarters. Although the entire Afghan army totalled a little more than one Soviet division slice, the army order of battle had ten infantry divisions, three armored brigades, three commando regiments, three mountain infantry brigades, and a paratroop regiment.

The major equipment holdings of the DRA Army were estimated to include 1,200 main battle tanks (200 T-34s, 900 T-54/T-55s, and 100 T-62s), 60 PT-76 light tanks, some BMP-1 armored fighting vehicles, 800 BTR-40 to BTR-152 armored personnel carriers, 900 artillery pieces ranging from 100 mm to 152 mm, 50 BM-13 and BM-16 132-mm multiple rocket launchers, 100+ mortars over 100-mm, 73-mm and 82-mm recoilless rifles, 76-mm and 100-mm anti-tank guns, and 350 anti-aircraft weapons (14.5 mm, 23 mm, 20 ZSU-23-4, 37 mm, 57 mm, 85 mm, and 100 mm).

The DRA Air Force had roughly 8,000 men, included its land-based air defense force. It had 160 combat aircraft and some Mi-24 armed helicopters. There was one regiment (three squadrons) of IL-28 light bombers, with 18 aircraft. There were eight fighter-ground attack squadrons (4 MiG-17, 2 MiG-19, 2 Su-7B). There were three air defense squadrons with MiG-21s. There were two transport aircraft squadrons and four helicopter squadrons with Mi-24s, Mi-4s, and Mi-8s. The air defense force had two surface-to-air missile brigades with 100 SA-2s and SA-3s. There was a radar brigade with three battalions, and an anti-aircraft brigade with 37-mm, 85-mm, and 100-mm guns.

The DRA's paramilitary forces in 1980 included KHAD, Sarandoy, and regional militia forces with a total of 30,000 men. Accurate estimates of these forces are not available. They had been radically reorganized under Amin and his Soviet-backed successor. The KHAD was being rapidly expanded as the old AGSA (Afghanistan da Gato da Satalo Adara or Afghan Interests Protection Association) was being cut back. The Sarandoy, which was technically part of the police, was in a state of near collapse. The same was true of the regional militias.[21]

The Soviet puppet government then began efforts to build up its forces. These had mixed success. The total number of progovernment forces may have reached 45,000 in 1981 and 55,000 in 1982. Mandatory recalls of veterans, along with relentless efforts at conscripting new recruits, partially restored army manning levels. Nevertheless, the best Afghan "divisions" averaged only about 2,500 men, or 25 percent of their proper strength by pre-1978 standards.[22] Soviet troops had to assume an increasing share of the fighting on the ground. Forced to take a longer range approach to reforming the Afghan army, the USSR began to train significant numbers of officers, warrant officers, NCOs, and special troops for long periods of time within the Soviet Union. During these lengthy training periods, the USSR carried out extensive indoctrination to try to produce a technically competent, ideologically trustworthy nucleus of a dedicated, pro-Soviet army. The DRA Army also increased the proportion of officers to troops in order to increase the number of relatively trustworthy individuals per unit.[23]

These Soviet efforts helped the Soviet-backed Afghan government forces to recover a moderate combat capability. While the core of the DRA Army's fighting strength dropped as low as 25,000 at the end of

1980, it built back up to 40,000 men in 1983, 46,000 men in 1984, and 47,000 men by the end of 1985. The government forces began to play a brigade-sized role in supporting Soviet offensives in 1982 and a division-sized role in 1983. They began to conduct independent brigade-sized actions in 1984 and division-sized actions in 1985. The government forces conducted a fully independent multi-regiment operation in the Kunar Valley in 1985 and fought at this level to the end of the war.

The total manning of the regular Afghan armed forces, however, remained unstable. According to one estimate, it rose to 75,000 in 1983. It then dropped back to 60,000 in 1984 and 55,000 in 1985.[24] In early 1986, the Afghan army was estimated to have 24,000 men in its 11 to 12 divisions; 6,600 men in its three armored brigades, mechanized brigade, two commando brigades, and paratroop regiment; 3,000 men in its artillery and two rocket regiments; 1,000 men in transport, engineer, and signals regiments; 1,950 men in Corps HQ and MOD staff; 3,500 construction troops; 1,000 administrative and maintenance troops; and 2,000 Army Schools.

Estimates differ sharply, but the regular Afghan forces seem to have suffered further internal upheavals in later 1986 and during 1987, and the total regular army and air force manning seems to have dropped to about 50,000 men. Estimates range from 40,000 to 55,000 at the start of 1988, with a drop to around 38,000 to 45,000 at the beginning of 1989. This total included the manpower in the army and some 5,000 men in the air force.[25]

In early 1989, the regular DRA Army had three corps with three armored and twelve infantry divisions, and one mechanized infantry brigade. These forces were sharply understrength, and some brigades were little more than a small regiment or reinforced battalion. The army also had one commando brigade (one commando and one parachute regiment), two mountain regiments, and one anti-aircraft brigade. The army was heavily equipped by regional standards, although its main mission was counterinsurgency.

The major equipment holdings of the DRA Army were estimated to include 450 main battle tanks (50 T-34s, 300 T-54/T-55s, and 100 T-62s), 60 PT-76 light tanks, 40 BMP-1s and BMP-2s, 700 BTR-40 to BTR-152 armored personnel carriers, 1000+ artillery pieces ranging from 100 mm to 152 mm, 50 BM-13 and BM-16 132-mm multiple rocket launchers, 1000+ mortars over 100 mm, 73-mm and 82-mm recoilless rifles, 76-mm and 100-mm anti-tank guns, and 600+ anti-aircraft weapons (14.5 mm, 23 mm, 20 ZSU-23-4, 37 mm, 57 mm, 85 mm, and 100 mm).

The DRA Air Force had roughly 5,000 men, including its land-based air defense force. It had 140 combat aircraft and 65 armed helicopters. There was one regiment (three squadrons) of IL-28 light bombers, with

18 aircraft. There were three fighter-ground attack regiments (1/30 MiG-17, 1/20 MiG-19, 1/13 Su-7B and 20 Su-22 Fitter J). There was one air defense regiment with 30 MiG-21F. There was an additional fixed wing air unit with 6 MiG-15UTI, MiG-17, 2 MiG-21U, and an IL-28U. The attack helicopter component had two regiments: one with 30 Mi-25s and one with 30 Mi-8s. There were two transport aircraft regiments. The air defense force had two surface-to-air missile brigades with 115 SA-2s and 110 SA-3s. There was a radar brigade with three battalions and an anti-aircraft brigade with 37-mm, 85-mm, and 100-mm guns.[26]

Up to the final days of its withdrawal from Afghanistan, the Soviet Union was still actively attempting to improve the regular DRA army and air forces by strengthening their equipment in preparation for its withdrawal. This "Afghanisation," however, had limited success in creating enough effective army units and air units to secure the country.

The Paramilitary Forces of the
Democratic Republic of Afghanistan (DRA)

The USSR and DRA came to rely heavily on paramilitary and intelligence forces to perform security and pacification tasks and to serve as a substitute for the regular DRA forces. Nevertheless, splits in these forces closely paralleled the deep split in the DRA's ruling communist party. When the Soviet invasion put Babrak Karmal's Parcham faction of the People's Democratic Party of Afghanistan (PDPA) in power, it was too weak to exclude the Khalq faction from the security forces. Members of the Khalq were put in charge of the Ministry of the Interior, which gave them control of the Sarandoy and police, and the former chief of Amin's secret police (the AGSA) was made a Deputy Prime Minister.[27]

This led Karmal to create a new secret police called the Khedemati-e-Dolati (KHAD, later WAD), whose forces were dominated by the Parcham faction. The KHAD was led by Mohammed Najibullah and later, when Najibullah became president, by his protege, Colonel General Ghulam Faruq Yaquibi. The KHAD (WAD) took on something of the character of the Soviet KGB. It acquired combat formations and was responsible for counterintelligence, suppression of opposition, control of the loyalty of the armed forces, terrorist attacks in Pakistan, and the assassination of defectors.

By 1988, some estimates put the KHAD (WAD) forces at 20,000 men.[28] The KHAD (WAD) was estimated to have an annual budget of roughly $116 million. At the peak of Soviet intervention, the KHAD had up to 1,500 Soviet advisors, many of them members of the KGB, and 4,000 officers trained in the USSR.[29]

other elements of the Mujahideen.

- *Hezb-i-Islami (Islamic Party) Yunis Khalis faction:* This group had a cadre strength of roughly 2,900–3,700 and a total strength of 10,000–20,000 supporters. It was a Sunni fundamentalist group which favored rule by the Islamic clergy. It was Pushtun, with elements from a number of tribes in eastern Afghanistan. It was supported by Britain, Pakistan, the PRC, Saudi Arabia, Egypt, and the U.S. It operated in Paktia (Jalaladin Haqqani), Kabul (Abdul Haq), Nangrahar province, Logar province, the Pagham hills, Kabul, Balkh, Fariab, Paktia, and Farah.
- *Harakat-e Ingelab-e-Islami (Islamic Revolution Movement):* A conservative-to-moderate Sunni group with roots back to Afghanistan's power structure before the revolution. It was led by Mohammed Nabi Mohammed, and had a hard-core strength of 2,500–3,000 and a total strength of 20,000. It was largely Ahmadzi Pushtun and operated in the tribal areas of southern and western Afghanistan.
- *Mahaz-e-Meilli-e-Islami Afghanistan (National Islamic Front of Afghanistan):* A Sunni monarchist movement, led by Pri Said Gailani. It had a hard-core strength of 2,500–4,000 and over 15,000 supporters. It was largely Pushtun and had a number of leaders who were ex-Afghan army officers. It received backing from the U.S. It operated in the Maidan Valley and Logar (Amin Wardak), Kandahar (Haji Latif) and Paktia (Rahmatullah Safi), and Pakita and Nimroz (Mohammed Nassim).
- *Jamiat-i-Islami Afghanistan (Islamic Society):* A Sunni fundamentalist movement favoring a government of Mullahs and led by Burhanuddin Rabbani. It had a hard-core strength of 6,000–8,000 and 24,000–30,000 supporters. It was largely Turkic, but had strong Pushtun elements. It received backing from Kuwait, Pakistan, the PRC, Saudi Arabia, and the U.S. It operated in the Panjshir Valley (Ahmad Shah Massoud); Herat, Farah, and Badghis provinces (Ismail Khan); and Balkh and Samagan provinces. It conducted small operations in Kabul, Badakshan, Fariab, Jowzjan, and Baghlan provinces.
- *Jabha-e-Nejat-e-Melli (National Liberation Front):* A conservative Sunni monarchist group led by Sibghatullah Mujadidi. It was traditional Pushtun. It had a hard-core strength of about 2,000 and a total strength of some 4,500–6,000. It operated in Kunar and Kandahar.
- *Islamic Alliance of the Afghan Mujahideen (Islamic Unity for the Liberation of Afghanistan):* A conservative Sunni group favoring an Islamic Republic and led by Abdul Rabbur Rasul Saif.

It had hard-core strength of about 1,000 and a total support of around 6,000. It was Pushtun and operated largely in Paktia and around Kabul. It had U.S. support and favored the unification of Afghan liberation movements.

- *Sepha-e-Pasdaran (Revolutionary Guards):* This movement was a conservative Shi'ite group which was strongly pro-Iranian and pro-Khomeini and was led by Mohsen Rezai. It had a cadre strength of some 5,000 and a total strength of around 9,000. It operated in the west in Ghowr, Helmand, Bamiyan, Jowzhjan, and Herat. It received substantial Iranian aid—more than any other Shi'ite fundamentalist movement.
- *Hezbollah (Party of God):* This movement was a conservative Shi'ite group which was strongly pro-Iranian and pro-Khomeini. It had a cadre strength of some 2,000 and a total strength of some 5,000. It operated in the west in Herat, Ghowr, and Helmand provinces and was affiliated with the Hezbollah in Iran and other countries.
- *Nasr:* This movement was a conservative Shi'ite group which broke with Iranian and pro-Khomeini groups. It had a cadre strength of some 1,700 and a total strength of some 5,000. It operated in the west in Ghowr, Helmand, and Bamiyan.
- *Shura:* A conservative Shi'ite group, led by Said Ali Beheshti, which favored an autonomous region in Hazara. It had a cadre strength of some 5,000 and a total strength of some 10,000. It operated in the west in Bamiyan, Baghlan, Balkh, and Ghazni provinces.
- *Harakat Islami (Islamic Movement):* A conservative Shi'ite group, led by Sheikh Mushini, which favored an Islamic republic. It had a hard-core strength of some 3,000 and a total strength of some 16,000. It was largely Hazara and Dari. It operated in the west in Fariab, Jowzjan, Balkh, and Badakshan.[35]

These Mujahideen factions were never able to unify into a government in exile before the Soviet withdrawal. They did, however, show some signs of improving unity. The main factions agreed to rotate the overall leadership of the Mujahideen council every three months, but various factions were still fighting each other in May 1988. The Mujahideen had also split in terms of their reliance on supply and support from the western and Arab groups supporting Pakistan and Iran.

The fragmentation among these groups made it very difficult for the Soviets and DRA to successfully attack their leadership or suppress them. It also, however, was a major factor that limited Mujahideen success. Some experts feel the Pakistani government helped to maintain this fragmentation rather than allow an Afghan government in exile to develop. These experts maintain that Pakistan feared its ability to control the Mujahideen and Pushtuns within its own borders and sought to strengthen the Sunni factions most under Pakistani influence.[36]

Although it is difficult to establish the exact number of fighters the various Mujahideen factions forces can deploy in the field, U.S. government estimates from early 1988 suggested the number of actual full-time active combat troops was around 90,000, with up to 110,000 more part-time forces, support elements, etc. Mujahideen forces, not surprisingly, claimed much higher figures. They also claimed an ability to mobilize 125,000 troops during times of need.

The Mujahideen began with little more than obsolete small arms. By 1988, they were armed with a wide range of foreign supplied and captured weapons. They then received steadily increasing aid from the West, Iran, and various Arab nations. Figures are not available for non-U.S. aid, but it seems to have roughly equalled U.S. aid. U.S. military aid was $30 million in 1980, $50 million in 1981, $50 million in 1982, $60 million in 1983, $140 million in 1984, $250 million in 1985, $470 million in 1986, $660 million in 1987, and $700 million in 1988.[37]

The peak levels of aid occurred toward the end of the Soviet invasion. In 1987, the U.S. provided $715 million in military humanitarian support to the resistance. About $670 million of this was covert aid managed by the CIA. The United States Agency for International Development (USAID) provided $30 million in economic aid and some $10 million in war surplus transfers. The U.S. budgeted $45 million in humanitarian aid in 1988 and rushed $300 million in military aid to the Mujahideen in 1988 to beat the 15 May 1988 deadline placed on U.S./Pakistani and Soviet military arms transfers that was to begin with the start of Soviet withdrawals.

By 1988, the Mujahideen were armed with some T-34 and T-55 tanks, some BMPs and BTR-40s and BTR-60s, 76-mm guns, 122-mm D-30 howitzers, 107-mm and 122-mm multiple rocket launchers, and Blowpipe, Stinger, and SA-7 light surface-to-air missiles. Other arms included AGS-17 30-mm grenade launchers; 51-mm, 60-mm, and 82-mm mortars; RPG-7 and SPG-9 rocket launchers and recoilless rifles; 40 GAI-BOI 200 AA guns; and 12.7-mm and 14.5-mm AA guns.

Much of the military aid to the Mujahideen was lost due to sabotage and thefts in the "pipeline." Actual transfer of the aid to refugees may have totalled as little as 30 percent of the total funding. These figures may seem exceptionally low, but they are typical of such operations in support of Third World conflicts. The need to plan for such problems in the management of aid transfers is a major lesson of recent low-intensity conflicts.[38]

The broader conditions under which the war was fought followed a familiar pattern in extended guerrilla conflicts. The USSR and DRA had a massive advantage in terms of firepower, air power, military mobility, and technology. They could control the cities, win most individual engagements, and secure part of the countryside and sufficient lines of communication to fight. The Mujahideen had the advantage of familiar terrain and enjoyed the support of most of the population.

The major disadvantages the Mujahideen faced included:

- *The lack of unification among the Mujahideen groups.* This led to a lack of coordination, separate truces with the Soviets, and even occasional fighting between groups. These divisions were exploited by Soviet and DRA intelligence agencies and occupation police with considerable effectiveness.[39]
- *The lack of ability to seize and hold a major city or defended objective.* The Mujahideen lacked the training, unity, and equipment to directly assault and hold any major city or Soviet/DRA objective. They lacked effective mass, coordination, and firepower. In spite of nine years in the field, they never developed a major capability for "regular" military operations.
- *A lack of adequate weapons and ammunition.* This problem was most acute at the beginning of the war, although critical problems existed until 1987 because of a lack of anti-tank and anti-aircraft weapons. Even mediocre weapons systems like the rocket-propelled grenades (RPGs) and SA-7s were in short supply. This situation changed in 1987 with the introduction of more arms and advanced light weapons like Stinger and Blowpipe.
- *A lack of a clear or structured chain of command.* The deaths of a small unit commander and his second in command could leave a guerrilla group temporarily leaderless. This was especially important when units were rendered leaderless in the middle of a battle with no time to iron out who would take over command.
- *Dependence on support from Pakistan and Iran—both of which are political, ideological, and religious rivals.* This helped maintain the splits between fundamentalist and moderate tribal groups and between Sunni and Shi'ite groups. It also made the Mujahideen vulnerable to outside restrictions of their supply lines, particularly in the face of growing Soviet pressure on Pakistan.
- *Inability to form a government in exile and compete for political*

legitimacy. The Mujahideen could not achieve formal recognition and political support as a government and were gravely weakened in seeking political control of the nation. Even in 1988, after the Soviets had begun their withdrawal, they were able to achieve only limited unity in proposing an alternative government to the DRA.

- *Low educational levels, lack of formal military training, and dependence on the local population for food, sanctuary, and medical recovery.*

Selected Chronology of the Afghan War

The history of the Afghan conflict was largely the history of three very different struggles. The first struggle was dominated by the Soviet Union. It invaded Afghanistan with the strategic objectives of securing a critical strategic area with a long border on the Soviet Union, creating a friendly government that could win popular support, restructuring the regional balance of power, and spreading Soviet ideology. These objectives were certainly desirable from a Soviet perspective, but the USSR soon learned that achieving them was far more costly than it could possibly have imagined when it invaded.

For nine years, the Soviet Union made a continuing attempt to find some combination of military tactics and technology, pacification techniques, political intimidation of Pakistan, and changes in the leadership and tactics of the DRA that could suppress the resistance of the vast majority of the Afghan people. The DRA was little more than a pawn in this effort, responding to Soviet direction and guidance as the USSR attempted to transform the DRA into a state that could win enough popular support to survive and manage an increasing portion of the burden of its own defense.

The second struggle was an often bewildering set of internal power struggles within the DRA government and its ruling party. The broad outlines of this conflict were simple and resulted in changes in the leader of the state. The struggles for power within the cabinet and military forces are far more complex. Their main impact in military terms, however, was to constantly weaken the government and undercut its ability to both win popular support and create effective military forces.[40]

The third struggle was the struggle of the Mujahideen to both win back control of the country and transform a wide range of competing tribal and religious groups into a viable government. During this struggle, the Mujahideen largely adapted or reacted to the Soviet Union. The various factions in the Mujahideen rarely attempted to dominate events through changes in strategy, tactics, or equipment. The most important changes affecting the Mujahideen's military capabilities came from the outside and consisted primarily of the sanctuaries and support provided by Pakistan and Iran and the weapons and funds provided by the West and the Gulf states. It was this support that allowed the Mujahideen to steadily improve their weaponry and military capability.

The Strategic Background to the Invasion

The Soviet invasion was the outcome of a long history of local rivalries and outside efforts to win control of the region. Throughout most of the nineteenth century, a complex struggle for control and influence over Afghanistan took place between Britain and Russia; it came to be called the "great game." At the same time, the competing factions in Afghanistan cooperated with one another to the extent that the country kept its independence for most of the colonial era, although it remained a basically tribal state with a thin gloss of urbanization and a weak and half-developed government and economy.

The central government was so weak that it could function only as long as it appeared to be strongly nationalist in character and did not challenge the traditions and customs of the people outside the urban areas, particularly the major tribal or Pushtun factions. The various ethnic and tribal groups in Afghanistan remained deeply divided. The Pushtuns were split between Afghanistan and Pakistan, and for many years, Afghanistan saw Pakistan as its main enemy and at least talked about creating a greater Pushtun state.

There were large Turkic minorities, divided among such groups as the Tajiks, Uzbecks, Turkomens, and Kirghiz. These non-Pushtun groups lived largely in the area near the Soviet border. Both the Pushtun and Turkic groups were divided into many different dialects and between the Sunni and Shi'ite branches of the Muslim faith. The result was an endless mix of rivalries and divisions. The only major unifying factor was the Muslim clergy, although it was often divided by sect and by the willingness of given groups of clergy to tolerate different degrees of modernization.

Afghanistan remained a monarchy until 1973. It was a monarchy which often had remarkably little real power to tax, enforce the law, or carry out most of the activities of a modern state. Roughly 90 percent of the population was illiterate, and industrial development accounted for less than one quarter of one percent of the GNP. Some tribal areas were virtually autonomous, and the role of women had changed little since the twelfth century.

A small urban elite governed the urbanized part of the country, and the largest institution within this elite was the armed forces, which had grown in size and influence largely in response to Afghanistan's rivalry with Pakistan over control of Pushtun territory. This Afghan elite was heavily influenced by the USSR, in part because the U.S. alignment with Pakistan made the USSR the natural source of aid and military assistance. Many of the younger members of the Afghan elite were trained in the USSR, and the growing Soviet influence in the country soon created radical political movements, the most important of which was the People's Democratic Party of Afghanistan (PDPA), which was created in 1965. This party participated in elections for a parliament, although 90 percent of the people did not bother to vote or seem to care about the result.

In 1973, a major prince named Mohammed Daoud carried out a coup against the king. He dropped his royal title and declared himself a President. Daoud, however, found it impossible to introduce effective reforms, and he did little more than create the climate in which far more radical political leaders could come to power under the banner of reform. At the same time, royalist and other factions continuously threatened Daoud, and coup attempts seem to have occurred in 1973, 1974, and 1976. A coup by the People's Democratic Party of Afghanistan (PDPA) in April 1978 succeeded in subverting key elements of the armed forces. After an attack on the palace by armored and air forces, Daoud, his brother, and a number of senior ministers and other officials were killed.

The People's Democratic Party of Afghanistan numbered only about 10,000 people at the time of the coup and was deeply divided between the Khalq (Masses) and Parcham (Flag) factions. The Khalq faction was led by Nur Mohammed Taraki and the Parcham faction by Barbak Karmal. Ideological differences did exist between Taraki and Karmal, but the key issues were personalities and power, although the Parcham faction was heavily influenced by intellectuals in the Tajik minority.

The leaders of the coup formed a Revolutionary Military Council on 28 April 1978. Within days, the Council announced the creation of the Democratic Republic of Afghanistan (DRA), with Nur Mohammed Taraki as the Prime Minister. This appointment did nothing to halt the bitter power struggles between the Khalq and Parcham, and the government showed little moderation in trying to ram through a series of ill-planned and highly ideological reforms. The government proceeded to alienate large parts of the population over issues such as land reform, religion, and the equality of women.

By June, armed resistance began to emerge in rural areas. In August, the government formed a new secret police called the AGSA. In July and August, the Khalq forced many of its Parcham rivals out of the government, and in August, it purged the military of many of its strongest leaders, including those that had helped bring the People's Democratic Party of Afghanistan to power. By October, rural violence was widespread, and the Sarandoy was almost completely ineffective. In addition, the government was forced to rely more and more on Soviet advisors for both its normal functions and internal security.

On 5 December 1978, the Khalq-dominated government signed a Soviet-Afghan Friendship Treaty that provided for Soviet-Afghan collective security efforts. The treaty almost immediately led the PRC to start significant arms shipments to the anti-government tribal rebels, or Mujahideen. This soon led to an anti-DRA coalition composed of the Mujahideen, the PRC, and Pakistan. The USSR had a strong motive to back Taraki and the Khalq. It had long treated Afghanistan as a key "buffer state."

The Soviet government had made various efforts to create a friendly regime in Afghanistan from the late 1920s onward. It actively involved itself in the divisions and squabbles in the People's Democratic Party of Afghanistan virtually from the day it was founded, and it had immediately supported an April 1978 coup that overthrew the quasi-Marxist remnants of the royal family and brought the People's Democratic Party of Afghanistan to power.

The growing ties between the DRA and USSR almost inevitably led to friction between the DRA and the U.S. This friction was made much worse early in 1979, when U.S. Ambassador Adolph Dubs was kidnapped by a group demanding that the DRA free three of its members. The government instead attacked the hotel where Dubs was being held, and he was killed in the shooting. According to some reports, the first covert CIA shipment of arms to Afghanistan arrived in Karachi in June 1979.[41]

The internal situation in Afghanistan deteriorated steadily throughout the first three months of 1979 with a growing internal power struggle between Taraki and Hafizullah Amin, who had acquired growing power as First Deputy Prime Minister, Foreign Minister, and a ruthless head of the Khalq's internal security effort. The government's attempts at reform led to an uprising in Herat in April and defections in the first troops sent to put down the uprising. The army and air force then succeeded in putting down the uprising by bombing and assaulting the city, but at the cost of 5,000 dead. Amin used the opportunity to further expand his power and became Prime Minister.

The USSR sent Army-General Alexei Yepishev to inspect the situation in early April, and he seems to have advocated building up the armed forces as a method of strengthening the government. This led to the rapid delivery of 100 T-62 tanks, a squadron of Mil-24 attack helicopters, some Mil-6 helicopters, twelve MiG-21 fighters, and some Su-20 fighter-bombers. The number of Soviet military and economic advisors rapidly grew from 1,000 at the start of the year to 5,000 in August, and the government and PDPA increasingly became identified with the USSR.[42] At the same time, attempts to use the army in fighting with the Mujahideen had little success, and elements of the Army continued to defect with their weapons.

During the period between April and September, the USSR continued to expand its advisory role and deliver more weapons. It assumed responsibility for security in key locations like Bagram airport after Mujahideen attacks. The DRA government also began to build up the AGSA as an alternative to the army and ruthlessly purged the leadership of the Sarandoy to create a pro-Khalq force. Amin became Minister of Defense on 27 July in what may have been an effort to consolidate power over all internal security forces. A major uprising in the Kunar Valley then led to still more defections to the Mujahideen by the regular forces, however, and the government increasingly became dependent on cadres of Soviet advisors in the army and attack helicopters to enforce its control.

Between September 11 and 14, Amin began to ruthlessly purge supporters of Taraki from the military. Taraki attempted to fight back with Soviet aid, and he seems to have tried to assassinate Amin. It was Amin who killed Taraki, however—although the death was not announced until October 9. Amin then claimed that 12,000 people had died during the previous year as a result of arrests he blamed on Taraki. He made limited attempts at political liberalization and seems to have tried to reduce Soviet influence. He forced the recall of the Soviet Ambassador, Alexander Puzanov, on November 8, which apparently aroused intense Soviet suspicion, in part because Amin had been educated in the U.S. and was considered highly suspect.

Amin had no real chance to consolidate power. In spite of Soviet protestations of friendship, the USSR seems to have begun considering military intervention almost immediately after Taraki's death. The Soviet Union apparently feared that any failure to intervene would force the entire PDPA elite out of power by anti-Soviet Mujahideen or would cause Amin to turn against the USSR and tilt toward Pakistan, the PRC, and/or the U.S.[43]

Pre–Soviet-Invasion Involvement

The USSR prepared for its invasion by following a pattern somewhat similar to its preparations to invade Czechoslovakia in 1968. The USSR began to organize for an invasion as early as August

1979, when Amin's actions suggested that he might oust Taraki. The USSR sent a small sixty-man planning unit under Army-General Ivan Pavlovsky to Afghanistan. This unit was able to travel freely through the country as part of a body of Soviet advisors that now totalled nearly 2,000.[44] Immediately after Amin's coup in October, the Soviet Operations Main Directorate gave responsibility for planning and organizing the invasion to First Deputy Defense Minister, Marshall Sergei Sokolov. This gave the USSR from October to December to plan the invasion.[45]

The USSR began to create the elements of what came to be called the 40th Army in early November. A headquarters was set up at Termez, on the Soviet border with Afghanistan, and two army groups were established: one in the Turkestan military district and the other in the Central Asian military district. The USSR faced the problem, however, that all of the major combat units in its Turkestan military district were low-grade reserve units, except for the 105th Air Assault (Airborne) Division. The situation in the Central Asian military district was roughly as bad, as its only two combat-ready units were deployed to meet the Soviet threat.

As a result, the USSR had to mobilize close to 100,000 men—most of which were Asiatic Russians such as Turkomens, Uzbecks, Tajiks, and Kirghiz—to bring its Category II and III reserve divisions up to strength. These units had severe shortfalls of officers and technicians, which forced a selective call-up of many key personnel from the reserves. The net result was to force the USSR to rely on a small cadre of elite airborne units which were not really organized for sustained independent operations and a low-grade mix of reserve forces unsuited for combat of any kind.

In early December, the USSR deployed battalion-sized airborne units as "security forces" for key airports and LOCs and sent in special security elements and advisors to "assist" Amin and his staff. Elements of the the 105th Guards Air Assault Division, which had been reinforced by regiments of the 103rd and 104th guards air assault divisions, began to arrive in Bagram on 6 and 7 December 1979. The USSR also disarmed potentially troublesome Afghan units like the 26th Parachute Regiment and put advisors in the local radio and power stations.

The USSR continued to conduct a deception operation, occasionally praising Amin and talking about reforming the PDPA. On 23 December, however, full-scale deployment of the 105th Guards Air Assault Division began. The USSR succeeded in persuading the 4th Armored Brigade to stay in its barracks and arrested additional officers in the 7th and 8th DRA divisions.

On 27 December, the USSR used its airborne and KGB units to "support" a coup that killed Amin and his supporters in the presidential palace. By this time, the USSR had two airborne divisions in Afghanistan, one at Bagram air base north of Kabul, securing the route from Termez in the USSR through the Salang Tunnel to Kabul, and one which it airlifted to Kabul airport on 24 to 26 December 1979. The USSR built this force up to nearly 60,000 men and 200 combat aircraft immediately after its new puppet president, Babrak Karmal, was given power. Karmal "invited" four motorized rifle divisions to move into Afghanistan.

The key events during this phase of the conflict were:

- 1953: Prince Mohammed Daoud becomes Prime Minister.
- 1955: Daoud turns to the Soviets for military assistance after the U.S. refuses. Khrushchev and Bulganin visit Afghanistan. Aid package includes construction of Bagram airport and Salang Tunnel. Afghan officers begin training in Warsaw Pact countries.
- 1963: Daoud resigns.
- 1965: People's Democratic Party of Afghanistan (PDPA) forms with Nur Mohammed Taraki as Secretary General. Other founders include Hafizullah Amin and Babrak Karmal, a suspected KGB agent.
- 1967: PDPA splits into two groups: the Khalq, led by Taraki, and the Parcham, led by Karmal. The split is caused by personality conflict and ideological disunity.
- 17 July 1973: Prince Mohammed Daoud overthrows King Zahir Shah while the king is abroad and introduces a pro-Soviet, quasi-Marxist regime, supported by both major factions of the Afghan Communist Party.
- 1975–1978: Daoud slowly removes key pro-Soviet officers and political figures from his government, seeks closer ties to Pakistan, and increases support for nonalignment.
- Mid-1977: Soviets force the two pro-Soviet Marxist factions, the Khalq led by Nur Mohammed Taraki and Parcham led by Babrak Karmal, to reunite as the People's Democratic Party of Afghanistan (PDPA).
- 15 April 1978: PDPA leader Mir Akber Khyyber is shot, and his death triggers major riots.
- 27–28 April 1978: The army, air force, and PDPA stage a coup and kill Daoud, who has been weakened by economic problems and his failure to provide the army with modern weapons and financial aid. MiG-15s fire rockets at targets in Kabul, attacking the Royal Palace, the Ministry of Defense and First Army Staff Head-

quarters. As many as 50 T-54 and T-55 tanks are involved in the attack, and a dozen tanks are destroyed. Two MiG-21s are shot down by ground fire and one MiG-17 crashes. Nur Mohammed Taraki becomes President and Babrak Karmal Vice-President.

- 30 April 1978: The USSR recognizes the new government.
- April–May 1978: Conservative officers are purged from the armed forces.
- 15 May 1978: The new government starts radical reforms that soon alienate a growing number of the people in rural areas.
- July 1978: Taraki creates a new secret police called the AGSA.
- August 1978: Several senior conservative Moslem leaders declare a Jihad (religious war) against the PDPA because of atheism, "land reform," and imprisonment of political opposition. The Mujahideen start a low-level war against the government using Lee Enfields, Martini Henrys, FN-FALs, and AK-47s.
- 17 August 1978: Taraki conducts another major purge of officers accused of plotting a coup attempt. Fighting escalates in the countryside. The Sarandoy almost ceases to function in many areas. The Khalqi PDPA faction ruthlessly purges the Parcham faction from power. Hafizullah Amin, the First Deputy Prime Minister and Foreign Minister, emerges as the steadily more powerful de facto head of the PDPA's internal security forces.
- 5 December 1978: Soviet-Afghan Treaty of Friendship and Cooperation is signed. Revolts occur in twenty-three of Afghanistan's twenty-eight provinces.
- February 1979: U.S. Ambassador Adolph Dubs is kidnapped and killed during a rescue attempt by Soviet-advised Afghan security police.
- 17 February 1979: Leaders of the Afghan resistance group Hesb-i-Islami claim they have spent the equivalent of 400,000 British pounds on weapons and ammunition. They claim approximately 2,270 men are undergoing guerrilla training in Pakistan.
- March 1979: Afghan soldiers join revolt in Herat, killing Soviet advisors and Afghan officials.
- 3 March 1979: Soviet and Afghan pilots use the Mi-24 helicopter gunship against guerrillas for the first time.
- 12 April 1979: Afghan rebels reportedly inflict heavy casualties on government forces and capture heavy military equipment and arms. The Nationalist Revolution Council claims to have seized eight armored personnel carriers, five cannons, two jeeps, and 120 machine guns in two engagements in Paktia province.
- 15 March 1979: A forced literacy campaign, combined with the impact of earlier attempts to abolish bride prices, sharply

increases Mujahideen activity in the Kunar Valley as well as rural unrest and major riots in Herat. The 17th Infantry Division, ordered to put down riots, deserts to the Mujahideen.

- 27 March 1979: Amin becomes Prime Minister as internal security becomes more and more the center of power.
- 6 April 1979: High-level Soviet military mission arrives in Kabul.
- 20 April 1979: Village of Kerala in Kunar Valley is destroyed by the DRA army; as many as 1,000 people are killed.
- 30 April 1979: Soviets send 12 "armored assault" helicopter gunships to Afghanistan. This is part of a package that includes 100 T-62 tanks, 12 MiG-21s, Su-22s, and Mil-6s. Rumors of chemical warfare are reported for the first time.
- 3 May 1979: Bombing and the 4th and 15th armored brigades are used to reassert control over Herat. Up to 5,000 people are killed. The retaking of Herat from rebellious army units involves MiG and Il-28 aircraft sorties. Some reports indicate a major movement of Soviet arms, including MiG-23s, occurs to reinforce troops in Nuristan. One report says as many as seven jets are shot down during the uprising.
- 11 May 1979: Afghan guerrillas claim to have downed three Soviet-built MiGs and to have captured anti-tank and anti-aircraft guns and some tanks.
- 17 May 1979: A brigade of the 7th Division deserts with all its equipment to the Mujahideen.
- June 1979: Eighteen more Mi-24 helicopters and more fighters are delivered to the DRA.
- July 1979: First Mujahideen rocket attack on Bagram air base occurs.
- 13 July 1979: Afghan army nearly disintegrates, torn apart by low morale and desertion; the countryside is largely under guerrilla control. The Afghan army becomes increasingly reliant on Soviet-built armor and helicopters; Soviet advisers number about 1,500. Afghan air force pilots are down to 500 from 2,000. Pilot training is now increased in the Soviet Union.
- 27 July 1979: Amin is appointed Minister of Defense.
- August 1979: The government's new land reform efforts trigger major new problems with rural unrest. Soviet military and economic advisors have risen from 1,000 to 5,000. The Sarandoy and AGSA are used in further large-scale purges of the officer corps of the DRA Army. A small Soviet team seems to have been sent to Afghanistan to study the possibility of seizing control of the government and armed forces.

- 5 August 1979: During an aborted coup by armored units in the Kunar Valley, Soviet-built Mi-24 helicopters are seen firing at lines of Afghan tanks. The Mi-24 is the weapon that has the most effect in attacking Mujahideen forces.
- 1 September 1979: The Afghan regime appears to regain confidence in the air force and some armored units. The pay of officers and NCOs has been doubled in the previous two weeks.
- 10–14 September 1979: Taraki visits Moscow in what is later rumored to be a meeting to plan the removal of Amin. Taraki returns to Kabul on 11 September. Amin purges four pro-Taraki ministers from the cabinet on 14 September.
- 14 September 1979: Government tanks in Kabul clash in a coup attempt that results in fifty to sixty deaths. Extra tanks are observed guarding key points in Kabul. Soviet advisers now number 3,000.
- 16 September 1979: Hafizullah Amin ousts Taraki. President Taraki is quietly murdered by Hafizullah Amin's guards just days after meeting with Brezhnev in Moscow and possibly attempting to remove Amin with the aid of Soviet Ambassador Alexander Puzanov. Amin becomes President. Taraki is initially said to have stepped down because of ill health. His death is announced on 9 October.

Late September–November 1979: Pre-Invasion Soviet Buildup

The Soviets responded to Taraki's murder and Amin's coup with a major military build-up involving an invasion force of one air assault division, two independent air assault regiments, and four motorized rifle divisions, with three more in reserve. Nearly 200 combat aircraft were committed to what later became the 40th Army.

The Soviets relied heavily on White Russian air assault troops backed by regular forces composed of central Asiatic troops, including Kazaks, Tajiks, Turkomens, and Uzbecks. The Soviets evidently believed they faced a short occupation and that Asian Muslim troops, with ethnic ties to the northern Afghans (Tajiks, Uzbecks, and Turkomens), would minimize cultural conflicts. The primary mission of these ground troops was to secure lines of communication (LOCs) and urban areas, although they had no special training or equipment.

Key events during this phase were:

- September 1979: The Soviet Operations Main Directorate begins organizing the invasion task force.
- 20 September 1979: State Department sources report increased military activity as part of the Soviet mobilization and

deployments that are necessary to create the invasion task force.

- October 1979: Amin announces the disbandment of the AGSA, blaming it and Taraki for the death of thousands of political prisoners. He creates his own new secret police called the KAM.
- 9 October 1979: The Soviets are believed to have as many as 4,000 troops guarding the Bagram air base near Kabul. The Mi-24 helicopter gunship is being used extensively against the anti-government guerrillas. The Soviets have sent 30 such gunships to Afghanistan, with 20 more in the pipeline. About 800 Soviet tanks and 800 APCs are in the country or en route. The USSR mobilizes five Category II and III divisions in Central Asia to allow it to concentrate Category I divisions for invasion.
- 14 October 1979: An attempted Afghan military takeover occurs involving tanks, helicopters, and jet strikes. Helicopters are observed flying from Soviet-controlled Bagram air base.
- 30 October 1979: Soviets establish a military base near Farah, 65 miles from Iran. Other air bases, such as the Afghan base at Shindand, are expanded. Soviet "advisory" presence is raised to 4,500.
- 2 November 1979: Government garrison troops at Gardez use artillery against surrounding guerrillas, but artillery takes 2.5 hours to zero in on guerrilla positions. The Soviets create the command structure for the invasion. The nucleus of the 40th Army headquarters is active at Termez. Separate invasion forces are forming in the Turkestan and Central Asian military districts.
- 13 November 1979: A government offensive uses 100 T-54 and T-62 Soviet tanks, about 100 APCs, and infantry supported by helicopter gunships to retake two-thirds of Paktia province. Estimates of casualties range from 800 to 1,000. The offensive was launched to relieve seventeen besieged posts and to clear roads. Guerrillas credit the government success to a new armored helicopter and return to besiege the positions in the wake of the offensive. A 60-truck convoy is captured in the fighting.
- 22 November 1979: Villages in Paktia, Nangarhar, and Logar are razed by assaults from the ground and air.

December 1979–January 1980: Soviet Invasion and Death of Amin

Soviet air assault forces and KGB troops launched a full-scale takeover of the capital, killed Amin, and seized control of the airport, radio stations, and key road junctions. A two-pronged invasion took place. One major thrust moved south from the Turkestan military district and went through the Salang Tunnel and across the Hindu Kush to Kabul. The second drove south from the Kushka and moved around the Hazara Mountains to seize Herat, Farah, and Kandahar. The Soviets effectively took control of the "modern" part of the country but made little effort to secure the many tribal areas and rural factions:

- Late November 1979: Following the model the Soviets used in Czechoslovakia, the Soviets infiltrate with Spetsnaz to seize key points inside the government and Kabul.
- 7–9 December 1979: Some 1,500–2,000 more Soviet forces move into Afghanistan. Soviet airborne troops from 103 Guards Airborne Division arrive at Bagram air base north of Kabul and send a forward detachment to secure the Salang Pass.
- 11 December 1979: Guerrillas acknowledge arrival of more than 100 Soviet Mi-24 gunships.
- 20–22 December 1979: Soviets reinforce the headquarters unit at Termez close to the Afghanistan border. Motorized rifle divisions are now ready to launch a two-pronged invasion. A regiment from the 104th Airborne Division arrives at Bagram. The regiment from the 103rd Guards Airborne Division secures Kabul airport, the rest of the Salang Tunnel, and the route from Termez in the USSR to Kabul.
- 24–26 December 1979: In a round-the-clock airlift of 75–125 flights of AN-22 and AN-12 aircraft per. day, with 350 sorties to Kabul and Bagram, 15,000 Soviet troops enter Afghanistan in 24 hours. The 105th Airborne Division completes its deployment to Kabul Airport from Fergana in the Turkestan military district. The forces from the 105th are airlifted in with their BMDs and use prepositioned fuel and trucks. They leave Bagram and Kabul airports on the evening of December 26 to begin taking control of the country. The DRA's 4th Armored Brigade, the key unit defending Amin, is persuaded not to intervene. Soviet soldiers and KGB arrest pro-Amin officers leading the 7th Division at Rishkoor and the 8th Division at Kargha and immobilize vehicles.
- 26–27 December 1979: Motorized rifle divisions cross the border. Pontoon bridges are put across the Oxus River at the border. Spetsnaz forces, sometimes using civilian clothing and DRA uniforms, seize key check points and work with much larger airborne forces to seize chokepoints and C^3 facilities. Soviet military advisors immobilize key equipment and neutralize key DRA personnel.
- 27 December 1979: "President" Amin is killed by KGB Spetsnaz and Soviet airborne forces. His palace is defended by eight T-54 tanks and troops, and an initial Spetsnaz raid fails. The

Duralamin Palace is overwhelmed by two battalions of Soviet paratroops. Babrak Karmal is made president. The four Soviet motorized rifle divisions already pouring into Afghanistan are "invited" by Karmal to help secure the country.

- 28 December 1979: President Karmal announces his new cabinet. He is forced to compromise with the Khalq and give them key internal security posts. He does, however, create a new Parcham-dominated security force called the Khedemati-e-Dolati (KHAD) under Mohammed Najibullah.
- 1 January 1980: 58,000 Soviet soldiers and 200 aircraft are operating in Afghanistan. Guerrillas have captured some Sagger and Snapper anti-tank missiles and a number of 132-mm rocket launchers from the Afghan army. In the first combined operations drive, the Soviets use white phosphorus incendiary devices against villages in Paktia.
- 3 January 1980: Karmal attempts to win popular support by announcing a moderate reform program and his respect for Islam. Many political prisoners are released from jail on 5 and 9 January, but a large number turn out to be members of the Parcham faction.
- 3–5 January 1980: Soviet 201st Motorized Rifle Division arrives at Jalalabad.
- 6 January 1980: Soviet military units have secured most key cities and important military airfields. These airfields are being fortified with SAM batteries and equipped with modern command and control facilities.
- 9 January 1980: Soviet Antonov aircraft make 4,000 separate flights into the capital during the first week of January. Soviet central Asian troops start to be replaced by more politically reliable and combat-ready troops from the western and eastern USSR.

    Large-scale defections take place from the Afghan civil service. It becomes increasingly apparent that Karmal's government is viewed by many Afghans who formerly supported the PDPA as a Soviet puppet regime.
- 13 January 1980: A major military convoy, including 156 tracked armored vehicles, 8 wheeled personnel carriers, 60 trucks carrying gasoline, and other trucks carrying supplies, is attacked and delayed for 24 hours in the Salang Pass area.
- 13–15 January: Marshall Sokolov commits his reserves to the invasion. The 5th Motorized Rifle Division is sent to Farah; the 54th Motorized Rifle Division to Herat and to seal the Iranian border. The 16th Motorized Rifle Division is sent to Mazar-i-Shariff via Termez. The headquarters of the Soviet 40th Army is

relocated from Termez to Bagram and then Kabul. Colonel General S. Magometov (and later Colonel General Alexander Mayorov) is appointed chief military advisor to Karmal and the Afghan Ministry of Defense.

Reports emerge of Soviet troops clashing with forces of the 8th Afghan Division and Afghan paratroops at Balar Hisar fort. The 30th Mountain Brigade of the 9th Division defects to the Mujahideen. Other units defect in the northeast. The Hazara resistance front establishes control over much of Uruzgan, Ghowr, and Bamiyan provinces.

- 15 January 1980: Local sources indicate 80,000 to 85,000 Soviet troops are in Afghanistan, including an advisory group in command of Afghan army units, an airborne division, and 5 motorized rifle divisions. At least 5 squadrons of MiG-21s, totalling 75 planes, and a squadron of MiG-23s are operating at Afghan air bases. Air units at Kandahar include Su-17 fighter bombers, and Yak-28s are used in reconnaissance.
- 20 January 1980: Convoy Number 58 from Tashkent to Kabul is ambushed by guerrilla snipers, causing four casualties.

January 1980–July 1980: Initial Soviet Commitment to War Against the Afghan Population

Major Mujahideen attacks began on Soviet units in the cities. The Soviets attacked "rebel" units using conventional air and armored attacks but rapidly became heavily dependent on the helicopter. The Soviet military presence shifted its role from securing the country to defending urban areas, key facilities, and lines of communication and conducting low-level small-unit action against the Mujahideen:

- 23 January 1980: U.S. State Department estimates Soviet troop strength at 85,000, with 1,750 tanks, 2,100 APCs, 500 combat aircraft, and 200 helicopters. No more than 45,000 DRA Army troops are still effective.
- 25 January 1980: More advanced types of MiG-21s are shipped from the Soviet Union, and Afghanistan receives MiG-23s with electronic surveillance equipment. Mechanized divisions with T-72 tanks, PT-76 light amphibious tanks, and BMP-1 personnel carriers are operational.
- 27 January 1980: Six parties of the Mujahideen announce the creation of the Alliance for the Liberation of Afghanistan in Peshawar. The parties rapidly divide into factions, however, and a bitter competition starts for Pakistani and PRC arms and funds.

- 28 January 1980: A Soviet armored column, trying to relieve a government garrison in Badakhstan province, comes under heavy guerrilla attack.
- 1 February 1980: T-72 tanks deploy along the Salang Pass and in the northern foothills of the Hindu Kush.
- February 1980: Guerrillas obtain increased quantities of the AK-47 automatic rifle, but the majority are still armed only with the traditional 303 Enfield. Some Israeli Uzi submachine guns and Czech rifles are seen. Ammunition is too expensive to allow weapons training for most of the guerrillas.
- 21 February 1980: DRA soldiers at the Ghazni airport, south of Kabul, are killed by helicopter gunship fire in retaliation for an uprising that killed 50 Soviet soldiers. A general strike in Kabul has some success.
- 24 February 1980: Reports indicate that Afghan air force gunners are often ineffective and civilians are often hit.
- 25 February 1980: In a battle near Kabul, Soviet fighters, including at least one MiG-23, bomb rebel DAR Army units with napalm.
- 28 February 1980: Soviet helicopter gunships play a major role in spotting snipers during general disorders in Kabul. Soviet anti-aircraft missiles appear at Kabul Airport for the first time. Five batteries of four missiles protect the Soviet army camp at the runway edge.
- 4 March 1980: First offensives start against Panjshir Valley. A combined Soviet and DRA Army offensive shatters large numbers of villages between Chaga Sarai, the provincial capital, and Asmar, site of a former government garrison in Kunar Valley. Casualties are estimated at 1,000 (civilians and insurgents). The strike force includes over 200 tanks and armored vehicles; over 50 helicopters, gunships, and cargo helicopters; and several squadrons of fighter bombers.
- 6 March 1980: Afghan guerrillas reportedly use a captured artillery piece to destroy tanks and a helicopter. Guerrillas ambush a Soviet patrol in the northern town of Abkul, killing fifty and forcing the remainder to withdraw.
- 8 March 1980: Soviet fighter jets and helicopters buzz the city of Kabul in a display of force to discourage impending civil unrest.
- 10 March 1980: The 357th Armored Rifle Brigade at Kargha military base conducts operations with T-62 and some T-72 tanks.
- 15 March 1980: Two Soviet infantry regiments, supported by aircraft with napalm, inflict 1,500 casualties in attacks on guerrilla targets in Asmar, Kunar province. The first Kunar

Valley offensive is largely completed, but the failure to use helicopters and assault forces to the rear of the Mujahideen generally allows their forces to escape. The offensive has little lasting impact.

- 29 March 1980: U.S. officials claim that mounting evidence exists of Soviet use of lethal gas in Afghanistan.
- April 1980: Fixed-wing, ground attack aircraft, such as the Sukhoi Su-17, are reported by guerrillas to be much less effective than rotary wing aircraft.
- 13 April 1980: The Central Committee of the PDPA meets but accomplishes nothing that wins added popular support. Growing economic strain is felt in Kabul as Mujahideen activity seriously disrupts the economy.
- May–June 1980: Mujahideen attempts and fails to create a Loyah Jirgah, or grand assembly, to unite various factions. The key conservative Islamic parties boycott the effort.
- June 1980: The 201st Motorized Rifle Division in Jalalabad starts new offensive operations in Paktia and Kunar. An entire motorized rifle battalion is ambushed on the Gardez-Khost road and virtually destroyed. The BTR-60P proves too vulnerable to fight in Afghan conditions, and T-55 tanks lack the gun elevation and depression to fight in mountains. The Soviets start to make far more use of helicopters, sometimes 16 to 18 against a single target. The Mujahideen begin repeated low-level attacks on Kabul and its outskirts.
- 19 June 1980: The Mujahideen attacks the key Soviet supply base covering the Salang road at Pol-e-Khumri. Ahmad Shah Massoud emerges as a key Mujahideen leader in the Panjshir.

July 1980–July 1981: Restructuring of Soviet Forces and DRA Internal Security Forces

The Soviet force became known as the Limited Contingent of Soviet Forces in Afghanistan (LCSFA). The 40th Army was subordinated to the Turkestan military district, and the First Deputy Commander of the Turkestan military district, Lt. General V.M. Mikhailov, became commander of the 40th Army.[46] The USSR began to realize that it faced a long war. Major efforts were made to improve the air bases in Afghanistan. An engineer regiment was deployed to improve defensive positions, and a pipeline was built from Termez to Pol-e-Khumri to reduce the problem of attacks on tanker trucks. A permanent bridge was built across the Oxus and Termez rivers. Many Soviet communications were shifted to land lines to improve communications through the mountains and improve security.

It became apparent that low-grade reserve motorized rifle divisions were unsuited for the large-scale guerrilla war taking place. Soviet forces needed to stress independent small unit tactics, and not the central direction of mass used in a major armored conflict. The 105th Guards Air Assault Division was disbanded and made part of a reinforced formation under the 103rd Guards Air Assault Division. This force was given added helicopter strength and relocated to a camp in the Darulaman area in southwest Kabul. The 360th Motorized Rifle Division, which had equipment ten to twenty years old, was disbanded and regrouped with other elements into the 180th Motorized Rifle Division, with regiments at Bagram and Khair Khana. Other forces were grouped under the 5th Guards MRD at Shindand, and the 201st MRD is reorganized and deployed to Kunduz.

Two specially formed motorized rifle brigades—the 66th and 70th—were set up at Jalalabad and Kandahar. These had four battalions, rather than three, and their own independent helicopter units.[47] A number of units were sent home on 22 June 1980. These included two tank regiments, the SA-4 missile unit, independent artillery brigade, some anti-aircraft units, surface-to-surface missile units, and other unnecessary support units. The changes were not completed until mid-1981, but the 40th Army was converted from a force that relied on seven regular motorized rifle divisions to one with three specially structured motorized rifle divisions, two independent motorized rifle brigades, and two independent motorized rifle regiments.

The Soviets shifted to lighter armor and more use of the helicopter. The number of helicopters in Afghanistan rose from about 60 to 300. Three complete helicopter regiments of 40–50 aircraft each were deployed to Bagram, Kunduz, and Kandahar. Fixed-wing air units with a total of about 130–200 MiG-31, Su-17/20, and MiG-23 fighters were set up at Bagram, Shindand, and Herat.[48]

Soviet forces continued the Panjshir offensives but struck more and more heavily at Mujahideen villages. It became clear that the USSR could not use low-grade Asian troops or trust them not to aid the Mujahideen. Soviet forces came to depend on White Russian combined arms reinforced battalions, support units, and air cover to try to drive the Mujahideen back into the mountains. The Soviets began to use Mi-24 helicopters intensively for attack missions and Mi-5 helicopters to land troops behind the Mujahideen forces. Increasing use was made of MiG-21 and MiG-23 fighters in close-air support roles.

The Soviets tried to use envelopment and pincer tactics and used company- and battalion-sized motorized rifle forces supported by engineer troops, light artillery units, and squads with portable anti-tank weapons: The key focus was on limited operations to secure areas like key towns, bases, and roads. The DRA Army continued to decline, but the DRA and Soviets gradually laid the groundwork for rebuilding its capability:

- 10 July 1980: Soviet IL-76 transports begin landing in the daylight for the first time. They off-load three types of light and mobile armored tracked vehicles: the BMD, BMP and BRDM. These evidently have been rushed to Afghanistan to replace less effective heavy armored vehicles and tanks.
- 15 July 1980: Fifty to sixty Afghan villages are demolished by Soviet jets, helicopter gunships, and armored vehicles in retaliatory raids against guerrilla ambushes. Observers suggest that an increased Soviet emphasis on air actions against pro-guerrilla villages is in evidence.
- 28 July 1980: Twenty-eight helicopter gunships and fighters head southwest from Kabul toward Ghazni to put down a revolt by the mutinous 14th Division of the DRA Army. Observers link the heavy use of Soviet gunship activity in and out of Kabul to increasing numbers of rebellions in the Afghan army.
- 3 August 1980: The active strength of the DRA Army may be as low as 30,000 men. The government announces a new call-up and drafts teachers. New officer courses are established with only three months of training (versus five years before the start of the war).
- 6 September 1980: A new penal law establishes penalties of four years for failing to respond to a call-up, six years for faking an illness to avoid the draft, and two to six years for being AWOL.
- Mid-September 1980: The Soviets' Panjshir 1 offensive is complete. The Mujahideen claim to have shot down ten helicopters. New Mujahideen attacks on Herat and Kandahar are reported.
- 16 September 1980: DRA government attempts to strengthen its local militias and revolution defense groups. The government makes more active efforts to buy the loyalty of local tribes and militias.
- Late 1980: The USSR divides Afghanistan into seven zones. Each is placed under a Soviet military officer and DRA political commissar. Soviet political and military tactics are adapted to the particular needs of each zone. Soviet and government forces increase the destruction of homes and villages and the removal of livestock in hostile areas.

Karmal vastly expands the role of the KHAD. East Germans

now play a major advisory role. Assadullah Sawari, the ex-head of the AGSA, is sent in exile as an ambassador.

- 16 October–4 November 1980: Karmal travels to Moscow for consultations and medical treatment.
- Late October 1980: USSR retaliates against Mujahideen raids by launching Panjshir 2 offensive.
- November–mid-December: More Mujahideen raids lead to a major Soviet offensive in the Logar area south of Kabul. Soviet heliborne air assault troops begin to make more effective use of cordon and search tactics. Air assault forces use the BMD armored vehicle successfully.
- January 1981: Heavy fighting in Logar, Kunar, and Panjshir. Soviets launch the Panjshir 3 campaign.
- 8 January 1981: New DRA conscription law goes into effect. Draft age is lowered from 21 to 20, and service time is extended six months.
- 14 January 1981: DRA begins to organize youth brigades.
- 22 January 1981: According to Pakistani sources, some guerrilla groups are getting relatively sophisticated weapons, such as rocket-propelled grenades and 12.9-mm machine guns. Only a very few have acquired or utilized shoulder-fired anti-aircraft rockets.
- Early 1981: The Wakhan corridor is occupied by the USSR.
- February–May 1981: Fighting is reported in Kandahar. Sporadic Mujahideen raids lead to constant low-level conflicts, although rumors of major battles are untrue. Similar sporadic fighting is occurring in Herat.
- March 1981: UN estimates that there are now 1,700,000 Afghan refugees in Pakistan and 400,000 in Iran.
- 10 April 1981: A new recruitment law is established to improve recruiting for the Sarandoy and other Ministry of Interior forces. The Sarandoy are reorganized and given a much stronger role in urban security. The Sarandoy's provincial forces are organized to provide operational battalions for convoy protection. (Eight of these formations exist by the end of 1981 in Balkh, Fariab, Farah, Helmand, Parwan, Takhar, Zabul, and Herat provinces.)[49]
- 13 April 1981: Mujahideen spokesmen claim that the Soviet helicopter gunship is the main Soviet military advantage against them.
- 14 April 1981: Mujahideen assassinate deputy head of KHAD in Kabul. This is part of a broad pattern of assassinations in April. Kabul's internal security remains poor.

Major improvements take place in the internal security of

Kabul. A Kabul security command is established with twelve fortified posts or security wards in the city. The 1st and 2nd Standby Regiments are organized as mobile internal security strike forces. Similar security commands are set up in other cites.

- Late April 1981: Growing splits exist between the moderate and fundamentalist Mujahideen groups.
- June 1981: Mass Soviet artillery fire and air strikes destroy much of Kandahar. More infighting in PDPA gradually leads to ouster of Brigadier Mohammed Rafi as Minister of Defense and de facto replacement by Major General Abdul Qadar.
- 9 June 1981: Guerrillas attack Soviet air base at Bagram and cause large-scale fires in ammunition and gasoline stores.
- 15 June 1981: Government holds Congress of "National Fatherland Front," headed by a Khalqi leader, in an attempt to co-opt other political groups to support the DRA. It has little impact in attracting groups from outside the PDPA.
- 20 June 1981: Government attempts new land reform program with little success.
- July 1981: 7th DRA Division is relocated from Kabul to Moqor, possibly to improve internal security of the capital.

July 1981–Early 1982: Continued Restructuring of Soviet Forces and DRA Internal Security Forces

The Soviets steadily improved their use of combined operations by independent brigades and regiments. They used combined arms task forces of Soviet and DRA troops supported by Soviet and DRA air units. The offensives became increasingly punitive. They generally began with a major air attack on target areas, often including villages known to be supporting Mujahideen forces. Heliborne assault forces were then landed to halt Mujahideen withdrawals and to attack from directions that achieved tactical surprise. Mechanized forces attacked into the areas supporting the guerrillas and often destroyed homes and crops, attempting to force the Mujahideen to retreat into the areas held by the helicopter assault forces:

- 4 July 1981: Soviets from 108th MRD attack Mujahideen bases in Sarobi Valley to protect the Kabul-Jalalabad road. Much improved use of air strikes and helicopter landings gives the Soviets unusual effectiveness.
- Mid-July–August 1981: More Mujahideen raids in Panjshir Valley lead to the Panjshir 4 campaign by Soviets, which makes more effective use of combined operations. It has some success but cannot keep the Mujahideen from successfully withdrawing.

Soviets attempt a major air assault on Mujahideen forces in the Marmoul Gorge near Mazar-i-Shariff. Soviet and DRA fighters spend a week launching air attacks, and then a battalion is landed by helicopter in the plain above the gorge. The battalion cannot fight its way down into the gorge and is withdrawn.

Soviet/DRA combined operations in the Panjshir and Farah and around Herat are more successful. Overall tempo of operations is low. Mujahideen operate relatively freely in Kandahar.

- 5–15 September 1980: Bitter but inconclusive fighting occurs in Farah province.
- 30 September 1981: Guerrillas in Panjshir claim to have a small number of anti-aircraft guns, forcing Soviet MiGs and gunships to enter Panjshir at high altitude.
- Early to mid-October 1981: Soviet and Sarandoy forces conduct some successful sweeps in the area around Herat.
- October 1981: DRA launches a recruiting drive in tribal areas; it has only limited success.
- Late 1981: Soviets launch air attacks into Pakistan on 4 and 22 October, 16 November, and 22 December in an effort to intimidate the Pakistani government into not supporting the Mujahideen. Soviets make massive use of air-dropped PRM-1 "butterfly" or "green parrot" mines to attempt to make Mujahideen supply routes unsafe. Colonel General Mayorov is replaced as senior Soviet advisor by Army General M. Sorokin.
- Late 1981: A new border guards force is organized under the Ministry of the Interior with five brigades. These brigades are located at Jalalabad, Khost, Kunduz, Nimroz, and Herat.
- Early December 1981: DRA Army forces fight with Soviet troops in major combined operations attacks in Nangrahar province. The DRA units have limited effectiveness.

Early to Mid-1982: Improved Weapons for Afghan
Freedom Fighters and Continued Soviet Offensives

By this time, the Soviets had a major "permanent" force in Afghanistan. The 40th Army headquarters remained in Kabul with the 103rd Guards Air Assault Division and the 108th Motorized Rifle Division. Bagram was a major Soviet air base and was the location of the 345th Air Assault Regiment and the 181st Motorized Rifle Regiment. Other forces were well deployed throughout the country. In the north, there was an air unit at Mazar-i-Shariff, along with the 187th Motorized Rifle Regiment. The 201st Motorized Rifle Division was at Kunduz, and the 866th Independent Motorized Rifle Division was at Faizabad. In the east, the 66th Motorized Rifle Brigade was at Jalalabad. The 191st Independent Motorized Rifle Regiment was south of Kabul at Ghazni. The 70th Motorized Rifle Brigade was in the south at Kandahar. There was an air unit in the east at Shindand, along with the 5th Guards Motorized Rifle Division.

The DRA was making slow progress in rebuilding the army but had expanded the KHAD to as many as 18,000 men with 182 zones of operations. According to one source, the KHAD had 312 Soviet advisors at this time. The KHAD steadily expanded its network of informers among the Mujahideen, tribes and villages, and refugee groups and provided the Soviets and DRA with information for many of their operations. This steadily expanded the power of Najibullah, the head of the KHAD, who also increasingly became involved with negotiating with the tribes. The KHAD was, however, solidly identified with the Parcham faction. Its efforts to enforce PDPA control over the regular armed forces met with considerable resistance, and it became a major rival of the Sarandoy. The KHAD also continued to have at least some internal security problems of its own.[50]

The U.S., Saudi Arabia, Egypt, and other Western and moderate Arab states stepped up their aid to the Mujahideen. Iran also provided aid to the Shi'ite Islamic fundamentalist groups in the west. The Soviets responded by increasing their forces, continuing major sweeps, and stepping up air attacks on the population. Division-sized Soviet sweeps occurred, one in the Panjshir and one in Herat. The Soviets continued to attempt to rebuild the DRA Army:

- January 1982: Western-made weapons, including American-made plastic anti-tank mines, appear in significant numbers in guerrilla forces for the first time. However, the guerrillas still lack heavy weapons, in particular effective anti-helicopter missiles.
- January–February 1982: Heavy fighting occurs in Herat. The Mujahideen make excellent use of tunnels and pick-up trucks to achieve protection and mobility in the relatively open area. The DRA forces lack the strength to be effective, but some 12,000 Soviet troops are deployed, with an MRD, elements of another MRD, two fighter squadrons, and a helicopter squadron. Repeated Soviet drives eventually inflict major casualties on the Mujahideen, and their activity level drops sharply, although the resistance retains many of its forces.
- January 1982: Sarandoy forces conduct ruthless sweeps for draft dodgers in all major cities. The DRA Army remains very weak, but elements of the 7th Division, 8th Division, 37th Commando Brigade, 38th Commando Brigade, and two armored regiments

in the Kabul area are capable of some degree of combat operations.

- 4 January 1982: Major-General Abdul Qadar becomes the acting Minister of Defense of the DRA.
- February 1982: The Soviets put LU-23 anti-aircraft guns in armored mounts on the back of LIL-135 trucks and use them as convoy escorts.
- Early 1982: Soviet forces increase to 105,000 men.
- February 1982: The Mujahideen begin to make frequent use of SA-7 surface-to-air missiles. Fighting occurs in Kandahar City.
- February 1982: Diego Cordovez of Ecuador is appointed personal representative of the new UN Secretary General Perez de Cuellar. He visits Kabul, Islamabad, and Tehran in April 1982 in the first round of what turn out to be six years of peace talks.
- March 1982: Soviet troops continue "beat the tiger" tactics of encirclement by troops and combined arms attacks on guerrilla villages. A typical attack on Paghman uses MiGs, helicopter gunships, 200 tanks, and multiple rocket launchers. Artillery and mass bombing attacks hit Kandahar and Herat. Thirty-mm AGS-17 automatic grenade launchers replace the 73-mm 2A20 cannon and Sagger ATGM launcher on some BMD airborne infantry combat vehicles.
- Late March 1982: The DRA 11th Division resumes active operations, signalling some improvement in the DRA Army.
- April 1982: DRA and Mujahideen forces fight in Baghlan and Kunduz areas. Soviets prepare for a massive division-sized operation against Massoud's Mujahideen forces in the Panjshir Valley.
- 25 April 1982: Mujahideen forces penetrate into Bagram Air Base and destroy twenty-three aircraft in one of the most successful raids of the war.
- May 1982: Soviet forces deliberately cross into Iran. The Iranians restrict Mujahideen operations and may be turning some Mujahideen over to the Soviets.
- 10–17 May 1982: Panjshir 5 offensive is the largest Soviet effort to date. Nearly 15,000 men are used, including 11,000 Soviets. DRA forces seal off the neck of the Panjshir Valley. Soviet fighters, including Su-17s, MiG-21s, and the new Su-25s launch massive air strikes against predesignated targets spotted by converted AN-12s. The bombing occurs only in the daylight, allowing the people and Mujahideen to operate at night. On 17 May, the bombing stops and heliborne landings by elements of the 103rd Air Assault Division start, concentrated around the center of the

Valley. A mechanized column then moves up the valley. T-62s—some equipped with bulldozers—slowly fight their way up the valley, supported by BTR-60Ps and Mi-24s. Another mechanized regiment attacks from the other end of the valley. The floor of the valley is under DRA control for the first time since 1978, and the Mujahideen lose roughly 1,000 dead to 300–400 for the Soviets. The DRA militia is then deployed into the valley, but it rapidly becomes apparent that most of the Mujahideen have simply withdrawn to the high ground. The DRA forces are soon forced to withdraw from the center of the valley.

- June 1982: DRA, Pakistan, and USSR begin peace talks in Geneva. Iran refuses to attend but asks to be kept informed.
- July 1982: PDPA attempts to create a party commissar system in the army and to strengthen political control.
- Mid-1982: The Soviets continue to intensify the use of air attacks, but guerrilla units inevitably return in force.

Mid-1982 to Late 1983:
Soviet Efforts to Control the Countryside

The Soviets steadily strengthened the defense of cities and bases, building bunkers and defensive rings and making extensive use of mines. They increased the number of guard posts along key lines of communications. Weapons were increasingly modified to deliver high rates of fire at very sharp angles of fire to improve their lethality in mountain combat. Convoy protection became more professional, and better use was made of helicopters and truck- or OAFV-mounted AA guns to provide protection. Some 200 Mil-6 and Mil-8 helicopters provided airlift.

Soviet offensive operations emphasized air power, and the USSR halted division-sized operations. The Soviets deployed significant numbers of new Su-25 attack aircraft and made extensive use of cluster bombs and retarded bombs with special fusing to ensure they could be used effectively in low-altitude attacks. The Soviets steadily increased their attack helicopter strength, used heliborne assault forces to provide new mobility, and used heavy bombers to try to suppress the population. There were few major offensives, but raids became deeper, and improved intelligence was used to pinpoint objectives. Far more use was made of helicopter firepower as a substitute for close-air support and artillery.

Scorched-earth tactics were increasingly used as a substitute for extensive and sustained Soviet military action in the field. These tactics improved the range of Soviet attacks against the Mujahideen and Soviet ability to strike at Mujahideen supply lines, but they had serious limitations. Soviet ground troops rarely tried to secure rural areas or to occupy the points they seized. The USSR won most military encounters in the field, but DRA forces usually could not fight unsupported, and Soviet victory did not mean significant long-term weakening of the Mujahideen.

The Mujahideen continued to improve their equipment and made some improvements in training. Press reports indicated that the CIA was providing roughly $30 to $50 million per year, and Saudi Arabia was also providing major funding. Some elements of the Mujahideen established training camps, and weapons like the SA-7, 82-mm mortar, 82-mm recoilless rifle, mines, 23-mm twin AA guns, and 12.7-mm and 14.5-mm anti-aircraft machine guns appeared in large numbers. The Mujahideen captured and used a few tanks, some BTR-60Ps, and medium artillery weapons. The Mujahideen remained divided, however, and often clashed:

- Mid-1982: Soviet conscripts begin to appear who have had special training for Afghanistan at camps in the Turkestan military district. Soviets no longer rely on training conscripts in units. The 54th MRD in Termez is also used to prepare troops. Infantrymen, bomb and mine disposal personnel, drivers, and gunners have up to 5 or 6 months of training. Training includes night and village warfare.
- Mid–late 1982: Several new weapons developments take place in Soviet forces. Rearward firing 7.62-mm machine guns are added to Soviet attack helicopters to shoot guerrillas who stand and fire in the wake of a gunship attack. The new family of AK-74 5.45-mm caliber small arms is in wide use by Soviet troops with a new and more lethal round, or "poison bullet" as the guerrillas refer to it.
- August–September 1982: The Soviets carry out the Panjshir 6 offensive. This is largely a repetition of Panjshir 5, with more extensive use of the Su-25 and a much faster tempo of operations. Once again, the Soviet forces are able to meet in the valley. This time, however, they carry out small follow-on pursuit attacks on the Mujahideen positions in the heights and tributary valleys. Each attack up the smaller valleys is preceded by the insertion of heliborne forces to block any retreat. In the interim, Soviet and DRA forces ruthlessly destroy homes, irrigation systems, and crops, thereby creating a large new wave of refugees. The Mujahideen forces under Massoud largely survive, but they have lost most of their infrastructure and 1,000–1,700 dead.

Other Soviet attacks take place in the Paghman hills near Kabul and the Marmoul Gorge area.

- 10 September 1982: 105 civilians hiding in an underground tunnel are reported killed when Soviet forces fill the tunnel with petrol and light it.
- Fall 1982: Soviets reportedly continue to use nerve agents, allegedly including SARIN and SOMAN and tricothecene toxin or yellow rain-using bombs and aerosol sprays. Chemical strikes are reported to cause 3,042 deaths. U.S. State Department estimates the number of chemical attacks at a minimum of 47.
- Fall 1982: A new heliborne military unit, the Soviet Air Assault Brigade, is being utilized, comprised of three battalions of paratroopers. This unit forms the cutting edge of many Soviet offensives.
- 10 November 1982: Brezhnev dies, and Yuri Andropov takes power. He tells President Zia of Pakistan that the USSR wants to leave Afghanistan.
- December 1982: The number of Afghan refugees in Pakistan reaches two million.
- Late 1982: The Mujahideen forces in the Pakistani border area are increasing sharply, drawing on the refugee camps and foreign arms for their expansion. Mujahideen forces now virtually besiege the DRA garrison at Khost.
- January-February 1983: A major struggle takes place to improve the security in and around Kabul. The Soviet-DRA effort seems to have some success. The Mujahideen find it steadily more difficult to operate freely in the city but manage to continue some rocket attacks and bombings.
- January 1983: Massoud agrees to a cease-fire in the Panjshir, evidently in an effort to rebuild his forces. The cease-fire allows the USSR to secure the Salang Pass road and to shift forces to operate against the Mujahideen in the Shomali area and other Mujahideen units near Kabul.
- 23 January 1983: British sources estimate that there are from 500 to 650 helicopters deployed in Afghanistan, including 200 Mi-24 Hinds.
- Early 1983: Convoy accident in Salang Tunnel causes major Soviet casualties.

  Cordovez shuttles between Tehran, Kabul, and Islamabad from 21 January to 7 February in search of a peace agreement. Obtains Soviet agreement in March to a new round of talks at Geneva.
- February 1983: Key resistance leader Massoud agrees to a truce with the USSR in the Panjshir.

- Mid-April 1984: The key initial Soviet operation in 1984 is an assault on the Panjshir Valley, the stronghold of the resistance forces of Massoud. The operation, which ends the sixteen-month truce, is a response to Massoud's increasing ability to cut important Soviet lines of communication, putting the Soviet's control of Kabul at risk.

  The Soviets launch the Panjshir 7 campaign with Tu-16 Badgers based in the Turkestan military district. This attack on the Panjshir Valley seems to have been the first major high-altitude bombing conducted by Badger bombers staging from bases in the southern USSR. Soviet motorized infantry advance up the valley, and air assault troops are helicoptered behind the resistance in an effort to cut off retreat. During this operation, Soviet forces carry out widespread assaults on villages and attacks on the civil population. The Soviets adopt a new tactic of forcing Afghans to leave their homes in order to end popular support of and assistance to the resistance forces.

  Soviet forces are deployed from the 66th Motorized Rifle Brigade and the 180th and 191st motorized rifle regiments, supported by DRA forces and Sarandoy. Massoud attempts preemptive raids of Soviet supply units but has only limited success. The Soviets use mechanized forces and heliborne assaults and attempt to block the tributary valleys to prevent Massoud's forces from escaping. The Soviet forces have a much faster tempo of operations than in the past. Elite forces of 500 to 1,500 Soviet and DRA troops use heliborne lift to surround entire villages. Soviet troops from the air assault forces (VDV) lead many of the key efforts.

  Both sides take relatively heavy casualties, but the Soviets secure the valley area. Rather than withdraw, they begin to build forts and strong points. They withdraw from the smaller valleys, but the Mujahideen are now forced to fight in the Panjshir Valley rather than the Salang Valley.
- April 1984: Diego Cordovez makes a new UN peace shuttle.
- June 1984: The Panjshir Valley campaign is followed by Soviet assaults on resistance forces in Herat in western Afghanistan, and a series of major operations in eastern Afghanistan are designed to cut insurgent supply routes. These actions increase casualties on both sides. The Soviet press acknowledges the likelihood of a prolonged and difficult conflict.
- June 1984: Soviet forces attack Mujahideen positions in the Logar with little success.
- 25–29 June 1984: Soviet and DRA forces conduct major sweeps

through the Koh-e-Safi plain east of Kabul as part of the broad effort to secure the region around the city. The militia and Sarandoy forces in the Kabul area are steadily expanded. The Mujahideen retaliate with more bombing and rocket attacks.

- Spring–Summer 1984: The USSR starts major Soviet operations in the field. Major air attacks destroy hostile villages and are followed by attack helicopter sweeps and major search-and-destroy troop sweeps which include heliborne BMD deployments. Soviet heliborne assault units more frequently take hills first to deny the Mujahideen good fire positions. The units also try to cut off key escape routes. Soviet forces launch offensive sweeps in attempts to secure Kunar Valley and Pakistan border area. Soviets use fuel air explosives and new burning agents.

  Food prices in Afghanistan have risen 145 percent since the Soviet invasion.

  The effectiveness of the Afghan resistance slowly improves, in spite of the fact that the 1984 military campaign is the largest and most aggressive Soviet offensive to date.

- July 1984: The USSR's actions in Afghanistan have resulted in a steady deterioration of Soviet relations with the government of Pakistan, which has been faced with accommodating 3,000,000 Afghan refugees. The Soviets present Pakistan with a demarche protesting Pakistan's aid to the Afghan resistance and cancel a scheduled meeting between foreign ministers.

- Mid-1984: U.S. sources indicate the total number of Soviet fixed wing combat aircraft rise to nearly 500 versus 430 in 1983, 375 in 1982, 300 in 1981, and about 175 in late 1979. A total of 150 Mi-8, 150 Mi-24, and some Mi-17 combat helicopters are deployed, bringing the totals to about 450 versus 375 in 1983, 325 in 1982, 275 in 1981, and 60 to 90 in 1980.

- August 1984: Afghan aircraft and artillery begin to conduct more frequent cross-border strikes against villages in Pakistani territory; these strikes will continue on through 1985. In view of the total Soviet control of the Afghan armed forces, such an escalation would be highly unlikely without direct Soviet authorization.

- Mid-1984: The fighting has now driven some 1,400,000 additional Afghans to flee to Iran and Pakistan, and at least 1,200,000 more have sought sanctuary in the relatively "secure" Soviet-held territories. There are estimated to be 3,500,000 Afghan refugees in Pakistan and 1,500,000 in Iran.

- August 1984: Soviet and DRA forces conduct the largest offensive in the Paktia area to date and relieve DRA garrison at Jaji. The

Soviet forces in Afghanistan are heavily committed, and forces are flown in from the 104th Guards Air Assault Division in the USSR to supplement them. The Mujahideen forces are temporarily forced back, but there are no lasting gains. Soviet forces relieve Qala in the Hazara Mountains after heavy fighting.

- 24–30 August 1984: The third round of Geneva peace talks takes place following the major Soviet offensive in Panjshir Valley and Pakistan's complaints of extensive Soviet and DRA air violations across its borders. The talks make little apparent progress.
- September 1984: The Mujahideen counter the improved security around Kabul and some other cities by introducing large-scale attacks using single PRC-made 107-mm rockets launched from crude launch rails. These rockets provide eight kilometers of range. The rebels also use limited numbers of PRC-made 122-mm rockets, captured BM-21 40 x 122-mm multiple rocket launchers, and 12-barrel PRC-made Type 63 107-mm rocket launchers.

    The Soviets respond by deploying additional BM-21 battalions. They attempt to suppress the Mujahideen with heavy artillery fire and seek to find targeting devices that can allow an immediate response to Mujahideen firings. In most cases, however, the Mujahideen simply leave the area or dig in before the Soviets can respond.
- 8 September 1984: The Panjshir 8 campaign begins. New heavy bombing by Tu-16s and selective heliborne raids by elite Soviet forces cause considerable Mujahideen casualties.
- Fall 1984: More Soviet troops enter Afghanistan, including Spetsnaz. Incursions into Pakistan reach the level of thirty-eight to fifty air flights and eight to twenty ground movements during the last four months of 1984. Refugee camps in Pakistan are hit, and the USSR starts to routinely patrol within 32 kilometers of the border.
- 28 October 1984: Soviet An-22 is shot down by rebel SA-7.
- 18–19 November 1984: Soviets launch a major operation in Paktia using up to five squadrons of Mil-6 helicopters. These are used to support sweeps through the plains in Khost, but the major guerrilla bases in the border area are not attacked.
- Fall–Winter 1984: Refugee columns are routinely attacked by air for the first time. Soviets destroy food supplies, small farms, and hamlets.
- Winter 1984: Soviet air attacks and heliborne sweeps continue as the USSR attempts to deprive the Mujahideen of a winter sanctuary.

- December 1984: The Soviets launch a major campaign in the Kunar Valley. Up to 8,000 Soviet and 6,000 DRA troops are involved. The Mujahideen retreat from their positions attacking the garrisons at Asmar and Barikot, but they return when Soviet and DRA forces withdraw.

Late 1984–December 1985: Soviet Attempts
to Seize Border Areas and Cut Off Mujahideen Supplies

The USSR continued much the same tactics on the ground and in the air, but it expanded the area of operations. Beginning in late 1984 and early 1985, the Soviets were far more aggressive in attacking Mujahideen forces in areas which once were virtual sanctuaries. To maintain control of the countryside and border areas, the Soviet and DRA forces attempted to create strings of forts and strong points rather than just conduct sweeps and maintain existing strong points.

The key cities were regarded as relatively secure, although Mujahideen rocket attacks continued and infiltrators occasionally hit key targets like Kabul airport. Major Soviet offensives tried to seal off the flow of supplies from Pakistan and Iran, and Soviet forces began to attack guerrilla bases and strongholds near the Pakistani border and in the Hazarajat. The Mujahideen suffered, but they began to create their own rear-area facilities and agriculture to replace dependence on the people. Mujahideen training continued to improve. Western and Arab arms flows increased:

- November 1984–January 1985: Soviets deploy 10,000 fresh troops along Afghanistan's borders with Iran and Pakistan. Airborne units lifted by Mi-6 helicopters attack rebel strongholds in the Tor Ghar mountain region of Paktia while 3,000 other troops move to the Iranian border area in Herat province. They manage to temporarily secure the Alingar and Alisheng routes, but not the Barikot route, to the Panjshir.
- January–February 1985: More Soviet troops move to the area near Rabat in Nimruz province as they try to reduce Mujahideen supplies from the southwest. Troops in Paktia on the Pakistani border are reinforced. Mujahideen raids on Bagram and Kandahar air bases destroy five to fifteen aircraft.
- March–May 1985: A United Nations report by Professor Felix Ermacora estimates that 50,000 Afghanis are held as political prisoners by the Soviets and DRA. The report documents Soviet attacks on three Afghan villages which kill 505 civilians. In their effort to seal off Pakistan, the Soviets commit 83 violations

of Pakistan's airspace in the first five months of 1985 (versus 88 in all of 1984).

- April 1985: President Reagan signs a national security decision directive (NSDD) ordering U.S. departments and agencies to use "all means available" to force the USSR to leave Afghanistan.[51]
- Early April 1985: Soviets attempt to clear the Maidan Valley west of Kabul. They make extensive use of Mil-24s and Su-25s. FROG-7 rockets are used for the first time with submunition warheads. BM-27 multiple rocket launchers are used in battery strength.
- 12 April 1985: The Mujahideen launch a major rocket attack on Kabul.
- 27 April 1985: Mujahideen mortar raid on Charikar, near Bagram.
- Late April 1985: DRA calls a Loyah Jirgah (great assembly) of leaders from rural areas, and attempts to persuade them to support local elections and a broader PDPA-led front. The KHAD acts as a major coordinating group in this effort.
- Spring 1985: Massoud's forces resume attacks on Salang convoys with considerable success.
- May 1985: DRA steadily builds up forces near border areas, deploying additional tanks and artillery. The number of border brigades has doubled since 1983.
- 19–28 May 1985: Soviets and DRA launch major offensives to secure the Kunar Valley and northern approaches to Jalalabad. Soviets make extensive use of heliborne air assault forces. DRA forces drive up the valley by land. The Soviet/DRA forces relieve the garrison at Barikot and drive Mujahideen forces out of the area temporarily.
- 25–31 May 1985: Cordovez makes another UN peace shuttle. Some progress is made on peace agreement by USSR and Pakistan.
- June 1985: Soviets launch massive air and helicopter attacks, using up to 10,000 troops, on villages and Mujahideen strong points in Kunar Valley in an attempt to cut off the Mujahideen from Pakistan. Another Soviet drive occurs in Paktia, and another penetrates deeply into the Hazarajat, Paghman, and Koh-e-Safi. The Soviets use paratroops to control the hills and make extensive use of napalm to clear strong points, villages, and brush. There are more cross-border raids, killing Afghans in Pakistan. A Soviet drive relieves an eleven-month rebel siege of Barikot in upper Kunar Valley. Soviet commandos are increasingly used to try to ambush Mujahideen supply lines elsewhere. An Afghan counter-ambush kills over fifty Soviet paratroops in upper Panjshir. Soviet helicopter sweeps increase from six to eight

helicopters per attack to as many as twenty. The Mujahideen increasingly move by night and disperse during the day.

Fourth round of peace talks takes place at Geneva, resulting in a deadlock on major points. There is some agreement between the West and the USSR on nonintervention and noninterference after Soviet withdrawal.

The Mujahideen groups with bases in Pakistan attempt to unify under the title of the Islamic Unity of Afghan Mujahideen. Iran becomes more active in attempting to create a unified pro-Khomeini group of Shi'ite Mujahideen movements in the west.

- 12 June 1985: Up to twenty aircraft are destroyed in an attack on Shindand air base. This seems to be sabotage, and KHAD executes DRA Air Force officers on the base.
- 15 June 1985: Mujahideen forces launch an exceptionally well coordinated attack on Pechgur base in the Panjshir, by penetrating minefields at night and storming the fort. It is the first time the Mujahideen take a major fort defended by minefields, artillery, and tanks.
- July 1985: Soviet and DRA forces launch Panjshir 9 as retaliation for the fall of Peshghowr. They retake Peshghowr, which the Mujahideen do not defend. Bombing raids and heliborne assaults have little punitive effect.
- July 1985: Rebel rocket attacks continue on Kabul. The Soviets normally fail to secure the countryside after their major sweeps against the Mujahideen in the mountains and rural areas. Two Afghan Mi-24 crews take helicopters to Pakistan. Afghan rebels counterattack in Panjshir. Up to 400 Afghan government troops are killed in an effort to recapture the Peshghowr military post.

  Rebels now widely cache arms in hiding posts, leave areas during Soviet sweeps, and then return later. Soviets provide increasing television coverage of war and seem to be trying to popularize war for first time. Soviet embassy in Kabul is hit with rockets.

  Mujahideen siege of Khost continues, but, although the Mujahideen have up to 7,000 men and multiple rocket launchers, they cannot take a heavily defended town.
- July 1985: Najibullah uses growing power over internal security to purge Sarandoy. Many remaining Khalqis are removed. The role of the KHAD is steadily expanded.
- 3 July 1985: Mujahideen successfully launch a serious raid on Herat.
- 25 July 1985: Soviets expand the responsibility of the Southern

TVD in commanding the operations in Afghanistan. Army General Mikhail Zaytsev replaces General Yuri Maksimov as commander. The Turkestan military district is now a major theater of operations.

- August 1985: Soviets launch a new offensive to break the Mujahideen siege of Khost in the southwest and succeed only in temporarily controlling the roads—a repetition of the outcome of a similar effort in 1984.
- 22 August–mid-September 1985: The Soviets and DRA launch a major offensive with 15,000 to 20,000 men to expand their positions in the Pakistani border area. A mechanized column drives up the Logar Valley, another force moves up through the mountains from Jalalabad, and a third forces moves into the area from Khost. The Soviet forces involve the 103rd Air Assault Division, a motorized rifle brigade, and a motorized rifle regiment. Heliborne assault forces land at nine different points in the Logar to block Mujahideen retreats. Some 100 Mujahideen are killed, but Soviet and DRA forces lose roughly 50–60 men. Soviets eventually seize a large supply dump near Hessarak but fail to take the major Mujahideen base at Zhawar, south of Khost. This leads the Mujahideen to feel the Soviets cannot take well-defended fixed bases.
- 21–26 August 1985: The fifth round of UN peace talks at Geneva collapse after DRA government attempts to insist on direct talks with Pakistan—which would imply the DRA is a legitimate government.
- September 1985: Soviets continue their effort to control the border areas. Soviet and Afghan government troops move into Azra Valley and Haji region of Paktia. Mujahideen take serious casualties, but so do Afghan government forces. Soviets increase the number of modern attack aircraft in the country. Soviets fail to relieve Khost after heavy Soviet and government casualties.
- September 1985: Another tribal Loyah Jirgah takes place in Kabul under the leadership of Najibullah. There are some indications of growing rivalry between refugee and Mujahideen groups and those that had stayed behind. DRA and PDPA seem to have some success in winning local loyalties.
- 3 September 1985: Afghan Airlines passenger aircraft is shot down, and more than 50 are killed. Kabul claims U.S.-made Stinger missiles were used in attack.
- October 1985: A new Soviet offensive occurs in Logar province as the USSR moves forces from Paktia and Wardak provinces and Kabul to the north. The third major Soviet offensive of the year

fails to secure territory or break up major rebel units. Soviet convoys are still being ambushed on Salang highway. The U.S. approves $200 million in extra aid to the Mujahideen in addition to $250 to $280 million already approved. Soviets again increase television coverage of war.

- October 1985: Soviets launch a series of air attacks at carefully selected targets designed to hit towns and hamlets friendly to the Mujahideen during the most critical phase of the wheat harvest.
- 3 October 1985: Further purges of Sarandoy leaders in Logar province take place. Najibullah continues to expand power.
- November 1985: Arms flow to rebels continues. The main impact of the Soviet offensives is to increase the number of refugees. Many arms movements continue by truck. U.S. covert aid to the Mujahideen since 1979 is reported to have reached $385 million. Saudi aid is said to be over $300 million and includes 300 anti-tank rocket launchers, 1,000 light anti-tank rockets, 10,000 machine guns, heavy guns and mortars (purchased from the PRC), and 20,000 boxes of ammunition. The PRC is reported to have 300 advisors working in Pakistan.
- November 1985: Bombings and helicopter raids continue. There are increasing reports of Soviet drug use and fights between ethnic Russian and central Asian troops (the latter have been returned to Afghanistan for the first time since early in the invasion). Gorbachev sends out feelers hinting at settlement. Soviet Spetsnaz forces are reported to have doubled since early in the year.
- 13 November 1985: UN votes 122–19 to demand withdrawal of foreign troops from Afghanistan. United Nations votes in favor of Soviet withdrawal from Afghanistan have increased from 111 in 1980 to 122 in 1985.
- December 1985: The war enters its seventh year. Soviet and rebel clashes continue. U.S. State Department estimates 33 to 50 percent of Afghan population of 13 million is dead, wounded, displaced, or in exile. Estimates of Afghan dead range up to one million, with four million refugees and many malnourished. More Gorbachev "peace" feelers are extended. Babrak Karmal calls for "national compromise," and appoints a non-party member prime minister and fourteen other non-communists to government. The Mujahideen again attempt to improve their unity. The Mujahideen are still able to move arms through Paktia and Nangarhar provinces. The fighting continues around Kabul and the surrounding provinces. The Mujahideen control most of the central Hazarajat region, and the Soviets are strongest in the north-central region from Sheberghan to Kunduz near the border.

Depopulation and the lack of food supply, rather than Soviet military action, remain the key problems affecting the Mujahideen, although the Soviets are more effectively using border posts to restrict supply through the Kunduz valley.

- 10–13 December 1985: U.S. agrees in principle to act as guarantor of UN peace agreement on Soviet withdrawal. Some agreement evidently is reached that the U.S. will halt aid to the Mujahideen if the Soviets withdraw.
- 16–19 December 1985: Sixth round of peace talks takes place in Geneva. There is an impasse over DRA insistence on direct negotiations with Pakistan.

1986–1987: Soviet Political Tactics and World Opinion

In 1986, the Soviets brought a new and more ruthless Afghan leader to power and made the Afghan government even more of a puppet state. Soviet political and military pressure on Pakistan increased, and the Soviets used peace initiatives and troop withdrawals to try to defuse outside hostility and to put still further pressure on Pakistan.

At the same time, the Soviets continued to attack the Afghan people as well as the Mujahideen. Soviet special forces and heliborne assaults continued to strike at civilian targets as well as resistance forces. The USSR continued its use of mass air and artillery strikes to conduct "scorched earth" attacks. More and more populated areas outside direct government control were mined, and the use of gas warfare continued.

In spite of steadily improving Soviet forces, equipment, and tactics, the war continued. Soviet troop strength was 45 percent higher than in 1982. Soviet deaths were estimated at 10,000 to 15,000 since 1979, and air losses were reported at 500 helicopters and aircraft.

Soviet troops suffered from morale and drug problems, even in elite units, but the USSR was able to limit the cost of the war by using Afghan troops in high-risk roles. It increasingly was able to buy partial support from tribal leaders in the north and create local militias. The USSR was able to recoup much of the $3 billion annual cost of the war and the $800 million in economic aid it has provided since 1979. About 85 percent of all military and economic aid was in the form of loans, and the USSR was making extensive use of Afghan gas and copper.

The Soviet and Afghan government security forces made increasing use of "carrot and stick" techniques such as bribery and subversion. They used these techniques to target Mujahideen forces for sudden Spetsnaz raids and to deprive them of their popular support and cut off their flow of medical services and supplies. Nearly 12,000 KGB and

NVD "advisors" were reported to be working with the KHAD (WAD), but they were forced to take an increasingly direct role in management and field operations.

Efforts to restructure the Afghan government and rebuild the Afghan forces had had only mixed success. Problems with the loyalty of the Air Force continued to surface. Najibullah's victory over Karmal did not make the Afghan government more popular, and the Afghan government seemed to remain divided into Najibullah and Karmal factions—raising the specter of another Parcham-versus-Khalq–like schism. The creation of a 50,000-strong youth corps and the training of 10,000 Afghans annually in the USSR did not seem to be creating reliable cadres.

Soviet attacks on the population—and increasing use of elite forces, helicopters, and air support—weakened the Mujahideen but could not defeat them. Some 30 to 50 percent of the total population was by now displaced or living as refugees outside Afghanistan. Food supplies were an increasing problem, as were paid spies within the Mujahideen. The USSR had effective security zones only around Kabul, Jalalabad, and Mazar-i-Shariff. Even these areas were the scenes of many low-level attacks, as were key economic areas of interest to the Soviets like the Ainak copper mines.

The Soviet forces and Afghan government spent much of the year concentrating on a mix of carefully targeted attacks, bribes, and other activities designed to win political control rather than defeat the Mujahideen in battle. This mix of ruthless "carrot and stick" tactics was more successful than the largely military tactics the USSR used earlier, but it still could not win control of the countryside. The war continued to be a grim war of attrition in which the Afghan people suffered.

Both sides made massive use of mine warfare. The Soviets and DRA continued to mine defended areas, and the Mujahideen had large supplies of mines of their own, including Italian-made anti-personnel mines.

The West reacted by furnishing more military aid to the rebels and providing a small amount of more sophisticated manportable surface-to-air missile weapons. As before, the Mujahideen still had to rely largely on their own courage and willingness to sacrifice.

While internal rivalry continued, some aspects of Mujahideen unity and coordination seemed to be improving in spite of growing divisions between the movements supported by Iran and Pakistan and the efforts at bribery and subversion by the Soviets and the Afghan government. The lack of any unified command or existence of a government in exile did, however, remain a major political and strategic problem:

- Winter 1985–1986: Soviet operations in 1986 begin with Soviet attacks aimed at shutting off the Mujahideen's supply lines from Pakistan in the two eastern provinces of Nangarhar, around the Khyber Pass area, and in Paktia. The Soviets score some successes. They also steadily increase the amount of "hot pursuit" attacks leading to air or artillery attacks on Pakistan's border areas—both for military and intimidation purposes. The Soviets do not, however, critically inhibit Mujahideen operations. Reports indicate the Soviets estimate that up to 85 percent of Afghan territory is still under Mujahideen or tribal control when Soviet forces are not present.

  The Mujahideen increasingly learn to take immediate cover when under air and helicopter attack and report that the primary Soviet air-to-ground weapons—guns on the Mi-24 and rockets on Soviet fighters—rarely score high kill rates. Nevertheless, the Soviet air threat is becoming increasingly more effective, particularly the Su-25, which seems to have high survivability against the SA-7.

  Soviets steadily increase their use of countermeasures against the SA-7. Aircraft increasingly routinely fire flares on take off. Soviet helicopters used in combat are reported to carry 30–50 magnesium flares.

- January 1986: Soviet officers execute twenty Soviet soldiers for refusing to fight.

  The KHAD (WAD) secret police are now part of a full Ministry of State Security under a Najibullah protege, Ghulam Faruq Yaquibi. The new Ministry takes over the provincial commands of the Sarandoy, but the Ministry of Interior continues to control some Sarandoy units, training, and administration. Provincial commands of the Ministry of State Security now command both KHAD and Sarandoy forces and intelligence groups. Soviet bombings and sweeps continue the effort to reduce the village population in Mujahideen areas.

- 24 January 1986: DRA and tribal militia forces fight Mujahideen in Nangrahar province. These forces are supported by elements of the 9th and 11th DRA divisions. The new combination of DRA and tribal forces drives the Mujahideen out of the area by mid-February, but the Mujahideen return the moment that the DRA and militia forces leave the area.

- Late January: DRA Army and Sarandoy forces conduct a small offensive in Herat near the Zendejan Pass.

- February 1986: Mikhail Gorbachev signals Soviet displeasure with the failure of the Afghan government to make progress in winning popular support and provide effective military forces by failing to meet with Babrak Karmal during his trip to the 27th Soviet Communist Party Congress in Moscow.

- 17 February 1986: Government press reports that Babrak Karmal does not appear to be in good health.
- 26 February 1986: The Reagan Administration breaks precedent with past covert operations and decides to send high-technology U.S. weapons to Afghanistan.[52]
- Spring 1986: USSR continues to build up its regional defense system around Kabul. It virtually depopulates a thirty-mile ring around the city. Three concentric security belts are created around the city, and a fourth will be under construction in the fall of 1986.

    In the field, the USSR continues to use scorched earth tactics and attack resistance food supplies by striking at farms, irrigation systems, and orchards. Use of "seismic" or trembler mines increases.

    An increasing amount of food for the Mujahideen must be brought from Pakistan. Shortages of food supply grow worse.

    Soviet attacks consist more and more of elite ground units in surgical strikes guided by infiltration and bribery of the resistance. The use of helicopter, fighter, and bomber firepower continues to increase.

- March 1986: Soviets begin attacks designed to destroy Mujahideen areas of occupation, or "no go" areas. These attacks will culminate in May in the Zhawar offensive.

    Spetsnaz forces begin large scale operations in Kuhistan area as spring thaw allows improved operations. Soviet efforts to buy support from elements of the Afridi tribe in the area near Jalalabad backfire, however, when the Afridi turn on the Soviets and then flee to Pakistan.

    Soviet forces attack Mujahideen units in Fariab province near the Soviet border, taking advantage of floods which make it difficult for the Mujahideen to escape in the relatively flat region. DRA forces include army, border guard, and Sarandoy units. The Soviets drive south from the USSR. The end result is a major defeat of the Mujahideen in the region with hundreds of dead and large numbers of defections.

- 21 March 1986: Four Pakistani troops are killed in the border area by an Afghan government jet.
- 27 March–early April 1986: Babrak Karmal delivers a brief speech to PDPA Central Committee meeting. Addresses the Revolutionary Committee meeting on April 2 and leaves for Soviet Union for "medical treatment."

- Late March 1986: Press reports appear that the U.S. has decided to send Stinger missiles to the Mujahideen. The Mujahideen's continuing lack of anti-aircraft capability and the growing Soviet reliance on helicopters for most operations had led the U.S. and the U.K. to conclude they must do something to deal with the Mujahideen's growing problems with Soviet air power.

    The reports of Stinger shipments are later confirmed, along with reports that various Arab governments delivered British-made Blowpipe systems equipped with proximity fuses. Temperature, rough handling, and poor training limit the initial effectiveness of Blowpipe.

    The Mujahideen are reported to have more success with 20-mm GAI-BO1 Oerlikon AA guns. These guns, made by Oerlikon Italiana to avoid violating Swiss neutrality laws, are paid for by U.S. and Saudi aid. The guns are relatively easy to operate and effective against helicopters. They can be disassembled into sections which can be carried by pack animals. Only forty guns, however, reportedly are delivered to Mujahideen forces. The Mujahideen also use PRC-supplied anti-aircraft guns, but these lack the range to be equally effective.

- April 1986: Soviets are reported to be using a total of seven Spetsnaz and seven airborne regiments with their own helicopter transport and attack helicopter support. Nearly 70 percent of all Soviet operations are reported to be heliborne, with Afghan forces doing the fighting on the ground.

    Spetsnaz and airborne units are reported to get near–real-time intelligence from Soviet intelligence officers working directly with Afghan intelligence. The number of Russian advisors working with the KHAD (WAD) is increasing significantly, and the KHAD (WAD) use of threats and bribes seems to be improving intelligence on the Mujahideen.

- 1 April 1986: The DRA government proposes a secret schedule for Soviet withdrawal during its talks with Pakistan—the first such schedule ever proposed. The schedule calls for a phased Soviet withdrawal in response to cessation of all Pakistani support to the Mujahideen.

- Early April–20 April 1986: A major DRA government offensive with up to 11,000 men plus 1,200 to 2,000 Soviet forces and heavy air support, begins. The DRA government forces are commanded by the Deputy Chief of Staff and include elements of five divisions plus a commando brigade and battalion. The Soviet combat forces include an air assault regiment. The Mujahideen base is defended by heavy armament by Mujahideen standards—including two

T-55s, three Bofors 40-mm AA guns, and heavy AA machine guns. This offensive has been in preparation since early February and draws on DRA forces throughout eastern Afghanistan. DRA forces attack up the valleys in the border area, and DRA and Soviet air assault and elite forces are air-lifted to Khost.

Three weeks of bitter fighting take place as the offensive slowly moves toward the major Mujahideen base in the border area at Zhawar. Soviet and DRA heliborne forces then land to try to seal the Mujahideen escape routes up the valleys. The Soviets use Su-25s with laser-guided bombs to attack hard points and to try to seal the tunnels used by the Mujahideen.

While the Soviet-backed DRA forces fail to take a base at Jaji Maydan and suffer heavy casualties in an airborne assault at Tani, they take Zhawar, a mile-long underground bunker and repair shop complex in Paktia near the Pakistani border, with Mujahideen losses estimated at 1,000 to 2,000. This Mujahideen defeat confirms long-standing fears that the Mujahideen cannot hold a fixed facility in Afghanistan. The Soviet forces use large-scale air attacks—sometimes more than twenty MiG-21, MiG-23, and Su-22 fighters in a single attack. They are reported to lose twelve helicopters and one fighter. The Mujahideen re-occupy the camp after Soviets leave but lose a major amount of supplies.

- Late April 1986: Mujahideen forces take significant losses in the area around Kandahar. Heavy fighting takes place around Khost and elsewhere in Paktia. Both sides take stiff losses, and at least one DRA unit—the 37th Commando Brigade—takes heavy losses. Large flows of serious Mujahideen casualties reach Pakistan.

  Reports surface of special Spetsnaz "hit teams" using helicopters to attack and kill Mujahideen leaders; the reports are not fully confirmed. It is clear, however, that Russians are now directing the KHAD (WAD) efforts to infiltrate the Mujahideen and direct heliborne Spetsnaz forces directly to their target in direct response to any major new intelligence on Mujahideen forces. The Soviets increasingly use dawn attacks of up to 30 helicopters to bring Spetsnaz assault troops right to their target.

- 25 April 1986: Babrak Karmal fails to give National Day address in Kabul. An editorial in Pravda criticizes Afghan government for poor leadership.

- 30 April 1986: Babrak Karmal is reported to be undergoing medical treatment in USSR.

- May 1986: A major Soviet-Afghan offensive in the border area attempts to cut Mujahideen supply lines from Teri Mangal in Pakistan. The offensive has temporary success, but Soviet forces

cannot remain in place, and Mujahideen supply activities rapidly
recover.

- 4 May 1986: Dr. Mohammed Najib(ullah), a 39-year-old medical
  doctor, is inaugurated as Secretary of the Afghan Communist
  Party. Babrak Karmal, who is reported to be dying of cancer, is
  allowed to "resign" on health grounds and is left in the nearly
  powerless post of President. Najib(ullah) is the head of the
  pacification program and KHAD (WAD), the secret police. He
  has run the KHAD (WAD)'s efforts to dominate the Mosques and
  the countryside. He also has led the Parcham's effort to dominate
  the more rural Khalq faction of the Afghan Communist Party.[53]

  Najib rapidly adopts a more Islamic public image, and DRA
  government speeches are suddenly given a more Islamic character.
  New incentive programs are set up for Afghan chieftains and
  leaders and for the refugees displaced by the Soviet scorched
  earth policy. These programs score some successes, particularly
  among Mujahideen leaders who have not won power or prestige
  and among the poor, who often become dependent on the Afghan
  government for survival.

- 19–23 May 1986: Seventh round of Geneva peace talks occurs.
  Little progress takes place as Soviet intensify efforts to secure the
  border areas and raids into Pakistan increase.

- June 1986: Soviet air attacks against Mujahideen supply depots
  and sanctuaries increase. It becomes clear that Soviet intelligence
  is improving.

  Soviet efforts continue to expand Afghanistan's military
  infrastructure in a few critical military areas. The 1.6-mile
  Salang Tunnel through the Hindu Kush north of Kabul is
  widened, and the Salang highway from the USSR to Kabul is
  improved. The port town of Hieratan on the Amu Darya in the
  border area is expanded.

- June 1986: Massoud increasingly operates outside of the Soviet-
  DRA dominated Panjshir Valley and conducts operations in
  Badakshan. He demonstrates the constant dilemma that Soviet
  and DRA forces face because of their inability to trap and kill
  large numbers of Mujahideen and win popular support in the areas
  they conquer. Tactical victories cannot be translated into lasting
  military or political victories.

- 18 June 1986: Reports of dissension within the seven main
  Mujahideen resistance groups highlight the inability of the
  Mujahideen to create a meaningful political entity. This prevents
  them from winning world recognition as an alternative to the
  DRA government.

- Summer 1986: DRA government troops conduct a major armored sweep in Logar province south of Kabul. Fighting continues into August with significant losses on both sides. The role of the bulk of the 80,000 Afghan government troops is still restricted to mop-up operations, but more DRA Army units take the field.

  U.S. military aid to Mujahideen is reported to have reached $400 million, with $100 million sent during the last year. Total military and economic aid in FY 1985 is reported to be $280 million. The CIA is reported to be training about 100 Mujahideen per month in arms smuggling and use.

  Conflicting reports surface about whether the Mujahideen are increasing their internal struggle for power—with a growing Sunni versus Shi'ite element—or increasing their cooperation.

  The U.S. agrees to sell restricted communications gear and computer equipment to Pakistan, in part to reduce its vulnerability to Soviet use of signals intelligence (SIGINT) during its efforts to support the Mujahideen and stop Soviet border raids and violations.

  Najib dismisses several key rivals, including Assadullah Sarwari, the DRA government's former Deputy Prime Minister and secret police chief. He promotes three loyalists to Politboro membership, including Ghulam Faruq Yaquibi, the new secret police chief.

- 1 July 1986: A Soviet troop transport is shot down, with losses of up to 100 DRA troops. Soviets increasingly send up helicopters to screen the area by firing flares before letting transports like the AN-26 take off. In spite of the security zone around Kabul, aircraft routinely fly evasive take-off and landing patterns to minimize their vulnerability.

- 6 July 1986: Mujahideen forces successfully ambush a major Soviet and DRA government convoy near Juma Bazar, northeast of Maimana. In general, however, most guerrilla forces now must remain in bases, in sanctuaries like mountain terrain and the other areas outside population centers, or in Pakistan. Only a relatively small portion of the 100,000–200,000 men in the various Mujahideen factions—largely consisting of small raiding parties—can operate in the field.

- Mid–late July 1986: A new Soviet offensive scores some victories near Herat but cannot dominate the countryside. The fighting continues at relatively high levels.

  A series of terror bombings in Pakistan's northwest border area are linked to Najib's political direction. Many are directed against buildings or areas used by the Mujahideen.

  Heavy fighting late in month destroys part of Herat.

- 28 July 1986: Gorbachev announces a limited Soviet withdrawal from Afghanistan. Says in Moscow that USSR will withdraw six regiments (about 6,000–7,000 men) from Afghanistan in late 1986. Gorbachev calls for the West to cut its aid by 6 percent.
- 30 July 1986: Further peace talks at Geneva make no progress.
- End of July–September 1986: Mujahideen forces remain active in the city of Kandahar. Soviet efforts to create a security zone in and around the city fail. The city is ruined, and the once rich agricultural areas nearby are devastated.
- August, 1986: Najib publicly admits that DRA Army desertions and avoidance of conscription continue. Outside experts rate the effective fighting strength of the Afghan army at only 40,000 men.

  The Mujahideen increasingly use the longer range PRC-made 130-mm rockets for long distance attacks, instead of the 107-mm rockets used since 1984. Some 30 rockets hit the Soviet complex in the Darulaman area of Kabul. The new rocket allows strikes from up to 10 km away and helps compensate for the improving Soviet security zones and ability to use helicopters.
- 11 August 1986: The DRA government charges that Pakistani militiamen are crossing the border to help Mujahideen. Reports again surface that Pakistan is holding back arms because of its fear of Soviet pressure.
- Mid-August 1986: Five guerrilla groups cooperate in capturing a major fort at Farkhar in the northeast under the leadership of Ahmed Shah Massoud—who shows he can operate successfully outside the Panjshir Valley.
- 25 August 1986: The DRA government charges that Iranian security forces have crossed the border to help the Mujahideen. Fighting is reported in Ghor, Herat, and Zabul.
- 26–27 August 1986: A major ammunition dump is blown up near Kabul. Mujahideen forces move within 3,000 meters and then attack the dump with 107-mm and 130-mm rockets.
- Fall 1986: The Mujahideen keep up their raids in the areas near Kabul in spite of growing Soviet efforts to suppress them. The Soviets conduct major operations in the Paghman district, with substantial Mujahideen losses. Mujahideen operations continue around Kandahar and Herat.

  Iran steps up its support of Shi'ite Mujahideen in the west and increasingly supports the three main pro-Khomeini Mujahideen groups operating in Herat, Farah, and Nimruz provinces. The Iranian government increases its criticism of Pakistan's lack of support and its ties with the West.

- 3 September 1986: DRA government announces a plan to resettle up to 300,000 civilians in the Pushtun and Pathan areas of the eastern provinces—areas where the Mujahideen have obtained much of their supply.
- 26 September 1986: According to one source, the U.S.-made Stinger missiles are used by the rebels for the first time, destroying three of four helicopters landing at Jalalabad airport.[54]
- October 1986: The Soviets claim to withdraw 8,000 troops out of 120,000. They actually remove three anti-aircraft regiments equipped with SA-8 missiles with no fighting role, plus one tank and two motorized rifle regiments which were sent to Afghanistan in September on rotation simply for later removal. The strength of Soviet elite special forces and mountain warfare units in Afghanistan continues to increase.

The first effective Mujahideen use of Stinger missiles is reported in the eastern province of Nangarhar. Other Soviet helicopters are then reported downed around Jalalabad and Kandahar and in the Rakhar region. Some reports indicate that the U.S. has provided 200 missiles under the conditions that two more missiles will be provided for each confirmed kill of a Soviet aircraft, but that anyone missing a target is to return for retraining. Other reports indicate only nine missiles have been transferred for firing as an initial test. Five Stinger missiles are reported to have been used during October, with two helicopter kills and one fighter kill. The Mujahideen also show increasing signs of properly handling and storing the Blowpipe missile and improving capability to use the Oerlikon 20-mm AA gun.

The Soviets continue to increase their bombing attacks on civilian towns and farms, using a combination of regular bombs, various burning agents, and mines. A major anti-population sweep of troops and aircraft is conducted in the Shomali region north of Kabul. Heavy fighting goes on around Jalalabad. New reports occur of the use of lethal gas in fighting in Paghman and Chesmibulbul, west of Paghman.

The Mujahideen report growing problems with Soviet mines, including butterfly mines. The large-scale use of mines over an extended period has created a growing need for simple but effective detectors. The Mujahideen have only a limited number of Soviet detectors.

Soviet air incursions into Pakistan reach 620 violations versus 420 in all of 1985. Nearly 30 percent of these incursions involve bombing or strafing. The U.S. discusses possible deployment or sale of an Airborne Warning and Air Control System

(AWACS) to Pakistan, plus new radars, anti-aircraft guns, and M-1 tanks.

- 22 October 1986: An Afghan pilot defects in his MiG-21 to Pakistan.
- Winter 1986: Two new Soviet divisions of 15,000 men are reported to be deployed to Afghanistan. Roughly one-third of all Soviet troops with mountain warfare training are now reported to be in Afghanistan. Soviet deserters in Afghan units are reported at 200.

  Heavy Mujahideen attacks continue. Desertions from the DRA Army continue.
- 10 November 1986: Reports surface that the USSR has deployed missiles into the Wakhan Corridor to cover a 180-mile stretch of the border with Pakistan under a still-secret agreement with the DRA government which allowed the USSR to annex the corridor in 1980. The political status of the Wakhan Corridor remains uncertain, but it becomes clear the Soviets began such deployments in 1981, and Soviet Scud B and FROG 3 deployments in the area are now confirmed. Five Soviet strong points, defended by barbed wire, 120-mm mortars, and AFVs, cover the key passes into Pakistan. A motorized rifle regiment with 2,500 men is present, and total Soviet troop strength is estimated at 4,000 men. This improves Soviet capability to limit arms flows into the nearby regions of Afghanistan from Pakistan and the PRC and to put military pressure on Pakistan.
- 5 November 1986: United Nations votes 122–20 for withdrawal of Soviet troops. A report by Felix Ermacora to the Human Rights Commission of the UN finds that more than 100 villages have been bombed and 10,000–12,000 civilians have been killed in the last nine months. The report concludes that Soviet and DRA government forces routinely use torture and decimate villages and that booby traps include mines disguised as toys. It states that the Mujahideen "command the support of the vast majority of the population." A third of the population is in exile. Total refugees are estimated at 1.9 million in Iran, 2.8–3.2 million in Pakistan, and 1.5–2 million displaced internal refugees. The flow of Afghan refugees to Pakistan is estimated at 6,000–8,000 a month. An Amnesty International report issued later in November confirms the UN report.
- 16 November 1986: New peace shuttle by Cordovez makes limited progress after talks in Moscow.
- 20 November 1986: Babrak Karmal is reported to have resigned from the presidency because of ill health.
- 23 November 1986: Mohammed Chamkani is appointed acting

president of Afghanistan, replacing Babrak Karmal. Chamkani is one of seven vice-presidents of the Revolutionary Council and is a titular non-communist. He is a tribal leader from Paktia and seems to be appointed as part of the Afghan government's effort to downplay its communist and anti-Islamic character and to win support from tribes in the Afghan-Pakistan border area.

- Late November 1986: The Mujahideen strengthen their hold on southern districts of Kandahar and areas to the south after a month of intensive fighting. Soviet and Afghan aircraft operating around the city fly far more intensive SAM-avoidance patterns, indicating that Blowpipe and Stinger are becoming more effective. Eleven helicopters and at least one MiG-23 are reported to have been shot down during the first two weeks of November.

- December 1986: Fighting continues in spite of the poor weather. A broader purge seems to be taking place within the Afghan government to ensure full loyalty to the USSR. Food and living conditions for the Afghan people still living inside the country reach their worst levels since the beginning of the war.

    As the war moves into its eighth year, there is no end in sight. The trends which will affect the fighting in 1987 are very similar to those which shaped the fighting in 1986.

- While internal rivalry continues to exist within the Mujahideen, some elements of unity and coordination seem to be improving. The Mujahideen are more unified in their attacks in spite of growing divisions between the movements supported by Iran and Pakistan, and in spite Soviet and Afghan government efforts at bribery and subversion. The lack of any unified command, along with a government in exile, remains the major political and strategic problem depriving the Mujahideen of political status and impact.

1987: The Year of the Mujahideen[55]

The fighting in Afghanistan reached its eighth year. The USSR had succeeded in keeping the Afghanistan conflict from becoming a "Vietnam." Nevertheless, the Soviets could not defeat the Mujahideen. Soviet exploitation of rebel internal divisions, scorched earth attacks, and conversion of most of Afghanistan's civil population to refugees temporarily "pacified" part of the population but did not defeat the Afghan people. The Soviets could not destroy the Mujahideen forces on the battlefield. The USSR was left reliant on an uncertain puppet regime.

As 1987 began, the USSR remained embroiled in a war it could afford to continue in military and economic terms, but which could go on for years without producing a political victory. The Mujahideen had gradually begun to seize the initiative from the Soviets and DRA and often dictated the place and pace of combat.

Soviet force increased slightly over the force levels in 1986. A few new artillery units arrived, and slightly higher existing personnel levels in units already in Afghanistan raised the total troop strength in the country to 120,000. Some 30,000 troops in the USSR continued to support logistics, combat operations, and air missions.

Most Soviet troops remained in static defensive deployments. The Soviets did, however, change their tactics as the Mujahideen got steadily greater numbers of Stingers and improved their air defense. Small sweep operations continued on the ground but no longer had large-scale air support. Two new types of 152-mm cannon, a new 122-mm howitzer, and a new 82-mm automatic mortar were sent to Afghanistan. The USSR relied much more heavily on artillery, and Soviet forces moved much more slowly. Heliborne assaults by elite troops and Spetsnaz decreased.

Aircraft losses rose to 150–200 per year. The Soviet air force flew higher and faster and spent far less time over target. Air strikes were much less effective. Helicopters and gunships took heavy casualties and could not operate effectively near Mujahideen units with Stinger or Blowpipe weapons.

The USSR began to shelter and revet more and more of its facilities. It built mountainside and underground bunkers. Security zones were expanded around Kabul and the other cities. The Soviets experienced growing morale problems and difficulties with dysentery, hepatitis, drugs, and alcohol abuse.

Major battles took place at Kunduz in the north; Barikot and Asmari on the Pakistani border; in the outskirts of Kabul and at Shomali and Paghman near Kabul; at Ali Khel, Gardez, and Khost near the border west of Kabul; and at Arghandab, Mahalajat, Kandahar, and Panjawi in the south. The Mujahideen captured positions near Kalafghan, Koran-va-Monjan, and Peshghowr, and expanded their forces in the Kunar and Salang valleys. The Soviets evacuated positions at Chaghcharan and Bamiyan.

The Soviets attempted to force Pakistan to halt its support of the Mujahideen with air raids and border incidents in Pakistan. There were major Soviet air raids on Bajour, Parachinar, and Miran Shah in Pakistan. This raised the total pattern of Soviet attacks on Pakistan to the levels shown in Table 2.4.

The level of fighting still varied by season but was consistently more intense than in past years, particularly in the winter. During the summer, combat was particularly intense in Kandahar, Paktia province, and the area of Kabul. The USSR made one last major effort

TABLE 2.4 Casualties Due to Border Violations by Soviet/DRA Forces and Terrorist Attacks in Pakistan: 1980–October 1987

Year	Air Attacks			Artillery Attacks			Terrorist Explosions			Total	
	Violations	Injured	Killed	Violations	Injured	Killed	Violations	Injured	Killed	Injured	Killed
1980	174	4	2	25	-	-	-	-	-	4	2
1981	94	3	5	17	-	-	-	-	-	3	5
1982	59	-	-	22	4	-	2	4	-	8	-
1983	93	2	-	41	8	-	47	27	4	37	4
1984	119	261	133	49	24	38	28	48	8	333	179
1985	256	38	19	121	19	25	118	173	96	230	140
1986	779	67	39	495	120	56	487	798	216	985	311
1987	574	437	183	517	130	50	450	953	198	1,520	431

SOURCE: U.S. Department of State, December 1987.

at pacification in December in the eastern part of the country, but by now the USSR, more than the Afghan people, had been worn down by the seemingly endless conflict:[56]

- January 1987: The Mujahideen make rocket attacks on Soviet culture center in Kabul. There are now 22,000 Soviet and 10,000 DRA troops in the area and three defensive rings extending up to 20 miles from the city.
- 15 January 1987: DRA announces unilateral six-month cease-fire, which is ignored by both sides. Najib begins active efforts at "national reconciliation."
- 1–15 February 1987: Soviet and DRA forces conduct operations against Mujahideen bases along the Pakistan border in eastern Kandahar province and south of Khost in Paktia province.
- 25 February–9 March 1987: The seventh round of UN peace talks in Geneva resume amid major Mujahideen offensives in the Pakistan border area. The Mujahideen increase their use of Stinger, and Soviet and DRA forces conduct retaliatory air raids. At the peace talks, there are differences regarding the timing of a Soviet withdrawal. The USSR reduces its period to eighteen months, but Pakistan insists on seven months.
- 8 March 1987: The Mujahideen rocket a factory in Pyandzh, a city in the USSR near the Amu Darya river border.
- 15 March 1987: In talks with Pakistan in Geneva, the USSR offers its first serious withdrawal plan, cutting withdrawal time from three to four years to eighteen months and insisting on a Kabul-dominated coalition. USSR and DRA offer to trade

noninterference for agreement that aid to Mujahideen will cease before Soviet withdrawal.

- April 1987: Snow slide destroys seventy-man Soviet outpost at Khenjan, north of Salang Tunnel. Bagram air base is hit by rebel rockets.
- 8 April 1987: Mujahideen attack Soviet border guard unit in USSR, killing two. The Soviets launch major counterraids and try to create a security zone in Kunduz and Takhar provinces.
- 10–25 April 1987: Soviet and DRA forces conduct sweeps against Mujahideen bases in southern Nangarhar province.
- 22 May–21 June 1987: Mujahideen attacks against Kandahar provoke three unsuccessful Soviet and DRA campaigns against Mujahideen-held areas outside the city. The first is at Arghandab (22 May–21 June). Mahalajat (5–21 July) and Panjawi (26 July–2 August) follow.
- 23 May–12 June 1987: Soviet and DRA forces, including a 5,000-man multi-regimental Soviet force, fail to capture Mujahideen base camps near Ali Khel along the Pakistan border in Paktia province. The Soviets fail even though they use tanks, OAFVs, and new 152-mm self-propelled artillery weapons. Spetsnaz assault troops are beaten back in direct face-to-face engagements. The Mujahideen successfully employ the Stinger in defending against Soviet aircraft, and intense Soviet bombing takes place at too high an altitude to be effective.
- Spring 1987: New fighting occurs around Herat. The west of the city is not secure, but Soviets tighten defenses by late in the year.
- June 1987: Iranians seize or buy sixteen to thirty Stinger missiles from a Mujahideen faction.

    Mujahideen shoot down two civilian AN-26 airliners in two weeks with Stinger or Blowpipe missiles, killing ninety-eight. Civilian airliners routinely start using evasion and countermeasure techniques. Air movement is no long safe anywhere in the country.
- 8 June–9 July 1987: DRA forces suffer two weeks of defeats in the Paghman area west of Kabul.
- Late June 1987: DRA drive up the Arghandab Valley, outside Kandahar, is halted by Mujahideen.
- 26 June–July 1987: Soviet forces operate in Paghman and in nearby Maidan Valley in response to DRA defeats. Mujahideen impose serious casualties using improved artillery and small arms and Stinger missiles.
- July 1987: Ismail Khan of Herat chairs the most broadly based Mujahideen effort yet to unite on strategy in a remote part of Ghor

province. Commanders and officials from several parties in western Afghanistan meet and issue a military communiqué asking for coordination and unity and chastising Mujahideen political leaders for their lack of unity.

- July 1987: Northern Council forces of Massoud storm Kalafghan, less than 50 miles from Soviet border, and take more than 100 DRA prisoners and large amounts of artillery and supplies.
- Early July 1987: Mujahideen attacks along the Kabul-Jalalabad highway destroy several Soviet outposts.
- 5–21 July 1987: Mujahideen attacks against Kandahar provoke three unsuccessful Soviet and DRA campaigns against Mujahideen-held areas outside the city; the second is at Mahalajat.
- 13 July 1987: Jamiat-i-Islami commander Massoud captures the battalion-sized garrison at Kalafghan in Takhar province.
- 15 July 1987: Najibullah extends unilateral cease-fire offer of 15 January 1987, announces a draft constitution, and offers selected ministries to opponents.
- 21 July 1987: Najibullah travels to Moscow for consultations. Lays wreath at tomb of unknown soldier.
- Summer 1987: Soviet forces evacuate garrisons at Bamiyan and Chaghcharan (capital of Ghor province) in central Afghanistan after several pro-Iranian Mujahideen assaults.
- August 1987: Intense Soviet attacks in forty-mile Shomali Basin cause new wave of refugees to flee to Kabul.
- 26 July–2 August 1987: Mujahideen attacks against Kandahar provoke three unsuccessful Soviet and DRA campaigns against Mujahideen-held areas outside the city. The third is at Panjawi.
- 7–15 August 1987: Mujahideen attacks on the outskirts of Kabul provoke a Soviet/DRA operation against the villages in the Shomali plain north of the city.
- 26 August–20 September 1987: Soviet and DRA forces from several parts of the northeast assist in the re-supply of the Faizabad garrison in Badakshan province.
- Late August 1987: DRA pilots mutiny at an air base north of Kabul and destroy up to fifteen planes. The thirty-five DRA pilots are reported to mutiny against orders to conduct low-altitude attacks in the face of Mujahideen use of Stinger and better AA guns.
- September 1987: USSR indicates it may accept withdrawal times shorter than eighteen months and will accept a coalition in which the DRA has only some key ministries. USSR and DRA insist on agreement that U.S. aid to Mujahideen through Pakistan will cease before Soviet withdrawal.[57]

- September 1987: The first confirmed capture of Stinger missiles from Mujahideen by pro-Soviet troops is announced.[58]
- September 1987: Soviet embassy complex in Kabul is hit by mortars.

  Thirty-five groups belonging to six of the Mujahideen factions conduct a coordinated attack and take many of the seventy Soviet/DRA security posts along a forty-mile stretch of the road from Kandahar to the Pakistan border.
- 7–10 September 1987: The fourth round of the seventh series of Geneva peace talks is held at the unprecedented request of the Soviet and DRA governments. No breakthrough occurs, but speculation arises that differences now exist between the Soviets and the DRA.
- 18 September 1987: *Izvestiya* describes Kandahar as "one big ruin."
- 27 September–26 October 1987: Soviet and DRA forces conduct large-scale sweep exercises in Logar province, south of Kabul.
- Autumn 1987: A 2,000-man DRA military group, under command of Arbab Ghani Teyurmi and responsible for security of the countryside along the Herat-Towraghondi road, defects to the Mujahideen near Herat with its equipment. Herat is a key unit in northwestern Afghanistan, and defection is a symbol of Soviet inability to use its troops and DRA troops and intelligence units to secure the countryside.[59]
- October 1987: The seven major elements of the Mujahideen elect Yunis Khalis, leader of the Hezb-e-Islami (Khalis) Party, as head of the alliance. There are still important divisions within the Mujahideen, but titular unity is improving.
- 8 October 1987: Iranian Revolutionary Guards, or Pasdaran forces, in the Gulf hit a U.S. helicopter with a Stinger they have bought from Mujahideen factions. The warhead fails to explode.[60]
- 14–21 October 1987: Soviet and DRA forces in Kandahar respond to Mujahideen attacks by deploying around the Mahalajat and trying to expand their defensive positions. They fail to do so, and follow-up attempts in early December and mid-January 1988 are equally unsuccessful.
- 22 October–2 November 1987: In a typical operation at this point in the war, Soviet and DRA air and ground forces strike at Mujahideen villages and forces in southern Logar province, eighty kilometers from Kabul. They attack in response to a Mujahideen ambush on 9 October that killed a local DRA militia commander. Two armored columns fail to entrap Mujahideen forces or even take their strong points. Heliborne assault forces and air and

artillery units are then called in. When assault forces fail to trap any Mujahideen and begin to take casualties, the Soviet forces use BM-27 MRLs to rocket villages in the area of Baraki Baraq. They kill numerous civilians but have negligible impact on the Mujahideen, which have left the target area.

- 31 October 1987: Massoud captures another battalion-sized garrison at Koran-va-Monjan in southern Badakshan province—a base astride a critical supply route to the Panjshir.
- Late October–November 1987: Mujahideen attack many outposts and strong points in Kunar Valley from Barikot to Kabul River. Barikot and Asmar come under siege but do not fall.
- November 1987: Najib offers a new approach to "national reconciliation." He changes his public name back from Najib to Najibullah to emphasize Islam (*Ullah* = *Allah*), drops the word "Democratic" from Democratic Republic of Afghanistan (DRA becomes RA) to ease Marxist taint, and offers to share power with seven major Mujahideen resistance groups. The sole remaining Khalqi leader in a high position, Interior Minister Mohammed Gulabzoi, is sent as ambassador to Moscow. Another Khalqi, Deputy Foreign Minister Abdul Ghaffer Lakanwal, defects in New York while visiting the UN.
- 20 November 1987: UN Assembly, in the largest margin yet (123–19, with 11 abstentions), passes a resolution calling for all foreign forces to withdraw from Afghanistan.
- 25 November 1987: A letter appears in *Pravda* stating, "There is talk the war in Afghanistan would have ended long ago if along with the sons of people, the sons of leaders were sent there as well."
- November–December 1987: Extensive Mujahideen shelling of garrisons in the Kunar Valley on the northeastern border with Pakistan results in Soviet and RA reinforcements from Jalalabad and Kabul.
- 1–10 December 1987: Heavy fighting in the Torkham–Khyber Pass area in eastern Nangarhar Province blocks highway traffic to the Pakistan border.
- 11 December 1987: Three RA air raids are directed against Mujahideen targets in Pakistan.
- 15 November 1987–25 January 1988: Large Soviet and RA forces operating from Gardez relieve the Mujahideen blockade of Khost in Paktia Province. Major operations begin on 15 December, and the Soviet and RA troops link up with the RA troops in the Khost garrison on 31 December. The basic operation, however, is a failure. The Soviets stall in the high mountain passes along the

eighty-mile route from Gardez to Khost. They break through only
after a flanking movement along another route. It is clear that
the USSR can no longer secure a route to the border area without
massive troop deployments and serious air losses.

1988–1989: The Years of Soviet "Withdrawal"

Soviet and DRA forces had won most of their individual
engagements in 1986 and 1987 but were gradually losing the war. In
spite of a vast Soviet effort, the DRA (now the RA) still lacked
popular support at the beginning of 1988 and could not secure the
countryside after any of its victories. The USSR and RA no longer
retained relative freedom of action in the air. They had little control
of the countryside outside densely populated areas like Herat and
Kandahar; the north-south highway to Kabul; key air bases and
cantonment areas like Shindand, Kabul airport, and Bagram airfield;
and the security perimeter of key cities like Kabul, Jalalabad, and
Mazar-i-Shariff.

In spite of the many individual Soviet tactical successes between
1984 and 1986, it became clear that Soviet deep raids and scorched
earth tactics could not suppress the Mujahideen. In early 1988, the
Mujahideen estimated that they had some 850 local and regional
commanders operating in the country and controlled some 80 percent of
the countryside.

Soviet pressure had not forced Pakistan to cut off its supply to the
Mujahideen, and Iran had increased its supply to the more radical pro-
Iranian Shi'ite factions of the Mujahideen. The USSR realized it was
unable to use the KHAD (WAD) and Sarandoy to subvert and suppress
the freedom fighters, and RA forces remained unreliable.

At the same time, the cost of the war and its broad unpopularity
created steadily more serious problems within the USSR. Gorbachev
and his advisors came to see it as a major political and financial
liability with little strategic purpose. In contrast, U.S. aid to the
Mujahideen was reported to be as high as $600 million a year and to
have totalled $2 billion since the start of the war. This was only part
of the aid pouring into the Mujahideen forces.[61]

As a result, the USSR finally agreed to withdraw from
Afghanistan, under an agreement reached under UN auspices whereby
it agreed to halt military support for the RA if the U.S. and Pakistan
agreed to halt or reduce their arms shipments to the Mujahideen once
the Soviet withdrawal began. The USSR began its withdrawals on 15
May 1988 and shifted from attempts to defeat the Mujahideen to a
combination of attacks and peace offensives designed to force them to
agree to a joint government with the PDPA.

Both the RA and the Mujahideen prepared for an all-out conflict after Soviet withdrawal, and immediate fighting began in the areas not occupied by Soviet forces. The RA gave up its garrisons in the lower Panjshir Valley and in Barikot in the Kunar Valley. It then attempted to hold the rest of the country rather than concentrate on defending fortified garrisons like Kabul and Jalalabad. While the USSR and the West and Pakistan continued to jockey for position and rush arms to their respective factions, fighting broke out in the Jaji Valley and for control of the major highways in the south. There was also fighting for Kandahar, the Kunduz-Talequan corridor, the Salang Valley, the Kunar Valley, Torkham, and control of the areas surrounding Kabul.

Soviet withdrawals after May 1988 did not lead to the immediate collapse of the RA in the areas formally under Soviet control. While the Mujahideen won many battles, the RA forces withdrew to those areas they felt they could hold. The Mujahideen had relatively little heavy equipment and found it difficult to penetrate the defenses of a well-supplied RA force equipped with air power and heavy weapons. The RA sometimes performed better than expected, and the Soviets provided reinforcements and airpower in emergencies.

The Soviet withdrawal proceeded more or less on schedule and was completed by 15 February 1989. The USSR attempted a major peace offensive and attempted to forge a coalition government before it left, but all peace efforts failed. The completion of the Soviet withdrawal on 15 February 1989 ended with the Soviet invasion being replaced by a civil war between the RA and Mujahideen.

- October 1987–February 1988: There are increasing signs the USSR will accept withdrawal on any face-saving terms.
- January 1988: President Zia of Pakistan reiterates his call for international peacekeeping forces to supervise Soviet withdrawal from Afghanistan.
- 1–2 January 1988: Soviet TV provides unusual full coverage of battle for relief of Khost.
- 26 January 1988–1 March 1988: Soviet and RA units temporarily occupy the Sangin area along the Helmand River north of Kandahar.
- 8 February 1988: Gorbachev announces a ten-month time frame for withdrawal, to begin sixty days after signing of accords. Fifty percent of Soviet troops are to leave in the first three months. Soviet withdrawal, he states, is no longer linked to the creation of an interim government. Debate focuses on symmetry of aid (whether U.S. agreement to halt aid to Mujahideen will be

matched by Soviet action). USSR claims U.S. should halt aid; its own aid is an internal matter.

- 11 February 1988: Hezb-i-Islami closes three offices in Iran after Iran puts pressure on Afghan refugees to fight for Iran.
- 15 February 1988: U.S. votes 77–0 in a "sense of the Senate" vote supporting Pakistan's refusal to sign a treaty with the pro-Soviet RA. The U.S. also supports Pakistan's insistence on a transitional regime to better assure Soviet withdrawal and the return of refugees to Afghanistan.
- 23 February 1988: The seven major factions of the Mujahideen propose an interim government which for the first time allows some ministerial posts to go to officials of the RA.
- 9–10 March 1988: USSR and RA government in Kabul rejects U.S. demand for cutoff of Soviet aid after withdrawal.
- 15 March 1988: USSR, Pakistan, and U.S. agree to nine-month withdrawal, reach no agreement on interim regime, and still disagree on symmetry of aid cutoff.
- March 1988: Twenty-one Mujahideen field commanders in Afghanistan condemn compromises in Geneva, claiming they aid the RA. Several of the more extreme Islamic leaders pledge to continue fighting, regardless of any pact.
- 17 March 1988: USSR announces it will withdraw even if no agreement is reached at Geneva.
- 21 March 1988: Mujahideen forces recapture border post at Zarmanki near Khost after heavy fighting.
- 23 March 1988: U.S. and Soviet officials discuss withdrawal arrangements as part of background to summit talks.
- 24 March 1988: Pakistan drops demand for interim government.
- Late March 1988: Soviet troops start transferring some of the responsibility for defense of the security perimeter around Kabul to RA forces. RA ministries are informed they will soon be responsible for their own security.
- April 1988: The U.S. uses C-5A flights to Pakistan to rush some $300 million worth of arms to the Mujahideen. Shipments include TOW missiles for the first time.
- April 1988: The Soviets announce they will leave behind up to $1 billion worth of arms. Soviet convoys of up to 400 vehicles carry new arms to RA. Soviet AN-12 flights carry arms to Kabul, and AN-26 aircraft then ferry supplies to smaller cities.
- April 1988: The Soviets begin to transfer posts in the Kabul area to the RA. The RA 1st Brigade replaces the Soviet garrison in the Darulaman area. Sarandoy forces assume the security responsibility northwest of Kabul. The RA Nangarhar fron-

tier force replaces the Soviet 66th Division in Nangarhar province.

- 7 April 1988: The USSR and RA announce in Moscow that all obstacles to a peace settlement have been removed and that Soviet withdrawal will start on 15 May 1988. Pakistan announces its agreement, stating that the USSR and U.S. have agreed on symmetry in aid and that both sides will be allowed to continue limited aid. The full details of the agreement are not released.

- 10 April 1988: Mujahideen shoot down an AN-26 civil airliner near the Soviet border, killing 29. Soviet forces strengthen protection of routes to Kabul in preparation for withdrawal.

  Leaking shell stored in an army ammunition dump in Rawalpundi blows up and kills 93. Nearly one-third of the $300 million in aid the U.S. has rushed to the Mujahideen is blown up, including 150 of the 300 Stingers sent so far in 1988.

- 11 April 1988: Soviets send a 1,000-vehicle convoy from the Soviet border to strengthen the ring defenses of Kabul.

- 14 April 1988: The Soviet withdrawal accords are signed at Geneva. The U.S. offers to match Soviet "restraint" in supplying arms to each side in Afghanistan.

- 18 April 1988: Soviets withdraw from provincial capital of Zabul province.

- 23 April 1988: There are some indications that the Soviets are strengthening Balkh and eight other northern provinces in order to create a pro-Soviet redoubt for the RA if the other parts of Afghanistan fall to the Mujahideen.

- 28 April 1988: Six are killed and forty-nine wounded by a truck bomb in Kabul. Najibullah announces in a two-hour press conference that Soviets will not leave arms behind; he claims the RA already has enough and says Soviet advisors will stay behind. He offers a coalition with the Mujahideen.

- 2 May 1988: It is confirmed that the first Soviet troop elements are already withdrawing from Afghanistan. Some 8,000 RA troops are deployed to help strengthen the defenses of Kabul.

- 3 May–June 1988: The Mujahideen begin to close in on Kandahar. They take a major outpost of the Achakzai Tribal Brigade that helps defend Kandahar and then attempt to take Spin Boldak near the border with Pakistan. The RA forces hold; they now include the 15th Infantry Division, the 7th Armored Brigade, the Achakzai Tribal Brigade, a Mari Baluch Tribal Brigade, and an Uzbeck Militia Brigade.

- Early to mid-May 1988: The Mujahideen launch a major campaign in the Jaji Valley, southeast of the "parrot's beak" on the

Pakistani border. They take Chamkani in the south and then gradually surround the town of Jaji. The Mujahideen are well equipped with rockets and multiple rocket launchers and can counter the firepower of RA forces. On 15 May, the Mujahideen forces flank the RA forces on both sides and force them to flee to Gardez, leaving much of their armor and support equipment. This opens up the supply route into Paktia and threatens the northern part of the routes from Kandahar to Kabul.

- 9 May 1988: Seventeen Mujahideen rockets hit Kabul, killing eleven civilians and wounding twelve.
- 11 May 1988: More Soviet troops withdraw. Some 15,000 troops have now been deployed to the north from the USSR to protect lines of withdrawal. Su-25 aircraft, flying from Kabul, cover convoys. Some seventy-six flights a day have left Kabul on each day since April 14. More than ten district centers have fallen to the Mujahideen in last two weeks, many in the center and the north and some near Jalalabad and Kandahar.
- 13 May 1988: Mujahideen launch constant low-level attacks on Soviet troops in Kandahar and mortar attacks on Soviet troops in Herat. Major Soviet garrisons are reported to have abandoned Kunar, Nangarhar, and Paktia provinces.
- 15 May 1988: Soviet troops stage farewell parade in Kabul and begin phased withdrawal. USSR formally starts a nine-month withdrawal, with 30,000 men to leave in the next two weeks. The Soviet plan seems to be to remove all sophisticated military equipment from the country and to move out along an axis from Shindand in the east to Kandahar in the center, north toward Kabul while removing forces from Gardez and Ghazni in the east, and then out of the country along the routes from Kabul to the USSR. The projected completion date is 15 February 1989, although the agreement allows Soviet advisors to stay in the country.[62]
- Mid-May 1988: Both the RA and Mujahideen exhibit continuing internal differences in spite of efforts at unity. Both arm for a major conflict.
- 16 May 1988: RA government agrees to allow UN officials to provide economic aid to areas not under the control of the government.
- 18 May 1988: First withdrawing Russian troops cross border into Russia. Mujahideen leaders from seven main groups meet in Afghanistan to discuss unified strategy for toppling RA after Russians leave.
- 19 May 1988: Soviet historian Eduard Rozentak says reports

of 12,000–18,000 Soviet dead in Afghanistan are more or less correct.

- Late May 1988: Three RA fortresses along the eastern border have fallen to the Mujahideen as Soviet forces begin to withdraw. These include Barikot (April 22), Chamkani (May 7), and Jaji (May 15). RA forces evacuate outlying bases they feel they cannot hold, like Mamakhel and Kagga, southwest of Jalalabad, and Tanbana, in the Panjshir Valley. The Soviets turn AN-12 transports over to the RA and suddenly provide large supplies of night vision devices and tactical radars. They begin flying bombing missions in support of RA forces threatened by the Mujahideen.
- Late May 1988: Soviet forces continue to pull out of the Nangarhar province and Kunar Valley. New long-range Mujahideen rockets hit Kabul. Mujahideen forces move toward Khost, Ghazni, Gardez, and Jalalabad. A major battle begins to shape up for Jalalabad, as a Hezb-i-Islami Mujahideen force attempts to take and hold a major city for the first time in the ten-year history of the war. Some 12,000 RA troops remain in Jalalabad. The Mujahideen decide against the attack as they discover the Soviets have returned some 2,000 men to the city after a highly visible withdrawal.
- 28 May 1988: One day before President Reagan arrives for the Moscow summit, the Soviet foreign ministry warns that the Soviets may slow down their pullout if Pakistan does not halt its "interference in the internal affairs of Afghanistan" and the U.S. does not reduce its "lavish supplies . . . of arms." Lt. General Boris Grimov, commander of the Soviet troops in Afghanistan, indicates that the USSR will leave $1 billion worth of equipment behind for the RA as it withdraws from Afghanistan. U.S. aid is now estimated to have reached $2 billion.
- 29 May 1988: Najibullah convenes Afghanistan's first parliament in fifteen years and urges the Mujahideen to take vacant seats in it.
- June 1988: The RA now has major problems in the west. The 25th Division is forced to defend Khost. The 12th Division has suffered major losses in the Jaji Valley campaign, and only the 14th Division (with a maximum of 5,000 regulars and militia) can cover the 200-mile road from Kandahar to Kabul. Mujahideen forces temporarily take towns and cities like Qara Bagh and Qalat. The southern highway becomes steadily less safe, and Kandahar becomes increasingly dependent on the route to the west from Herat and on air supply.

- 7 June 1988: Najibullah says at the UN that he might ask the Soviets to delay their withdrawal if Pakistan does not halt the follow of arms to the Mujahideen. He states that the Soviets have already withdrawn 34,000 troops. Pakistani officials say the figure is closer to 15,000, and a Soviet Deputy Foreign Minister says 13,000.
- Early June 1988: The seven-party Mujahideen alliance in Peshawar is unable to develop a coherent policy toward the RA. The Mujahideen field commanders become more and more powerful, but remain divided. Pakistan's support of Gulbuddin Hekmatyr's radical Islamic Party creates fears that a strongly anti-Soviet Islamic fundamentalist group might take over. Various field commanders strengthen their power in their own areas: Ismail Khan in Herat in the west, Abdul Haq in the region around Kabul, and Ahmad Shah Massoud who heads an alliance of commanders in seven northeast provinces.
- 18 June 1988: Qalat, the provincial capital of Zabul in southeastern Afghanistan, falls to the Mujahideen after a seventeen-day siege. It is the first city to fall into their hands, but a 300–400 man RA fortress continues to fight.
- 19 June 1988: The seven-party alliance names a cabinet of two vice-presidents and eleven ministers, divided between Islamic fundamentalists and moderates. Ahmad Shah, a U.S.-educated engineer, is named president of the transitional government. The U.S. considers sending an envoy to the Mujahideen because of growing problems in the flow of information through Pakistan and Pakistan's alignment with radical Islamic factions.

    The Mujahideen attack on a key RA border defense point called Spin Boldak fails. The Mujahideen siege cannot drive well-supplied RA troops out of a heavily fortified position.
- 24 June 1988: Mujahideen forces infiltrate the defense perimeter around Kabul and destroy eight Su-25 fighters.
- 25 June 1988: The RA retakes Qalat after Mujahideen factions start fighting over control of the city. The RA garrison makes effective use of its artillery, and the Mujahideen cannot penetrate the RA minefields. The RA's combination of superior firepower, fortifications, and mines becomes a key factor limiting Mujahideen success.
- Late June 1988: Bitter fighting continues in Kandahar. The RA garrison, with 6,000 men (1,000 conscripts and 5,000 militiamen), fights well against up to 20,000 Mujahideen. The RA forces have a well-protected base with dug-in tanks and some twenty fortified strong points. High-flying Soviet aircraft provide

extensive air support beyond the range of the Stinger. The only long-range Mujahideen weapon is the B-12 rocket.

- 27 June 1988: President Zia of Pakistan charges that the WAD is carrying out large-scale bombing attacks and terrorism in Pakistan. The Soviets claim to have cleared 1,518 of the 2,131 minefields they laid in Afghanistan and to have turned 100 more minefields over to the RA. The Soviets are estimated to have laid some 10 million to 16 million mines in the country. Many are booby traps or are not in plotted minefields.[63]

- July 1988: UN negotiator Diego Cordovez conducts a nine-day shuttle to Kabul, Tehran, and Islamabad in an unsuccessful effort to achieve a cease-fire by 1 September and form a new government through a Loyah Jerga.

- Early July 1988: In spite of reversals in attacking major strong points and cities, the Mujahideen have now occupied nearly 100 garrison points once held by Soviet and RA forces. The effort to interdict supply along the Pakistani border is largely abandoned. The Mujahideen get steadily larger supplies of 122-mm rockets with ranges up to twelve miles, plus 120-mm mortars.

- July 1988: Mujahideen forces move on Kandahar from the west and the Arghandab Valley in the north. They are halted by Soviet high-level bombing and take significant losses.

- 9 July 1988: Diego Cordovez of the UN calls for a halt to the fighting and to efforts to create a coalition government.

- 12 July 1988: Mujahideen forces leave Maidan Shar, capital of Wardak province, after a brief occupation. The Soviets bomb the town and say they will continue until the Mujahideen leave. The Soviets accuse Pakistan of violating the Geneva accords by continuing to provide high volumes of supply to the Mujahideen and encouraging them to attack Soviet troops; they say there were at least 250 violations of the accords since 15 May.

- 16 July 1988: Pakistan, under heavy pressure from the U.S., says it will cut the flow of supplies to the Mujahideen. The Mujahideen fire twenty-one rockets into Kabul from their positions roughly six miles outside the city, killing twenty and wounding thirty-four. The Soviets move troops back into the area and counterattack the Mujahideen positions.

- 25 July 1988: The Soviets say they will still withdraw 50 percent of their troops by 15 August, but the figures are uncertain. The Soviets say they have now withdrawn 32,000 troops, but the U.S. believes the figure is 25,000. The Soviets have previously said they had 100,300 troops in the country on 15 May, when the U.S. estimated the figure at 115,000.[64]

- August 1988: The U.S. has now begun shipping arms to the Afghan field commanders directly, often using trucks moving from Pakistan. The U.S. is doing this in part to sharply reduce control by Gulbuddin Hekmatyr and the fundamentalist Hezb-i-Islami Party over the flow of arms and to ensure that moderates can play a strong role in any future government.[65]
- 4 August 1988: Pakistani F-16 shoots down the third RA or Soviet aircraft that Pakistan has intercepted intruding into Pakistani air space.
- 5 August 1988: The USSR announces that all Soviet troops have left Kandahar. The city is reinforced by RA troops.
- 8 August–early September 1988: The Mujahideen have long controlled most of Kunduz province, except the cities of Kunduz, Talequan, and Faizabad. The Soviets withdraw from Faizabad and Kunduz by 8 August. They leave only the 19th RA Division which is forced to cover the entire road from Faizabad to Kunduz. The Mujahideen attempt to take Kunduz during 10–14 August and occupy most of the city but cannot take the air field. Kunduz is on one of the two main roads north from Kabul to the Soviet border. (Most Soviet forces are moving along the other route to Hieratan and Termez.) The USSR airlifts in Soviet troops and RA reinforcements at night, including special KHAD troops. Soviet fighters provide up to thirty sorties a day of air support. A column of the 20th RA Division is sent north from Baghlan. Kunduz is relieved on 19 August, but the Mujahideen then capture Khanabad, Talequan, and Keshem in the northeast. The RA forces recapture Khanabad but cannot take Talequan. The 20th Division has taken heavy losses during its offensive, and the RA 19th Division is now trapped in the border area in Faizabad.
- 10–11 August 1988: Mujahideen rockets hit a Soviet supply dump at Kalagay, along the Salang highway about 100 miles north of Kabul. Some reports say the major supply dump of the Soviet 40th Army is destroyed and 109–598 Soviet troops and 112 civilians are killed. Some reports say that up to two years' worth of ammunition and much of Kabul's fuel storage are lost. Lt. General Boris Grimov denies any such losses.[66]
- Mid-August 1988: The Mujahideen have still not taken Khost near the Pakistani border after a siege of more than eight months. The Soviets and RA provide air supply by night, and the combination of minefields, artillery, and fortress positions cannot be overcome. The Soviets use large numbers of flares at night to help counter the Stinger.
- 13 August 1988: The fighting for Kunduz continues as the

Mujahideen take the city on 13 August, but lose it the next day. The Soviets have rushed out of the city in an effort to meet their goal of a 50 percent reduction. Control of the city remains uncertain until 18 August. The Soviets return to the city by late August, when it becomes apparent that the RA cannot hold it alone.

- 14 August 1988: The USSR charges that a regular Pakistani army unit has fought in support of the Mujahideen near Spin Boldak.
- 15 August 1988: The Soviets announce that they have cut their troops by 50 percent. The Soviet commander, Lt. General Boris Grimov, announces that the USSR will leave the RA with $250 million worth of buildings. He says Soviet troops will now remain concentrated in six provinces, including Kabul, Kapisa, Baghlan, and Samangan. This covers the area around the capital and the route north. Soviet forces stay in Farah province in the west, probably to keep the air base at Shindand.[67] The RA is having increasing trouble maintaining a presence in the northeastern provinces of Takhar, Kunduz, and Kunar.
- 17 August 1988: President Zia of Pakistan, U.S. Ambassador Arnold Raphael, the U.S. military attaché, and several Pakistani generals are killed as their C-130 explodes in midair shortly after taking off from Bahawalpur. Pakistani investigators later claim sabotage, but are unable to trace the exact cause or determine who is responsible or whether those involved have external backing. Pakistan immediately says it will continue its support of the Mujahideen. On 22 August, *Pravda* denies any role in Zia's death.
- 27 August 1988: A new wave of Mujahideen rocket attacks takes place on Kabul. Some twenty rockets hit the airport. Soviet and RA troops immediately attempt to sweep the area.
- 31 August 1988: The U.S. charges that the USSR has violated the Geneva accords and is bombing Afghan targets using aircraft based outside the country. The fighting around Kunduz continues. The RA has provided some 3,000–4,000 reinforcements, and Soviet troops have returned to the city. (Only the use of aircraft in Afghanistan is forbidden by the accords.) The Soviets say they are only responding to Pakistani violations of the accords.
- 1 September 1988: A massive ammunition dump at Kabul explodes. Vast amounts of munitions and some aircraft are destroyed. The Mujahideen now seem to have towed 122-mm multiple rocket launchers and are able to deliver significant fire much more accurately.
- 2 September–November 1988: The Soviets withdraw from

Kandahar. The loyalty of the Achakzai Militia Brigade and two RA battalions defending Spin Boldak collapses, and the Mujahideen take Spin Boldak and the road up to Taktahpul on the southeast outskirts of Kandahar. Up to 500 Soviet troops and 18 helicopters re-deploy to Kandahar to reinforce its defenses. Mujahideen forces capture several towns near the Soviet line of retreat, including Istaleef, Mir Bacha Kot, and Qara Bagh, north of Kabul. Kalakin, Kariz e Mir, and Qala Murad Beg are under fire. An RA government counterattack is beaten back on 15 October, and only a Soviet supply column from Herat, the deployment of more Uzbeck forces, and Soviet air support in the form of MiG-27 fighters and Backfire bombers can secure the city.

- 12 September 1988: Najibullah abolishes the National Reconciliation Commission he had set up in 1987.
- 23 September 1988: Pakistan reports the fourth RA air raid of the month on Pakistani territory.
- 27 September 1988: Soviet Foreign Minister Eduard Shevardnadze issues a veiled threat that the Soviets will halt their pullout if attacks on their forces and key RA strong points do not cease.
- 28 September 1988: The State Department announces the U.S. has asked the Mujahideen to stop harassing Soviet forces and let them withdraw in peace. Rebel rocket and bombing attacks on Kabul continue.
- 30 September 1988: Abdul Wakil, the Afghan Foreign Minister, accuses the U.S. and Pakistan of violating the Geneva accords.
- 30 September–15 October 1988: The militia garrison at Asmar, which supports the key RA unit securing the Kunar Valley—the 9th RA Division—defects to the Mujahideen. The RA government is forced to rapidly withdraw the 9th Division from Asadabad, which is about to be cut off, and relocate it to Jalalabad.
- Late September 1988: The seven-party rebel alliance in Peshawar turns down new Soviet offers of negotiating a coalition government.
- October–November, 1988: Mujahideen capture a number of strategic military posts controlling the main supply routes across the Pakistan-Afghan border and securing the Jalalabad-Kabul highway.
- 5 October 1988: The Soviet command in Afghanistan complains that rebels continue to rocket Kabul and lay siege to Khost.
- 9 October 1988: A special meeting of the People's Democratic Party of Afghanistan takes place in Kabul. In fact, Najibullah calls for a purifying purge of the party. His proposal follows new signs of a division between the dominant Parcham faction and its

rivals in the Khalq. Afghanistan's Prime Minister, Mohammed Hassan Sharq, who is not a member of the party, states that "the Afghan people do not have much confidence in the ruling People's Democratic Party or in the Mujahideen."[68] The Soviets praise Sharq in a sustained media campaign, and he travels to Moscow to meet Gorbachev. Rumors surface that Najibullah may step down so Sharq can take his place, as the USSR searches to find some way of creating a political solution to the conflict. The Soviets suddenly start to praise Ahmad Shah Massoud, evidently reaching out to the more moderate factions of the Mujahideen.

- Early October 1988: The Mujahideen are reported to have taken thirty-eight military posts in Paktia from RA forces and to have captured eighty vehicles and large quantities of weapons.
- 19 October 1988: Another special meeting of the People's Democratic Party of Afghanistan takes place in Kabul. It is clear that ten to fifteen arrests and detentions of senior party officials have taken place. Two members of the twelve-man Politburo are removed—one from the Khalq and one from the Parcham faction. Rebel shelling of Kabul continues.
- 21 October 1988: At a PDPA party plenum, Najibullah calls for negotiations with the Mujahideen. Deigo Cordovez calls upon the former king of Afghanistan, Mohammed Zahir Shah, to act as a mediator.
- 26 October 1988: RA government claims three U.S. "military advisors" are killed by a land mine in Paktia.
- Late October 1988: Three senior Pakistani intelligence officials are reported to have visited Massoud to offer him help. Massoud is reported to be forming regular forces to strike at the RA in urban areas once the Soviets leave.

  First Deputy Foreign Minister Yuli Vorontsov is evidently given the responsibility of trying to help the RA government negotiate to form a coalition with the Mujahideen. Army General Valentin Ivanovick Varenniknov, First Deputy Chief of Staff of the Soviet Armed Forces, is evidently put in charge of the withdrawal of Soviet troops within the Soviet Ministry of Defense.[69]
- 28 October 1988: U.S. intelligence sources state that the USSR has deployed thirty new MiG-27 attack jets at Shindand. The MiG-27 is an advanced attack aircraft with significantly superior range-payload and attack avionics to the MiG-23. Backfire bombers, flying from Mariy in the Turkestan Republic of the USSR, bomb Mujahideen positions. The Backfires carry twelve to eighteen

bombs each and fly above the range of the Stinger missiles. Su-24 fighter-bombers attack from closer to Afghanistan.[70]

- 30 October 1988: President Najibullah calls on the UN to organize an international conference that would endorse nonaligned status for his country. It is announced that Prime Minister Mohammed Hassan Sharq will address the United Nations. This seems to be part of a Soviet campaign to build him up as a non-party compromise leader.

    The seven-party Mujahideen alliance announces it will hold elections in January to select a President and to negotiate a cease-fire with the RA. They do, however, rule out communist participation in a government.

- November 1988: Soviets claim that the Mujahideen are now holding 313 Soviet prisoners of war.

    A major Mujahideen concentration is building up around Kandahar. The city can be safely supplied only by air, and Mujahideen 107-mm and 120-mm rockets regularly hit the airport. The 15th RA Infantry Division and substantial militia forces are under virtual siege in Kandahar.

    Various Mujahideen factions announce a new offensive to hit Soviet forces as they withdraw from the country. Raids continue on the Salang highway, sometimes halting traffic. Massoud has reacted to the deployment of the MiG-27 and Scud by ending his policy of letting the Soviets withdraw. The RA has committed all of its reserves to defending Kunduz and can do little to defend the main supply route to Kabul. Bread and fuel begin to become scarce.

    Rocket attacks and raids continue in the Kabul area. The Mujahideen now have Egyptian, PRC, and Soviet rockets with ranges up to thirty kilometers. Mujahideen forces have de facto control of Logar south of Kabul and Kunar and Kapisa to the northeast. Ariana Afghan Airways and Aeroflot are now the only airlines flying to Kabul. Kabul is swollen from a city of one million to nearly two and a half million as pro-RA groups evacuate the countryside. Food becomes steadily more scarce, and the city is almost totally dependent on imports from the USSR.

- 1 November 1988: Scud B (SS-1E) long-range missiles, with a range of up to 180 miles, are paraded through the streets of Kabul, evidently as a symbol of Soviet support to the RA and a tacit threat to Pakistan. Tass indicates the missiles will be used against rebel bases, munitions depots, and rocket launch zones. U.S. reconnaissance photos show Scud and FROG missiles have been deployed where they can fire into Pakistan.

- 2 November 1988: Pakistan claims to have shot down one of two RA Su-22s that flew ten miles into its airspace. The Soviets fire at least ten Scud missiles at Mujahideen positions near the Pakistani border.

  The Mujahideen have spent months capturing the local garrisons around Torkham on the road from the Pakistani border to Jalalabad. They now take Torkham. The RA is forced to deploy the 11th Division and the 9th Division, which it has withdrawn from Kunar, to launch a counterattack.
- 4 November 1988: First Deputy Foreign Minister Alexander Bessmertnykh announces the Soviets are suspending their pullout from Afghanistan and may slip their 15 February 1989 deadline unless they are allowed to withdraw peacefully and unless an honorable compromise is reached between the Mujahideen and the RA. He claims there have been 555 attacks on Soviet forces since the 14 April accords, including 26 on Soviet aircraft. President Reagan threatens to stop encouraging the Mujahideen to show restraint and to stop providing U.S. support for restraining the flow of arms to them.
- 5 November 1988: The Soviet press does not repeat Bessmertnykh's remarks and only notes that Soviet forces whose tour is completed are being partially replaced and more up-to-date equipment is being provided.
- 7 November 1988: The USSR has already fired eight Scud missiles against Mujahideen bases near the Pakistani border. The USSR continues to fly MiG-27s from Shindand and Backfires from the USSR against the Mujahideen forces surrounding Kandahar. Mujahideen sources claim that MiG-27 raids have killed 66 and wounded 193 in Kandahar, virtually all civilians.[71]

  RA Deputy Foreign Minister Abdul Ghaffar Lakanwal defects while attending a meeting at the UN with Afghan Prime Minister Mohammed Sharq.
- 9 November 1988: Afghan Prime Minister Mohammed Hassan Sharq calls for demilitarization of Afghanistan under international supervision and for a UN conference to ensure Afghan neutrality.
- 10 November 1988: A spokesman for the Mujahideen coalition in Peshawar says that Mujahideen will attack withdrawing Soviet forces in retaliation for missile strikes and bombings. Press reports say that the U.S. will no longer urge restraint on Mujahideen, but the U.S. privately urges Mujahideen not to attack Kandahar until after Soviet withdrawals are completed.
- 11 November 1988: Afghan Deputy Prime Minister Mangal warns

that Afghanistan faces a desperate struggle and that the "intensiveness" of military operations will double or triple once the Soviet forces leave.[72]

- 11–13 November 1988: CPSU Central Committee Secretary Baklanov tells Soviet servicemen in Afghanistan that they will be withdrawn in "strict accordance with the time frame set by the Geneva agreements."[73]
- 14 November 1988: RA troops and militia reopen the Jalalabad-to-Tor Khan highway through the Khyber Pass after a week of fighting with Mujahideen.
- Mid-November 1988: Soviet and RA 9th and 11th Division forces retake a key base at Torkham on the Kabul-Jalalabad highway. The USSR continues to try to use limited military action and threats to force the Mujahideen to reach a settlement with the RA. The Mujahideen charge new uses of chemical warfare by the Soviets.

  Continuous fighting takes place for Torkham. A shipment of Milan anti-tank weapons is given to the Mujahideen, who destroy a company of tanks and cause 185 RA soldiers to surrender. Torkham is held securely by the Mujahideen on 25 November.
- 15 November 1988: Ten Soviets are killed and eleven wounded by rebel rocket attacks on Kabul civilian airport when a rocket hits an Aeroflot airliner. Lt. General Lev B. Serebrov, the head of intelligence in the LCSFA threatens that the USSR will escalate its attacks on the Mujahideen if such rocket attacks continue.
- 19 November 1988: Gorbachev warns that the U.S. and Pakistan may be attempting to scuttle the Geneva accords and calls for them to accept "new approaches to international affairs."
- Late November 1988: Mujahideen successes, such as the retaking of Torkham, force the Soviets to agree to one-on-one talks with the Mujahideen in return for an agreement to reduce attacks on retreating Soviet forces, particularly in the Salang Valley.
- 3–5 December 1988: Soviet and Mujahideen representatives meet in Saudi Arabia to discuss the withdrawal and cease-fire. Some compromises seem to be reached on POW exchanges and on halting attacks on Soviet forces and on 7 December, First Deputy Minister Yuli Vorontsov states the Soviet withdrawal from Afghanistan will be completed by 15 February and "probably before." They do not reach any agreement on a settlement with the RA.
- 7 December 1988: At UN, Gorbachev calls for a cease-fire in January, a halt to arming all belligerents, a UN peacekeeping contingent, and an international conference on neutrality and

demilitarization of Afghanistan. Mujahideen later call for holding elections in January 1989 to elect a head of state who can negotiate a cease-fire.

Afghan Foreign Minister Wakil publishes an interview in *Pravda* calling for "securing neutral status" for Afghanistan and talks of Austria and Switzerland as "perfectly acceptable" precedents.

- 8 December 1988: RA Vice-President Abdul Hamid Mohtat states that a lasting cease-fire is the government's top priority.
- 18 December 1988: A Mujahideen spokesman in Peshawar says the Soviets must bring specific proposals to the next meeting if any progress is to be made on a cease-fire. Reports surface that the Mujahideen might agree to a cease-fire if the Soviets halt bombing, agree to leave by 15 February and pay reparations after the war.
- 22 December 1988: First Deputy Minister Yuli Vorontsov and First Deputy Foreign Minister Bessmertnykh meet with U.S. Ambassador John Matlock, Jr., to discuss Afghanistan.

Major food shortages begin to build up in Kabul as city swells in population and food shipments into the city from the USSR are reduced.

- 24 December 1988: First Deputy Minister Yuli Vorontsov meets with former Afghan king Zahir Shah in Rome. Tass report of the meeting talks about the potential role of the ex-king in a dialogue of "all political forces."[74]
- 31 December 1988: Najibullah announces a temporary unilateral cease-fire. Soviet Foreign Ministry announces similar cease-fire for Soviet forces.

First Deputy Foreign Minister Bessmertnykh meets with U.S. Ambassador Matlock on Afghanistan.

RA announces another temporary cease-fire. Soviet Foreign Ministry announces a similar cease-fire for Soviet forces and warns that it will end after four days if not observed by Mujahideen.

- 2–4 January 1989: Vorontsov meets with Iranian Foreign Minister Velayati and talks of a possible meeting with the eight largest Iranian-backed Mujahideen groups in the west.
- 3 January 1989: RA announces it has carried out a "retaliatory strike" because the Mujahideen do not observe the 31 December cease-fire offer.
- 3–4 January 1989: Iranian Deputy Foreign Minister Larijani meets with Gorbachev as a personal representative of Khomeini.
- 4 January 1989: Vorontsov meets with Pakistani officials in

Islamabad and talks about meetings with representatives of the seven largest Mujahideen groups in the east.

- 15 January 1989: Soviet commander in Afghanistan, Lt. General Boris Grimov, again says that Soviet forces will complete withdrawal on schedule.

    Food and fuel shortages in Kabul are reaching the crisis point; some rioting is reported.

- 20–23 January 1989: Soviets conduct major bombings and heliborne sweeps in an effort to secure Salang highway from attacks by Mujahideen led by Massoud. Hundreds of Mujahideen and civilians are killed.

    Soviets relieve food crisis in Kabul by using IL-76s and military transports to fly in some 3,000 tons of food supplies. Each flight requires fire flares and up to four helicopters to surround the aircraft during takeoff and landing.

- 26 January 1989: *Izvestiya* carries an article expressing doubts about RA forces' ability to defend Kabul.

- 27–28 January 1989: Soviet Minister of Defense Yazov visits Kabul. RA reports say he gives Gorbachev's "assurance" that the USSR will "not abandon its friends." The Soviets do not carry this report of the meeting.

- 29 January 1989: Moscow TV criticizes the Afghan government for not moving food and supplies to Kabul the previous summer, saying the government is "not just" and "perhaps a criminal design" was behind this failure.

- 30 January 1989: Soviet commander in Afghanistan, Lt. General Boris Grimov, says that Soviet bombing in support of the RA will cease when Soviet forces complete withdrawal.

- Early February 1989: RA government arms some 30,000–50,000 members of the PDPA. The "Palace Guard" defending Kabul and the RA regime is said to total 20,000–25,000.[75]

- 4 February 1989: The Mujahideen launch rocket attacks on Bagram air base.

- 5 February 1989: Mujahideen seize RA military camp in Qarah Bagh area as smaller RA outposts continue to fall.

- 5–7 February 1989: Soviet Foreign Minister Eduard Shevardnadze makes no progress in two days of talks in Pakistan in persuading the Mujahideen to accept a coalition government with the RA.

- 7 February 1989: The U.S. now estimates that there are 3.5 million Afghan refugees in Pakistan and 1.5 million in Iran. It also estimates that there are 10 to 30 million land mines in Afghanistan, and its estimate of the impact of Soviet and RA military attacks on Pakistan is 450 dead and 800 wounded plus 500 dead and 2,000 wounded from some 900 terrorist attacks.[76]

- 8 February 1989: Seven main Mujahideen groups in Peshawar continue debate on how to attack Kabul. Efforts to compromise on giving each group an equal voice fail. Leaders like Abdul Haq cannot forge any unity on key issues.
- 9 February 1989: A Soviet soldier dies in one of the few Mujahideen attacks on a Soviet convoy leaving Afghanistan during the final month of Soviet withdrawal.
- 10 February 1989: Bush Administration reaches decision to continue supplying arms to Mujahideen in spite of growing concern that Mujahideen may divide into civil war between moderate and extremist Islamic factions and along tribal and ethnic lines.
- 11 February 1989: A shura, or consultative council, of the seven major resistance groups based in Afghanistan meets, but some elements boycott meeting and little real unity is achieved.

   Najibullah accuses Pakistan of planning to invade Afghanistan and annex the country in an effort to end Mujahideen ties to Pakistan.

   An RA Air Force pilot defects to Mujahideen. Shelling and minor clashes take place in Kandahar, Helmand, Paktia, and Nangarhar.
- 12 February 1989: Soviet forces in LCSFA now remain in only two Afghan provinces.
- 13 February 1989: The last Soviet soldier in the capital, private Vyacheslav Ryabinin, leaves Kabul. Soviet forces are now deployed only in the border towns of Towraghondi, near Kushka, and Hieratan opposite Termez.
- 15 February 1989: Last Soviet members of LCSFA leave Afghanistan. Fifty armored personnel carriers and 400 men cross Friendship Brigade between Khairaton and Termez. The last Soviet soldier leaves when the LCSFA's commander, Lt. General Boris Grimov, walks across the bridge to Termez. USSR announces that some 250 Soviet "diplomats" and a "small cadre" of Soviet military advisors stay behind.

   Both Soviet and RA governments reiterate the fact that Soviet air power will not be used to help the RA after the withdrawal. Mujahideen now have up to 30,000 men around Kabul and 15,000 around Kandahar. Mujahideen forces also surround Jalalabad, which has several thousand RA army troops and up to 2,000 WAD, Sarandoy, and militia forces.

   Pravda reports that a Soviet airlift has brought 7,000 tons of emergency supplies into Kabul and that the airlift is continuing.

Tass reports a large supply convoy has reached the city through the Salang Pass. *Trud* reports looting and desertions by the RA Army.

- 16 February 1989: Mujahideen fire ten rockets at Kabul and kill seven. Mujahideen use rockets and mortars on Herat, Ghazni, Gardez, and Khost. Salang highway is cut intermittently by Mujahideen forces.
- 18 February 1989: A shura of the seven major Islamic guerrilla movements, with 400 delegates, announces it has agreed on a government in exile with a moderate president, Mohammed Nabi Mohammed, and conservative Premier, Ahmad Shah. They fail, however, to agree on a cabinet, and dissent breaks out over the nomination of Ahmad Shah.
- 18 February 1989: Najibullah declares a state of emergency. He seems to have given up on a coalition government. He strengthens his own powers and prepares to rule with loyalists. Civil rights are suspended. A Shi'ite, Sultan Ali Kishtman, replaces a potential rival to Najibullah, Mohammed Hassan Sharq, as Prime Minister. Najibullah, however, presides over the new Council of Ministers.
- 23 February 1989: Low-level fighting occurs between RA and Mujahideen forces in Kandahar and Herat and along the Kabul-Nangarhar highway. Food rioting continues in Kabul. The RA government makes new efforts at forced conscription.
- 24 February 1989: Shura of the seven major Islamic guerrilla movements, with 400 delegates, again announces it has agreed on a government in exile with a moderate intellectual, Sibgatullah Mojadedi, as president and offers amnesty to most RA officials. They choose Abdul Rabbur Rasul Saif, a strict fundamentalist conservative, as Premier and nominate Ahmad Shah to the cabinet. They fail, however, to agree on a cabinet, and dissent breaks out over the nomination of Ahmad Shah. The cabinet is elected and includes three key fundamentalists: Yunis Khalis, Gulbuddin Hekmatyr, and Burhanuddin Rabbani. New reports surface of Mujahideen squabbling on strategy and influence leading to delays in the attack on Jalalabad. Debates surface over whether Pakistan should be allowed to transfer U.S. aid, given its tendency to favor the fundamentalist and anti-Western movement led by Hekmatyr's Islamic Party.
- 5 March 1989: New fighting in the Salang as Mujahideen fire on RA convoys to Kabul.

The Key Lessons from Soviet Withdrawal
and Future Trends in the Afghan Conflict

As Figure 2.1 shows, the USSR succeeded in keeping the Afghanistan conflict from becoming as costly and divisive as the U.S. intervention in Vietnam. Nevertheless, the Soviets repeated many aspects of the American experience in that conflict. They were able to win most military encounters, but they were not able to occupy the countryside, and they faced an insuperable military problem: They could not defeat an aroused people and were committed to backing a government that lacked popular support.

The Democratic Republic of Afghanistan was incapable of becoming a popular government, and its power base was too small to allow it to become a successful tyranny. As a result, Soviet military victories could make the situation worse but not better. Nothing short of destruction of the people could allow Soviet forces to defeat the enemy in the countryside and outside the major urban areas and military strong points. Nothing short of a truly massive Soviet military presence five to six times the forces the USSR deployed could have allowed them to occupy the territory they gained temporary control of through tactical victories. Yevgeny Primakov, a member of the Central Committee and director of the Soviet Institute of World Economic and International Relations, admitted shortly before the final Soviet withdrawal, "Our mistake was thinking this government (the DRA) can control the situation around the country. We were mistaken in these ideas."[77]

There were several other factors that denied the USSR success. The Soviets were never able to cut the Mujahideen off from "sanctuaries" in Pakistan and Iran and their external sources of supply. The USSR seems to have initially had a very exaggerated idea of its ability, through pacification and relocation campaigns, to use troops and airpower to reduce the Mujahideen's ability to obtain local supplies of food and shelter. It placed far more importance than was justified on forcing an entire people into compliance and submission by air, artillery, gas, mine, and infantry attacks on the population.

The Soviets learned three major lessons of modern war in much the same hard way the U.S. learned them in Vietnam: First, it is virtually impossible to defeat a popular guerrilla army with secure sources of supply and a recovery area. Second, it is extremely difficult—if not impossible—to use modern weapons technology to cut off a guerrilla force from food and other basic supplies. Third, the success of pacification techniques depends on the existence of a popular local government, and the techniques must be seen as the actions of the local government and not of foreign military forces.

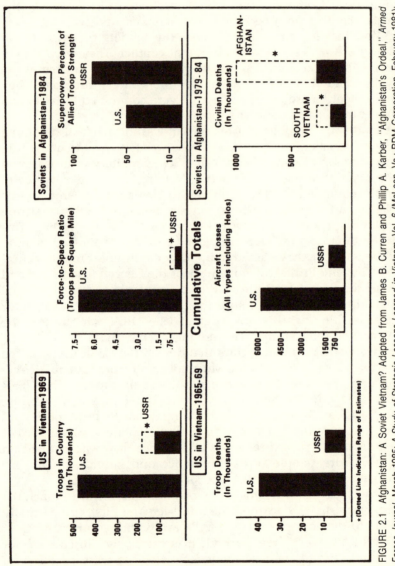

FIGURE 2.1 Afghanistan: A Soviet Vietnam? Adapted from James B. Curren and Phillip A. Karber, "Afghanistan's Ordeal," *Armed Forces Journal*, March 1985; *A Study of Strategic Lessons Learned in Vietnam*, Vol. 6 (McLean, Va.: BDM Corporation, February 1981); Gunther Lewy, *America in Vietnam* (New York: Oxford University Press, 1978); conversations with U.S. Department of State officials, November 26–28, 1984; and "News in Brief," *International Defense Review*, March 1984.

The RA government remains deeply divided at this writing. While Najibullah's Parcham (Banner) faction is still in control and dominates the KGB-trained KHAD, it is the Khalq (Masses) faction which is most popular and which has the most influence outside Kabul. The Khalq also still has the most influence over the army. Both factions still attack each other and seem to have conducted some assassinations during the start of Soviet withdrawal. The Soviets may be willing to accept a non-party government as a trade for stability, and the future status of the entire communist party in Afghanistan is now uncertain.

It is far from clear, however, that Soviet withdrawal will bring the Mujahideen a decisive victory, or which—if any—mix of factions in the Mujahideen will take power. The Mujahideen controlled only about one-third of the country on 15 May 1988—the day Soviet withdrawal began. They were deeply divided in terms of religion, tribe, and their approach to running a state. The leadership of the Republic of Afghanistan was also deeply divided, however, and may be unable to unite against the Mujahideen, even in the face of Soviet withdrawal.

Since the Soviet withdrawal, the Mujahideen have failed to emerge as a cohesive fighting force, or one strong enough to take a single major RA-held city. Massive continuing Soviet aid has kept the RA government alive and allowed RA land and air forces to become more effective. Improved Soviet countermeasures have given the RA Air Force and Soviet air transport aircraft much greater ability to survive Stinger attacks. Soviet supply of over 500 Scud missiles, each with 1,600-pound warheads, has given the RA an effective "terror weapon" that cannot be halted with the Stinger.

The Mujahideen's efforts to seize Jalalabad in a siege lasting four months between March and June 1989 devastated the city after strikes by nearly 130,000 Mujahideen-fired rockets. The Mujahideen never succeeded in breaching more than part of one ring of Jalalabad's defenses, however, and suffered serious casualties. They also failed to improve their ability to coordinate their attacks and lacked the artillery and anti-armor capability to penetrate RA minefields and active defenses. In addition, they had to reduce operations in many areas to mass a force of only 5,000–14,000 men; the RA force in Jalalabad alone totaled 15,000 to 20,000.

The future of the Mujahideen effort will depend on the flow of aid and technology. The U.S. and Pakistan cut their aid effort in the first five months of 1989 because they thought the RA government would rapidly collapse. The USSR, meanwhile, provided an airlift of 25 to 40 IL-76 aircraft per day to the RA, plus aid at a rate of over 300 million rubles ($490 million) per year. The Soviets also gave the RA

Air Force Antonov 12 transports converted to act as bombers that can fly above the range of the Stinger and drop up to 30,000 pounds of bombs.

In mid-1989, the RA still had roughly 55,000 men in the Army and Air Force, 35,000 in the Ministry of State Security secret police, 25,000 men in the Sarandoy, 25,000 in various irregular militias, and an additional 20,000 in PDPA and party youth militias. It had a new Special Guards Corps defending Kabul, with a strength of three brigades consolidated from the 37th and 38th commando brigades, the Presidential Guard Brigade and elements of the Sarandoy. This Guards force had up to 10,000 men. The RA also steadily expanded its minefields and defensive rings around Kabul and other key cities.

The RA armed forces received large numbers of Soviet weapons from the Soviet forces evacuating Afghanistan in January and February 1989. These included BTR-70 armored personnel carriers, BMP-2 armored infantry fighting vehicles, 122-mm self-propelled guns, BM-27 multiple rocket launchers, and AGS-17 automatic grenade launchers. The Soviets delivered a further massive convoy of T-54 and T-62 tanks, APCs, and artillery to Afghanistan in late May 1989. The Soviets also left the RA Air Force with a strength of 80–90 Su-22 and other Sukhoi fighter-bombers, 15–20 MiG-27s, 50 MiG-21s, 20 MiG-17s, 30 Mi-24s, 60 Mi-8s and Mi-17s, 35–40 AN-26s and AN-32s, and 12 AN-12s.

This array of equipment gave the RA much the same firepower advantage against the Mujahideen that the Soviets had had before their withdrawal. The RA government was content to hold a few key cities while pressing for some form of coalition government. It became more popular the moment it stood on its own, while the Mujahideen remained divided and often fought each other over spoils they had not yet won. Rather than give the Mujahideen a quick victory, the Soviet withdrawal had the initial effect of leaving much the same divisions in Afghanistan that existed at the time of the Soviet invasion.

To succeed, the Mujahideen must now unify, convert their forces to conduct regular operations, acquire a major new source of firepower, cut off the RA's internal lines of communication, and limit Soviet resupply. In contrast, the RA can succeed only if it can somehow break the Mujahideen's will to resist or can create a coalition government in which the RA still plays a major role. It is difficult to rule out the alternative of a bloody stalemate lasting several years.

The future role of external powers is equally uncertain. The USSR is attempting to preserve its influence by massive military resupply of the RA, expansion of economic ties to the country, and creation of pro-Soviet local governments in the northern part of the country. The USSR may or may not succeed. This may leave the West with little choice other than continuing military resupply of the Mujahideen. Iran's role in the future of Afghanistan and its internal religious differences is equally uncertain. While the Afghan conflict with the USSR seems to be ending at this writing, the Afghan civil war is still in progress.

The Terrain

Terrain and weather are two key factors which helped prevent the USSR from conquering Afghanistan and which shape the outcome of the lessons of the war. Afghanistan is an arid, landlocked country, with cold winters and hot summers. The terrain is largely mountainous, with plains in the north and southwest. As Figure 2.2 shows, Afghanistan has a rugged and mountainous terrain with a number of valleys. Only 12 percent of the land is arable, and there are few areas with permanent crops. Another 46 percent consists of meadows, 3 percent is forest and woodland, and 39 percent is other types of terrain. Even before the war, the land suffered from overgrazing, deforestation, and desertification.

The total area of the country is about 647,500 square kilometers. It is roughly the size of Texas, and it has 5,510 kilometers of land boundaries. The longest border is with Pakistan, although there are also long boundaries with the USSR and Iran. The narrow northern Wakhan Corridor provides direct access to China and separates the USSR from Pakistan.

The mountainous core of the Hindu Kush Mountains and the Himalayas push into central Afghanistan in a general northeast-to-southwest direction within a hundred miles of the Iranian border. Many passes cut through these central mountains and provide the primary routes toward the main routes north and south.

The northern boundary with the Soviet Union is over 1,500 miles long. This boundary begins in the east on the high plateau of the Pamir and follows the course of Amu Darya (also known as the Oxus River) for more than 600 miles to Kham-i-Ab. After Kham-i-Ab, the Afghan border with the Soviet Union turns southwest through the Turkmenian steppes until it reaches the Zulfikar Pass at the Iranian border.

The northern section between the mountainous region and the Amu Darya is partly fertile. Water is sufficient here, and the soil is good. This border area lying between Afghanistan and the Soviet Union is referred to as the Turkestan Plains. The northern foothills drop abruptly from 6,000 to 4,000 feet (1,830 to 1,220 meters) into stony plains about 1,200 feet (370 meters) above sea level. The rolling semi-desert Turkestan Plains are north of the Hindu Kush mountains. More semi-desert and desert areas lie south of these mountains, while the eastern part of the country has Afghanistan's only forests.

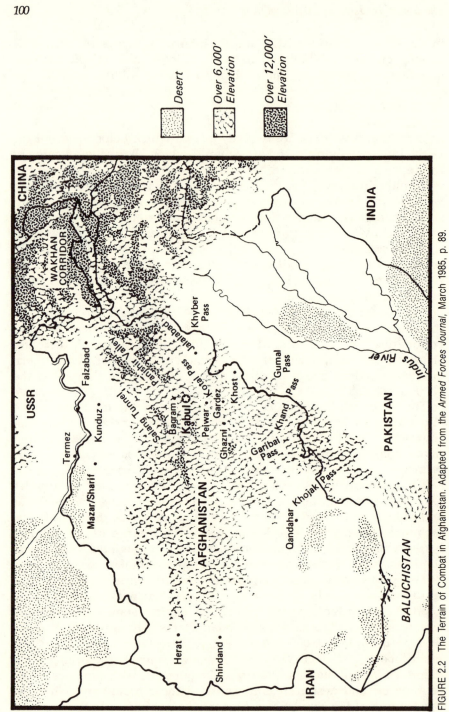

FIGURE 2.2 The Terrain of Combat in Afghanistan. Adapted from the *Armed Forces Journal*, March 1985, p. 89.

Weather problems and the special difficulties of mountain warfare must be given careful consideration in evaluating Soviet and Mujahideen performance in Afghanistan. In many ways, the Afghan conflict has been a test of Soviet ability to adapt to mountain warfare. The Soviets were not particularly well trained for such operations prior to the Afghan invasion, but they did much to change their capabilities. They greatly improved their training, technology, tactics, and troop strength, although these improvements were not enough to result in any form of victory.

The mountains are inhospitable and contain numerous defiles which are ideal for snipers and difficult for vehicles. There is, however, considerable nakedness to the terrain, and one observer has noted, "Bare rock dominates dramatically everywhere above 14,000 feet or 4,270 meters."[78]

There are no jungles or marshlands to conceal troop movements. The harsh mountainous topography channels both transportation and communication lines.

As Figures 2.3 to 2.6 show, there are a relatively limited number of urban areas and population centers and major lines of communication to secure. The USSR seized control of virtually all of these at the start of the war and had the advantage of a far shorter logistic pipeline than has been required in any recent Western intervention in a major Third World conflict.

Afghans raised in the local environment possessed the important advantage of knowledge and skill in their ability to conceal themselves behind rocks and within crevices along the Afghan landscape. They could operate in the mountainous areas which dominate the valleys and roads in the country. The Soviets generally had to move by helicopter or use road-bound vehicles. When they did move by foot, they usually moved short distances and for specific tactical purposes. They could not occupy or dominate the countryside and usually lacked the manpower to dominate a given area. The Afghan insurgents had the benefit of launching attacks on Soviet forces travelling through valleys. Most of the guerrilla operations were concentrated in the mountainous areas where heavily populated cities and towns are located.

At the same time, the conflict was a war for control lines of communication. This kind of war is more familiar to Soviet forces but involves complex terrain factors. The transportation infrastructure in Afghanistan is limited. The only rail links are short (nine- to fifteen-kilometer lines). One runs from Kushka (USSR) to Towraghondi, and another from Termez (USSR) to Kheyrabad, a transhipment point on the Amu Darya. The only major waterway is the river, which is 1,200

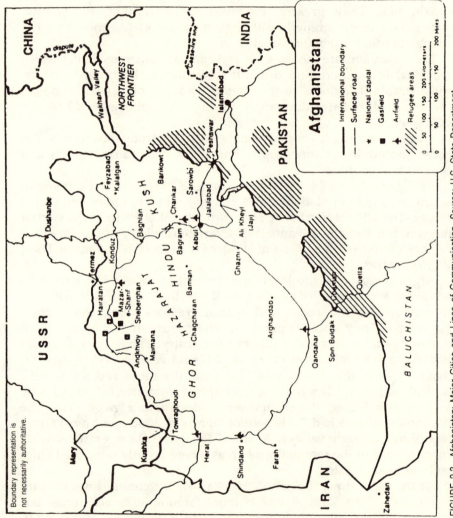

FIGURE 2.3 Afghanistan: Major Cities and Lines of Communication. *Source:* U.S. State Department.

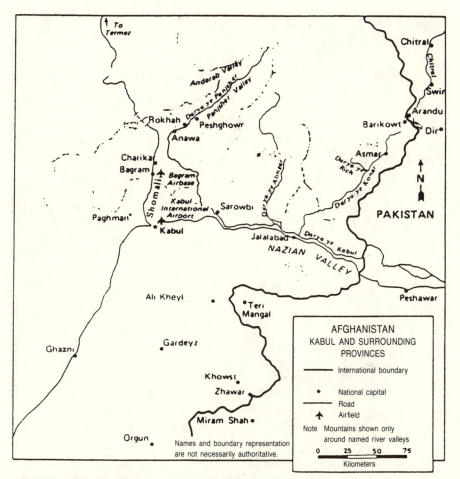

FIGURE 2.4 Afghanistan: Kabul and the Surrounding Provinces. *Source:* U.S. State Department.

kilometers long and can take steamers up to 500 metric tons. There are three ports, and Shir Khan is the largest.

Estimates of the present road system are uncertain, but there seem to be 21,000 kilometers of roads, with about 2,800 with hard surface and 1,650 of improved earth and bituminous treated gravel. The remaining 16,550 consists of unimproved earth and tracks. There are five major civil airfields and a total of forty-two. Thirty-four of these are usable, and twelve have permanent surface runways. Nine have 2,440–3,659 meter runways, and fifteen have runways of 1,220 to 2,439 meters. The key communication links are described in Table 2.5, which gives a good picture of the problems the USSR faced in highway defense.

FIGURE 2.5   Afghanistan: Military Areas in the Northeast. *Source:* U.S. State Department.

When the war began, the nation had only 31,200 telephones, five AM stations, one TV station, and one earth satellite station. The nation relied on subsistence agriculture and small manufacturing. The GNP was only $3.52 billion in 1985. Per capita income was $250. Exports totalled about $780 million and civil imports $900 million. The only major export was natural gas through a 180-kilometer pipeline to the USSR.[79]

Threat Assessment Technologies

The most important calculations the attacker can make in war are the probable cost of the conflict and its ultimate military and political

FIGURE 2.6 Afghanistan: Soviet Major Combat Unit Deployments in December 1987. *Source:* U.S. State Department.

outcome. One of the most consistent lessons of war is that these calculations are almost invariably wrong, and they are far more likely to err in underestimating risks and costs than in overestimating. By and large, war enforces its own logic on grand strategy, and politics becomes an extension of war by other means.

There is no way to be sure how seriously the Soviets underestimated the political and military consequences of their initial invasion, but it is virtually certain that they did not expect most of the nation to rise up against them, nor did they expect nearly a decade of intensive guerrilla war. A secret communist party circular has admitted this mistake, and Aleksander Bovin, a prominent political writer for *Izvestiya*, has criticized the Soviet invasion of Afghanistan as a reflection of an excessive tendency to use force.[80]

This Soviet underestimation of the risks of backing a coup d'etat with massive amounts of force could not have been the result of shortfalls in human intelligence (HUMINT) collection. The Soviets virtually controlled the key power centers and officials in Kabul long before their invasion, and they had vast experience with the tribal

TABLE 2.5 Key Lines of Communication in the Afghan Conflict

Termez/Jeyretan to Naebabad: Route 4

Length: 60 km. Construction: bituminous asphalt. Obstructions: none. Remarks: Key road connecting Soviet border with Afghan road systems, particularly roads to Pol-e-Khomri depot and beyond.

Mazar-i-Shariff to Pol-e-Khomri: Route 3

Length: 230 km. Construction: bituminous asphalt. Obstructions: 20 (+) bridges, including Qonduz River bridge 5 km outside Pol-e-Khomri; extensive valleys, gorges, and mountain curves. Remarks: major road route from border to key junction at Pol-e-Khomri.

Shir Khan to Kabul: Route 2

Length: 425 km. Construction: bituminous asphalt. Obstructions: 40 (+) bridges, Salang Pass 2700 m long, many snow galleries. Remarks: Soviet built highway; key route south from Soviet border; however, subject to extensive guerrilla interdiction due to bridges, rugged mountain road network, and adverse conditions during winter.

Kabul to Tour Khan/Khyber Pass: Route 1

Length: 285 km. Construction: concrete. Obstruction: about 15 bridges, eight tunnels, all with snow galleys, extensive switchbacks. Minimal passing room in pass/gorge areas, landslides common. Remarks: famous Khyber Pass route to Kabul. Rebuilt in 1960s by United States. High mountains and river gorge conditions from Jalalabad to Pakistani border; periodically interdicted by guerrilla groups. Previously the major trade route out of the country.

Herat/Macqandak to Kabul: Route 12

Length: 800 km.(+). Construction: gravel or unsurfaced. Obstructions: improvised bridges where streams cross gravelled or unimproved dirt road sections; extremely poor road conditions throughout route. Remarks: only east-west central access road; however, not passable in many areas during winter due to extreme snow/ice conditions; during spring and autumn, it is subject to flash flooding, blocking access for as long as a few days. Summer heat conditions dry and dusty; any season requires four-wheel drive military vehicle use only. Mountain areas have landslides and earthquakes; very sparsely populated region.

Kushka to Herat: Route 10

Length: 115 km. Construction: bituminous concrete. Obstructions: a few bridges, otherwise good road through open plains. Remarks: third main connecting road from Soviet Union to important western trade route city of Herat (center of all major Persian-Afghan trade).

Herat to Kandahar: Route 13

Length: 600 km. Construction: concrete. Obstruction: 30 (+) bridges, including bridges over Harirud and Farah rivers. Mostly open valleys and plains, except for hills surrounding Delaram city. Remarks: built by Soviet Union in 1960s. Main access to major Soviet bases established at Shindand (controlling western sector of country) and Kandahar (southern sector). All roads in these two sectors are wide open and without any hill or mountain grades to restrict vehicle speed. Two lanes throughout; some areas subject to flash floods; extremes of heat conditions from summer to winter temperatures require constant road repairs. Small earthquakes are common.

(continues)

TABLE 2.5 (*continued*)

Kandahar to Chaman (Pakistan): Route 14
   Length: 120 km. (est.). Construction: bituminous asphalt. Obstructions: a few small bridges, including one over Darya-ye Arghandad (river) near Kandahar. Mostly low hills and open plains all the way to Pakistani border. Remarks: U.S.-built road, intended to provide a southern route into Pakistan for transshipment of trading goods out of country.

Jalalabad to Barg-e-Matal (Asadabad): Route 23
   Length: 250 km. (est.). Construction: gravel, concrete, etc. Obstructions: 20 to 30 small bridges, some along Darya-ye Kabul (river) which track with road route up the river valley. Remarks: scene of extensive guerrilla and Soviet attacks and counterattacks. Extensive road curves common to river valley roads with rugged mountains.

Khanabad-Faizabad-Eshkashem-Wakhan Corridor: Route 7
   Length: 800 km. Construction: bituminous asphalt, gravel, stone, unpaved. Obstructions: some small bridges between Khanabad and Eshkashem, from Eshkashem to Chinese border extensive curves along rugged mountains of the Hindu Kush. Remarks: Afghanistan's only access route to China. From Khanabad eastward, road becomes increasingly steep, with sharp mountain curves and deep ravines. Beyond Eshkashem, road is unpaved to small town of Qaleh-ye Panjeh (360 km). Mostly pack animals from here to border, in spring and autumn. Light military 4x4 vehicles can partially use in summer (restricted access).

SOURCE: Adapted from G. Jacobs, "Afghanistan Forces: How Many Are There?" *Jane's Defence Weekly*, June 22, 1985.

and political groups in the country. It did, however, represent a major strategic failure in political and intelligence analysis.

The Soviet effort to assess the Mujahideen threat that developed in Afghanistan after the Soviet-backed coup in Kabul illustrates another set of intelligence problems—and ones that can occur when sophisticated intelligence assets have to be employed against unsophisticated infantry targets operating in small groups which lack large, detectable assets or electronic emissions.

Soviet Army forces are organized to rely on signals intelligence (SIGINT) for virtually all of their tactical intelligence. Photo intelligence (PHOTINT) and human source intelligence (HUMINT) are normally supposed to provide only a small fraction of such data. The war in Afghanistan required very different priorities, and showed that intelligence sensors designed to gain information about a sophisticated opponent are often tailored to indicators that often do not exist in the operations of unsophisticated opponents. As a result, the Soviets faced a problem as challenging as that faced by the U.S. in Vietnam.

Although the populations of Afghanistan and Vietnam are similar and both number roughly 17 million, Afghanistan is four times larger in area. The USSR chose to deploy only 100,000 to 130,000 men to cover Afghanistan versus a peak of 450,000 men for the U.S. in Vietnam. The Soviets were forced to rely on local forces of only 25,000 to 65,000 men versus over 200,000 in the Army of the Republic of Vietnam (ARVN). This gave the USSR a force-to-space ratio of about 0.75 men per square mile versus a maximum ratio of 7.5 men per square mile for the U.S. in Vietnam.[81] Afghanistan did provide less ground cover for the Mujahideen than Vietnam did for the Viet Cong and North Vietnamese Army (NVA) forces, but the terrain in Afghanistan was rougher and the population was less centralized and urbanized.

The Mujahideen were split into seven major factions, which made it difficult to attack any given faction and dominate the war. While full-time actives may have totaled only 90,000 to 120,000 men, these factions could draw on a pool of reserves that may have been as high as 180,000 to 210,000 men. The Mujahideen's primitive equipment, lack of coordination, and division into eight different geographic areas further complicated the intelligence problem—just as similar ethnic and regional divisions greatly complicated Israel's intelligence problem in Lebanon.

Photo intelligence (PHOTINT), SAR, SLAR, and other airborne sensors had limited value to the Soviets in dealing with most Mujahideen targets, which were normally small roaming bands of rebels or civilian trucks. Soviet sensors may have had more value in major offensives against entrenched rebels in the various Afghan towns and valleys, but even then, their value was largely in mapping terrain and targeting villages and built-up areas.

The Soviets did improve their use of photo intelligence during the war and made better use of their Su-17 fighter-reconnaissance and AN-30 Clark photo reconnaissance aircraft. It is important to note, however, that Soviet reconnaissance and intelligence cameras, data links, and/or on-board data banks and processors on the aircraft deployed in Afghanistan seem to have lacked the near real-time correlation analysis needed to rapidly identify small shifts in movement or potential infantry groups. The USSR must have used advanced airborne sensors, unattended ground sensors, other special PHOTINT systems, and radar aids to deal with this situation, but no details are readily available. It is clear that the Soviets' sensors did not provide a reliable way of locating Mujahideen forces for either intelligence or targeting purposes. When the USSR withdrew from Afghanistan, Afghan forces still moved with relative impunity at night and often could move in the daytime when they were in rough terrain or out of line of sight of Soviet forces.[82]

Signals intelligence (SIGINT) assets were of limited initial use to the Soviets because the Mujahideen lacked radios, were divided into numerous factions, and fought as small, independent groups. After 1985, as the Mujahideen made more and more use of captured Soviet radios, the value of Soviet SIGINT assets increased. Soviet attempts to detect Mujahideen electronic emissions (ELINT) also often failed until 1985–1987 because the Afghans made limited use of such equipment. Likewise, Soviet attempts to intercept rebel radio communications often failed unless an agent was able to provide specific times and frequencies. In addition, the rebels often used messengers.

According to some Egyptian reports, Soviet SIGINT and ELINT capabilities improved further in 1987, when outside aid gave the major Mujahideen groups large numbers of HF and VHF radios. Although these radios had commercial-quality voice encryption, they evidently were not secure. This highlights the need for rugged, light, manportable secure communications gear that Western and friendly forces can use in low-intensity combat without risking the capture or decryption of sensitive technology and methods.

With regard to tactical threat assessment, the Soviets seem to have made limited use of ground surveillance radars (GSRs) and used artillery radars to target the source of rockets and mortars. The Little Fred and SNAR-10 (GS-13) Soviet radars seemed to combine both artillery targeting and limited battlefield surveillance capabilities. The Little Fred Radar is normally mounted on a BMP and can track incoming artillery fire at ranges up to seven to twelve kilometers. The SNAR-10 is also mounted on tracked vehicles. It has an artillery tracking range of ten to twenty kilometers and a possible surveillance range of twelve to fifteen kilometers.[83]

There are environmental and terrain problems in Afghanistan, however, that may often have made such radars only marginally effective as threat assessment devices. This is especially true in the more mountainous regions of Afghanistan where the rebels tended to operate. The problems affecting GSRs in such areas included dead space, multiple reflection of echos, and the shielding of radar waves.

The Soviets and DRA had to rely heavily on nontechnological means of intelligence gathering. This was a situation the U.S. faced in Lebanon in 1982–83 and which may well characterize future Western intervention in Third World political crises and civil wars. Human intelligence (HUMINT) involving agents in the field was of particular importance to the Soviets since technology could not be applied to Soviet threat assessment problems in Afghanistan. The Soviets and

DRA used classic "divide and conquer" techniques exploiting ethnic and regional tensions and payments to informers and tribal leaders.

The Soviets made a special effort to recruit reliable pro-government Afghans and use them to infiltrate the various Mujahideen groups. To accomplish this, the Soviets are reported to have taken many of Afghanistan's most promising young officers and placed them in the KHAD (WAD), Afghanistan's intelligence service. Indeed, the best students of the Afghan military academies were almost always considered for appointment to the KHAD (WAD).[84]

From 1980 to 1989, the KHAD (WAD) became one of the most efficient branches of the DRA government. Throughout its development, the KHAD's leaders maintained close links with the Soviet KGB and its leadership. The KHAD developed a complex network of informers and operated a significant agent network which it operated through the Department of Tribal Affairs in the Ministry for Nationalities. In undertaking their intelligence duties, KHAD (WAD) personnel usually worked within their own native areas and made considerable use of their own ethnic, family, and tribal ties. Often the KHAD (WAD) devoted special attention to recruiting tribal dignitaries despite the lack of a "progressive" orientation.

Agent networks employed by KHAD (WAD) officials were associated with several notable intelligence successes for the DRA. In the Panjshir Valley, KHAD (WAD) officials are reported to have succeeded in recruiting the cousin of rebel leader Ahmad Shah Massoud as well as one of Massoud's senior military commanders. Massoud eventually discovered this, but only after considerable information had been passed on to the Soviets and Massoud's own safety was imperiled.[85] This and other intelligence successes are believed to have occurred due to the large sums of money the KHAD (WAD) was able to provide for its agents.

At the same time, it is important to point out that the Soviet tactic of trying to rely on local intelligence forces in many ways failed. The USSR was never able to fully penetrate the major Mujahideen factions, although they were far more divided and subject to bribery and intimidation than a unified force like the Viet Cong. In many cases, KHAD (WAD), Sarandoy, and militia forces acted as agents for the Mujahideen. The Mujahideen also had superior HUMINT throughout the war, and were able to monitor most Soviet operations and detect Soviet and DRA vulnerabilities with great success. The fragmentation of the Mujahideen into so many groups, their concentration on direct action, and their ability to take the initiative in small operations denied the USSR the success it needed to allow a mix of firepower, mobility, and reliance on local forces to achieve successful economy of force.

The Soviet experience with threat assessment in Afghanistan has some clear implications for the West, since the West and the Soviet Union use many of the same types of sensors to collect intelligence (although they use different systems). In particular, the war in Afghanistan underscores the need for more efficient forms of intelligence gathering in counter-guerrilla environments. The ephemeral nature of guerrilla formations virtually requires theater assets that can respond to commanders in near real time. This lesson is reinforced by the examinations of the Iran-Iraq War and the 1982 fighting in Lebanon in other volumes in this set.

It is clear that no Western state can use the Soviet tactics of repression as a substitute for intelligence. Since 1982, the USSR increasingly attacked Afghanistan's rural population. It used carpet bombing, ground sweeps, attacks on refugees, and the destruction of farms and hamlets to deny rebel forces a sanctuary and to try to force the collapse of the Mujahideen. As Vietnam clearly demonstrated, Western governments cannot risk the domestic and foreign reaction to even more benign forms of pacification as a substitute for intelligence. The West must make every possible use of intelligence sensors, fusion, and processing.

The threat assessment by the Mujahideen was almost exclusively confined to HUMINT, although some support may have been provided by other countries. As was the case with the Viet Cong in Vietnam, this did not mean that the Mujahideen lacked effective intelligence. They do not seem to have had the consistent ability to penetrate the highest levels of command, intelligence, and decision making that characterized NVA and Viet Cong intelligence operations throughout the Vietnam war, but they often had excellent intelligence on everything but the precise purpose and direction of major Soviet offensives and deep strike operations.

The Mujahideen became expert at the use of local intelligence and forward observations, and they took advantage of the fact the USSR often followed repetitive patterns in launching given types of attacks and offensives. They also took advantage of the Soviet reliance on static defenses, often without aggressive patrolling, and the slow tempo of many Soviet operations.

PHOTINT was not available to the Mujahideen, and the Mujahideen made only crude attempts to exploit SIGINT by intercepting Afghan government and clear Soviet transmissions. Many Mujahideen groups were without the technical expertise or spare parts to repair and maintain captured Soviet radios which might have been used to intercept hostile message traffic. There is also some evidence to suggest that the Mujahideen did not treat the gathering of SIGINT as a significant military task, even when captured equipment and operators who defected were often available. See Figure 2.7.

Effective and Secure C³

The most important problems in command, control, and communications in the Afghan conflict were the human and organizational problems in command and control, rather than problems in communications and technology. Soviet forces had a monopoly on modern communications technology but still had to restructure their organization or "control" to meet the specific contingency needs of the campaign. The DRA government forces suffered from deep internal political divisions, uncertain loyalty, a lack of command cohesion, and the division of the regular and internal security forces into often competing groups. The Mujahideen forces often fought with each other, and lacked command unity, tactical control, and communications technology.

Soviet Doctrine

The Soviets began the war with standard Soviet control and communications techniques. The centralized nature of the standard Soviet command structure is shown in Figure 2.8, and typical Soviet key communications gear are shown in Table 2.6. The Soviets stress concealment, dispersal, hardness, mobility, and redundancy of C³ assets in conducting C³ operations. Normal Soviet communication assets include radio, troposcatter, SATCOM, and land lines. The latter asset was significant because the Soviets rapidly converted much of their communications system in Afghanistan to overcome the transmittal problems inherent in mountain operations and to improve security. They also were able to use existing civilian lines to supplement military-laid lines.

The special operating conditions in Afghanistan had mixed effects on Soviet ability to use this mix of doctrine and assets. Some operated to ease the normal burden on Soviet C³. The Soviets could operate in an ECM-free environment. No serious effort was required to deal with Afghan jamming. Evidence compiled by one analyst also suggests that the Mujahideen did not consider ESM (i.e., radio intercept) and imitative manipulative deception (i.e., entering the enemy's radio network) as forms of warfare they could understand or conduct.[86] The Mujahideen's lack of communication equipment and interest in early warning gave the Soviets an extremely favorable environment for their C³, although the Mujahideen did strike at C³ assets and try to destroy them.

The Soviets did, however, have to make organizational changes

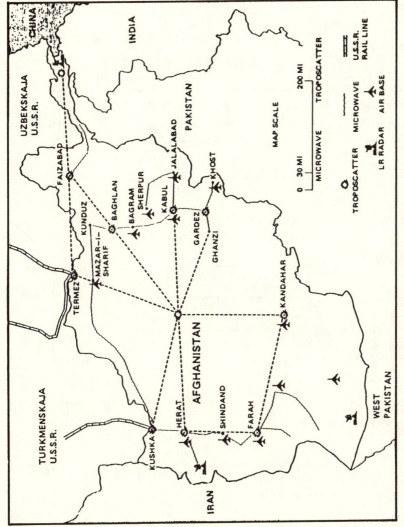
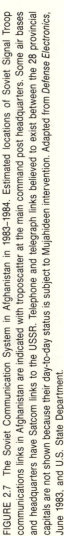

FIGURE 2.7 The Soviet Communication System in Afghanistan in 1983–1984. Estimated locations of Soviet Signal Troop communications links in Afghanistan are indicated with troposcatter at the main command post headquarters. Some air bases and headquarters have Satcom links to the USSR. Telephone and telegraph links believed to exist between the 28 provincial capitals are not shown because their day-to-day status is subject to Mujahideen intervention. Adapted from *Defense Electronics*, June 1983, and U.S. State Department.

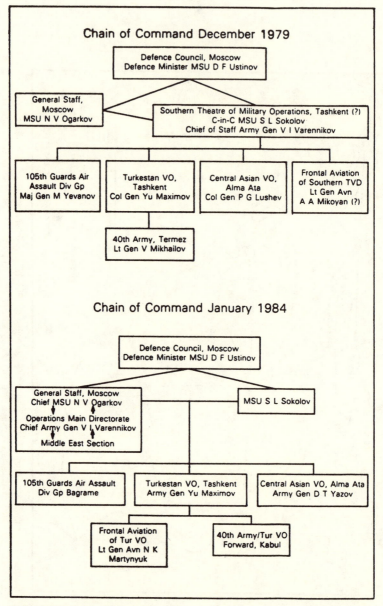

Chain of Command December 1979

Defence Council, Moscow
Defence Minister MSU D F Ustinov

General Staff, Moscow
MSU N V Ogarkov

Southern Theatre of Military Operations, Tashkent (?)
C-in-C MSU S L Sokolov
Chief of Staff Army Gen V I Varennikov

105th Guards Air Assault Div Gp
Maj Gen M Yevanov

Turkestan VO, Tashkent
Col Gen Yu Maximov

Central Asian VO, Alma Ata
Col Gen P G Lushev

Frontal Aviation of Southern TVD
Lt Gen Avn A A Mikoyan (?)

40th Army, Termez
Lt Gen V Mikhailov

Chain of Command January 1984

Defence Council, Moscow
Defence Minister MSU D F Ustinov

General Staff, Moscow
Chief MSU N V Ogarkov

Operations Main Directorate
Chief Army Gen V I Varennikov

Middle East Section

MSU S L Sokolov

105th Guards Air Assault Div Gp Bagrame

Turkestan VO, Tashkent
Army Gen Yu Maximov

Central Asian VO, Alma Ata
Army Gen D T Yazov

Frontal Aviation of Tur VO
Lt Gen Avn N K Martynyuk

40th Army/Tur VO Forward, Kabul

FIGURE 2.8 The Soviet Chain of Command in Afghanistan. The flow charts represent simplified structures showing key positions of command. Some elements and positions have not been included. Adapted from *Jane's Defence Weekly*, January 12, 1985, p. 72, and work by David Isby.

TABLE 2.6 Typical Soviet Army Tactical Field Communications Equipment Early in the War[a]

Organization	Communications Systems			
Moscow	Satcom	Land lines		
40th Army	Satcom	Tropo	R-401	R-405
Division	Tropo	R-401	R-405	
Regiment	R-123	R-107	R-311	
Battalion	R-123	R-107	R-311	
Company	R-123	R-107	R-126	
Platoon	R-123	R-126		
Squad	R-123	R-126		

[a]Telephone and telegraph equipment are not listed.
SOURCE: *Defense Electronics*, June 1983, p. 106.

and adapt their command and control systems to new tactical conditions of the Afghan conflict. At the same time, the Soviets had to make changes in allocating and using their communications equipment to adapt to the shifts in the structure of their forces. For example, the Soviets had to make more and more use of relays, often by satellite, ground unit, or airborne unit. They had to improve tactical communications at every level from the forward combat forces to the rear. Many older radios like the R-126 lacked the range to be effective, and mountains were a major problem in maintaining communications links until the Soviets deployed helicopters and aircraft as relays and added a satellite communications link.

The Soviet Command Structure

The major changes in the Soviet command structure during the war have been described in the previous chronology. The Soviets seem to have initially structured the command of the Limited Contingent of Soviet Forces in Afghanistan (LCSFA) and 40th Army as a temporary command designed largely to move forces into the country and seize key urban objectives and lines of communication for a short period of time. This command seems to have reported directly to the Soviet Operations Main Directorate for major decisions and to the Southern TVD and Turkestan military district for specific types of operation or support.

Once the major fighting began, however, the command seems to have been transferred to the Soviet Southern TVD high command. At the same time, the LCSFA was transformed into a major command with close links to the Turkestan military district which grew steadily throughout the war as the Turkestan military district was transformed into a major support area for air operations, support, training, and occasional military attacks that penetrated into Afghanistan.

By the early 1980s, the LCSFA command was roughly equivalent to a military district, but it had to deal constantly with the DRA and had no military council or military educational facilities. It was purely a combat command. The exact relationship between this command and the 40th Army is unclear, but the LCSFA may have had overall authority over the 40th Army, the military aspects of the political and pacification effort, air operations, and operations involving forces from outside the country.

The Soviets also made steady changes in their order of battle to reflect the need for new command and control concepts that stressed small combat unit operations, combined arms, combined operations, and combinations of mechanized land offensives and heliborne assault forces. These changes began in the spring of 1980, when it became clear that the Soviets, rather than the Afghans, would have to do most of the fighting.[87] The Soviets had initially deployed the 105th Airborne Division and four regular motorized rifle divisions (MRDs) of largely Central Asian troops to Kabul. These MRDs were equipped as a regular Soviet Army and were designed for armored and mechanized operations.

As the previous chronology has described, the Soviets quickly discovered that much of this force structure, including some of the army's organic support troops, was unsuitable to fighting a guerrilla war. The USSR sent home a number of units in mid-1980. These units included the 40th Army's artillery and surface-to-air missile brigades, a tank regiment (probably belonging to the 360th Motorized Rifle Division), and several FROG battalions, totaling about 10,000 men. Successive mutinies by the Afghan 8th (January 1980) and 14th (July 1980) armored divisions then led the Soviets to adopt a separate C^3 system from that of their supposed allies.

The Soviet subordinate command structure also changed. Soviet attempts to combine a rigid and over-centralized tactical C^3 structure with conventional tactics resulted in a number of defeats. This led to an increasing Soviet emphasis on decentralized support and more independent operations by reinforced battalions and regiments with organic artillery, engineer, and helicopter backup. Combat forces increasingly were organized with dedicated support forces, to provide the instant responsiveness lacking in the standard Soviet system, and with integral helicopter and artillery forces.

Late in 1980, the Soviets seem to have established two "test bed" brigades (66th Motor Rifle Brigade in Jalalabad and 70th Motor Rifle Brigade in Kandahar). These brigades were used for integrated heliborne/mechanized operations. An air assault brigade of four rifle battalions (two of which were parachute trained) was established at Shir Khan. Elements from the Air Assault Division at Bagram were used in this role. Despite some regimental heliborne operations, the reinforced battalion became the standard element for these landings. The Soviets altered the number of divisions in Afghanistan. The 16th Motor Rifle Brigade may have been pulled back into the Central Asian VO (military district), the 346th Motor Rifle Brigade to Kushka (Turkestan VO), and the 66th Motor Rifle Division to Samarkand (Turkestan VO).

The Soviets attempted to use their new force mix to mount large offensives (division-sized task forces) against the guerrillas around Jalalabad (March 1980), Herat (winter 1981–82 and April 1984) and the Panjshir Valley (1980–82 and 1984). The Panjshir stronghold received repeated assaults because the Mujahideen continuously threatened the Soviet's key supply line, the Kabul to Mazar-i-Shariff road as it passes through the Salang Pass. The Soviet used formations as large as 20,000 men in their attacks on the Panjshir Valley. These large-scale offensives also required changes in the high command. In 1982, the Soviets created two operational commands, one at Kabul and one at Termez, and seven to nine territorial commands. This allowed them to decentralize major operations and make them more efficient.

These changes in the Soviet force and command structure helped Soviet forces break up large Mujahideen formations in many of the valleys and settled areas and force the Mujahideen to use smaller and more dispersed formations. This, however, created new pressures. The Soviets rapidly found that a large-unit–oriented C^3 system was difficult to use in a mountain environment and slowed the tempo of operations. As a result, they altered the chain of command to create subordinate command structures for deep operations in which the operation commander had more authority. They also tried to steadily increase the independence of action of small units and lower-ranking officers, although with mixed success.

The Soviets also found it necessary to create smaller combined arms units and to vary their organization and force mix to suit different terrain and tactical conditions. They gained extensive experience in linking battalion-sized artillery units to these combined arms units and in providing batteries for close support of mobile strike forces. They made increasing use of mortars in deep raids and small detachments, partly because of the command and control problems inherent in artillery mobility and rear-area reaction times.[88] At the same time, the Soviets adjusted their command structure to make steadily greater use of transport, assault helicopters, attack helicopters, and close air support. This required steady improvements in their C^3 arrangements for land-air operations.

It was not until 1984–1986, however, that Soviet C^3 arrangements became sufficiently flexible to give field commanders full authority in calling in fixed-wing air support, and Soviet ability to quickly adjust operations became evident. Even then, the best performing Soviet units were almost all airborne, air assault, and reconnaissance forces or motorized rifle units with special training and organization.

The Soviets came to emphasize reliance on flexible small-unit tactics involving the increasing use of helicopters, Spetsnaz, and other ranger-type forces, along with simultaneous efforts to cut the Mujahideen off from their supply routes through Pakistan and deny them major bases or sanctuaries while securing urban areas and major lines of supply. The USSR also increasingly allowed major task group commanders to call in air support on a quick reaction basis and to avoid clearing such requests through higher levels of command. It never, however, gave them sufficient authority to use airpower with maximum effectiveness.

The standard Soviet doctrinal solution to providing communications support also affected command and control. The standard Soviet solution was to issue more radios and to establish (when possible) more retransmission sites.[89] This solution quickly proved inadequate in Afghanistan and generated a debate about the role of junior leaders in mountain terrain. The result of this debate was to slowly expand the leadership responsibilities of NCOs, warrant officers, and junior commissioned officers so that they were able to take greater initiative in combat situations. By 1984, there were signs that the Soviets were implementing this decentralization of command and control in the forces opposing NATO. Soviet exercises and doctrine increasingly stressed speed of maneuver and independence of action in other theaters.

The USSR seems to have had some success in establishing the command and control links necessary to use the new Su-25 Frogfoot as a fixed-wing close support aircraft and to use more mobile artillery. The command and control interface between small combat arms elements and the attack or assault helicopter became the key to tactical success. The Soviets adapted their C^3 system, but this adaptation focused more on devolving command authority to lower echelons of command than on changes in technology.

The USSR also had to adapt its command system to make increasing use of DRA informers and joint operations with DRA forces. As time went on, the USSR also increasingly had to coordinate bombing operations, movements up the valleys by mechanized forces, and rapid heliborne assaults and blocking operations. The exact changes required in the Soviet force structure needed to do this were unclear, but from 1982 onward, the commanders of such operations became steadily more proficient. Further, the coordination between fixed-wing air support and bombing operations steadily improved with time.

The basic problem the Soviets faced was that they could never locate the Mujahideen effectively, or develop a rapid enough tempo of operations, to destroy the Mujahideen forces in a given area (rather than merely suppress their operations temporarily or force them to change location). It is unclear that there is any solution to a problem in which a limited military force must wage war on virtually the entire population of a nation. The Soviet command structure also faced the fact that it was attacking a target that was extremely difficult to locate and kill. The USSR had to spend vast resources to kill small numbers of Mujahideen, who could be rapidly replaced, and could not find a way in which technology or proxy forces could protect it from high casualties.

By 1987, the Soviets were also forced to change their command and control system to reflect the changes in Mujahideen tactics. The Mujahideen steadily increased in strength and weaponry without presenting a clear and easily defined set of targets that the USSR and DRA could attack. The DRA could not win popular support, and the improving air defense capabilities of the Mujahideen forced the Soviets to restrict their use of helicopters. The Soviets could continue small sweep operations on the ground, but these no longer could take advantage of survivable air support—which had been an essential Soviet method of establishing control and communications. The Soviets made more use of artillery and tanks, but this meant that the tempo of operations slowed down. Heliborne assault operations also had to be cut back as casualties increased.

During 1987 and 1988, many Soviet operations reverted to the use of relatively large and road-bound armored/artillery/mechanized infantry formations. Aircraft flew higher and faster and were much less effective. This tended to channel Soviet operations into predictable lines of communication and made them relatively slow at a time when the Mujahideen were steadily improving their ability to use new weapons. It forced the Soviets back onto the defensive. The Soviets were forced to pull out of isolated areas and to devote far more forces to routine defensive operations to try to secure urban areas.

Command and Force Mix and Training Issues

The USSR used troop rotations and changes in their training methods to help deal with morale and ethnic problems in command and control. LCSFA units quickly lost their central Asian "flavor" as national servicemen replaced reservists. Although central Asian troops returned to the Afghan front, every effort was made to reduce the risk of units becoming disaffected or causing morale problems among the White Russian troops.

In mid-1982, the USSR began to send in troops that had been specially trained for warfare in Afghanistan, and a major training center was established at Ashkhabad, with other training groups at Termez and Kushka.[90] The USSR began to realize that effective command and control were impossible without the special training needed to perform specialized tasks. Special training facilities like typical Afghan villages and strong points were set. Mountain warfare training was improved. Heliborne assault training was improved, and specialists like drivers and gunners were give five to six months of training.

The USSR also came to realize that effective command and control required high-quality manpower, and that quality was more important than mass. This lesson was slow to be absorbed. Until 1984, most conscripts did six-month tours, and many were still sent to their combat units without any major combat training, although some then stayed longer. The Soviets began to provide two to six months of special training to many conscripts and other ranks before sending them to Afghanistan. They also came to make more and more use of highly disciplined professional airborne and Spetsnaz troops in key combat roles. The USSR learned that in unit training, an over-rigid reliance on routine training and rotation cycles could lead to serious problems in military effectiveness.[91]

The Soviets never, however, were able to overcome a pattern of hazing and mistreatment of new troops by the more experienced forces. One of the more peculiar aspects of the Soviet force structure was the tolerance of a system in which enlisted men with longer service were allowed to use new replacements to do menial tasks, routinely mistreat them, and often use physical abuse. This problem was more common among garrison troops but also affected combat troops in the field. While this kind of procedure was relatively common in nineteenth-century armies and was often used to force new recruits to adapt themselves to army life, other forces have found it has no place in modern combat where even the newest troops have to operate sophisticated weapons and military systems and where competence—not time in service—is vital to effective command and control.

The lack of an effective career NCO force that was trained to act with a considerable degree of authority and independence also damaged Soviet ability to exert effective command and control, but this situation also improved after early 1982. In common with standard Soviet practice, NCOs served for six months in a training division before posting to Afghanistan. A large number of the NCOs sent to the LCSFA were trained in Ashkhabad in the Turkestan MD (VO). The 280th Training Division stationed in Ashkhabad had extensive ranges and battle training areas. More and more enlisted men also received specialist training at this center as time went by. Many, but not all, Afghanistan-bound troops were instructed at Ashkhabad; one captured sergeant did his NCO course in a training division in Lithuania.

Officers were kept on longer rotations, as were the career soldiers in elite units, but officers were given exceptionally fast promotion. Afghanistan became a "fast track" for promotion at every echelon from the commander of the 40th Army down to junior officer. This was particularly true of helicopter unit commanders, air assault troops, and Spetsnaz. Unlike Soviet conscripts, many of the officers and elite troops emerged as excellent battle-hardened troops, showing excellent leadership and initiative and good abilities in command and control. The Soviet officer corps that emerged from Afghanistan was scarcely perfect but it was far more competent and flexible than the corps that began the war.

Many commanders serving in Afghanistan went to higher posts in Category I units in eastern Europe and the Far East.[92] The overall impact of the war has been to improve Soviet experience and capability at the command level, although estimates that 50,000 to 66,000 officers now in Soviet forces served in Afghanistan may be exaggerated.[93]

The Soviet C[3]I system also reinforced command and control with a heavy internal security element. Air Assault Division personnel and paratroops were given an important role in guarding the government. There are some indications that the Air Assault Division forces were under the command of Southern TVD or Turkestan VO rather than the forward headquarters in Kabul, but this is unclear. Other security missions were performed by detachments of internal security troops, and a regiment of KGB security troops protected Afghan political leaders, senior Soviet personnel, and key installations. A number of border detachments (brigades of about 1,500 men each) belonging to the KGB's Main Border Troops' Directorate helped to secure the frontier and operated in Afghanistan.

These changes in Soviet command and control reflect an important lesson: changes in force mix, training, troop quality, and tactics may be far more important in shaping C^{3}I for low-level wars and special conditions of combat than are changes in technology. At the same time, it is interesting to note the comments of one of the major Mujahideen combat leaders, Abdul Haq, regarding Soviet command and control and troop quality:[94]

> At the beginning, young reservists were deployed. Later on, older and better trained and equipped forces were used, particularly paratroopers, but they haven't succeeded in stopping us either. In Afghanistan, you need quick decisions and still Russian officers cannot decide for themselves without going back to their higher commands. The Soviets have improved their tactics and have much more experience, but they are only here for no more than two years, while most of the Mujahideen have been fighting since the start of the war.

As for communications *per se*, the Soviets did not radically alter their pattern of communications technology, although they did gradually deploy steadily more sophisticated communications systems. The Soviet C^3 presence also took on a more permanent character. The Soviets began with troops in temporary structures, including a tent city. By 1983–1984, key Soviet C^{3}I units were in permanent buildings with a number of fixed communications sites and fixed antenna arrays. Soviet engineers established a number of elaborate communication centers throughout the country as well as in a central headquarters north of Kabul. The Soviets also replaced some of their twin plate system antennas for troposcatter communications with twin dish antennas. While these systems substantially reduced site mobility, they nevertheless improved the volume of communications and Soviet command and control capability within Afghanistan.[95]

DRA C^3 Capabilities

The C^3 capabilities of the DRA were modeled and equipped on the basis of Soviet forces. The Ministry of Defense had three corps headquarters and division headquarters under the corps. These exerted command on a largely geographical basis. Air operations were centralized in Kabul, often leading to a one-day wait in obtaining air support.

The DRA system was subordinated to Soviet forces, and there were Soviet advisors at virtually every level of command. The Soviets also had political and intelligence advisors working in the government, KHAD (WAD), Sarandoy, and some border guard and militia units. The DRA had no independent secure communications links. The USSR had long realized that control or oversight of host country communications is critical in many Third World countries, and Soviet advisors were able to shift from advisory supervision to direct control of most major DRA operations in Afghanistan.

Mujahideen C^3 Capabilities

Mujahideen command and control technology were usually simple to the point of being primitive. Although the Mujahideen gained an increasing number of radios beginning in 1984–1985, they still made extensive use of messengers when Soviet withdrawal began.[96] One official source has said that many of the Mujahideen who did have radios used the R-132M HF/VHF-FM transceiver and older Soviet-built R-105 and R-126 radios. It has since become clear that the Mujahideen also captured many smaller Soviet R-392A transceivers. Nevertheless, these radios are bulky and can be easily located with direction-finding equipment.[97]

The Mujahideen do seem to have acquired improved radio systems and a limited degree of secure communications gear after 1986. The extent of such improvement is unclear, however, and "sophisticated" gear of any kind seems to have been confined to a few major command headquarters. The experience of the Mujahideen illustrates the need to be able to equip friendly forces in the Third World with more modern and easy-to-operate systems and with secure voice and counter-DF techniques like burst transmission. These systems are available commercially and have been used by the Marxist rebels in El Salvador. A small number of similar systems may have been supplied to some of the Mujahideen after 1985, but this is unclear.

Combined Arms

Many of the features of combined arms operations in Afghanistan have already been described. It is important to stress, however, that the Soviets steadily improved their use of combined arms as the result of their operations in Afghanistan. These improvements took place in two distinct forms of combat and affected two different approaches to combined arms. The first approach involved mountain warfare, and the second involved warfare in the valleys and more open areas of the country.

In both cases, the Soviets relied on steady increases in force levels and fire power, along with more sophisticated tactics and complex uses of C^3I technology. They relied on mass firepower and large-scale air attacks to minimize Soviet casualties and on attacks on the Afghan people to compensate for an inability to target and destroy the Mujahideen.

*The Initial Soviet Experience
in Mountain Warfare: 1980–1981*

In 1980, the first Soviet combined arms operations relied heavily on tank and motorized rifle (mechanized infantry) units designed for warfare in central Europe. The Soviets emphasized the same kind of artillery support from field guns, howitzers, mortars, and multiple rocket launchers that they emphasized in deployments against NATO. Soviet forces emphasized the control of LOCs and strong points and underemphasized the need to use combined arms to control territory and the role of helicopters and infantry.

Even in the mountains, Soviet forces tended to move in slow formations or convoys and to stay vehicle bound. This tendency was reinforced by their equipment. Soviet APCs/IFVs are equipped with firing ports and in some cases heavily armed, although the armor initially deployed to Afghanistan provided poor visibility and angles of fire. Soviet troops tended to fight within their vehicles regardless of the tactical situation, even when exposed Mujahideen targets were available. Soviet forces made little effort to secure the high ground along the routes they followed and were very poor at carrying out ground reconnaissance.

Soviet tank units were also used in the mountains despite the problems in maneuvering and using tank firepower. This combination of forces failed to achieve effective military results in the mountain areas. The Mujahideen quickly learned to fire at the lead and last vehicle in a column and at selected targets before withdrawing.

By the beginning of 1981, these problems in combined arms had led the Soviets to reevaluate their doctrine on mountain warfare. The Soviets had reduced the role of tank units in mountain combat and emphasized the use of air mobile (helicopter), motorized rifle, airborne, and Spetsnaz units. They also had begun to introduce large numbers of anti-aircraft guns for sweeping the mountainsides in which the Mujahideen hid.[98]

As time went on, the Soviets learned to use combined arms reinforced battalions (CARBs) and infantry sweeps in conjunction with helicopter lift and heavy combat helicopter support. They stopped set piece attacks and road-bound movements and started hit-and-run operations. They emphasized the use of lighter APCs and AFVs, including the use of BMDs airlifted by Mi-6 Hook helicopters.[99]

They introduced vehicles that encouraged more flexible and less vehicle- and road-bound operations. These include the BTR-70, and later the BTR-80, armored personnel carriers and new variants of the BMP and BMD, with 30-mm cannon rather than 73-mm anti-tank guns.

They shifted their emphasis on artillery support to lighter artillery such as 160-mm mortars and 76-mm mountain guns. These weapons proved particularly useful in supporting mountain operations.[100] They steadily improved infantry firepower with weapons like the AK-74 assault rifle, the AGS-17 automatic grenade launcher, and Vasilek rapid fire automatic mortar.

The Soviets created artillery firebases about fifteen to twenty kilometers apart during 1981. They deployed large numbers of howitzers and MRLs, using them to cover APC-oriented infantry attacks and movements—which sometimes were able to move rapidly while shifting coverage from one firebase to another. They used firepower as a substitute for both maneuver and control of the countryside. This change in combined arms helped protect Soviet and DRA troops from Mujahideen small arms fire. The USSR also began to pay more attention to using heliborne forces to seize control of the high ground.

The Mujahideen, however, were generally more accurate in using their light weapons and were far better able to exploit mountain terrain in a firefight. The continued Soviet emphasis on armored vehicles also made Soviet troops vulnerable to anti-tank and heavy machine guns (which could penetrate BTR, BMP, or BMD armor). Soviet forces moved slowly and could rarely purse Mujahideen forces successfully.

The Initial Soviet Experience in Valley Warfare: 1980–1981

The Soviets adapted somewhat different techniques in their large-scale combined arms operations in campaigns like the Panjshir Valley. In 1980, the Soviets attempted to rely on securing strong points and LOCs and using the DRA Army and informers to target the Mujahideen. These campaigns were slow moving, armor heavy, road bound, and poorly executed. The resulting "convoy mentality" made Soviet armor vulnerable to Mujahideen anti-tank rocket launchers and led to numerous successful ambushes of Soviet and Afghan forces. Soviet tactics allowed the Mujahideen to dominate the countryside and many key towns and cities.

By 1981, however, the Soviets began to expand their effort to dominate the large towns and started to make much better and more intensive use of artillery and air power against rebel-held towns, villages, and strong points. The Soviets also used a mixture of propaganda, informers, and quasi-political efforts in the areas where they and the DRA could achieve some influence. They began a brute force approach in the areas firmly under Mujahideen control. The

USSR also attempted to use air-scattered mines, booby traps, and possibly chemical warfare to limit Mujahideen operations in the countryside and force the population to seek refuge in "secure" towns and cities.

Soviet Combined Arms in 1982

The USSR continued to use large offensives in 1982 but began to make steadily more aggressive use of small unit actions, particularly those using attack helicopters and helicopter assault forces. Rather than using air-mobile troops to support infantry operations using armored fighting vehicles, the Soviets often landed forces that supported the air mobile units. Small unit tactics drove the tempo of operations.

The USSR made more use of offensive tactical airpower, in part because airpower offered maximum mobility and in part because the Mujahideen had only a limited number of AA guns and a few early versions of the SA-7. Soviet and Afghan combat aircraft strength had already increased from around 200 aircraft in 1980 to 300 in 1981. It increased to nearly 400 aircraft in 1982. Helicopter strength increased from about 100 in 1980 to 210 in 1981 and 310 in 1982.[101]

The Soviets steadily increased their use of heliborne assaults and dismounted troops in mountain combat.[102] This involved some important changes in their motorized rifle brigades. Eventually, every third trooper came to have an airborne assault role. According to one source, the 70th Motorized Rifle Brigade eventually evolved into a largely air-mobile heliborne assault unit.[103]

Once the Soviets began these operations, they also rapidly increased helicopter fire support, provided large numbers of AA guns for firepower support, and made use of specialized anti-sniper units which entered into terrain that was not passable by APCs. The Soviet infantry units which were expected to dismount were given special training, were more professional, and were equipped with additional sources of firepower to compensate for a lack of armor and heavy artillery. The AGS-17 automatic grenade launchers proved to be a particularly good form of mobile firepower. The characteristics of the AGS-17 system are shown in Table 2.7.

The Soviets still, however, generally restricted their operations to enhanced division-sized attacks. They avoided mass sweeps of the countryside and did not systematically occupy towns, villages, and refugee areas. They relied on major offensives against key rebel areas, continued use of Afghan government forces, political attempts to weaken the rebels, increased use of gas and mines, and brute force artillery/air operations against the population in selected towns

TABLE 2.7 Characteristics of Crew-Served AGS-17 Automatic Grenade Launchers

Caliber (mm)	30
Weight (kg)	17 (launcher)
loaded	43 (on tripod)
Rate of fire (rd/min)	60 +
Elevation	up to 85°
Crew	3
Length (m)	.80
Ammunition	30 mm, HEAP, HEAT, incendiary
Range	
Maximum (m)	1,700
Effective (m)	800–1200

SOURCE: *The Soviet Army: Troops, Organization and Equipment*, FM 100-2-3 (Washington, D.C.: GPO, July 1984).

and urban areas. These tactics limited Soviet losses and defense expenditures but again failed to control the countryside or weaken rebel influence.

Soviet Combined Arms in 1983

In 1983, the Soviets added as many as 20,000 more ground troops and deployed about 100 more combat aircraft and 100 more helicopters.[104] They increased the use of small Soviet heliborne infantry and light mechanized infantry operations, although they still tended to rely on major offensives and "reaction" operations. They conducted steadily more sophisticated search-and-destroy operations and began far more aggressive attempts to block Mujahideen withdrawals. They extended patrols and helicopter sweeps to secure the areas around towns and cities. They also continued to use their air supremacy and combined operations (land/air) as a substitute for combined arms.

The Soviets also began to make extensive use of Tu-16 and Su-24 bombers for mass area bombings in support of operations like the Panjshir offensives and the new Su-25 Frogfoot, Su-17, MiG-21, MiG-23, and MiG-27 in search-and-kill operations in direct support of ground operations. Mi-8 and Mi-24 helicopters were used as on-call firepower, along with heavy use of AA machine guns to provide area and suppressive fire. Soviet artillery was also used extensively against the farms and small villages which made up the agricultural infrastructure supporting the Mujahideen, and Soviet infantry became more aggressive in leaving their vehicles and road areas and in pursuing light AFVs off road.

A Mujahideen commander described the changes in the situation as follows:[105]

> . . . at the beginning of the war it was easy, we could walk into (Kabul) and attack where we wanted. We had our bases 2 to 3 kilometers from the enemy positions, even at 6 to 7 kilometers from the biggest Soviet base of Darlahman. . . . In 1982, they had a 3 kilometer security belt, but it wasn't very effective . . . eventually we received 207 mm rockets with 8 kilometer range, and targets inside the capital were constantly under fire.
>
> . . . eventually, they spread out around their belts of outposts, trying to control an area around the city wide enough to keep it out of range of our rockets. In spite of the three rings of defensive positions they built, we are still regularly slipping through and our operations are still going on. . . . Of course we have to be very professional now. All operations have to be carefully planned. We have to have a lot of protection groups because all positions in their area must be engaged . . . routes must be clearly known. Alternative retreat routes have to be studied. We have to take care of mines, booby-trapped illuminating flares that give away our positions, even dogs.

The DRA Army remained ineffective, in spite of Soviet efforts to introduce an improved commissar and secret police element and to train cadres in the USSR. The Soviets continued to find they lacked the combination of Soviet and DRA strength to occupy space and secure rebel areas. The Soviets attempted to use the KHAD, Sarandoy, and various militias as a substitute for the DRA Army but had only mixed success. They also found their HUMINT could not provide reliable operational and targeting data (in part because of the impossibility of dealing with small independent cell-like Mujahideen forces, seven different rebel groups, and more than twenty linguistic groups) and never found an adequate intelligence/targeting technology to act as a substitute.[106]

Soviet Combined Arms in 1984

In 1984, the Soviets faced the choice of a massive troop build-up of the type the U.S. used in Vietnam or of finding some alternative way to control the countryside. This essentially was a choice between a "low cost" war, producing limited casualties and consuming 1 to 2 percent of Soviet defense spending, and a massive national effort of the kind the U.S. had launched in Vietnam. They also faced the problem that the Mujahideen now had substantially larger numbers of SA-7s, and Soviet forces were losing some of their freedom in using tactical aircraft and helicopters as a substitute for combined arms.

The Soviets chose to increase their reliance on a brute force approach to using firepower, rather than make major increases in troop levels. They greatly increased the use of the Tu-16 regiment and four tactical Su-24 bomber squadrons in the Turkestan military district to provide area bombing against small hamlets and the agricultural infrastructure the rebels depended on to survive. They raised the attack altitude for fighter strikes and equipped their helicopters and fighters with decoy flares to counter the SA-7.

They backed this increased use of airpower with aggressive "counter-population" ground operations against agricultural areas and with the first major attacks on refugee movements and camps. They used helicopters and heliborne operations, including heliborne BMDs, to close in on the rebels and steadily improved ground-helicopter-air coordination, helicopter tactics, and use of vertical assault techniques.

In the fall of 1984, the USSR introduced additional troops and stepped up its attacks on Mujahideen food supplies, particularly in the Panjshir. This often led to strange patterns of attack. Artillery fire was used against agricultural areas in ways that seemed closer to random fire than a planned concept. The same was true of bombing. Villages and small areas were devastated, but nearby areas often suffered minimal or low damage. The net effect was often to hurt innocent civilians without having any real impact on the Mujahideen.

The Soviets made more use of airborne (VDV), reconnaissance (*razvedchiki*), Soviet (DShB) and DRA air assault units, and Spetsnaz to seize key hills before attacking with land forces.[107] They increased their helicopter flights from roughly six to twenty helicopters per sortie to shock Mujahideen units and saturate their defenses. They struck heavily at refugee movements and camps, treating all civilians and livestock as military targets. By early 1985, as many as 5.6 million Afghans were refugees (1.1 to 1.4 million in Iran, 2.6 to 3 million in Pakistan, and 950,000 to 1.2 million in cities in Afghanistan) and 500,000 to 1 million civilians were dead. Many rural areas were without food, seed, grain, livestock, or any form of medical treatment.[108]

It is tempting to criticize the USSR for its slowness in improving its combined arms/combined operations against an enemy with no real combined arms of its own. At the same time, the USSR did keep its total casualties and defense expenditures relatively low and must have had considerable reluctance to "Sovietize" the campaign and adopt tactics which had serious potential consequences. Some estimates put Soviet casualties from 1979 to 1984 as low as 10,000, versus 40,000 for the U.S. in Vietnam from 1965 to 1969. There was a more general acceptance of the fact that the war cost about 1 to 2 percent of

Soviet defense expenditures in 1984, versus 23 percent of U.S. expenditures for the Vietnam war in 1969. Even if one compares losses at the end of the war, the USSR estimated Soviet casualties from 1979 to mid-1988 as 13,310 killed, 33,478 wounded, and 311 missing in action. This compares with 58,135 killed and 153,303 wounded for the U.S. in Vietnam.[109]

Soviet Combined Arms in 1985 and 1986

The USSR largely retained its existing approaches to combined arms in 1985 and 1986, although operations became deeper and lasted significantly longer. As the previous chronology has shown, the USSR developed advanced heliborne tactics for mountain warfare to attack the Mujahideen in formerly secure positions. It used security zones, scorched earth, Afghan government troop sweeps, longer-range mass artillery fire against towns and agricultural areas, and bombing to try to deny the Mujahideen popular support and food. It struck repeatedly at border areas and Mujahideen supply activities. It also made progressively more ruthless use of the KHAD and Sarandoy and of bribery, assassination, and divide-and-conquer techniques. It is important to note that this form of paramilitary operation had become just as important as part of combined operations as it did during the U.S. intervention in Vietnam and is virtually certain to be a critical aspect of any major guerrilla warfare operation.

In 1986, the USSR added a new political dimension. It substituted a new and more compliant Afghan leader and began to focus on "national reconciliation" and peace offers as means of limiting the Soviet commitment and achieving victory. The USSR increasingly emphasized political warfare in its mixture of combined arms. It again stepped up its use of bribes, infiltration in the Mujahideen, and threats. It sought to use these means to divide the Mujahideen, develop the near real-time intelligence necessary to make strikes by Soviet elite troops more effective, and force popular dependence on the Afghan government.

The USSR began an active "hearts and minds" campaign and started sending small agitprop units into villages. The USSR reinforced these efforts with continued air and artillery strikes on hostile population centers. It steadily increased its political and military pressure on Pakistan and continued to cloak the ruthlessness of its military activities with "peace" and "troop withdrawal" initiatives.

The USSR also made an attempt at "Vietnamization." It tried to give DRA forces more and more independent responsibility and to use them to replace Soviet forces in perimeter defenses and in guarding lines of communication. The result was mixed. There were some successes, but the DRA forces as a whole were very slow to act on their own, and problems with desertion and operational failures continued.

The basic principles of Soviet combined arms were still to make maximum use of firepower, limit casualties and troop numbers, emphasize helicopter firepower and mobility, create an effective HUMINT network, defend cities and high-value targets, destroy the agricultural and other infrastructure of hostile areas in the countryside, interdict Mujahideen supply routes, and attempt to force Pakistan to reduce its support of the Mujahideen.

In contrast, the Mujahideen were limited by their divisions, lack of technology, and lack of heavy weapons and helicopters. They lacked the military cohesion to adopt effective combined arms, tactics, and political credibility as a government in exile. This greatly aided the USSR. There was no single or effective entity that the West could aid, train, or equip. Unlike other guerrilla movements, the Mujahideen cannot evolve into a more effective fighting force without radical political changes.

It is interesting, however, to read the comment of a leading Mujahideen leader on Soviet combined arms in 1983–1986,

> Scorched earth tactics began in 1983. . . . At the beginning we were really scared of the Mi-24 gunship helicopters. They were hitting us hard with rockets and Gatlings, and we had no proper weapons to defend ourselves. Eventually we learned to wait on mountain tops, shooting when the helicopters were flying lower down to strike at valleys.
>
> . . . Since the Soviets have a lot of equipment, everything can be effective against us. Certainly mines are a very serious problem. They are using a lot of new models . . . heliborne paratroop operations could be described as the most effective Soviet tactics. Slowly we had to learn: keeping permanent pickets on hill-tops. . . . We would have a force ready to engage the paratroopers when they came, giving time to the rest of the Mujahideen to organize themselves. It is crucial to move very fast, always trying to take high ground positions, from which to counter-manoeuvre. . . . We also used to put anti-tank mines in the places where helicopters could land.[110]

Such Soviet combined arms tactics may have been more "cost effective" in a guerrilla war than U.S. tactics and efforts to control the countryside or "win the hearts and minds of the people" were in Vietnam. At the same time, the USSR found that it could not cripple the Mujahideen or achieve its political goals in pacifying the country, and it gradually begin to encounter improved Mujahideen air defenses and ability to fight in coordinate assaults.

The Soviet approach to combined use of the KHAD (WAD) and Sarandoy with tactics like carpet bombing also involved morale and political costs no Western nation can bear. Nevertheless, they may provide a pattern for future wars. Like the Soviet use of Cuban proxies in earlier Third World conflicts, the USSR adopted a "low-cost" solution to the use of force that the West can only match with regional allies, the use of advanced technology, and far more sensitivity to moral and external political conditions.[111]

By late 1986, the USSR began to encounter growing military problems as well as political ones. The Mujahideen had learned how to take shelter in the face of Soviet air and artillery attacks and to withdraw in the face of deep Soviet penetrations and use of Spetsnaz. During 1987, the Mujahideen continued to improve their air defenses to the point where the USSR lost its freedom of action in using helicopters in the assault and close-air-support role. Although the Soviets increasingly began trying to push the DRA into conducting their own independent operations, the continued weakness of the DRA meant the USSR could not shift the burden of defending the countryside to local troops.

Soviet Combined Arms in 1987

Soviet combined arms tactics changed again in 1987, but in many ways, they were a reversion to older methods. The Soviets added artillery units and increased the strength of army combat units to compensate for their increasing problems in using helicopters. The USSR raised their total troop strength to 120,000.[112] The USSR had to shift from using Hinds to using MRLs to provide close support.

Both Soviet and DRA forces sharply increased their artillery strength. The Soviets poured artillery into the country as a substitute for airpower, including two new types of 152-mm cannon, a 122-mm howitzer, and a new automatic 82-mm mortar. They reduced the frequency of small sweep operations and made major cuts in air and helicopter support, particularly after they began to take major helicopter losses during their June 1987 offensive in Paktia.

The Soviets sharply cut the number of heliborne assaults by elite troops because of rising casualties. They withdrew exposed units and outposts that depended heavily on helicopter support and air cover. The Soviets deployed more troops to the perimeter defense of cities and key bases and used more of the 30,000 troops in the USSR to defend their rear areas and lines of communication. They began to heavily shelter and revet all fixed installations as the Mujahideen steadily improved their long-range weaponry, and they constructed underground and mountainside bunkers for fuel and ammunition. Several airports were given added runways and improved perimeter defenses.

Even so, the growing Soviet problems in securing air movements affected supply and movement. The Soviets suffered more because of Afghanistan's limited transportation network outside the border area, particularly in exposed positions where the Soviets were forced to defend long roads or fight convoys through to provide resupply.

Aircraft losses rose to unacceptable levels, and Soviet and DRA forces often lost an aircraft a day. Total losses reached 150–200 for the year, not counting accidents and damage. These losses were particularly high at the start of 1987 and only declined when the Soviets flew higher and faster and spent far less time acquiring and pursuing targets. Helicopter losses were serious in any mission that brought them into areas defended with Stingers and the Mujahideen's improved air defense guns. Attack helicopter losses were so high that the USSR started substituting fixed-wing aircraft. These not only were inherently far less effective, but Soviet and DRA pilots failed to press many attack sorties home.

The airborne, assault, reconnaissance, and other elite heliborne troops lost some of their effectiveness as their air cover and helicopter support declined and the Mujahideen adapted their tactics. Casualties rose, morale suffered, and the Mujahideen increasingly were able to fight elite Soviet forces, rather than retreat, and occasionally defeat them. One rebel leader stated:[113]

> . . . Spetsnaz[114] are trained for specific targets, but we aren't a conventional force with secret bases and special aircraft or equipment for them to destroy. They are skilled at moving at night and in hiding, but in Afghanistan there are no jungles where they can travel undetected. Mujahideen are moving at night as well and it isn't easy for the Spetsnaz to move around . . . they mostly come in by helicopter, perhaps eventually marching for a while to a nearby area where they intend to operate, but they are forced to do practically the same job as paratroopers. They try to attack us, but to do that their numbers must be significant. In fact, they don't operate in small four or five man teams. Their smallest group is 50-strong, even when they organize observation posts. We learned relatively easily how to face them.
>
> . . . I believe the Spetsnaz . . . are the only Soviet troops who can think for themselves and take quick decisions. However, we discovered that they are good on the attack, but they can't do much when we attack them. . . . They can't take along tanks, IFVs, or other hardware. . . . It's simpler for us to fight them, especially on a terrain we know better. . . . Spetsnaz operations decreased (beginning in 1986).

In spite of cuts in the amount and tempo of land combat and the use of relatively slow moving armored columns supported by artillery, Soviet casualties reached at least 3,000 in 1987, with many killed. The Soviets had made considerable improvements in their combined operations during 1982–1985, but even before the Stinger and Blowpipe inhibited their use of airpower, they could not make firepower, or the use of airpower and airlift, a substitute for the ability to occupy space and win the support of the Afghan people. Like the U.S. in Vietnam, they could not find a substitute for an effective host government and strong support from local forces. While there were many other defects in Soviet combined arms, the key lesson was that while war may succeed as an extension of politics, only total war can be a substitute for politics. This was a level of conflict and combined arms activity that the USSR was not prepared to engage in.

Soviet Combined Arms in 1988 and 1989

Soviet combined operations in 1988 and 1989 were increasingly dictated by two major considerations: withdrawing Soviet troops and preserving the DRA government in power long enough to force a coalition government with the Mujahideen. In practice, this meant that the Soviets attempted to move in sufficiently overwhelming force to avoid Mujahideen attacks and then to stay in garrison areas while using the maximum amount of high-flying airpower and artillery to provide both security and support for DRA forces.

The Soviets exploited the fact that the Mujahideen had only limited amounts of long-range firepower and that there were severe altitude limits on the range of the manportable surface-to-air missiles in Mujahideen hands. They also exploited the fact that Mujahideen forces now had to take predictable and defensible targets like cities and strong points. This allowed sudden sweeps out of garrisons and cities, the use of artillery fire, and the use of area bombing in areas where the Mujahideen were likely to be located. Beginning in mid-1988, the Soviets increasingly threatened the Mujahideen with the destruction of any major towns they captured and provided emergency reinforcements when such cites seemed likely to fall to Mujahideen forces. They increasingly used bombers flying from the USSR, and in November 1988, the Soviets started firing Scud missiles as a means of delivering both a terror weapon and fire support without exposing manned aircraft. Similarly, the USSR would use long-range artillery punitively to attack towns friendly to the Mujahideen, or captured by the Mujahideen, to force them to withdraw.

It is difficult to appraise the effectiveness of these Soviet tactics. The USSR was still forced to undertake a major combined arms offensive to secure the Salang road and could do nothing to prevent major Mujahideen concentrations from building up around Kabul, Kandahar, and Jalalabad. The Soviets essentially attempted to force the Mujahideen to wait to attack the DRA until the Soviets had left and secured their own withdrawal, at the same time negotiating for some kind of coalition. By and large, the Soviet bombing only rarely hit major Mujahideen forces. The major targets remained civilians friendly to the Mujahideen, rather than Mujahideen forces.

Infantry

Despite the importance of Soviet combined arms tactics, it was the interaction of Soviet, DRA, and Mujahideen infantry forces which played the most critical role in determining the actual outcome of most tactical encounters. This emphasis on infantry was a result of the political structure of the conflict, the terrain, the organization and equipment of non-Soviet forces, and the way the Mujahideen were forced to fight.[115]

Soviet Regular Infantry and Problems in Infantry Quality

The Soviets began the war with severe problems in infantry quality that they could never fully overcome. Even after the USSR replaced the largely Asian motorized rifle troops with ethnic Russians and other non-Asian troops, the bulk of the manpower in regular infantry and motorized rifle units lacked training. Conscripts were often sent to Afghanistan because they failed to pay bribes—a problem that characterizes many aspects of the corrupt Soviet conscription system for criminal action. Others were sent because they were regarded as problem soldiers. Health services were poor, and drugs, alcoholism, and medical problems were common.

Until 1982, most conscripts had little or no combat training before they entered combat units in Afghanistan. They were expected to train in the unit in combat. Even after 1982, most ordinary troops outside select motorized rifle units and assault and combat support units had inadequate training and were expected to learn on the job. Many support forces were central Asians who did not read or speak Russian and were treated as menials.

There were serious disciplinary problems, hostility between new and older troops, theft, and problems with looting and atrocities. Many of these same problems had occurred with the more poorly led U.S. forces in Vietnam, but the Soviet problems were far more severe. Most ordinary infantry did not, however, go into units which were expected to play an aggressive combat role. They were put into garrison roles and used in defensive, support, and convoy missions.

Officers, NCOs, and specialists were generally of significantly higher quality than their troops. Good officers were often given high pay and rapid promotion. Some officers were, however, sent to Afghanistan as punishment, and many Soviet units seem to have experienced problems with low-grade NCOs and officers who remained distant from their troops.

The regular Soviet infantry forces that did serve in combat had to steadily change their tactics, particularly during the first three years of the war. Soviet infantry, including airborne troops, relied far too heavily on their armored personnel carriers at the beginning of the war and tended to stay in their vehicles and on the roads. This made it almost impossible to see and kill the Mujahideen, made the Soviet infantry ideal targets as the Mujahideen obtained rocket launchers and other heavy weapons, and tied troops to predictable routes while leaving most of the terrain to their enemy.

As a result, the Soviets had to change both the quality and the training of their motorized infantry. Most of the Soviet troops entering Afghanistan before 1983 had negligible mountain warfare training, even in rudimentary skills like driving and maintaining vehicles in mountains, and little or no air assault training. By 1983–1984, an increasing number had special training in mountain warfare—some in the mountains of Bulgaria. The troops assigned to key combat units had improved night warfare training and training in independent air mobile operations before they arrived.[116]

Several lessons can be drawn from this experience: Infantry must be trained for combat before it is deployed, or it takes heavy losses and loses much of its effectiveness. Infantry must be specially trained and equipped for the specific conditions and missions under which it will fight. Untrained infantry lose battles and take casualties, and low-grade infantry consume more resources and create more morale problems than they are worth.

Equally important, successful infantry operations require good leadership and close human relationships between junior officers, NCOs, and enlisted men. Forces in which officers stand aside from their men and NCOs and older troops are allowed to bully or exploit ordinary soldiers lose much of their effectiveness. If infantry forces are to be effective, discipline must consist of concern and leadership, not punishment.

Soviet Elite Infantry Operations

The Soviet force structure, however, cannot be understood simply by examining the Soviet treatment of conscripts and ordinary units. Some of the most important changes in Soviet infantry were the steady growth of elite forces such as Spetsnaz, reconnaissance troops, airborne troops, and heliborne assault troops. Estimates differ as to the size of the various elite forces in Afghanistan. Some estimates indicate that they reach a peaked of 15 to 20 percent of the total Soviet force and that they consisted of 18,000 to 23,000 troops. Virtually all sources agree that these elite forces not only raised the quality of Soviet forces, but their deployment reflected a deepening understanding of the role mobile infantry can play in effectively containing a guerrilla movement.

The Soviets generally refer to these elite forces as *desant* forces, which the USSR defines as "forces specially prepared and landed or designated for landing on the enemy's territory for the purpose of conducting combat actions." Soviet *desant* forces included several major types of forces. The most important in terms of the Soviet experience in Afghanistan are the airborne forces, or VDV, and the assault troops, or DShB. The USSR also made good use of reconnaissance troops or scouts (*razvedchiki*), and various forms of special purpose forces or Spetsnaz (*spetsialnoye naznachenie*), including raiders (*raydoviki*), infiltration troops (*vysotniki*), and other specialized forces.[117]

The VDV are *vozdushno-desantnaya-voiska* or air landing troops, and all such units have the distinction as being referred to as "Guards" forces. The VDV forces are the most elite of the elite troops and have the most demanding selection and training. The DShB are *desantno-shturmovyata brigada*, or landing-assault brigades, and only some units are referred to as "Guards." The DShB also have good training, but some are less select. Independent DShB units seem to have special uniforms and be identical in elite status to the VDV and possibly a branch of the VDV.

Other DShB troops are specially trained battalions in regular divisions and independent brigades. These are specially selected and trained forces but do not have the same elite status as the previous forces. The reconnaissance forces are not a special branch of the *desant* forces or infantry, but are rather company- or battalion-sized elite elements within all combat elements. The reconnaissance elements of the VDV and DShB are the most elite elements of these forces.[118]

The Spetsnaz involve a wide range of elite elements with very different organization and training, and some are KGB. They can range from forces that include specially selected and trained conscripts to all-career units similar to the U.S. rangers, and they include forces which are specially trained in behind-the-lines operations and sabotage.

Soviet Airborne Operations

The airborne forces were deployed in Afghanistan from the start, and virtually all airborne forces were well trained before they arrived in country. Following the model that Soviet forces first used in Czechoslovakia, airborne elements and Spetsnaz began to enter the country weeks before the Soviet coup. According to some estimates, the entire 103rd and 105th Guards Airborne divisions were involved during the initial invasion, along with at least one regiment of the 104th Airborne.

During 1979–1980, the airborne forces saw only limited action. The 105th Division was disbanded, except for one regiment. The two regiments of the 103rd Guards Airborne became the key airborne formations in the country. Airborne forces became steadily more active during 1981–1982 but made little use of actual parachute drops.

The Soviets also found that large airborne formations became too slow and inflexible to keep up with the Mujahideen. They often violated Soviet doctrine, which requires such troops to have high tactical mobility and conduct rapidly moving combat once they enter an area, not simply be mobile in the initial assault phase. While these forces often were valuable in seizing specific points, they could not effectively pursue the enemy and had a much slower tempo of operations than was desired.

In 1983, the Soviets shifted to using small airborne elements acting independently or spearheading combined arms elements. These forces played a key role in securing passes and key areas, although they sometimes ran into Mujahideen ambushes. The airborne forces increasingly made heavy use of helicopters, followed by rapid terrain movements and assaults, many of which were pressed home in running or moving attacks.

By the Panjshir 7 offensive of 1984, a regiment from the 104th Airborne had been added to the total airborne strength. The other airborne elements were two regiments from the 103rd Division and the one former 105th regiment.[119] These forces conducted a wide variety of night operations, mountain warfare missions, and other special-purpose assault missions. Some elements were extremely competent and aggressive and considerably impressed the Mujahideen.

The problem the Soviets could never fully correct in their airborne forces before they began their withdrawal in 1988 was the inability of such troops to stay in the field for extended periods and constantly seek out the enemy. Small airborne units tended to win small battles but failed to have a decisive tactical effect in a war where there was a very high ratio of area to population and where the Soviets had too low a force density. The airborne forces also failed to achieve decisive results because they lacked the endurance to pursue the Mujahideen for days or weeks after the initial shock phase and several days of mobile battle.

Soviet Air Assault Operations

Soviet air assault and air mobile (DShB) forces were also deployed to Afghanistan from the start.[120] The 66th (56th?) Air Assault Brigade was deployed in 1980 and played a major combat role throughout the conflict. This brigade was reported to have about 4,000 men in three DShB and three infantry battalions. Another independent battalion (40th) and DShB forces from the USSR were used, as were specially trained elements of the motorized rifle divisions. These forces tended to be White Russian, Ukrainian, or Belorussian.

The DShB forces used helicopters to strike at points with company-sized operations anywhere from 20 to 200 kilometers deep into enemy territory. They also sometimes used BTRs, BMPs, and other armored vehicles without heliborne assault. They often performed quick surgical raids and conducted night ambushes and counter-ambushes. They stressed the use of tactics designed to draw Mujahideen forces into tactical traps.

As time went on, the DShB steadily changed several aspects of their operations. They increased the armament of their lift helicopters, they added attack helicopter support, they added heavy infantry weapons and artillery, and they added heavy lift helicopters such as the Mi-26 Halo. According to some reports, they also made increasing use of the BMD rather than the BTR and BRDM because the latter vehicles proved to be too vulnerable and were hard to fight from.

Like the airborne forces, the DShB became steadily more mobile and flexible with time and were used increasingly in small independent operations. They were particularly valuable in suddenly assaulting key strong points, mountain areas, and other high-value targets. Like the airborne troops, they could win most operations and secure a small area while they were in place but could not occupy and hold a large area.

In some ways, the overall Soviet tactics were self-defeating in terms of the outcome of this kind of operation. They helped ensure that small splintered opposition groups existed throughout most hostile regions. The often arbitrary Soviet air and artillery attacks on the population ensured a source of support and recruitment, and it was easier for the Mujahideen to recover from most tactical defeats than for Soviet forces to recover from most tactical victories.

*Reconnaissance and Raider Troops
and "Spetsnaz" Operations*[121]

The precise nature of the reconnaissance and raider operations in Afghanistan is not clear. In many cases, specially trained elements of regular units seemed to have been called Spetsnaz. What is clear is that some of these troops performed very well, and some did not. The Afghans were often deeply impressed by the scout and raider troops, some of which outfought the Mujahideen on their own terrain—both in the mountains and in the desert.

These operations became particularly important during the start of the offensives in 1984. Spetsnaz troops conducted a wide range of small special operations against key Mujahideen targets and played a blocking and scouting role. They operated extensively at night and often attacked or ambushed Mujahideen supply routes. They supported DRA forces and the DRA militia as advisors and de facto commanders, and they seem to have performed at least some assassinations.

Other key missions included setting up observation posts and small forts on mountain tops and along supply routes, conducting rescue operations and mountainside assaults, and performing other operations involving small forces operating independently in enemy territory. Some Soviet reports refer to operations at heights of 3,000 meters and operations in hostile territory lasting up to a month.

The tempo of their operations began to drop in 1986, however, as it became clear that the Soviets could not halt the Mujahideen in this manner. There are some indications these forces also tended to take high casualties and that their operations were cut back to reduce losses. There is no question, however, that Soviet ability to conduct well-targeted classic counterinsurgency operations improved significantly over time.

Soviet Infantry Weapons and Firepower

The Soviets improved their marksmanship; provided infantry with more RPGs, mortars, and grenade launchers; and made increasing use of anti-sniper techniques as the war progressed. This Soviet emphasis on improved infantry firepower is reflected in the deployment of the new 5.44-mm AK-74 assault rifle. The AK-74 is a cheap, reliable, and more effective weapon than the 7.62-caliber AKM and AK-47. The AK-74 is lighter, has 20 percent more effective range, is easier to aim, fires a smaller flat-nosed round with excellent tumbling characteristics once it hits something denser than air, and produces a more lethal wound. This last characteristic led to the Mujahideen referring to it as "poison bullets."[122]

The AK-74 is easy to control in full and semi-automatic fire and is capable of withstanding considerable abuse when subjected to dirt, sand, and mud. This reflects a continuing emphasis on "worst case" operability in Soviet assault rifles that is not always found in Western counterparts.

The Soviets improved the use of suppressors for night combat and gave selected infantry forces silenced weapons. The Soviets also deployed another version of the AK-74 called the AKMS. It was a cut-down weapon designed for easy operation from within armored vehicles, and it proved successful in some operations. A cut-down form of the AK-74, called the AKSU, was deployed to replace to AKMS. It too was used inside armored vehicles, by artillery and helicopter crews, and increasingly as a substitute for pistols.

Soviet forces were given increasingly large numbers of light machine guns and used vehicle-mounted turrets and AA guns to "hose" the Mujahideen with automatic weapons fire. This kind of area fire seems to have been far more effective in suppression and casualty-producing effect than assault rifles. The Soviets also issued a smaller caliber machine gun, the RPK-74. The RPK-74 is the squad machine gun version of the AK-74. It fires the same ammunition as the AK-74, is equipped with a bipod, and has a longer magazine.[123] It has proved highly mobile and very effective in mountain combat.

Soviet infantry in Afghanistan were widely equipped with BG-15 40-mm grenade launchers for their assault rifles. They were given large numbers of AGS-17 tripod-mounted automatic grenade launchers that could fire a magazine of 29 grenades at ranges of 500–1,200 meters.[124] These weapons proved to be excellent in breaking up attacks, conducting night defensive combat, and attacking the small rock forts or defenses used by the Mujahideen. The Mujahideen, in turn, often used captured AGS-17s on Soviet troops.

During the early 1980s, the Soviets deployed an improved and more compact version of the RPG called the RPG-18. This weapon is somewhat similar to the U.S. LAW. It is a small manportable weapon with a disposal casing that acts as the launcher. It has a diameter of 64 mm and can defeat up to 375 mm of armor at an angle of 90 degrees. Later in the war, the USSR deployed an improved version of the RPG-18 called the RPG-22. This system proved to be particularly useful against Mujahideen strongholds, although the Mujahideen captured enough of the system to use them against the government. It has a telescopic tube which is 805 mm long when extended and has simple pop-up sights set for ranges of 50, 150, and 250 meters with a temperature-compensating rear sight. The RPG-22 fires an 80-mm rocket with a chemical explosive warhead capable of penetrating 480 mm of armor at 90 degrees.[125] The RPG-22 has a range of 0–250 meters (versus 135–200 meters for the RPG-18) and can penetrate 390 mm of armor (versus 360 for the RPG-18).

The Soviets also improved their RPG-7 portable rocket launcher. The RPG-7 is a small folding form of the RPG-7 which was originally designed for use by airborne forces. The launcher uses a PGO-7V range-finding sight with ranges of 200 to 500 meters in increments of 100 meters. The sight has 2.5 magnification and a thirteen-degree field of view. It uses a smaller projectile with a cone diameter of 70 mm. It is designed largely as an anti-personnel or anti–light-armor weapon, and an extended-range version is available. This new round was used extensively against resistance strong points and supply units.

Combat troops were given large numbers of disposable single-shot RPO grenade launchers and flame grenades, with ranges up to 400 meters. A lighter version of this weapon called the RPO-A was also deployed, as were BG-15 single-shot grenade launchers. These proved to be light enough for mountain combat and were very effective area weapons. The RPO was particularly effective because it could fire an incendiary grenade with persistent burning characteristics up to 200 meters. The RPO-A could fire a similar round up to 1,000 meters.[126] One of the key lessons the Soviets learned was the need to keep improving the range and lethality of highly portable infantry weapons. No artillery or crew-served weapons could serve as a substitute in either mountain or ambush conditions because of the need for instant direct fire capability.

Like U.S. forces in Vietnam, the Soviets also steadily expanded their use of light body armor. Bulletproof vests became standard Soviet issue for combat soldiers, and relatively crude metal linings were soon replaced with more modern composites.[127] The effectiveness of these vests in reducing casualties in Afghanistan is not known, nor is there credible information on how often the Soviet troops actually wore these vests. It seems likely, however, that they were as effective as the similar equipment issued to U.S. forces in Vietnam and Lebanon.

Soviet Sniper and Anti-Sniper Operations

Early in the war, Soviet writers complained about the poor standards of marksmanship in the Soviet military.[128] There was pressure to raise military standards regarding marksmanship, which led to improved training and to equipping troops with the area weapons just discussed as a substitute for accuracy. It also led the USSR to make increased use of specially trained "counter-snipers, and to triple the normal number of sniper's rifles in their combat units."[129]

The Soviets also found that some of the Mujahideen with European rifles could shoot infantry at distances out of the effective range of their assault rifles. This led to the use of special sniper suppression squads that were the first to dismount from vehicles. These squads were equipped with long-range rifles with scopes and RPG-18s to provide heavier fire.[130] This point is interesting because Western forces equipped with automatic weapons may well face similar problems with snipers.

The Role of DRA Infantry

The DRA Army was so subordinate to the Soviet forces during most of the fighting that it is difficult to talk about the performance of most troops. The key issues were more political than military, and the central problem underlying DRA behavior was the fact that the bulk of the ordinary troops were conscripts and had only lukewarm support for the government as long as it was Soviet controlled. The Soviets paid more attention to "Afghanisation" throughout the war than the U.S. did during most of the fighting in Vietnam, however, and had some success. This was largely, however, in organizing and training forces to defend fixed points and urban areas.

The DRA Army created some effective elite units. These units were not immediately effective, however, perhaps because they were first regarded as dangerous by the USSR and then extensively retrained. They became active with the advent of major unconventional warfare operations in 1984 and were closely integrated with Soviet forces. They were sometimes employed as platoons in Soviet combined arms reinforced battalions (CARBs) and acted as scouts and infiltration forces.[131]

The Soviets do not seem to have been able to rebuild the 26th Airborne Regiment after it mutinied in 1980, but a successor does seem to have been set up. They did create relatively effective forces out of the 37th and 38th commando brigades in Kabul, along with the 446th Commando Battalion in Kandahar.[132] The USSR also helped create a number of "divisions" that acted as effective forces in defensive positions and which could occasionally counterattack effectively even without Soviet support.

The political weaknesses in the rest of the DRA infantry forces help explain the growing role of Soviet infantry during the early and mid-1980s. These weaknesses also show why the USSR eventually faced a no-win situation. The broad political conflicts within the DRA government, and its unpopularity, affected infantry combat. The Mujahideen often gave Afghan army troops the opportunity to surrender prior to an operation, and government troops frequently took this option. They often joined the Mujahideen or at least turned their weapons over to them. This option, however, was usually not offered Afghan troops that had just killed Mujahideen soldiers. No Afghan troops wanted to surrender with a rifle that had been fired and an empty clip of ammunition. Captured Afghan government officers were also subjected to torture and execution and often showed little interest in pushing their troops into combat where their units might break up and lead to their capture.

The Role of Mujahideen Infantry

The Mujahideen infantry were divided along tribal and religious lines, a major disadvantage. They lacked effective combined arms and combined operations support and were normally forced to fight in small units of no more than 50–75 men. They normally had no opportunity to mass and act as a "regular" army, and until they received the Stinger in September 1986, they had to fight a 300–400 meter war. To succeed, they had to move that close to Soviet or DRA units or risk being wiped out by air or artillery fire. The same distance also represented the maximum effective range of their 12.7-mm and 14.5-mm machine guns and RPG-2s and RPG-7s. The Afghan Mujahideen, however, did have three significant advantages over the Soviets in terms of infantry warfare. The first was the support of the people. The second was their division into many small independent groups with access to sanctuaries in Pakistan and Iran. They could be defeated only in detail and could then recover in secure areas. The third was their familiarity with the terrain and weather conditions under which they were required to operate.[133]

Unlike the Soviets, the Mujahideen did not have to "unlearn" the techniques formulated to wage a war in Europe. They were acclimatized to the weather and were experts on the terrain. They instinctively understood the value of the high ground, and they steadily improved their ability to take cover and shelter in the mountains as time went on. The Mujahideen were masters of mountain survival techniques and were familiar with the flora and fauna of Afghanistan.

The Mujahideen were able to deploy and disperse more quickly in mountain terrain on foot than the USSR could by air, and they developed similar tactics for fighting and dispersing on the plains and around cities and strong points. They began as small squads, but after 1984, they gradually began to cooperate more and more in operations in which a mixture of forces could suddenly assemble from different directions, with one element securing the rear and flanks while the other attacked. The Mujahideen also learned through years of experience how to use small-unit tactics and improve their use of mortars and heavier weaponry.

After 1985, the Mujahideen began more formal efforts at training. They developed rudimentary communications for some units and factions and created new heavier fighting units or strike groups of twenty-five to fifty men each. Special teams and crews were trained in the use of heavy weapons such as mortars, heavy machine guns, recoilless rifles, and 107-mm and 122-mm rockets. Similar training eventually was provided to the Stinger units. Some factions also trained cartographers, medics, and mine warfare and demolition and explosives experts. Some Mujahideen groups provided ideological and literacy training.[134]

The Mujahideen began to plan attacks on a formal basis. They created models of their targets and carried out extensive intelligence mapping and planning sessions. This allowed them to achieve well-planned surprise attacks in spite of the improvement in Soviet infantry tactics. Some Mujahideen forces set up a more formal administrative system, and many units created self-supporting rural rear areas.

The Mujahideen, however, remained a largely improvised and changing guerrilla force through mid-1989. As one of the most successful leaders, Ahmad Shah Massoud, said, "The important thing in operations . . . is that they should be effective. . . . If we can't be sure they'll be effective, we don't make them. . . . Our struggle is based on our experience inside the country and on a study of external experiences. But mostly, our thinking is based on a study of domestic experiences."[135]

The Mujahideen ability to utilize terrain to maximum advantage was particularly evident in their defense against Soviet offensives into the various strategic valleys in Afghanistan. The Mujahideen were adept at calculating where terrain would channel Soviet troops and arranged ambushes accordingly.

These skills were apparent in the 1982 Soviet offensive in the Panjshir Valley (known as Panjshir 5). In this battle, the Mujahideen consistently made use of high ground for observation of Soviet activities. The Mujahideen then exploited the terrain to counterattack and ambush division-sized Soviet forces. Soviet T-62 tanks acting as a route security patrol were knocked out with a minefield and ambushed at Bazerak. As the Soviet column progressed, more Mujahideen ambushes occurred in terrain which acted as choke points. These ambushes slowed the advance of the column and created stationary vehicular targets. The Mujahideen then split up into "side valleys" and forced the Soviet forces to divide and advance into more areas. The final result of Panjshir 5 was that the Soviet column bogged down and was unable to link up with troops inserted by helicopter.

In contrast, the 1984 Soviet drive into the Panjshir Valley reflected far greater use of helicopter lift, off-road use of AFVs, on-call air and attack helicopter support, and bomber destruction of friendly farms and hamlets. The Soviets tried to counter tactical expertise and knowledge of the terrain with area fire. The Mujahideen, however, learned to cache their weapons and disperse and improved the quality of their ambushes. They gradually improved their use of rocket launchers and SA-7s and started to let Soviet sweeps pass by and then regrouped to hit at rear echelon units.[136] The Soviets took their objectives, but their tactical victories were strategically and politically meaningless.

This pattern of infantry combat poses obvious lessons to Western forces like USCENTCOM. Superior firepower and command and control can hold an objective such as a city or a key line of communication, but Western forces may have to deploy in the middle of civil conflict and deal with guerrilla forces similar to the Mujahideen with superior knowledge of the terrain. As discussed in another volume in this set, in the case of the Iran-Iraq War, knowledge of terrain can be effective in larger-scale conflicts and can present similar challenges to mechanized forces.

Mujahideen Infantry Weapons

The Afghans had only a limited number of modern weapons at the beginning of the Soviet invasion. Many guerrillas were armed with bolt-action Lee Enfield .303 rifles or locally produced copies of these weapons. Others had old Martini-Henrys. A few looted AK-47s and Pakistani-supplied FN-FALS were available, but these more effective weapons were relatively rare.[137]

The Afghan guerrillas rapidly obtained large numbers of light weapons after the near collapse of the DRA forces in 1980, however. They continued to upgrade their weaponry from 1981 to 1988, although they still had significant gaps in anti-armor and anti-air weapons. They now have many AK-47s, some AK-74s, SKS 7.62-mm rifles, Iranian 7.62-mm G-3s, 9-mm Sten guns, shot guns, and Chinese-made Type-56-1 assault rifles. Light machine guns include the 7.62-mm RPD and RPK, plus the 7.62-mm PKM and some older Czech weapons like the ZB-36.

The shortage of light machine guns and ammunition was a continuing problem until large-scale outside supply began to be effective in 1985–1986. The Mujahideen also had 12.7-mm "Dasha" and 14.5-mm "Zigriat" medium and heavy submachine guns and 20-mm AA guns. The former two heavy machine guns made up the bulk of the Mujahideen air defense force until 1985–1986. The number of such weapons then increased steadily. There were only 13 heavy machine guns in the entire Panjshir Valley in 1982, but 250 in 1984. By the late 1980s, the Mujahideen were virtually saturated with infantry weapons.[138]

The Mujahideen gradually acquired large numbers of RPG-2s, RPG-7s, and Type 59 tank grenade launchers, plus many other Soviet infantry weapons. These were used in increasing numbers after 1982. The rebels found these systems to be extremely useful but bulky, with ammunition that was difficult to move. They would have liked lighter systems with light ammunition. The Mujahideen had some old towed AA guns, 107-mm and 130-mm rocket launchers, mortars, SA-7s, Blowpipes, and Stingers.

It is interesting to note that the primary weapon in Mujahideen forces in late 1988 was still the rifle, with the older men preferring the accuracy of the .303 or sniper rifles and the younger men preferring the volume of fire from assault rifles. Sniper weapons were of critical value to the Mujahideen, who often could kill Soviet troops from outside the effective range of the Soviet assault rifle.

The improvement in Mujahideen weaponry was due partly to foreign suppliers, including Egypt, China, Pakistan, Iran, Saudi Arabia, and the United States, and partly as a result of capturing weapons. The levels of U.S. aid to the Mujahideen have already been described. They also had substantial aid from such diverse sources as the PRC and Saudi Arabia. Aside from such specialized infantry weapons as Stinger and Blowpipe, these sources of aid provided 14.5-mm machine guns, large numbers of 107-mm and 122-mm rockets, and an increasing number of light long-range mortars.

Other deliveries included an increasing number of SA-7s, up to 70 percent of which came from the PRC. They included about $35 million worth of PLO and other arms captured by Israel during the 1982 fighting in Lebanon plus Soviet weapons from Egypt and other Soviet-supplied Third World states. The U.S. began to furnish a single-barreled Oerlikon 20-mm towed AA gun in 1985–1986. This gun weighs 545 kilograms, but it can fire 1,000 rounds per minute and is usable against both air and ground targets.[139]

Only a portion of these infantry weapons, however, found their way into the hands of the Mujahideen in the field. As has been discussed earlier, this was partially because the Pakistanis were under pressure from Moscow to restrain the Mujahideen. It appears, however, that the Pakistani government equipped elements of its army and police forces with weapons that were to be delivered to Afghan rebels. The Pakistanis then passed on their older army rifles to the guerrillas.[140]

The Afghan guerrillas also made use of various homemade weapons, including explosives, Molotov cocktails, and homemade grenades. The activities of the Mujahideen reflected considerable resourcefulness, which poses yet another warning of how effective guerrillas and saboteurs can be using unconventional warfare and homemade weapons to disrupt heavily armed regular forces.[141]

In terms of lessons, it is interesting to note that at the time Soviet withdrawal began, the most significant concerns of the Mujahideen were the need for modern, man-portable, anti-aircraft weapons that might be useful against Soviet helicopters like the Stinger. They were also concerned with obtaining more anti-aircraft machine guns and more effective land-attack systems like the TOW and Dragon anti-tank guided missiles (ATGMs). They also stressed the need for light long-range artillery with ranges in excess of eight kilometers.

Tanks and Armored Vehicles

When the Soviet Union invaded Afghanistan in December 1979, it did so with an army and an air force that had been trained and equipped to fight in Europe. The Soviets called upon many of their tactical systems to perform a variety of functions for which they were not designed. This led to the painful process of adaptation described earlier, in which the Soviets tried to cope with the requirements of guerrilla warfare.

Tanks

Soviet attempts to use main battle tanks in Afghanistan proved to be troublesome early in the fighting because Afghan terrain was not suited to the use of such large and cumbersome combat vehicles in many areas, except to defend roads and main areas of concentration. Soviet armored troops were faced with a situation where the use of tanks was often inappropriate.

The most obvious problem involved the inability of tanks to maneuver through much of Afghanistan's mountainous terrain. Other problems arose even when tanks were able to maneuver. Soviet articles on tank maintenance point out that T-55 and T-62 tanks experienced frequent clutch problems in hilly terrain and lost their tracks on rocky ground. Further, the additional strains on the vehicle caused by having to traverse steep slopes could cause tank engines to overheat unless the quantity of coolant was doubled or tripled. Fuel expenditure on such terrain was 30 to 50 percent more than that expended traveling on flat ground.[142]

Equally important, Soviet tank guns did not prove particularly effective against most infantry targets in rough terrain. This was particularly true of the T-55, which lacked the gun elevation and depression to be effective in mountain combat.[143] Soviet tanks lacked sights with the wide visual coverage and targeting aids necessary to easily locate typical Mujahideen targets or allow tank crews to deal rapidly with infantry ambushes. Commanders could not fight from open turrets, however, without taking losses. Tank guns also could not be elevated to the degree required or tracked with sufficient speed, and crews experienced severe discomfort and fatigue problems because of the poor human engineering and ventilation of Soviet tanks.

The Soviets did retain their tanks throughout the war and deployed additional numbers of T-62s and some T-72s to replace some of their T-55s. According to some reports, they also deployed modernized variants of these tanks with improved armor after 1983, probably using them largely in the plains or in convoys. They shifted to more modern tanks with the enhanced frontal armor used in Soviet forces in eastern Europe after 1983. Soviet tanks also seem to have had some parts and track modifications to improve their performance in mountain areas—a warning that other nations may have to broaden the testing of their tanks to include similar mountain and desert conditions if they are to operate properly under such conditions.[144]

The main change in the Soviet approach to armor during the conflict was to emphasize lighter armored fighting vehicles and armored personnel carriers. This gave Soviet forces a higher degree of maneuverability and effectiveness in mountainous terrain where problems with ambushes were especially acute. At the same time, the Soviets rapidly learned in 1980 that tanks can survive against guerrilla forces with rocket launchers only under more favorable terrain conditions if they have properly combined arms support.

The Soviets did continue to use tanks from 1980 to 1983, but Soviet tank forces were used largely in supporting other arms under favorable terrain conditions or along main routes. Beginning in 1984, the Soviets made increasing use of tanks as spearhead elements for the offensive forces that moved by land. The tanks advanced slowly, supported by heliborne forces on the heights, and normally with extensive artillery support. This reduced the tanks' vulnerability, but it slowed the tempo of operations and was suitable only for efforts like opening main lines of communication, relieving besieged garrisons, and attacking Mujahideen strong points.

Tanks took on a new role in 1987–1988 as air cover and helicopter support was curtailed. The tank was used to provide low vulnerability in a number of operations. By and large, however, tanks avoided direct combat and would reserve or halt and allow artillery fire to be called in to saturate Mujahideen positions. This lack of aggressiveness may have stemmed from a desire to avoid losses during the evacuation phase of the war, but it also seemed to stem from the fact that the tanks could not survive without extensive artillery and suppressive fire support.

Other Armored Vehicles

The main lesson the Soviets learned in using their other armored vehicles during the war was that troops cannot fight successfully from such vehicles in many types of terrain and tactical conditions. They adopt static tactics, and the fireports of such vehicles sharply limit the ability to see and engage the enemy. These problems were partly due to the Soviet concept of training troops in units before 1984 and partly a result of the fact that the vehicles often made ideal targets for even lightly armed infantry and could not engage infantry successfully.

The Soviets steadily improved the training of their infantry from 1984 onwards. They sharply increased the amount of infantry firepower for dismounted combat. As has been discussed earlier, this included grenade launchers, rocket launchers, flame grenades, and machine guns. They also provided steadily increasing amounts of fire support from artillery, mortars, and AA guns.

The Soviets used a wide variety of other armored vehicles (OAFVs) during the war, including BTR-60PBs, BTR-70s, BTR-80s, BMP-1s, BMP-2, and BMDs. They constantly altered their mix of other fighting vehicles during the war and modified the weapons and other equipment on these vehicles. Like the U.S. in Vietnam, they found that vehicles designed to fight in central Europe had to be adapted and modified to suit the special conditions of combat.

For example, the Soviets replaced many of their BMPs—which were too large for mountain trails, subject to frequent breakdowns, and difficult to service in the field—with BMDs and BMD-2s. The BMD is a family of light armored vehicles, including the APC, MICV, and light tank/self-propelled (SP) gun. It has a maximum speed of at least 40 mph and can carry three crew members and six infantry troops. The light, air-dropable BMD has been of considerable importance to Soviet mountain operations. The BMDs deployed in Afghanistan may also have been given improved armor and were secure against machine guns even at close ranges—although this would not have been true if the Mujahideen had had the armor-piercing ammunition common to better equipped forces.[145]

Many Afghan mountain routes were not passable to the larger BMPs, BTR-60s, BTR-70s, or BTR-80s. These OAFVs proved more useful in the cities, for LOC protection, as armored ambulances, and in defending strategic crossroads.[146] Another important difference that made the BMD more useful than the BMP in mountain warfare was the BMP's highly visible exhaust trail. This was caused partly by an over-enrichment of the fuel mixture which occurs for the BMP at high altitudes. BMP breakdowns in the mountains were frequent. The BMP also required an improved ventilation during the war to deal with gas buildup from firing, and the road-wheels had to be modified to make them more reliable.[147]

These problems seem to have been compounded by the fact that Soviet BMP crews engaged in poor preventative maintenance and showed relatively poor ability in repairing these vehicles once they broke down.[148] While BMD crews may have been no better, their vehicles endured less punishment in the mountains. The one advantage the BMP did seem to have over the BMD in mountain conflict was that the BMP had less difficulty crossing swift mountain rivers.[149]

The light tank/SP gun variant of the BMD proved to be useful. It is a well-armed vehicle which was designed primarily for use by Soviet airborne forces. It has a turret identical to the larger BMP. It normally includes a 73-mm smooth-bore gun with a Sagger missile on the gun's launch rail. It also has at least two 7.62 machine guns. Both the gun and missiles were used against mountain targets, hardpoints, and villages.

The Soviets also armed such infantry-fighting vehicles in Afghanistan with a rapid-fire 30-mm cannon in place of the standard low-pressure 73-mm smooth-bore anti-tank gun. This new 30-mm cannon was first seen on a BMP in Afghanistan in mid-1981. It was later observed on BMDs as well. This shift in weapon allowed Soviet troops to adjust their armament to meet an infantry rather than an armored threat. The Soviets found they often did not need an anti-tank or hard point kill capability but did need long-range anti-infantry area fire and suppressive fire capability. They also found they needed machine guns and cannon which could "hose" targets with high rates of fire, easily track targets (unlike slow-moving heavy guns), and be easily hyper-elevated. Some OAFVs used vehicle-mounted mortars and a modification of the Soviet 30-mm AGS-17 rapid-fire grenade launcher as a main armament to provide rapid surge fire and direct fire support.[150]

The Soviets did use the BMP to accompany tanks and in independent operations, and it worked reasonably well in suitable terrain, but the original BMP gun could elevate only 33 degrees and the 73-mm gun lacked the rate of fire and area coverage the Soviets needed. It was often replaced with the BMP-2, which had a turret with a 30-mm rapid-fire cannon that could be elevated by 50 degrees.[151] The Sagger missiles on the system also were useful against Mujahideen forts and sheltered troops. There were still reports of a fairly high mechanical breakdown rate in the mid-1980s, however, and the vehicle proved to be very vulnerable to anti-tank rocket launchers. It caught fire, or "brewed up," very easily, and the combination of internal gear and fuel cells on the rear doors led to spalling and often secondary explosions.[152]

The Soviets also used the BMP to solve a special communications problem in mountain warfare. They created a control-management detachment to maintain the continuity of communications in mountain areas. This included a BMP-KshM (command staff vehicle) and two GAZ-66 mounted communications vans. These had the communications gear to ensure high-level capability to preserve control and management from the rear while maintaining contact with the main elements of Soviet forces. They were used by the spearhead forces of both the regular mechanized troops and Spetsnaz, and they had the ability to communicate independently on the HF nets used at the regiment level and above. Unlike similar units in other Soviet forces, where the GAZ-66 act as independent transceiver units, the ones in Afghanistan acted primarily as relays.[153]

The older Soviet BTR-60 transport and reconnaissance vehicles were heavily utilized by Soviet and regular Afghan troops and occasionally by the Mujahideen. Virtually all of the BTR-60s were the BTR-60PB version with an armored roof. Open vehicles proved not to be survivable in mountain and rough terrain combat. The BTR-60s are built for speed rather than protection and proved relatively easy for the Afghans to handle. The standard armament for the BTR-60 is a 12.7- or 14.5-mm gun, and from one to three 7.62 machine guns. The main weapon had to be quickly modified after the early years of the war because it could elevate only by 30 degrees, versus the 60–70 degrees that was desirable.

Firing ports were also available for use by the infantry within the armored personnel carrier (APC), although these ports were so small it was virtually impossible to acquire concealed targets and aim infantry weapons. The BTR-60 had a maximum speed of around 50 mph and was amphibious. It had a crew of two and was capable of carrying sixteen troops.

The main problems with the vehicle were its light armor and relatively poor tires, which had only marginal survivability against hits. The BTR-60PBs often had their fuel burn when they were hit, particularly when they carried external fuel, and they were extremely difficult to evacuate. They had only two small roof hatches, and the infantry had to jump from these hatches under some combat conditions. This required specialized training, and accidents were common. It also exposed infantry to fire.

To obtain these vehicles, the Mujahideen tried to kill the vehicles' drivers by directing small arms fire at the unarmored forward wheel well. They also reportedly tried to destroy the tires, although this often proved difficult because of the tires' automatic reinflation system. If the tires could be destroyed, Soviet troops were forced to leave the vehicle and become vulnerable to small arms fire from the Afghans.

The newer BTR-70 was a more successful design. The BTR-70 allowed faster entrance and exit than earlier models of the BTR and had slightly improved firing ports—although overall visibility from a buttoned-down vehicle remained poor. The engines were more powerful, and the vehicle was much easier to maintain. Troop and crew space was larger and better engineered. There were larger roof hatches and triangular doors in the middle on each side. It could vary tire pressure more efficiently to suit the terrain, and it usually was better armed.

The Soviets often used versions with 14.5-mm machine gun turrets and variants using two roof-mounted AGS-17 grenade launchers. This reflects the fact that rapid area fire cover is crucial in dealing with infantry attacks. The BTR-70 suffered from many of the same problems in burning as the BTR-60PB. Evacuation was easier, but it was still a serious problem.

The BTR-70 vehicle was sometimes modified to serve as a command vehicle through the addition of two extra whip antennas (for a total of three). The BTR-70 was often seen in the company the BAZ-66 signal vehicle. Together these vehicles were believed to form part of the C³ equipment for a regimental or brigade-level headquarters.[154] BTR-70s in Afghanistan were also fitted with AGS-17 30-mm automatic grenade launchers while retaining both the 14.5-mm KPVT machine gun and the 7.62-mm PKT machine gun. The addition of a rapid-fire grenade launcher added a great deal of firepower to these systems since the AGS-17 had a rate of fire which could saturate a hostile position.

The BTR-80, which was first deployed in 1980 and appeared in Afghanistan in 1983, was even more capable. It used a single 260-horsepower V-8 diesel engine instead of the two 115-horsepower V-6 petrol engines in the BTR-60 and BTR-70. This made it less prone to burn. It had more road speed and range. The manually operated one-man turret was similar to that on the BTR-60PB and BTR-70, but the 14.5-mm machine gun could elevate to +60 degrees rather than +30 degrees. Some BTR-70s were retrofitted with this weapon because elevation proved critical in mountain combat.

To improve the BTR-80's capability to escape from ambush, smoke canisters were mounted on each side which could be fired from within (the T-72 and BMP-2 used similar devices). A new two-door side hatch arrangement between the second and third axles, similar to the Cadillac Gage Commando series, had the top open to the front, and the bottom became a step. Infantry could rapidly dismount from either side on the run. There were firing ports in the front of the vehicle angled to fire obliquely forward so the BTR-80 could cover the dead ground which was created in the BTR-70 by relying only on firing from side ports. There were also firing ports for the commander and in the two roof hatches. The main problem with the BTR-80 was its comparatively light armor, and some Soviet troops evidently still complained about the problems in evacuating the vehicle.[155]

The DRA forces used armor largely as an extension of Soviet doctrine and organization. They began the war with large numbers of BTR-152 wheeled armored cars. They rapidly found that these vehicles had to be replaced because they lacked the mobility and endurance to operate effectively in Afghanistan and were too vulnerable. The open tops allowed the Mujahideen to snipe into the vehicles, and they could be easily defeated with rocket launchers and other light weapons like grenades. The Soviets largely replace the BTR-152s with BTR-60PBs, but this scarcely solved the DRA's problems.

The Mujahideen used its limited armor defensively and largely in the rear. Captured tanks were used largely as artillery weapons. This was not a critical problem during most of the war, since main force concentrations could not survive. The Mujahideen found, however, that they could not assault many strong points after the beginning of the Soviet withdrawal in 1988 because they lacked armored mobility and protection in the assault phase.

Precision-Guided and Specialized Land Munitions

Anti-tank guided weapons have been utilized in Afghanistan. The Afghan rebels had little or no armor and no airpower at which the Soviets could direct their PGMs. Despite this, anti-tank guided missiles (ATGMs) were often of good use to the Soviets. The Soviets used such weapons, particularly the AT-3 Sagger, mounted on BMD vehicles as a way of compensating for a lack of tank firepower when attacking hard targets. They also used light crew-portable versions of such weapons and fired others from helicopters.

The Sagger had a range of 300 to 3,150 meters and a 2.7-kilogram warhead. It was a first generation system that required the operator to simultaneously track the missile and target while guiding the missile by wire. More advanced systems were deployed on Soviet helicopters.

Like the ZSU-23s, anti-tank guided missiles could be used in the direct fire mode and aimed directly at rebel positions. As previously noted, the main guns on tanks and BMPs could not always be elevated to the point where they could place accurate fire on Mujahideen attacking from hill crests. ATGMs proved particularly effective in long-range fire against stone houses and the small stone hill forts used by the Mujahideen. A parachute-equipped version was also used to carry communications lines over rough terrain.

The Soviets exercised tight control over their allocations of anti-tank guided weapons. The presence of unnecessary anti-tank guided weapons in the hands of Soviet troops created the problem that if these troops were defeated, the weapons fell into the hands of the Mujahideen. The risk of losing such weapons was even more acute with DRA troops, since many defected to the Mujahideen with their weapons. This led the Soviets to demand that a number of portable anti-tank guided weapons in DRA forces be turned over to Soviet authorities. The hand-held SA-7 surface-to-air infrared missiles were also removed from the inventory of DRA government forces in 1980.[156]

RPG-7 anti-armor rocket launchers were in heavy use on both sides during the war and were often the primary firepower available to the Mujahideen. The Soviets have also brought some of their newer RPGs into Afghanistan, particularly the RPG-16, although some RPG-18s were used as well.[157] The differences between these rocket launchers and the RPG-7 are noted in Table 2.8.

The RPG-16 replaced the RPG-7 in Soviet hands but was not issued to the DRA forces until 1988. Some were captured by the Mujahideen. The round was only two-thirds the length of the RPG-7, and the weapon was smaller in diameter and easier to handle. It was, however, more lethal and effective at ranges up to 500–800 meters versus 300–500 meters for the RPG-7. It also was more accurate and more stable. The RPG-16 round was heavier in spite of its smaller size: 3 kilograms versus 2.5 for the RPG-7. The units deployed in Afghanistan often had improved night sights—reflecting the growing Soviet emphasis on night warfare.[158]

The RPG-18 was a single-shot weapon that seems to have been adapted from the U.S. M-72A Light Anti-Tank Weapon (LAW).[159] The light weight and shorter range of the RPG-18 made it particularly desirable for rough terrain combat, and it was modified to use a longer missile, a shaped charge warhead, and bigger charge. This reduced its effective range to about 140 meters but made it more effective in firing at Mujahideen concealed among rocks. Unlike the RPG-7 or RPG-16, the RPG-18 was not assigned to a specific person within the Soviet squad organization and could be used by a variety of individuals who did not

TABLE 2.8 Soviet Rocket-Propelled Grenade Launchers

	RPG-7	RPG-16	RPG-18	RPG-22
Warhead caliber (mm)	85	58.3	64	72
Armor penetration (mm)	330	up to 375	up to 375	up to 400
Grenade	rocket-assisted heat	rocket-assisted heat	rocket-assisted heat	rocket-assisted heat
Weight (kg)	7.9 (empty)	10.3	2.7 (grenade and launcher)	—
Rate of fire (rd/min)	4–6	4–6	NA (disposable weapon)	—
Range (m)	300–500	500–800	200	250

SOURCE: *The Soviet Army: Troops, Organization and Equipment*, FM 100-2-3 (Washington D.C.: GPO, 1984), pp. 5, 72–75.

have special training as anti-tank grenadiers. It was in wide use by Soviet airborne troops.[160]

A larger version of the RPG-18, called the RPG-22, with a heavier warhead and 80-mm diameter, seems to have entered service in Afghanistan in 1986. The larger warhead was useful in dealing with Mujahideen forts. The Soviet Army also used heavier weapons like the RPG-9 73-mm recoilless gun (with a range of 800 meters and a round weight of up to 4 kilograms).

Tube Artillery, Multiple Rocket Launchers, and Mortars

Artillery has been used extensively by the Soviet Army and Afghan army and occasionally by some of the larger Mujahideen groups, such as those found in the Panjshir Valley. The Soviet and DRA governments, however, had a near monopoly on artillery and long-range firepower during most of the war.

The Soviets used their artillery to support their offensives and to help neutralize centers of urban resistance. They made heavy use of mass fire for suppressive purposes in most of their valley campaigns and to solve the problem of warfare in built-up areas. After 1982, Soviet artillery was often used to destroy the rural infrastructure the Mujahideen depended upon and to destroy rural villages and farms. It was used to create civilian panic and to reduce the risk of exposing Soviet troops.

The Soviets also used artillery to protect slow-moving formations and as a substitute for maneuver and a rapid tempo of operations. From 1981 onwards, the Soviets made heavy use of firebases to provide cover for moving convoys and armored formations. The Soviets also began to deploy more self-propelled artillery and to shift from generalized mass fire to carefully targeted mass fire. They made very heavy use of artillery barrages to suppress the Mujahideen in assaults and movements and to attack towns and camps. They also combined such fire with air strikes in a number of major offensives. Multiple rocket launchers proved more useful than tube artillery, however, in delivering sudden mass bursts of fire and catching the Mujahideen before they could move. Soviet barrages sometimes went on for three to five hours but often served little real purpose after the first minutes of attack.

During 1983, the Soviets also created smaller artillery groups and allowed them to work much more flexibly with armored and infantry units. They also established firebases with overlapping coverage to provide support for both defensive forces and attacking units. These shifts toward mobile and carefully target fire made Soviet artillery far more tactically effective after 1983–1984.

Artillery was increasingly used after mid-1986 as a substitute for air cover and attack helicopter support. This became even more common in 1987 and 1988. Both Soviet and DRA forces found that artillery often gave them a decisive edge over Mujahideen forces when the Mujahideen had to attack strongly defended positions. The Soviet and DRA forces also used the shelling of towns, or the threat of shelling, to force the Mujahideen to abandon some towns they captured.

Tube Artillery

The Soviets deployed steadily greater numbers of artillery weapons as time went on. They reinforced their artillery forces in 1987, once the Mujahideen began to use Stinger missiles to suppress Soviet helicopters. They provided field troops with a new automatic 82-mm mortar and deployed a new 122-mm howitzer and two new 152-mm cannons.

During 1980–1983, the USSR seems to have made use of improved anti-personnel rounds and fusing specially adapted to maintain conditions. It also increased its deployments of battlefield radars and sophisticated targeting devices, although effective Soviet counter-battery fire was rare. The Soviets do not seem to have made wide use of centralized and computerized fire direction. They relied heavily on forward artillery controllers, area fire, and line-of-sight targeting.

The Soviets made increasing use of self-propelled artillery to accompany troops and armor in the valley campaigns. They deployed the 2S1 SO-122 (M-1974) self-propelled howitzer (15,300-meter maximum range) and the 2S3 SO-152 (M-1973) self-propelled howitzer (18,500-meter maximum range). They found the 2S5 (M-1981) 152-mm self-propelled gun to be of particular value. It replaced the 130-mm towed M-46 field guns in units like the Soviet 40th Artillery Brigade outside Kabul. The 2S5 offered greater range (HE projectiles to 27,000 meters and rocket-assisted projectiles to 37,000 meters). It could be used to substitute for airpower at longer ranges. It could move with units and could be taken in and out of action more quickly. The towed M-1976 version of this gun was also deployed to Afghanistan.

The Soviets also used artillery in combination with mines. They extended their defensive perimeter around key areas like Kabul to 30 kilometers and created three concentric defensive rings of mines and artillery positions to limit Mujahideen ability to use mortars to attack Soviet targets.[161]

By and large, Soviet artillery was not particularly effective in terms of effect per round. Those heavier artillery units which were not in direct support were comparatively slow to react and shift fires. The Soviet literature on Afghanistan is far more impressed with the impact of Soviet artillery fire than are any of the reports on Soviet artillery fire by the Mujahideen. Mujahideen interviews consistently show more concern with mines, assault infantry, Spetsnaz, mortars, and attack helicopters.

Some special problems in using artillery in mountain warfare became apparent to Soviet troops operating in Afghanistan. Most Soviet heavy and medium artillery weapons could not be elevated high enough to fire at guerrillas operating from mountain crests. Another problem was the weight and bulk of such weapons, which made movement difficult, even for most self-propelled weapons. One Soviet solution was to switch to lighter weapons such as the 76-mm mountain gun. The Soviets also tried to use tanks and AFVs as more mobile artillery for mountain warfare, although this did not prove particularly effective.

The 76-mm mountain gun was in service within both the Soviet and the DRA armies, and captured 76-mm weapons were in the hands of the Mujahideen. The mountainous terrain throughout much of Afghanistan gave this system special importance. Its characteristics are shown in Table 2.9. The relatively light weight of the system made it especially effective for travel in the mountains.

The Mujahideen generally relied on captured artillery, although they did not develop high proficiency in using such weapons or deploy

TABLE 2.9 The Characteristics of the Soviet 76-mm Mountain Gun (M-1966)

Weight	
Firing position (kg)	780
Travel position (kg)	780
Length, travel position (m)	4.80
Width, travel position (m)	1.50
Height, travel position (m)	1.40
Fire control	direct fire sight and panoramic telescope
Ammunition (types)	Frag-HE, HEAT
Crew	7
Performance	
Elevation (°)	-5 to +65
Traverse	50 total
Maximum range (m)	10,500–11,500
Muzzle velocity (m/sec)	600 (Frag-HE)
Rate of fire	
Maximum (rd/min)	15
Sustained, 1st hr (rd)	100
Armor penetration (mm @ 0o obliquity @ 1,000 m)	300 (HEAT, any range)
Unit of fire (rd)	140
Date of initial inventory	1966

SOURCE: *The Soviet Army Troops, Organization and Equipment,* FM 100-2-3 (Washington, D.C.: Government Printing Office, July 16, 1984), pp. 5–46.

tube artillery in large numbers. They did, however, have large numbers of rockets and mortars.[162]

Multiple Rocket Launchers and Rockets

The Soviets also made extensive use of multiple rocket launchers in Afghanistan, particularly towed and vehicle-mounted variants of the BM-21. The BM-21 carried up to forty rockets per weapon. These could fire eleven to twenty kilometers and each had a nineteen-kilogram warhead. The Soviets also used the BM-14, with sixteen to seventeen rounds, a range of 9,800 meters, and a 19.8-kilogram warhead.

Multiple rocket launchers were considered particularly valuable in rapid mass fire since they could be used to saturate Mujahideen positions and destroy area targets such as rebel villages without warning. Their lethal effects were further enhanced in mountain or rocky areas by the rock splinters that result from the impact of the blast. Their main disadvantage related to the continuing problem Soviet systems had with elevation. Soviet BM-21 and BM-14 MRLs had a problem clearing nearby mountain crests because of their limited elevation.

While the Mujahideen used large stocks of Chinese 107-mm rockets, these initially involved very primitive fire techniques. The rocket was propped up in a wooden cradle, aimed with a quadrant, and fired with a battery. Although the rocket had a 8.5-km range, 1.26-kg warhead, and a contact fuse, its inaccuracy restricted its use to area fire targets.[163]

After 1985, the Mujahideen made increasing use of the Chinese Type 63 wheeled, 12-round, 107-mm multiple rocket launchers. While the Mujahideen initially had problems operating these systems (for example, they forgot to remove the traveling wheels prior to firing), these comparatively light towed systems proved to be far more effective than single rockets. Beginning in 1987, the Mujahideen also began to make extensive use of 122-mm multiple rocket launchers. These were harder to move but much more accurate and effective than the 107-mm rockets.

The value of rockets to the Mujahideen was particularly clear during the fighting from 1986 onwards. The Mujahideen were often able to use rockets to attack urban and military base targets in spite of improving Soviet security zones. The Mujahideen used both the Type 63 and BM-13 multiple rocket launchers and heavier 130-mm rockets as well as 107-mm rounds. They also used longer-range Egyptian rockets and U.S.-modified 122-mm multiple rocket launchers that had been modified so they could be split apart and carried by mule rather than by a motor vehicle.[164] In spite of these improvements, the Mujahideen never massed enough artillery to be able to compete with regular Soviet and RA forces in firepower.

Mortars

The Soviets also found that a variety of mortars, including the 81-mm (3,040 meters maximum range, 3.4 kilogram round weight, 56 kilograms weapon rate), and the 120-mm mortars (5,700 meters maximum range, 15.4 kilogram round weight, 275 kilograms weapon rate), were highly effective weapons in mountain warfare.[165] They made steadily greater use of light mortars. The mortars organic to Soviet airborne and motorized rifle units do not present elevation problems and are man-, crew-, or helicopter-portable in even the roughest mountain terrain.

The larger 160-mm mortars (8,000 meters maximum range, 42 kilogram round weight, 1,300 kilograms weapon rate) and 240-mm mortars (9,700 meters maximum range, 100 kilogram round weight, 3,600 kilograms weapon rate) were rarely used, although there are some reports that they were deployed down to small-unit level for special combat purposes.

The Soviets also deployed the new AM2B9 Vailyek automatic 82-mm mortar. This is a battalion-level weapon with a direct-fire range of 1,000 meters and a maximum effective range of 5,000 meters. It can elevate to 80 degrees. It uses a horizontally fed four-round clip. The weapon was deployed in towed form and on a variety of different OAFVs. Its key advantage was very high rate of fire, allowing several rounds to be brought on target very quickly. This greatly improved the suppressive effect of the weapon. It also could deliver large amounts of smoke.

Some use was also made of the SO-120 2S9 self-propelled gun mortar and the SM-240 2S4 (M-1975) self-propelled mortar. The former weapon was used to provide heavy firepower in the Salang Pass area, and the latter was used north of Kabul and in the Panjshir area to destroy villages and deliver fire against caves.[166]

The Mujahideen relied heavily on mortars but had mixed success. The main problems the Mujahideen had in using mortars were supply, lack of range, and lack of training. The Mujahideen claimed they needed a weapon with a range of at least ten to twelve kilometers to strike from outside artillery-protected perimeter defenses. It also needed to be accurate or lethal enough for strikes on air bases. They noted that any increase in weapon or ammunition size presented major logistic problems. This explains why they often shifted to longer-range 107-mm and 122-mm rockets as the war went on.

According to some reports, the Mujahideen found that the U.S. 82-mm mortar had substantially more effective range than the obsolete Soviet 81-mm mortar. Although the Mujahideen could solve part of their range problem with rockets, they found these to be too inaccurate and too bulky for many missions. As a result, the U.S. began to provide light 120-mm mortars in late 1987. These weapons had a range of roughly six kilometers and used new rocket-propelled line-charge anti-mine munitions designed to help the Mujahideen penetrate minefields. They were employed successfully in an attack on the Soviet special forces camp at Chrag Sari in the Kunar Valley on 17 January 1988.[167]

The Mujahideen also used captured Soviet artillery of several types, but they had very erratic training in using artillery, and most weapons crews initially had no training at all. They often had to fire their entire stock of mortars or artillery rounds to zero in on any area target. This situation began to improve significantly during 1987, and the U.S supplied at least some modified 120-mm Spanish mortars equipped with satellite tracking systems to allow very precise location of mortars for indirect fire against point targets.[168] It is clear, however, that any future Western support of guerrilla forces should entail more formal training in the use of weapons like mortars and careful attention to problems like the weight and packaging of the weapon and ammunition.

Surface-to-Surface Rockets and Missiles

Surface-to-surface rockets and missiles were used only sporadically in the Afghan war before the Soviet withdrawal in February 1989, although the Soviets deployed them at the start of their invasion, used FROG 7 systems occasionally from 1984 on, and deployed and used Scuds during the final months before their withdrawal. The Soviets apparently tried the FROG 7 on several occasions early in the conflict and then decided not to use these systems further because of their limited potential for dealing with the tactical situation in Afghanistan.[169]

The Soviet decision not to use FROGs during the period between 1980 and 1984 involved four interrelated factors:

1. Soviet control of the air and the corresponding ability of the Soviets to bomb any area of the country with more cost-effective systems;
2. the relatively low lethality per warhead against the target mix involved;
3. the lack of standard SSM targets such as staging areas for conventional forces; and
4. the inaccuracy of these systems.

The Soviets do, however, seem to have begun to use an improved FROG 7 in 1984. This missile used cluster bomb warheads to improve its lethality as a conventional weapon.[170] It is unclear that this improved warhead made the FROG 7 much more effective in conventional combat than the normal HE warhead, and there are no Mujahideen reports of it having any impact on the tactical situation.

The FROG 7, which is also called the R65A or Luna, was designed for nuclear attack and has only limited effectiveness as a conventional weapon. It has a single-stage solid propellent rocket motor. It was first exhibited in 1967. It is 9.0 meters long and 61 centimeters in diameter and weighs 5,727 kilograms. There is no guidance system other than a spin-stabilized ballistic trajectory. If any trajectory correction is made after launch, it will begin during boost. After boost, the trajectory is ballistic.

The FROG's warhead weight is 455 kilograms, and its maximum range is 60–70 kilometers. It is normally mounted upon, and launched from, a wheeled erector launcher called the ZIL-135. The main nozzle is surrounded by a ring of much smaller nozzles, and the system is far superior in reliability and accuracy to early FROGs. Nevertheless, the operation CEP is between 300 and 900 meters, assuming perfecting targeting. As a result, the missile has a very low kill probability except against a very large area target.[171] The FROG's lack of weapons accuracy, lethality, and targeting capability make it largely a terror weapon in a war like the conflict in Afghanistan, and even then its value its dubious. An attack with virtually any fighter-bomber would normally be far more effective.[172]

The Soviet Union also deployed some version of the Scud missile in November 1988 and soon fired a few systems in the direction of Mujahideen based in the border area near Pakistan. It then very publicly transferred some missiles to DRA forces. The main Soviet motive in deployment and use of the Scud seems to have been more political than military. The Scuds did offer the USSR a way of avoid the use of aircraft, which would expose its fighters to improved Mujahideen air defenses. The USSR could achieve far more effectiveness, however, by using the Tu-26 Backfire bombers it also employed during this period or high flying attack fighters like the Su-24.

The Scud was far more sophisticated than the FROG 7. All variants of the Scud were true guided missiles. They had a strap-down inertial guidance using three gyros to correct ballistic trajectory, and they used internal graphite jet vane steering. They had a warhead that detached from the missile body during the final fall toward target. This provided added stability and allowed the warhead to hit at a velocity above Mach 1.5.

It is not clear what variant of the Scud the USSR deployed to Afghanistan. The missiles seemed to be ordinary Scud Bs, which first became operational in 1967, and which the Soviet Union designated as the R-17E or R-300E. The Scud B missile was 11.25 meters long and 85 centimeters in diameter and weighed 6,300 kilograms. It had a single-stage storable liquid rocket engine and was usually deployed on the

MAZ-543 eight-wheel transporter-erector-launcher (TEL). The Scud C was a larger missile than the Scud B and had more range. It was 12.2 meters long and one meter in diameter and weighs 10,000 kilograms. The Scud D (SS-1e) was designed to deliver submunition buses and was more accurate than previous Scuds. It entered Soviet service in the early 1980s and would have been the most logical weapon to employ in Afghanistan, although the USSR might well have been reluctant to transfer such a system to the DRA, given the risk that it would fall into Mujahideen, and probably Western, hands.

The Scud B had a range of roughly 280 kilometers, a 1.0-kilometer CEP, and a 1,000-kilogram throw-weight. The Scud C had a range of up to 550 kilometers, a CEP of roughly 0.3 kilometers at short to medium ranges, and a 600-kilogram throw-weight.[173] The Scud D had roughly the same range as the Scud B and a 0.3 kilometer CEP. Even the Scud D would have lacked the combination of accuracy and targeting capability to have much military effect against anything but town-sized targets. The Scud did have more shock and terror value than the FROG 7 and raised the tacit threat of the use of chemical weapons—given the recent example of the Iran-Iraq War. It is unclear, however, that it did much in Soviet hands to intimidate the Mujahideen. In fact, Massoud actually claimed to have resumed attacks on withdrawing Soviet forces because the Soviets had escalated the conflict.

The Scud became far more important after the Soviet withdrawal because the USSR shipped large numbers of these missiles to the RA. They had shipped over 500 Scuds by June 1989, and RA forces had fired over 350 missiles against Mujahideen formations around Kabul and Jalalabad and other targets. Scud units in Kabul had the range to hit targets near Jalalabad, and even though the missiles created only limited casualties, they had a major terror effect. The Mujahideen had no defenses and only seconds of warning, and the missile strikes often left them with a sense of helplessness.

Mines and Barriers

Mines were important to both sides in the Afghan War, and Mujahideen estimates of the number of Mujahideen and civilians killed or maimed by mines reach 25,000–50,000 persons. These numbers made mines by far the largest cause of Mujahideen casualties. The Soviets made very extensive use of them. In mid-1988, the Soviets claim to have cleared 1,518 of the 2,131 minefields they laid in Afghanistan and to have turned 100 more minefields over to the DRA. These claims, however, referred only to plotted minefields; the Soviets seem to have used mines in many other areas. Many mines were booby traps or were air dropped or scattered outside plotted minefields.[174] The Soviets laid well over 30 million mines, and some estimates run as high as 50 million. Mines of widely different types were used from all over the world, and many were nonmetallic and extremely hard to detect.[175]

The Soviets utilized air- and land-deployed mines and submunitions to reduce movement between Pakistan and Afghanistan and as perimeter defenses of everything from strong points to urban areas. In some cases, minefields were also used to secure DRA garrisons and prevent desertions.[176] Alef Gulf, a Mujahideen commander at Barri, near Khost, described the impact of mines as follows: "Our great problem here is mines. There are mine fields all around the town, and it is very difficult for us to attack. If we cannot find a way to clear mines, the DRA government forces can stand up to us."[177]

The Soviets made particularly heavy use of mines to interdict supply routes and the guerrilla trails which were used to support the Mujahideen in the field. This activity produced many casualties but was relatively ineffective in reducing the flow of supply, since the Mujahideen were willing to deploy and expose troops in creating and defending mine barriers. A more sustained Soviet effort might have been more successful in limiting Mujahideen activity, but Soviet mines had largely a harassment effect, and most casualties were civilian.

Many types of mines were used, although the Soviets soon learned to avoid using anti-tank mines because the Mujahideen dug them up and used them against Soviet and RA forces. The mine warfare effort got steadily more sophisticated with time. The Soviets used large numbers of MON-50s, which are copies of the U.S. M-18A1 Claymore. These mines have a matrix of corrugated internal fragmentation material which is set in plastic explosive. They can cover a 60-degree arc out to ranges of 50 meters. The Soviets also used large MON-100, MON-200, and MON-500 mines. The MON-100 is a cylinder with a concave face that can be set on a tripod or mounted on a tree or rock wall. It has 450 steel fragments set in five kilograms of plastic explosive. It can spray these fragments as far as 100 meters. The MON-200 is 52 centimeters in diameter and has a 12-kilogram plastic charge. These large mines could have considerable lethality but were easier to detect.

The Soviets also used new PMN-2 mines, which are about the size of small fruitcake tins and are buried, and UMK remote-control mines or "wave mines" (upravlyaemoye minnoye kompleks). These latter mines, first used in 1985, exploded as the result of either vibration or remote triggering by an electric signal. There was a central sensor system tied to a simple battery-powered discrete transistor circuit and triggered by up to four wires and possibly an acoustic trigger. The UMK could be connected by wires to a number of mines. This allowed traps to be set on major logistic routes or paths which could trigger a number of simultaneous explosions.[178]

Many of the mines the Soviets placed on the trails between Afghanistan and Pakistan appeared to have been dropped from helicopters. The PFM-1 "butterfly" or "green parrot" mine was widely dropped. This mine appears to be a copy of the U.S. BLU-43B mine. It is cased in plastic, filled with liquid explosive, and weighs approximately twelve grams. "Wings" extend outward from the lower portion of the fuse well and serve to stabilize and disperse the mine. The PFM-1 butterfly exists in green, tan, and possibly white versions. It is camouflaged to look like stone or sand. It self-defuses after several hours or days, but self-defusing often fails, and fields can remain active for months or years. It is virtually impossible to detect with conventional gear. Up to one million of these mines may have been dropped on Mujahideen lines of communication during the first seven years of the war. The Soviets also seem to have developed a new air-droppable mine with a self-deploying trip wire, but the details of this development are unclear.[179]

The Soviets dropped various booby-trapped explosives which exploded if they were touched. These booby traps were disguised as watches, coins, ink pens, matchbooks, clothing, compasses, toys, leaves, and even rocks. According to Afghan sources, the Soviets cleared these mines from trails relatively soon after they were dropped and replaced them at approximately two-month intervals.

The Mujahideen had serious and continuing problems in dealing with mines. They were forced to expose themselves as they tried to slowly clear a path with a long pole with a metal "rake" end. They also drove animals into minefields, threw rocks, used professional mine hunters, or simply walked single file into minefields, taking the loss of the leading men. One of the more ingenious—if ineffective—methods of clearing mines was to shoot at them from a safe distance with a slingshot. The Mujahideen also used mortars and rockets to set off mine fields, but they also consistently sought more advanced mine-clearing equipment. Throughout the war they were without effective mine-detecting and -clearing devices, but they did receive some Lightfoot mine-breaching systems. These systems used a mortar device that fired a small rocket dragging a one-half-inch cable about 1,000 feet. The cord exploded on contact, clearing a six-foot-wide path through about 80 percent of the anti-personnel mines used in Afghanistan. The Mujahideen usually fired the systems in groups of three or four to clear a secure path and leapfrogged from one fire point to another. These systems were effective in breaching the minefields around DRA and Soviet strong points.[180]

The Mujahideen also used forward observers to map Soviet minefields as they were laid. Over time, they trained explosives and demolition experts to locate mines by sight or touch, and they learned to scout minefields at night before attacks. As a result, the Mujahideen improved their minefield penetration operations as time went on, particularly in attacking defended strong points and cities.

The Soviets tried to counter by deploying concentric rings of mines up to 3,000 meters from the Mujahideen's defensive perimeter, increasing the density of mines per square kilometer, adding flare mines to minefields to indicate penetration, deploying advanced mines with acoustic and seismic sensors, and improving troop surveillance of mined areas. The results of this duel were grim. Soviet and DRA mining did not prevent Mujahideen operations, but it did cause substantial casualties and forced far more careful Mujahideen planning and coordination.[181]

The Mujahideen also made extensive use of mines. The Mujahideen acquired most of the DRA's stock of Soviet TM-46 anti-tank mines early in the war. Other mines were retrieved from Soviet minefields while others were supplied from external sources. These imported mines included the British-designed Mark 7 anti-tank mine, a foreign-made variation of the U.S. Claymore, and the Italian-made Technovar TC/6 anti-personnel mine, or "Eastercake."[182]

The Mujahideen came to make extensive use both anti-armor and anti-personnel mines. Additionally, the Mujahideen were reported to have used unexploded Soviet aerial bombs to make mines.[183] One of the reported uses of such mines was to disrupt the movement of Soviet military convoys.

The Soviets were forced to use combat engineers and sappers to clear mines virtually from the very start of the conflict. They began with UAZ-469 jeeps equipped with mine detectors and rapidly shifted to putting mine detectors on tanks when snipers started picking out the mine-detecting jeeps. Columns often could not move without mine-detection units and sappers. Hand-held mine detectors became common.

The Mujahideen reacted by getting better mines. The Mujahideen began to get significant supplies of nonmetallic mines by 1982.[184] After 1982, the Mujahideen mining effort was relatively sophisticated. The scale of the Mujahideen mining effort is indicated by the fact that one sapper battalion of the 201st MRD claimed to have cleared 30,000 mines over a five-year period, covering some 1,000 kilometers of roads. When the Soviets took the Mujahideen fortress at Zhawar on the

Pakistani border, they found 6,000 anti-tank mines and 12,000 anti-personnel mines.[185]

By 1984, Soviet publications had begun to warn about enemy mines that could not be detected by their conventional induction mine detectors. In fact, the Soviets seemed to be as concerned as the U.S. about the lack of adequate field-deployable technology for detecting mines made of plastic. They did, however, have some success with trained dogs. According to Afghan sources, the Soviets made use of a small nondescript breed of dog to detect mines by smell.[186] The sapper crews involved generally used BTR-70s.

Dogs did not work with mines buried underground but seem to have worked for surface booby traps and mines. Flat Parrot mines, which are known to have been used in Afghanistan, would meet the latter description.[187] The Soviets may also have used animals to set off the mines by walking on them.

Another way the Soviets dealt with mines after 1983 was to place rollers in front of their tanks to detonate mines along roads or in other terrain which could be traversed by tanks. The Soviets removed the turrets from some of their T-55s and IT-1 tank destroyers and used "sheepsfoot" mine rollers. The converted T-55 was designated the M-1987/1 and was armed with a 12.7-mm heavy machine gun. There also was a converted IT-122 tank destroyer converted into a mine sweeper called the M-1987/2. This had a roller and a turret-mounted 12.7-mm machine gun.[188]

The Mujahideen countered minerolling with at least two types of mines using PRC- and Italian-made pneumatic fuses which came closer to setting off the mine with each vehicle that rolled over them. The Mujahideen also learned to vary the number of vehicles required by varying the depth of the mine and by creating cone-shaped holes above the mine's trigger device. There also were at least some remotely triggered mines.[189]

There is no way to assess how effective each side was in using mines to impact on supply, defense, and operations, but mines did produce large numbers of casualties. Some lessons both sides learned, however, was that concealment and camouflage were critical, that big mines were relatively easy to spot, that detection was no substitute for active penetration and detonation, and that the use of conventional mine detectors was ineffective.

All-Weather and Night Target Acquisition Systems

Soviet and RA forces normally remained on the defensive at night. All-weather and night vision systems, and individual night vision devices such as infrared binoculars and drivers' night vision devices, played an important role in the Afghan conflict. The NSP-2 night observation system and the TVN-2 infrared night driving device were standard equipment for Soviet units in Afghanistan. These systems can be used actively or passively. In the active mode they produce emissions which can be identified by adversaries using infrared sensors. This weakness, however, had little relevance in Afghanistan. Soviet tanks were equipped with night observation devices which could include sighting equipment for the main gun and a searchlight that could be fitted with an infrared filter. Targets could be identified at up to 800 meters with these systems.

Soviet illumination devices included cartridges, rockets, shells, bombs, flares, mines, motor shells, searchlights, and tracer shells. These active devices were employed not only to illuminate the battlefield but also to temporarily blind the enemy. Illumination was both continuous and periodic. Periodic illumination was often used against the Mujahideen. Continuous illumination may have occurred during periods of especially intense offensive action, but it was relatively rare.

The Soviets fought a number of large-scale night battles in Afghanistan, but their success in using their technical "edge" was uncertain. Guerrilla sources in Pakistan, for example, claimed that troops of Ahmad Shah Massoud killed over 300 Soviet commandos in a 11 July 1984 night battle near the village of Bayarakan in the Panjshir Valley. This was the first act of resistance by Massoud since the signing of an earlier truce with the Soviet government. Since that time, the Soviet forces seem to have improved their tactics and readiness but were still surprised by night infiltration and ambushes. They seemed to lack any wide-area night surveillance systems and sensors, and the Mujahideen capitalized on their superior HUMINT and knowledge of terrain.

The extent to which illumination and/or night observation devices were used by the Mujahideen is not known. It is clear, however, that the guerrillas were very capable of moving and fighting at night. Knowledge of terrain and tactical skill often proved as effective as advanced technology.

Anti-Aircraft Artillery

The Mujahideen lacked effective anti-aircraft (AA) guns throughout most of the fighting, and Soviet and Afghan government forces did not need them in the anti-aircraft role. The Mujahideen also found that the Soviets steadily improved the Mi-24 Hind's survivability and used increasing numbers of attack and armed helicopters to reduce individual exposure and overall vulnerability. This made it increasingly dangerous to fire ordinary machine guns, which often did little more than target Mujahideen forces.

From 1981 onwards, this led the Mujahideen to actively seek more and better surface-to-air missiles and better AA guns. It is unclear how general a lesson this experience provides, but it is clear that Mujahideen forces felt that destroying the Hind and other Soviet helicopters had the highest possible priority.

The U.S. initially sought to improve Mujahideen capabilities by buying heavier PRC 14.5-mm AA machine guns and by furnishing the Afghans with a single-barreled 20-mm Oerlikon-Buhrle GAI-BO1 cannon. This cannon weighs 545 kilograms but is cart-transportable by mule teams as well as road- or river-portable. The Oerlikon gun has about a 12,000- to 18,000-meter effective range and fires 1,000 rounds per minute.

About forty such guns from the Italiana branch of Oerlikon were deployed in 1985. They were shipped from Genoa via Iran and Pakistan. Substantially more may have been in service by 1988. While the full details of the Oerlikon's use in Mujahideen hands are unclear, it seems to have required more training than most Mujahideen forces possessed. It produced both helicopter and MiG kills and was useful against land targets, but it also had serious limitations.[190] Although the gun could be broken down into 50 kilogram loads, it was still difficult to move and had no guidance system. This led to problems in moving ammunition as well as the weapon and sharply reduced its lethality. Neither the Oerlikon nor the 14.5-mm AA machine guns were sufficiently lethal against helicopters or fighters. Furthermore, the Mujahideen tended to use guns against ground targets and missiles against air targets.[191]

Even in 1988, after the delivery of the Oerlikons and deliveries of well over 300 Stinger systems, the Mujahideen were still forced to rely on heavy machine guns and light AA guns to attack Soviet helicopters in many operations, and these weapons still dominated their anti-aircraft armament by a ratio of at least eight to one.

These smaller-caliber weapons lost effectiveness during 1984–1987, due to the improved protection and armor plating found on Soviet helicopters. It is believed that the areas of plating on the undercarriage of the Hind D and E helicopters are titanium and completely resistant to 7.62-mm caliber fire. There were, however, occasions when the Mujahideen fired down on helicopters performing reconnaissance work in valleys.[192]

The Mujahideen use of 12.7-mm and 14.5-mm guns became much more effective after 1986–1987, when the Stinger and noise detectors began to be provided in significant numbers. The Soviets could avoid the Stinger by flying low, but the helicopters did not perform well in flying nap-of-the-earth techniques. The Hinds and other helicopters had to fly at altitudes that made them easy to spot and often brought them well within range of the heavy Mujahideen AA machine guns. The U.S. also began to supply a 12.7-mm round that had a tungsten penetrator that could punch through Soviet cockpit armor and a phosphorous charge to start fires on any aircraft it hit.[193]

Some Mujahideen groups favored mass fire by 12.7-mm and 14.5-mm AA machine guns and RPD-51 machine guns over the use of the SA-7. This may have been because they lacked adequate training in using the SA-7 or found it easier to use automatic weapons in curtain fire rather than as point-defense weapons. Unfortunately, insufficient operational details are available to clearly determine why some Mujahideen groups differ over the value of guns versus missiles.

In contrast, the Soviets deployed ZU-23 twin AA guns on BMDs, truck-mounted AA guns (particularly to guard the Salang Pass route), M-1939 37-mm AA guns, and many 14.5-mm AA machine guns.[194] They often found AA guns to be useful both as a long-range direct fire suppression weapon and as a means of giving infantry the mobile firepower that modern "armor heavy" forces lack. Soviet dual purpose anti-aircraft guns played a critical role in the ground fighting. These systems were used as direct-fire weapons against Mujahideen rebels and their battle positions. The AA guns served as partial replacements for tank guns, which could not be elevated high enough to be effective against Afghans firing down from the crests of hills or mountains, and they provided excellent area saturation fire with good ricochet and secondary effects. This was particularly important in protecting convoys, which were frequently guarded by ZIL-135 trucks with armored mounts housing twin 23-mm anti-aircraft guns.[195]

Surface-to-Air Missiles

The Soviets deployed surface-to-air missiles, seemingly because of the fear of an attack on main bases by the Pakistani air force. The missiles included the SA-2 and SA-3 in DRA forces before the Soviet invasion. The Soviets deployed into Afghanistan with SA-4s but then withdrew them. They kept SA-8s and SA-13s in the country. For reasons that are not clear, Soviet troops deployed into the field with SA-7s.

The USSR retained at least some of its heavier surface-to-air missile systems within Afghanistan despite the lack of an air threat.

The associated fire control, target acquisition, and IFF radars were also deployed. No lessons emerged regarding these systems in combat since they were not employed against hostile aircraft.[196]

The Mujahideen increasingly utilized manportable surface-to-air missile systems once these became available in early 1982.[197] The technical specifications of these missiles are shown in Table 2.10. They began by using early variants of the Soviet SA-7 Grail to try to counter the threat of Soviet attack helicopters. As already noted, the Soviets prudently removed these weapons from the hands of the Afghan army. This effectively ended one source of resupply for the rebels, but the Mujahideen were able to obtain such systems from outside sources, including the United States and Egypt.[198]

While the SA-7s were clearly an asset when the rebels could obtain them, they had significant shortcomings.[199] The early models of the SA-7 had a maximum range of 3.7 kilometers and a warhead with a simple fuse and 0.37 kilograms' worth of explosive. The improved Strela 2Ms had a filter to reject extraneous IR sources, simple counter-countermeasures, a more powerful motor, a range of 5.5 kilometers, and a larger fragmentation warhead.[200]

Both models of the SA-7 had serious defects. The SA-7 required a very hot target and could home only on the exhaust of engines. This meant it was effective only in a tail-chase mode. It was too slow to catch most fighters. If it was aimed within 20 degrees of the sun, it would fly toward the sun. The seeker could be saturated by solar reflection off clouds, and even sun-backed rocks could deflect the seeker if the missile was fired at low altitudes. The SA-7 left a trail of white smoke which enabled pilots to find the firing positions without much difficulty. The Soviets could defeat them with flares dropped from their helicopters.[201] Some of the Soviet helicopters, particularly the Mi-24 Hinds, had fairly cool-running engines, which made them less susceptible to attack with heat-seeking missiles.

These missiles also had serious reliability problems and high misfire rates, although the frequency with which these difficulties occurred is unknown.[202] It is also unclear why the Mujahideen had such major problems with SA-7 misfires. A similar rate of misfire does not seem to have occurred in the other conflicts under study. The rebels' problems may have been related to the types of SA-7s supplied to them, poor handling, or firing without obtaining a sighting good enough for the missile to track. Older systems and Chinese or Egyptian copies of the SA-7s may have contributed to the unusually high rates of misfire.

Even when the SA-7 did not misfire, its warhead was not highly lethal, and terminal accuracy at the target was often poor. It weighed

TABLE 2.10 Major Shoulder-Fired Surface-to-Air Missiles that Impacted on the Fighting in Afghanistan

Maker	Type	IOC Date	Missile Weight (kg)	System Weight (kg)	Range (km)	Warhead Weight (kg)	Guidance Type	Cost in $U.S. 1987	
								Missile	Launcher
PRC[a]	Hong Ying 3	1973	9	15	3.5	1.7	IR	22,200	12,000
Egypt[a]	Sakr Eye	1985	9	15	3.3	1.7	IR	28,000	12,000
U.K.	Blowpipe[b]	1972	11	21.3	3	2.2	Command	21,000	94,000
	Javelin	1984	11	22.5	4.5	2.2	Semi-auto Command	24,000	100,000
U.S.	FIM-43A Redeye	1964	8.5	13	3	2	IR	24,000	14,000[c]
	FIM-92A Stinger	1978	10.1	15	5.5	2	IR	35,000	15,000
	FIM-92B Stinger POST	1984	10.1	15	5.5	3	IR/UV	42,000	15,000
	FIM-92C Stinger RMP	1987	10.1	15	5.5	3	IR/UV	42,000	15,000
USSR	SA-7/Strela 2[d]	1966	9.2	13.37	3.6	1.1	IR	—	12,000
	SA-7B/Strela 2M[d]	1972	9.97	14.68	4.5	1.1	IR	22,000	12,000
	SA-14/Gremlin[e]	1978	10.5	15	6.0	2.0	IR	32,000	15,000
	SA-16	1984	12	18	4-7	2.0	Laser	32,000	15,000

[a]Copy of SA-7.
[b]Manual guidance option.
[c]Reconditioned and second hand.
[d]Copy of U.S. Redeye.
[e]Copy of U.S. Stinger.

SOURCES: Adapted from Aaron Karp, "Blowpipes and Stingers in Afghanistan: One Year Later," *Armed Forces Journal International*, September 1987, pp. 36–40; and *Jane's Defence Weekly*, January 23, 1988, pp. 139–141, and June 4, 1988, p. 1116.

only 9.2 to 9.97 kilograms, depending on the missile type, versus 14.5 kilograms for the U.S. Redeye. Even the warhead of the improved SA-7 used a maximum of 1.1 kilograms of HE, and its homing system and fusing was grossly inferior to the Redeye, Stinger, and Stinger Post.

This led a number of U.S. and British experts to press for supplying the Stinger and Blowpipe to the Mujahideen. Some experts seem to have called for such deployments as early as 1980, but the effort became serious only in 1985, after the U.S. decided on a major supply effort for the Mujahideen. Part of the reason was that the deployment of Stinger was sharply resisted within the CIA because of a fear it would provoke Soviet attacks on Pakistan and the missiles would fall into terrorist hands.

As a result, the CIA concentrated on increasing the supply of SA-7s. When this did not work, the CIA decided to order 300 British Blowpipe missiles.[203] The Blowpipe is a relatively lightweight man-portable weapon consisting of a missile in a launching canister and an aiming unit. Unlike most sight and track IR guided systems, it is radio controlled and has a two-stage rocket. The operator controls it after launch with a thumb control to keep the missile on the line of sight to the target. He must simultaneously track the target and steer the missile.

The order was placed in 1985, and the Mujahideen received about 225 of the 300 missiles that were shipped. They were trained to use the missile with some success, but the Blowpipe required a far more skilled operator than the other "fire and forget" light surface-to-air missiles that might have been sent to the Mujahideen. It also required careful handling and cool storage. It therefore proved to be too sophisticated for many operators and difficult to handle under many Afghan combat conditions.[204]

The problems with the Blowpipe again raised the issue of providing Stinger. The CIA continued to resist on security grounds and the agency's belief that the Mujahideen were too unsophisticated to use the Stinger system. In late 1985, however, pressure from the State Department and Pakistan led to a decision to deploy the Stinger system. The CIA was slow to act, and the first shipment of 150 Stingers did not arrive in Mujahideen camps until the summer of 1986. While some reports exist of Stinger kills as early as May, these may have been Blowpipe. The first firm confirmation of Stinger kills seems to have occurred on 26 September 1986, when three Hind helicopters were shot down near Jalalabad.[205]

The Stinger is a U.S. Army manportable system that began manufacture in 1978.[206] It weighs 34 pounds, is 5 feet long, and has a maximum range of 5.8 kilometers and a maximum target altitude of 3.5

kilometers, both of which are better than that of Redeye. It is much faster than the Redeye or SA-7 and has a maximum speed of Mach 2.2, which enables it to kill departing jet fighters. It has a maximum maneuverability of around eight "G" and can kill most evading fighters. It uses a passive infrared seeker and a proportional navigation system, and it can kill aircraft from the sides and even head-on under some circumstances.

Stinger has a highly explosive warhead and dual-thrust rocket motor. The warhead is relatively advanced and has good immunity to flares and other countermeasures. While Blowpipe can be fitted with a proximity warhead, the Stinger's warhead has a more limited lethal area. The Stinger, however, is effective at flight altitudes as low as thirty feet.

The U.S. Army requires 136 hours of Stinger training, but the weapon proved relatively simple for the Mujahideen to operate—largely because they had no interest in technical training or complicated IFF procedures and shot largely under relatively simple fair-weather tactical conditions. The first four-man Mujahideen teams did receive eight weeks of training from U.S. advisors, but other Mujahideen later used the missiles with only limited training. The system was particularly easy to use when ambushes were set up near air bases or areas where the Mujahideen could pick their targets and fire under optimal conditions, rather than having to select their targets while under fire.[207]

The first Mujahideen use of Blowpipe led the USSR to use their air forces with far more caution, but the deployment of Stinger almost immediately changed the course of the fighting. Although claims that 90 percent of the missiles scored a kill are false, the missile did prove highly lethal in comparison with previous manportable or light surface-to-air missile systems.

The Stingers soon killed enough Soviet fixed aircraft to force them to greatly increase attack air speed and stop spending time over target. The Stingers also forced fighters and fighter-bombers to increase their attack height from 2,000–4,000 feet to around 10,000 feet. Soviet combat helicopter and fighter losses went up to 1.2 to 1.4 aircraft a day during late 1986 and early 1987 and dropped only after the USSR cut back sharply on its air operations.[208]

Because of aircraft losses, the deployment of Stinger forced the USSR to severely restrict its use of AN-12 and AN-26 air transports until it developed the tactic of using three to four helicopters firing flares to cover a take-off or landing. Most Soviet aircraft landing and taking off in Afghanistan eventually had to take evasive measures.

The key target of the Stinger was helicopters, which accounted for roughly 80 percent of 1,500–2,000 aircraft the Soviets lost in Afghanistan.[209] The Soviet and DRA forces soon lost strong points and operational flexibility and mobility because of the lack of air cover for helicopter assault and close air support missions, and they were forced to retreat from exposed positions. This forced them to give up their attempt to expand their control of the countryside in a number of key areas.[210]

The USSR did make increasingly successful attempts to use active and passive countermeasures. As early as 1984, Soviet helicopters began to make extensive use of IR suppressors, flares, and terrain masking, and Soviet fixed-wing aircraft made extensive use of high-altitude bombing, stand-off tactics, and night flying. In many cases, both bombers and fighter-bombers started bombing at over 50,000 feet. The USSR also began to use infrared jammers similar to the AN/ALQ-144, AN/ALQ-147, or AN-ALQ-157.[211] Even after the Soviets changed tactics, however, the Mujahideen seem to have gotten one kill for every three missiles. Further, the RA aircraft and helicopter pilots do not seem to have been given as much training and countermeasure capability as the Soviet pilots and rapidly proved far less willing to fly as many missions or as demanding or high-risk sortie profiles.[212]

It is important to note that the Blowpipe and Stinger missiles almost certainly accounted for less than 50 percent of the losses in Afghanistan.[213] They did, however, sharply decrease the ability of fixed-wing aircraft to find and kill targets, and they allowed the Mujahideen to move through the country far more easily and restore their supply lines. They also forced Soviet helicopter pilots to fly low and use techniques that brought them within effective range of the Mujahideen's 12.7-mm and 14.5-mm anti-aircraft machine guns.

One Mujahideen commander described the impact of Stinger as follows:[214]

> The British in the Falklands had aircraft with air-to-air missiles, they had Stinger, Blowpipe, and Rapier missiles, and still the Argentines could attack. Still they could sink ships. How could we stop all the Soviet aircraft because we have 25 to 30 Stingers? No, it is impossible. . . . We have hit their morale. They have changed their flying, they use different aircraft and their best pilots. This is the effect, but we cannot stop them completely. Conventional armies cannot do it with all their equipment, and we cannot do it with Stinger. . . . "What is the need for Spetsnaz if they cannot be used for reconnaissance or attacks if they cannot move or hide? They have to move in helicopters for operations like heliborne troops. The loss of one heliborne soldier is like the loss of ten conscript soldiers, while the loss of one Spetsnaz soldier is like the loss of ten heliborne troops.

Once the U.S. finally realized how successful the Stinger system was, it quickly shipped more Stingers. Roughly 150 more arrived in 1986, at least 600 more in 1987, and substantially more in early 1988. At least 1,000 were shipped by the time of Soviet withdrawal in February 1989.[215] The U.S. also developed a highly sensitive sound detector that allowed the Mujahideen to detect helicopters from miles away. It also improved their readiness to fire and their ability to cope with low-flying Soviet helicopters.[216]

According to U.S. Army estimates, the Mujahideen scored 269 hits out of 340 Stinger firings during the period before Soviet withdrawal. This was a hit rate of 79 percent, including misfires and gunner errors. The U.S. estimates that 90 percent of the Stingers were fired at crossing targets, 10 percent at incoming targets, and a few at outgoing targets.

The main impact of the Stinger was not the number of targets killed, however, but the fact that the Soviet and RA loss of the ability to control the air environment in combat gave the Mujahideen far greater freedom of action. In combination with the transfer of longer-range weapons like mortars, rockets, anti-tank weapons, and recoilless rifles, the Stinger also allowed the Mujahideen to engage the Soviet and RA forces at ranges greater than 400 meters.

It is important to stress that the Stinger alone scarcely forced the USSR to withdraw from Afghanistan. The sheer dedication and persistence of the Mujahideen did that. The Stringer did, however, tip the air balance. Its success also demonstrates how even a relatively simple weapons system can have a major impact on combat and particularly on air and helicopter operations. While the Stinger was only one factor in the Mujahideen successes in 1987 and 1988, there is no question that it had a powerful tactical, if not strategic, impact on the Soviet decision to withdraw from Afghanistan.

Even after Soviet withdrawal, Soviet transport aircraft resupplying the RA had to land and take off in bases with extensive perimeter defenses, fire large numbers of preemptive flares, and fly tight spirals near the landing strip. These actions kept them out of the range of Mujahideen "gunners" firing the Stinger but severely curtailed the flexibility in Soviet air operations.

RA pilots had to use similar countermeasures, dropping most of their bombs from very high altitudes or flying sudden mass fighter-bomber sweeps at very low altitudes—substituting rapid overflight and mass bombing for the ability to kill their target. These techniques worked largely because the Soviets supplied the RA with Antonov-12 transports converted to act as bombers. They could fly above the effective range of the Stinger and carry up to 30,000 pounds of bombs. Although these aircraft were not very accurate or capable of providing flexible and rapidly responsive air support, they were effective in attacking any easily locatable large concentration of Mujahideen attacking an RA-held city.

The Soviet Air Buildup in Afghanistan

The key phases of the Soviet air buildup in Afghanistan are shown in Figure 2.9. The Soviet air units in Afghanistan built up to as many as 250 aircraft and 245 combat helicopters and in the Transcaucasus military district increased from about 200 to 525 combat aircraft. The USSR seems to have deployed about 100 additional bombers to the region from Soviet Long Range Aviation beginning in 1984.[217] The DRA government also had an air force which included over 115 combat aircraft and around 15–30 armed helicopters, but it flew a relatively limited number of combat missions.[218]

The Soviets built up a massive structure to support large-scale air operations in Afghanistan. Major Soviet bases included Bagram, Kabul International, Mazar-i-Sharif and Jalalabad (currently used by helicopters and transports), and especially Herat, Shindand, Farah, Lashkar Gah, the Serden Bank, Askargh, and Kandahar. All of these air bases had long, paved runways.

Smaller Soviet bases existed at Kunduz, Maimana, Dilaram, and other cities and towns. These bases could operate helicopters, transports, and even tactical fighter-bombers. MiG-23s and the MiG-27s (Floggers) operated from most of the major air bases in Afghanistan and reach Pakistan, much of the Gulf, and Iran. The Soviets also operated forward helicopter and transport aircraft bases of various sizes, some of which could be expanded to operate tactical aircraft.[219]

The conduct of the military operations in the eastern provinces of Afghanistan provided the Soviets with the opportunity to test and evaluate many of their new air weapon systems under combat conditions. In early 1981, the Soviets deployed six preproduction Su-25s to Bagram for operational test and evaluation missions. In the summer of that year, they deployed an operational squadron of 15 Su-25s. By late 1982, the Soviets already had a second operational squadron in Shindand.

In late 1984, Soviet Frontal Aviation (FA) forces in Afghanistan included 30 to 45 MiG-23s (based in Bagram), 75 to 90 MiG-21s, 75 to 90 Su-17s, 30 Su-25s, as well as temporary deployments of 6 to 12 MiG-25s (Foxbat B and D) for local and regional reconnaissance missions. An additional 36 Su-17s were deployed to Herat in early April 1984. These forces may have been deployed only as part of the spring

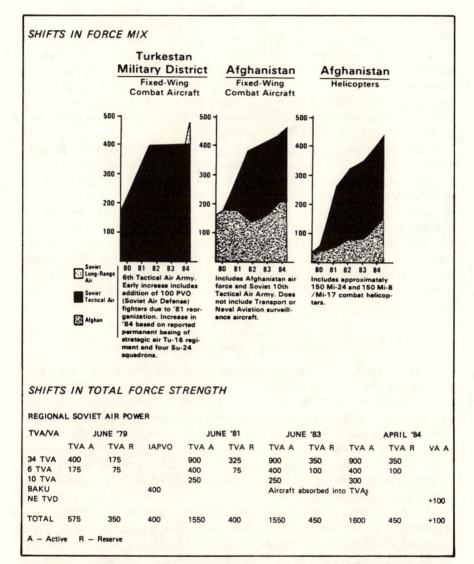

SHIFTS IN FORCE MIX

Turkestan Military District
Fixed-Wing Combat Aircraft

Afghanistan
Fixed-Wing Combat Aircraft

Afghanistan
Helicopters

Soviet Long-Range Air

Soviet Tactical Air

Afghan

80 81 82 83 84
6th Tactical Air Army. Early increase includes addition of 100 PVO (Soviet Air Defense) fighters due to '81 reorganization. Increase in '84 based on reported permanent basing of strategic air Tu-16 regiment and four Su-24 squadrons.

80 81 82 83 84
Includes Afghanistan air force and Soviet 10th Tactical Air Army. Does not include Transport or Naval Aviation surveillance aircraft.

80 81 82 83 84
Includes approximately 150 Mi-24 and 150 Mi-8 /Mi-17 combat helicopters.

SHIFTS IN TOTAL FORCE STRENGTH

REGIONAL SOVIET AIR POWER

TVA/VA	JUNE '79			JUNE '81		JUNE '83			APRIL '84		
	TVA A	TVA R	IAPVO	TVA A	TVA R	TVA A	TVA R	TVA A	TVA R	VA A
34 TVA	400	175		900	325	900	350	900	350	
6 TVA	175	75		400	75	400	100	400	100	
10 TVA				250		250		300		
BAKU			400			Aircraft absorbed into TVAs				
NE TVD										+100
TOTAL	575	350	400	1550	400	1550	450	1600	450	+100

A — Active   R — Reserve

FIGURE 2.9   The Soviet Air Buildup in Afghanistan. Adapted from "Soviet Air Force in Afghanistan," *Jane's Defence Weekly,* July 7, 1984, p. 1105; *Armed Forces Journal,* March 1985; and David C. Isby, "Soviet Tactics in the War in Afghanistan," *Jane's Defence Review,* Vol. 4, No. 7, 1983.

offensive, but may also have remained as a reinforcement of the local FA deployment.

In late 1985, Soviet air strength in Afghanistan seemed to include 80 MiG-21, 40 MiG-23, 80 Su-17, and 30 Su-25 attack aircraft, along with 15 MiG-21R and 12 MiG-25 reconnaissance aircraft. In addition, the Soviets used the assets of the DRA Air Force, which acquired large numbers of aircraft as a result of a 1957 arms agreement with the USSR. These aircraft included 45 MiG-21s, 60 to 75 Su-7s, 90 MiG-17s, 45 L-39s, and 45 Il-28s—although many had been lost or were no longer in flying condition. A new Afghan air regiment of 35 Su-22s was being organized by the Soviets in Bagram.[220]

Soviet force strengths in the country may have dropped in 1987 and 1988. In early 1988, Soviet air strength may have been as low as several units of MiG-21, 45 MiG-23, 10 Su-17, some Su-22, and 90 Su-25 attack aircraft. The major combat elements of the DRA Air Force had 30 MiG-17s, 30 MiG-21s, 35 Su-17s, and 18 11-28s. There were other combat aircraft including MiG-15s, MiG-17s, MiG-19s, MiG-21s, and MiG-23s. In late 1988, however, the USSR deployed 30 new MiG-27s back to Afghanistan and began to use Backfire and Su-24 bombing attacks from the USSR. This was a reaction to constant Mujahideen attacks on withdrawing Soviet forces and the fear the DRA government might collapse.[221]

Fixed-Wing Close Air Support

It is important to note that none of the Soviet aircraft and helicopters deployed to Afghanistan were designed to fight there. The Mi-24 helicopter and the MiG-23 jet fighter are good examples. Both systems were developed for use in European combat. Like the U.S. in Vietnam, the USSR had to adapt its air systems to meet the special needs of the terrain and of guerrilla war. For example, there were no Mujahideen tanks in Afghanistan and relatively few fixed hard targets. There were a few heavily defended fixed sites, but these were rarely part of Mujahideen tactics.

The fixed-wing aircraft employed by the Soviets in Afghanistan included both high-altitude bombers and close support aircraft. They included Tu-16 and Tu-22 bombers, and Su-17, MiG-21, MiG-23, MiG-27, Su-24, and Su-25 fighters and fighter-bombers. The fighter-bombers provided extensive direct support of Soviet ground forces. They initially dropped conventional bombs, many of which failed to arm and which had little lethality in the rough ground and unique terrain conditions in Afghanistan. During 1983, however, Soviet forces changed the fuses on most of their bombs, and many began to drop retarded cluster bombs with drogue chutes and then fire 57-mm rockets. These cluster bombs included the RBK-250, each of which carried 60 bomblets with roughly the lethal area of an 81-mm mortar round. Some estimates of the total lethal area of the weapon reached 200,000 square feet.[222]

Soviet close support virtually always involved preplanned strikes and normally involved the use of both fixed-wing aircraft and helicopters. The fighters would hit fixed targets while the helicopters provided direct air support and landed heliborne troops. Soviet forces generally received more air support than DRA forces. However, DRA government ground forces were sometimes supported by cadres of elite Soviet sub-units, to provide a "quality edge," and these operations received stronger fixed-wing aircraft and close air support.

The key targets for the fixed-wing aircraft were hardened mountain locations, which controlled the heights as well as narrow ravines. Soviet aircraft tended to attack either when there were known resistance forces or assets or in preemptive moves designed to deny their use to the resistance when the Mujahideen threatened military operations on the ground. The Soviets made heavy use of MiG-23s, Su-17s, and Su-25s for these missions.

By 1982, the Soviets began to conduct longer-range strikes. Su-24s, together with Su-17s and MiG-23/27s, were engaged in intensive bombing of known installations and in attacking concentrations of the resistance in and around the valleys. Daily sortie rates are estimated to have exceeded 100. The Fencers and Floggers operated from bases inside the Soviet Union, like Termez in the Urbekistan Republic, just across the border. Other bases included Mary and Kushka. Most of the Fitter sorties were flown from Bagram.[223]

Soviet close-air tactics changed between 1982 and 1984 to place growing emphasis on FACs, or forward air controllers. These normally operated from helicopters. According to one 1984 report, Soviet air attacks on the Mujahideen tended to adopt the following model:

- Generally, air activity is restricted to the mornings, ceasing at noon. Antonov 12s fly daily reconnaissance flights, circling hourly over mountain positions to gather information for air strikes. Helicopter attacks represent the most numerous form of air strike and generally start with two Mi-4 Hounds attacking with unguided rockets and machine gun fire, followed by four Hind Ds which continue the strike with rockets and cannon. Meanwhile the Hounds circle, ejecting heat decoy flares at regular intervals.
- Fighter ground attack (FGA) appears in the form of MiG-21s sometimes preceded by two Mi-4 Hounds, which, having tested

the Mujahideen defenses, call in the jets. They attack individually, taking it in turn to rocket or bomb the Mujahideen positions. Having released their ordnance, they each eject three sets of four heat decoy flares as they climb away.[224]

This "model" of a Soviet air attack conforms to the other information that has since become available. The use of helicopters for the spotter and first-shot role appears to be logical, given Soviet reliance on helicopters, as does the need to flush out the enemy through Hind attacks. Early morning attacks tended to catch the Mujahideen in a fixed position and make heliborne assaults most effective. The use of the MiG-21 aircraft, however, suggests the author witnessed an attack against a routine target with low to medium priority. After 1983–1984, the Soviets tended to attack targets with more sophisticated Soviet aircraft such as the MiG-23 and Su-25 Frogfoot.

The MiG-21 was a proven Soviet "war-horse," and its reliability, turning radius, and relatively low airspeed provided useful advantages in the ground-attack mode. However, the MiG-21 could not function with high effectiveness in a counter-guerrilla role. Such a role required aircraft with high loiter time and relatively low airspeed. The model MiG-23, and similar Soviet fighters, also faced the problem of excessive airspeed but could partly compensate by using their more advanced attack avionics.

The MiG-23s and Su-17s normally carried out close-air support missions where only general accuracy was required, such as reaction to ambushes on specific ridges. They delivered munitions with aerial effect (cluster and chemical munitions) and helped provide area denial. Both the MiG-23s and the Su-17s normally used 57- and 80-mm unguided rockets. The Su-17s also used various bombs, including the multipurpose 500-kg cluster bombs (these are chemical, anti-personnel, and incendiary bomblets, usually a combination).

Mujahideen sources rated Soviet accuracy in using MiG-21, MiG-23, and Su-17 fighters as comparatively low, particularly with unguided rockets. According to many reports, however, attacking Soviet aircraft rarely pressed home their attacks at low altitudes even in the period before the deployment of Stinger and Blowpipe, and they tended to stand off at ranges of about 2,000 meters, which inevitably degraded their accuracy. The MiG-21s also lost effectiveness because they dropped 250-kilogram bombs from such altitudes and fired 57-mm rockets from beyond their useful range. All these tactics led to more inaccurate and ineffective strikes, and this suggests that at least some Soviet pilots were not well trained and/or did not receive adequate coordination from other units such as spotters in Mi-4 helicopters.[225]

According to other reports, many Soviet bombs failed to properly deploy and scatter, which conforms to other information about such failures of Soviet ordnance.[226]

MiG-21, MiG-23, and Su-17 fighters were more effective against other fixed targets in quasi-interdiction missions. These targets included villages, hardened mountain locations, controlling heights, and narrow creeks leading toward main villages. They used area weapons such as chemical warfare agents, napalm, and cluster bombs.[227] Attacks on villages, however, increasingly involved medium bombers such as the Su-24 and presumably Tu-16 Badgers. The smaller fighters lacked the payload for such large targets. Such fighters became steadily less effective after 1985, however, as the Mujahideen learned how to conduct even more of their movement by night and began to use deeper shelters.

The most effective Soviet close-air support fighter in Afghanistan until the Mujahideen acquired large numbers of manportable surface-to-air missiles seems to have been the Su-25 Frogfoot, which first entered combat in 1982 and was based at Bagram.[228] The Su-25 flew at relatively low air speeds (880 km/h maximum). It had an armored cockpit protected by two slabs of armor and was armed with a 30-mm Gatling-type gun system in the port side of the nose for use against armor. Its wings had 10 pylons to carry armaments and could carry up to 9,920 pounds of arms. There were two small outboard pylons for AA-2 or AA-8 air-to-air missiles. It had a nose-mounted laser range finder and marked target seeker, a Sirena-3 radar warning system and SRO-2 IFF system, and a chaff/flare dispenser in the tail cone. The Su-25's gross takeoff weight was approximately 36,000 pounds. It could fly up to 608 miles per hour, and the aircraft's nominal hi-lo-hi combat radius with 4,410 pounds of munitions was 345 miles.

The Su-25 used armored panels for protection and had two Tumansky R-13-300 turbojets—each with 11,240 pounds' thrust. It seems to have reached full operational capability in 1984. The Frogfoot seems to have had a slightly higher overall payload capability in such a role than the A-10.[229] It was particularly well equipped for saturation attacks against Afghan urban centers and key hard points.[230] The ordnance used in Afghanistan included 57-mm and 80-mm rockets and 1,100-pound incendiary, anti-personnel, and chemical cluster bombs.

The Su-25 was used both against specific point targets and for air support in land and helicopter attacks on point targets. The Su-25's primary role is said to have been in providing low-level close-air support in coordination with MiG-21 and Su-17 fighters and Mi-24 support gunships, particularly in hitting at Mujahideen mortar and rocket positions. The Su-25s, like other Soviet fighters, generally operated in loose pairs. After 1985, one would go in very low and attack separately. Another would circle and fire flares as a counter-measure against SAMs and try to suppress any Mujahideen response. The Mujahideen often reported on the accuracy and lethal effectiveness of the Su-25.[231]

The initial Frogfoot operations in the Soviet autumn offensive in the Panjshir Valley of 1983 were effective, but their performance in offensives during 1984–1986 seems to have been better. The accuracy of the Su-25 improved considerably, and the Soviets seem to have made effective use of AN-12 transports and other aircraft as spotter aircraft.[232] Su-25s reportedly destroyed concealed fortified objectives in 1984, 1985, and 1986—targets they could rarely kill in 1983—and could hit targets in rough terrain with great accuracy. They released munitions at longer ranges with growing accuracy, although there is still no indication that "smart munitions" were used.[233]

This may indicate that Soviet pilots improved their training and learned from experience, but this improved accuracy may also have resulted from improved avionics. The Soviets may have begun to use more advanced fighter targeting and delivery aids, and there are some indications that the MiG-23 and Su-25 Frogfoot employed in Afghanistan used laser range finders, low-light television, infrared sensors, radars, and computers. Another explanation is the use of more advanced heads-up display and bombing computers. U.S. pilots experienced major increases in their accuracy in similar missions after deployment of the advanced displays in aircraft like the A-18. It is doubtful whether they could have improved their performance without improved avionics.[234] Soviet fighter pilots generally had to fly very demanding attack approaches because of the terrain and risk of anti-aircraft defenses.

Soviet air ordnance also improved. After the summer of 1983, the Soviets are reported to have used 225- to 500-kilogram cluster bombs and 500-kilogram fuel-air explosives. According to some sources, they also began to use container bombs about the size of 500 kilograms to dispense a black tarlike incendiary which falls in droplets on the ground and bursts into flame on contact with a foot or vehicle, often after a period of months. The USSR is also reported to have used fuel-air explosives in Paktia, Ghazni, Logar, and Wardak provinces. Many of the explosives were delivered by Su-17s.[235]

Other new bombs included a combination of incendiary, anti-personnel, and blast using a combination of small anti-personnel shrapnel buried in a thick dark brown burning agent surrounding a HE core. This explodes well above the ground scattering a persistent fire and killing shrapnel. Another fire bomb has been reported in the form of a 2.5-meter drum with a blast-incendiary core surrounded by about six magnesium and phosphorous rods two meters long. The intense heat is said to have produced "a localized fire storm" in an Afghan village and caused a chain reaction of collapsed and burning buildings. Finally, the Soviets seem to have begun to make effective use of laser guided bombs against targets like tunnels, cave mouths, and hard-to-reach strong points no later than 1986.[236]

The use of these new weapons was tied to changes in Soviet tactics. Soviet and Afghan forces began to actively harass Mujahideen units in 1984 and try to force them into villages or known hiding points. The Soviets would use assault troops, helicopters, artillery, and mortar fire to try to drive Mujahideen units. They would then use fighter bombers or long-range bombers to hit at towns or hiding points. In other cases, Soviet Spetsnaz and intelligence and Afghan KHAD (WAD) units would pick towns and target them for air attacks. Infiltrators, spotters, and small border units were used to target caravans or Mujahideen supply units. These techniques seem to have been refined steadily during 1984 to 1986, although Mujahideen reports do not seem to regard Soviet fighters and bombers as being as dangerous as the threat from helicopters.[237]

The basic problem with many of these tactics was that it was impossible to deploy enough force to destroy an entire countryside. In addition, the purpose behind many air strikes was unclear. The Soviets often hit at villages or farms with no Mujahideen presence, and they may have done as much to drive more people to the Mujahideen cause as hurt them.

As has been discussed earlier, however, Soviet close-air support tactics changed again in 1987 and in 1988. The USSR cut back sharply on missions requiring low altitude and close support. They relied more on artillery, and they increased the altitude and speed of their attack aircraft. Although they deployed a number of IR countermeasures and evasion techniques, they could not find an effective counter to the Mujahideen deployment of Stinger and Blowpipe. As a result, they emphasized area bombing and shifted to attack profiles using advanced attack aircraft like the MiG-27 fighter, which the USSR deployed to Shindand in late 1988.[238] They also used high-altitude Su-24 and Backfire attacks since these aircraft could fly above the operational ceiling of the Stinger.[239]

The MiG-27 ground attack aircraft offered the USSR its best ability to deliver air-to-ground ordnance with reasonable accuracy while flying low-altitude attack profiles at high speed and maneuvering to avoid hits by surface-to-air missiles. The MiG-27 is a single-seat fighter which has a number of features in common with the MiG-23 but differs in a number of important details. It has roughly the same engine as the MiG-23MF, but the R-29-300 engine is rated at 25,350 lbs. static thrust using afterburner, and the aircraft has a fixed-engine air intake and two-position afterburner nozzle to improve low-altitude transonic performance. There are two variants of the MiG-27—the Flogger D and Flogger F—and both seem to have operated in Afghanistan.[240]

The Flogger D and F each has a gross weight of 44,300 pounds and a maximum external load of 9,920 lbs. It has a maximum speed of Mach 1.7 at medium altitude and Mach 1.1 at sea level. It has a ceiling of 52,000 feet. Its lo-lo-lo combat radius is 240 miles when loaded with two AA-2 air-to-air missiles, four 1,000-lb. bombs, and a belly tank. The ferry range is 1,550 miles.

The Flogger D has a nose design that is optimized for air attack rather than interception, as is the case with most MiG-23s. The nose is sharply tapered in terms of its side elevation and has a small window with a laser range finder and a radar ranging antenna. The Flogger D has a doppler navigation radar. The seat and canopy are raised to improve the pilot's view, and the sides of the cockpit are armored. It has a six-barrel 30-mm Gatling gun under the belly and a bomb/JATO rack under the each side of the rear of the fuselage. There are five pylons for external stores on each wing. The aircraft can deliver tactical nuclear weapons, and a variety of laser-guided bombs and air-to-surface missiles, including the AS-7 Kerry, AS-10 Karen, AS-12 Kegler, and AS-14 Kedge. A bullet-shaped missile guidance radar antenna is located above each glove pylon. A radar warning receiver blister is on each side of the fuselage.

The Flogger J was first identified in 1981. It has a new nose with a lip at the top and a blister fairing below it. It has electro-optical sensors with a rearward laser designation capability to allow the aircraft to deliver laser-guided bombs more effectively. It does not have the bullet-shaped missile delivery antennas or external armor on each side of the cockpit. There are two 30-mm gun pods with depressible gun barrels to provide more effective ground attack capability.[241]

It is unclear how the MiG-27 performed in dealing with Stinger, what countermeasures it used, and what losses the USSR incurred. It is important, however, that the USSR seems to have concluded that its other less-capable fighters could not fly effective attack sorties against the improved Mujahideen air defenses and that the use of the Su-25 had to be sharply curtailed even when the USSR had over a year to try to find countermeasures to the Stinger.

Interdiction and Long-Range Air Attack

Beginning in 1983 and 1984, the Soviets emphasized high-altitude aerial attacks on area targets and made intensive use of "carpet bombing." Beginning with the Panjshir offensive of April 1984, the Soviets flew up to thirty Tu-16 sorties per day against small villages.[242] These were usually followed up by coordinated attacks by fighter bombers, helicopters, and artillery.

These Soviet air strikes against civilian targets were an attempted solution to the stalemate in the countryside. They allowed the USSR to attack the Mujahideen's socioeconomic infrastructure. Such attacks take time and massive amounts of airpower to be effective, however, and the Afghan population was dispersed throughout the country in rural, small village settings that did not offer concentrated targets.[243] Nevertheless, the attacks seemed to be achieving part of their objective during 1984–1986. Their psychological and economic impact was reflected in the gross number of refugees in Pakistan (approximately three million) and the number of recent additions to the Afghan urban populations.

The attacks in 1985 involved an even more brutal policy of carpet bombing as part of a coordinated air and ground assault. As one source put it:[244]

> Recently in the Panjshir Valley as many as 100 Soviet Tu-16 Badger bombers and Su-24 Fencer fighters saturated the area with high altitude carpet bombing. In their wake came some 80 M-24 Hind assault helicopters, more than 500 tanks and armored personnel carriers, and 20,000 troops.

The primary bombers used in carpet bombing were the Tu-22 Blinder, the Tu-16 Badger, and the Su-24 Fencer. The Tu-16 Badger made its first public appearance in the Soviet Union in 1954. Approximately half of the 2,000 built remain operational. The Tu-16 is designated for use in theater strike operations, and it can carry both nuclear and conventional weapons.[245] Its performance characteristics are summarized in Table 2.11.

The Tupolev Tu-22 "Blinder D" is also reported to have been engaged in bombing missions in Afghanistan. Because of the high performance characteristics of this aircraft, it was employed against area targets in carpet bombing tactics. The Tu-22 first appeared in public in 1961, when it was heralded as the Soviet Union's first supersonic bomber. The Blinder is a medium bomber designated in the theater strike role. It has Mach 1.4 (920 mph) dash speed capability,

TABLE 2.11 The Tu-16 Badger

Type:	Twin-jet medium bomber and reconnaissance/attack aircraft
Wings:	Cantilever high mid-wing monoplane
Fuselage:	All metal semi-monocoque structure of oval cross-section
Power Plant:	Two Mikulin AIM-3 turbojet engines, each rated at 85.8 kn (19,285 lb. st) at sea level, in early Tu-16s. Later aircraft fitted with RD-3M turbojets, each rated at 93.19 kn (20,950 lb. st)
Accommodation:	Crew of six
Armament:	Seven 23-mm NR-23 cannons. Bomb load up to 9,000 kg (19,800 lb.) delivered from weapons bay
Avionics and Equipment:	Radio and radar aids
Dimensions:	Wing span 39.93 m (108 ft.), length overall 34.80 m (114 ft.), weight empty 37,200 kg (82,000 lb.), normal T-O 72,000 kg (158,000 lb.)
Performance:	AM03 engines; maximum level speed at 19,000 ft., 535 kns; service ceiling, 12,300 m (40,350 ft.), range with 3,790 kg, 2605 NM. (4,800 km, 3,000 me), (8,360 lb.) bomb load

SOURCES: Bill Gunston, *Modern Soviet Air Force* (New York: ARCO, 1982), pp. 116–119; *Jane's All the World's Aircraft*; and *Air Force Magazine*, various editions.

but a range of only 1,400 miles (2,250 kilometers) unrefueled. The Tu-22 is powered by two afterburning turbojets, circa 1977, but modifications may have included the use of turbofan engines, which would make it much more fuel efficient. Its performance is summarized in Table 2.12.

The Su-24 Fencer was used extensively in bombing raids against area targets such as villages. The Su-24 aircraft, and its generic predecessor, the Su-19, functions in the high performance fighter bomber role. Its mission is analogous to that of the American F-111, and it complements the Su-25 Frogfoot in the high-speed attack role.

The Su-24 Fencer-D is a formidable aircraft. It is a two-man aircraft (pilot and weapons/navigation officer side by side). It has three position-variable geometry wings and in-flight refueling capability. It has a very high-range payload and is equipped to deliver a wide range of air-to-surface missiles, including the AS-14. It has a maximum speed of Mach 2.2 at medium altitude and Mach 1.2 at sea level. It has a ceiling of 54,100 feet. Its hi-lo-hi combat radius is 805

TABLE 2.12 The Tu-22 Blinder D

Dimension:	Wingspan 90 ft., 10 1/2" (27.70 m), length 132 ft., 11 1/2" (40.53 m), height, 35 ft. (10.67 m)
Weights:	Empty: about 85,000 lb.; Maximum: 185,000 lb.
Armaments:	One 23-mm NS-23 in. radar-directed barbette in tail; internal weapon bay for 20,000 pounds of free-fall bombs or other stores

SOURCES: Bill Gunston, *Modern Soviet Air Force* (New York: ARCO, 1982); *Jane's All the World's Aircraft*, and *Air Force Magazine*, various editions.

miles when loaded with 6,600 pounds of armament and two external tanks.[246]

Its features include ventral fins, double-shock side inlets, full-span flaps, and double-sided flaps. It has modern avionics, including a multi-mode attack radar, Doppler, laser ranger, and comprehensive EW/ECM components. It has an advanced long-range navigation system and electro-optical delivery systems for night and poor weather attack. It has an estimated night and poor weather accuracy (CEP) of 180 feet. Its features are summarized in Table 2.13.

According to resistance leaders and Western diplomats, Soviet area bombing did massive damage to villages, crops, livestock, and irrigation systems in Mujahideen areas. The Soviet objective was to strain the rural support network, and the strikes resulted in widespread food shortages in rural areas. The bombing campaign also greatly increased the number of civilians leaving the countryside for Soviet-dominated cities which were more susceptible to Soviet military control.

After August 1984, resistance leaders began to report that the destruction of crops and irrigation systems had caused serious food shortages and malnutrition in some areas. There is little doubt that the carpet bombing tactics also eroded the effectiveness of the resistance at this time. Masoud Khalilil, a spokesman for the Jamiat-i-Islami stated, "In some places, resistance fighters are retreating from their fighting positions not so much because of Russian military pressure but because of hunger."[247] The bombing also undoubtedly created strains between the guerrillas and their civilian base.

The problems with Soviet bombing, however, were that it made even more enemies for the USSR and DRA, failed to have a decisive impact on the Mujahideen even in limited areas, and simply drove many civilians from the country. In those areas where the bombing was

TABLE 2.13 The Su-24 Fencer

Type:	Two-seat multi-role combat aircraft.
Engines:	Two afterburning turbo-fan or turbojet engines, probably two 24,500 lb. Lyulka AL-21F3.
Dimensions:	Wingspan (spread at 220°), 56 ft., 3"; swept (72°), 31 ft., 3"; length: 69 ft., 10" (21.9 m); weight: empty 35,000 lb. (estimated), maximum loaded, 70,000 lb.
Performance:	(Estimated): maximum speed, clear 950 mph, 1.25 at sea level, 1,650 mph (Mach 2.5) at altitude. Initial climb over 40,000 ft./min. Service ceiling: about 60,000 ft. Combat radius 500 miles, with maximum weapons.
Armament:	One 23-mm twin-barrel cannon in lower centerline, at least six pylons on wings for wide-ranging ordnance.

SOURCES: Bill Gunston, *Modern Soviet Air Force* (New York: ARCO, 1982); *Jane's All the World's Aircraft*, and *Air Force Magazine*, various editions.

intensive, the Mujahideen learned to disperse better and more quickly, started their own agricultural system, and improved their ability to bring food in from the outside.

Further, the Soviet execution of long-range bombing was at best erratic. Scattered areas were attacked and others left untouched. Relatively innocent villages were hit, and pro-Mujahideen villages were destroyed. The damaged areas could usually obtain supplies from nearby areas that were not affected. The Soviet attempt to deny the Mujahideen access to the population may have done as much harm as good, particularly once the Mujahideen went on the offensive in the countryside in 1987.[248]

The Soviets were, however, able to solve some of these problems when they resumed bombing Afghanistan from outside the country in late 1988. Most of the bombing was done against known targets, and heavy use was made of both the Tu-16 and Tu-26.[249] Targets often included Mujahideen forces attacking DRA strong points and large Mujahideen force concentrations. The result was a natural increase in effectiveness, although there were few signs it was likely to change the outcome of the war.

It is unclear why the Soviets made use of the Tupolev Tu-26 (Tu-22M) Backfire bomber at this time. It may have been because of the advanced avionics on this bomber and its superior high-altitude bombing capability, because they were seeking to intimidate Pakistan and the Mujahideen by deploying a new aircraft, or because the USSR wished to test its conventional strike capabilities. The Backfire has a maximum speed of Mach 2.0 at medium altitude and Mach 0.9 at sea level. It is normally configured for nuclear strike or anti-ship missile attacks, but it can carry multiple racks of twelve to eighteen bombs under its air intake trunks and some 26,450 pounds of conventional bombs or mines. It has very advanced ECM and ECCM gear. Its maximum combat radius is 2,485 miles.[250]

Air Reconnaissance, C³I, IFF, and AC&W

The Soviet air command and control system also had to adapt to the conditions in Afghanistan. The Soviet Army's initial lack of aviation helicopters and forward air controllers created a need for both specially trained ground observers and smoother liaison and communications between army and air force personnel at divisional headquarters. Considerable confusion resulted from the layering of command and communications during the first year of the war.[251]

The USSR improved its land-air coordination after 1982 and developed the equivalent of forward air controllers (FACs) on "on call" support. It still, however, had to continue to rely on HUMINT and reconnaissance methods. The main Soviet improvements in air reconnaissance and command and control came from the increasing use of attack and combat helicopters in direct support and armed reconnaissance roles. The heliborne assault brigade and Spetsnaz came to play a steadily growing role in search-and-destroy missions.

The use of air assault brigades in Afghanistan was also an acknowledgment of the need for flexibility in helicopter operations emphasizing tactical mobility. As many as five of these brigades may have operated in the country, although most have the same designation as conventional motorized rifle brigades. According to one source, these brigades included a regiment of sixty-four assault helicopters, a squadron of Mi-26 heavy lift helicopters, and three air-assault rifle battalions. Also, according to this source, each army-level formation had a helicopter transport regiment used to lift infantry units. One battalion in three motor-rifle regiments was reported to be trained for helicopter operations.[252]

At the same time, however, the USSR did perform steadily more reconnaissance missions and seems to have tried to improve its sensors to find the kind of small targets used by the Mujahideen. It seems to have had some success in use slow-flying spotter and targeting aircraft until the Mujahideen acquired large numbers of manportable surface-to-air missiles, and then seems to have made use of advanced electro-optical systems to provide a target and surveillance capability at longer ranges. It is unclear, however, that such systems ever provided any stand-off capability. This increasingly forced the USSR to use high-altitude reconnaissance and high-altitude area bombing against preplanned fixed Mujahideen targets, which deprived Soviet airpower of much of its operational flexibility, time-urgent strike capability, and ability to conduct effective missions in close-air support and against supply units. The need for survivable surveillance of small unit operations is a key lesson of the Afghan conflict.

Helicopters

The helicopter soon became one of the most dominant Soviet combat systems of the war. While there is little agreement on precise strength figures, the USSR seems to have increased its helicopter deployments at twice the rate it increased its deployments of combat aircraft. During most of the war, helicopters played an even more important role in combat missions than fixed-wing aircraft did. Helicopters also dominated Soviet air losses. Any estimates of such losses are controversial, but the USSR probably lost well over 800 rotary wing aircraft. This compares with U.S. losses of approximately 4,000 helicopters in Vietnam. It is interesting to note that virtually all U.S. losses occurred to small arms and to the same 12.7-mm, 14.5-mm, and 23-mm anti-aircraft machine guns that the PRC supplied to the Mujahideen.[253]

The Soviet invasion of Afghanistan occurred at a time when the Soviets were just beginning to acquire attack helicopters and rethink their concept of heliborne mobility. The Soviets first integrated combat helicopters into their combat operations in mountainous terrain in early 1976, in the course of the KAVKAZ-76 exercise. Helicopters became a basic part of the Soviet concept of operations, and combat helicopters played a central role in the initial Soviet direct intervention in the fighting in Afghanistan in April 1978. At the time of the invasion, however, the Soviets used only a limited number of armed helicopters, some of which were Aeroflot Mi-8s converted to carry rocket pods.

The Buildup of the Helicopter Force

The Soviets did not plan to use helicopters extensively when they first invaded Afghanistan. In January 1980 there were only about 15 to 20 Soviet helicopters in country. Following the introduction of the second wave of Soviet forces, these numbers grew to 30 to 40 in February

1980. They grew to 45 to 60 during the spring offensive in June 1980. Soviet helicopter deployment to Afghanistan then increased dramatically in the summer of 1980. There were 175 to 200 Soviet helicopters in Afghanistan by July. In September 1980 the number reached 250 to 300 helicopters. Deployments increased at the rate of 100 helicopters per year. While fighter deployments tended to level off in 1981–1982, the rate of helicopter deployment actually increased in 1983–1984.

Following the completion of the reorganization of the Soviet Army forces in 1983, the Soviets relied more and more on combat helicopters. While the exact numbers and types of helicopters deployed were always controversial, the Soviet arsenal in Afghanistan at the start of 1984 seemed to include some 140 Mi-24s (11 squadrons), 105 Mi-8s and Mi-17s (17 squadrons), 40 Mi-6s (three squadrons), and an assortment of Mi-2s, Mi-4s, and Mi-8s for special duties. There were also a few Mi-26 Hook heavy-lift helicopters in Afghanistan after 1983, probably in special formations.[254]

There also were roughly 30 Mi-8s and 30 to 40 Mi-4s in the DRA Air Force in 1984. These were organized in three composite regiments, and the Afghan Commandos were reorganized and heavily equipped with Mi-17s. The DRA, however, took very heavy losses. Out of the 70 Mi-17s delivered to the DRA in 1984, 26 were destroyed by 1986 and 14 had been pulled back to the USSR. Ten of the 16 Mi-25s delivered to the DRA in 1984 were lost by 1986.[255]

An additional 35 to 40 helicopters were deployed to Soviet units at Bagram in preparation for the spring offensive of 1984. From 1984 to early 1988, there were roughly 140 Mi-24 attack and 130 Mi-8/Mi-17 combat helicopters in Afghanistan, plus up to 200 heavy lift and transport helicopters.[256] These estimates are uncertain. Other estimates put the total number of helicopters at 275 in Afghanistan in 1986–1987, with 100 more in support in the USSR.[257]

Until the deployment of Stinger and Blowpipe in 1987, the attack helicopter allowed Soviet forces to take the initiative away from the guerrillas by confronting them directly with superior technology that they generally could not defend against or evade and by denying them the ability to exploit their often superior off-road mobility and knowledge of the ground. The Soviets used helicopters to attack enemy forces and equipment, gather intelligence, target artillery fire, insert assault troops, evacuate the wounded, deliver supplies, and transfer weapons and equipment in untrafficable areas.[258]

This Soviet strength began to be cut by early 1988. One estimate of Soviet helicopter strength counts 270 combat helicopters, with 140 Mi-24 Hinds, 130 Mi-8 Hips, and additional Mi-6 Hooks and Mi-2

Hoplites. Some Mi-26s were present. Reports of test deployments of Mi-28 Havocs was uncertain. Estimates of DRA helicopter strength in 1988 are controversial, but the DRA seems to have had 12 Mi-4s, 25 Mi-8s, and 13 Mi-25s.[259]

Helicopter losses were also the most significant air losses. At the start of 1986, nearly 1,000 aircraft had been lost as a result of the fighting in Afghanistan and most were reported to be helicopters. Another 400 aircraft are estimated to have been lost during 1987 and early 1988. Most of these were helicopters. About half of all Soviet helicopter losses seem to have been due to accidents.[260]

Changes in Helicopter Tactics

The increase in helicopters was accompanied by a major change in Soviet tactics, which shifted from an emphasis on armored vehicles to a new focus on tactical mobility.[261] The Soviets, however, were slow to adapt the pop-up and terrain-hugging tactics of the U.S. During 1980, they usually exposed the Hind A in straight runs in at Mujahideen targets, often with several helicopters slowly closing in on the target from different directions (the spokes in a "wagon wheel" formation). This made their operations predictable and led to increasing losses. This tactical rigidity partly reflected the fact that most Soviet helicopter pilots and commanders had limited and relatively rigid training and had to learn combat techniques on the job.[262]

By late 1980, the more survivable helicopters like the Hip and Hind were used as scouts and forward observers. They would fly high outside of gun range and call in both combat helicopters and fixed-wing helicopters. Mi-4 Hooks would be used to mark targets with rockets and act as battle managers for the attack helicopters. These battle management tactics steadily improved in 1984, as the USSR deployed Hips and Hooks equipped to act as command posts with special sensors and communications gear. Soviet helicopter pilots also made steadily greater use of contour or ground-hugging flight beginning in 1981, although Soviet helicopters do not allow such flight as easily as U.S. models do.

The DRA government forces had made effective use of the guns on the Soviet Hind A armed helicopter in 1979, before the Soviet invasion.[263] The Soviets built upon this experience during the course of 1980 and 1981. They began attacking Mujahideen villages in June 1981, using groups of sixteen to eighteen armed helicopters against a single village. They had only forty-five to sixty helicopters in the country at this time, but they soon began to rapidly increase the number of helicopters. They also provided dedicated helicopter assets to brigade and regimental assault units, since they found that it was essential for ground combat commanders to have direct control over at least some of the helicopters they used in small unit actions. The key problem was ensuring immediate response by the helicopter lift and attack forces used in the assault phase.[264] The Soviets also made extensive use of helicopters for mobility to cope with the long distances between cities and lack of security on the roads. (It is 425 kilometers from the Soviet border to Kabul and 600 kilometers from Kandahar to Herat.)

The Soviets began to conduct large-scale helicopter operations in the Panjshir beginning in 1982, with flights of twelve to sixteen helicopters, although the normal formation was four. Resistance sources said that the helicopters seemed to be everywhere, participating in every military activity. The Soviets do, however, seem to have taken major helicopter losses, and the Hind A was withdrawn from Afghanistan and replaced with the Hind B in 1983.

Soviet helicopter attack tactics also changed. Pilots began to use flares and other countermeasures against the SA-7 in 1983. They started their runs at 7,000 to 8,000 meters and rarely closed to more than 1,500 meters against defended targets. They came in at very low altitudes, popped up to 20–100 meters to fire, and turned rapidly away in evasive maneuvers. Helicopters on reconnaissance missions stopped flying predictable paths. Combat helicopters stopped flying alone or side by side. One would stand by as guard while the second closed in on potentially threatening areas.

The Soviets never made extensive use of the Mi-8 and Mi-24 in night combat. Most of the versions of these helicopters deployed to Afghanistan lacked night target acquisition capability and night vision aids such as FLIR. The Soviets seem to have used night vision goggles to fly helicopters, but this is uncertain. Soviet pilots began to fly night combat missions in 1982. Night missions became more common in 1983, generally with flares used for illumination. Soviet pilots may have shifted to night vision goggles and away from the use of illumination flares during 1984–1985. Most night missions remained restricted to interdiction, foray and supply missions, airfield defense, reconnaissance, reaction, and training until Soviet withdrawal. Most Soviet night missions were defensive in character.

Major convoys began to receive helicopter support after 1983, often with armed Hips. On-call Hinds were used to respond to Mujahideen ambushes and often did so very successfully.

During 1984, Soviet pilots began to fly spiral approaches to landing in combat zones; by 1986, they were doing this all over the country. They began to fly at maximum ceiling to avoid fire while on ferry missions. Heavy lift missions declined in combat areas, although the

Hook and Halo had often been a useful way to move BMDs and artillery into difficult areas.

The most striking characteristic of Soviet helicopter operations during this period was their growing sophistication and integration into the overall ground operations. Every move that Soviet units made on the ground was accompanied by strikes by combat helicopters against sources of hostile fire and threatening points to the flanks of these forces.[265]

These helicopter strikes were initially carried out by small formations of two to six helicopters, mainly Mi-24s (Hinds), but formations increased to a maximum of twenty helicopters in 1985 and reached thirty helicopters in 1986. The Soviets also came to keep Hinds permanently on station and available for quick reaction. Earlier in the war, most Soviet helicopter strikes were rigidly preplanned. The shift to more mobile Soviet tactics created a need for quick reaction strikes, and Soviet helicopter forces increasingly seemed to operate on an on-call basis.

Part of the Soviet success in using both both aircraft and helicopters in support roles during 1984–1986 can be attributed to improved intelligence operations and links to the KHAD (WAD) and to better use of forward air controllers (FACs) and changes in FAC tactics. The Soviets made large-scale use of heliborne FACs beginning in 1984. These observers flew in retrofitted Mi-4s (Hounds) and Hinds, in either singles or pairs, although there have been some unconfirmed reports of the use of the Mi-28 Havoc in this role.

When such observers identified the objectives or targets of opportunity, they shot smoke and/or white phosphorus rockets to designate them. These designations were usually followed immediately by an aerial strike by helicopters, aircraft, or both. The Mujahideen learned to use these smoke rockets as a warning sign of an impending aerial strike and had time to disperse. After the 1984 Panjshir Valley offensive, the FAC helicopters began to mark targets only seconds before the aerial strike so that the Mujahideen forces had less time to escape. The effectiveness of properly spotted aerial strikes was often high.

A report by Yossef Bodansky provides a good picture of Soviet helicopter operations in the period before they were inhibited by the use of Blowpipe and Stinger and heavier AA gun defenses.[266] On 21 April 1984, the Mujahideen destroyed much of the upper structure of the Mattok bridge on the Ghorband River, south of Salang Tunnel. When they concentrated for a repeated attack on the bridge, the Soviets launched a surprise heliborne operation that wiped out a Mujahideen force estimated to be 1,500 to 2,000 strong. Other

Mujahideen tried to hide during the day in a valley, but the Soviets landed two companies, some 200 troops, on two mountains which controlled the back exit from the valley and blocked it. Almost immediately, the trapped Mujahideen forces were subjected to aerial bombardment by helicopters and aircraft. Attempts to advance out of the valley were blocked by the Soviet troops.

Reports during 1984–1985 emphasized the growing ferocity of similar Soviet helicopter attacks and the high level of Mujahideen casualties. The growing aggressiveness of Soviet helicopter attacks is reflected by reports that such attacks were sometimes carried out too close to the heliborne troops and produced casualties.

In another attack in 1984, when the main Soviet and Afghan Army formation advanced toward Rokhen, the Soviets launched a heliborne operation that landed troops on a series of controlling heights. They then provided them with massive helicopter fire support. These forces advanced and protected the flanks of the main forces during their advance in the most critical part of the Panjshir Valley. This operation was mainly preemptive, and it succeeded because there was no serious attempt to interfere with the advance of the force. The Soviets consistently proved in 1985 and 1986, however, that they could rapidly envelop a Mujahideen unit and inflict serious casualties.

The Soviets made steadily increasing use of helicopters to land airborne troops on various mountain tops. Small detachments of troops, usually companies, were landed by Mi-8s and Mi-17s (Hips). These forces were provided with extensive fire support from Hips and Hinds. Upon landing, they started to chase resistance forces from the edges of the valley into killing zones where the Mujahideen forces were subjected to helicopter or fighter attacks. Other heliborne forces were used for border and supply interdiction roles, quick reaction against ambushes, and convoy and LOC protection.

The impact of the Stinger and Blowpipe has been described earlier. Beginning in 1987, the Soviets often lost an average of more than one helicopter a day. They had to abandon many small strips and forward locations because the Mujahideen would ambush them with Stingers when they took off, and according to some reports, Soviet helicopters had to be pulled out of Jalalabad and Samarkhel airfield in 1987 because of these problems.[267]

The Soviet Hind Helicopter

The performance characteristics of Soviet helicopters are shown in Table 2.14. It is clear that the Mi-24 Hind helicopter has been refined from an armed transport helicopter into one of the best operational

TABLE 2.14 Specifications of Soviet Military Helicopters

	Mi-2	Mi-4	Mi-6	Mi-10/10K	Mi-8 Mi-17	Mi-24	Mi-24/27	Mi-28
Code Name	Hoplite	Hound	Hook	Hare	Hip	Hind-Al	Hind E	Havoc
Maximum Speed (km/h)	200	160	300	200	260	275	275	300
Range (km)	170	250 - 400	250 - 404	250 - 450	298	300	300	240
Weight (kg) Empty	2,365	5,268	27,240	24,680	6,816	6,500	6,500	3,700
Loaded	8,157	7,800	42,500	38,000	12,000	11,500	11,500	7,100
Crew	2	2	3	3	2	2	2	2
Trooplift	8 - 10	8 - 11	68	28 - 40	28	8	8	N/A
Payload (kg)	800	1,800	12,000	9,000	2,800	2,300	2,300	1,200
Armament Guns	Optional	Optional	1x12.7mm	None	Gunpods	1x12.7mm	4 Barrel Cannon Turret	23mm Cannon
Missiles	4xAT-3 or AT-5	None	None	None	4xAT-2 or 6xAT-3	4xAT-4	6xAT-6	16xAT-6M 8xSA-14
Rockets	Pods	Pods and Bombs	None	None	Rockets or 4 Pods	250kg Bombs or Rockets	Bombs or Rockets	N/A

SOURCES: Adapted from *Jane's All the World's Aircraft, 1984/1985*; *The International Defense Review*, October 1984, p. 1456; and Bill Gunston, *Military Helicopters* (New York: ARCO, 1981).

attack helicopters in the world. It began as a heavily armed and armored transport used to carry a squad of eight assault troops. There was titanium armor on the belly, heavy armor around the engine and critical drive components, and bullet-proof glass over the cockpit. The Hind A could carry up to sixteen troops.

Before the Soviet invasion of Afghanistan, various exercises suggested that the Hind would be used in both the attack role and to protect troop-carrying helicopters like the Mi-8. The Hind, however, was then redesigned to use a stepped cockpit with a weapons operator in tandem, and the attack models of the Hind A were replaced in 1983 with the Hind D and then the Hind E.

The Hind D and E were designed to carry fuel and a flight mechanic instead of troops. Both were modified to carry 1,500 kilograms of internal fuel, providing a fully combat loaded mission radius of 165 kilometers. They could carry a full reload of munitions in the cabin and used external tanks with some munitions to extend their range to 224–288 kilometers. Their heavy weapons load and armament was adjusted to be steadily more effective in the close-fire support role, and it proved effective in troop escort/combat assault, anti-armor, and anti-helicopter missions.[268]

The Hind Ds used during most of the fighting in Afghanistan normally employed four AT-2 Swatter anti-tank guided missiles and four UV-32-57 pods with 128 57-mm rockets, but it can carry mine dispensers, bombs, and cluster bombs. The Hind D version carries a chin-mounted 12.7-mm Gatling gun with an approximate range of 1,500 meters. The Hind D is capable of speeds in excess of 165 knots, and can still carry up to eight fully equipped troops. The Hind Es used in Afghanistan carried four AT-6 Spiral anti-tank missiles. This missile reportedly has a longer range and greater velocity than U.S. TOW missiles. They also carried UV-32 57-mm rocket pods.[269]

The Hind D and E have self-sealing fuel tanks, intake plugs to reduce their IR signature, titanium belly armor, and landing gear for rolling take-offs. They have a precision low-speed air speed sensor for rocket firing, a laser range finder, IR imaging, and low-light television. Some may have a Doppler radar. The export version given to the DRA did not have many of these features, however, and could not use the Swatter ATGM.

In Afghanistan, Hind helicopters often carried PFM-1 mine dispensers, incendiary bombs, anti-personnel bombs, and chemical munitions. Napalm bombs appear to have been dropped only by fixed-wing aircraft. Helicopters have, however, been reported to have used flechette munitions which have reportedly been extremely effective.[270] The Mujahideen do report, however, that the 12.7-mm

Gatling cannon fire from the Hind D and E is often inaccurate and has comparatively low lethality.

The variants of the Hind D and E employed during most of the fighting in Afghanistan proved highly survivable against machine guns, and they often engaged the Mujahideen from a low-altitude hover during the first years of their deployment in Afghanistan. Later, however, their weak points were attacked by the rebels. These weak points included lack of good flight performance at low altitudes and speeds, inability to fly sustained nap-of-the-earth flight profiles, lack of aids for night flight and target acquisition, and vulnerabilities such as their broad beam, air intake openings, rotors and rotor blades, tail unit support at the side fin, missile support, and the space between the rotors and the missile support (where tanks are located).

The best armored portion of the Hind helicopter is the under-fuselage tunnel. The windows of the helicopter are also armored. This means the Hind has its greatest vulnerabilities on top of the system, which led the Mujahideen to try to shoot down on helicopters from elevated points in the mountains. Soviet pilots modified their attack tactics, however, to dive from 1,000 meters and break away with evasive turns and terrain-hugging flight.

In other instances, several Hinds circled the ground in the wagon-wheel pattern described earlier. When this still led to losses, the Soviets started using scout helicopters and attacking 7,000 to 8,000 meters away from the target. They then would run in hugging the earth and then pop up to 20–100 meters to launch their munitions. This pop-up occurred at the maximum range of the weapons system. Other tactics included using one helicopter to attack while another acted as a wing man to draw fire and strike at any group shooting at the first helicopter. The Soviets were limited in what they could do because no variant of the Mi-24 or Mi-25 is as maneuverable as U.S. AH-1 or AH-64 attack helicopters, and they have far less sophisticated sensors.

Hinds escorting convoys also came to carry assault troops that would land at suspected ambush points, while other Hinds carrying attack munitions would circle a column and its flanks. The troop-carrying units would leapfrog from point to point, and helicopter commanders were given increasing personal initiative as time went on.[271]

The Soviets steadily improved the survivability of the Hind D and Hind E after the Mujahideen began using advanced manportable surface-to-air missiles. The Hinds were given improved engine exhaust IR suppressors and fuselage-mounted flare dispensers, and the Hinds often came to eject flares at regular intervals horizontally and slightly forward to both right and left in an effort to counter the SA-7, Blowpipe, and Stinger. The Hinds also were given an IR pulsed jammer countermeasures system, perhaps one similar to the AN/ALQ-144. During 1987–1988, the maneuverability of new production Hinds was improved to allow more rapid turns and to allow sustained flight at nap-of-the-earth altitudes, which the Soviets define as five meters. . Two winglet sensor packages were added to each side of the cockpit, and the instrument display was rearranged to make night flight easier. An upgraded electro-optical system for target acquisition and a much improved laser designator were added. The Hinds that had been modernized with TV systems were given an improved TV telescope to allow use of the new AT-6 Spiral tube-launched air-to-surface missile, giving them a strike range of up to eight kilometers, which is beyond the range of existing manportable surface-to-air missiles. Some experts believe that the telescope has a FLIR capability, but this is very uncertain.

All engine intakes were covered with vortex debris extractors. The troop-carrying space in the Hind E and F was converted to reload carrying space, the central wing spar was strengthened, and a flight mechanic was added as a third crewman. Because the earlier models of the Hind forced a trade-off between added internal fuel and munitions carrying capability, the later Hinds were modified to carry up to four external 300-kilogram fuel tanks on strong points on the wings. This increased the maximum combat radius from 160 kilometers to 224 kilometers with two tanks and 288 kilometers with four. Existing Soviet and RA Hinds were also upgraded when they were sent back to the factory for major overhauls after 500 hours of flight.

The Soviets also deployed a new variant of the Hind called the Hind F, which incorporated all the above improvements. Early Hind Fs had a twin-barreled GSh 23-mm cannon, UV-19-57 rocket pods, PFM-1 mine dispensers, and AT-6 Spiral missiles. Later Hind Fs had 30-mm twin-barreled GSh cannons of the kind fitted to new BMP-2 and BMD-2 fighting vehicles. Rails were also added to allow launch of SA-14 and SA-16 missiles (SA-7 launch capability was retrofitted to the Hind E). All Hinds were given the option of using pods with the new UV-21-75 or UV-21-76, whose increased range also allowed them to fire at rangers outside the reach of existing manportable surface-to-air missiles.

Finally, there are reports of a follow-on version of the Hind called the Mi-27, which may have been tested in Afghanistan. Variants have both twin bubble canopies and a single streamlined canopy for the crew. They have more powerful engines in external square section pods, a vastly improved rotor assembly with what seems to be a target acquisition pod on top, many of the subsystems developed for the new Mi-28 Havoc, and further improvements in night flight and nap-of-the-earth flying techniques. The Mi-27 is expected to replace the present honeycomb aluminum rotor with glass fiber blades. The stub wings are swept and slightly lower than those of the previous Hinds. Each has three strong points and a wing-tip end pylon.[272] These steps undoubtedly improved the survivability of the Hind, but it is difficult to determine their effectiveness. It is clear that by late 1987, the USSR no longer was willing to take significant losses. Systems like the Stinger continued to present an unacceptable threat, if only because Mujahideen infantry actions had worn the USSR down to the point where it no longer maintained its strategic commitment to the conflict.[273]

The Soviet Mi-28 Havoc Helicopter

There is considerable debate over exactly what mix of new attack helicopters the Soviets will deploy as a result of the lessons they have learned in Afghanistan and changing mission requirements in Europe. The new Soviet Mi-28 Havoc seems to be the prime candidate for large-scale deployment, although it has a competitor in the new Kamov Ka-136.

The Mi-28 Havoc is lighter, more maneuverable, and more stealthy than the Hind and does not have a bulky compartment. It may have undergone test operations in Afghanistan from late 1985 through 1988, and it reflects virtually all of the lessons the USSR learned regarding Hind vulnerability and performance. It was designed as an attack helicopter, unlike the Hind and the Mi-8 Hip C, which were originally designed as transport helicopters.

The Havoc is a twin-engined helicopter using more powerful versions of the Isotov TV-3-177 engines used in the Hind. It has a copilot gunner in the front compartment, with the pilot behind on an elevated seat. It is slightly shorter than the Hind and has a much narrower beam. It has a maximum speed of 162 NM/h (300 km/h) and a combat radius of 130 nautical miles (240 km). It has integral armor around the cockpit area. The Havoc uses a glass fiber main rotor and has an X-shaped rear rotor similar to the one on the U.S. AH-64. It has the heavy 30-mm gun used in the Hind F in an undernose turret. There is a pylon under each wing for ATGMs or rockets, and its wing-tip pylon tubes can carry air-to-air missiles. It has upward-deflected jet pipes and foreign-object deflectors forward of the air intakes. The Havoc has large infrared suppressors on the exhausts, and all the exhaust is deflected vertically downwards.

The Havoc has improved decoy dispensers and will use an improved infrared countermeasures system. There is extensive use of internal composite armor. The armored glass windows are relatively small, but both visibility and maneuver are greatly improved over the Hind. The Havoc can maneuver at –0.5G to +3.5G. The newly designed seats and landing gear can protect the crew in the event of crash landings at speeds up to 15 meters per second, and the crew can evacuate through a door in the side. The Havoc also has improved nose-mounted night vision systems and a nose-mounted radar. This may be for guidance of the AT-6 air-to-surface missile, but some experts argue that it has an air-to-air combat capability with a detection range of 17 miles and a tracking range of 12 miles. The gunner's sight is in the undernose turret and is a plain direct-vision optical device with a built-in laser for range finding. The pilot in the rear seat has a fixed heads-up display.

The Kamov Ka-136 has not entered production and may be developmental. It has most of the advanced features of the Mi-28 but is lighter and may fly at speeds of up to 189 NM/h (350 km/h).[274]

The Soviet Mi-8 and Mi-17 Hip Helicopters

The Mi-8 Hip E, and its follow-on derivative the Mi-17 Hip H, proved successful in escort duty roles with road convoys, and the Soviets built up their helicopter strength to the point where they had roughly 150 of these aircraft in Afghanistan in 1983.[275] These aircraft, and the heavy-lift Mi-6 helicopters, were routinely used to support heliborne assault operations of 500–2,000 men from 1984 to the point where the Blowpipe and Stinger began to pose a major threat.

Although the Mi-8 and Mi-17 were far more vulnerable than the Mi-24 and Mi-26, they still carried considerable fire power. The Soviets often used Mi-8 Hip Es to insert troops on mountain tops in advance of a convoy. These tactics were referred to as "cresting the heights." Such escorts normally operated in pairs, using four per convoy.

The Hip (Mi-8) medium utility helicopter may be the world's most heavily armed transport helicopter. The latest E version carries one flexibly mounted 12.7-mm machine gun, up to 192 rockets, plus four Swatter missiles. It can also lay chemical blocks or carry two mine dispersal units and sow up to 144 PFM-1s or other mines. The Hip can travel at speeds in excess of 135 knots. The Hip E has a crew of three and is capable of carrying up to 28 troops or 8,250 pounds of cargo. The Hip C is the basic assault helicopter version.[276]

The Mi-17 or Hip H, an upgraded version of the Hip E armed with an additional 12.7-mm machine gun that fired to the rear, was also utilized in Afghanistan. It seemed to be a response to guerrillas firing from behind attack helicopters on strafing runs, presumably exposing their positions by standing to fire. Combinations of Hips and Hinds lifted whole battalions up to fifty kilometers beyond the front line.

The Mi-17 was more maneuverable than the Mi-8, which was relatively slow flying, and may have had more lift at high altitude—where the Mi-8 was marginal.

Both types of Hips had defects. They performed badly at high and very low altitudes and had exposed non–crash-worthy fuel lines, limited rotor and engine life, and poor trim controls.[277]

The Soviet Mi-4 Hound Helicopter

The Mi-4 Hound was also used extensively as a multi-role helicopter—particularly by the DRA. It dates back to 1952, and several thousand of these craft were built. It has served as the utility helicopter work-horse of the Soviet military. The Hound is powered by a 1,700 horsepower Shvetsov A Sh-82V 18-cylinder two-row radial engine, turning a 68-foot, four-blade main rotor. The maximum loaded weight is 17,200 pounds with a cargo capacity of about 6,000 pounds. The Mi-4's cruise speed is about 100 mph and the range is about 250 miles with eight passengers or 155 miles with eleven passengers.[278]

The army assault version of the Hound uses a fixed or movable machine gun or cannon in front. It can include weapon pylons for rocket or gun pods. In Afghanistan, it was used largely for spotting or as a scout. The normal transport versions, which were the ones used most often in Afghanistan, have large rear doors for artillery, missiles, and small vehicles and space for fourteen equipped troops. It has proved very useful as a low-cost spotter for ground troops, other helicopters, and fighters.[279]

The Soviet Mi-6 Hook Heavy Lift Helicopter

The Mi-6 was used extensively as a heavy lift helicopter and often to ferry in Soviet forces from the USSR. It was used extensively in Paktia in November 1984. The Soviets found that such heavy lift helicopters were very valuable in providing rapid troop lift in large-scale air-assault operations. The helicopter is, however, very vulnerable to light surface-to-air missiles and very easy to detect. It is obvious that a higher speed, less noisy, and more survivable system is needed to provide heavy lift in most modern combat situations.

The Mi-6 dates back to early 1957. A crane version is called the Mi-10K or Harke. The Mi-6 was the world's largest lift helicopter when it was introduced and set lift records that stood until the USSR deployed the more powerful Mil-12 Homer. The Mi-6 can carry up to 12,000 kilograms internally. Its normal maximum speed is 186 mile per hour. Its service ceiling is 14,750 feet. Its range with half payload is 404 miles (650 kilometers) and 155 miles (350 kilometers) with a 12,000 kilogram (26,460 lb.) load. It can carry up to 68 troops and combat vehicles like the BDRM. Over 1,000 of these craft were built, although nearly half are in civil use.[280]

Tactical and Defensive Changes

As has been discussed earlier, the Soviets came to use mixed forces of attack and escort helicopters and made heavy use of flares. They often began an attack with Mi-24s making dawn strafing runs over a suspected guerrilla stronghold such as an encampment or a village. The Soviets then deployed troops using both Mi-8s and Mi-24s. Jet fighters, such as the MiG-23 or Su-17 and the new Su-25 Frogfoot, were used to soften up the target when major resistance was expected. The assault helicopter attacks were increasingly followed by heliborne landings in surrounding areas in an attempt to surround guerrillas and choke off supplies. This tactic, often referred to as the "cordon and search," consisted of a methodical search-and-destroy effort in closed-off areas.[281]

The Soviets had far more landing sites in Afghanistan than the U.S. had in Vietnam. In some ways, however, they became trapped by the helicopter. They never refined their infantry tactics to fight in the mountains without helicopter support, and they came to depend on the helicopter for many of their movements, firepower, and protection of their lines of supply.

The Mujahideen were poorly equipped to take advantage of this over-dependence until 1987. As has been described earlier, they had some SA-7s, but these could be decoyed with flares, and most had to rely on machine guns and old AA guns. More and better AA guns helped, but it was the Stinger and Blowpipe that made a major difference.[282]

The Soviets also seem to have been exceptionally slow in deploying effective countermeasures to Blowpipe and Stinger, although they were quick to deploy countermeasures per se. The Hinds and other helicopters were rapidly equipped with dorsal-mounted IR jammers, and the Hinds were given improved stub-wing IR flare dispensers and intake/exhaust shrouds. The USSR also had an active IR jammer called "Hot Brick." Some sources say this was deployed in 1987, but others indicate it was not deployed until 1988.

The Hinds also were given improved armament. A Hind F variant appeared with GSu-23 23-mm twin mountings to replace the 12.7-mm Gatling gun on the Hind D and E. AT-6 Spiral missile launchers and nose-mounted guidance systems provided improved accuracy and long-range firepower. It is unclear how these changes might have affected the impact of Stinger if they had been deployed earlier in large numbers.[283]

Combined Operations

There is considerable debate over the quality of Soviet combined operations in Afghanistan. Many operations were slow to develop, were overly centralized, were slow moving in tempo, and made limited use of both maneuver and quick-reacting air power. Even in 1988, there were still complaints about the grindingly slow reaction time in getting air missions approved. Fully armed and ready Hinds would be sitting on an airfield under attack and still be waiting for command permission to fly defensive missions. Similar complaints continued about delays in getting command authority for fully ready helicopters or fighters to defend convoys. There was virtually no armed reconnaissance by fixed-wing aircraft, and it was only late in the war that pilots were allowed targets of opportunity.[284]

At their best, however, Soviet combined operations in Afghanistan increasingly involved close coordination between Soviet intelligence and the Soviet Army and Air Force. In its most elaborate form this consisted of intelligence collection by special KGB and NVD units associated with the KHAD (WAD). This was followed by an initial assault on an objective by Soviet fixed-wing aircraft, followed in turn by an attack by Soviet maneuver elements supported by Mi-24 Hind attack helicopters and assault and transport helicopters.[285]

The first of these operations began in 1981, largely as punitive raids. The Soviets would begin by assembling their air attack assets and conducting an extensive air bombardment of the target area. They would then land helicopter forces to stop the withdrawal of Mujahideen units and to attack from directions that the Mujahideen could not predict or defend. The Soviets would launch mechanized forces into the area. They would destroy both the villages and the agricultural infrastructure in the area and attempt to force the Mujahideen to retreat into the positions held by the heliborne forces.

These operations were continued with variations until the end of the war. In the process, the Soviets learned they had to steadily increase the tempo of operations, stress independent small-unit action, increase the number of heliborne assault forces, and mix ranger and strike forces with holding forces. They had to double and then triple the tempo of their mechanized operations and steadily increase the amount of infantry, artillery, and heliborne firepower directly under the unit commander actually in the battle area. Central or rear-area control was tantamount to ineffectiveness or defeat, as was any attempt to rigidly execute preplanned operations or use low-grade or untrained troops in critical roles. Young aggressive junior commanders given considerable freedom of action and direct control over the use of combined operations assets by flexible field grade officers became the key to success.

The Soviets steadily improved these capabilities, although such combined operations did not gather full momentum until 1983–1984, and the USSR still experienced major problems in making them effective well into 1986. The best examples of these types of operations in Afghanistan were in the strategic valleys such as the Logar and Shomali and especially the Panjshir and Kunar. Soviet combined operations continued to improve during 1984–1986, and this was especially true in regard to the offensives against the large rebel-held valleys. Pre–ground-attack aerial bombardment by fixed-wing aircraft increased in volume and accuracy. This increasing use of air power eased the task of the ground elements and reduced casualties.

After 1984, the Soviets improved their support of ground forces with fixed-wing bombardment in large offensives by initiating action with medium bombers. They followed up with bombing runs by high-speed strike fighters such as the MiG-21 and Su-25.[286] Medium bombers were increasingly used to destroy villages, towns, and other potential supply areas.

Strike fighters were used against specific targets of tactical importance. To carry out these missions, Soviet fighter pilots changed their tactics to nap-of-the-earth, low-level attack missions. In such attacks the Soviet fighters used cluster bombs with drogue chutes. The purpose of these chutes was apparently to help permit bomblets to disperse.[287]

The ability of assault helicopters to support ground operations increased steadily from 1982 to 1986. This was important with regard to both the large-scale offensives and the smaller-scale mountain operations and proved to be a practical validation of Soviet exercise doctrine dating back to the first Soviet assault helicopters used in integrated combat operations in mountainous terrain, which occurred during the KAVKAZ-76 exercise in 1976.[288]

Helicopters provided the third wave of support for ground troops after the medium bomber and close-strike forces. They helped to meet the immediate air support needs of the ground troops. In the mountains the helicopters were also used as a substitute for artillery, which could not always be transported into the more rugged areas of the mountains.[289]

The key remaining problems in the Soviet approach to combined operations before the Mujahideen acquired Stinger and Blowpipe were the lack of flexible maneuver in large-scale ground troop operations, the failure to develop flexible infantry forces that could sustain themselves on foot and dominate the countryside, and the failure to fully integrate air operations into ground operations in a way that gave field commanders direct control over all their air assets.[290]

As for the Soviet shift back to reliance on armor and artillery once the Stinger and Blowpipe were deployed, the resulting combined operations were not particularly impressive, with the exception of some well-planned operations in the Salang area and around Kandahar and Jalalabad. The Soviets often did not seem to be able to step up the tempo of their air operations or to find solutions like laser illumination or other targeting aids that would allow aircraft to reduce their vulnerability and still hit their targets. Artillery continued to react slowly in many cases, and accuracy was relatively poor unless the Soviet forces took a comparatively long time to deploy artillery-locating radars and similar assets.

It is difficult, however, to interpret the reversion to slow-moving advances dependent on artillery fire. By mid-1987, the USSR may well have decided to minimize casualties and withdraw and may have tailored its tactics accordingly. There was little point in "winning" pointless tactical encounters during 1988 and 1989, when the Soviets were clearly committed to withdrawing.

Logistics and Support

The Soviets began the war with the advantage of having nearly 1,000 Soviet advisors helping the Afghan government forces maintain sophisticated weapons like the Mi-24, Su-7B, and T-62. They shipped roughly 100 more T-62 tanks and 30 Mi-24 helicopters to Afghanistan in June 1979 to help the government deal with the rising Mujahideen threat, and they increased their maintenance personnel as they built their forces up just before the invasion. Interestingly enough, only a few days before the Soviet invasion in December 1979, Soviet maintenance personnel had the batteries removed from the tanks in the Afghan army under the guise of "winterizing" the tanks—a trick which sharply limited the effective armored strength of Afghan government forces.[291]

During 1979 and early 1980, the Soviets initially treated their presence as temporary and did little to create a permanent logistic base for combat. They secured the Salang Tunnel, created supply dumps, and established a secure line of strong points along the routes from the Soviet border to Kabul. After 1980, however, they steadily upgraded their maintenance and support facilities, improved critical aspects of the road system, and built up the major series of air bases discussed earlier.[292]

Once intensive fighting began, the Soviets rapidly began to experience serious repair and maintenance problems—particularly with equipment taken from Category II and Category III reserve status, or in Soviet Asian, as distinguished from White Russian, forces. The units had far more maintenance and support problems than Soviet Category I units. Asiatic technicians, for example, often had trouble even reading repair manuals written in Russian. The resulting logistics and maintenance burden was another factor that led to Soviet withdrawal of tank and other units with equipment that was not of immediate value in combat.

Further, the Soviets found that the Soviet-supplied equipment in DRA government forces required about two to three times as much maintenance as the equipment in Soviet forces. Once it was actively used in combat, the Soviets often had to assume much of the maintenance burden. The need to deploy repair shops and spare parts with any mobile force or invasion force was one of the major lessons the Soviets drew from the fighting.

The Soviets initially depended largely on the maintenance battalions in their ground units for most service and repair work. In a motorized rifle division, the battalion had 19 officers, 275 enlisted men, and 75 major vehicles, including cranes, armored recovery vehicles, PARM repair shops, and jeeps. A Ural-375 truck was often used as a tractor. Each combat regiment also had its own maintenance company with four officers, 62 other ranks, and a crane, two armored recovery vehicles, and 14 trucks. Each combat battalion relied on tents and field facilities. Other units relied heavily on hand tools and substitution of parts.

This organization did not prove adequate for operations in Afghanistan. New technical personnel and equipment had to be added. For example, a senior technical specialist was added to each repair company. Further, the repair system within combat regiments proved too rigid. The system was supposed to use a forward deployed technical observation point to evacuate or repair equipment to a repair evacuation point in the rear, but this proved too slow and too rigid except in a few Warsaw Pact–style armored operations like those in the Panjshir Valley. More and more repair assets had to be deployed forward on an on-call basis, and the Soviets had to provide most of the skilled repair work for the Afghan government forces.

Radios and other communications gear proved to be a particular problem, and the Soviets had to shift from repair in the rear to adding communications technicians and special repair vans like the M-2 mobile radio workshop to forward deployed units—particularly in large-scale offensives.

The Soviet Army also had to build up a network of spare parts and repair facilities, which had to be increased to compensate for two serious problems in Soviet force quality. First, most regular Soviet troops served in Afghanistan on six- to twelve-month tours. This led to constant rotation, and many Soviet repair, logistics, and support forces were rotated just when they had fully developed the special expertise necessary to deal with the service and combat repair problems typical of combat in Afghanistan. Further, Soviet forces did not have career cadres of NCOs and enlisted men in repair units and depended on conscripts serving only two years.

This lack of skilled and experienced manpower meant many added repairs had to be sent to the rear to repair depots. It also led to a fair amount of equipment being abandoned to the Mujahideen during both Soviet attacks and Mujahideen ambushes of Soviet convoys. Soviet forces had limited capability to repair armored and other vehicles under fire, and vehicles that a more adequate system could have recovered had to be abandoned.

After 1984, the Soviets built up major permanent repair shops and facilities. These were supplemented by the integration of Soviet depots and Afghan industrial facilities after mid-1985. This gave the Soviet 40th Army the facilities of a permanent garrison. Major repair depots were set up at Jalalabad and Herat, and a major vehicle workshop was created at Kabul. The facilities in Kabul were reported to be able to handle up to 900 trucks and 300 oil transports per day. In late 1986, there were seven to nine major Soviet vehicle repair and overhaul facilities in Afghanistan.

The Soviet Aviation Engineering Service (AES) had similar problems at the start of the war. It had to organize new repair facilities as part of the 10th Tactical Air Army the Soviets deployed to Afghanistan—although the heavy Soviet reliance on older MiG-21 and Su-17 fighters somewhat simplified the AES's task.

From 1980 to 1982, the Soviets set up field repair stations using UPS-16-T inflatable tents at most of the active air bases outside Kabul, replacing them in mid-1982 with fixed facilities. The Soviets also steadily increased the sophistication of their main repair facilities at Bagram as they began to deploy additional fighter types like the Su-25. By 1986, these new fighter types included the MiG-23, MiG-25B/D, and MiG-29, and repair facilities at Bagram were expanded to be able to handle major combat repairs normally done in Soviet depots.

The Soviets transferred functions like sheet metal repairs of fighters, which are normally done in major workshops in the rear, to forward air bases. They created special trailers with aircraft repair equipment—including a welder, drills, grinders, power source, and patching material. These were tailored to perform the relatively light repairs required to deal with the Mujahideen AA guns and SA-7 threat. Further, the Soviets developed special field kits for helicopter and aircraft repairs in remote areas. These kits included equipment such as portable argon-arc welders. Even at the time of the Soviet withdrawal, sophisticated equipment like FLIR and other critical avionics were repaired on a box substitution or SWAP basis.

The USSR improved the repair facilities at the major Soviet air bases in the border area, and airfield and repair shops at facilities like Karshi-Khanabad, Mary, and Chardzhou in Turkestan began to bear some of the major maintenance burden. Shindand and Kandahar were given the capability to service bombers once the Soviets started to use the Tu-16 and Su-24, and Jalalabad was given specialized repair facilities for transport aircraft and helicopters.

Soviet helicopters generally proved easy to repair in the field, and their large gear boxes and the easy accessibility of communications and radar reduced the burden at the field level. Some had very short rotor lives. They required more frequent major overhauls than Western helicopters, but predictable maintenance is easier to handle than unscheduled maintenance, and the overall operational availability of Soviet helicopters was high.

The Soviets steadily improved their forward maintenance and repair capability as a result of the lessons they learned during the war, but it is unclear whether or not this led to a broader change in Soviet forces. The Soviets also improved the level of maintenance training in the Asiatic units they returned to Afghanistan, but it is unclear whether this reflected special training for the units sent to the war or an overall improvement in Asiatic units. The general problems the USSR had with its high rotation rate and severe shortages of career NCOs and enlisted men with repair training seemed to remain unchanged.

The Soviet approach to the maintenance of complex ground equipment in Afghanistan reflects a vastly different form of tasking than that found in Western armies. Highly trained officers perform nearly all preventive and corrective maintenance, while enlisted personnel perform only the most basic maintenance functions. This practice appears to have been carried on in Afghanistan with respect to most major systems.[293]

The logistics lessons from the war are also significant. The Soviets were largely successful in making their supply push or forward delivery system work, but they never fully solved the problem of how to fight the highway war (*dorozhnaia voina*) and find the best mix of road and helicopter movement. While the Soviets relied heavily on airlift until 1987–1988, most supplies arriving in Afghanistan from the Soviet Union were still moved by truck convoys. These convoys involved 100 to 300 vehicles, about 30 percent of which were convoy defense vehicles. The remaining vehicles were evenly divided between POL (petroleum, oil, and lubricant) carriers and supply carriers.

The Soviet convoys generally formed at the main Soviet Kairaton Transhipment Complex at Termez or at Kushka on the border to the east. They moved south along routes to Herat or to the Pol-e-Khomri Logistic Facility. The convoys using the latter route from Termez to Kabul had to travel 450 kilometers, including the 2,700-meter long Salang Tunnel. Further, the difficult mountain conditions required 70–90 percent more gasoline than routes in Europe and 30 to 40 percent more diesel fuel.

These conditions provided a severe test of the new Soviet material support battalions that were replacing the motor transport battalions and separate supply elements that had previously supported line divisions. The USSR was eventually forced to deploy over thirty such battalions and a transport brigade and to create more than a dozen major depots in Afghanistan and nearby areas of the USSR. It soon became apparent that reservists and ordinary conscripts could not handle the workload, that these routes required carefully trained drivers, and that only the KamAZ trucks held up on these routes. The USSR also began to form the equivalent of material support brigades to allocate the work more efficiently.

Soviet convoys represented lucrative targets to the Mujahideen and served as the weak link in the Soviet logistical system. This increasingly led the Soviets to build up fire bases and strong points along all major supply routes, to use larger convoys, and to escort convoys traveling through dangerous areas with helicopters.[294] The Soviets also attempted to reduce the need for convoys by increasing river traffic where possible and building two pipelines along the Termez-Salang-Kabul road. These pipelines were so vulnerable, however, that a brigade of special pipeline construction troops had to be deployed to try to keep them open. The USSR also had to establish more than fifteen POL storage sites.

The Mujahideen became expert at using rock slides, fires, bridge demolitions, mines, and mortars and in attacking from high ground. They learned to create caves and attack from several directions at once. It took two weeks to complete the round trip from Termez to Kabul, and the maximum number of trips any driver could normally make in a two-year enlistment was eighty. The trips were so dangerous that pennants for "courage and valor" were awarded for twenty, forty, sixty, and eighty trips.

The Soviets responded by strengthening the forces escorting each convoy and improving all key transit links to reduce transit time and vulnerability. Large convoys came to have military escorts in front, within, and behind the convoy. Special support elements were set up to tow, repair, or destroy vehicles while in transit. ZU-23 23-mm twin-barreled AA guns were mounted on KamAZ trucks to provide support fire.

The USSR also increased the number of strong points along each route and set up roving patrols and sapper, traffic control, and repair units to deal with problems and attacks. They systematically strengthened the coverage of major routes, and they deployed a Soviet airborne unit of battalion size, an Afghan battalion, and Afghan militia to protect the Salang Tunnel. The sappers found mine removal to be a full-time job and used armored mine rolling vehicles, mine detectors, mine probes, and possibly mine-sniffing dogs.[295]

The Soviets often used helicopters to resupply units that had been cut off by the rebels. One Soviet account of the war, for example, mentions Soviet helicopters transporting water to an isolated Afghan battalion. Without this water, the account claims, the battalion would have perished. One additional component of the Soviet logistics system was the use of various local militias to help guard supply routes. This use of local forces helped keep routes free of mines, obstacles, and booby traps, in addition to helping prevent the Mujahideen from preparing ambushes and positioning themselves in locations enabling them to fire upon Soviet or DRA convoys.[296]

Like the U.S. in Vietnam, the Soviets also made constant use of heavy lift helicopters and fixed-wing transports from the day they arrived until the day they left. Air resupply was essential for rapid troop movement, reinforcement of threatened cities, response to Mujahideen attacks on roads, and a host of other problems than no land-based supply system could deal with. As early as 22–26 December 1979, for example, the Soviets flew over 350 Antonov and Ilyushin heavy transport sorties to Kabul. Airlift became essential in many areas during 1980, as the Mujahideen improved their capability to interdict road movement. It was still essential in 1983, when the Soviets had to donate some 1,500 KamAZ trucks to the DRA to make up for its losses in road movement. The USSR did, however, have major problems in organizing efficient airlift in many instances. It could take up to one and one-half hours simply to refuel an AN-12.[297]

The story of Mujahideen supply effort is familiar from the world press. It was largely a saga of man-packed supply and the occasional use of trucks in grueling infiltration efforts across the Iranian and Pakistani borders, small stockpiles, growing food and sanctuary problems, and an almost total lack of medical care. The main lessons of this effort are:

- The virtual impossibility of sealing off infiltration by guerrillas in a country where the guerrillas control the countryside and have popular support.
- The acute medical effects on both guerrillas and the local populace of having to operate without proper medical care. There is a clear need for light emergency medical packs with very simple instructions for use and emergency aid kits for doctors tailored to the weapons and wound characteristics of the war to reduce rebel casualties.
- The unexpectedly high mobility of guerrilla forces and logistics throughout in spite of draconian Soviet efforts to cut off supply.
- The critical importance of munitions and weapons size and weight. Many weapons are marginally too heavy, and the Mujahideen often ran out of ammunition, particularly for mortars and RPGs, simply because of manpower limits. Similarly, there is a critical need for "low training" point-and-kill or shoot-and-hit weapons which can be broadly disseminated to popular forces with little or no training and limited native literacy.
- The inability of modern sensors to track and inhibit infiltration which can take advantage of night and rough terrain and shelter in population areas.

In short, the Mujahideen experience closely parallels the Viet Cong experience in Vietnam. While a small, relatively homogeneous country like Israel can limit guerrilla supply, regular armed forces operating over a larger alien territory cannot. The population must be won over, destroyed, or driven into exile to shut off guerrilla supply.

Chemical/Biological Weapons and Defensive Systems

The Soviet Union seems to have made at least limited use of chemical agents (possibly nerve agents), and may possibly have used biological agents (possibly trichothecene mycotoxin). It also seems to have experimented with a wide range of delivery systems. These included aircraft, artillery, and multiple rocket launchers. Soviet use of such weapons seems to have been reduced after 1982 and to have halted after 1986. All of the evidence surrounding Soviet use of chemical weapons is controversial, however, and the major source for reports of Soviet use are U.S. government reports which cannot be independently verified.[298]

Mujahideen reports of Soviet use of chemical weapons and toxins began shortly after the start of the war. These reports included incidents in the northwest near Herat, in three areas near Kandahar, in areas near Gardez and north of Kabul, and in the border areas in Paktia. The U.S. State Department later stated it had evidence to confirm most of these Mujahideen reports. It also indicated that the Soviets and DRA government began to use chemical agents against Mujahideen groups nearly six months before the invasion of 27 December 1979.[299]

The first reports of a major use of chemical weapons occurred on 16 November 1979, when Afghan government Il-28 bombers were reported to have dropped chemical bombs along with conventional bombs on targets in Farah and Herat and in Badghis province. Afghan defectors reported that Soviet advisors provided both special training and supplies of lethal and incapacitating agents.

From 1979 to the summer of 1981, the U.S. government received reports of 47 separate chemical attacks with a claimed death toll of over 3,000. In 24 of the cases, there was independent evidence of the use of chemicals, and in 20 cases Soviet or Afghan combat operations were confirmed to be in progress in the areas and at the time where the use of chemicals was reported.

The bulk of the initial attacks were reported to be on villages or sheltered areas where the Mujahideen were believed to have dispersed. While none of these agents was firmly identified, the medical reports on victims found symptoms of paralysis, blisters, bleeding, and other neurological effects. The symptoms included death and were far more toxic than riot control agents like CN, CS, or Adamsite.

Ten separate chemical attacks were reported in the first months of 1980, largely in northeastern Afghanistan. Helicopter attacks were particularly common, and symptoms were often similar to those suffered by Hmong refugees in Cambodia. By the spring and summer of 1980, chemical attacks were common in all areas of resistance. These attacks increasingly seemed to be designed to drive Mujahideen forces into the open where they could be hit by conventional weapons or attacked by heliborne and air-assault units. One Dutch journalist reported the use of Mi-24s to deliver gas agents, and other Afghan sources reported similar Mi-24 attacks. During this period, attacks were reported near Herat, and a Soviet chemical warfare battalion is known to have set up decontamination facilities in Shindand.

The Soviet attacks in 1981 were reported to be similar. The Soviets continued to use Mi-24 helicopters, although they also seem to have used RPK cluster bombs with gas-armed bomblets. The targets of the attacks also seem to have broadened to include supply movements. Soviet soldiers are reported to have made use of CW hand grenades. These grenades were used to attack Mujahideen operating in tunnels and caves. It is not known whether the agents employed in conjunction with these grenades were lethal or merely incapacitating.

Soviet troops appear to have pumped some form of CBW agent from armored vehicles in Logar province.[300] Soviet helicopters are also reported to have dropped bombs containing toxic chemicals and to have made use of spray devices. These latter spray tanks have been used to poison crops, although they could also conceivably have some role in applying anti-personnel agents.[301]

Reports of Soviet gas attacks continued in 1982, and these attacks produced the chronology shown in Table 2.15. The Soviets may also have shifted from mustard and nerve gases to the use of weapons which produced more terrifying physical symptoms. These agents seem to have included "yellow rain," trichothecene mycotoxins, Tabun, Phosgene or Phosgene oxide, and other agents. The mycotoxins like yellow rain, "sleeping death," and "Blue X" seem to have been used in considerable amounts.

The use of yellow rain leads the victim to experience intense burning sensations, vomiting, headaches, spasms, and convulsions. Internal bleeding follows, followed by the destruction of the bone marrow. The skin then turns black as necrosis sets in and immediately becomes gangrenous. The time from exposure to physical decomposition may be a matter of hours. Sleeping death causes instant death to the victim without affecting the central nervous system. Victims have been found in their fighting positions, holding their rifles, their eyes open, their finger on the trigger, and with no apparent cause of death. The agent seems to be odorless and extremely lethal. Blue X is a non-lethal agent dispensed in aerosol form and dropped from aircraft. It renders the victim unconscious for eight to twelve hours.[302]

Soviet gas attacks were increasingly conducted in coordination with Soviet air assault operations and used to try to force the Mujahideen into exposed killing areas that could be exploited by Soviet troops flown into the area in Mi-8 (Hip) helicopters.[303] The use of pumped gas in September 1982 was evidently to try to poison underground waterways where the Mujahideen were hiding. Cuban sources outside of Afghanistan have confirmed the existence of such equipment.[304]

According to most reports, the Soviets cut back sharply on their use of chemical warfare after 1982. If available reports are correct, the Soviets seem to have made increasing use of air burst bombs and cluster munitions during 1984–1986, when they did deliver gas agents. They seem to have preferred the use of helicopters because these allowed

TABLE 2.15 Soviet Gas Warfare Attacks in 1982

Date	Village / Location	Method of Attack	Form of Material	Persons Killed	Wounded
Early Feb.	North of Shindand	aircraft	yellow substance	4	?
4, 5 Feb.	South of Shindand	helicopter	yellow substance	0	?
19 Feb.	Badakhshan Province	aircraft	yellow crystals	?	?
May– June	Kandahar Province	helicopter rockets	black, yellow, white gasses	3	15
June	Farah Province	aircraft bombs	red, black, white smoke	?	?
11 June	Kandahar Province	aircraft bombs	?	15	30
June	Baghlan Province	helicopter	?	?	?
July	Panjshir Valley	aircraft	nerve gas	0	0
12–13 Sept.	Logar Province	pumped from armored vehicle	gas	73	0
Sept.	Logar Province	?	?	7	?
Late Sept./ Early Oct.	Baghlan Province	aircraft bombs	?	?	?

SOURCE: U.S. Department of State, *Chemical Warfare in Southeast Asia and Afghanistan: An Update*, Special Report No. 104 (Washington, D.C.: GPO, November 1982).

quick but accurate delivery. They also developed a helicopter tactic in which the helicopters dropped chemical bombs and then fired air-to-ground rockets into the chemical cloud to increase dispersion.[305] The Russians continued to use artillery as well, however, and on at least one occasion they may have caused losses to the "friendly fire" of gas shells.

Soviet forces seem to have made particularly heavy use of chemical weapons during the fighting in Paghman and Chesmibulbul in October and November 1986. Canisters were also dropped into irrigation shafts and tunnels, producing symptoms similar to that of cyanosis. Some weapons also seem to have been used in the Nazian border district at this time.[306] Although scattered reports of the use of chemical agents occurred after this time, the Soviets seem to have reduced or ended their use of such agents.

There are several possible explanations. First, only a relatively few reported uses of chemical weapons seem to have had much effect on the Mujahideen. Most reports involved casualties largely among non-combatant villagers and refugees. Second, worldwide publicity may have affected Soviet behavior. Third, the Soviet shift to mass bombing in 1983–1984, along with the use of burning agents and new bombs, may have produced a more effective killing mechanism with far less negative publicity. Finally, the use of gas weapons involved complex weapons handling and decontamination and restricted troop operations in the vicinity.

The Mujahideen could do little to defend against Soviet CBW attacks. They had no protective masks or collective protection equipment. One interesting solution, supposedly suggested by Chinese advisors, involved the use of rubber materials to encircle Afghan encampments exposed to the threat of chemical warfare. When these encampments were attacked with CW agents, the Afghans then set the rubber on fire. The burning rubber supposedly put up a thermal barrier between the target and the chemical agents. In addition, the cloud of carbon (soot) was supposed to absorb the agent in the air and thus reduce the downwind danger.

It is interesting to note that gas had less impact as a terror weapon in Afghanistan than in Iran and that Mujahideen accounts of the most devastating weapons focus on butterfly mines or fuel-air explosives and incendiaries. Like the Iran-Iraq War, the Afghan War also indicates that a fairly wide range of alternative military methods are as militarily effective as gas. While Mujahideen reports often refer to gas warfare, the more believable accounts of its use do not imply that such use accounted for large numbers of killed and wounded in Afghanistan.

Nuclear Weapons

The Soviets did not use nuclear weapons in Afghanistan. They might, however, have been useful in some circumstances. They could have been employed as part of the campaign to destroy the rural infrastructure or against fixed Mujahideen strong points. The Soviets were believed to possess artillery shells and bombs with enhanced radiation options. These would have been particularly effective in producing population kills without major physical damage or lingering radiation.

Conclusions

The lessons that the Soviet Union learned in Afghanistan are so complex, and involve so many details, that it is difficult to generalize. In fact, Marshall Kilikov, then commander-in-chief of the Warsaw Pact, said in 1987, "There is no war there in a conventional sense. It is difficult to apply experience there in a war as might be applied to Europe. War in Afghanistan is very strange."[307]

The irony is that the most important lesson that the USSR has learned from the war is very similar to the lesson the U.S. learned in Vietnam: It should never have been fought. Force is a very uncertain means of saving a people from itself or a truly unpopular or incompetent and/or unpopular leadership from its people. As Aleksander Bovin, a leading commentator in *Izvestiya* put it, "We clearly overestimated our possibilities and underestimated what could be called the resistance of the environment."[308] It is doubtful that this belated wisdom will ever be much consolation to the Soviet casualties in the war or to the people of Afghanistan.

Notes

1. This estimate is based upon Mark Urban, *The War in Afghanistan* (London: St. Martin's Press, 1988), pp. 42, 47, 48, 55. To put this strength in perspective, the USSR invaded Czechoslovakia with roughly 250,000 men.

2. James C. Bussert, "Signal Troops Central to Soviet Afghanistan Invasion," *Defense Electronics* (June 1983), p. 104.

3. Stephen T. Hosmer and Thomas W. Wolfe, *Soviet Policy and Practice Toward Third World Conflicts* (Lexington: Lexington Books, 1983), p. 120.

4. This estimate is based upon Urban, *The War in Afghanistan*, pp. 66–67.

5. Department of Defense, *Soviet Military Power* (Washington, D.C.: State Department, 1985), p. 116; Craig Karp, "Afghanistan: Eight Years of Soviet Occupation," *Department of State Bulletin*, Vol. 88, No. 2132, pp. 1–24 (March 1988); *Jane's Defence Weekly* (April 23, 1988), p. 793.

6. Estimates differ sharply. For example, the State Department estimates that Soviet forces in late 1987 included the 5th 201st, 108th, and 103rd guards and the 40th Division, plus the 3rd Spetsnaz Brigade and the 866th, 375th, 66th, 191st, and 70th brigades (U.S. Department of State, 12-87, INR/GE 7363). David Isby estimates that the Soviet order of battle was 103rd Airborne Division (NW Camp, Kabul); 108th (NE Camp, Kabul), 201st (Kunduz), and

5th guards (Shindand), 357th (Kushka, USSR) and 360th (Termez, USSR) motorized rifle divisions; 70th (Kandahar) and 66th (Jalalabad) motorized rifle regiments), 191st (Ghazni) and 866th (Faizabad) motorized rifle regiments; 56th Air Assault Brigade (Gardez); three Spetsnaz brigades (Kabul, Shindand, Kandahar); 375th Guards Airborne Regiment (Bagram); 40th Airmobile Battalion (Kabul), 40th Airfield Defense Battalion (Bagram); 40th Heavy Artillery Brigade (Kabul), and two KGB mobile border guard groups (Kabul and Herat). David C. Isby, *Weapons and Tactics of the Soviet Army, Fully Revised Edition* (London: Jane's, 1988), pp. 34–35.

7. The initial invasion forces were largely Kazaks, Tajiks, Turkomens, and Uzbecks.

8. Captain Charles G. Wheeler, "The Forces in Conflict: Perspectives on Afghanistan," *Military Review* (July 1987), pp. 52–72. Albert A. Stahel and Paul Burcherer, *Afghanistan: Five Years of Resistance and Guerrilla Warfare* (Washington, D.C.: Freedom Policy Foundation, 1986), pp. 8 and 11.

9. *Washington Times* (November 14, 1985, and January 15, 1986); *New York Times* (November 2, 1985). Some U.S. intelligence experts believed the functioning strength of the Afghan army had dropped to 30,000 men in early 1984. See *New York Times* (May 15, 1984). Karp, op. cit., p. 15.

10. *Jane's Defence Weekly* (July 7, 1984).

11. This estimate of land and air strength is based on the figures in International Institute for Strategic Studies (IISS), *Military Balance, 1987/1988* (London, 1989), p. 43; and in Department of Defense, *Soviet Military Power, 1987* (Washington, D.C.: GPO, 1987).

12. The Soviet-backed regime was called the Democratic Republic of Afghanistan (DRA) at the beginning of the war but changed its name to the Republic of Afghanistan (RA) at the end of the war in an attempt to reduce its identification with a Marxist-dominated regime.

13. ACDA, *World Military Expenditures and Arms Transfers, 1987* (Washington, D.C.: Government Printing Office, 1988), p. 48.

14. IISS, *Military Balance*, various years.

15. Mark Galeotti, "Afghan Army Elite Forces," *Armed Forces* (September 1988), pp. 424–425.

16. Edgar O'Ballance, "Soviet Tactics in Afghanistan," *Military Review* (August 1980).

17. For examples of mutinies, see Reuters Dispatch, "Afghan Army Unit Reported to Rebel in Four-Hour Battle," *New York Times* (August 6, 1979); Michael T. Kaufman, "Afghan Guerrillas Boast of Success in Struggle Against Soviet Backed Regime," *New York Times* (August 14, 1979); "Afghan Generals Arrested," *Jane's Defence Weekly* (January 18, 1986), p. 43; *Baltimore Sun* (June 26, 1985); and *Washington Times* (June 26, 1985).

18. Selig S. Harrison, "Dateline Afghanistan: Exit Through Finland," *Foreign Policy*, No. 41 (Winter 1980–81), p. 170.

19. Ibid. See also Jonathan R. Adelman, "The Soviet Uses of Force: Four Cases in Soviet Crisis Decision Making," *Crossroads*, No. 16 (1985), pp. 47–81; and Geoffrey Warhurst, "Afghanistan—A Dissenting Appraisal," *RUSI Journal* (September 1980), pp. 26–36.

20. Some sources put full-time active manning as low as 20,000. Hosmer and Wolfe, op. cit., p. 119; and Drew Middleton, "Three Soviet Drives Reported in Afghanistan," *New York Times* (July 25, 1984), p. 43.

21. Anthony Arnold, *Afghanistan's Two-Party Communism* (Stanford, Calif: Hoover Institution, 1983), p. 84.

22. IISS, *Military Balance, 1985*, p. 95, and *1986*, p. 119. The air force strength is difficult to estimate since large numbers of Czech and Cuban "advisors" served in a 7,000-man force, and Afghan air force officers had to be shot for sabotaging Soviet aircraft. See *Washington Times* and *Baltimore Sun* (June 26, 1985).

23. The DRA army, like the Soviet army, has a grade of junior lieutenant (i.e., third lieutenant).

24. These trend estimates are based on Karp, op. cit.

25. Estimates are based on various editions of the IISS *Military Balance* and John Hill, "Afghanistan in 1988: Year of the Mujahideen," *Armed Forces Journal International* (March 1989), pp. 72–80.

26. These figures are based on IISS estimates. They do not include correction for the up to 9,000 weapons the Soviets reported leaving behind.

27. The officials involved were Mohammed Gulabzoi and Assadullah Sawari.

28. Estimates are based on various editions of the IISS *Military Balance* and Hill, op. cit.

29. Rosanne Klass, "Afghanistan: The Accords," *Foreign Affairs* (Summer 1988), pp. 922–945.

30. See Mark Urban, "A More Competent Afghan Army," *Jane's Defence Weekly* (November 23, 1985), pp. 1147–1151, and "That's a Russian in Disguise," *The Economist* (October 26, 1985), pp. 46–48; "Russia's Costly Bargain in Afghanistan," *The Economist* (November 30, 1985), pp. 37–38; and Anthony Arnold, "The Stony Path to Afghan Socialism," and Robert L. Canfield, "Islamic Sources of Resistance," both in *Orbis*, Vol. 29, No. 1 (Spring 1985), pp. 40–71.

31. This estimate is based on the figures in IISS, *Military Balance, 1988/1989*, pp. 150–151; the *Washington Post* (May 1, 1988), p. A-24; and Hill, op. cit.

32. Adapted from printouts furnished by the U.S. Arms Control and Disarmament Agency.

33. See *Jane's Defence Weekly* (November 5, 1988), p. 1156.

34. Ethnic estimates of Afghanistan are highly controversial. A July 1987 estimate by the CIA puts the total population at 14,184,000, with an annual growth rate of 1.44 percent. This included an estimate subtracting refugee movements to Iran and Pakistan in recent years, but not back to 1979. The population was estimated to be 50 percent Pushtun, 25 percent Tajik, 9 percent Uzbeck, and 9 percent Hazra. Other ethnic groups included Chahar Aimaks, Turkomens, Baluchi, and others. The religion was 74 percent Sunni, 25 percent Shi'ite, and 1 percent other. The language was 50 percent Pushtun, 35 percent Afghan Persian (Dari), 11 percent Turkic languages, and 4 percent about thirty minor languages, including Baluchi and Pashai. No recent estimates exist of

the labor force. In 1980, it was 4.98 million, with 68 percent in agriculture, 10 percent industry, 6 percent construction, 5 percent commerce, and 9 percent other. Life expectancy was about 42 years, and literacy was 12 percent.

35. These strength estimates are very uncertain and show the levels in 1988. They are based upon Karp, op. cit., p. 15; Urban, *The War in Afghanistan*, pp. 241–244; and Hill, op. cit.

36. *Washington Post* (January 13, 1985); *Houston Chronicle* (December 23, 1984); *USA Today* (January 14, 1985); *Washington Post* (September 4, 1985). Also see Alex R. Alexiev, "Soviet Strategy and the Mujahideen," *Orbis*, Vol. 29, No. 1 (Spring 1985), pp. 15–20.

37. Estimates differ sharply by source. The data seem to be reasonable estimates but also seem to be in fiscal rather than calendar years. See Tim Weiner, "The CIA's Leaking Pipeline," *Philadelphia Inquirer* (February 28, 1988), pp. 1–A and 12–A.

38. Michael Yardley, "Afghanistan, A First Hand View," *International Defense Review*, Vol. 20, No. 3 (1987), pp. 275–277; *Christian Science Monitor* (December 8, 1987), p. 15.

39. See A Nearby Observer, "The Afghan-Soviet War: Stalemate or Evolution," *The Middle East Journal* (Spring 1982); and Major John M. Hutcheson, "Scorched-Earth Policy: Soviets in Afghanistan," *Military Review* (April 1982), p. 36.

40. For a good introduction to the interparty struggles see Arnold, *Afghanistan's Two-Party Communism*.

41. Urban, *The War in Afghanistan*, pp. 29–30.

42. Ibid., pp. 32–34.

43. It is important to note that there is considerable evidence that the Soviet decision to invade Afghanistan was taken by a cadre of three or four civilian leaders and that more of the Politburo did not know of the decision until the invasion had taken place. Members of the Central Committee went out of their way in 1988 to indicate that the approval of the invasion was not made by the Committee or any formal Soviet decision process. This may, of course, have been intended to decouple the current leadership with the leadership that had started the war. *New York Times* (March 30, 1988), p. 11.

44. *International Herald Tribune* (September 21, 1979), and *Washington Post* (January 2, 1980).

45. Urban, *The War in Afghanistan*, p. 39.

46. Ibid., p. 66.

47. Some elements of the 105th Guards Air Assault Division may have been included in the 70th Motorized Rifle Brigade. Urban, *The War in Afghanistan*, p. 67.

48. The lower figure seems likely to be more accurate. The higher figure is a U.S. State Department estimate.

49. Urban, *The War in Afghanistan*, p. 81.

50. Some senior personnel may have defected to Pakistan in late 1982.

51. *Washington Post* (February 12, 1989), p. A–1.

52. Ibid.

53. Najibullah was born to a white-collar family in 1947 and joined the

Communist Party while in secondary school. He studied medicine at Kabul University and was jailed twice for subversive activities. He was an early ally of Karmal and the Parcham faction. He joined the Central Committee in 1975 and then the Revolutionary Council created after the Communist takeover. He changed his name to Najib to remove its religious character (Ullah=Allah). He served as ambassador in Iran and was then expelled for plotting against the rival Khalq faction. The USSR brought him back to Afghanistan in 1979 and made him a senior official in the Khad. He assumed the rank of lieutenant general and became a full member of the Afghan Politburo in 1981. He was appointed to the ruling secretariat in December 1985.

54. *Washington Post* (February 12, 1989), p. A–1.

55. The author would like to thank several members of the Defense Intelligence Agency for an informal review of the data for 1987–1988. He has also drawn heavily on the work of Richard P. Cronin of the Congressional Research Service and his series "Afghanistan Peace Talks: An Annotated Chronology and Analysis of the United Nations–Sponsored Negotiations," CRS 88-149F (Washington, D.C.: Congressional Research Service, 1988), and on Karp, op. cit..

56. Based on interviews by the author and on Karp, op. cit., p. 15.

57. The U.S. had tentatively agreed to act as the guarantor of such an agreement and halt its aid if the Soviets withdrew in December 1985. There was then little prospect of such withdrawal. It later became clear that such agreement did not have President Reagan's approval. *New York Times* (February 11, 1988), p. 12.

58. *Washington Times* (September 10, 1987), p. A–10.

59. Herat is a major junction city, with the Soviet border 100 kilometers north and Kahriz some 150 kilometers to the west on the Iran border. There are road links to Kabul and Kandahar. The unit's equipment is interesting. It had a BM-21 122-mm MRL, two 82-mm mortars, two 14.5-mm and eleven 12.7-mm AA guns, four 7.62-mm machine guns, 500 AK-17 rifles, 350 carbines, 200 .303 Enfield rifles, five pistols, extensive small arm ammunition, five R-105 field radios, two vehicles, and nearly 200 tons of food. *Jane's Defence Weekly* (January 9, 1988), p. 7.

60. *Washington Post* (February 12, 1989), p. A–1.

61. Richard P. Cronin and Francis T. Miko, "Afghanistan: Status, U.S. Role, and Implications of Soviet Withdrawal," Congressional Research Service, IB88049 (January 1989), p. 1.

62. *Washington Times* (April 11, 1988), p. 1; *Washington Times* (June 28, 1988), p. A–7.

63. *New York Times* (August 14, 1988), p. 9.

64. *New York Times* (July 26, 1988).

65. *Washington Post* (August 31, 1988), p. A–19.

66. Mohibullah Khan, the Mujahideen leader making these claims, also claimed to have destroyed 20 dumps of fuel, 20,000 tons of food, 113 armored vehicles, 137 trucks and jeeps, and four helicopters. *Washington Times* (August 24, 1988), p. 9.

67. *Washington Post* (August 15, 1988), p. A–1.

68. *New York Times* (October 19, 1988), p. A–3.

69. *Jane's Defence Weekly* (November 5, 1988), p. 1156.

70. *Aviation Week* (November 7, 1988), p. 21; *New York Times* (October 29, 1988), p. 1.

71. *Washington Times* (November 7, 1988), p. A–1.

72. *Izvestiya* (November 11, 1988).

73. *Pravda* (November 13, 1988).

74. Tass (December 27, 1988).

75. *Washington Post* (February 7, 1989), p. A–1.

76. *Wall Street Journal* (February 7, 1989), p. A–24.

77. *Washington Times* (November 18, 1989), p. 8.

78. Louis Dupree, *Afghanistan* (Princeton: Princeton University Press, 1980).

79. Adapted from CIA, *The World Factbook, 1987* (Washington, D.C: Government Printing Office, 1988), pp. 1–2.

80. *New York Times* (June 17, 1988), p. A–1.

81. James B. Curren and Phillip Karber, "Afghanistan's Ordeal," *Armed Forces Journal* (March 1985), pp. 78–103.

82. *Washington Post* (January 16, 1986); *New York Times* (November 3, 1985); *Jane's Defence Weekly* (July 7, 1984); Yossef Bodansky, "New Weapons in Afghanistan," *Jane's Defence Weekly* (March 9, 1985), p. 412.

83. Isby, *Weapons and Tactics of the Soviet Army, Fully Revised Edition*, pp. 489–490.

84. Oliver Roy, "Afghanistan: Four Years of Soviet Occupation," *Swiss Review of World Affairs*, Vol. 32, No. 12 (March 1984), p. 11.

85. William J. Eaton, "Key Afghan Rebel Reportedly Eludes Capture," *Los Angeles Times* (May 2, 1984), p. 10. Massoud was the most well known commander of the Afghan resistance.

86. Bussert, op. cit.

87. Much of the following analysis in this section, and the sections on combined arms and infantry, is adapted from the various writings of David C. Isby, including an advance copy of Chapter Six of his revised edition of *The Soviet Army* (London: Jane's, 1988). Other works cited include Amphibious Warfare School Conference Group on Afghanistan, "Battle Study: The Soviet War in Afghanistan," *Marine Corps Gazette* (July 1986), pp. 58–65; Mark L. Urban, "Soviet Forces in Afghanistan," *Jane's Defence Weekly* (January 12, 1985), and "Afghanistan: A New Horizon for the Soviets," *Jane's Defence Weekly* (February 8, 1986), pp. 209–211; and Ian Kemp, "Abdul Haq: Soviet Mistakes in Afghanistan," *Jane's Defence Weekly* (March 5, 1988), pp. 380–381. Extensive use is also made of Mark Urban's *The War in Afghanistan*.

88. See Yossef Bodansky, "Learning Afghanistan's Lessons," *Jane's Defence Weekly* (February 20, 1988), pp. 310–311.

89. *The Soviet Army: Specialized Warfare and Rear Area Support*, FN 100-2-2 (Washington, D.C.: Government Printing Office, July 1984).

90. Urban, *The War in Afghanistan*, p. 132.

91. It is far from clear that this short tour of duty system worked, and the Soviets did improve conscript training and alter tours of duty to increase the amount of experience in their forces as time went on. Drug addiction became

a major problem, and Soviet officer reports reflect an increasing problem with "irregular relations" (homosexuality). Some Soviet soldiers even defected to the Mujahideen. The Soviets failed to properly improve living conditions or provide adequate food and medical care for ordinary troops, and they did little to solve the morale problems of conscript forces. For typical reports toward the latter period of the war, see Alexander Alexiev, *Inside the Soviet Army in Afghanistan*, Santa Monica, RAND R-3627-A, 1988, pp. 5–14 and 35–60; the *Boston Globe* (January 31, 1987), p. 1; *Jane's Defence Weekly* (October 18, 1986), pp. 888–889; and the *New York City Tribune* (July 8, 1987), p. 1.

92. It is interesting to note that Colonel General D.A. Dragunskiy, the author of a new book on tactics against NATO called *Motorized Rifle (Tank) Battalion in Combat*, has written a text which reflects a number of lessons from Afghanistan, including the need to increase the tempo of operations, emphasize speed, and give the battalion commander more emphasis, particularly in selecting the equipment and methods necessary to achieve his objectives.

93. Urban, "Afghanistan: A New Horizon for the Soviets," pp. 209–210.

94. Haq was a commander of the Hezb-i-Islami forces near Kabul. Almerigo Gritz, "Abdul Haq: My Fight with the Red Army," *Jane's Defence Weekly* (February 7, 1987), pp. 181–182.

95. If anything, there are some indications that the Soviets developed jamming capability against Pakistani C^3 facilities in the border area at some point in 1985.

96. "Resistance Leader Tactics of Groups Operations Surveyed," *L'Express*, Paris (February 23, 1984).

97. "U.S. Aid Question Divides Administration," *Washington Times* (July 20, 1984), p. 7A.

98. Some ZSU-23-4s were rebuilt to allow higher elevation for firing at targets on mountainsides.

99. *The Soviet Army: Specialized Warfare and Rear Area Support*, p. 3-1; Lt. Kip McCormick, "The Evolution of Soviet Military Doctrine," *Military Review* (July 1987), pp. 52–72.

100. *New York Times* (November 3, 1985); "BTR-70 in Afghanistan," *Jane's Defence Weekly* (June 16, 1984), pp. 956–958; and "BTR-80 Armored Personnel Carrier," *Jane's Defence Weekly* (February 15, 1986), p. 261.

101. Such estimates are very uncertain. See "Soviet Air Force in Afghanistan," *Jane's Defence Weekly* (July 7, 1984); David C. Isby, "Soviet Tactics in the War in Afghanistan," *Jane's Defence Review*, Vol. 4, No. 7 (1984).

102. David C. Isby, "Afghanistan 1982: The War Continues," *International Defense Review*, Vol. 15, No. 11 (November 1982), p. 1524; Yossef Bodansky, "New Weapons in Afghanistan," *Jane's Defence Weekly* (March 9, 1985), p. 412.

103. Lars Gyllenhall, "Soviet Tanks in Afghanistan," *Armed Forces* (February 1987), p. 88.

104. Significant differences of opinion exist over the extent to which the USSR added troops rather than rotated new troops in and old troops out. General Alexei Lizichev, head of the Army and Navy's Chief Political

Directorate, stated on 25 May 1988 that Soviet forces in Afghanistan totalled only 103,000 men. This is about 12,000 (or 10 percent) less than U.S. estimates. *Armed Forces* (August, 1988), p. 347.

105. Gritz, op. cit. Abdul Haq was a commander of the Hezb-i-Islami forces near Kabul.

106. *Washington Post* (January 15, 1986); *Jane's Defence Weekly* (May 26, 1984), p. 819, (July 2, 1985), pp. 1104–1106, and (April 2, 1985), p. 412; and James Coyne, "Frontal Aviations One-Two Punch," *Air Force* (March 1985), pp. 48, 112.

107. The VDV are *vozdushno-desantnaya-voiska* or air landing troops. The DShB are *desantno-shturmovyata brigada* or landing assault brigades. The VDV forces are by far the most elite troops and have the most demanding selection and training. The DShB also have excellent training but are less select. The reconnaissance forces are company- or battalion-sized elite elements within the VDV and DShB forces and other Soviet divisions. The DRA Army had up to three regiments with reconnaissance/airborne troops and one air assault regiment in 1979. Little mention was made of the use of these units until 1984, perhaps because they were first regarded as dangerous by the USSR and then extensively retrained. They became very active with the advent of major unconventional warfare operations in 1984 and were closely integrated with Soviet forces. They were sometimes employed as platoons in Soviet combined arms reinforced battalions (CARBs) and acted as scouts and infiltration forces. Alexiev, *Inside the Soviet Army in Afghanistan*, pp. 15–18 and 25–35.

108. *New York Times* (November 3, 1985); *Washington Post* (January 13, 14, and 15, 1986); *Washington Times* (December 26, 1985); *Baltimore Sun* (January 10, 1986).

109. Curren and Karber, op. cit., pp. 88 and 94; "Russia's Costly Blunder in Afghanistan," *Economist* (November 30, 1985), pp. 37–38; *Armed Forces* (August 1988), p. 347.

110. Gritz, op. cit.

111. For an interesting argument that the Afghan War radically affected overall Soviet senior command assignments and modernized Soviet training and tactics, see Yossef Bodansky, "General of the Army D.T. Yazov: Victor in Afghanistan," *Jane's Defence Weekly* (March 31, 1984), p. 485; and Urban, "Afghanistan: A New Horizon for the Soviets," op. cit., pp. 209–210.

112. Soviet sources report 103,000. *Armed Forces* (August, 1988), p. 341.

113. Gritz, op. cit.

114. The term was used generically to describe Soviet elite forces, few of which were, in fact, Spetsnaz.

115. The Mujahideen captured some T-34/85s, BTR-40s, and BTR-60s but rarely employ them in combat.

116. *Jane's Defence Weekly* (March 12, 1988), p. 471.

117. A good generic history and description of all Soviet desant forces can be found in Major James F. Holcomb and Dr. Graham H. Turbville, "Soviet Desant Forces—Parts 1 and 2," *International Defense Review* (September 1988), pp. 1077–1082, and (October 1988), pp. 1259–1264. This description is

based on Soviet force organization in the USSR and does not track in detail with reporting on Soviet organization and activity in Afghanistan. The reader should also be aware that even experts in this area disagree sharply on the role of Spetsnaz forces and the size of the forces in Afghanistan. Two leading experts, David C. Isby and Alexander Alexiev, disagree sharply on which forces should be called Spetsnaz and the size of such forces the USSR deployed in Afghanistan. Isby, *Weapons and Tactics of the Soviet Army, Fully Revised Edition*, pp. 389–398. Alexiev, *Inside the Soviet Army in Afghanistan*, pp. 15–18 and 25–35. Isby states that three Spetsnaz brigades were deployed in Afghanistan, but Alexiev doubts the existence of more than small intelligence-oriented elements. Many other sources tend to call all assault troops Spetsnaz.

118. Experts do not agree on the relative importance of Soviet elite forces. These comments represent the author's judgments based upon uncertain data.

119. No firm agreement exists about unit designations. See Urban, *The War in Afghanistan*, pp. 148–150, for a different assessment of the units involved.

120. The distinction between air mobile and air assault seems to be that air assault formations are slightly large and include parachute battalions in the brigades, rather than simply heliborne units. The meaning of the distinction in terms of Soviet performance in Afghanistan is not clear.

121. See Isby, *Weapons and Tactics of the Soviet Army, Fully Revised Edition*, pp. 389–398; and Alexiev, *Inside the Soviet Army in Afghanistan*, pp. 15–18 and 25–35.

122. Urban, *The War in Afghanistan*, p. 133.

123. *The Soviet Army: Troops, Organization and Equipment*, FM 100-2-3 (Washington: Government Printing Office, July 1984); and David C. Isby, "Afghanistan 1982: The War Continues," pp. 1523–1528.

124. This weapon was also mounted on AFVs and the Mi-8 helicopter.

125. *Jane's Defence Weekly* (December 3, 1988), p. 1425.

126. Urban, *The War in Afghanistan*, p. 133.

127. Nancy Peabody Newell and Richard Newell, *The Struggle for Afghanistan* (Ithaca: Cornell University Press, 1981), p. 137.

128. Drew Middleton, "In Afghan War, Soviets Learn from Guerrillas," *New York Times* (January 23, 1983), p. 6.

129. These marksmen are sent to a sniper school or receive 40–60 days of extra training. *New York Times* (November 3, 1985); *Washington Post* (January 13, 14, and 15, 1986); *Washington Times* (December 26, 1985); *Baltimore Sun* (January 10, 1986).

130. Middleton, "In Afghan War, Soviets Learn from Guerrillas."

131. See Galeotti, op. cit.

132. Mujahideen references to the 444th and 666th commando brigades seem to refer to battalions subordinate to the 37th and 38th brigades.

133. For a good summary description of the composition of the Mujahideen, see David C. Isby, "Jihad in Afghanistan," *Soldiers of Freedom*, Vol. 3, No. 1 (February 1987), pp. 16–24.

134. *Washington Post* (December 21, 1987), p. A–1, and (December 26, 1987), p. A–1.

135. Massoud was a major leader of the Jamiat-i-Islami. *Washington Post* (December 21, 1987), p. A–1.

136. *New York Times* (January 23, 1983); *Economist* (November 30, 1983), pp. 37–38; *Washington Times* (December 26, 1985 and February 12, 1986).

137. Edward Girardet, "Afghans Lament Lack of Guns," *Christian Science Monitor* (May 13, 1980), p. 3; Urban, *The War in Afghanistan*, p. 18.

138. Amphibious Warfare School Conference Group on Afghanistan, op. cit., pp. 65–70.

139. *Washington Post* (December 20, 1985); and "International Defense Digest," *International Defense Review* (November 1986), pp. 1733–1734.

140. Edward Girardet, "Arming Afghan Guerrillas: Perils, Secrecy," *Christian Science Monitor* (November 20, 1984), p. 15; "Corruption Bleeds U.S. Aid," *USA Today* (January 14, 1985); "Foreign Report," *The Economist* (December 20, 1984); *Washington Post* (January 13, 1985); "Corruption Diverts U.S. Aid," *Washington Post* (December 20, 1985); *Houston Chronicle* (December 23, 1984); *Foreign Report* (December 20, 1984), pp. 1–2; and *Wall Street Journal* (December 27, 1984). Similar press reports surfaced repeatedly in 1985 and 1986.

141. *Jane's Defence Weekly* (December 22, 1984 and August 17, 1985); *International Defense Review* (November 1986), pp. 1733–1734; *Time* (October 6, 1986), pp. 42–43; *Economist* (October 25, 1986), p. 43; and *Jane's Defence Weekly* (August 16, 1986), p. 239.

142. *The Soviet Army: Specialized Warfare and Rear Area Support*, p. 71; Donald M. Hart, "Low Intensity Conflict in Afghanistan: The Soviet View," *Survival*, Vol. 24 (March–April 1982), p. 62.

143. Urban, *The War in Afghanistan*, p. 63.

144. Lars Gyllenhaal, "Soviet Tanks in Afghanistan," *Armed Forces*, Vol. 6, No. 2 (February 1987), pp. 86–88.

145. Ibid.

146. "Soviets Adopt New Tactics in Afghan Battles," *Washington Star* (December 25, 1980), p. 14; and Marcia Gauger, "Year in Afghanistan Frustrates Russians," *Washington Star* (December 27, 1980), p. A–7.

147. Isby, "Afghanistan 1982: The War Continues," p. 524, and *Weapons and Tactics of the Soviet Army, Fully Revised Edition*, pp. 406–408.

148. Isby, "Afghanistan 1982: The War Continues," p. 524.

149. Ibid.

150. Curren and Karber, op. cit., pp. 96–97.

151. Urban, *The War in Afghanistan*, p. 120.

152. Isby, *Weapons and Tactics of the Soviet Army, Fully Revised Edition*, p. 187.

153. *Jane's Defence Weekly* (October 17, 1987), p. 889.

154. "BTR-70 in Afghanistan," *Jane's Defence Weekly* (June 16, 1984), p. 956.

155. *Jane's Defence Weekly* (February 15, 1986), p. 261.

156. See Isby, *Weapons and Tactics of the Soviet Army, Fully Revised Edition*.

157. Isby, "Afghanistan 1982: The War Continues."

158. Isby, *Weapons and Tactics of the Soviet Army, Fully Revised Edition*, pp. 194–201.

159. One German source reported that Afghan guerrilla groups captured quantities of the RPG-18. See "Soviets Throw Away Antitank Weapon in Service in Afghanistan," *Soldat und Technik*, 91, Vol. 24, No. 7, p. 53.

160. *Jane's Defence Weekly* (August 16, 1986), p. 239.

161. *Jane's Defence Weekly* (November 14, 1987), p. 1113; and Karp, op. cit.

162. *Washington Post* (February 12, 1989), p. A–34.

163. *Jane's Defence Weekly* (August 17, 1985), p. 295; *Baltimore Sun* (January 10, 1986); *Foreign Report* (December 20, 1984), pp. 1–2.

164. *Time* (October 6, 1986), p. 43; *Washington Post* (February 12, 1989), p. A–34; Urban, *The War in Afghanistan*, pp. 152–153.

165. A new 2S12 120-mm mortar may also have been deployed.

166. Isby, *Weapons and Tactics of the Soviet Army, Fully Revised Edition*, pp. 254–257; William P. Baxter, "New Soviet Airborne Artillery," *Jane's Intelligence Review* (September 1988), pp. 18–20.

167. It is unclear whether the weapons were Spanish or Israeli or captured Soviet equipment obtained in Grenada. *Washington Post* (January 28, 1988), p. A–25; *Jane's Defence Weekly* (February 13, 1988), p. 250.

168. *Washington Post* (February 12, 1989), p. A–34.

169. *Jane's Defence Weekly* (March 30, 1985), p. 531, and (May 11, 1985), p. 794. There were also reports that the SS-12 was deployed at Shindand air base.

170. Urban, *The War in Afghanistan*, p. 165.

171. This estimate is based upon General Dynamics, *The World's Missile Systems*, 7th ed., General Dynamics, Pomona, California, Division (April 1982), pp. 65–66.

172. Scott James, "Does Western Technology Offset Larger Soviet Numbers?" *Defense Electronics* (February 1981).

173. Isby, *Weapons and Tactics of the Soviet Army, Fully Revised Edition*, pp. 294–297; *Washington Post* (November 2, 1988), p. 5.

174. *New York Times* (August 14, 1988), p. 9.

175. *New York Times* (August 14, 1988), p. 9, (October 8, 1988), p. 3; *Washington Post* (June 19, 1988), p. A–27.

176. Urban, *The War in Afghanistan*, p. 138.

177. *Washington Post* (August 21, 1988), p. A–22.

178. David C. Isby, "New Non-Contact Mines in Afghanistan," *Soviet Intelligence Review* (September 1988), pp. 21–22.

179. *The Soviet Army: Troops, Organization and Equipment*, pp. 5–122; *Los Angeles Times* (August 18, 1985); Urban, *The War in Afghanistan*, pp. 91 and 186.

180. *Washington Post* (February 12, 1989), p. A–34.

181. The Mujahideen sometimes used wooden pitchforks to obtain Soviet mines.

182. *Jane's Defense Weekly* (February 18, 1989), p. 279.

183. See Major P. Studenkin, "From an Afghan Notebook: In the Land of

Mountains and Hopes," *Pravda* (April 14, 1981), translated in *Strategic Review* (Summer 1981), pp. 80–81.

184. Isby, *Weapons and Tactics of the Soviet Army, Fully Revised Edition*, p. 1528.

185. Urban, *The War in Afghanistan*, pp. 187 and 193.

186. E.S. Williams, "Mine Warfare in Afghanistan," *Armed Forces* (October 1988), pp. 451–454.

187. George P. Shultz, *Chemical Warfare in Southeast Asia and Afghanistan: An Update*, Special Report No. 104 (Washington, D.C.: Department of State, November 1982); Williams, op. cit.

188. *Jane's Defence Weekly* (February 18, 1989), p. 279.

189. Williams, op. cit.

190. *Jane's Defence Weekly* (November 28, 1986), p. 1259.

191. Harrison, op. cit, p. 16; *Jane's Defence Weekly* (March 16, 1985), p. 439, (February 1, 1986), pp. 152–153; *Washington Post* (January 16, 1985); "Barrage and Counter Barrage," *Time* (October 6, 1986), pp. 42–43.

192. Edward Girardet, "Arming Guerrillas: Perils, Secrecy"; *Washington Post* (January 13, 1985), (January 16, 1985); *Baltimore Sun* (January 10, 1986); *USA Today* (January 14, 1985); *Foreign Report* (December 20, 1984).

193. *Washington Post* (February 12, 1989), p. A–34.

194. The Soviets deployed radar-guided ZSU-23-4 23-mm AA guns for airfield protection but never used them for this purpose.

195. Drew Middleton, "In Afghan War, Soviets Learn from Guerrillas"; *New York Times* (November 3, 1985); *Washington Times* (December 26, 1985); and Isby, "Afghanistan 1982: The War Continues," p. 1527.

196. A recent CBS news film taken inside Afghanistan shows Kabul airport surrounded by SA-2 guideline missiles.

197. Urban, *The War in Afghanistan*, p. 96.

198. Harrison, op. cit., p. 16; *Jane's Defence Weekly* (March 16, 1985), p. 439, (February 1, 1986), pp. 152–153; *Washington Post* (January 16, 1985); "Barrage and Counter Barrage."

199. The PZRK, or 9M32 Strela 2, is known in the West as the SA-7 Grail. It began development in 1959, after the appearance of a similar U.S. system: the FIM-43A Redeye. It was developed by the Toropov OKB-134 design team in Tushino, which had designed the 9M9 Kub (SA-6 Gainful) and had completed reserve engineering of the AIM-9 Sidewinder as part of creation of the VVS RS-3/K-13 (AA-2 Atoll). The original design called for a scaled-down Sidewinder, complete with Gyros. This design proved to be too large and complex, and the missile was given stabilization with pop-out fins and a simpler Gyro. Considerable debate took place over whether to design an all-aspect missile or a simpler tail-pursuit system with proportional guidance like the Redeye. After trials, the USSR selected a system unaided by proportional guidance in spite of the acute fuel inefficiency that resulted.

Development was completed in 1965, and the missile entered service in 1966. The 9M32 missile was deployed in a 9P53 gripstock launcher, which is delivered to the field in a wooden box with two missiles and four thermal batteries. In combat, a small protective plastic cover is removed to activate the uncooled lead-sulfide IR seeker. The problems in the original design led to the development of the Strela 2M with the 9M32M missile and 9P58 launcher. This system was first deployed in 1972. The older model SA-7 has a maximum effective range of 3,600 meters and a maximum altitude of 3,000 meters. The improved model SA-7 has a maximum effective range of 4,500 meters and a maximum altitude of 5,500 meters.

The best statistical kill data on the Strela comes from Vietnam. One data sample shows that 350 incidents, using 528 missiles, produced 48 kills. The highest target altitude was 2,600 meters and the lowest 25 meters. This led to the rapid deployment of countermeasures. In 1973, the Israelis estimated that up to 5,000 Strelas were fired for two confirmed kills and a maximum of six. Some 28 more aircraft were damaged. The Strelas did, however, prove very effective in 1975, at the end of the Vietnam War, when used against the slow-flying A-37s and other aircraft of South Vietnam. The SA-7 is being replaced by the SA-14 and SA-16. The SA-14 is infrared and the SA-16 is laser beam riding. The SA-14 has a more powerful motor, digital electronics, more battery power, more coolant, all-aspect engagement, faster reaction time, more reliability, a much better IR seeker with built-in IR countermeasures, a larger warhead, a range of 6,000–7,000 meters and a ceiling of more than 5,000 meters. See "Versatile Soviet Strela Air Defense Missile," *Jane's Defence Weekly* (January 23, 1988), pp. 139–141, and *Jane's Defence Weekly* (June 4, 1988), p. 1116.

200. In Soviet forces, the Strela 2M is deployed with a small radio receiver mounted on the operator's helmet, which picks up aircraft transmissions and acts as a kind of early warning device.

201. It is unclear whether the Soviets made much use of electronic IRCM or "hot brick" jammers.

202. "The Secret Intelligence War Inside Afghanistan," *London Sunday Times* (April 5, 1981).

203. *Washington Post* (January 13, 14, 15, and 16, 1986), (February 12, 1989), p. A–34; *Jane's Defence Weekly* (January 31, 1987), p. 131.

204. *International Defense Review* (May 1987), p. 546.

205. For an excellent account of the U.S. decision to deploy the Stinger, see John Walcott and Tim Carrington, "CIA Resisted Proposal to Give Afghan Rebels U.S. Stinger Missiles," *Wall Street Journal* (February 16, 1988), p. 1.

206. *Washington Times* (February 26, 1988), p. F–3.

207. Andrew Cockburn, "Afghanistan Rebels Using Stingers with Deadly Accuracy," *Defense Week* (June 1, 1988), p. 7; and *Washington Times* (February 26, 1988), p. F–3.

208. Michael Mecham, "U.S. Credits Afghan Resistance with Thwarting Soviet Air Power," *Aviation Week* (July 13, 1987), pp. 26–28.

209. The Soviets had already lost about 1,000 aircraft before December 1986, when large numbers of Stingers reached the battlefield.

210. Some sources claim one kill for every two to four missiles.

211. James W. Rawles, "Stinger: Requiem for the Combat Helicopter," *Defense Electronics* (November 1988), pp. 30–34; Guy Willis, "Hind Weapons and Countermeasures Fit," *International Defense Review* (February 1989), p. 136.

212. The Afghans were still able to kill three Soviet helicopters in a single day on 2 January 1988. The lack of Soviet success in deploying effective countermeasures through May 1988 came as a surprise to many American experts. A vastly improved form of Stinger (the Stinger FIM-92B POST [Passive Optical Seeker Tracker]), which was not sent to Afghanistan, was developed in large part because of the fear that Soviet acquisition of the designs for the Stinger from traitors in Greece had given the USSR the ability to counter the system. The Soviets had obtained their data on the Stinger in 1984 from Michael Megaleconomou, an electronics expert in the Greek branch of ITT and a Greek officer. The Soviet SA-14, or Gremlin, missile is largely a copy of the Stinger.

The Stinger POST was replaced after only 559 were produced, however, because of the development of the Stinger FIM-92C RMP (Reprogrammable Microprocessor) with a software reprogramming capability that allows the guidance and control functions to be tailored to given threats and countermeasures. It has rosette pattern scanning (selective scanning of parts of the target) and a two-channel seeker covering both IR and ultraviolet to defeat countermeasures. It can distinguish between low-infrared targets, flares, and background clutter. *Washington Times* (October 29, 1987), p. A–10; *Defense News* (January 25, 1988), p. 35; Rawles, op. cit.

213. *Washington Post* (February 12, 1989), p. A–1; Rawles, op. cit.

214. *Jane's Defence Weekly* (March 5, 1998), pp. 380–381.

215. Many Stingers were lost to Pakistani diversion, some were stolen or seized by Iran, and some were captured by the Soviets and DRA. Roughly 600 missiles, out of 800 shipped, reached the Mujahideen between October 1986 and August 1987. *Jane's Defence Weekly* (July 25, 1987), pp. 153–155, (October 10, 1987), p. 785; *New York Times* (July 7, 1987), p. 6; *Washington Post* (July 20, 1987), p. 1, (February 12, 1989), p. A–34; *The Economist* (July 4, 1987), pp. 41–42; *Defense News* (January 25, 1988), p. 35; Aaron Karp, "Blowpipes and Stingers in Afghanistan: One Year Later," *Armed Forces Journal International* (September 1987), pp. 36–40.

216. *Washington Post* (February 12, 1989), p. A–34.

217. IISS, *Military Balance, 1985/1986*, p. 29. The Soviet air units involved come under the Southern or "Near Eastern" Strategic Theater (GTUD) with its headquarters at Tashkent.

218. IISS, *Military Balance, 1983/1984*, p. 87, and *1985/1986*, p. 119.

219. *The Economist* (October 26, 1985), p. 48; *Jane's Defence Weekly* (March 31, 1984), pp. 481–483.

220. For background on the debate over the size of Soviet air forces in Afghanistan at this time see *Jane's Defence Weekly* (January 12, 1985), (February 9, 1985, and June 2, 1985).

221. IISS, *Military Balance, 1987/1988*, p. 151.

222. Urban, *The War in Afghanistan*, p. 121; David C. Isby, "SOF Counts Coups in Afghanistan," *Soldier of Fortune* (October 1984).

223. Soviet sources indicate that the Su-24 and Tu-16s were kept out of Afghanistan because of the fear of Mujahideen rocket attacks on air fields.

224. See Bussert, op. cit., p. 105.

225. John Gunston, "Afghanistan USSR Terror Attacks," *Jane's Defence Weekly* (March 31, 1984), pp. 481–484.

226. Ibid.

227. For an early account of a typical attack on a village reported by a Japanese photographer, see "Soviet Air Strikes and Armored Assaults Fail Against 3 Afghan Towns," *Baltimore Sun* (November 7, 1980), p. 7.

228. The Su-25 appears to be a partial copy of the Northrop A-9 design that competed for selection against the U.S. A-10.

229. See John W. R. Taylor, "Gallery of Soviet Aerospace Weapons," *Air Force Magazine* (March 1984), p. 118. Conservative recent estimates put the armament weight at 8,820 pounds. This report does not accept any evidence of heavy calibre guns on the Su-25 Frogfoot. It suggests that the Su-25 is more like the Northrop A-9A than the A-10. More recent reporting is provided in "Sukhoi Su-25 Frogfoot," *Jane's Defence Weekly* (March 2, 1985), pp. 362–363.

230. See Henry Trewhitt, "Soviets Begin Afghan Bombing Drive," *Baltimore Sun* (April 25, 1984), and John R. Taylor, "Gallery of Soviet Aerospace Weapons," *Air Force Magazine* (March 1986), p. 89. On the massing of bombers preliminary to the spring campaign, see Walter Andrews, "Soviets May Intensify Fight on Afghanistan," *Washington Times* (April 18, 1984).

231. Capt. Anthony A. Cardoza, "Soviet Aviation in Afghanistan," *Proceedings* (February 1987), pp. 85–88; Isby, *The Soviet Army*, Chap. 6; Amphibious Warfare School Conference Group, op. cit., pp. 65–70.

232. Urban, *The War in Afghanistan*, p. 102.

233. Reports that the Soviets were dissatisfied with Su-25 and slowed production are inaccurate. It is entering Czech and Hungarian units, as well as Soviet front-line units in Europe, and will be used in conjunction with the Mi-28 and Mi-24 attack helicopters. The aircraft is produced at the Tbilisi aircraft plant. *Air Force Magazine* (March 1986), p. 89.

234. See Bussert, op. cit., p. 105, and Richard Mackenzie, "The Afghan War," *Air Force Magazine* (September 1988), pp. 140–153.

235. *Newsday* (June 13, 1988), p. 13.

236. Yossef Bodansky, "New Weapons in Afghanistan," *Jane's Defence Weekly* (March 9, 1985), p. 412; Urban, *The War in Afghanistan*, p. 193.

237. See *Jane's Defence Weekly* (May 20, 1984, and March 9, 1985); *Washington Post* (January 15, 1985); *New York Times* (October 31, 1985, and December 27, 1985); *Time* (October 6, 1986), pp. 43–44; and *Economist* (October 26, 1986), p. 43.

238. Thirty of the new fighters were deployed. *Washington Times* (November 3, 1988), p. 1; *Washington Post* (November 1, 1988), p. A–27.

239. Cardoza, op. cit.; Isby, *The Soviet Army*, Chap. 6; Amphibious Warfare School Conference Group, op. cit.

240. The so-called Flogger F and Flogger H are export versions of the MiG-23 with far less attack mission capability. *Aviation Week* (November 7, 1988), p. 21.

241. Adapted from *Air Force Magazine* (March 1988), p. 76, and *Jane's All the World's Aircraft* (London, 1988).

242. The first major such Tu-16 raid seems to have occurred on 20 April 1984.

243. Charles Bork, "Soviet Planes Attack Towns in Afghanistan Despite Resistance," *Washington Times* (July 18, 1984), p. 42; Jonathan Broder, "Soviet Offensive Puts Rebels on Run," *Chicago Tribune* (July 16, 1984), p. 1; Gunston, op. cit.; James Rupert, "Depopulation Campaign Brutally Changes Villages," *Washington Post* (January 15, 1986); "Worried Pakistan Limits Arms to Afghan Rebels," *Washington Post* (July 23, 1986), p. A–1; *Time* (October 6, 1986), p. 42.

244. *Time* (May 7, 1984), p. 44. See also Mary Bine Weaver, "Big Soviet Drive in Afghanistan Reflects Tougher Chernenko," *Christian Science Monitor* (May 10, 1984), p. 9; *New York Times* (July 12, 1985); and *Washington Times* (July 18, 1985).

245. In Soviet forces, these bombers are supported by a few Tu-16 refueling tankers. Approximately ninety of these aircraft (the Badger Hand J) are tasked with ECM missions and fifteen are for reconnaissance.

246. Data adapted from *Air Force Magazine* (March 1988), p. 76, and *Jane's All the World's Aircraft*.

247. Jonathan Broder, "Soviets Open Afghan Drive," *Chicago Tribune* (August 12, 1984), p. 35.

248. On the use of "migratory genocide" to denude the countryside, see Roger Fontaine, "Migratory Genocide Considered Part of Moscow's War Strategy," *Washington Times* (July 17, 1984), p. 1. For a less pessimistic analysis based on Western intelligence assessments, see Drew Middleton, "Soviet Target: Afghan Areas Aiding Rebels," *New York Times* (July 15, 1984), p. 7. For a description of the impact of bombing toward the end of the war, see Cardoza, op. cit.; Isby, *The Soviet Army*, Chap. 6; Amphibious Warfare School Conference Group, op. cit., pp. 65–70.

249. *Aviation Week* (November 7, 1988), p. 21; *New York Times* (November 6, 1988), p. 11.

250. Data adapted from *Air Force Magazine* (March 1988), p. 76.

251. Bussert, op. cit., p. 107. See also C. J. Dick, "Soviet Operational Maneuver Groups," *International Defense Review*, No. 6 (1983), p. 771. According to the author, the Soviet's Group of Soviet Forces Germany (GSFG) "now has an excellent system of vectoring and controlling close air support—a significant departure from the previous lack of interest in CAS . . ." (close air support) for both helicopter and dedicated fixed-wing support. The author supplies no details, however, and it is not at all clear to what extent the new system has penetrated through the old values of control rigidity.

252. Isby, "Afghanistan 1982: The War Continues," p. 1527. See also "Soviet Helicopters on the Afghan Battlefield," Guoji Hangkong (Beijing), *International Aviation*, Vol. 83, no. 16, pp. 18–19.

253. Urban, *The War in Afghanistan*, p. 217.

254. There is little agreement on the precise numbers and mix of Soviet helicopter forces.

255. Isby, *Weapons and Tactics of the Soviet Army, Fully Revised Edition*, pp. 436–439.

256. IISS, *Military Balance*, various years; Drew Middleton, "In Afghan

War, Soviets Learn From Guerrillas." There seem to be indications that Mi-24s were supplied to Afghanistan by early May 1979. See "Afghans Said to Obtain Soviet Copter Gunships," *Washington Post* (May 4, 1979). According to one source, the number of Soviet helicopter gunships in Afghanistan quadrupled to about 240. See Hosmer and Wolfe, op. cit., p. 243.

257. Isby, *Weapons and Tactics of the Soviet Army, Fully Revised Edition*, pp. 436–439.

258. Cardoza, op. cit.; Isby, *The Soviet Army*, Chap. 6; Amphibious Warfare School Conference Group, op. cit., pp. 65–70.

259. This analysis draws heavily on "Soviet Air Force in Afghanistan," *Jane's Defence Weekly* (July 7, 1984). Also see IISS, *Military Balance 1985/1986* and *1987/1988*. The counts are very uncertain.

260. Isby, *Weapons and Tactics of the Soviet Army, Fully Revised Edition*, p. 439.

261. See the discussion on helicopter tactics in the following: Colonel Franz Freistetter, "The Battle in Afghanistan: A View from Europe," *Strategic Review* (Winter 1981), p. 41; Drew Middleton, "In Afghan War, Soviets Learn from Guerrillas." For an important analysis of the command and control issue with respect to helicopters, see Bussert, op. cit., pp. 102–108. For Soviet views on the lessons of Vietnam pertinent to the helicopter role, see I. Ye. Shavrov, General of the Army, *Lokal'nye Voiny: Istoriya i Souremenost* (Local Wars: History and Present Day) (Voenizdat, 1981), pp. 79–84. Also see Roger Fontaine, "Soviets Recasting Strategy to Crush Afghan Resistance," *Washington Times* (December 26, 1985); Edward Girardet, "Rebels Struggling to Adapt," *Baltimore Sun* (January 10, 1986); Drew Middleton, "Russians in Afghanistan: Changes in Tactics," *New York Times* (November 3, 1985); and "That's a Russian in Disguise," *The Economist* (October 26, 1985), pp. 46–48.

262. One of the most famous of the combat helicopter pilots, Lt. Colonel Nikolai I. Malyshev, called the training obsolete, over-rigid, and unrealistic. He noted that Soviet regulations forbade the maneuvers that pilots had to use to escape the Stinger missile. *Jane's Defence Weekly* (July 9, 1988), p. 47.

263. The Mujahideen then had no anti-aircraft weapons of any kind. Urban, *The War in Afghanistan*, p. 37.

264. Urban, *The War in Afghanistan*, pp. 63 and 67.

265. This analysis draws heavily on Yossef Bodansky, "Most Feared Soviet Aircraft in Afghanistan," *Jane's Defence Weekly* (May 19, 1984); "Soviet Air Force in Afghanistan," *Jane's Defence Weekly* (July 7, 1984); and Curren and Karber, op. cit.

266. Bodansky, "Most Feared Soviet Aircraft in Afghanistan"; "Soviet Air Force in Afghanistan," *Jane's Defence Weekly* (July 7, 1984).

267. Isby, *Weapons and Tactics of the Soviet Army, Fully Revised Edition*, p. 439.

268. Deborah G. Meyer, "What's in the Soviet Arsenal?" *Armed Forces Journal International* (May 1982), p. 42; *Jane's Defence Weekly* (January 30, 1988), p. 182.

269. See comments by Brig. Gen. Ellis D. Parker (Army Deputy Director of Requirements and Aviation Officer in the Office of the Army Deputy Chief of

Staff for Operations and Plans) in "Soviets Stress Helicopter in Anti-armor Role," *Aviation Week and Space Technology* (January 16, 1984), p. 92. Also see Guy Willis, "Hind Weapons and Countermeasures Fit," *International Defense Review* (February 1989), p. 136.

270. See *Jane's Defence Weekly* (March 31, 1984, July 7, 1984, and February 1, 1986); *Air Force* (March 1985), pp. 48 and 112; *New York Times* (November 3, 1984); *Washington Times* (August 20, 1986), p. 5A; and *Washington Post* (July 23, 1986), p. A–1.

271. Anthony A. Cardoza, op. cit., pp. 86–87.

272. Yossef Bodansky, "Havoc and Super Hind," *Defense Helicopter World* (April–May 1989), pp. 28–32, and "Havoc Learns Afghan Lessons," *Jane's Defence Weekly* (June 17, 1989), p. 1235; Peter Adams, "Afghan Rebels' Stingers Teach Soviet Pilots Vital Lessons," *Defense News* (May 15, 1989), p. 12.

273. Parker, op. cit.; Willis, op. cit.

274. *Jane's Defence Weekly* (February 1, 1986), p. 152.

275. Urban, *The War in Afghanistan*, pp. 120 and 149.

276. Ibid. Some sources have suggested that advanced models of the Mi-24 include low-light television and infrared sensors and new radars. For example, see O'Ballance, op. cit.

277. Cardoza, op. cit., pp. 86–87.

278. Amphibious Warfare School Conference Group, op. cit.

279. Bill Gunston, *Modern Soviet Air Force* (New York: ARCO, 1982), p. 138; *Jane's Defence Weekly* (March 31, 1984), pp. 481–483.

280. Bill Gunston, *Helicopters* (New York, ARCO, 1981), pp. 90–93.

281. Isby, "Afghanistan 1982: The War Continues," p. 1526.

282. Soviet helicopters were seen deploying mass groups of infrared flares. One Soviet aircraft launched four groups of seventeen flares each after an SA-7 attack on a Soviet helicopter. *Jane's Defence Weekly* (March 16, 1985), p. 439.

283. *Jane's Defence Weekly* (November 14, 1987), p. 1113, (January 30, 1988), p. 1988.

284. Cardoza, op. cit., pp. 85–88; Isby, *The Soviet Army*, Chap. 6; Amphibious Warfare School Conference Group, op. cit., pp. 65–70.

285. "The Bear Descends on the Lion," *Time* (May 7, 1984), p. 44.

286. "Su-24s, Tu-16s Support Soviet Ground Forces," *Aviation Week & Space Technology* (October 29, 1984), p. 40.

287. Ibid.; *Time* (October 6, 1986), p. 42; *The Economist* (October 25, 1986), p. 43.

288. "Soviet Air Force in Afghanistan," *Jane's Defence Weekly* (July 7, 1984), p. 1105.

289. Captain Steven A. Frith, "Soviet Attack Helicopters: Rethinking the Threat," *Military Review* (March 1981), p. 55.

290. Douglas M. Hart, "Low-intensity Conflict in Afghanistan: The Soviet View," *Survival*, Vol. 24, No. 2 (March/April 1982), p. 64.

291. Col. A. Khrobrykh, "One Mountain Pass After Another—From the Afghan Notebook," *Aviatsiya I Kosmonautika*, No. 10 (Trans-Soviet Press, March 1981), p. 73. For a comprehensive review of Soviet logistics in

Afghanistan, see "Soviet Maintenance in Afghanistan" (Parts 1, 2, and 3), *Jane's Defence Weekly* (February 23 and March 1, 1986).

292. Cited in David Rees, *Afghanistan's Role in Soviet Strategy*, Conflict Studies No. 118 (London: Institute for the Study of Conflict, May 1980), p. 1.

293. See "Helicopter Repair in Afghanistan," *Flight International* (July 2, 1983), p. 11; and James C. Bussert, "Soviet Military Maintenance Looks to ATE for Solutions," *Defense Electronics* (March 1983).

294. For a good description of the resulting combat, see Graham H. Turbiville, Jr., "Ambush! The Road War in Afghanistan," *Army* (January 1988), pp. 32–42.

295. Khrobrykh, op. cit. For a comprehensive review of Soviet logistics in Afghanistan, see "Soviet Maintenance in Afghanistan," op. cit.; and Turbiville, Jr., op. cit.

296. See A Nearby Observer, op. cit., p. 159.

297. Urban, *The War in Afghanistan*, pp. 44, 64, 120, 158.

298. For an argument that the Soviets did not use chemical weapons, see Urban, *The War in Afghanistan*, pp. 56–57.

299. See U.S. Department of State, *Chemical Warfare in Southeast Asia and Afghanistan: An Update*, Report No. 104 (Washington, D.C.: Bureau of Public Affairs, November 1982).

300. Ibid.

301. "Soviet Use of Gas and Booby Traps in Afghanistan," op. cit.

302. Amphibious Warfare School Conference Group, op. cit., pp. 60–61.

303. Isby, "Afghanistan 1982: The War Continues," pp. 1526–1528.

304. *USA Today* (November 30, 1982), p. 9; *Wall Street Journal* (November 30, 1982), p. 7; *Baltimore Sun* (November 30, 1982), p. 4; Nicholas Rothwell, "Soviet Rain," *American Spectator* (October 22, 1982), pp. 8–10; *Time* (December 13, 1982), p. 57; Franklin L. Lavin, "Yellow Rain," *Human Events* (October 22, 1982), p. 11; *Washington Times* (December 30, 1982), p. 11.

305. William A. Ross, "Primary Role for Soviet Air Forces in the Delivery of Chemical Weapons," *Jane's Defence Weekly* (July 30, 1988), p. 1053.

306. *Jane's Defence Weekly* (November 22, 1987), p. 1206; Stockholm International Peace Research Institute, *SIPRI Yearbook, 1987* (Oxford: Oxford Press, 1987), p. 106.

307. Isby, *Weapons and Tactics of the Soviet Army, Fully Revised Edition*, p. 80.

308. *New York Times* (June 17, 1988), p. A–1.

3

THE FALKLANDS WAR

The Combatants

The Falklands War is the only war under study in which one side was a major Western power. It is also the only war in which both sides fought at the limits of their power projection capability. The Falklands were roughly 400 miles from the nearest major naval and air bases in Argentina and 3,750 miles from the nearest British staging point at Ascension Island. Both sides had relatively sophisticated land, air, and sea forces, but both had great difficulty in deploying their forces effectively and could not use their tactical air power to maximum effect.

The Falklands War is also the only war in which both sides had high levels of Western technology, the training and organization to use it, and suitable C^3I, battle management, and support capability. Although the other wars discussed have involved advanced Western and Soviet technology, one or more sides in those conflicts lacked the proficiency in training and organization to use this technology.

At the same time, the Falklands conflict is a limited war involving unique conditions in terms of terrain, sea, weather, logistics, and lines of communication. The fighting in South Georgia was very limited and was more a contest in comparative deployment capability than a true military struggle. The fighting for the Falklands was more a contest between a British naval task force and land-based Argentine air forces than a struggle between armies. The Argentine surface fleet never directly threatened British forces, and the Argentine army never displayed the aggressiveness and determination necessary to utilize the size of the land forces deployed or match that of British forces.

A detailed chronology of the conflict reveals just how much of the war consisted of unique episodic encounters between forces organized and trained for other missions. In many cases, the outcome of the encounter might have been reversed by a single hit or bomb, minor shifts in weather, or the command decisions of small units and forces.

Clear concepts of operations do emerge from such a chronology, but any "lessons" drawn from the war must be tempered with the reservation that each lesson must be reviewed in terms of the specific event or events upon which it is based.

The Falklands War: Chronology of Key Events

While the Falklands War had a long political prelude, the actual fighting lasted only seventy-four days, from 2 April to 14 June 1982. This fighting began with an Argentine invasion of the Falklands, then became a naval struggle followed by a British amphibious landing and counterinvasion, and ended with British recapture of Port Stanley on 14 June. The chronology of the war is summarized below, and it reflects a pattern of political and military escalation that moved from the demonstrative use of force to a large-scale clash between air, naval, and ground forces.[1]

- 19 March 1982: Argentine scrap-metal workers from the Argentine Navy transport *Bahia Buen Suceso* landed at Leith Harbour on the north side of South Georgia Island. South Georgia is about 800 miles east-southeast of the Falkland Islands and is on the same latitude as Cape Horn. The island is about 105 miles long and 18 miles across at the widest point. South Georgia is not part of the Falkland Islands but is a direct dependency of the United Kingdom.

  The scrap-metal workers were in the employ of Constantino Sergio Davidoff, who had a contract with an Edinburgh firm to remove scrap left by abandoned whaling stations. Thirty-five scientists of the British Antarctic Survey were also present on South Georgia at Grytviken, about 20 miles east of Leith Harbour. Four of these scientists discovered the presence of the scrap-metal workers and noticed that they had raised the Argentine flag. The Argentines were told they did not have authority for the landing, and the British Antarctic Survey team reported the landing to the Governor of the Falkland Islands.
- 20 March 1982: The *Bahia Buen Suceso* departed from South Georgia, leaving some scrap-metal workers at Leith Harbour. The HMS *Endurance* was dispatched from Port Stanley with twenty-two Royal Marines and instructions to arrange for the departure of the Argentines. The HMS *Endurance* was an ice patrol ship and carried two Wasp helicopters and two 20-mm guns.
- 23 March 1982: The HMS *Endurance* was ordered to put into Grytviken and await further orders.

- 26 March 1982: Over 100 Argentine troops were landed at Leith Harbour by the *Bahia Paraiso*, a 9,600-ton polar transport ship. The landing was witnessed by a British officer on covert assignment, and London was informed of the invasion. Two Argentine frigates sailed from Puerto Belgrano. These were French Type A-69 frigates originally intended for South Africa, commissioned between 1978 to 1981. Several other Argentine Navy ships also sailed.
- 27 March 1982: The *Bahia Paraiso* departed Leith Harbour, leaving Argentine troops ashore. The HMS *Endurance* was ordered to patrol the coast and assure that the *Bahia Paraiso* did not return to Leith Harbour. The *Endurance* discovered that the *Bahia Paraiso* had gone to only the three-mile limit. London ordered the *Endurance* not to take action.
- 28 March 1982: The British survey vessel *John Biscoe* was en route to Port Stanley in the Falkland Islands from Montevideo, Uruguay, with forty-three Royal Marines aboard. The Marines were a relief detachment for the Falklands garrison that was about to complete its twelve-months duty.
- 29 March 1982: Forty-three Royal Marines from the *John Biscoe* landed at Port Stanley, reinforcing the remaining twenty-five of the resident detachment. The nuclear submarine HMS *Spartan* was ordered to embark stores and weapons at Gibraltar.
- 30 March 1982: More ships of the Argentine navy, including the aircraft carrier the *Veinticinco de Mayo* (the former HMS *Venerable*) and two destroyers, put to sea. An Argentine C-130 Hercules aircraft scouted the Falklands. HMS *Endurance* was ordered to sail for the Falklands, leaving the Royal Marine detachment on South Georgia. The British nuclear submarine *Splendid* was ordered to deploy to the South Atlantic.
- 31 March 1982: Seven RAF C-130 Hercules transport planes left for Gibraltar. Some unloaded supplies for ships including the frigates HMS *Broadsword* and HMS *Yarmouth*. Other planes proceeded to Ascension Island. The UK began to secretly prepare a task force for South Atlantic operations.
- 1 April 1982: The nuclear hunter-killer submarine HMS *Spartan* departed from Gibraltar. The transport, *Fort Austin*, departed for the South Atlantic conveying Special Air Service (SAS) and Special Boat Squadron (SBS) forces.
- 2 April 1982: Argentina invaded the Falklands in Operation Rosanio. Argentine forces, consisting largely of untrained conscripts in summer uniform, were poorly equipped and lacked an effective supply system. Some units, however, had a full year's

training and were largely professional, including the 25th Infantry Brigade, 3rd Artillery Infantry Brigade, 5th Marine Brigade and 601 and 602 commandos. About 120 Argentine commandos landed by helicopter at Mullett Creek about five miles southwest of Port Stanley before dawn. They had two objectives: to seize the marine barracks at Moody Brook (about two miles west of Port Stanley) and to capture the government house in Port Stanley. One group arrived at the marine barracks at 6 A.M. but found them deserted. At the same time, the second group found the government house defended by 33 Royal Marines and attacked. Sixteen Royal Marines combined and attempted to relieve the government house without success.

Argentine reinforcements went ashore at a location about two miles northeast of Port Stanley and just north of the airstrip. They were landed by the only tank landing ship (LST) in the Argentine navy. Standing outside York Bay were the Argentine frigates *Drummond* and *Granville*, the destroyers *Santissima Trinidad* and *Hercules* (British Type 42 ships), and the *Almirante Irizar*, an Antarctic support ship. This Finnish-built ship had been fitted to carry helicopters and landing craft and serve as a troop ship. About 600 Argentine marines, 280 army and air force personnel, and eighteen armored personnel carriers landed. The British destroyed one armored personnel carrier with a round from a Swedish-built 84-mm Carl Gustav shoulder-fired anti-tank weapon but then faced massive Argentine superiority.

The British Governor, Rex Hunt, was then forced to surrender to Admiral Carlos Busser, deputy commander of the invasion force. There were no casualties on the British side. Casualties on the Argentine side were five killed (two confirmed, including a captain in the commandos) and seventeen wounded (two confirmed). The Argentines then brought in reinforcements by air, using seven Lockheed C-130 Hercules transports and ten Fokker F-27 aircraft.

The British logistic landing ship *Sir Geraint* left Plymouth with a cargo of heavy equipment. Sea Harrier aircraft started to land aboard the HMS *Hermes*. Sea King helicopters embarked on the HMS *Invincible*.

The Soviet Union launched Cosmos 1347 reconnaissance spacecraft into a 364 × 181 km orbit inclined at 70.4 degrees. It had the capability to return film to earth at intervals during missions and at the end of the mission. At its high inclination it could cover the South Atlantic.

- 3 April 1982: Argentina invaded South Georgia. The Argentine frigate *Guerrico* and the *Bahia Paraiso* arrived at Grytviken in South Georgia. Argentine marines were sent ashore in Alouette helicopters. Royal Marines directed their fire at a Puma helicopter, which was damaged and withdrew. The *Guerrico* then entered the harbor, and the Royal Marines fired on it. Three rounds from the *Carl Gustav* hit home: one hit the ship's side, one hit an Exocet launcher, and a third hit the gun turret. The *Guerrico* shelled the British position with its 100-mm gun. The British surrendered. Argentine casualties were four killed and one wounded; one Royal Marine was wounded.

British Prime Minister Margaret Thatcher announced that a large Royal Navy task force would sail for the South Atlantic as soon as preparations were complete and that the task force would include the HMS *Invincible,* which would leave port on 5 April. The first Royal Air Force (RAF) transport aircraft was deployed to Ascension Island.

The land-force units in the task force, which were charged with the recapture of the islands, included the 3rd Commando Brigade, composed of three battalions of Royal Marines and two battalions from the Parachute Regiment. President General Leopoldo Galtieri of Argentina promised that not one meter of the Falklands would ever be given back to the "invaders."

The UN Security Council adopted Resolution 502 (by vote of ten to one with four abstentions) demanding an immediate cessation of hostilities, the withdrawal of all Argentine forces, and a diplomatic solution to the crisis. This resolution was adopted under Chapter 7 of the UN Charter, which makes it mandatory and which allows Britain to take measures of self-defense in response to armed attack.

- 5 April 1982: The first British task force ships sailed from the United Kingdom. Rear Admiral John F. Woodward was appointed to command the task force. HMS *Invincible* and HMS *Hermes* put to sea from Portsmouth, followed by the support tanker *Pearleaf.* The *Hermes* carried twelve Sea Harriers and fifteen helicopters. The first of many merchant ship requisitions was announced. The P&O cruise liner *Canberra,* P&O ferry *Elk,* and several British Petroleum tankers were requisitioned.
- 6 April 1982: Argentina created a new South Atlantic command headquarters at Puerto Belgrano.
- 7 April 1982: Britain declared a maritime exclusion zone with a 200-nautical-mile radius which was centered on a point near the middle of the Falkland Islands. This zone was to be effective at 0400 hours GMT on 12 April.

The P&O liner *Canberra* arrived in Southampton to undergo military coversions that included the addition of two helicopter landing platforms. The 3rd Battalion of the parachute regiment and Royal Marine Forces embarked on the *Canberra*.

Nine French technicians from Dessault-Breguet, who were currently at Bahia Blanca military base to check the airworthiness of five Super Etendard aircraft delivered to Argentina, were instructed to stop giving technical support. The departure of an Aerospatiale team from France to check the fitting of the Exocet missile to the Super Etendards was canceled.

- 8 April 1982: Soviet Union launched the Cosmos 1349 navigation satellite into a 1,025 × 984 km orbit inclined at 83 degrees.
- 10 April 1982: The composition of the British task force was announced; see Table 3.1.
- 12 April 1982: The 200-nautical-mile maritime exclusion zone went into effect around the Falklands.
- 13 April 1982: Four Vulcan bombers and five flight crews were detached from Strike Command and assigned to the task force.
- 14 April 1982: The Cunard container ship *Atlantic Conveyor* (14,946 tons) was requisitioned. It was to be adapted for the sealift of Harrier aircraft. The HMS *Intrepid*, the sister ship of HMS *Fearless* and the only other amphibious assault ship in the Royal Navy, was put back into commission.
- 15 April 1982: Orders were given to begin detailed planning for the recapture of South Georgia. The task force for this mission was to include the HMS *Antrim*, HMS *Endurance*, and the tanker *Tidespring*.

  The first conference was held aboard the HMS *Fearless* to plan "Operation Corporate" and the retaking of the Falkland Islands.
- 16 April 1982: Units of the Argentine navy sailed from Puerto Belgrano. These included the carrier *Veinticinco de Mayo*, the cruiser *General Belgrano*, two destroyers, and three submarines.

  The first elements of the Royal Navy Task Force passed Ascension Island on their way to the Falklands.

  The Soviet Union launched Cosmos 1350 reconnaissance platform into a 380 × 185 km orbit inclined at 67.2 degrees. It later maneuvered down to a 292 × 163 km orbit, presumably for better resolution.
- 17 April 1982: British commanders met aboard *Hermes* to plan an amphibious landing and the first phase of British attack. The two British aircraft carriers arrived at Ascension Island.
- 18 April 1982: Part of the British task force sailed south from Ascension Island. The HMS *Fearless* and planners stayed behind,

TABLE 3.1 Composition of British Task Force: 1982

Aircraft Carriers	
Hermes	23,900 tons
Invincible	19,500 tons
Amphibious Assault Ship	
Fearless	11,060 tons
County-Class Destroyers	5,400 tons
Antrim	
Glamorgan	
Type 42 *Sheffield*-Class Destroyers	3,500 tons
Sheffield	
Glasgow	
Coventry	
Type 22 *Broadsword*-Class Destroyers	3,500 tons
Broadsword	
Brilliant	
Type 21 *Amazon*-Class Frigates	2,750 tons
Antelope	
Arrow	
Alacrity	
Type 12 *Rothesay*-Class Frigates	2,280 tons
Yarmouth	
Plymouth	
Fleet Oil Tankers	
Bayleaf	40,200 tons
Pearleaf	25,790 tons
Olmeda	36,000 tons
Tidespring	27,400 tons
Supply Ships	
Fort Austin	23,600 tons
Resource	22,890 tons
Stromness	16,792 tons
Logistic Landing Ships	3,250 tons
Sir Galahad	
Sir Geraint	
Sir Bedivere	
Sir Percivale	
Sir Tristram	
Requisitioned Merchant Ships	
Canberra	44,807 tons
Elk	5,463 tons
Requisitioned Sea-Going Tugs	
Salvageman	1,598 tons
Irishman	686 tons
Yorkshireman	686 tons

SOURCE: Ministry of Defence, London.

as did the *Canberra* and the troops. *Veinticinco de Mayo* returned to port with "engine trouble."

- 19 April 1982: Argentine Super Etendard aircraft departed from Bahia Blanca for a base farther south at Rio Gallegos, 475 miles from Port Stanley.
- 20 April 1982: One thousand more British soldiers, including a battalion of the Parachute Regiment, sailed for the Falklands. Merchant Navy support of the task force reached 35 ships. Sixteen of these ships were requisitioned and nineteen chartered.
- 21 April 1982: The first contact between British and Argentine forces occured when an Argentine Boeing 707, on a surveillance mission, penetrated within twelve miles of the British task force before retreating. Royal Air Force Harrier aircraft were equipped with Aim-9L missiles in a crash retrofit. RAF pilots underwent training for ski-jump take-off procedures required for operations from the British carriers.

  HMS *Antrim* and HMS *Endurance* arrived at South Georgia Island to reconnoiter the strength of the Argentine forces at Grytviken and Leith Harbour. The main landing force was kept 200 miles offshore in the tanker *Tidespring*. Members of the British Antarctic Survey team avoided capture, and one was contacted by the British forces. The scientist argued against the plan to land thirteen members of the Special Air Service on Fortuna Glacier west of Leith Harbour, miles from Grytviken. The plan proceeded anyway, and the force was landed by two Wessex 5 helicopters.

  The Soviet Union launched Cosmos 1352 from Tyurtam into a 383 × 216 km orbit, presumably for broader coverage.
- 22 April 1982: The Special Air Service force on Fortuna Glacier suffered from frostbite and hypothermia and required evacuation. A Wessex 3 and two Wessex 5 helicopters were sent to remove them. In the attempt, all seventeen men squeezed into a five-passenger Wessex 3 and returned to the HMS *Antrim*.
- 23 April 1982: The British government warned Argentina that any approach by Argentine ships or aircraft which could amount to a threat to the task force "would be dealt with appropriately." Two Special Boat Squadron squads returned to the HMS *Endurance*. They had gone ashore southeast of Grytviken trying to cross Cumberland East Bay and reach Grytviken in inflatable Gemini boats. Ice floes punctured their boats, and they had to be rescued by helicopters.

  Special Air Service forces went ashore at Stromness Bay between Grytviken and Leith Harbour in five Gemini boats. These forces represented the first major successful special forces effort. They found that the Argentine forces were small and had limited combat capability.

The Soviet Union launched the Cosmos 1353 into a 269 × 218 km orbit inclined at 82.3 degrees.

- 25 April 1982: A Wessex 3 helicopter from the HMS *Antrim* found the Argentine submarine *Santa Fe* on the surface about five miles from Grytviken and dropped depth charges. Lynx helicopters from the HMS *Brilliant* and Wasp helicopters from the HMS *Endurance* renewed this attack. They fired As-12 missiles that hit but passed through the *Santa Fe* without exploding. The *Santa Fe* reached King Edward Harbour, near Grytviken, where it was beached, listing and leaking oil. The 1,870-ton *Santa Fe* was an old submarine which was commissioned as the USS *Catfish* in 1945 and then sold to Argentina in 1971.

  The British now concluded that they could attack South Georgia Island even though their main landing force was 200 miles away. A force of 75 men, including Royal Marines, special air service, and special boat squadron forces, landed at Hestesletten, which was separated from Grytviken by a 1,000-foot ridge. The HMS *Antrim* and HMS *Plymouth* bombard Grytviken with 4.5-inch guns. Upon reaching the top of the ridge, British forces found white flags flying. The Argentines had already surrendered.

- 26 April 1982: All Argentine forces surrendered at Leith Harbour, with 137 prisoners taken. The 10,650-ton cruiser *General Belgrano* sailed from Argentina's southernmost port, Ushuaia. The HMS *Intrepid*, sister ship to the HMS *Fearless*, sailed for the South Atlantic.

- 28 April 1982: Four Vulcan bombers flew to Ascension Island. The British announced that an expanded blockade of all air and sea routes within the 200-nautical-mile exclusion zone around the Falklands would go into effect on 30 April. This blockade applied to all ships and aircraft, both military and civilian, within the zone which did not have transit authority from the Ministry of Defense in London.

  The Soviet Union launched the Cosmos 1354 navigation spacecraft into an 829 × 759 km orbit inclined at 74 degrees.

- 29 April 1982: The Soviet Union launched Cosmos 1355 from Tyuratam into a 402 × 128 km orbit, which was a standard orbit for a Soviet ocean-surveillance system that could pinpoint ship locations. Its inclination allowed it to fly over the Falkland Islands where recorded data showing positions of the British and Argentine vessels could be played down to Soviet ground stations.

The British warned that all Argentine vessels shadowing the task force were subject to attack.

- 30 April 1982: The British total exclusion zone, or blockade, went into effect. The United States announced its support of the British position on the Falklands, implemented military and economic sanctions against Argentina, and offered military supplies to Britain.
- 1 May 1982: The fighting started in the Falklands. In a pre-dawn attack, a single Avro Vulcan bomber dropped twenty-one 1,000-lb. bombs on Port Stanley airfield after a nine-hour flight from Wideawake airfield on Ascension Island. The attack was of limited success. One bomb cratered Port Stanley runway but did not deny use of the airfield to Argentine Hercules or Pucara aircraft. The crater was partly repaired. The mission, called Black Buck 1, required inflight refueling on both outbound and inbound legs from Handly Page Victor tanker aircraft. Ten Victors and one back-up Vulcan were required to support a single Vulcan in this mission because the Victors required refueling in some cases. Limited parking space at Wideawake restricted British to sixteen Victors. Only one Vulcan at a time could be supported all the way to Port Stanley.

The Vulcan attack was followed by an attack by Sea Harriers which concentrated on attacking the ends of the runway to make it too short for use by Argentine jet fighters. Sea Harriers also attacked the airstrip at Goose Green, about fifty miles west of Port Stanley. The Port Stanley airfield was bombarded by frigates of the task force, which in turn were attacked by Argentine aircraft. The HMS *Arrow* was slightly damaged.

Argentina admitted the loss of two Dagger fighters (an Israeli-built export version of the Mirage 5). An attack by Argentina using English Electric Canberra bombers resulted in one Canberra being shot down by a Sea Harrier and damage to a second. This showed Argentina that its only bomber was too obsolete to survive in combat against the Harriers.

Special Air Service and Special Boat Squadron units were put ashore on East and West Falkland by helicopter to reconnoiter possible landing sites. A four-man SBS squad found no Argentine forces in the San Carlos area.

The Argentine submarine *San Luis* fired a torpedo at a British ship at a range of 1,200 meters and escaped from the ensuing hunt by frigates and two helicopters.

- 2 May 1982: At 4 P.M., at a range of less than three miles, the British submarine HMS *Conquerer* fired Mark VIII torpedoes at the cruiser *General Belgrano*. One torpedo struck on port bow and a second hit the stern, and the *General Belgrano* sank within forty minutes. The Argentine destroyers mounted an attack on the HMS *Conqueror*, but it escaped. About 368 members of the crew of the *General Belgrano* perished. Some survivors were not rescued for thirty hours after the attack. The *General Belgrano* was about 35 miles outside the exclusion zone at the time. The attack was ordered by the War Cabinet. The British claimed that the *General Belgrano* and the two accompanying destroyers, *Piedra Buena* and *Hipolito Bouchard*, were proceeding toward the exclusion zone and were a threat to the task force. The Argentines claimed that *General Belgrano* was 50 miles southwest of the exclusion zone, was sailing west toward the Argentine mainland, and had orders not to enter the zone.

  The 4,400-ton *Conqueror* was one of three nuclear attack submarines of the *Churchill* class commissioned in 1971. The *General Belgrano* was commissioned in 1939 as the USS *Phoenix*, a *Brooklyn* class cruiser, and was a survivor of Pearl Harbor. It was sold to Argentina in 1951 for $7.8 million. There were some indications that the *Belgrano* was not operating in a water-tight combat mode with all compartments sealed and that it sank because of this.

  A Sea King helicopter was fired on by an Argentine patrol ship about 90 miles inside the exclusion zone. The patrol ship was then attacked and destroyed by a Westland Lynx helicopter from the HMS *Coventry*, which fired two Sea Skua missiles. The ship, which may have been carrying mines, exploded.

- 3 May 1982: The *Queen Elizabeth 2* was requisitioned to take the 5th Infantry Brigade to the South Atlantic. This brigade was a reconstituted unit because two of the 5th Brigade battalions were already in the South Atlantic (the 2nd and 3rd parachute battalions). Two regular units of the 5th Brigade, the 7th Duke of Edinburgh's own Gurkha Rifles and the 4th Field Regiment, Royal Artillery, were joined by the 2nd Battalion Scots Guards and the 1st Battalion Welsh Guards. The reconstituted unit had conducted a major training exercise, code name "Welsh Falcon," in late April to prepare for operations in the Falklands. Other ship requisitions included the two 6,500-ton Townsend Thoresen North Sea ferries, *Baltic Ferry* and *Nordic Ferry*, and the Cunard container ship *Atlantic Causeway*, a sister ship to the *Atlantic Conveyor*. The aircraft carrier HMS *Bulwark*, which was waiting to be scrapped, was to be put back into service as a barracks and landing platform for the Falklands garrison.

- 4 May 1982: A Type 42 British destroyer, the HMS *Sheffield*, was struck by a single AM-39 Exocet air-to-surface missile launched by an Argentine navy Super Etendard aircraft at a range of about 23 nautical miles. The *Sheffield* was on radar picket duty southeast of the Falklands and about 20 miles in front of the rest of the fleet. Two Super Etendard aircraft approached the British task force and fired two missiles, possibly at two separate targets. One target may have been the HMS *Hermes*, which was beyond the missile's range. In any case, the second Exocet hit the *Sheffield* about six feet above the waterline amidships and penetrated at an oblique angle to the main engine room and near fuel tanks, where it burned. The fire and explosion instantly cut off most electric power, communications equipment, and all pressure to the *Sheffield's* fire hoses. Within twenty seconds the Sheffield was filled with suffocating fumes from the burning PVC coating on the exposed portion of four miles of electrical wiring in the ship. The fire could not be controlled, and the order to abandon ship was given about five hours after the attack. Twenty members of the 286-man *Sheffield* crew were killed and 24 injured.

  Reports that the Super Etendard aircraft that attacked the *Sheffield* failed to return to base after running out of fuel were denied by the Argentines. They claimed that they lost no Super Etendard aircraft during these actions and that all planes returned after being refueled by Hercules aircraft. Reports that the Exocet did not detonate but that damage was caused by unconsumed propellant have since been denied by the French. The Argentines now had three Exocet missiles remaining in inventory.

  A single RAF Vulcan again bombed the Port Stanley airfield in mission Black Buck. It dropped twenty-one 1,000-lb bombs at an altitude of about 15,000 feet, but they did not damage the airstrip. Sea Harriers again attacked Port Stanley airfield. One Harrier was shot down by ground fire, possibly by a Roland missile.

- 5 May 1982: The Soviet Union launched Cosmos 1356 into a 684 × 632 km orbit inclined at 81.2 degrees. It was capable of monitoring radio transmissions and could cover the Falkland Islands area.

- 6 May 1982: Two Sea Harriers disappeared while on patrol in bad weather, probably due to a collision.

- 7 May 1982: The British extended the exclusion zone around the Falklands to twelve miles off the Argentine coast. A new squadron of Sea King helicopters was commissioned. Britain asked the U.S. for KC-135 tanker aircraft.

- 8 May 1982: Eight Sea Harriers and six RAF Harriers flew from the United Kingdom to Ascension Island in nine hours with in-flight refueling by RAF Victor tankers. The fourteen aircraft were taken to the Falklands from Ascension Island aboard the *Atlantic Conveyor*. Additional RAF Harriers flew to the *Hermes*, using aerial refueling.

- 9 May 1982: British warships shelled Port Stanley from 13 miles offshore. An Argentine Puma helicopter was shot down near Port Stanley. Sea Harriers intercepted and attacked the fishing vessel *Narwal*, which was being used to shadow the task force. The ship was secured by a Royal Navy boarding party and found to be seriously damaged.

- 10 May 1982: The *Sheffield* sank while under tow outside the military exclusion zone. Argentine C-130 Hercules aircraft, escorted by Mirage fighters, attempted to reach Port Stanley but were turned away by Sea Harriers. Royal Navy ships, standing off the east coast of the islands, again bombarded Port Stanley.

  The British imposed a controlled airspace of a 100-nautical-mile radius around the Wideawake airfield on Ascension Island.

  The Argentine submarine *San Luis* fired several torpedos at large from a range of 5,000 meters. One torpedo was said to have hit but not exploded.

- 11 May 1982: A British attempt to interdict supply routes between East and West Falkland across Falkland Sound resulted in the sinking of the transport *Cabo de los Estados* by gunfire from the Type 21 frigate, HMS *Alacrity*. The Argentine ship, carrying fuel and ammunition, exploded. British naval bombardment of Port Stanley continued.

- 12 May 1982: Thirty-five hundred troops of the 3rd Infantry Brigade sailed on the *Queen Elizabeth 2*. The new Sea King helicopter squadron embarked on the *Atlantic Causeway*.

  The Argentine air force started major attacks on the British task force. Four Argentine A-4 Skyhawk aircraft attacked two British ships. Two were shot down by Sea Wolf missiles, while a third crashed into the sea while taking evasive action. A second wave of A-4s attacked. A third wave of A-4s broke off the attack.

  The HMS *Glasgow* was struck by a bomb which failed to explode. The decision was made for a landing at San Carlos, and suitable orders were given.

- 13 May 1982: Britain attempted to resume the Black Buck Vulcan missions against Port Stanley airport, but was forced to cancel the mission because the headwinds were too strong for safety, given the Vulcan's fuel reserves.

- 14–15 May 1982: Twelve four-man teams of the Special Air Service carried out a raid on Pebble Island, north of West Falkland Island. They blew up an ammunition dump and eleven parked Argentine aircraft. The destroyed aircraft included six Pucara twin turboprop counterinsurgency aircraft and several Skyvan light transports.
- 16 May 1982: Sea Harriers attacked two blockade-running Argentine ships in Falkland Sound. One was abandoned by its crew off Port King. The special boat squadron units were removed from San Carlos.
- 18 May 1982: The *Atlantic Conveyor* arrived with a cargo of Sea Harriers and RAF Harriers. The aircraft were transferred to the *Hermes* and the *Invincible*.
- 19 May 1982: A Sea King helicopter was lost while ferrying troops between ships.
- 20 May 1982: See Table 3.2 for the additional ships added to the Falkland Islands task force. Another Sea King helicopter was lost in bad weather.
- 21 May 1982: British raids were launched on Port Louis, Goose Green, and Fox Bay. These raids were supported by Harrier strikes and naval bombardment, in an effort to mask the concentration of British forces off San Carlos. Although there were no Argentine forces at San Carlos as recently as 16 May, a four-man patrol from the HMS *Brilliant* discovered a group of Argentines on Fanning Head, which dominates the north entrance to San Carlos Water. A special boat squadron eliminated this Argentine force before the main landing.

The British plan called for the 40th Commando and the 2nd Battalion of the Parachute Regiment to land on either side of San Carlos. The 45th Commando was to land near Ajax Bay, and the 3rd Battalion of the Parachute Regiment was to land at Port San Carlos. The pump filling the embarkation dock of the HMS *Fearless* broke down, and, at considerable risk, the dock gate was opened to allow the sea to flood in. This delayed the departure of the 40th Commando. The men of the 2nd Parachute Battalion had great trouble climbing off the *Norland*, which has no dock at all, and then set off in the wrong direction until corrected. Nevertheless, forty commandos liberated San Carlos and found thirty-one islanders, most of whom had fled Port Stanley. The 2nd Battalion of the Parachute Regiment took Sussex Mountain to protect the beachhead from the south, the 45th Commando

TABLE 3.2 Additional Ships for the Falkland Islands Task Force

WARSHIPS

    Amphibious Assault Ship
      Intrepid   11,060 tons

    Type 82-Class Light Cruiser
      Bristol   6,100 tons

    Type 42 *Sheffield*-Class Destroyers   3,500 tons
      Exeter
      Cardiff

    Type 21 *Amazon*-Class Frigates   2,750 tons
      Active
      Avenger

    Leander-Class Frigates
      Minerva   3,200 tons
      Penelope   3,200 tons
      Andromeda   2,962 tons

REQUISITIONED AND CHARTERED SHIPS

Liner		
Queen Elizabeth 2	Cunard	67,000 tons
Cargo Ships		
Atlantic Causeway	Cunard	14,946 tons
Baltic Ferry	Stena Cargo Line	6,455 tons
Geestport	Geest Line	7,730 tons
Lycaon	China Mutual United Steam Navigation Co.	11,804 tons
Nordic Ferry	Stena Cargo Line	6,455 tons
Saxonia	Cunard	8,547 tons
Tankers		
Alvega	Silver Line	33,329 tons
Vinga Polaris	Vinga Tankers	8,000 tons
Cable Ship		
Iris	British Telecom	3,873 tons
Supply Tug		
Wimpey Seahorse	Wimpey Marine	1,599 tons

SOURCE: Ministry of Defence, London.

secured an unused refrigeration plant at Ajax Bay, and the 3rd Parachute occupied Port San Carlos to find evidence that about forty Argentine soldiers had just left. Thinking that all was clear, a Sea King helicopter lifting Rapier missiles and accompanied by a Gazelle helicopter took off for Port San Carlos. The two helicopters were fired upon by the retreating Argentines. The Sea King escaped but the Gazelle was downed, apparently by a Blowpipe missile. A second Gazelle was downed the same way.

Argentina responded with fifty-four attack sorties against British shipping. The first attacks were by Pucara aircraft from Port Stanley. Two Pucaras were shot down but the frigate HMS *Argonaut* was damaged. Twenty-one minutes later, Argentine Skyhawks and Mirages began the first of seventy-two sorties against the British task force on that day. The HMS *Ardent* was hit by two 1,000-lb. bombs on the aft deck, knocking out all major systems. Ten more bombs were dropped on the *Ardent*, which was not previously listed as a member of the task force. The HMS *Argonaut* was also badly damaged by a hit on the flight deck by two bombs. The *Argonaut* was immobilized and was towed into San Carlos Water. The *Antrim* and *Brilliant* were hit by bombs that failed to explode. The *Canberra* was not hit, and the Argentines claimed that they had not been trying to hit it. Sixteen fixed-wing Argentine aircraft were shot down during these attacks (nine Mirages, five Skyhawks, and two Pucaras), as well as four helicopters. A RAF Harrier was lost away from San Carlos Bay.

The British succeeded in landing considerable heavy equipment: 105-mm guns of the 29th Commando Brigade, Royal Artillery; armored fighting vehicles (Scimitar and Scorpion), and Rapier air defense missiles. A detachment of Sea King helicopters demonstrated the value of heliborne lift by ferrying 520 troops and 912,000 pounds of stores.

- 22 May 1982: Argentine air attacks were limited to two Skyhawks, which were quickly chased off by Harriers. The British took advantage of the lull to land equipment and supplies and establish batteries of Rapier anti-aircraft missiles. By the end of the day, 5,000 British troops were ashore and occupied an area of ten square miles. Under the cover of darkness, the *Canberra* was removed from Falkland Sound to South Georgia Island. Two Harriers attacked and severely damaged an Argentine patrol craft.
- 23 May 1982: Intensive Argentine air attacks resumed. The HMS *Antelope* was struck by two 1,000-lb. bombs that lodged in the engine room but did not explode. The ship sailed into San Carlos

Water for repairs and to have its bombs defused. One bomb then exploded, an uncontrollable fire broke out, and the ship was abandoned. Five Mirages and one Skyhawk aircraft were shot down. In separate actions, Harriers destroyed one Puma and one UH-1 Iroquois helicopter and strafed a second Puma, which was forced to land. Harriers attacked the Goose Green landing strip. A Sea Harrier was lost on take-off.

- 24 May 1982: The HMS *Antelope* sank. Argentina renewed its air attacks with twenty-four Mirage and Skyhawk sorties. A Sea Harrier claimed the first doublekill of the conflict, downing two Mirages with two Sidewinder missiles. A total of eight Argentine jet aircraft were lost. The logistics landing ship, HMS *Sir Galahad*, was hit by an unexploded bomb through the side and had to be evacuated. Her sister ship, HMS *Sir Lancelot*, was also hit. Since the start of the action at San Carlos, ten British ships had been sunk or hit by bombs that failed to explode. Overall, only about 20 percent of Argentine bomb hits exploded.

- 25 May 1982: Argentina located a large ship heading toward Falkland Sound and decided to attack it with Exocet missiles. The British ship, ten miles north of Pebble Island, was screened by the HMS *Coventry* and HMS *Broadsword*, which were guarding the entrance to Falkland Sound. These ships were attacked by Skyhawk aircraft and Exocet missiles. The British hoped that the *Coventry*, a sister ship to the *Sheffield*, could be protected by the Sea Wolf missiles of the *Broadsword*. The Sea Wolf, however, was a point defense system and not effective at protecting other targets. Earlier in the conflict, both the *Broadsword* and the *Brilliant* had been hit by direct attacks, and the Sea Wolf had failed to provide direct point defense. This experience was repeated. The HMS *Coventry* was hit with three 1,000-lb. bombs and capsized within twenty minutes. The HMS *Broadsword* also was hit but suffered no casualties and remained operational. Four Skyhawks were shot down.

Two Super Etendard aircraft then attacked the first major ship to appear on their radars. Each fired one Exocet missile. The *Atlantic Conveyor* was hit and subsequently abandoned with the loss of twelve lives. The cargo and weapons lost with the *Atlantic Conveyor* included three Chinook helicopters, six Wessex-5 support helicopters, two Lynx helicopters, tents to accommodate 4,000 men, mobile landing strips for the Harriers, and a water-desalination plant. The Chinooks, each capable of carrying up to eighty troops, were to have played a crucial role in carrying troops and cargo for the land war.

The Soviet Union launched the film recovery earth resources spacecraft Cosmos 1369 into a 269 × 229 km orbit inclined at 82.3 degrees.

- 27 May 1982: One RAF Harrier was lost to enemy fire.
- 28 May 1982: The 2nd Parachute recaptured Darwin and Goose Green. Troops of the 2nd Battalion, Parachute Regiment, under the command of Lt. Col. Herbert ("H") Jones, launched an attack at 2:30 A.M. in pouring rain on the Argentine forces holding Goose Green. This attack later raised questions, as the main objective of the campaign was Port Stanley. Some critics thought Goose Green might have been bypassed without hazard.

British intelligence regarding the size of Argentines forces at Goose Green proved faulty, and the 450 British troops did not know that Argentine forces outnumbered them by four to one until the end of the battle. The British troops carried 56 machine guns (double the normal number) and "throwaway" 61-mm anti-tank rockets and were supported with 105-mm artillery and Milan-guided missiles. They had asked for light tanks but were told they were required for "other priorities." The HMS *Antrim* was offshore to the west in Brenton Loch for support but had some problems with its 4.5-inch guns.

Goose Green and Darwin, which is about two miles to the north of Goose Green, are on a narrow north-south isthmus which is only 400 yards wide at its narrowest point. Entrenched Argentine troops held the high ground of Boca Hill on the west and Darwin Hill on the east. Three British companies of 110 men each moved forward, one to attack each hill and one in the center. By dawn at 6 A.M., neither hill had been taken. HQ forces joined the attack on Darwin Hill, but the attack failed. Support artillery was then brought forward, and the British moved troops up on Boca Hill, using the cover of an eighteen-foot lip above the beach. Boca Hill was hit from two sides, and the Argentines surrendered in a matter of minutes. The Milan missiles proved very effective against the Argentine strong points.

Darwin Hill was secured at the same time. Darwin village was bypassed, and the British decided to take the Goose Green airstrip and school house, a strong point between Darwin and Goose Green. This target was assigned to the reserve company. They were attacked by two Pucara aircraft that narrowly missed the troops with napalm. One of the aircraft was shot down with a Blowpipe missile.

As the weather cleared, three Harriers dropped anti-personnel cluster bombs on Argentine guns on a narrow spit of land east of Goose Green and put them out of action. The Argentines had been holding 112 civilians captive in Goose Green for 30 days, and the British opened negotiations. The first conversations led to the surrender of a 50-man Argentine air force contingent. The other Argentine forces then surrendered. The British had lost 18 killed and 34 wounded. Argentine losses were about 250 killed and 120 wounded. One British Scout helicopter and four Argentine Pucara aircraft had been shot down.

The British tried to launch Black Buck against the Argentine radars in Port Stanley. The Vulcan carried four Shrike AGM-54As on its wing pylons and extra fuel in its bomb bay. The mission was aborted due to problems with the fuel probe on the lead Victor tanker.

The Soviet Union launched the imaging reconnaissance satellite Cosmos 1370 into a 290 × 203 km orbit inclined at 62.8 degrees.

- 29 May 1982: The 3rd Battalion, Parachute Regiment, completed a 26-mile march in full kit and total darkness to Teal Inlet. The 45th Commando left for Douglas. Elements of the 42nd Commando attempted a helicopter landing on Mount Kent (near Port Stanley) that nearly ended in disaster when the sole surviving Chinook helicopter inadvertently touched down in water in a storm and lost a wheel and a door before returning to Port San Carlos.

Major General Mario Menendez sent a message to Buenos Aires warning that his forces would not win.

An Argentine air force Hercules aircraft attacked the British petroleum tanker *Wye* north of South Georgia Island with eight 500-lb. bombs. One bomb struck the deck but failed to explode. The *Wye* was carrying 21,000 tons of fuel but continued on undamaged.

A flight of two Super Etendard and four A-4C Skyhawk aircraft attempted to attack the HMS *Invincible*. They struck at a target about ninety miles east of the Falklands. The Argentines reported that they had identified and hit the aircraft carrier *Invincible*. The British claimed the Argentines struck at the HMS *Avenger* and the HMS *Exeter* and the *Avenger* destroyed an Exocet with its guns. Two Argentine A-4 aircraft were reported to be shot down.

The final tally for the Exocet missiles was five firings and two ships sunk. The French denied the British claims that the Exocet was fooled by chaff and that the *Atlantic Conveyor* was not the primary target during the attack of 25 May. The British continued to insist that only one Exocet hit the primary target

(*Sheffield*), and the Argentines continued to insist that they had hit the *Invincible*.

- 30 May 1982: The 45th Commando and 3rd Parachute Brigade secured Douglas settlement and Teal Inlet on the north side of East Falkland Island. Elements of the 42nd Commando and units of the Special Air Service succeeded in landing on Mount Kent and Mount Challenger. Mount Kent, 1,504 feet high, is only ten miles from Port Stanley. British warships bombarded positions around Port Stanley. An RAF Harrier was lost to the enemy.

  The British flew a Black Buck mission in a second attempt to use the Vulcan with Shrike against the TPS-43 radar at Port Stanley. The mission failed when the radar stopped emitting during a diversionary Harrier attack.

- 1 June 1982: The Soviets launched an intelligence spacecraft, Cosmos 1371, into an 833 × 793 km orbit inclined at 74.1 degrees. The British 5th Infantry Brigade landed at San Carlos.

- 2 June 1982: A Sea Harrier was lost to enemy fire. Black Buck failed when the Argentines shut off their radars and no lock-on was possible. The Vulcan refueling probe was damaged, and it was forced to divert to Galao airport in Brazil. The Vulcan was allowed to return to Ascension, but Brazil kept the Shrike.

- 4 June 1982: Forces of B Company, 2nd Battalion, Parachute Regiment, landed by helicopter at the undefended settlements of Fitzroy and Bluff Cove, 36 miles from Goose Green.

- 5 June 1982: The British started to move 1,200 members of the Scots and Welsh guards to the Fitzroy–Bluff Cove area. The Scots Guards were taken to Lively Island near the mouth of Choiseul Sound aboard HMS *Intrepid*, but could not go farther for fear of attack by land-based Exocet missiles that had been deployed at Port Stanley. They proceded to Bluff Cove in landing craft. Due to the atrocious weather, they took five hours to reach Bluff Cove, and the trip was further lengthened by a challenge from HMS *Cardiff*, which must not have known of their presence. Five Harriers (two Sea Harriers and three RAF Harriers) landed at the forward operating base at San Carlos.

- 6 June 1982: Welsh Guards were embarked on the *Fearless*, but the weather was so bad that landing craft could not get out of Bluff Cove. Two landing craft on the *Fearless* were filled with troops and sent ashore. The remaining troops returned with the *Fearless* to San Carlos Water. The landing of the 5th Brigade was completed, and the British had about 8,000 troops ashore. A British Gazelle helicopter was lost.

- 7–8 June 1982: The Argentine air force attacked British ships at

Pleasant Bay. At Fitzroy, the *Sir Galahad* joined her sister ship, the HMS *Sir Tristram*, which earlier had brought supplies and equipment. Unloading of the two ships took much longer than expected because the beach at Fitzroy settlement was very narrow. In addition, the Welsh Guards were not anxious to disembark, since getting to Bluff Cove involved a twelve-mile march that could be avoided if the landing craft could provide transport. Although Fitzroy and Bluff Cove are only four miles apart, the bridge across the inlet that separates them had been blown up by the Argentines. At 2:10 P.M., *Sir Galahad* and *Sir Tristram* were attacked by two Skyhawks and two Mirages. The ships had been within range of the Argentine radar atop Sapper Hill near Port Stanley. The British suffered fifty-one killed and forty-six injured. The attacks occured before the Rapier surface-to-air missile defenses were fully established. Helicopters were in the process of ferrying Rapier equipment ashore at the time of the attack.

The frigate HMS *Plymouth* was attacked by five Mirage aircraft at San Carlos and struck by four bombs, none of which exploded. One passed through the ship's funnel and another set off a depth charge, starting a fire that was put out in an hour. The *Plymouth* remained operational. Seven Argentine aircraft were shot down. One RAF Harrier was lost.

- 10 June 1982: Mount Harriet, Two Sisters, and Mount Longdon were fully secured. British 105-mm guns commenced bombardment of Port Stanley from positions high on Mount Kent. Each of the five batteries (six guns each) was given 1,200 shells.
- 11 June 1982: The final Black Buck mission struck at the Port Stanley airport without success. Only one of seven Vulcan missions had succeeded in causing significant target damage.
- 11–12 June 1982: Following three days of artillery bombardment, the British launched the first phase of the attack on Port Stanley. The 3rd Parachute Battalion was assigned to take 600-foot Mount Longdon five miles west of Port Stanley, while the 2nd Paratroops, the Welsh Guards, and two companies of the 40th Commando were held in reserve. The fighting was sharp, and on many occasions British forces could advance only because of close naval gun support from the HMS *Avenger*. The British losses during this battle were twenty-three killed and forty-seven wounded. The Argentines lost fifty killed and ten wounded as well as thirty-nine taken prisoner.

The Argentine forces had an edge in night combat. They were equipped with effective night sights (passive night goggles). The

British forces had a few dozen pair, but the Argentines had hundreds.

The 42nd Commando was ordered to take the 900-foot Mount Harriet and the 750-foot Goat Ridge. They received naval gun support from the HMS *Yarmouth*, and the Scots Guard and Gurkhas were in reserve. They achieved their objectives. Argentine losses were unspecified but heavy. About 200 prisoners were taken. The British troops found the Milan missile to be a very effective way of dislodging entrenched troops (but expensive at $35,000 each). The 45th Commando attacked the Two Sisters range just west of Port Stanley, with naval gun support from HMS *Glamorgan*. It achieved its goal with the loss of four men.

HMS *Glamorgan* was struck by a land-launched Exocet missile. The Argentines did not possess the land-launched version of the Exocet, but they removed one from their shipboard Exocets and mounted it on a flatbed trailer. The *Glamorgan* attempted to shoot down the Exocet with a Sea Cat missile but failed. The missile exploded in the area of the helicopter hangar, destroying a Wessex-3 helicopter and resulting in thirteen killed and seventeen injured. The ship remained operational.

The Argentine air force launched its final air attacks, losing one aircraft to a Sea Dart Missile.

- 14 June 1982: The second phase of the attack on Port Stanley was launched before dawn. The 2nd Battalion, Parachute Regiment, took Wireless Ridge with little direct opposition but experienced considerable difficulty because of 155-mm Argentine artillery fire. Light tanks (Scimitars and Scorpions) were used in support of the advance for the first time.

The Scots Guards attacked Tumbledown Mountain and found it defended by an elite Argentine marine battalion. The Scots Guards were supported by Harriers using cluster and laser-guided bombs. They took Tumbledown Mountain with a loss of nine killed and forty-one wounded. Argentine losses were estimated at thirty killed. The Gurkhas took Mount Williams with little resistance. The Welsh Guards took Wireless Ridge and Sapper Hill with little resistance, but made a six-hour crossing of a minefield under artillery fire to reach it.

Port Stanley was now exposed to British attack. After the Argentines expressed willingness, Captain Roderick Bell and SAS Colonel Michael Ross arrived in Port Stanley for conversations with General Menendez. General Menendez struck the word "unconditional" but did surrender all Argentine forces in East and West Falkland together with their equipment to Major General

Jeremy Moore, commander of the 5th British Brigade. The last Argentine C-130 aircraft departed from Port Stanley hours before the surrender.

- 18 June 1982: The Liner *Canberra* with 4,200 prisoners and the ferry *Norland* with 2,000 prisoners sailed from Port Stanley for Puerto Madrym. The British had taken a total of 11,400 prisoners.
- 20 June 1982: The Argentine scientific base on Thule Island, one of the South Sandwich Islands which stretch from 250 to 500 miles southeast of South Georgia Island, surrendered to the HMS *Endurance* and its warship escort.
- 21 June 1982: The burnt hulk of the logistics landing ship *Sir Galahad* was towed from Fitzroy and sunk at sea. The Port Stanley airstrip was opened for operations by British Hercules transport aircraft.
- 25 June 1982: Governor Hunt returned to Port Stanley.
- 12 July 1982: The military aspects of the Falkland Islands conflict ended with the announcement that Britain was satisfied that active hostilities were ended, although Argentina did not agree to the end of conflict. The British total exclusion zone and economic sanctions remained in effect.
- 13 July 1982: The British announced that Britain would not sell the HMS *Invincible* to Australia. Australia would get a new carrier of the *Invincible* class and was offered the lease of HMS *Hermes* while the new carrier was being built.
- 22 July 1982: Britain lifted the total exclusion zone but warned Argentina to keep military ships and aircraft away from the Falklands.

The Forces Engaged

The forces engaged on each side are shown in Table 3.3. It is important to note that Argentina had superior land and air power, while Britain was able to deploy superior sea power. It is also important to note that neither side deployed forces or technology that were procured for such a conflict. Britain was in the final stages of phasing out its global power projection capability when the war began. Argentina had procured and trained its forces for regional status, internal political purposes, and potential conflict with Chile.

Great Britain and Argentina fought without allies, although the United States provided considerable material and logistical support to the British. This support is summarized in Table 3.4.[2] The U.S. began major assistance to Britain in April 1982, long before the U.S. National

TABLE 3.3 Falklands War: Forces and Force Ratios[a]

British Falklands Task Force	Argentine Assets Available to Repel a British Invasion
NAVAL FORCES	
44 warships, including	110 ships
5 fleet submarines	1 aircraft carrier
1 Oberon-class submarine	1 heavy cruiser
2 ASW carriers	7 destroyers
7 guided missile destroyers	12 frigates
15 general purpose frigates	19 other ships
9 Corvette/patrol ships	4 diesel submarines
2 assault ships	1 assault ship
6 logistic landing ships	5 logistics landing ships
22 auxiliaries	45 merchant ships
NAVAL AIR	
20–28 FRS-1 Sea Harriers	10–12 A-4 Skyhawk
106–150 various helicopters	5–10 Super Etendard
	8–10 MB-339 Aeromacchi
AIR FORCE	
8–14 GR-3 Harriers	50–68 A-4 Skyhawk
5–9 Vulcan B	20–21 Mirage III
1–4 CH-46 Chinook	20–26 Mirage V (Dagger)
	30–60 IA-58 Pucara
	5–9 B-62 Canberra
ARMY	
	12–20 helicopters
TOTAL FORCES	
33–55 fixed wing aircraft	148–216 fixed wing aircraft
107–154 helicopters	12–20 helicopters
GROUND FORCES	
9,500 troops:	12,150 troops:
3rd Commando Brigade	8,400 in Port Stanley defense
(5 battalions, 3 Royal Marine,	force (5 regiments, 1 Marine
2 Parachute)	battalion)

(continues)

TABLE 3.3 *(continued)*

British Falklands Task Force	Argentine Assets Available to Repel a British Invasion
GROUND FORCES (continued)	
5th Infantry Brigade	1,600 in Goose Green/Darwin
(3 Army battalions)	defense force (2 regiments)
2 artillery regiments	1 105-mm howitzer regiment with
(30 howitzers)	30 guns
1/2 armored squadron	1 1.55-mm howitzer battery with
(12 Scorpions, 18 APCs)	4 guns
Several hundred SAS and SBS	1 armored car company with 15
special forces	armored cars
1 engineer regiment	1 Marine special forces company
combat support forces	(recce) with 125 men
	2 engineer companies
	other support forces

[a]Sources differ widely, in part because of counting rules. The range shown for the air force is the low and high estimate in British and Argentine sources. Many of the forces listed could not be committed to combat.

Security Council decided that the U.S. would firmly back Britain in a meeting on 1 May 1982. This commitment followed U.S. Navy studies indicating that the UK task force had so fragile a logistics tail that it might well lose the war. Secretary of Defense Caspar Weinberger steadily strengthened this commitment after consulting with President Ronald Reagan.

The U.S. set up a central clearing house in the Pentagon to provide a 24-hour response time for release of goods from inventory. The U.S. provided additional water purification and accommodation on Ascension Island, released its strategic stockpiles on the island, and diverted a U.S. tanker. A total of 12.5 million gallons of U.S. aviation fuel was provided for British Vulcan bombers, Victor Tankers, Nimrod reconnaissance planes, and C-130 transporters. The U.S. provided drop containers for British C-130 air drops on the islands and air refueling parts.

The weapons supplies listed in Table 3.4 proved critical. The Aim-9L air-to-air missiles gave Britain's Harriers a decisive edge against Argentine fighters. The U.S. supplied the matting necessary to convert Widewake airport for Harrier operations. The Shrike anti-radiation missiles came with Argentine radar frequencies. Other important

TABLE 3.4 Material Supplied to Britain by the United States During the Falklands War

200 Sidewinder Aim-9L air-to-air missiles	350 torpedo exhaust valves
Harrier-Sidewinder adaptor plates	Satellite dishes and encrypting facilities
8 Stinger anti-aircraft systems	Submarine detection equipment
Vulcan Phalanx air defense gun system	Flare cartridges for M130 dispensing systems
Harpoon anti-ship missiles	60-mm illuminating mortar rounds
Shrike air-to-ground radar-seeking missiles	40-mm high-explosive ammunition
18 CTU-2A air drop containers	Other assorted ammunition
4,700 tons airfield matting	Night vision goggles
1 C-47 helicopter engine	Special mess heaters
12.5-million gallons aviation fuel	Long-range patrol ration packs

SOURCES: *The Economist*, March 3, 1984, and U.S. Department of Defense.

equipment included Stinger surface-to-air missiles for SAS, night vision goggles, Chinook engines, several thousand mortar rounds, a Vulcan-Phalanx anti-missile gun system, long-range patrol radiation packs, and a host of other equipment.

Later in the war, the U.S. also moved a military satellite to cover the Falklands. The National Security Agency provided signals intelligence to the British intelligence center at Cheltenham for U.S. listening stations in the South Atlantic, as well as the technology to decrypt Argentine codes for use by British intelligence ships like the HMS *Endurance*. The U.S. also allocated some of its military satellite channels to the UK and sold some $4 million in satellite dishes and encryption equipment for use by the commander of the task force, British submarines, and the British fleet headquarters at Northwood. The decision to allow the HMS *Conqueror* to sink the *General Belgrano* seems to have been made using U.S. satellite gear.

The U.S. also drafted a contingency plan to transfer an American amphibious assault ship to Britain in the event it lost either of its carriers, the *Hermes* or the *Invincible*. This ship was the USS *Guam*. In contrast, Argentina quickly found itself isolated and unable to obtain resupply of critical weapons like the Exocet or technical advice in electronic warfare.

The continuing tension on the Chilean-Argentine border forced Argentina to keep some troops on the border in case Chile took advantage of the opportunities provided by the Falklands War. The Argentine troops remaining on the border included two elite battalions of mountain commandos which were stationed at Comodor Revadaria. Many of the elite Naval Infantry Corps troops (Marines) who initially invaded the Falklands were subsequently transferred to the Chilean border. Their replacements were poorly trained conscripts of the Argentine Army who generally proved to have very poor organization, leadership, and training.

In spite of the ad hoc character of the war, the British performance was impressive. The British recaptured the Falklands in a combined operation using rapidly assembled elements of their army, navy, and air force which had to be deployed over 8,000 miles from Britain on very short notice. All were drawn from units designed for combat in support of NATO. Much of their equipment reflected past strains on the British defense budget and the need to reduce the cost of sophisticated weapons systems. British ground force equipment, however, was generally superior to that of the Argentines (see Table 3.3). Further, Britain was able to draw on stocks of material earmarked for use against the Soviet Union in a European war.

One of the critical differences between each side was the relative character of their land forces. The British troops were all career volunteers who were well motivated and led by experienced officers and professional NCOs. The Argentine forces consisted largely of conscripts who were not trained for the unique terrain, weather, and sea conditions of the Falklands. The Argentine officers were often promoted more for political reasons than for military expertise. They tended to look down upon conscripts, who were often mistreated as a result of such contempt. Argentine tactical planning was poor, and only the Argentine air force exhibited high morale and a willingness to take casualties.

The Argentine military government had engaged in a substantial military buildup before the conflict and had purchased many modern European weapons systems. This buildup is reflected in Table 3.5. It began in 1976–1977, shortly before Argentina's near-war with Chile over the Beagle Channel in 1978. Indeed, part of the reason the Argentines chose to initiate the Falklands invasion was that their massive expenditures on arms imports after 1974 had (along with many other factors) severely damaged the Argentine economy. The invasion of the Falklands was intended to shore up an unpopular military government.

Despite this buildup, the Argentine military had serious structural flaws. The army lacked any significant mobile assault forces and had failed to carry out detailed and realistic plans to seize the Falklands or properly train most of the forces it included in its improvision.[3]

Individual Argentine units fought well, particularly in prepared defensive positions. Argentine units with good training and experienced leadership, such as the marines, 25th Infantry, 3rd Artillery, and 601 and 602 commandos, showed they could fight as the

TABLE 3.5 Argentine Military Buildup

| | Military Expenditures | | Armed Forces |
Year	In millions of U.S. dollars	With dollars held constant at 1981 level	In hundreds of thousands of troops
1972	792	1541	140
1973	932	1716	160
1974	1173	1386	150
1975	1658	2575	160
1976	1948	2863	155
1977	2259	3134	155
1978	2617	3381	155
1979	2758	3285	155
1980	2739	2995	155
1981	3186	3186	155
1982	4,147	NA	175
1983	3,139	—	175
1984	2.676	—	174
1985	2,368	—	129

SOURCES: U.S. Arms Control and Disarmament Agency, *World Military Expenditures and Arms Transfers,1972–1982* (Washington, D.C.: GPO, 1983), p. 17; 1987 edition, p. 49.

equals of British units such as the Welsh and Scots guards. Nevertheless, Argentine forces had poor overall leadership, organization, and C^{3}I. The Argentine officer corps was divided and corrupt. Interservice rivalry was extensive and debilitating, and army training was poor. The Argentine "dirty war" against domestic "terrorism" had shifted the military from a combat organization to a torture and internal security organization. The Argentine commander of the Falklands was a product of this reorientation. Major General Mario Menendez had a reputation as a hard and effective commander because of his conduct against Argentine opposition movements, but his experience was political rather than military and had little value in a campaign against regular troops with equal or superior weaponry. In fact, Menendez's failure to plug the gaps in his defense of Port Stanley, particularly around Mount Kent, and his hasty retreat from Fitzroy and Bluff Cove were major errors contributing to the speed of the Argentine defeat.

The Argentine officers leading most conscript troops remained isolated from their troops, made no effort to improve their training once they had landed, left them in summer uniforms, and often left them poorly housed and supplied. In contrast, British officers worked closely with their troops and showed great concern for their equipment and welfare. While Argentine troops did little training, the British troops fired about "37 1/2 years' worth" of their normal training ammunition during their voyage to the Falklands.

These differences between the two sides affected much of the outcome and helped limit the cost of the fighting. In spite of the relatively large forces and weapons involved, the war caused the least bloodshed of any of the conflicts under examination. The resulting casualty figures are listed in Table 3.6. There were only 256 British and 746 Argentine dead.

The Terrain

The military terrain of the Falklands campaign included the island of South Georgia and the sea around it, the East and West Falkland islands, and the sea surrounding these islands. The Falklands are 400 miles from Argentina and 3,750 miles from the British staging area at Ascension Island. Initial operations, however, took place at South Georgia. This island is 800 miles farther southeast from the Falklands.

The Falklands coastline is rocky and virtually barren of trees. The interior is mountainous and boggy, and most vehicles cannot move. The climate and terrain are equally harsh. The weather is always unpredictable, and the fighting occurred just before the onset of winter when there is frequent mist, rain, and snow. Serious problems existed in terms of exposure and frostbite. There were also unexpected problems with trenchfoot. The harsh weather conditions and rough terrain occasionally reduced normal marching speed to about two miles per hour. The British seem to have lost two Harriers because of a collision in poor weather, and visibility over the Falklands was so poor that the Argentine air force did not launch attack aircraft on thirteen days because of its inability to acquire targets.

There were also a number of problems on the Falklands that made it difficult to use field artillery in the proper manner. These included cloud cover and rain, high winds that reduced accuracy, and cold temperatures that made it extremely difficult to screw fuses into shells. The peat-laden soil reduced the explosive and fragmentation effect of shells and increased the importance of airbursts.[4]

This combination of weather and terrain conditions constantly affected amphibious operations. Both Argentina and Britain took advantage of nighttime to make amphibious landings. The Argentines succeeded in the initial assault on Port Stanley by eighty troops from the *Santissima Trinidad* because they hit the beaches at night and suffered no casualties. The Argentine force that landed at South

TABLE 3.6 Falklands War: Casualties and Losses

	British	*Argentine*
A. CASUALTIES		
Killed	256	746
Wounded	777[a]	1,336
Total	1,023	1,550–1,750
Captured	80	11,400
B. EQUIPMENT LOSSES		
	2 Destroyers	1 Heavy Cruiser
	2 Frigates	1 Submarine
	1 Assault Ship	1 Patrol Vessel
	1 Container Ship	5 Navy A-4 Skyhawks
	6 Sea Harriers	40 Air Force A-4 Skyhawks
	4 GR-3 Harriers	27 Mirage III/V
	3 CH-46 Chinook	3 B-62 Canberra
	24 helicopters	3 MB-339 Aeromacchi
		21 IA-58 Pucara
		10 Army helicopters
		8 non-combatant aircraft
C. DIFFERENCES OVER AIR LOSSES		
	British Air Force personnel losses (according to Argentine sources):	36 officers killed 14 NCOs killed 5 soldiers killed
	British Air Force equipment losses (according to Argentine sources):	12 to 14 aircraft 12 helicopters
D. COST OF THE FIGHTING		
	$1.6 billion	$1.85 billion

[a]of whom over 700 fully recovered

SOURCES: Jeffrey Ethell and Alfred Price, *Air War: South Atlantic* (New York: Macmillan, 1984); *The Falklands Campaign: The Lessons* (London: Her Majesty's Stationery Office, 1982); and Nora Kinzer Stewart, "A Study in Cohesion: South Atlantic Conflict 1982," *Military Review*, April 1985, p. 31.

Georgia in the daytime did suffer casualties. The British took advantage of nighttime and cloud cover, plus the fact that the Argentines lacked fighters equipped for night attack missions, during their landing at San Carlos. The landing conditions were so difficult,

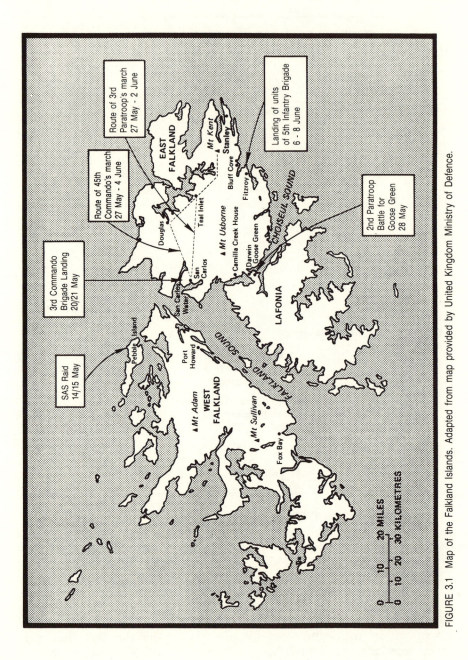

FIGURE 3.1 Map of the Falkland Islands. Adapted from map provided by United Kingdom Ministry of Defence.

however, that the British ships could not meet their schedule and the Argentine air force eventually inflicted significant causalties. At the same time, the terrain made movement so difficult that this was a key factor preventing Argentine troops from trying to halt the British landings at the beachheads.[5]

The rough terrain of the Falklands led to extensive mountain warfare. The British avoided mountain combat during the landing at San Carlos through their rapid seizure of Mount Kent. (See Figure 3.1.) The Argentines established their main defense line around Port Stanley, however, in the mountains on a line including Mt. Harriet, Mt. Longdon, Two Sisters, Tumbledown, and Sapper Hill. The weather was extremely cold in these heights. Fortunately for the British, it was not as cold as British planners expected, and the British troops were relatively well equipped. The Argentines, however, were not equipped with adequate and sufficient cold-weather gear, and this may have affected their performance.[6]

Maintenance personnel were forced to struggle with the problems associated with extreme cold and humidity. These problems were equally bad at sea due to the severe weather conditions in the South Atlantic. Harrier cockpits, for example, were sometimes drenched, thus affecting the integrity of the electronic systems. This forced Britain to rely heavily on ad hoc maintenance solutions. For example, Clingfilm was used to cover a display panel. In another case, a bath edge sealing compound was used to prevent water seepage through the pilot tube to the Blue Fox radar in the nose cone. Excellent discipline was required to avoid losses and accidents due to the punishing sea. British performance was outstanding in this regard.

Threat Assessment Technologies

The invasion of the Falkland Islands and South Georgia by Argentine forces on 2 April 1982 came as a political and military surprise to Britain. This surprise was the result of British policy rather than a lack of intelligence data or technical means. British government studies after the war made it clear that Argentina should not have achieved surprise in invading the Falklands, and that the failure to react was the result of political rather than intelligence failures.[7] Britain might have benefited if it had had an ability to deploy its own PHOTINT, SIGINT and COMINT satellites, but there is every indication that Britain had sufficient warning indicators to act without such sensors. In fact, there are strong indications that Britain had access to Argentine diplomatic and military communications as well as the more overt indicators.[8]

This experience reinforces U.S. experience in Vietnam, Angola, and Lebanon and reflects the broad history of the indications and warning (I&W) problem in modern warfare. The key problem in warning is rarely the collection and processing of indicators; it is generally a combination of the failure to (a) organize collection and processing technology in a way that integrates the warning indicators which occur in unexpected areas, (b) devote adequate analytic resources, and (c) overcome the prejudices of senior intelligence officials and policy makers. No intelligence system or technology can compensate for policy level direction and senior management that does not seek, or cannot accept, warning that disagrees with existing policy. The warning problem is almost inevitably the result of policy, and not intelligence, failures.

Once the Argentines had invaded the Falklands, British threat assessment suffered severely from a lack of up-to-date data on Argentine military forces and capabilities.[9] This was partially due to inadequate British attaché resources and reporting on Latin America, but it was also the result of the priority British intelligence analysts gave to a European war scenario. The British entered the war knowing surprisingly little about the Argentines' order-of-battle, military personalities, readiness, and technical capabilities for a nation that had provided Argentina with nearly 10 percent of its arms imports over the preceding five years.[10] As the previous chronology shows, the UK failed to estimate the total size of the Argentine threat and had to rely on U.S. intelligence and special forces scouting for local reconnaissance. This scouting often produced dated or incorrect results.

Satellite reconnaissance by the Soviet Union occurred throughout the war. The U.S. had SIGINT listening posts in the region and later shifted the orbit of a U.S. photo-reconnaissance satellite to provide Britain with better cover.[11] The range of coverage is illustrated in Figure 3.2. Figures 3.3 and 3.4 show the ground tracks (and hence the photographic targets of American and Soviet satellites) of satellites launched at key points during the war. The dates of each orbit are indicated. It is almost certain that the U.S. provided Britain with copies of the photographs it took and with relevant U.S. COMINT and ELINT from a wide range of sources, possibly including SR-71 "Blackbird" aircraft. The Argentines emphatically deny that they received any similar support from the Soviet Union, but there are indications that at least some data were provided.[12] What is more uncertain is the value of such satellite coverage. The weather largely precluded effective satellite coverage during most of at least fifteen days during the time British forces were preparing to land, landing, and taking control of the island.

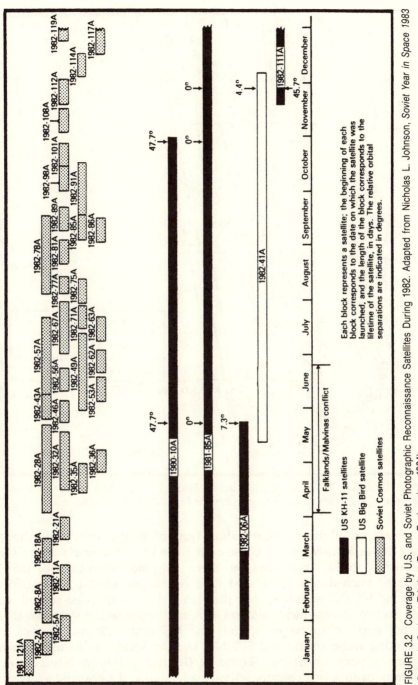

FIGURE 3.2 Coverage by U.S. and Soviet Photographic Reconnaissance Satellites During 1982. Adapted from Nicholas L. Johnson, *Soviet Year in Space 1983* (Colorado Springs: Teledyne Brown Engineering, 1984).

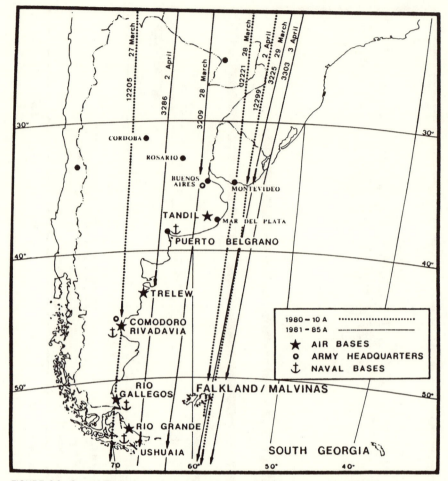

FIGURE 3.3 Ground Tracks over Argentina and the Falklands. Adapted from Nicholas L. Johnson, *Soviet Year in Space 1983* (Colorado Springs: Teledyne Brown Engineering, 1984).

Intercepts of the near-saturation flow of British communications from the task force to the UK would have been extremely revealing and useful to the Argentines, but there is no indication that the USSR obtained such data or provided it to Argentina, although the USSR did send SIGINT satellites over the area. Britain had access to both its own secure communications and U.S. military satellite systems. It is almost certain, in contrast, that the UK and U.S. had access to Argentine radio traffic and SIGINT, but the level and value of such access is very uncertain. There is limited value in intercepting communications in a country whose leadership and commanders are so politicized that they fail to communicate honestly and objectively.

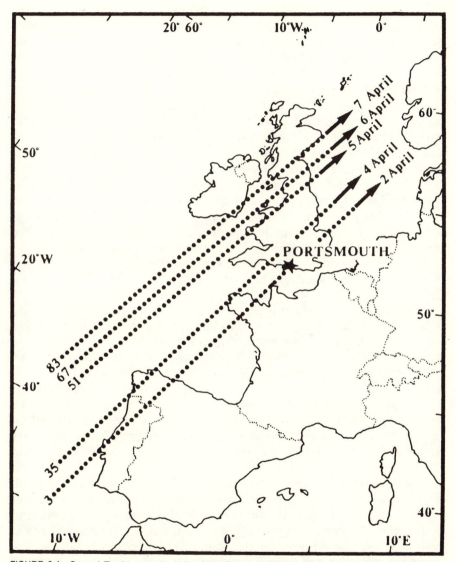

FIGURE 3.4 Ground Tracks over the U.K. of the Soviet Satellite *Cosmos*. Adapted from Nicholas L. Johnson, *Soviet Year in Space 1983* (Colorado Springs: Teledyne Brown Engineering, 1984).

Much of the information Argentine officers communicated consisted of misinformation or outright lies.[13]

It is unclear that the USSR could track British naval movements except on the most episodic basis, and the ground forces involved on both sides were too small, too lightly equipped, and too infantry dominated for either side to track most combat movements. Only the British naval forces at San Carlos, the key land beaches and dispersal strips, and the fixed Argentine defenses and airport at Port Stanley offered highly lucrative targets for PHOTINT satellites.

The Argentines also claim they successfully deceived British reconnaissance aircraft and presumably U.S. satellites after the Vulcan attacks on the runway at Port Stanley airport. The second Vulcan sortie is reported to have dropped twenty-one 1,000-lb. bombs, none of which cracked the runway. The Argentines claim they then put circles of sand and earth on the runway that looked like craters, and the British attacks stopped. The Argentines did not, however, operate any first-line combat aircraft from the airport at Port Stanley, although they used C-130s to resupply. The runway may well have been blocked for first-line fighter operations; at any rate, British ability to sustain the Vulcan in long range sorties was so marginal that it seems unlikely that Argentine deception was the key factor halting further missions.[14]

In short, the same general problems that affect other low-level wars emerge regarding the value of satellite intelligence coverage. There were unquestionably important targets for satellite coverage, but the resulting PHOTINT and SIGINT were often far less valuable than usual; and satellites failed to take the place of dedicated theater air assets, or other sensors, that could have provided continuous or sustained coverage of key collection targets in critical combat areas. Further, significant prewar HUMINT was needed to allow interpretation of collection given the unique nature of each country's forces, capabilities, political system deployments, vulnerabilities, and C^3I systems.

In other areas of threat assessment, early warning for the British fleet had to be provided, largely by shipborne radar backed by Harrier fighters and Sea King helicopters with limited sensor capability and endurance. Shipborne early warning proved inadequate because of the way in which the Argentines attacked and for technical reasons. The Argentine Mirages and Skyhawks were able to fly just above sea level and could avoid surface ship detection until they were within 25 to 30 nautical miles. under optimal conditions and within visual or missile range of their targets, when they could "pop-up" from land cover. The HMS *Sheffield*, for example, was on radar picket duty when it was sunk by an Argentine Super Etendard using an Exocet missile. The British fleet's lack of airborne early warning proved to be an extremely serious shortcoming.

The British situation was made worse by the sensor and C^3I limitations of the key British ships deployed to the Falklands. The British attempted to maintain a radar picket screen about 220 kilometers from the main task force. However, no class of British ship has been designed for duty as a radar picket or for survivability against multiple air and/or air-to-surface missile attacks in such a role. None has been designed for area defense with a mix of long- and short-range air defense systems, highly sophisticated C^3I capabilities and integration, the "fusion" of radar and electronic support measures (ESM), and the ability to rapidly pass sensor and fire control data from other ships. All recent British vessels have been cost constrained in terms of both their initial designs and later cost compromises that reduced their overall sensor, C^3I, and/or air defense capabilities.

One special C^3I problem may have existed because of the need to rely heavily on satellite communications. Britain has confirmed that it had shut down the radars on the *Sheffield* when it was hit by an Argentine-launched Exocet. Some reports indicate these radars were turned off both to minimize the risk of detection and to allow satellite transmissions. Reports also indicate that the *Sheffield* was relying on electronic support measures that could not operate effectively during satellite transmission. It is far more likely, however, that British ESM gear failed because of technical limitations or because it was set to regard the Exocet missile as friendly.[15]

It is clear that British ships sometimes failed to detect either Argentine radar scanning or Exocet lock-on. It is also clear that British surface ships also lacked the ability to rapidly process radar and air defense data and transfer it to air defense weapons systems both within a given ship and on a task force basis.

The radar range on British surface ships was limited to 30 to 35 nautical miles of coverage at low altitudes under any conditions because of the curvature of the earth, but British ships also faced the problem that they had to combine surveillance and warning with air and missile defense. This presented a problem because some radars, like the Type 965R air search radar, proved to have poor low-altitude coverage beyond 12 to 15 nautical miles. While short-range radars like the 992Q provided good coverage to the horizon line, this coverage still furnishes so little warning that it is clear the British had inadequate time in which to react.

This inability to react was particularly bad in those cases in which a British ship lacked fully automated and integrated fire control. The British Type 42, for example, had a manual sensor integration and fire control system, which required detection on the air search radar, redetection on a target indication radar, and transfer of data to the Sea Dart missile guidance radar. This made it very vulnerable to multiple low altitude attacks of the kind that sank the *Conventry*.

The Type 22 did have the Sea Wolf defense missile and radars and fire control designed for defense against sea-skimming missiles, but both the missiles and radar had very short ranges and limited reload capability. The Sea Wolf also functions at such short ranges that it must be fired almost immediately once a target is detected and must rely heavily on automated sensor and fire control linkage. This severely limited the ability of the Type 22s to combine area surveillance with area defense. The Type 22s had to stay very near the other ships in the task force to provide any area defense coverage. Although the Type 22s generally performed well, and the Sea Wolf scored significant hits against aircraft, they were not tested against missiles and exhibited serious limitations in dealing with multiple low-altitude air attacks.

British Type 21 ships had the Sea Cat missile and 4.5-inch and 20-mm guns, and they were better designed for saturation combat, but they still failed to deal with saturation attacks. The *Ardent*, for example, was sunk in a simultaneous attack by four Argentine aircraft. This example provides an important warning for the future: The attacking aircraft used conventional iron bombs, and many Third World countries are capable of mounting such saturation raids.[16]

These problems in British naval sensor, C^3, and defense capabilities provide several important lessons:

- No Western sensor, ESM, or air defense system can afford to be tailored to Soviet threats. The proliferation of Western arms in Third World nations means that virtually all Western equipment must be included in the "threat" in designing modern weapons and sensors.
- The "area defense" concept of the Aegis class of U.S. vessels was largely validated even for "low-level" wars. There is no question that the British would have been far better off with a ship that had a fully integrated mix of long- and short-range sensors and defenses.
- Western ships must be designed to survive low-altitude and sea-skimming missile attacks. Over 100 countries now have such missiles, and the number is growing steadily. While specialized ships without such defense may be able to operate as part of

integrated task forces, they lack independence of action and cannot safely be deployed to project sea power.

- The need for adequate fusion of sensors and of warning and fire control will grow steadily as threat systems improve and increase in numbers. Many of today's ships fail to adequately integrate their sensors and weaponry.

- Ships cannot substitute for airborne early warning. They lack the range to provide adequate warning of missile and low-altitude air attacks either in the open sea or in areas near shore where terrain can mask such attacks. This repeats a lesson provided during the latter phases of the Pacific campaign of World War II, when radar picket ships consistently failed to either survive saturation attacks or provide adequate warning. At the same time, it should be noted that the Falklands experience indicates such ships and aircraft should have good ESM and good radar coverage of low-altitude aircraft flying over land. The problem is one not simply of air defense but of mission capability in broader intelligence and warning roles.

The British did attempt to use their Sea Harriers to provide more extended warning, but they were limited by both aircraft numbers and the capabilities of the radar on the Sea Harrier. There were only twenty-eight Sea Harriers deployed, and the fourteen RAF Harrier GR-3s lacked radar capability. The Blue Fox radar on the Sea Harrier FRS-1 did not provide good look-down or area surveillance coverage over the ocean, and its low-altitude coverage was poor over land. Such radars may have been adequate to support the individual air-to-air combat missions for which they were designed but were not suited for broader mission roles. The fuel limitations of the Harrier also meant that it became increasingly limited in endurance at ranges above 100 nautical miles.[17]

The British tried to correct this shortcoming by modifying Sea King helicopters to accept the long-range Searchwater radar of the Nimrod aircraft.[18] Unfortunately for the British, the modifications were completed a week after the war ended. Even if they had been completed in time, it is doubtful that such a system could have provided 24-hour surveillance because of the poor fuel economy of helicopters and their limited loiter time, combat radius, speed, and ceiling. Britain has since modified Searchwater radars for its Sea King helicopters and plans to equip all of its British aircraft carriers with an organic heliborne AEW capability.[19]

The British were more successful in modifying the Nimrod MR.1/2 for long-range maritime surveillance missions. In-flight refueling probes were developed and operational over the Falklands within 24 days. The British flew over 130 sorties from Wideawake airfield on Ascension. One of the sorties remained airborne for 19 hours. Some Nimrods were equipped with Harpoon and others with two or four Aim-9L to allow attacks on Argentine B-707 surveillance aircraft and for self-protection. This variant of the Nimrod was called the MRZP but was never used its armament in combat. The Nimrod's Searchwater radar may have played a detection role in spotting fighter attacks, but it had little look-down capability against fighters. The Nimrods have extensive ELINT capability, but the role this played is unclear.[20]

The British flew fighter reconnaissance missions, but these could not substitute for heavy reliance on human and naval reconnaissance. Airborne sensors and processing could not monitor small Argentine movements or establish readiness and infantry locations, and weather and cloud cover were a constant problem. The British made extensive use of elite reconnaissance troops throughout the fighting. These troops included the Royal Marines, the Special Air Service (SAS) and the Special Boat Squadron (SBS) troops that were landed on the islands to gather intelligence. The elite force operated in advance of the main body of troops in order to gather intelligence and to conduct raids. This British effort was often successful but could have benefited from improved collection systems, remote sensors, night vision aids, secure radios, and special mission ships and helicopters.

The British also suffered during the war from inadequate fusion and flow of information. Senior British ground commanders consistently lacked data available to British planners in London. For example, the British had obtained SIGINT data in London that gave the entire Argentine order of battle at Goose Green. This would have told British commanders that there were nearly 1,050 Argentine troops in the area rather than the less than 100 that they expected. The Royal Navy also failed to provide good data flow to British land commanders. This highlights the need for total fusion of command and intelligence data at every level of operational command in wartime operations.

Argentine threat assessment was much less sophisticated than that of the British, although it was often effective. The Argentines used two mobile air defense radars (TPS-43 and TPS-44) to detect British naval movements and to direct some of their air attacks. These systems remained operational throughout the war, although the British made a considerable effort to destroy them with Shrike (AGM-45) and anti-radar missiles (ARMs). These facilities escaped either because they switched off their transmissions or because of the limited reliability of the anti-radar missiles used.

The Argentines carried out airborne reconnaissance with a Boeing 707 and flew maritime patrol missions early in the war, but they rarely exposed these aircraft to the threat of British Harriers once heavy combat started. This normally forced Argentine fighters and ground forces to operate without adequate threat assessment and reconnaissance data, although such data could have had great impact in improving anti-ship operations and ground defense. Argentine fighter aircraft lacked the advanced on-board avionics that would have improved their performance in attack and air combat missions; they also lacked sophisticated ELINT and ESSM systems.

The Argentine attack aircraft relied heavily on the TPS-43 radar facility at Port Stanley. Although this facility performed well, significant gaps existed in its range and coverage which limited its function as a combat information facility. At best, the TPS-43 provided only low-altitude coverage out to the horizon, or about 26 nautical miles at sea level and less than 35 nautical miles at altitudes below 500 meters.

In addition to this central facility, the Argentines made limited use of HS-125 aircraft as high-altitude communication relay posts. These aircraft passed information on the Sea Harrier patrols from the command center at Port Stanley to low-flying attack and transport aircraft.[21] The Argentines also used a combination of radars to provide range information, electronic support measures to detect the radar emissions from British Harriers, and ships to get air activity and range data. There are some reports the Argentines used ESM in targeting their use of Exocet, although it is unclear whether this ever went beyond simple intercept of unsecure communication or identification of the frequency of ship-mounted radars.[22]

The Argentines also made extensive use of electronic support measures to detect British radar emissions. They used airborne ESM gear to detect and characterize the emissions from British ships, then used brief radar scans to get range information, and finally used radar to fire their Exocets. This technique was limited, however, to characterizing and targeting British ships actively involved in picket duty or air defense. Argentina does not seem to have been able to use ESM to characterize and target emissions from the other ships in the British task force.[23]

Both sides would have benefited from a long-endurance airborne or aerostat tactical intelligence platform with systems like SAR, SLAR, IR, ELINT, and ESM. Both sides lacked suitable theater-deployable airborne systems, particularly with the proper combination of survivability and endurance.

Effective and Secure C³I

Tactical command of both the British land and sea forces was exercised by Rear Admiral Sir John Woodward until the headquarters of the commando brigade was established at San Carlos Bay. Admiral Woodward did, however, retain tactical control of the Harriers and the 200 helicopters in the force.

British C³ during the Falklands campaign had many of the same advantages that the Soviets enjoyed in Afghanistan. The British had access to U.S. military communications satellites and secure communications gear. The British were able to operate their C³ assets in an atmosphere in which they did not have to contend with equally sophisticated EW assets in the hands of the enemy, and they had U.S. support in decrypting Argentine communications.[24] The comparative lack of hostile Argentine jamming or deception did not, however, mean that there was no electronic activity, since the C³ of the British fleet is known to have been monitored by the Soviet Union. This monitoring was engaged in by Soviet Cosmos satellites and Primori class intelligence gathering ships.[25] Soviet Bear aircraft, operating from Cuba and West Africa, provided a further threat. These aircraft were able to survey the Ascension Island area but were unable to reach as far as the Falklands.[26] In addition, Argentina had some airborne ESM and SIGINT capability, and its radio direction finding equipment was sufficiently advanced to present a real threat to British land assets.

The British also suffered from uncertain organization of their high command, and British land commanders assumed command at San Carlos without proper briefings and preplanning. British land command and communications often broke down in rough terrain or even at moderate distances near the beach. It was small-unit initiative, and not central C³I, which led to most British successes in the land fighting. This success was similar in many ways to the Israeli experience in 1982 and highlights the lesson that good training for independent action will often be far more important than any conceivable improvement to C³I systems.

The British would have faced major problems without the use of U.S. satellite communications. Their ships lacked the C³I capacity to handle combined operations, and the British had to rely on satellite communications to link the task force with higher authorities in the UK. According to the British White Paper on the Falklands, these assets did not always work well, and there were times when they could not accommodate the traffic that the British tried to handle. This parallels U.S. experience in Vietnam and could affect other contingencies in which military operations must suddenly be conducted in Third World areas.[27]

The White Paper goes on to state:

> The vital importance was shown of satellite communications in operations conducted at great distance. There were times during the Falklands Campaign when the flow of signal traffic to the task force threatened to exceed the capacity of the available systems. This never delayed the transmission of important operational messages but it did affect some other traffic. We currently plan to acquire a new British military satellite and to provide a terminal in all major surface warships, which will be a significant improvement.
>
> As the task force sailed south it became increasingly important to receive frequent detailed situation reports from the area of operations, both as general background for decision makers in Whitehall and as the essential basis for early and accurate announcements to Parliament and the media on events in the South Atlantic. Hard pressed local commanders were not always able to provide these and for the future we are considering how they might be enabled to do so. It will not, of course, be the intention to impose any detailed direction of actions in the field, which must remain the responsibility of the commander on the spot.[28]

The assault ship HMS *Fearless* functioned as an important command center during operations. The *Fearless* was specifically designed for the task and employed 36 radio circuits; her communications dealt with up to 3,500 signals per day.

At a lower level of operations, the British also discovered they needed improved communications gear for special operations. While there is no clear evidence that Argentina ever successfully identified the transmissions of SAS and SBS personnel operating in the Falklands, Britain did develop a clipboard-sized 50-watt transceiver for long-range voice and data burst communications. This unit, the MEL PRC-319, weighs 8.1 lbs. and can transmit a precoded 10-second burst at 300 bits per second using a two-frequency simplex system. It breaks down into small components for concealment and has a separate 1.5-lb. message unit to record coded data in the field for later burst transmissions. This device is of special interest because it is obviously designed to improve communications by special forces operating near or in enemy territory, and it tends to confirm rumors that SAS personnel operated in or near Port Stanley during much of the final phase of the fighting.[29]

The Argentines seem to have had four separate C^3I links: (a) a high-level politico-military system that operated with a highly politicized view of reality, (b) an army system centered in the Falklands with poor leadership and organization and weak tactical and theater communications, (c) a navy system unsuited in scale and sophistication for fleet operations, and (d) an air force system that was highly professional but lacked the assets and technology to provide sensor and communications coverage of the Falklands. It is unclear how the Argentines (much less British intelligence) could get a coherent result from these four different and poorly coordinated systems.[30]

As was noted earlier, Argentine command and control suffered greatly from interservice rivalry and an unwillingness of officers in the field to exercise leadership of their troops in any meaningful way.[31] Only the air force and naval air branches seem to have used their C^3 assets effectively. It is not clear to what extent the Argentines even tried to maintain any kind of centralized control over their major combat formations and assets in the Falklands.

Britain seems to have been able to monitor the communications of Argentine aircraft and ships, many of which communicated in the clear. This often gave the British several minutes of additional warning of air attack. The Argentines seem to have had a limited amount of secure communications gear, although at least some elements of the air force and army air defense forces used proper communications discipline and practiced careful emitter control. The British lacked secure air communications but practiced careful communications discipline.[32] The British clearly had access to at least some Argentine "secure" communications at both the diplomatic and high-command levels. It is unclear, however, whether this provided great tactical benefits. Discussion with Argentine sources indicate that most ground force and diplomatic traffic probably had limited operational value except to reveal some aspects of the efforts to resupply the Falklands and that data on host air operations could not have been obtained from such sources.

Combined Arms

Combined arms operations in the Falklands involved extensive use of infantry and artillery forces. The British also made limited use of light tanks and AFVs, but the Argentines made little use of any armored vehicles in combat. The British made more use of combined or "joint warfare" operations, land/air, air/sea, and sea/land than of combined arms and probably made more effective use of all their military resources than any other force in the campaigns under study.

The British displayed a thorough understanding of how to use the combined arms they had as well as an ability to improvise and display flexibility in combat situations throughout the campaign. The Argentines, on the other hand, defended some positions with courage, but the Argentine senior commanders showed little imagination and insight into the optimal use of combined arms. The Argentine army relied on a preconceived decision that Britain would not attempt a landing outside Port Stanley and then relied on rigid plans to defend in place. It showed little flexibility and technical capability to combine its infantry and artillery resources.

Infantry

Land combat during the Falklands war was dominated by infantry fighting. The Argentines made little use of their armored vehicles, and the British were restricted to limited use of the Scorpian and Scimitar light tanks and had to rely heavily on forced marches and close infantry combat. The British infantry troops participating in the fighting included elements of the Special Air Service (SAS), Special Boat Squadron (SBS), the Royal Marines, paratroopers, the Gurkha Rifles and Welsh and Scots guards. Since the terrain of the Falklands was generally too rough for armored personnel carriers (APCs), all of these troops fought as dismounted infantry despite the fact that many of them had been trained to fight using APCs. The Argentine infantry forces included some members of the Argentine army and Naval Infantry Corps. Some of the problems associated with these Argentine forces have already been discussed.

According to the British White Paper, the Falklands campaign "underlined the importance of night operations and aggressive patrolling." The fighting also, however, demonstrated the value of superior infantry weaponry and equipment. British paratroopers faced well-dug-in Argentine infantry at Goose Green. The Argentine positions were well prepared with good overhead cover. They were, therefore, in a good position to resist a British advance. When British troops assaulted these positions, they took substantial casualties from riflemen, machine gunners, and occasionally 35-mm anti-aircraft guns. The British paratroopers had to contend with the fact that Argentine rifles had greater range and muzzle velocity than British submachine guns. In some cases, British troops were reported to have discarded their own small arms for Argentine rifles.

This experience highlights a continuing lesson of World War II, Korea, Vietnam, and many other conflicts. No command can predict what weapons capability it will need most from its basic infantry weapons: portability, range, volume of fire, or hitting power. There is a natural tendency, however, to pick one capability over the others and to downplay improving the lethality of the rifle and automatic rifle for an emphasis on heavier weapons and more advanced technologies. In practice, however, the rifle and machine gun continue to dominate most low-level combats. Western forces still need advanced rifles and other infantry weapons that can combine all four of the critical features listed above.

The British paratroopers assaulting Goose Green also used 66-mm light anti-tank weapons, 84-mm medium anti-tank weapons, and machine guns to break up the Argentine defenses. They used these weapons for long-range fire and closed quickly on the Argentine positions and raked them with submachine-gun fire. Another favorite tactic was to toss hand grenades into trenches. These British infantry tactics were complemented by the effective use of artillery and naval gunfire and air support during good weather. According to the British White Paper, the British infantry could not have accomplished their mission without this support. The White Paper also called for training all infantry personnel in helping to direct and target indirect fire support. This is a lesson all armies should emulate, given the value that a similar approach would have had during the Arab-Israeli and Iran-Iraq conflicts.

It is important to note, however, that most targeting for British fire support either was based on firing at known Argentine positions or involved line-of-sight target acquisition by the artillery unit or visual "spotters." There were no major counterbattery exchanges, and targeting against targets beyond line of sight was generally based on maps, scouting, and earlier photo or air reconnaissance. The British were able to take advantage of classic World War II sea power and artillery techniques because the Argentine ground forces usually lacked the equipment to fire back. The situation would have been far different if the Argentines had had significant numbers of radar-operated guns or shore-to-ship missiles near the British landing areas. If any new lesson emerged from this experience, it consists largely of the need for fusing and shells that would be effective in bogs, marshes, and wet terrain as well as on relatively dry hard surfaces.

The fighting did demonstrate clearly the advantage of prepared lines, deep bunkers, protected firing positions, mines, and pre-surveyed fire lines that could be directly covered by mortars and heavy machine guns. It also showed that fixed infantry positions remain as important as ever. The Argentines reported that their deep bunkers were totally immune to air support, naval gun fire, and artillery and that they did not suffer a single casualty in such positions. The Argentine trenches seem to have provided Argentine troops with near immunity to indirect fire, except for mortars, although such fire may have had considerable shock effect.

One weapon the British might have found useful in storming trenches is the automatic grenade launcher. The anti-tank weapons discussed earlier, as well as British machine guns, were all direct-fire weapons. A short-range indirect-fire weapon such as a grenade launcher might have been useful in killing troops within trenches. The British did possess a few grenade launchers (American-made M-79s), but these were in the hands of the SAS and SBS.

The British infantry advance on Port Stanley involved the most serious fighting in the war and required extensive mountain combat. Thirty-three company-sized Argentine units were dug into positions in the surrounding mountains which they had been fortifying and improving for six weeks. The Argentine infantry defending these positions were equipped with heavy machine guns and recoilless rifles, and their positions were protected by minefields and artillery.

The British infantry had to storm trenches in overcoming these Argentine defenses and also had to deal with deep bunkers and minefields. This resulted in several tough battles in which the British infantry was again supported primarily by artillery and naval gunfire. In carrying out these attacks, the British generally met the most determined resistance along the first layer of defense. Individual Argentine fighting men fought well but lacked leadership, reinforcement, and tactical flexibility. The Argentines were far less effective fighters once the British had broken through. Resistance often continued however, and some Argentine troops fought to the death. Argentine troops fought fiercely at Mount Longdon, and some died from bayonet wounds.[33]

Most of the more than 10,000 Argentine troops in the Falklands were conscripts with limited time in service in their units. They were still in their summer uniforms and were poorly supplied. Their effectiveness was also severely degraded by Argentina's outdated "Prussian style" training, poor C^{3}I, a failure to fully complete the circumferential defenses of Port Stanley (Mount Kent and Mount Challenger were not properly defended), and lack of aggressive leadership. Elements of units such as the 25th Infantry Brigade and the 3rd Artillery Brigade, whose conscripts had served in the unit for more than a year, fought more effectively, as did the marines and Argentina's equivalent of the SAS, the 601 and 602 commandos. By and large, however, it was the lack of competence and aggressiveness in so-called professional officers, their constant posturing and failure to communicate effectively, even with junior ranks and NCOs, and their rivalry and politics that crippled the army's performance.

The poor performance of the Argentine army is noted in a number of sources. The best indication of Argentine failures, however, has emerged in the changes in the army since 1982. While many have occurred for political and economic reasons, a major effort has been made to bridge the gap between officer, NCO, and conscript. Conscripts have been reduced from 60,000–80,000 annually to 30,000–40,000. Many now serve only 180 days. The rest get adequate training for the first time. Officers now must meet minimal training standards, although overall professional education of the officer corps remains very poor by Western standards. The concentration of officers and command centers in urban and resort areas is being reduced. A mobile assault brigade is being created to help compensate for the rigid World War II level of infantry and army unit organization. This again illustrates the critical impact of human factors and politicization on military effectiveness. In fact, these were the dominant factors shaping the performance of the Argentine forces in the Falklands.[34]

The Argentine army also has drastically reduced its inefficient and heavily politicized corps-level organization and put more emphasis on effective command and readiness at the unit level. Tactical maneuver units have been brought up to full strength at the expense of bloated regional commands and area support activities. Air defense, communications, and engineer units have been reorganized and reequipped to improve mobility, field performance, and responsiveness to combat units. Most units are now less subject to central or high command interference and are better organized to emphasize a mission-oriented chain of command.

As for Argentine infantry armament, the Argentine army had a general superiority in night-vision devices, machine guns, artillery, mortars, and mines. Argentina is procuring a new rifle as the result of the fighting in the Falklands, but the reasons are as yet unclear. In general, the Argentines had a striking superiority in weapons numbers as well as in total manpower.

It is difficult to draw detailed lessons from the infantry combat in the Falklands except in regard to: (1) the excellent performance of Britain's well-trained regulars, particularly the commandos and parachute units, in adapting to conditions for which they had limited training; (2) the general importance of infantry combat capability; and (3) the need for suitable weapons. There was, however, a clear need for improved light infantry fire power such as rifles, machine guns, and grenade launchers which could provide the combination of range and high volume of fire needed for such combat conditions. The Falklands campaign also indicates that both sides would have benefited from a light multiple rocket launcher capable of high surge rates of fire and helicopter or light vehicle mobility.

Tanks and Armored Vehicles

Armored warfare was severely constrained during the Falkland Islands campaign by the absence of serviceable roads and by terrain that was so boggy that it could barely support the use of Land Rovers, much less main battle tanks or self-propelled artillery. While the British were able to use the BV-202 arctic transport vehicle, and their eight Scimitars (30-mm gun) and Scorpions (76-mm gun), to move from San Carlos to Port Stanley, they were far short of the numbers needed to provide either adequate mobility or fire power. This meant they had to rely heavily upon helicopter mobility (when possible) or marching with full pack. No main battle tanks were used in any phase of the Falkland Islands fighting.

The fighting in the Falklands did not, however, involve a complete absence of armored units. British strategy at Port Stanley relied on the extensive use of dismounted infantry supported by light armor, and the British made good use of the Scorpion and Scimitar light tanks they had available in the final stages of the fighting. These weapons have a ground pressure less than that of a man. About a half-squadron (eight) of these vehicles were deployed with the Blue and Royals, although it is unclear whether they had much tactical effect until the last few days of combat. The British might have made more extensive use of light tanks and AFVs if it had not been for the sinking of the containership *Atlantic Conveyor* which contained most of the CH-47 Chinook helicopters that could have been used to airlift light tanks.

The Scorpion light tank is an Alvis-built system equipped with a 76-mm gun and high-quality night vision equipment. The Scimitar is a light armored tank equipped with a 30-mm cannon. The basic characteristics of these light tanks are shown in Table 3.7. Apart from the size of their guns, there is no significant physical difference between the Scimitar and Scorpion. The Scimitar is used more for reconnaissance. Scorpion and Scimitar tanks did travel an average of 350 miles per vehicle over difficult terrain during some phases of the war. They also provided some degree of protection for their crews. One Scorpion withstood an artillery shell that landed less than five feet away while another ran over a mine which severely damaged the vehicle but left the crew unharmed.[35]

The lack of suitable terrain for armor did create some problems for those units of the British army which had been trained to fight from APCs rather than in nonmechanized infantry combat. The Welsh Guards were a case in point. Having spent several months on ceremonial duties prior to the fighting and having been trained for

TABLE 3.7 British Land-Based Armor in the Falklands

Scorpion Light Tank	Scimitar Light Fighting Vehicle
Weight	Weight
17,500 lbs. (aluminum alloy armor)	17,100 lbs.
Firepower	Firepower
76-mm gun	30-mm Rarden gun
Range	Range
1,600–3,500 meters	1,000–2,000 meters
Speed	Speed
Approx. 50 mph max. road	Approx. 50 mph max. road
(with 4 mph in water)	(with 4 mph in water)
Operating Temperature	Operating Temperature
-32 to +50°C	-32 to +0°C
Ground Pressure	Ground Pressure
5 psi	5 psi

SOURCE: *Aviator Recognition Manual*, FM1-402 (Washington, D.C.: Department of the Army, 1984), pp. 7-24–7-25.

mechanized combat, this unit found itself unable to conduct foot marches that were seen as relatively untaxing by other units.

The Argentines made no use of tanks or armored vehicles in maneuver warfare, although they did have twelve Panhard 90 armored cars on the island and may have used the 90-mm guns on their Panhards for fire support during the final phases of their defense of Port Stanley. This lack of emphasis on armor may relate directly to the Argentines' lack of interest in offensive maneuver combat. The Argentines also used a company of LVTP-7 landing vehicles during their initial invasion of Port Stanley, although these World War II vintage systems were later withdrawn. These vehicles have only machine gun armament, 30 mm of frontal armament, and 7 mm of side armament. The one anti-tank round that hit an LVTP-7 was fired by the small 25-man Royal Marine contingent at Port Stanley and killed not only the vehicle but most of the men aboard. The Argentines tried to rely on an attrition-oriented defense to grind down the British attackers. This helps account for the fact that the Argentines only once attempted a serious counterattack.

Precision-Guided and Specialized Land Munitions

The comparatively small numbers of armored vehicles used in the Falklands War meant that the war served as a poor environment for examining the performance of anti-armor precision-guided munitions (PGMs) against enemy tanks. No Milan anti-tank PGMs were used against any Argentine vehicle, although they proved lethal against Argentine machine guns and infantry posts. The Wombat recoilless anti-tank guns (which are not PGMs) in the possession of the British 3rd Paratroop Battalion were not even off-loaded from the British ships. Accordingly, the key role of PGMs during the land portion of the Falklands fighting was the British use of Milan anti-tank missiles against hard-point targets where troops used rock or built-up defense posts. This use of ATGMs parallels the Soviet experience in Afghanistan, the Israeli experience in Lebanon, and both Iranian and Iraqi experiences during the Iran-Iraq War. It reinforces the need to design ATGMs for a broader tactical role as hard-point killers in land combat.

Milan missiles and regular anti-tank rockets were also used extensively by the British to assault Argentine strong points and fortifications at Port Stanley. They served as a mobile source of firepower for small units which often lacked adequate on-call artillery support. The fact that the Milan was a direct, rather than indirect, fire weapon gave it the advantage of being a "surgical" weapon that could supplement mortar and/or artillery fire with greater accuracy and faster "time on target."

The SAS used Milans, machine guns, and mortars in one of the early actions against the Argentine garrison at Darwin. Milan units were, however, scattered throughout the entire British order-of-battle and participated in the British advance across the Falklands. These units became a priority target for Argentine snipers and indirect fire. Over 150 Milans were fired throughout the war.[36] The British also occasionally fired Milans at low-flying Mirage and Pucara aircraft. No aircraft kills occurred as the result of such actions, but the Argentine planes may have had to maneuver to avoid being hit. This seems to have given British infantry added time to disperse.[37]

Tube Artillery

The British used a variety of artillery systems throughout the war, including helicopter-portable 105-mm light guns and the 4.5-inch naval guns which the fleet used to support ground troops (see Table 3.8). The limited naval gun capability of Royal Navy ships became clear during the war. Each naval 4.5-inch gun had the same output per minute as an entire six-gun 105-mm battery. These guns fired about 8,000 rounds in support of ground operations, and any malfunction threatened

TABLE 3.8 The Artillery of the Falklands War

Type of Artillery	Specifications	
	Range	Rate of Fire
105-mm Light Gun		
(British-made)	2,500 meters minimum	3 rounds/minute sustained
	17,000 meters with super charge	6 round maximum
155-mm Field Howitzer Model 50		
(French-made)	18,000 meters	3–4 rounds/minute
105-mm Model 56 Pack Howitzer		
(Italian-made)	10,200 meters	8 rounds/minute
Oerlikon Twin 35-mm Anti-aircraft/		
Gun Type GDF-001	4,000 meters	550 rounds/minute
Rhein Metal Twin 20-mm		
Anti-aircraft Gun	2,000 meters	1,000 rounds/minute

SOURCES: See *Aviator Recognition Manual,* FM1-402 (Washington, D.C.: Department of the Army, 1984); and Bryan Perret, *Weapons of the Falklands Conflict* (Dorset: Blandford Press, 1982).

to leave British troops without adequate artillery support. According to the British White Paper:

> The infantry would not have been able to carry out their objectives without the support they received from artillery and Naval bombardment. The ability of the 105 mm light guns to bring down instant and accurate fire at night or through smoke and fog contributed significantly to the final collapse of Argentine morale. The importance was underlined of all ranks being trained and able to call for fire.[38]

The British also were able to make good use of their 105-mm light guns and Model 56 pack howitzers. These reached fire support levels of up to 500 rounds per day, and the British were able to use helicopters to move both their guns and their ammunition. The British also used their artillery aggressively. They moved weapons and shifted fire to support the tactical situation, while the Argentines were slow to move their guns and react. The lack of Argentine counterbattery fire allowed the British to use their artillery with considerable security, and a combination of training, use of high ground, and laser range finders allowed the British to fire at directly observed targets and with great accuracy. British artillery spotters also improved the RAF's ability to provide close-air support.

Despite the fact that the Argentines were fighting a defensive war, they made relatively poor use of artillery. They had significant resources near Port Stanley. These included four 155-mm howitzers for artillery support, thirty Italian Model 56 105-mm howitzers, 81-mm mortars, twelve MAL-90 armored cars, and twin 20-mm and 35-mm AA guns. This may not have been an adequate number to support broad area defense, and the Argentines experienced some lethality problems because the peat and wet soil sometimes absorbed shells and reduced their effects. Nevertheless, the Argentines had more firepower than the British, and weapons numbers were not the real issue. The Argentines failed to organize and effectively use the weapons they had and relied heavily on textbook theory. They often fired in defensive patterns when they should have aggressively sought out and called in specific targets, and they failed to rapidly concentrate fire.

Surface-to-Surface Rockets and Missiles

Heavy surface-to-surface rockets and missiles were not used during the Falklands War. No tactical surface-to-surface rockets and/or missiles were available to the Argentines, and the British elected not to use any of their sea-based missiles against land targets. The dual-purpose missiles in British possession were more appropriate to anti-ship warfare than shore bombardment, which was left to the 4.5-inch gun on various fleet destroyers and frigates.

Mines and Barriers

Extensive use was made of mine warfare and barriers during the Falkland Islands campaign. The Argentine carried out a great deal of defensive preparation between the time when they seized the Falklands and the arrival of British troops. They mined a number of land defense areas and laid smart bottom mines which can discriminate between small craft and warships in the approaches to Stanley. Although the British navy never directly attacked Port Stanley, the British White Paper on the Falklands called the extensive use of mines by the Argentine army "a notable problem."[39] Although they did not keep precise records, the Argentines seem to have laid at least 4,000 anti-tank mines and 11,000 anti-personnel mines and booby traps. The Argentine army now estimates the total number of mines at 25,000 to 30,000.

The Argentines, however, faced a difficult task in trying to effectively mine the broad defensive areas they used to defend key positions, and they failed to provide fire support, aggressive patrolling, and direct fire coverage to prevent relatively rapid mine clearing by the Royal Engineers and/or penetration of their minefields. More aggressive patrol and fire support action might have had a significant effect since the plastic mines could not be detected and had to be removed by hand. The impact of mines might also have been much worse if the Argentines had not expected the British to land at Port Stanley (instead of San Carlos where they actually did land). The beaches around Port Stanley were heavily mined.

Nine types of land mines were laid by the Argentines. These included:

1. the Israeli number 6 anti-tank mine (which is a copy of the Soviet TM-46 mine);
2. the Israeli number 4 plastic anti-personnel mine (based on a West German design);
3. the World War II vintage U.S. M-1 anti-tank mine;
4. the Italian MISAR SB-81 anti-armor mine (which has a plastic case and can be buried in the ground up to 100 mm deep);
5. the Italian MISAR SB-33 scatter dropped anti-personnel mine (which can be dropped from a helicopter, is small and irregular, and is difficult to locate when emplaced on the ground or beach);
6. the Spanish C-3-B anti-tank mine (a plastic mine with some metal);
7. the Spanish P-4-B anti-personnel mine;
8. the Argentine FMK-3 anti-tank mine; and
9. the Argentine FMK-1 anti-personnel mine (which was laid without its detector ring).[40]

These Argentine mine defenses represented a mix of old and new technologies. The older mines did not represent much of a challenge to British mine detection, but the newer, plastic mines presented so formidable a set of detection problems that a number of Argentine mine fields in the Falklands have had to be fenced off and left in the post-war period. This is because the problems associated with disarming these weapons were such that Britain has had to abandon its efforts to clear them. The No. 4 SB-33, P-4-B, and FMK-1 mines proved almost impossible to detect, particularly because many were laid without the detector ring that would have enabled the Argentines to pull their own mines. In spite of some £7 million in research and four years of effort, the British have not found any means to detect such mines. British mine detectors are designed to work under magnetic conditions in the northern hemisphere and have not functioned well with the iron ore and other magnetic materials in the local soil. Attempts to use low-level radiation and chemical soil treatments have also failed, and

British sappers had to be equipped with special mine-proof boots as a partial substitute for improved mine detectors. This indicates similar mine detection problems could raise serious difficulties in future wars.[41] The British also had both naval and land mines, but had no serious reason to use them.

All-Weather and Night Target Acquisition Systems

Extensive night fighting took place during the land battles. This was particularly true during the final British attacks on Port Stanley, where the British chose to attack at night in order to help compensate for the well-prepared Argentine defense. The British made considerable use of night observation equipment, although some problems arose. Supplies were badly inadequate and night goggles had to be obtained on an emergency supply basis from the U.S. Some of the older British equipment malfunctioned and became temporarily useless after a bright explosion or flash. The British called this phenomenon "bloom out," and it closely parallels Soviet problems with their night vision devices and the U.S. experience in Vietnam. Night vision devices must be able to cope with flares and artillery fire to be effective. A key system that did not develop problems with "bloom out" was the second-generation night fighting sight associated with the British light tanks.

The shortage of high-quality night vision devices also led to a situation in which illumination devices such as hand-held Shermulley flares assumed particular importance. The British acknowledged a generalized need to improve and expand their inventories of night fighting equipment after the war. The British White Paper on the Falklands stated: "Since the conflict we have placed orders for the procurement of general purpose night-vision goggles for the infantry and night flying goggles for the Army Air Corp. Further purchases of both types are planned."[42]

All-weather and night acquisition systems for close support and interdiction missions were not available to the Argentine air forces. Argentine aircraft did not have advanced target acquisition systems for the land attack role and depended solely on visual target acquisition and avionics alignment to target. They did not undertake night missions or fly in bad weather.

The situation was significantly better for the Argentine troops on the ground. Night vision equipment was procured and extensively used for the defense of static positions. Much of this equipment was American made. Passive sights and night goggles were particularly effective in the hands of Argentine snipers around Mount Longdon.[43]

The Argentine troops had far more devices than the British and might have used them to inflict more night casualties if they had been more aggressive and the British had not made good use of indirect fire weapons for infantry suppression.

Anti-Aircraft Artillery

The Argentines used anti-aircraft guns in the Falklands war against both aircraft and non-aircraft targets. These guns seem to have been reasonably well deployed, but the RAF lost only five Harriers to ground fire (largely to missiles) in spite of relatively high numbers of close-air support sorties. The Argentines concentrated their guns for air base defense and seem to have been more successful in deterring such attacks than achieving actual kills. The British did not use anti-aircraft guns.

The Argentines had two major anti-aircraft gun positions, one near Port Stanley and another at the Condor air base near Goose Green in the East Falklands. The force near Port Stanley had two types of guns, the Oerlikon twin 35-mm gun (type GDF-011) with the Super Fledermaus gun-laying radar and the Rheinmetal-Oerlikon twin 20-mm anti-aircraft gun with Israeli-made Elta short-range radars. The force at Port Stanley originally had two batteries of 35-mm guns and one battery of 20-mm guns. This was later reinforced with added 20-mm guns, another 35-mm battery, a Skyguard radar director, Tigercat and Roland launchers, and SA-7 missiles.

The main role of the AA units at Port Stanley was to guard the runway. By the time the first British air raid took place on 1 May, there were 16 twin-barrel guns in place. The Argentine radars were somewhat disturbed by the ALQ-101 jamming pods used by the Vulcan but were otherwise operational. The 35-mm guns were effective to 10,000 feet and the Tigercat and Roland to 12,000 to 15,000 feet.

Despite repeated Argentine claims, however, only one clear AA gun hit occurred when a Harrier was damaged on 1 May. The guns may have deterred Harrier strikes on the airfield or disrupted them, but they had little kill effect.

The Argentine anti-aircraft gun positions at Condor included two SA-7 launchers, six 20-mm twin guns with Elta launchers, and two 20-mm twin guns with Skyguard. These were coordinated to provide protection corridors for the Pucaras at Goose Green. The guns did achieve one kill of a Harrier on 4 May and succeeded in forcing the Harriers to stay out of the air. Harrier air defense suppression missions on 16, 17, and 18 May failed, and efforts to use naval guns to "walk in" on the Elta radars failed when the Argentines moved the radars. Another

Harrier was hit on 27 May, but on 28 May British ground forces began to close in. Mortar fire knocked out some guns, and the others were used in the ground defense role until the Argentine forces had to surrender.

The British army reports indicate that British troops did experience problems with both the 35-mm and the 20-mm gun during the fighting at Goose Green. Radar-controlled 20-mm guns firing from the eastern tip of Goose Green settlement were able to bring very heavy amounts of fire on the ridge overlooking the settlement. This initially denied British paratroopers the use of this key terrain, but the guns were eventually destroyed by mortars and direct assault.[44] This again illustrates the value of AA guns as dual purpose weapons.

Surface-to-Air Missiles

Surface-to-air missiles (SAMs) were used extensively in the Falklands War. These included several British naval systems which will be discussed later: Sea Wolf, Sea Dart, and Sea Cat. The SAMs used by British land forces included the Rapier, Blowpipe, and Stinger. The first two systems, which are British, were used more extensively than the third system, which is American.

It is difficult to put the role of these land-based missiles in perspective. The Argentines report they executed 445 combat sorties, not counting sea-air rescue and transport sorties. They do not indicate how many sorties were flown over land and report only 34 Mirage and Skyhawk kills (42 percent of the deployed force) from any cause. British estimates claim 20 kills by the Harrier, 8 by Sea Cat, 8 by Sea Dart, 5 by Sea Wolf, 14 by Rapier, 8 by Blowpipe, and 8 by Stinger and other missiles. These British data indicate that 72 kills came from aircraft and SAMs and that 29 percent came from land-based SAMs. Other estimates of Argentine losses go as high as 109 with a total of 41 losses to SAMs and 7 to small arms, friendly fire, and British Naval 4.5-inch guns.

The key British land-based surface-to-air missiles, the Rapier and Blowpipe, were well tested prior to the Falklands conflict. Both were well suited to the combat conditions involved. They are light, portable, optically guided air defense weapons which are simple to operate manually. Regardless of the uncertainties involved, they had considerable success, destroying up to 23 aircraft. The Rapiers destroyed up to 14 aircraft with only 45 missiles fired, whereas about 10 missiles were fired for each kill by a Blowpipe.

The British-made Rapier weighs 43.6 kilograms, is 2.25 meters long, 12.7 centimeters in diameter, and has a 2.7-kilogram, high-explosive warhead. It has a two-stage, solid-propellant rocket motor and flies at

Mach 2 plus. It can engage aircraft at ranges up to 6 kilometers. The operational sequence is as follows: An enemy aircraft is picked up by a surveillance radar; it is then interrogated by IFF (identification of friend or foe). If the target is unfriendly, the operator begins tracking the target by radar. A computer signals when the target is within range. The operator then fires, and the fire control radar, tracking the Rapier as well as the enemy aircraft, applies corrections to the Rapier's trajectory by means of a microwave-command transmission. The missile may also be directed to its target optically, with the operator keeping the target in his line of sight while a television unit tracks the missile's tail flares. The tracking unit then sends course-correction signals to the missile.[45]

Rapier was the land system called up most often for the air defense of both ground forces and ships deployed within the defensive envelope of the system. Ground-based Rapiers downed up to 14 Argentine aircraft during the conflict. The main problem with the Rapier during the conflict was that the version of the system used in the Falklands was not mobile. Other problems involved inadequately prepared crews and severe maintenance problems. Nevertheless, the British considered the Rapier to be one of their most effective weapons. They also planned a strategy in which ships at anchorage were to be protected by the combined abilities of the navy and the shore-based Rapiers. The Rapiers were therefore among the first weapons to be placed ashore following the British landing at San Carlos. The sites for these weapons had been selected by computer at the British Ministry of Defense.

The San Carlos battle involved combat conditions which may be important in other port defense and mountain warfare contingencies. These are well described in an analysis by William J. Ruhe:[46]

> [The] Rapier land batteries were mounted on high ground overlooking the landing area. Although this frequently required a missile interception at the maximum range of six kilometers (resulting in some missiles not striking targets crossing in front of the battery), such missile attacks nevertheless disturbed the Argentine pilots as they delivered their bombs. Moreover, because of the extremely low levels at which the Argentine pilots approached the British ships, many of the kills made by Rapiers were ones where the missile was fired down at the attacking planes. Fortunately, the Rapier used a contact fuse in its warhead rather than a proximity fuse; this provided some measure of protection against hits by friendly forces. Additionally, when the Rapier's radar tracking system was saturated with land and sea returns when pointed down at the low-flying aircraft, it was possible to fire the Rapiers by using the secondary optical tracking system.

The Rapier system and the British strategy for using Rapier, however, had several flaws. The delicate electronics within the system itself proved to be overly sensitive to the harsh handling that took place within the wartime environment. In addition, the British needed more mobility. Of twelve Rapiers established to protect the fleet at San Carlos, as many as eight launchers were unserviceable at any one time during the first day. Problems continued to arise throughout the fighting with the maintenance and repair of these systems. The Rapiers experienced interference between their tracking radars and IFF systems and sometimes had to shut down their tracking radars and use their optical tracking systems. Furthermore, the Rapier generator needed so much gasoline that there were sometimes fuel shortages at the beachhead.

Another operational problem was that the British Rapier operators were not at the peak of their proficiency since their live-fire exercise was not recent, and it took time for them to again get comfortable with their weapons system. The tendency for the Argentines to fly as low as possible also complicated visual tracking. The resulting combination of problems with the Rapier and a lack of adequate anti-aircraft weapons on board British ships created serious problems in defending the beachhead. This was reflected in the large number of ships damaged or destroyed by Argentine bombs.

The Blowpipe is an optically guided system and is far less sophisticated than Rapier. Blowpipe is a manportable shoulder-fired system and weighs 12.7 kilograms in its fiberglass container. An aiming unit is clipped to the cannister. The missile is 1.39 meters long, 19.6 centimeters in diameter in its container, and 26.7 centimeters in diameter with its wings extended. It has a maximum range of 6.5 kilometers, an effective range of 3 kilometers, and can identify aircraft using an IFF attachment on the firing cannister. It was derived from the U.S. Redeye. It achieved a maximum of 8 kills for roughly 100 missiles fired. This is an optimal kill probability of 0.125 versus 0.31 for the Rapier. At the same time, the portability of the Blowpipe and the case with which it could be dispersed in large numbers meant it had an important effect in discouraging or degrading Argentine attack sorties. Ironically, the British had sold the Argentines the Blowpipe, and one British Harrier may have been killed by the system.

The Blowpipe's firing sequence is simple. An explosive charge expels the missile from its container. The exploding debris is ejected from the rear end of the cannister and serves as a hazard to those near the blast. When the missile has left the tube and its sustainer motor has ignited, the operator, sighting on the missile's tail flares through a monocular sight, guides the missile with a thumb-operated flight controller. The missile follows directions broadcast to it from a small transmitter in the flight controller unit. The missile has a two-kilogram warhead which is exploded by a proximity fuse when it nears an aircraft.

The Blowpipe had a number of technical limitations which may have reduced its kill probability in the Falklands. It can home only on the exhaust heat of low-flying aircraft. It is easily decoyed by flares. Its warhead is too small to be highly lethal, and its 1.5 Mach maximum speed and limited range mean it can engage only subsonic aircraft. The thumb control on the launcher is awkward and any movement across the operator's line of sight makes it almost impossible to continue manual guidance.

The system also requires the operator to have free movement. British troops often had to expose themselves to Argentine fire to use the Blowpipe. Although the Argentines did not take advantage of this opportunity, a more aggressive enemy infantry might have killed a number of Blowpipe operators. The Blowpipe also was criticized for the fact that it was "wholly ineffective against a crossing rather than an approaching target."[47] This criticism, however, is valid for virtually all light manportable SAMs and reflects limits imposed by current guidance and rocket propellent technology which badly need to be overcome.

Unfortunately, the British have so downplayed the role of the U.S.-made Stingers they deployed to the Falklands that it is not possible to assess how much the Stinger's superiority to Blowpipe affected its performance.[48] Unlike the Blowpipe, the Stinger is an all-aspect, fire-and-forget system with improved IR sensors and a built-in logic to distinquish between aircraft and decoys like flares. It is also slightly heavier than Blowpipe at 15.8 kilograms and has enough speed to attack supersonic targets.

The Stinger was deployed in limited numbers but seems to have had a higher kill probability than Blowpipe. For the most part, the Stingers were carried by elite reconnaissance units such as the SAS. The Stinger met the SAS's need to cover territory without being burdened with any of the heavier systems. The forces carrying Stinger were not subjected to extensive air attacks, however, and only one Argentine aircraft was clearly destroyed with the Stinger system.[49]

It is clear that British troops benefited from the comparatively high numbers and wide dispersal of such systems. It is also possible that part of the reason the Argentines failed to use their Pucara ground attack aircraft effectively was the result of a fear that the Blowpipe and the Stinger would be used against them when they attacked at low altitudes. While a number of these aircraft were destroyed in the successful British raid on Pebble Island, the surviving Pucaras were rarely successful in hitting ground targets and often failed to aggressively seek out and penetrate to such targets.

This confirms the value of broadly dispersing manportable SAMs throughout a force and deploying as many launchers as possible. It is also significant that the British found the IFF on Blowpipe to be of value in spite of the limited number of aircraft they deployed and the comparatively limited number of Argentine attack sorties. The British have also significantly improved some aspects of Blowpipe, including counter-decoy action and the ability to deal with crossing targets, by providing a semiautomated TV guidance system.

The Argentine side used shoulder-fired anti-aircraft weapons as well as the British Blowpipe. In December 1982, the Argentine journal *Aerospacio* reported that Argentine forces had used Soviet SA-7 Grail missiles during the war which had been obtained from Peru or Libya. These missiles were commented upon very unfavorably.[50] This is hardly surprising considering the lack of combat kills that can be attributed to Argentine shoulder-fired missiles. Only one British plane may have been lost to such a system. Ironically, the system that destroyed this plane may actually have been a British-made Blowpipe sold to Argentina.[51] What is not clear is how well equipped Argentine forces were with such missiles, how well they were trained, and how well their systems were deployed. It seems likely that British air losses would have been much greater if Argentine troops had had large numbers of more modern systems like Blowpipe and Stinger.

The Argentines also had Roland, and a considerable debate has emerged as to whether or not this French radar-aided optically guided system achieved any kills and how lethal it was. At least seven Roland missiles exploded near British Vulcans and Sea Harriers, and they did so in spite of the Vulcan's use of ECM and the Harrier's use of radar wakening and chaff. The British claim, however, that a maximum of one aircraft was lost to Roland, and even French manufacturers claim only three to five kills. This is a surprisingly poor performance given the size and sophistication of the system. The Roland has a maximum range of 6 kilometers, a radar range of 16 kiometers, and an HE warhead with a proximity fuse. The system has a Mach 1.5 cruise speed, a 63-kilogram launch weight, and a command microwave radio link. It has a monopulse tracking radar and should have been relatively countermeasure resistant. Unfortunately, both the UK and French have made so many claims and counterclaims that it is difficult to firmly establish the facts.

The full details of the role of electronic warfare in surface-to-air missile suppression during the Falklands War are unclear. The U.S. did provide Shrike missiles and full details of Argentina's radar frequencies and other electronic order-of-battle data to Britain. The British ships had extensive electronic warfare gear, but the Harriers did not and proved highly vulnerable to Argentine air defense radars. As a result, the British had to rapidly improvise a self-protection jammer called Blue Eric in a modified Harrier gun pod. Existing pods like the British Marconi Sky Shadow and the U.S.-made Westinghouse ALQ-101 pods were too heavy. Similarly, the British had to rush efforts to fit the ALE-40 chaff and infrared decoy dispenser. It is interesting that this series of modifications was rushed into service between 6 May and 18 May 1982. It never, however, saw service. Blue Eric did not arrive in the Falklands until 8 June, and by the time weather permitted the system's use, the Argentine radars had been cleared from their positions.[52]

Ground Attack and Close Air Support

The British air base and main air defense sites in the Falklands are shown in Table 3.9. The air war in the Falklands involved many unique conditions. The weather blocked air combat for days at a time. British air power consisted largely of the ability to fly one Vulcan bomber sortie every two days from Ascension Island and the 28 Sea Harriers and 14 RAF Harrier GR-3s with the task force. The Royal Navy had only 34 Sea Harriers and came close to exhausting its inventory. The RAF pilots deployed to the Falklands had never previously trained on ships. Nevertheless, the British were able to support over 1,500 Sea Harrier and 150 GR-3 sorties, and some estimates go as high as 2,376 sorties and 2,700 hours of flying time.[53]

The British also helped compensate for their lack of fixed-wing aircraft with helicopters. The Royal Navy has released data which indicate it flew some 12,757 sorties for a total 23,724 flying hours. A break-out of this data clearly reflects the importance of rotary wing aircraft (see Table 3.10).

The British Ministry of Defence has stated that no Harriers were lost in air-to-air combat and that only five were lost to ground fire. It claims a total of seven Harriers were lost under combat conditions and four in accidents. While a debate still goes on about the exact causes and numbers of British losses, it is important to note that the range of uncertainty in this debate is less than five aircraft.

The data on the Argentine side of the air war are more uncertain. The Argentines had about 120 jet combat aircraft and 45 jet turboprop light attack aircraft. The Argentines employed U.S.-made A-4B,

TABLE 3.9 British Air Base and Air Defense Facilities in the Falklands

	Location
MAIN AIRFIELDS	
Pebble Island	W. Falkland
Dunnose Head Settlement	W. Falkland
Goose Green	Lafonia/E. Falkland
Cape Pembroke	E. Falkland
AIR SEARCH RADARS	
Pebble Island	W. Falkland
Byron Heights	W. Falkland
Port Stanley	E. Falkland
MAIN CONCENTRATIONS OF ANTI-AIRCRAFT WEAPONS	
Port Howard	W. Falkland
Fox Bay	W. Falkland
Darwin	E. Falkland
Port Stanley	E. Falkland
Cape Penbroke	E. Falkland

SOURCE: Adapted from Jeffrey Ethell and Alfred Price, *Air War: South Atlantic* (New York: Macmillan, 1984), pp. 80–81.

TABLE 3.10 British Helicopter Sorties and Flying Time

	Flying Time (Hours)	Sorties
Sea Harrier	2,675	2,376
Sea King	11,922	5,552
Wessex	5,090	2,054
Lynx	3,043	1,863
Wasp	994	912
Total	23,724	12,757

A-4C, and A-4Q Skyhawks and Naval 1 Skyhawks; British-made Mark-62 Canberra bombers and I-58 Pucara light turboprop attack aircraft; French-made Super Etendard fighter bombers and Mirage IIIEAs; Israeli Daggers or Mirage Vs; and Italian-made Macchi MB-326 and MB-329 lighter jet fighters.

Estimates of Argentine numbers vary sharply. The Argentines now say they employed 81 A-4s, Mirage IIIs, and Daggers; 5 Super Etendards; and 15 Naval A-4Q Skyhawks. They also may have employed 8 Macchi MB-326 and 8 Macchi MB-329 light jet fighters on the Falklands and up to 45 Pucaras. This would have given the Argentines a total of 117 to 120 fixed-wing jets plus the 45 Pucara turboprops. Other, less official, breakdowns include 76 A-4s, 26 Daggers, 16 Mirage IIIs, 9 Canberras, and 5 Super Etendards plus the Pucaras and Macchis.[54]

The Argentine air force claims that 505 sorties were planned, 445 were actually executed, and 302 actually reached their objective. It reports its combat aircraft flew a total of 2,782 flying hours. This is a remarkably low sortie rate, given the British Admiralty's claim that 28 Sea Harriers flew 2,376 sorties and a total of 2,675 flying hours. While distance and weather were clearly a factor, the Argentines would have been severely hurt by their low sortie rate. Reports since the war indicate it was a function of (a) the lack of targeting and recce data, (b) weather, (c) the navy's failure to risk its aircraft in close-in sorties, (d) poor command use of aircraft in the Falklands, and (e) support problems.

Estimates of Argentine losses differ, but the British claim they included 109 aircraft of all kinds, including 31 A-4 Skyhawks and 26 Mirage IIIs and Daggers. The Argentines admit the loss of 34 Mirage and Skyhawk fighters and report their total losses of aircraft of all types at 102. The numbers and causes of these losses will be discussed shortly.

It is important to note that neither side was really flying a modern air force. Both sides lacked the most modern AEW, C³I and recce assets and could not deploy a balanced force of such assets. Both sides lacked the proper combination of avionics and missiles for effective beyond-visual-range (BVR) combat. The British lacked fighter numbers and endurance, and the basic design of the Harrier was then almost 25 years old. The British Vulcan bombers were scheduled to be scrapped, and the Argentine Canberras and A-4B and A-4C Skyhawks were obsolete by the middle 1970s. The A-4Qs were only marginally better. The Mirage III and Daggers were "day fighters" lacking in sophisticated avionics and munitions for air-to-air combat and attack missions, and the Super Etendards lacked the radar and avionics sophistication to properly target their Exocet missiles beyond visual range.

The Argentine air force also suffered from the fact that it had never really planned or trained to fight at sea. Brigadier General Ernesto Crespo, who later became the chief of staff of the Argentine air force, put it this way,

Before the war, we were prepared for air-to-ground combat. We had never operated at sea, although we had trained for in-flight rendezvous and refueling, using the Omega navigation system, and we had never thought about the possibility of a war of this type. We had to learn on the spot the tactics and modes of operation to be employed by the Air Force because we were not adequately armed. . . . We have (since) done all we possibly can to transform force from a simple act of violence to one of scientific intelligence. Our Air Force is doing its utmost to become truly professional . . . to adopt intelligence and well thought out responses, instead of explosive reactions.[55]

At the same time, it is important to understand that air power was critical to logistics as well as to combat. The British flew five times as many transport and supply sorties as they did combat sorties, and they flew some 5,600 troops and 7,500 tons of cargo on long-range flights to Ascension Island. This involved over 1,700 flying hours by C-130 and VC-10 transports. The RAF also flew 35 air drops by C-130 aircraft over the Falklands, plus 150 Nimrod sorties to monitor naval activity along the Argentine coast. The Argentines claim they flew 446 SAR sorties, or almost exactly their number of combat sorties. They were able to continuously land at Port Stanley until the end of the war, and they claim that Argentine aircraft delivered 435 tons of cargo by air to Port Stanley after 1 June and evacuated 264 wounded.

Air-to-Air and Anti-Ship Air Wars

The ground attack and close air support aspects of the Falklands conflict can be divided into three major aspects: the role of British forces, the role of Argentine forces, and the impact of air-to-surface missiles. The air war in the Falklands was largely a war between Argentine attack aircraft attacking naval targets at low altitudes, with a minimum of fighter escort, and British Harrier fighters flying air defense and ground-attack missions. Although the outcome of the air-to-air battle was decisively in favor of the British, the Argentines had other primary objectives. The Argentines showed great courage and skill in executing air attacks on British naval forces. While the figures involved are controversial, it is possible to make a reasonably good estimate of the causes of the air losses on each side. This estimate of air losses is shown in Tables 3.11 and 3.12, and the size of Argentine losses makes it clear that the Argentine air force persisted in the face of very heavy casualties.

If one assumes the total of 102 aircraft is correct, Argentina lost 32 aircraft to the Harrier. Twenty-eight of these kills were by the Sea Harrier and 25 were in air-to-air combat, with 18 kills by Aim-9L, 5 kills by 20-mm cannon, 1 by Aim-AL or cannon, and 1 during evasion

TABLE 3.11 Argentine Aircraft Losses by Type/Cause

Type	Number	Cause
PUMA (ARMY)	1	small arms
	1	Sea Dart missile
	2	Harrier GR3 (30-mm cannon)
	1	Sea Harrier
PUCARA	1	operational accident
	1	Sea Harrier (cluster bomb)
	1	Sea Harrier (30-mm cannon)
	2	Blowpipe
	6	ground action
	1	Stinger
MIRAGE	2	Sea Harrier (Sidewinder)
DAGGER	8	Sea Harrier (Sidewinder)
	1	Sea Cat
SKYHAWK	4	operational accident
	6	Sea Harrier (Sidewinder)
	3	MHS *Brilliant* (Sea Wolf)
	2	multiple weapons
HMS *Exeter* (Sea Dart)	1	Bofors 40 mm
	1	Sea Harrier (30 mm) and small arms
HMS *Ardent*		
	1	Sea Harrier (30 mm)
MACCHI 339	1	operational accident
	1	Blowpipe
CANBERRA	1	Sea Harrier (Sidewinder)
	1	HMS *Exeter* (Sea Dart)
C-130 HERCULES	1	Sea Harrier (Sidewinder)
TURBO MENTORS	4	ground action
LEAR JET	1	(unknown)
TOTAL LOSSES BY CAUSE:		Sidewinder 18 (Harrier)
		30-mm cannon 5
		Sidewinder & cannon 1
		cluster bombs 2

SOURCES: Jeffrey Ethell and Alfred Price, *Air War: South Atlantic* (New York: Macmillan, 1984), pp. 234–242; Bruce W. Watson and Peter M. Dunn, *Military Lessons of the Falklands War* (Boulder, Colo.: Westview, 1984), pp. 31–33; and Jesus R. Briasco and Salvadore M. Huertas, *Falklands, Witness of Battle* (Valencia, Spain: Frederico Domenech/S.A. Gremis, 1985), pp. 164–167.

TABLE 3.12 British Aircraft Losses by Type/Cause

Type	Number	Cause
Sea Harrier	2	ground anti-aircraft fire (1 Roland)
	3	operational accident
Harrier GR3	2	ground anti-aircraft fire (1 small arms fire)
	1	operational accident
Sea King	4	operational accident
Lynx	2	air attack
Wessex	6	Exocet (lost on Atlantic conveyor)
	2	operational accident
Chirooks	3	Exocet (lost on Atlantic conveyor)
Scout	1	air combat
Gazelle	1	missile
	2	small arms

SOURCES: Adapted from Jeffrey Ethell and Alfred Price, *Air War: South Atlantic* (New York: Macmillan, 1984), pp. 248–251; and Bruce W. Watson and Peter M. Dunn, *Military Lessons of the Falklands War* (Boulder, Colo.: Westview, 1984), pp. 31–33. British and French sources disagree over whether one or two/three aircraft were lost to Roland missile fire.

under attack. The Sea Harrier killed 3 aircraft on the ground: 2 by cluster bomb and 1 by cannon fire. The RAF Harriers killed 4 aircraft, all on the ground; 3 kills were by 30-mm cannon and 1 by cluster bomb.

Ground- and sea-based weapons killed twenty Argentine aircraft. Four of those kills were caused by multiple weapons during the attack on San Carlos Water. Nine were killed by sea-launched missiles: one by Sea Cat, five by Sea Dart, and three by Sea Wolf. Seven were killed by land-based systems: five by Blowpipe, Stinger, and small arms; one by Bofors 40-mm cannon; and one by Rapier. As for the other Argentine aircraft losses, eleven were lost in the SAS raid on Pebble Island, six were lost in operational accidents, one was lost with the *General Belgrano*, and thirty-two were captured on the ground, including fifteen from the Air Force, three from the Navy, two from the Coast Guard, and 12 from the Army.

The Argentine air force lost a total of sixty-three aircraft, twenty-seven of which were based in the Falklands and thirty-six of which were land based. The aircraft in the Falklands included twenty-five Pucaras and two Bell 212s. The aircraft based on the mainland included eleven Daggers, nineteen Skyhawks, two Canberras, one Learjet, one C-130H, and two Mirage IIIs. The Argentine navy lost three mainland-based A-4Qs, one Alouette helicopter on the *Belgrano*, five Macchi 339s and four Torbo-Mentors in the Falklands. The coast guard lost two Skyvans and one Puma in the Falklands, and the army lost two Chinooks, eight Pumas, nine Bell UH-1Hs, and three Augusta 109s in the Falklands and South Georgia.

The British lost thirty-four aircraft. Eleven were lost to operational accidents, one was abandoned, and thirteen were lost with the ships they were on. One Scout helicopter was shot down by a Pucara: the only Argentine air-to-air kill. Eight were lost to ground fire: three to 20-mm or 35-mm AA guns, three to small arms fire, one to a Roland, and one to a missile of unknown type. The fleet air arm lost twenty-three planes: six Sea Harriers, nine Wessex HAS.31H.U.5, five Sea King HAS.5/HC.4, and three Lynx HAS.2. The Royal Marines lost one Scout AH.1 and two Gazelle AH.1s. The Royal Air Force lost four Harrier GR3s and three Chinook HC.1s. The Army Air Corps lost one AH.1.

These data scarcely reveal a clear kill pattern. They do indicate, however, that the Harriers scored about thirty-one kills, with twenty-four by missile (largely Aim-9L) and seven by guns, or roughly 25 percent of all Argentine losses. The British claim no Harriers were lost in air-to-air combat and that their only air combat loss was one Scout helicopter to a Pucara during the battle of Goose Green. This pattern of losses does reveal the effectiveness of the Aim-9L and the British emphasis on air defense compared with the Argentine emphasis on attacking naval targets.

The British Experience in Air Combat

This difference in mission emphasis, however, makes it difficult to draw lessons from the air-to-air combat. Air combat consisted largely of the Sea Harrier against Argentine fighters that deliberately chose not to engage and that lacked the radars, avionics, and missiles for effective air combat. The Sea Harriers also interacted with British ship-based sensors and ship-to-air missiles and acted as an air defense screen in a role neither the Harrier nor British ships were designed for. It is important to note that the outcome might have been radically different if the Argentines had had (a) the range and endurance to engage the Harriers, (b) the U.S. Aim-9L or an effective BVR engagement capability, (c) bombs which exploded after hitting a ship, (d) more Exocets and launch air craft, or (e) the capability to time mass raids to saturate the limited multiple engagement capability of British ships and the limited number of Harriers that could engage at any given time. Nevertheless, the outcome of the war is still a notable tribute to the reliability of the Harrier and the skill of British pilots.

The Sea Harrier was conceived in the mid-1950s and was originally designed as a close support aircraft for operation in the V/STOL mode off light aircraft carriers. It entered Royal Navy service in July 1969. It was powered by a Rolls Royce Bristol Pegasus Mark 103 vectored thrust turbofan rated at 21,500 pounds of static thrust, and it was the world's first operational fixed-wing, vertical-lift fighter craft. The Sea Harrier fighters also carried two sidewinder Aim-9L missiles and 30-mm cannon. The Harrier GR3 had a maximum payload of 8,000 pounds and could carry 5,000 pounds on five pylons in close air support missions. A typical attack payload consisted of two 30-mm cannon pods, a 1,000-pound bomb, and two matra 155-rocket pods.

The Sea Harrier has a top speed of 737 mph or Mach 0.972 at low level, a climb speed (VTOL) of 50,000 feet per minute at sea level, and a service ceiling of 50,000 feet. The Harrier's combat radius is 260 miles. All RAF Harriers are fitted with laser range finders and marked target seekers in a chisel nose.[56]

The Sea Harrier incorporated comprehensive communication and navigation/attack equipment. It is unclear what role equipment such as the Blue Fox radar on the Harrier played in air combat, but the British seem to have made extensive use of its target acquisition, ranging, and fire control capabilities.[57] Other equipment included the Ferranti FE541 inertial navigation and attack system (INAS), the Smith electronic head-up display, the Smith air data computer, and the Ferranti laser ranger and marked target seeker (LRMTS).[58]

There is no question that British pilots feel that they operated under a handicap because they lacked both any form of AEW aircraft or AWACS and advanced avionics on the Sea Harrier. The lessons of the Falklands explain much of the development of the follow-on Sea Harrier FSR-2, which will have a much more advanced computer and all-weather radar called the Sea Vixen. This radar will allow the aircraft to carry up to four advanced AMRAAM air-to-air missiles and engage in beyond-visual-range combat. The Sea Harrier FSR-2 will have multiple target engagement, track-while scan, and shoot-down and look-down capabilities. These are all features and British pilots felt could have greatly improved their performance in the Falklands, particularly in dealing with large A-4 raids.

Other lessons reflected in the Sea Harrier FSR-2 are the 1553B data bus and provision for a secure joint tactical data distribution system, a much lower workload cockpit with a hands-on throttle and stick control, and a much improved autopilot system. The FSR-2 also has an improved radar warning receiver and will be able to carry more fuel. This will allow it to maintain a 1-1/2-hour combat air patrol at a range of 185 kilometers (100 miles) from a ship.

Even so, the first FSR-2s were delivered in 1988, some six years after the war. They still lack operational Blue Vixen radars and are not expected to be fully operational until 1992. This is not a quick reaction to the lessons of the Falklands, and the Royal Navy is already complaining that it needs an FSR-3 with even more advanced avionics, more speed, and a much greater range. It is clear that advances in the threat in both Warsaw Pact and Third World forces are making the lessons of the Falklands steadily more important—if also steadily more expensive to act upon.[59]

The primary Argentine air force targets of the Harriers were the three Argentine variants of the U.S. Navy's McDonnell Douglas A-4B Skyhawk. These attack bomber aircraft were powered by a 7,700 pound thrust J65-W-16A engine. The U.S. Navy version of the A-4 has an AN/APG-53A radar, Marconi-Elliott AVQ-24 head-up display, and electronic countermeasures. The Argentine A-4B and A-4C did not have such sophisticated avionics and did not carry countermeasures equipment, although the A-4Q had a radar suited for anti-ship targeting and attack.

The armament on the A-4s included two 20-mm Mark 12 cannon with 200 rounds each, plus provision for an external load of up to 1,800 to 2,000 kilograms on hardpoints. The A-4s could carry a wide range of ordnance including HE bombs, air-to-air and air-to-surface rockets, Sidewinder AAMs, Bullpup ASMs, ECM pods, gun pods, and torpedoes. At normal loaded weight, the A-4 has a top speed of 646 mph, it can climb 10,300 feet per minute, and it has a service ceiling of 49,000 feet. The educational combat range of the A-4 with a 4,000-pound bomb load is about 460 miles.

The primary fighters the Argentines used for their relatively few cover and air defense missions were the Mirage III and the Israeli Nester version of the Mirage III. Both aircraft are very similar. The Dagger is powered by an Atar 9C engine in the Nester configuration. According to one source, this version of the Mirage III has a top speed of 1,460 mph or Mach 2.2 at 39,000 feet, a climb speed of 12,000 feet per minute, and a service ceiling of 75,450 feet. Its combat radius is estimated at 745 miles, or at about 600 miles with two 500-pound bombs.

It is not clear whether the radar used in the Argentine (Nester) Mirage was the Israeli Elta-built version of the Cyrano used in the

Mirage IIIEAs or a simple ranging sight based on Aida II.[60] The Dagger typically carried two 30-mm DEFA cannon and two 1,000-pound bombs. The Argentine air force Daggers carried Matra R.530 air-to-air missiles, older versions of the Sidewinder air-to-air missile.[61] The Argentine Mirages and Daggers were faster and more maneuverable than the Harriers at medium to high altitudes but were slower when maneuvering at low altitudes and had serious avionics limitations in supporting low-altitude missile and gun combat.

Data are not available on the number of sorties each side flew per day, ratios per day, or sortie type. It is clear, however, that British aircraft numbers were very limited. The British initially deployed twenty Sea Harriers, which sailed with the fleet in mid-April 1982, and eight reinforcement Sea Harriers arrived later. There also were fourteen RAF Harrier GR3s, but these were designed as ground attack aircraft. They were fitted with Aim-9L Sidewinders to provide some on-board protective capability,[62] but they were not used in the air defense screen. The total number of British air defense sorties thus had to be relatively limited.

This makes the British air-to-air kill performance even more impressive. Once again the numbers are controversial, but Argentine naval and air force Skyhawk, Dagger, and Super Etendard fighter-bomber units flew a total of 180 sorties from the mainland. In all, the British estimate nineteen Skyhawks and Daggers were destroyed. According to one British source, these losses break down as follows: twelve to action by Sea Harriers, five to surface-launched missiles and gunfire, one shared between ships' fire and a Sea Harrier, and one shot down in error by the Argentines.[63]

The key statistic affecting air combat performance is that eighteen to nineteen of the Harrier's twenty-three kills were the result of using the Aim-9L missile, although there is some question as to the exact figure. For example, one British report claims that twenty-four aircraft were destroyed for twenty-seven Aim-9L missiles fired and that the aircraft was destroyed in every case of a missile lock-on.[64] On the other hand, another British source cites the total number of kills at twenty-three, seventeen of which were the result of Sidewinders. This variance does not contradict the point that the missile was extremely effective. These results dovetail closely with the experience of the Israeli air force in the June 1982 war in Lebanon. The Sidewinder kill rate in that conflict was also approximately 80 percent.

It is also notable that most of the Sea Harrier kills were accomplished against relatively high performance Argentine fighters. While these Argentine fighters did not heavily engage the Harriers, they were flown skillfully and in attack profiles, making it unlikely the Harriers could have been anywhere as effective without the Aim-9L. Most of the engagements occurred between 50 and 500 feet and involved high load factors maneuvering at around 550 knots in an essentially horizontal plane.

British pilot reports also indicate that the Aim-9L proved to be very reliable and that once the aircraft's avionics indicated a "lock on," the results of a launch were almost certain to be a confirmed kill.[65] This performance may, however, have been augmented by the avionics on the Harrier aircraft. One source asserts that Harrier aircraft sensors provided data which enabled the Aim-9L missile to be fired at greater target angles than normally possible, and this data allowed maximum use of the missile's all-aspect guidance system.[66] This report must be viewed with skepticism, however, given the relatively old and unsophisticated avionics then on the Sea Harrier.

No Sea Harriers or GR3s were lost due to air combat, although several aircraft were destroyed by ground fire, one to ditching on takeoff, and "one over the side" in heavy weather. The Harrier pilots did not really test the value of the special maneuver or jinking ("viffing") capabilities of the aircraft. They normally conducted straight intercepts against opponents who did not engage them in air-to-air combat.[67] According to one Argentine source, the prescribed tactic was to avoid air combat. "We were briefed to avoid dogfights and escape at low level and alone," recalled Ruben Zini, who flew with Group 5.[68] There is no doubt, however, that some of the VTOL capabilities of the Harrier aircraft had considerable value. They gave the aircraft the flexibility to operate from small aircraft carriers, once the exclusive domain of helicopters, and to take off and land in extremely difficult environments such as helipads on merchant ships in heavy weather and temporary landing facilities on the beach.[69]

The Argentine perception of British capabilities also indicates a healthy respect for the Harrier. One Argentine officer stated,

> What were we briefed to do if jumped by Sea Harriers? Well, we had a lot of experience of air combat maneuvering, but in the A-4 there was not much choice. Not only were we too slow, but we knew very well we could not outmaneuver the Sea Harrier. All we could do was try to escape at low level at full throttle. . . . We never mounted Sidewinders on our Skyhawks because our mission was always one of attack, never air-to-air combat. The Sidewinder-L is a very, very effective missile and our older models could not hope to equal them.[70]

This same Argentine pilot's assessment of the A-4 Skyhawk shows much less confidence in the aircraft than Israeli pilots show in describing more advanced versions of the aircraft, i.e., the A-4N.[71]

This aircraft was manufactured as recently as 1979, and the Israelis expect to use advanced versions until the 1990s. The Argentine aircraft, on the other hand, used the Matra 530 air-to-air missile, which was not comparable because it lacked low-altitude engagement ability.[72]

Nevertheless, it must be stressed that the results of the Falklands fighting do not show how the Harrier or the variants flown by the U.S. Marine Corps would have performed against a modern fighter aircraft.[73] The Harriers encountered Argentine fighters which could make only limited maneuvers while they carried out a single attack pass against the British ships.[74] The Mirages and Daggers were normally very pressed for fuel, operating as they were at the far end of their operational range. They had only about two minutes over the target area in strafing runs in the Strait of San Carlos or bombing against Royal Navy units. Interestingly enough, at least one source claims that the British feared the Mirages most and that the Harriers were initially supposed to use their viffing ability to avoid combat with the Mirage.[75]

Argentine Skyhawks also generally did not engage the Harrier, although this might have been an interesting test of VSTOL performance versus the kind of less-capable fighters operated by many Third World states. Both planes are comparable in speed and turn capability, although the A-4 Skyhawk is much slower at low altitudes, by approximately 100 knots, and lacks air combat avionics. The U.S. Marines have tested both aircraft extensively. According to at least one Marine, however, the match-up is not even close; the Harrier can outfly and outgun the Skyhawks and do so on a two-to-one basis.[76] The Harriers did not have to maneuver protectively in most encounters and could do their best to destroy the attackers through simple optimal interceptions. Their most difficult task was not dogfighting but detecting and locating enemy aircraft flying low-altitude profiles, although they had the advantage that the Argentine aircraft had to fly predictable attack profiles. Argentine attack planes were compelled to fly low to escape British shipborne SAMs like the Sea Dart missile. This meant that the Harriers did not need to give chase at higher altitudes, where the A-4 or Mirage's speed would be optimal, and expend precious fuel in the climb.[77]

Argentine Air Combat Experience
in Anti-Ship Attacks

The Argentine air force's performance in anti-ship attacks was in some ways a remarkably successful case of adapting a force structure to new combat conditions. At the same time, it was an effort by an air force that had never trained or equipped itself for the mission and had many defects. Brigadier General Ernesto Crespo, who later became the chief of staff of the Argentine air force, described the problems the Argentines faced during the fighting as follows:

> The Air Force was not prepared for such a war, whose characteristics only became apparent abruptly on the spot. Technical capabilities play a fundamental role in this conflict. We had to create or invent all the procedures we used in the Malvinas progressively as events unfolded. We learned little by little from each blow which we received and from which we suffered. We then coined a phrase which we kept repeating: "To learn, one must first pay." . . . Our previous weapons were designed for a surface-air confrontation, but not for coping with a frigate, which is really a floating electronic station. . . . It is for these reasons that we are now developing sophisticated systems . . . we have taken all necessary measures for responding more effectively to a similar conflict in the future.[78]

The tactics that Argentine aircraft did use against British ships were inherently limited in their effectiveness. The Argentines had uncertain ability to coordinate mass attacks and faced major problems in aircraft range, aircraft avionics, munitions, aircraft operability, and aircraft sustainability.[79] Although the Argentines often flew large numbers of sorties on a given day, the aircraft normally arrived over the fleet or naval targets in relatively small groups. Instead of attempting to overwhelm British defenses with large numbers of aircraft, the Argentines usually attacked ships a few planes at a time. This normally allowed the British to focus all of their anti-aircraft defenses on a comparatively few intruders.

The Argentines also had to use low-altitude attack runs as a result of their respect for the British Sea Dart missile system and other British ship-based air defenses which functioned optimally at mid- to high altitudes. Neither the Mirage IIIEs nor the Israeli-built Daggers had advanced weapons delivery avionics or the kind of advanced radar that can track and characterize surface targets. Although some of the Argentine A-4s had been modified with Ferranti D126R Isis weapons arming systems, they were not comparable to modern attack aircraft like the F-16 or F-20A and had serious problems in delivering ordnance at such low altitudes.[80]

Although there is some controversy over the exact impact of the range limitations involved, there is little doubt that the Argentine air force had to operate at the extreme end of its aircrafts' operational radii even when these could be refueled. According to one source, only 81 Argentine aircraft out of a total of 225 could fly from Argentine bases to within range of the British ships. These included the Mirage IIIs, the Mirage Vs, the A-4 Skyhawks, and Argentina's obsolete and slow-maneuvering Canberra bombers. Of these, only the A-4B and A-4C Skyhawks were air-refuelable, and only two KC-130 tankers were available.

Argentina's five Super Etendards had a maximum range of only 375 miles, although they were equipped with a buddy refueling system which provided some extended range capability which was used effectively in several missions. This refueling technology, however, limited the bomb load of the aircraft. The Mirages had no refueling ability and could make only one pass over the island even with external fuel tanks.[81] These problems were often compounded by head winds, weather, and target acquisition problems. Even a few extra minutes of combat or high power maneuver often brought all types of Argentine fighters to the point of no return.

This raises the important lesson of the need to be able to base as far forward as possible in any remote-area conflict. The Argentines failed to recognize the advantage of rapidly building up a forward basing capability at Port Stanley airport at the point when they could have done so without opposition, and they never recovered from their mistake. While some controversy remains over whether or not the RAF cratered the runway enough to block it, it was only 4,000 feet long. Argentine Pucaras and MB-329s could use this runway length safely, but not the A-Hs, Daggers, or Mirages. The only other fields in the Falklands had grass strips, and the only strip fully suitable for MB-339 and Pucara operations was at Pebble Island. Even then, light attack aircraft could not operate off this strip when fully loaded with bombs. Ironically, the Argentines had the construction equipment necessary to extend the strip at Port Stanley and considerable land-based air defense resources to protect it. They had aluminum runway extension material but failed to ship it while large ships could still move to the Falklands.

In contrast, the British clearly recognized the importance of forward basing. They lengthened the runway at Port Stanley, and the first British Phantoms landed there on 17 October 1982, after a nine-hour flight from Ascension which required seven in-flight refuelings.[82] As will be discussed shortly, however, the Argentine fighters were still able to inflict a very significant amount of damage to the ships of the British fleet. If Argentine pilots had been better instructed on the exact bombing profile they should have used, or their bombs had been adjusted to explode on contact, they would have been able to inflict much higher losses on the British.

The Role of British Air Attack Forces

The only major long-range air attacks during the Falklands War were carried out by Vulcan bombers striking at the Port Stanley airfield. These attacks required several air refuelings enroute from Ascension Island and also seem to have involved the only major use of electronic warfare against Argentine radars and SAM defenses.

According to the British White Paper:

> In the longest range bombing missions yet flown Vulcan bombers attacked Port Stanley airfield, but with only 1,000 lb. bombs they were unable to close the runway for more than a short period. The need was underlined for an advanced airfield attack weapon such as JP 233.[83]

These Black Buck missions were at the extreme limit of the Vulcan's capability, even with refueling, and the quality of the military planning behind such raids seems to have been somewhat uncertain. The objective of incapacitating the runway was certainly valid, but the number of bombers and tankers was marginal at best, and the munitions available were insufficiently accurate and/or lethal. The RAF was lucky that even one Vulcan reached its target and that even one bomb dropped close enough to damage the runway enough to firmly prevent heavy transport of Mirage and A-4 fighter operations.[84]

The Vulcans carried out their one successful mission on 1 May 1982. They had to fly a total of 7,860 miles and carry out six refuelings, five on the attack leg and one on the return. The flight each way was a minimum of eight hours and 3,886 miles (the distance from London to Karachi). The initial attack involved two Vulcan B-2 bombers (one in reserve) and eleven supporting Victors (one in rescue). All the reserve aircraft had to be used. The attacking Vulcan and remaining Victors consumed far more fuel than planned and had serious refueling problems.[85]

The Vulcan also experienced problems with its avionics but attacked with all key systems operating. It penetrated at a height of about 500 feet with a "pop-up" to an attack altitude of 10,000 feet. It began to receive radar warning pulses from the TPS-43 radar at Port Stanley about 50 miles from target, although it then was still at 500 feet. The Vulcan carried twenty-one 1,000-pound bombs since Britain's JP-233 runway cratering munition was not then operational. It had to fly at a 30° angle to the runway and drop bombs at 50 yards (0.25 second intervals) to have a reasonable probability of hitting with even one bomb. The 10,000-foot altitude was necessary both to give the bombs sufficient momentum to create a deep crater and reduce the Vulcan's vulnerability to short-range air defense systems (SHORADS).

The Vulcan employed ALQ-101 jamming pods fitted under the starboard wing and a British on-board jamming system. It also could carry a pair of Shrike AGM-45 anti-radiation missiles, although these seem to have been used only on later missions. Two were fired and one seems to have hit the radar or an anti-aircraft gun.[86] The Vulcans also carried chaff but employed it only on later missions.

None of the other Black Buck missions was successful. The first air defense radar suppression mission was flown on 31 May; it struck at night and at 16,000 feet. This attack seems to have hit an AA gun radar but was otherwise a failure. A second attack on 3 June failed because the Argentines switched off their radars when the Vulcan came within nine miles of the target. The Vulcan then dropped down to 10,000 feet to force the Argentines to use their radars to defend, but they only turned on their Skyguards. Two Shrikes were fired, but their effect was uncertain and the Vulcan experienced critical fuel problems and had to land in Brazil. The British adapted the Harrier GR3 to carry Shrike by mid-June, but it was not used successfully in combat.

In spite of these problems and failures, the British experience does tend to validate the numerous NATO studies showing the value of long-range strike aircraft that can carry high payloads of effective anti-runway weapons, such as the French Durandel or an effective cluster bomb system. It is also clear that the British could have achieved decisive results using nuclear bombs in the Falklands from the strategic focal point of Ascension Island as well as from submarines and carrier-based aircraft. Although such nuclear capabilities are only hypothetically relevant, the loss of one or more British carriers might have made their use more viable. In the same context, the acquisition by Third World countries of bombers which are more advanced than the Argentine B-57 Canberra and the Iraqi Badger bombers might well lead such countries to use nuclear weapons if they acquire them. It is interesting to note that both Iraq and Argentina are considered by the U.S. government to be capable of acquiring nuclear weapons within the next decade.

Most of the ground attack missions during the Falklands fighting were performed largely by the Harriers.[87] Up to 500 ground attack sorties were flown by this aircraft. They resulted in the loss of only five aircraft, an attrition rate of only about 1 percent.[88] As has been discussed earlier, anti-aircraft guns and small arms seem to have claimed four Harriers, and one aircraft may have been lost to a Roland missile.

The Harrier provided this close air support with conventional bombs, rockets, and cannon fire, and it also undertook day and night reconnaissance.[89] It carried a maximum of three 1,000-pound bombs in the close air support/ground attack mission. Many ground attack sorties were used to destroy hard targets in lieu of artillery support, which was often in short supply. The Harriers performed well in these missions, but some doubt remains concerning the accuracy achieved in bombing runs.

The battle at Goose Green was heavily affected by Harrier aircraft attacking ground positions. However, ground fire was responsible for downing two of the Harriers. This was due partly to the low-altitude flying tactics utilized by the British and partly to the necessity of making multiple passes on ill-defined and camouflaged targets.[90] Indeed, the Harriers met much more serious enemy opposition than the Sea Harriers; they encountered the enemy on almost every mission. As a result, the Harriers took hits both from gunfire and from missiles.

The Harriers were also successful in hitting point targets, at least some of which were laser designated or called in by FACs using laser designators. For example, they were successful in hitting 35-mm guns in the Goose Green area. Attacking with cluster bombs and two-inch rockets, the Harriers eliminated several 35-mm guns and raised the morale of the British paratroopers in the vicinity. The attack again took place at low altitudes of 50 to 100 feet and came as a surprise to the Argentines.[91]

Harriers from the HMS *Hermes* and HMS *Invincible* also attacked the Port Stanley airfield with three 1,000-pound bombs on 24 May in a coordinated attack. These attacks on the runway were conducted at extremely low altitudes. The Harriers first launched a salvo of 1,000-pound bombs with radar airburst fuses to suppress the Argentine air defenses. Five Sea Harriers then attacked buildings and aircraft with 600-pound cluster bombs and the runway with 1,000-pound parachute-retarded bombs. Succeeding Harriers were forced to fly through bomb debris, but this did not result in any material damage to the aircraft.[92] Fortunately for the British, most of the attacking aircraft approached from behind the coverage of Argentina's main TPS-43 radar, with the result that there was minimal ground fire. The effect of these attacks on the runway at Port Stanley is open to question. The Argentines reported that damage was minimal but they tried to make the runway appear as if the runway were severely damaged:

> We had no real runway hits in the 45 days of combat. This, all sources agreed, was due to some of the poor strike techniques employed by first

the RN Sea Harriers, and then the RAF's Harriers. They were coming in on fast, low deliveries which were inaccurate, or tosslobbing their bombs ineffectively. Significantly, many of the sub-munitions used in the anti-airfield bombs failed to detonate, causing problems for the British, as, of course, bomb failures were to cause problems for the Argentineans. The Argentines report that when the RAF Harriers came in it seemed as though they were determined to do the job on the airfield which the RN had failed to do, but in the end resorted to exactly the same delivery techniques as the RN.

This Argentine statement conflicts with assessments like those of Bryan Perret, who claims that the Harrier attacks did major damage:

Harrier after Harrier flew the length of the airfield to release a combination of delayed action high-explosive and cluster bombs; the former caused deep craters in the runway while the multiple bursts of the latter wrecked parked aircraft, damaged installations and started fires among the stockpiled stores.[93]

Other British experts, however, support the Argentine view. Regardless of the conflicting nature of these assessments, the fact remains that the Harriers did not fully knock out the runway, although they did considerable damage to the airport facilities. This failure again highlights the need for more effective anti-runway weapons with "smart" warheads and standoff range.

The RAF Harriers also showed they could rapidly establish forward basing as well as adapt to operations at sea. After the buildup of the San Carlos beachhead, a forward-operating base was constructed on the north shore of San Carlos Water. GR3s flew ground-support missions from this base. Harrier pilots "planned" their missions from their cockpits and typically responded in about 25 minutes to requests from ground units. The San Carlos base handled as many as nine Harriers at one time, and over 150 operational refuelings were achieved. When needed, replenishment and rearming of the Harriers were done back on board ship.

This ability to operate off relatively unimproved runways could be of major importance in a future conflict. It is interesting to note, however, that Britain found it needed improved precision, path indication (PAPI), approach, and carrier helicopter approach path (CHAPI) equipment for night and poor weather operations. This may be an important lesson, as few Western forces have light, rapidly portable equipment to handle the air control and C^2 task for either fighters or helicopters, and both Israel and Iraq have found forward area C^2 for helicopters to be a serious problem. [94]

Argentine Performance in Attack Missions

The Argentines flew Mirage and A-4 sorties in support of the land battle but concentrated on using their fighters to attack the British fleet. Argentina also conducted a limited number of attacks on British infantry using their Pucara light attack aircraft. These attacks were often pressed home at very low altitudes and with considerable expertise, but they lacked the payload lethality to have much effect on dispersed infantry forces. Argentina's light attack aircraft did little aside from shooting down a Scout helicopter and inflicting minor damage and casualties on the HMS *Argonaut*. All thirty-four aircraft on the islands were lost, and they seem to have inflicted only minimal casualties on British ground forces. The Argentine performance with the Pucara scarcely validates the advocates of cheap, light attack aircraft. The Pucaras were flown aggressively and showed relatively low vulnerability to light SAMs and ground fire. Still, they really could not survive over a defended battlefield.[95]

The Pucara is a small, twin-engined, counterinsurgency-designated aircraft with a maximum level speed of 270 knots/1,500 km per hour at 9,845 feet. It has the capacity for 1,620 kg/3,571 lb. of external ordance or other stores and a range of 3,042 km/1,890 statute miles. Its most obvious limitations are speed: At 270 knots it is only marginally faster than an attack helicopter such as the UH-1. The Pucara aircraft proved rugged enough to sustain hits from small-arms fire and could return to base with only one live engine. However, soldier-fired British Blowpipe missiles seem to have been effective in destroying the Pucara, and Argentine aircraft failed to use flares and other IR countermeasures and make proper use of chaff.

The obsolete Canberra was also utilized in the ground attack role. The Canberras flew from bases on the mainland but experienced major losses. The Argentine air defenses at Port Stanley also provided a good lesson in the value of good IFF when they mistakenly shot down a Canberra that flew over Port Stanley after the RAF Vulcan attack on 1 May. The Canberra's range/payload/bombing accuracy limitations and vulnerability to the Harrier-Sidewinder made Argentine pilots extremely reluctant to fly such missions.

As has been discussed earlier, the main Argentine air attacks using the A-4A, A-4B, Mirages, and Daggers concentrated on surface warships in or near the San Carlos Bay area, which were supporting and off-loading British troops and supplies in the area. The effectiveness of such Argentine air attacks can be measured in terms of the number of ships lost or damaged. The Falklands experience showed that dedicated pilots using conventional weapons and avionics can destroy missile-defended surface ships if they have suitable range and endurance, even if adequate warning time is not available and protective avionics and other measures are not effectively employed.

In fact, the Argentines would have been far more lethal in such attacks if they had had the ability to refuel their Daggers and Mirages and had been able to solve their bomb delivery profile and fusing problems. There is still some debate over whether the problem was the result of fuses designed to use propeller sensors which armed only in World War II-type dive bombing attacks, the failure to release the bombs at the proper moment, or the failure to "pop up" and raise delivery altitude. In any case, several British ships were hit by bombs that did not explode. Some even passed through and lodged within the hull, as in the case of HMS *Argonaut*.

The full list of British ships hit by bombs that failed to detonate is somewhat startling. It includes the HMS *Argonaut*, HMS *Glasgow*, HMS *Sheffield* (missile), HMS *Antrim*, HMS *Ardent*, HMS *Antelope*, HMS *Sir Bedivere*, HMS *Broadsword*, HMS *Plymouth*, and HMS *Glamorgan*. It seems at least possible that if these bomb hits had resulted in explosions, they might have forced the British task force ships to withdraw or had a political effect on the course of the war. They certainly indicate the vulnerability of well-equipped task forces to typical Third World air weapons.[96]

The Role of Air-Launched Precision-Guided Munitions

Although the Argentines conducted at least nineteen successful air strikes on British ships using bombs and guns and damaged or sank sixteen ships, it was the Argentine use of Exocet that captured the world's imagination. At the beginning of the war Argentina was in possession of six or seven AM-39 air-launched Exocet missiles and a somewhat larger stock of MM-38 ship- and land-launched Exocet missiles.

Three Exocets are known to have done significant damage to the British fleet. Two Exocets were fired at the frigate *Sheffield*, one of which struck and sank her. The *Atlantic Conveyor*, a huge, well-stocked container ship, was sunk by an Exocet fired from a Super Etendard on 25 May. The destroyer *Glamorgan* was hit by a shore-based Exocet on 12 June but managed to survive the attack. Britain also shot down one of the Argentine Exocets on 1 June 1982 with its Sea Wolf point defense system. The loss of the *Sheffield*, the most unsettling in terms of technological questions involved, was the result of a hit by a dud Exocet missile. It was the resultant fire, and not a warhead explosion, that eventually forced the abandonment of the warship. A cheap and somewhat dated sea-skimming air-to-ship missile specifically designed for air and missile defense had destroyed a British warship.

The air-launched version of the Exocet is called the AM-39. The AM-39 has been operational since 1977 and has a 47-mile range and 364-pound target. The AM-39s were not launched from ships during the war, although some were fired from land and one hit a target. The AM-39 weighs 654 kilograms and has a 165-kilogram warhead designed to explode after penetration. It is 4.69 meters long and 0.35 meters in diameter. It has a dual thrust rocket propulsion system. The booster burn time is 2.1 seconds, and the main rocket burns for 105 seconds. It flies at 600 mph (Mach 0.93). The missile altitude is controlled by a radio altimeter, and its course is determined by an inertial guidance system programmed by the launch aircraft. It flies at about 15 meters high to within 12 kilometers of the target. The radar acquisition system in the missile nose then activates and homes in on the target. The missile then drops to a sea-skimming height of 2 to 5 meters. The proportional navigation system in the missile allows it to home on the center of the ship rather than the tail.

The history of the first AM-39 strike, which sank the *Sheffield*, is fairly clear. On 4 May 1982, the Argentine Naval Air Command responded to reconnaissance reports from a Neptune patrol aircraft and ordered a Super Etendard strike against ships sighted about 100 miles south of Port Stanley. Two Super Etendard aircraft, each carrying external fuel tanks and a single Exocet missile, were refueled by KC-130 Hercules tankers 15 minutes after take-off. After approaching their target at medium altitude, they dropped to 50 feet. The aircraft then pulled up to 120 feet to obtain a radar fix on the target. They launched their combined total of two Exocets, at a range of about 23 miles, and withdrew at high speed. Neither pilot had a visual sighting on the designated target. They relied on radar sightings and used a command panel in the Super Etendard's avionics which enables the pilot to input operational data, such as aircraft speed and altitude and target distance and bearing within one to two degrees of azimuth. These inputs are provided primarily by the Thomson-CSF Agave Monopulse radar unit, which tracks and designates the target during the brief period in which the aircraft "pops up" to search for the target. After target acquisition, tracking is automatic.[97]

The Exocet missile impacted at 680 mph and punched a 30-foot hole in the *Sheffield*'s side. Some sources claim the warhead did not explode and the rocket motor started a fire. It is also possible that the warhead burned rather than exploded. In any case, the missile penetrated the hull and then started an intensely hot fire.[98] The crew fought the blaze for four hours after the attack, but the ship eventually had to be left to burn itself out after the fire threatened the magazines. The other Exocet missile, fired in the same attack, passed close to the frigate *Yarmouth* before it crashed into the sea. The only uncertainties about what happened are the exact operational state of the *Sheffield*'s radar and ESM gear. Current reports indicate that the ship had its radar off and was relying on ESM for aircraft and missile detection. As has been mentioned earlier, this ESM seems to have been shut down because it could not function while the *Sheffield* was using its satellite communications gear. The ship's Abbey Hill ESM gear and other electronics may also have been programmed to treat the Exocet as a "friendly" system, although this is unclear.

One obvious lesson from this sinking is that ships need to have fully integrated sensor and fire control systems, some form of "close in" protection, and as much active and passive protection as can be provided. Even simple defensive measures might have saved the *Sheffield*. Some later Exocet attacks seem to have been thwarted by chaff rockets which blanked out the main target.[99] Another obvious lesson is that modern naval surface fleets must be protected by ongoing airborne early warning. This must include a look-down radar capability to detect sea-skimming missiles launched and low-altitude attack aircraft.

It is also clear that shipboard air defense systems need to be thoroughly and realistically tested against the threat in a battlefield environment with all the electronics systems functioning in both normal and defense warning modes. The *Sheffield* should have been able to detect the incoming missile without interfering with its defense communication systems. The Exocet radar homing head transmits actively in the final five miles of flight and should have been easy to detect. Even at 600 mph, the ship should have had at least 30 seconds in which to react and normally should have detected the moment of launch. This would provide about 120 seconds of warning. Nevertheless, the *Sheffield* proved incapable of responding to the attack.

The *Sheffield* also did a remarkably bad job of coping with the fire. The AM-39 was not really designed to "kill" ships as large as the *Sheffield*, but it hit in an area which proved so vulnerable that it crippled the ship's damage control capabilities within minutes of impact. The missile hit the galley and started an oil fire which spread along the cable runs and piping and filled the ship with dense black smoke. The ship's plastic partitions and furniture also burned, and the smoke from the PVC-covered cable runs was toxic. Even the crew had problems because their basic uniforms were polyester. The ship also had limited and overcentralized damage-control and fire-fighting capability. While this damage was partly the result of a fluke hit, it is still a warning that the need to pack modern warships with as many weapons and electronics as possible can make them very vulnerable.

The British regard both the potential impact of improved air-to-ship and ship-to-ship missiles and ship vulnerability as two of the key lessons of the war. According to the British White Paper:

> The Campaign showed the potential of air-launched, seaskimming missiles. We have already equipped a number of Nimrod aircraft with the Harpoon anti-ship missile and we will further improve our existing capability in this area by the early acquisition of the advanced Sea Eagle missile, which has a longer range and more discriminating capability than Exocet.[100]

The British reinforced this lesson by using their own light air-to-ship missiles against Argentine ships. These included two systems which were lighter and less smart than the Exocet: the AS-12 and Sea Skua.

The AS-12 is a "semi-smart" guided missile system with a maximum range of six kilometers. It was mounted on Lynx helicopters and scored the first missile ship kill of the war when a hit forced the Argentine submarine *Santa Fe* aground at South Georgia Island. It may also have been used against small craft later in the war. The AS-12 had to be guided by a crew member using a joystick who simultaneously had to sight the target and missile. Nevertheless, this "first generation" weapon did force warships aground and proved effective at ranges of several kilometers.

The Sea Skua had nearly twelve kilometers of range and could home on a target illuminated by the Sea Spray radar in British Lynx helicopters. It had a radar altimeter for sea skimming and a terminal maneuver to reduce vulnerability during the last seconds of its attack. Although it had only a 30-kilogram warhead, it seriously damaged at least two Argentine patrol boats, the *Alferez Sobral* and *Comodoro Somellera*, and one eventually sank.[101]

This experience is still further evidence that relatively cheap air-to-ship missiles can kill expensive warships. This conclusion is reinforced by the fact that many of the air-to-ship missiles now in service have longer ranges, heavier warheads (most Soviet ASMs have warheads which are at least equal in weight to the entire Exocet missile), and much more sophisticated and automated guidance and avionics packages than the Exocets used in the Falklands. The Exocets in the Argentine inventory required an optimal attack angle of 90° to obtain a proper radar and needed exceptionally accurate manual programming for its Adac homing radar head to acquire the target. As many as half the AM-39s fired may have failed to reach their target for this reason. For example, two of the AM-39s fired on 30 May 1982 failed to fully track their targets, and a third was hit by the 4.5-inch gun on the HMS *Avenger*.[102] Many Third World forces now have, or have ordered, more sophisticated weapons than the variant of the AM-39 used in the Falklands, and most Warsaw Pact and NATO forces have considerably more lethal technologies.

The Impact of Other Air Munitions

The Harriers carried laser-guided bombs, iron bombs, cluster bombs, and 30-mm cannon. The British found the three-meter accuracy of laser-guided bombs greatly aided close support missions. At the same time, the British had fusing and lethality problems similar to those of Argentina. The final battle of Port Stanley was preceded by an attack by two Harriers using two Paveway laser-guided bombs each. These attacks were conducted in close cooperation with forward air controllers, but the pilots' lack of familiarity with the equipment put the first attempts off target. Only the third attempt resulted in a direct hit with a 1,000-pound bomb.[103] British iron bombs were frequently duds, and their cluster bombs often did not fall as designed. It is unclear how the British experience in this area relates to the Argentine experience. Some of the Argentine bombs were well beyond their effective shelf life, and improper delivery angle and fusing were important reasons for Argentine failures. The reasons for the British problems, however, are unclear.

Both sides clearly would have benefited from better operational testing of the munitions. Both sides would also have benefited from more sophisticated stand-off weapons technology and improved area ordnance. The British were operating with late-1970s aircraft (the Harriers) with bombs dating back to the Vietnam era and before. Although the use of conventional iron bombs was often successful, the attack experience on both sides strongly encourages the use of precision-guided weapons such as the Maverick (laser-guided, TV-guided, or IR version) or submunitions dispensers in standoff delivery systems. The American experience in Vietnam and the Israeli experience in the October 1973 and 1982 Middle East wars provides similar lessons regarding the need for advanced air-to-ground technology.

Air Reconnaissance, C³I, IFF, and AC&W

As has already been stressed, Britain badly needed adequate AEW resources.[104] Adequate AEW would have been especially important in reducing the impact of Argentine strikes on British ships deployed near land barriers which masked attacking aircraft. Britain might have been able to destroy the Super Etendard in flight, rather than having to try to destroy the Exocets after they had been launched. Britain also badly needed a platform to provide better imagery to support ground operations. According to the British White Paper:

> The absence of a dedicated overland air reconnaissance capability was a handicap in the Campaign, and the resulting lack of precise information on enemy dispositions presented an additional hazard to ground forces. We plan to improve our tactical reconnaissance capability.[105]

Many detections of Argentine air attacks were made through visual or limited range contact by Sea Harrier pilots, who had only an average of twenty operational minutes on station in the combat air patrol role.[106] Very few low-flying attackers were detected by the Blue Fox radar. The lack of an AWACS/AEW aircraft also made task force air defense operations almost impossible. It was unusual for a Sea Harrier to receive air control data from surface units during the San Carlos Bay action. In general, the British system of combat air patrol had to be very inefficient, providing only a few aircraft in position to intercept attackers at any one time. This experience is a serious warning to the U.S. Marine Corps, which plans to operate the AV-8 and AV-8B with even less sophisticated avionics.[107]

It also seems clear that even aircraft dedicated to low-level wars need something more sophisticated than Blue Fox radar.[108] The Harrier lacked the ability to discriminate low-altitude aircraft from their radar background. This performance is not surprising, given the fact that the Blue Fox was never designed to be a true look-down radar. Nevertheless, the British clearly needed such a capability on several occasions. This emphasizes the need for the Blue Vixen update and the more advanced Blue Falcon radar that Ferranti is developing for the Sea Harriers, plus the possible need to retrofit the U.S. Marine Corps' AV-8s and AV-8Bs with the most advanced radar package possible if there is any risk they will not have extensive air cover from other fighters.[109]

There also was a clear need for all-weather recce systems that could have given British and Argentine commanders near-real time information. The Argentines lacked advanced recce aircraft of any kind. The British had to fly reconnaissance missions from Ascension Island, and had full all-weather capability only against ships. This island had to act as the main "forward" land base for Nimrod aircraft even though it was approximately 3,886 miles, or a minimum of seven hours flying time, from the scene of the fighting.[110] Victor and Vulcan aircraft did provide a capability for the extremely long-range mission reconnaissance but had limited all-weather capability, had to be dedicated to other missions, and provided little data on Argentine activities and troop dispositions.[111] Such long-range Vulcan missions also had very slow reaction times and very high costs. The British might have done much better with RPVs, or long-range versions of an SR-71 type aircraft.

Neither the British nor the Argentines had an aircraft capable of combined maritime surveillance and low-altitude air defense and warning capability. Argentine S-2E and SP-24 maritime reconnaissance aircraft lacked the radar range to cover the task force and remain clear of its air defenses, although they do seem to have used electronic support measures (ESM) to obtain some data on the fleet and for Exocet targeting.

More broadly, neither side seems to have entered the war with any clear concept of how to support its field forces with intelligence at any distance from a land air base or with air intelligence assets suitable for low-level infantry action. The British had ample assets for a NATO environment but could not deploy them in the Falklands and did not seem to have trained or equipped its air reconnaissance units for low-level wars. They did make good use of helicopters for scouting missions and Harriers for light recce missions, but they lacked sophisticated sensors, interpretation capability, and proper fusion of operational planning and all-source intelligence. The Argentine commander also lacked sophisticated assets and failed to use the aircraft he did have to scout and patrol aggressively and conduct deep penetration missions. This was a command failure, and it is unclear whether any technology or changes in organization would have compensated for it.

Helicopters

British helicopters performed both attack and mobility functions during the conflict. As has already been mentioned, Sea Skua missiles fired from Lynx helicopters damaged the patrol boats *Alferez Sobral* and *Comodoro Somellera*. Both helicopters were from No. 815 Squadron from the HMS *Coventry* and HMS *Glasgow*.[112] In land action, Gazelle and Scout helicopters were repeatedly used to attack military targets. Although the Scouts were armed with obsolete SS-11 missiles with first generation manual guidance systems, they knocked out enemy bunkers and even gun positions near Port Stanley and attacked troops on the Lafonia Plains.[113]

The mobility mission was far more critical, however, and was essential to British success. Although Britain lost its three heavy lift helicopters with the sinking of the *Atlantic Conveyer*, the Naval Air Command reports that it still flew 10,381 helicopter sorties for a total period of 21,049 flight hours (5,552 Sea King, 2,054 Wessex, 1,863 Lynx, and 912 Wasp sorties).[114] This is over 80 percent of all sorties flown on the British side and nearly 90 percent of the total flight hours. Well over 80 percent of these missions were to provide mobility or transport.

British helicopters provided this extensive logistics support, moving men and equipment in some of the most adverse weather conditions possible. They flew off slippery and frigid decks in cross-deck and ship-to-shore operations and across rugged mountainous terrain ashore. They also maintained extraordinarily high sortie rates per helicopter. The high professionalism of British pilots and maintenance crews provided a classic demonstration that readiness and training can substitute for force numbers.

In fact, the helicopter has seldom played a more important role, because ongoing military operations have rarely been conducted in such extremes of weather, geography, and combat. The virtues of helicopter mobility, reconnaissance, and transport have been known for some time, beginning back in the Korean War, and they were largely operationalized in the American military experience in Vietnam. The Falklands, however, serves as an important demonstration of flexibility of helicopter technology.

The Special Air Service attack on South Georgia Island on 12 April 1982 provided a particularly interesting picture of the strength and limitations of helicopters in extreme weather conditons. Experiencing white-out in an extreme gale, the pilot of a Wessex V crashed in an effort to rescue a beleaguered SAS team struggling to survive in the weather. Later, another Wessex III crashed in similar conditions on the same rescue mission. However, the situation was salvaged by remarkable flying when a third Wessex (type III) flew seventeen personnel out from the two previous crashes. The next day, a helicopter retrieved a landing party adrift on a raft in the frigid Atlantic. Clearly, this testifies once again to the mobility and life-saving capabilities of the helicopter.[115]

Throughout the war, British helicopters repeatedly showed the ability to insert special forces teams in isolated and rugged environments. On 8 May and 14 May 1982, two Sea Kings were used to insert commandos in a successful raid on an Argentine air base on Pebble Island. This action resulted in the loss of several Argentine ground-attack aircraft by ground assault. Unfortunately for the British, about this time a Sea King helicopter crashed into the sea after colliding with an albatross. This resulted in the deaths of all twenty-two men on board.[116]

The British experienced remarkably few losses in carrying out these missions. They lost a total of about 24 helicopters, depending on the source. Ten of these (one Lynx, six Wessex, and three Chinook) were lost with the sinking of the *Atlantic Conveyer*. This means only 14 were lost in combat operations, or a loss rate of one per 742 sorties. Only 3 were clearly lost to combat fire, 2 to ground fire and 1 to Pucura. These are amazingly small combat losses per sortie and clearly reflect the static and passive nature of most Argentine ground operations. Experience in other recent wars indicates that helicopters are far more vulnerable.

The Argentines also used helicopters effectively in transport and mobility missions but failed to use them as effectively for special operations, aggressive scouting, or to support efforts to halt the British landings. The Argentines did attempt to resupply their garrison during the battle of Goose Green, using a single Chinook and six Huey helicopters, but were successfully warded off by artillery fire. No reinforcements landed to save the Argentine positions.[117]

Combined Operations

The British conducted combined operations more effectively than any other combatant in the five wars under examination. British troops advancing on the ground were effectively supported by elements of the air force and navy. While Argentina largely failed to carry out successful air support, the UK was successful in using air power and heliborne lift in urgent tactical situations. The use of cluster bombs to neutralize various Argentine strong points was especially important in ensuring the advance of troops on the ground. The destruction of several Argentine anti-aircraft guns that were pinning down British infantry at Goose Green was also particularly important in solving a time-urgent practical problem.

Naval gunfire from the 4.5-inch guns of the British fleet was also important throughout the Falklands campaign, having been used to hold the fleet at bay off Port Stanley. Unfortunately for the British, these guns were countered by heavy artillery. The gunfire was useful for breaking up Argentine defensive positions prior to an assault, and one of the major British lessons learned from this experience was the need for more and larger naval guns to be used for shore support. At Goose Green, for example, serious problems ensued when the HMS *Arrow's* 4.5-inch gun jammed. This problem was compounded by the fact that the rifle companies had not brought their 2-inch mortars into combat on this occasion because of the difficulty in transporting them.[118]

It is also significant that some important combined operations involved coordination between small elements of the different services. The raid on Pebble Island was carried out by twelve four-man teams from the SAS with the support of naval gunfire. This raid served as an important demonstration of the value of special forces. It destroyed an ammunition storage site and eleven Argentine aircraft. It was described by Admiral Woodward in the following way:

> Pebble Island was successfully raided in the most atrocious weather and provided just the right political and military boost to morale. In my view, this single operation is easily the best example of a successful "All Arms" special operation we are likely to see in a very long while. A short notice operation carried out with speed and dash.[119]

Nevertheless, it must be stressed that the British succeeded in using relatively small forces against a relatively static enemy. They did not succeed in creating effective fusion of intelligence and operations at the higher command level, and they never fully resolved the role of higher officials in London in shaping combined operations. It is far from clear whether the British would have done as well against a more aggressive or better coordinated enemy or in the larger-scale conflicts analyzed earlier. The Falklands is no indication that Western forces have the combined operations capability needed to deal with most low-level wars. Indeed, the U.S. experience in Lebanon and the Israeli experiences in 1973 and 1982 indicate that this may be a critical weakness of Western organized forces.

As for Argentine efforts at combined operations, it is clear that Argentina suffered badly from serious coordination problems at every level. A report on the lessons of the war by the Argentine air force chief of staff, Brigadier General Ernesto Crespo, made devastating criticisms of Argentina's performance.

The report found that there was no effective coordination between the air force south command and the South Atlantic command. It found that the navy entered the war without any real war plan and then refused to engage in joint planning. In fact, the Crespo report concluded that Argentina had no real doctrine for joint operations and that "there [were] three forces totally different in their conception and strategy for joint action."

The detailed criticism in the Crespo report includes the failure of the navy to organize effectively for maritime reconnaissance missions and alleges false reports by navy pilots that led to missions against nonexistent targets. It found that coordination by the army and navy was so bad that the air force had to organize its own reconnaissance and targeting effort and had to operate without adequate intelligence over the Falklands.

The Argentine command structure knew so little about combined operations that it continued to deny the possibility of a major British operation at San Carlos until the British fleet was fully committed. It could not effectively allocate tankers to refuel the Super Etendards, and missions were either delayed to the point where they became ineffective or had to be cancelled.

The navy failed to take minimal protective measures to deal with air or submarine attack and lost the *General Belgrano* and *Santa Fe* in part from failure to evaluate the risk operations by British aircraft or submarines. The air force never fully planned or trained for fighting in the Falklands, and the army had no doctrine for mobility. It remained static behind its lines and depended on the air force for both resupply and communications. It had "low combat morale" and dealt with its positions as "fortresses."

It should also be noted that one of the combined arms problems that affected the war was the fact that Argentina's carrier, the *Veinticinco de Mayo,* was never really equipped and trained to support combined operations. Her flight deck was expanded in 1980–1981, and her catapult was strengthened, but the ship could do only 24 knots and could not reliably operate the Super Etendard fighters needed to use air-to-ship missiles effectively. The electronics on the ship were British and were not fully compatible with the electronics on the Argentine navy's four MEKO 360 destroyers. Even in 1988, the carrier was just entering a two-year refit in an attempt to give it diesel engines to replace its gas turbines and bring its speed up to the point where it could allow the carrier to operate Argentina's fourteen Super Etendard aircraft on a regular basis. The carrier's effective complement was limited to eighteen A-4Q Skyhawks and S-2Es and four Sh-3D Sea Kings and A-103 Alouette IIIs.[120]

The Crespo report concludes with recommendations that are virtually the mirror image of the reasons for Britain's success. It suggests that:

- The responsibilities of each service must be clearly defined.
- Intensive permanent joint planning and training must be fully institutionalized.
- Joint planning at all levels must be implemented in the form of an integrated command, control, and training organization.
- Operations must be commanded on the basis of a joint command for a specific theater of operations.[121]

Logistics and Support

Both sides faced massive logistics and support problems. The British faced the problem of an 8,000-mile supply line which was vulnerable to the threats posed by Argentine planes and submarines. In describing the difficulties inherent in such an operation, Admiral Sir John Feldhouse, who presided over operational headquarters in London, stated, "I hope that people realize that this is the most difficult thing that we have attempted since the second World War."[122]

The British White Paper outlined four major lessons associated with the logistical requirements of the campaign:

First: Rates of usage, particularly of ammunition, missiles, and anti-submarine weapons were higher than anticipated. Last year we announced plans to increase substantially war reserve stocks in order to improve staying power; scalings will be reviewed in the light of experience in the Falklands Campaign.

Second: We need to consider the level of logistic support maintained for 'out of area' operations. Since the late 1960s there has been a steady reduction in the Services' capability to support large forces outside the NATO area. All the demands of the task force were met, but only by giving it first call on resources and by using some stocks earmarked for NATO operations. The Services' logistic capability to support 'out of area' operations has to be considered in the light of the Government's overall policy for such operations. . . .We shall, however, review the size and composition of the special stockpile being created to support 'out of area' land operations. We shall also consider whether logistic support could be organised as part of a flexible system able to support forces whether inside or outside the NATO area.

Third: Air-to-air refuelling is vital in supporting operations at long range. For example, RAF Harriers flew non-stop to the South Atlantic from Ascension Island with tanker support. In the operations from Ascension Island, the relatively small amount of fuel carried by the Victor tanker aircraft resulted in a large proportion of the available tanker force being used for each Vulcan, Nimrod and Hercules sortie. Large capacity strategic tanker aircraft are needed to provide greater operational flexibility in the future. . . .

Finally, the Campaign brought home the significant contribution which civil resources can make to the nation's strength in a crisis. . . . Our intention to review the use of national logistic and manpower resources in this way has now been given even greater impetus. The smooth and rapid implementation of existing contingency plans to use merchant shipping in support of the Services was a major success story of the Campaign. Some 45 ships were taken up from trade, from passenger liners to trawlers. They provided vital support across the entire logistic spectrum. Tankers carried fuel for ships, aircraft and land forces. Liners, such as the *QE2* and *Canberra*, and ferries gave service as troop carriers. Cargo ships, such as the *Atlantic Conveyor*, carried helicopters, Harriers, heavy equipment and stores. Other vessels were taken up as hospital ships, repair ships or tugs. All these ships were manned by volunteer, civilian crews, supplemented by small Naval or RFA parties.[123]

The British succeeded only because of U.S. willingness to support the British task force in the areas described earlier, plus their ability to rapidly organize a massive naval logistic effort, assemble and modify commercial cargo ships and tankers, and then support them with helicopters and fixed-wing aircraft. The British were eventually forced to use one support ship for every combat ship in the task force and experienced severe endurance or "at sea" problems because of the limited supplies and fuel their smaller combat ships could carry. This "little war" involved fifty requisitioned ships totaling over 673,000 tons capacity, plus 398,958 tons of capacity from ships in the Royal Fleet Auxiliary. It meant organizing and loading cargo for combat use on very short notice and with 21-day sailing times. It then meant some 600 airborne refueling operations and over 2,000 operations for replenishment at sea, 1,500 of these involving tankers.[124] The remaining 500 operations required transfer of over 15,000 packet loads to user vessels. The full scale of this effort is illustrated in Table 3.13.

This experience is a powerful validation of the U.S. Navy's emphasis on improving its fast deployment capability on nuclear power and long endurance combat ships and of the general emphasis the U.S. has placed on strategic mobility. It also is a lesson regarding the value of a strong NATO merchant marine and naval transport reserve. It is extremely doubtful that the UK could ever have considered intervening in the Falklands without a strong merchant marine crewed largely by British sailors and operating under the British flag.

Part of the reason that the British managed to overcome their logistical problems was their ability to use Ascension Island as a staging point for logistical operations. Ascension Island is a British possession, although its airfield and facilities have been leased to the United States. The U.S. provided the auxiliary airfield at Wideawake and other facilities on Ascension Island to the British for use in the Falklands campaign in accordance with a 1962 exchange of notes between the U.S. and UK.[125] The British also used the target ranges at Ascension for some much-needed target practice for the light tanks. Equally important, Ascension served as a convenient pick-up point for American-supplied war materials. In this regard, Secretary

TABLE 3.13 British Naval Logistics Effort in the Falklands Conflict

	Private		Royal Fleet Auxiliary		Total	
	No. of Ships	Tons Capacity	No. of Ships	Tons Capacity	No. of Ships	Tons Capacity
Troop Transports and Equipment Ferries	13	215,339			13	215,339
Supply Ships	4	35,616	5	109,772	9	145,387
Support Ships	15	49,912	5	20,835	20	70,744
Tankers	23	374,172	10	271,954	33	646,126

SOURCE: Adapted from data in Bruce W. Watson and Peter M. Dunn, *Military Lessons of the Falklands War* (Boulder, Colo.: Westview Press, 1984), p. 168.

of Defense Weinberger took personal charge of the effort to get ample supplies to the British. This use of Ascension serves as an important example of the value of similar staging bases to U.S. Central Command (USCENTCOM) such as Diego Garcia and Masirah.

Once British troops landed in the Falklands, they found that manpower was as critical as technology to logistics. This was sometimes a matter of sheer supply. For example, British troops routinely fired four to five times their estimated daily consumption rates per weapon, reflecting a long-standing British failure to update ammunition expenditure plans because of fiscal constraints in meeting more realistic goals. Other problems were a function of terrain, location, and the need to transfer all supplies by sea or air. The choice of San Carlos as a landing site for debarking troops meant that British troops were faced with long marches over rough terrain, which strained British movement and logistics. This choice was made because both Berkeley Sound and Port Stanley had to be eliminated as potential landing sites because of a fear of strong Argentine defenses that would produce high casualties.[126]

The British lack of vehicles, and the severe problems in using most vehicles in the Falklands, made helicopter use a natural choice. Unfortunately for the British, they did not have a chance to fully utilize helicopters in the logistics role because they lost all but one of their Chinooks and a squadron of their Wessexes when the containership *Atlantic Conveyor* was hit on 25 May 1982 and sank three days later. This left the task force with one CH-47, twenty Sea Kings, and seventeen Wessexes, although four more CH-47s arrived on 10 June. These helicopter losses required the use of additional and vulnerable landing craft, made the timing of critical operations dependent on the state of the sea, prevented vertical envelopment by land, and led to additional delays due to problems with loading and launching amphibious ships. These problems provided yet another lesson in the difficulty of using amphibious forces and in the superiority of helicopter lift. At the same time, they helped force the main landing ships, *Sir Galahad* and *Sir Tristam*, to sail right into Bluff Cove, where *Sir Galahad* was burned. This meant the British could not move artillery flexibly by helicopter and that either supply ships had to be put at hazard or logistics plans were constantly disrupted as ships were moved to reduce their vulnerability. In addition, it disrupted effective C^3/BM control of logistics and helped force extensive troop movement using full packs. This illustrated the importance of dispersing helicopter lift and logistics assets in naval task forces. The British might well have experienced serious operational problems, or even been unsuccessful, if they had suffered major further helicopter losses.

The Royal Marines and Royal Army did demonstrate the value of all-terrain vehicles. They had a few tracked Snowcats and Volvo-tracked vehicles; these were the only land vehicles capable of negotiating the terrain. The Volvo-tracked vehicles (known as Bvs) played an important role in carrying heavy weapons and radios. They also played an important role in the recovery of stragglers. The Snowcats appeared to have similar functions but were much less reliable and frequently broke down.

As for support capabilities, it is important to note that the British achieved high sustainability for all their forces and proved that operations and maintenance (O&M) or "tail" can be as important as "teeth." Britain maintained good on-line availability for all key combat systems. Ship readiness was very high, and most high technology weapons and electronics had high operational availability rates. The extraordinarily high British sortie rates per aircraft have already been discussed. It is notable that the Harriers flew well over 90 percent of their sorties with fully operational main avionics.

The Falklands also produced some useful insights about the value of arming support vessels with modular air defense and equipping them with Arapaho-like dock conversions for VTOL and helicopter landings. The British certainly benefited from their ability to use helicopters on a wide range of larger support vessels. They now plan to provide a Harrier deck kit and at least some modular terminal defense for their larger cargo and support ships in future conflicts.

When considering the logistical problems of the Argentine forces, one has to consider the distances between the islands and the mainland as well as the inter-island logistics. Those distances allowed the British to gradually isolate the Argentine force in the Falklands through a blockade which permitted only limited operations by small craft and cargo aircraft. In addition, destroying Argentina's inter-island logistical connections helped the British slowly isolate the individual Argentine garrisons into unsupplied and noncooperative entities.

Inter-island logistics proved to be a major shortcoming in Argentine operations, although many of these problems had nothing to do with the British effort to disrupt Argentine logistics. While the Argentine air force maintained some communications by aircraft and helicopter, the Argentine army failed to exploit such resources effectively. The incompetence and dereliction of duty by various Argentine officers contributed greatly to these problems as well as problems in allocating the stockpiles in the Port Stanley area. When the British troops entered Port Stanley, they were shocked by the huge stockpiles of weapons (and the presence of large numbers of troops) that had never been sent to the front. Another problem with Argentine logistics resulted from political decisions at the highest levels of Argentine command. Rather than deploy their troops in a carefully planned defense, the Argentines airlifted in huge numbers of troops in the hopes that a British invasion could be deterred by sheer numbers of personnel.[127]

The British effort to blockade the Falkland Islands and prevent Argentine supplies from being brought in from the mainland seems to have been a relative success, although it never really halted the Argentines' logistics movements. Supplies were flown in up to the last days of the war, and Britain's success in blocking first-line fighter operations from Port Stanley airport did not halt Argentine C-130 sorties. This again illustrates the value of developing more advanced airfield suppression systems.

Naval Systems

The fighting in the Falklands provides only limited lessons regarding the performance of naval systems. The Argentine navy was not employed aggressively and did not play any significant role in the conflict after the sinking of the *General Belgrano*. The British navy was employed far more aggressively, but the combat ships in the task force consisted of a hastily improvised mix of ships headed for scrapping and retirement and modern ships tailored to very different missions supporting other NATO forces in the defense of the Atlantic.

Nevertheless, some important lessons did emerge from the fighting. One was the need to give far more careful consideration to surface ship vulnerability and to providing the proper mix of defense and survivability. A second was the need for integrated long- and short-range air and missile defense and the ability to deal with saturation attacks. Other less critical lessons emerged regarding given weapons systems and ship design.

Naval Surface Forces

Although both sides employed submarines and had extensive surface forces, the naval battle was essentially a battle between British ships and Argentine aircraft. The Argentine navy was involved in combat, but only in a limited way. Eight Argentine ships were involved in combat; see Table 3.14. One, the *General Belgrano*, was sunk by a submarine. The other seven were hit by aircraft or missiles launched from helicopters. Four were hit by Harriers and three by helicopter-launched AS-12 or Sea Skua air-to-surface missiles. All of these air strikes involved routine applications of air warfare, and none provide significant lessons.

The Argentines also faced the problem that their surface forces were built around a carrier, the *Veinticinco de Mayo*, which was nearly forty years old. This carrier often could not develop speeds over 15 knots, which meant it could not launch fully loaded Super Etendard fighters (a speed of 30 knots is needed for such operations). This confronted Argentina with a dilemma after the war because there was no obvious solution to improving surface fleet capabilities other than buying advanced long-range surface-to-surface missiles. Argentina instead chose to buy six West German type 1700 submarines and cut fleet days at sea from 120 days before the war to 30 days in 1986.

The British experience in naval warfare is more interesting. Twenty to twenty-one British ships sustained combat damage; see Table 3.15. All but four of these were hit by bombs. Two were hit and sunk by Exocets, one was hit and damaged by Exocets, one was strafed, and the other seventeen were hit by bombs, many repeatedly and thirteen seriously. Three were sunk by these bombs and a fourth was hit by bombs and had to be scuttled. Nine other ships were hit by bombs which failed to explode but might have sunk or crippled the ship if they had exploded. The British problem with ship vulnerability was

TABLE 3.14 Argentine Ships Lost or Damaged in the Falklands War

	LOST:	
25 APRIL	*SANTA FE* (submarine)	DAMAGED BY ASW HELICOPTERS. LATER RUN ASHORE AND ABANDONED.
2 MAY	*GENERAL BELGRANO* (cruiser)	TORPEDOED AND SUNK BY NUCLEAR SUBMARINE.
3 MAY	*COMODORO SOMELLERA* (patrol boat)	SUNK BY SEA SKUA MISSILES FIRED BY A LYNX HELICOPTER.
9 MAY	*NARWAL* (trawler attached to Argentine navy)	BOMBED AND STRAFED BY HARRIER AIRCRAFT. ABANDONED BY HER CREW, SHE SANK UNDER TOW THE NEXT DAY, AFTER BEING CAPTURED BY THE BRITISH NAVY.
16 MAY	*BAHÍA BUEN SUCESO* (freighter)	STRAFED BY SEA HARRIERS. LATER ABANDONED AND BLOWN AGROUND.
16 MAY	*RIO CARCARAÑA* (freighter)	BOMBED AND STRAFED BY SEA HARRIERS. ABANDONED BY CREW.
22 MAY	*RIO IGUAZU* (Coast Guard patrol boat)	STRAFED BY SEA HARRIERS; DAMAGED AND RUN AGROUND.
	DAMAGED:	
3 MAY	*ALFEREZ SOBRAL* (patrol boat)	SERIOUSLY DAMAGED AFTER BEING HIT BY SEA SKUA MISSILES FIRED BY A LYNX HELICOPTER.

SOURCE: Adapted from Max Hastings and Simon Jenkins, *The Battle for the Falklands* (New York: Norton, 1983), p. 381, and material provided by the British Ministry of Defence.

far greater than British losses indicate; see Table 3.16 for British ship losses.

There are no precise data that put British losses into perspective in terms of Argentine sortie survival rates or rates per hit or kill.[128] It is clear, however, that an air force using fighters without advanced attack avionics and modern attack munitions, flown by pilots trained only for land attack missions, can inflict very significant damage on a modern and alert naval task force. This is particularly true when aircraft can take advantage of the lack of airborne AEW or radar masking by land barriers.

What is less clear is how the limited British experience in the

TABLE 3.15 British Ships Damaged in the Falklands War

1 MAY	HMS *ARROW* (frigate) HMS *GLAMORGAN* (destroyer)	BOTH SHIPS SUFFERED MINOR DAMAGE FROM ATTACKS BY DAGGER AIRCRAFT.
12 MAY	HMS *GLASGOW* (destroyer)	SUFFERED MODERATE DAMAGE DURING AN ATTACK BY SKYHAWKS.
21 MAY	HMS *ARGONAUT* (frigate)	HIT TWICE BY 1000-LB. BOMBS THAT FAILED TO EXPLODE BUT NEVERTHELESS SERIOUSLY DAMAGED THE SHIP.
	HMS *ANTRIM* (destroyer)	HIT ASTERN BY 1000-LB. BOMB THAT FAILED TO DETONATE BUT NEVERTHELESS SERIOUSLY DAMAGED THE SHIP.
	HMS *BROADSWORD* (frigate)	SUFFERED MINOR DAMAGE IN TWO SEPARATE STRAFING INCIDENTS.
	HMS *BRILLIANT* (frigate)	SUFFERED MINOR DAMAGE IN A STRAFING ATTACK.
24 MAY	RFA *SIR LANCELOT* (Royal Fleet Auxiliary) RFA *SIR GALAHAD* * (Royal Fleet Auxiliary)	BOTH SHIPS SUFFERED MODERATE DAMAGE WHEN THEY WERE HIT WITH 1000-LB. BOMBS THAT FAILED TO EXPLODE.
25 MAY	HMS *BROADSWORD*	SUFFERED MODERATE DAMAGE WHEN HIT BY 1000-LB. BOMB THAT FAILED TO EXPLODE.
8 JUNE	HMS *PLYMOUTH* (frigate)	SUFFERED SERIOUS DAMAGE WHEN HIT BY FOUR 1000-LB. BOMBS. NONE EXPLODED BUT ONE HIT A DEPTH CHARGE AND STARTED A SERIOUS FIRE.
	RFA *SIR TRISTRAM* (Royal Fleet Auxiliary)	SEVERELY DAMAGED BY SKYHAWKS OFF FITZROY.
12 JUNE	HMS *GLAMORGAN* (destroyer)	HIT BY A LAND-BASED EXOCET MISSILE THAT FAILED TO EXPLODE BUT CAUSED SERIOUS DAMAGE.

 * *LATER LOST*

SOURCES: Adapted from Max Hastings and Simon Jenkins, *The Battle for the Falklands* (New York: Norton, 1983), p. 381, and *The Falklands Campaign: The Lessons* (London: HMSO, 1982), p. 45.

TABLE 3.16   British Ships Lost in the Falklands War

4 MAY	HMS *SHEFFIELD* (destroyer)	SUNK BY EXOCET MISSILE FIRED BY SUPER ETENDARD.
21 MAY	HMS *ARDENT* (frigate)	DAMAGED BY CONVENTIONAL BOMBS. ABANDONED AND SUNK.
23 MAY	HMS *ANTELOPE* (frigate)	DAMAGED BY TWO UNEXPLODED BOMBS. WHEN ONE BOMB EXPLODED DURING LATER ATTEMPTS TO DEFUSE IT, THE SHIP WAS LOST.
25 MAY	HMS *COVENTRY* (destroyer)	SUNK AFTER BEING HIT BY THREE 1000-LB. BOMBS.
	ATLANTIC CONVEYOR (container ship)	SUNK BY EXOCET MISSILE FIRED BY SUPER ETENDARD.
8 JUNE	RFA *SIR GALAHAD* (Royal Fleet Auxiliary)	SCUTTLED AFTER BEING SEVERELY DAMAGED BY SKYHAWKS.

SOURCE: *The Falklands Campaign: The Lessons* (London: HMSO, 1982), p. 46.

Falklands can be translated into specific lessons regarding the proper trade-offs in ship armor, active defenses, and damage control. It can be argued that all the British combat ships hit by aircraft suffered from weakness in their air and missile defenses that were the result of prior design trade-offs and cost constraints that increased their vulnerability. This, however, raises the issue of whether the Royal Navy would have been better off with fewer and better-armed ships or should have sacrificed capability in its primary missions to deal with the risks of a relatively low probability contingency.

It also is not always clear what the precise pattern of vulnerability was. The total sample of combat ship kills consists of one Exocet kill and four bomb kills. The Exocet kill of the *Sheffield* has been discussed earlier. The *Atlantic Conveyer* was not a combat ship, and the only other Exocet hit was a strike by a land-launched missile against the destroyer *Glamorgan* on 12 June. This Exocet warhead did not explode, although the missile still did considerable damage. The other ships that were sunk or abandoned were generally hit by multiple strikes. The *Ardent* was hit by three separate sets of air strikes and one bomb that exploded in the engine room; the *Antelope* was hit with multiple strikes and had to be scuttled. This is scarcely a common pattern.

One thing is clear: Aluminum was not a major cause of ship

vulnerability. Three ships were critically damaged by fire: the *Sheffield*, *Ardent*, and *Antelope*. The *Sheffield* had no aluminum, and its fire was far more the result of the use of modern plastics than that of metals. The *Ardent* and *Antelope* did have aluminum super- structures, and aluminum does present some risks. Past accidents to U.S. ships, such as the *Belknap* and *Worden*, had shown that aluminum can spall or deform in intense heat, which led to confused speculation that the aluminum superstructures of the two British ships had "burned."[129]

Follow-up studies have also shown that British vulnerability would have increased, or mission capability would have been lost, if such ships had traded the weight savings inherent in aluminum for steel. Further, past studies have shown that proper insulation and protective anti-spalling coatings can compensate for whatever vulnerability aluminum may have because of its lower melting and deformation temperature. The British White Paper seems fully correct in its comments on this issue.

> Aluminum was used in the superstructure of the Type 21 class of frigate and to a small extent in a few other classes but not in the Type 42 destroyers such as HMS *Sheffield*. By use of aluminum it is possible to make significant savings in the weight of ships above the waterline, but it has been recognized that this metal loses strength in fires and therefore its extensive use in the construction of RN warships was discontinued several years ago. Nonetheless, there is no evidence that it has contributed to the loss of any vessel.[130]

The major weaknesses of the Type 21 frigates were probably due more to their use of plastics, the inherent vulnerability of turbine design, and their historical evolution at a time of serious defense budget constraints than their metallurgy. The Type 21s had an uncertain reputation in the British fleet before the Falklands because the commercial builder, Vosper Thorneycroft, originally conceived them as relatively low performance ships for foreign fleets such as that of the Shah of Iran. The Royal Navy then made the decision that they would be acceptable as lower-cost replacements for the *Leander* and the Broad-Beam *Leander* class frigates. The Type 21s were armed only with four Exocet launchers, one four-missile Sea Cat launcher, one 4.5-inch gun, and two 20-mm AA guns. They were relatively light 3,250 ton vessels and were integrated into the fleet more to meet budget constraints than for military requirements.

The post-Falkland recriminations against the craft thus tended to assume an "I told you so" tenor. Nevertheless, the alternative would have been to build slower ships. The Olympus and Tyne gas turbines and the ship's light weight make the Type 21 a very fast ship which may acquit itself admirably when it is called upon to perform its primary mission of anti-submarine warfare.

The Type 42 destroyers were also subjected to criticism prior to the fighting because of the impact of budgetary constraints on their design. They were armed with updated versions of the Sea Dart, but a 30 percent reduction in ship size for cost reasons early in their design precluded the addition of the highly capable Sea Wolf "close in" anti-missile system. All three of the Type 42 destroyers acting as pickets were hit. *Sheffield* and *Coventry* were sunk, and *Glasgow* was damaged when a bomb passed through both sides of the ship. Since these ships were explicitly designed for anti-aircraft picket duty, the losses seemed to add credibility to charges that the Type 42s were underarmed.[131]

Another interesting problem that emerged in regard to surface ships relates to the severe damage done to these ships by single bombs or missiles. Even bombs that did not explode sometimes inflicted grave damage to British surface craft. This vulnerability seems to have been at least partly the result of the British emphasis on defensive electronics, which they believed were more cost effective than damage control, damage supression, active defense, and armor. The electronics were meant to neutralize a Warsaw Pact missile threat before the ship was harmed, while armor and damage control could only minimize damage after the impact of a hit. This design emphasis on a preventive versus remedial capability seems suitable in dealing with a limited number of high technology strikes. It has little value, however, against mass air attacks. The defenses were consistently overwhelmed in the Falklands.

British damage control facilities were also affected by budget cuts, and some were badly overcentralized. This problem was particularly apparent with regard to the *Sheffield*. The hit on *Sheffield* left the ship with no power and no pumps. This created an extensive damage control problem that previously utilized safeguards (e.g., alternative sources of power, duplication of pumps forward and aft, and secondary lighting) could have managed possibly with more success.[132]

The British White Paper states some of these points:

> Some important lessons have been learned about the rapid spread of fire and smoke in ships, and about the use of materials which can prove hazardous in fires. Cabling fitted in older ships can prove inflammable; this hazard will be greatly reduced in new ships. Urgent studies are now in hand aimed at improving the survivability of existing ships and incorporating lessons in future designs. Examples of measures which will be taken include improved fire zones; changes to the design of watertight doors and hatches; the provision of more escape hatches;

making bulkheads more smoke-tight; the re-siting of fuel tanks; reductions in inflammable materials; and additional fire pumps, breathing apparatus and personal breathing sets.[133]

In broader terms, the Falklands War presented some useful insights regarding the value of aircraft carriers. While the British ASW/VSTOL carriers proved to be invaluable throughout the war, the need to protect them placed severe limitations on the circumstances under which they could be used. A basic premise of British operations was that no greater disaster could occur than the loss of an aircraft carrier. This meant British carriers normally had to be deployed to ensure maximum protection for the carrier rather than maximum effectiveness of the aircraft. This premise, however, was more the result of the lack of airborne warning and air superiority assets than of the inherent vulnerability of the carrier.

Once again, it is important to stress, the British fleet suffered severely from its lack of airborne early warning (AEW) or AWACS capability to defend the carriers. The Harrier's primary mission was close support, and it was not designed to provide an air defense screen for the carrier. The Falklands experience thus validates the need for heavy carriers that can mount and sustain an extensive long-range air defense cover. It also indicates that light assault carriers must have friendly air cover and extensive AEW/AWACS assets to survive even in Third World conflicts. It is also important to note that the threat to British carriers was sharply reduced by the fact that the Falklands were barely within fighter range of Argentina, by the lack of Argentine extensive training for naval war, and by the lack of suitable bombs and/or attack munitions. Both sides could easily have fought very different wars if the Argentines had been slightly better equipped, and the British carriers would have been far more vulnerable.

Submarine Forces

The Falklands was not an important test of submarine warfare, although the submarine had a critical tactical effect. It is still unclear whether or not the Argentine navy would have played an aggressive role against the British navy if British submarines were not present. The Argentine navy was highly politicized, had good reason to fear the effectiveness of British surface forces and naval airpower, and had limited experience in fleet operations. Nevertheless, the sinking of the *General Belgrano* by the nuclear attack submarine *Conqueror* effectively knocked the Argentine navy out of the war. The Argentines kept their ships in port and claimed that their carrier had suffered a breakdown. The limited naval reconnaissance reduced Argentine resupply of the Falklands to small ships and one container ship which took advantage of bad weather and high seas to resupply Port Stanley after the British landing at San Carlos. They allowed the British fleet to concentrate almost solely on supporting amphibious landings and air defense.

The British White Paper describes the impact of British nuclear submarines as follows:

> The SSNs were flexible and powerful instruments throughout the crisis, posing a ubiquitous threat which the Argentines could neither measure nor oppose. Their speed and independence of support meant that they were the first assets to arrive in the South Atlantic, enabling us to declare the maritime exclusion zone early. They also provided valuable intelligence to our forces in the total exclusion zone.[134]

The sinking of the *General Belgrano* is also interesting because of several problems that the British and the *Conqueror* experienced during the engagement. The first is the problem of unanticipated escalation. The *Belgrano* was not closed up when it was struck, and the captain had failed to take the basic precautions essential in operating in a war zone. The debate over the ship's course and precise position relative to the exclusion zone is unimportant since the British had declared all Argentine warships were prospective targets. The British had no way of knowing the Argentine failure to secure the ship's watertight compartments. Although the *Belgrano* took two hits in areas that normally would not have sunk the ship, the aft hit occurred in an area that led to progressive flooding through its unsecured compartments, and eventually it sank.[135] This was a key factor in ensuring that no peace settlement was possible and in shaping the pattern of escalation that rapidly led to the sinking of the *Sheffield* and forced a major British landing.

This inability to select a controlled step in the "ladder of escalation" provides an important lesson about the difficulty in managing escalation in limited wars. It is easy to theorize about the effects of a given tactical action, but the political and military effect can easily escalate far beyond a given side's intentions. In many ways, the "fog" or "friction" of escalation is even more dangerous that the "fog" or "friction" of war.

The *Conqueror* also experienced torpedo problems of a kind that have plagued the British and U.S. navies since the early days of World War II. The *Conqueror* was armed with Mark 24 wire-guided Tigerfish torpedos and Mark 8 conventional torpedos. The Tigerfish was the most modern torpedo type available to the British, yet it was considered unreliable. During its sea trials in 1967, for example, a test Tigerfish independently changed its course by 180 degrees and almost hit its launch submarine. It also missed the *Sir Galahad* when it had to be destroyed as a result of damage during the fighting in the Falklands. This reputation for unreliability may have been an important factor in the decision by the *Conqueror's* commander to use World War II vintage Mark 8 torpedos. In addition, the Tigerfish torpedos were designed primarily for use against other submarines. They have a fairly small warhead and are not an ideal weapon for sinking or disabling a heavy cruiser. Nevertheless, the failure to use the Tigerfish raises similar issues about the value of several U.S. Navy designs, several of which have had troubled development histories. The British have since developed a Tigerfish Mark 24 Mod-2 quiet long-range heavy torpedo which has been proven in some fifty test firings, but this is still an area where independent NATO trial, and test and evaluation, could have considerable value.[136] The British have modified the original Tigerfish by adding the computer and homing technology used in the lightweight Stingray torpedo. The Tigerfish is wire guided with an integral sonar and computer for final approach. It is designed to explode beneath a ship and break its back. The new Tigerfish will replace the Mark 8 over the next five years. A totally new torpedo, the Spearfish, will be deployed in the early 1990s. It is smarter, faster, and deeper diving, but it is noisier and is best suited for use against Soviet SSNs; see Table 3.17.

It is also interesting to note that the Argentines seem to have been far more effective in pursuing the *Conqueror* after the strike on the *General Belgrano* than would normally have been expected. The *Conqueror* had not attempted to hit the two former U.S. escorts sailing with the *Belgrano*. Both were equipped with relatively modern long-range sonars, either the SQS-4 or some similar type. A British diary that was leaked after the war indicates that these sonars allowed the escorts to track and attack the *Conqueror* with far more effectiveness than should have been possible. It seems clear that Argentine depth charges came close enough to shock the crew. This Argentine success may have resulted, however, from the fact that the *Conqueror* closed to unusually short ranges in an attempt to limit damage. The accuracy of the leaks regarding Argentine pursuit of the *Conqueror* is unclear. Neverthless, many Third World nations now have similar sonars and ASW capabilities, and the incident may be an important warning about the limitations Western nations will face in using SSNs in limited conflicts.

The war might also have taken on a different character if Argentina's three submarines had been more modern and better armed

TABLE 3.17   Differences in Submarine Technology

	GUPPY II CLASS	VALIANT CLASS
STATUS	*WORLD WAR II VINTAGE USED BY ARGENTINA DURING THE FALKLANDS WAR*	*1960–1970s VINTAGE USED BY UK DURING THE FALKLANDS WAR*
POWER	*CONVENTIONAL*	*NUCLEAR*
SPEED SUBMERGED	*15 KNOTS*	*28 KNOTS*
TORPEDO TUBES	*10 – 21 IN* *6 FWD 4 AFT*	*6 – 21 IN* *26 RELOADS*
COMPLEMENT	*82 – 84*	*103*
RANGE (MILES)	*12,000 AT 10 KNOTS*	*UNSPECIFIED BUT CON-SIDERABLE, GIVEN THE NUCLEAR REACTOR*
TORPEDOES	*UNGUIDED*	*UNGUIDED AND WIRE-GUIDED TIGERFISH*

and if one had not been surprised on the surface. Two of these three submarines were modern light or "coastal" submarines of the *Salta* class which were manufactured in West Germany and commissioned in 1974. They were 1,185-ton vessels with eight 21-inch torpedo tubes and a submerged speed of 22 knots. They are silent and difficult to detect but have limited endurance, and only one seems to have been fully operational. The third was the *Santa Fe*, an ex-U.S. *Guppy* class submarine. This ship was much larger (2,420 tons submerged), had ten 21-inch torpedo tubes, and had more endurance. Its maximum underwater speed was only 15 knots, however, and it was far noisier and easier to detect. The *Santa Fe* was forced aground by a hit from helicopter-launched missiles during the fighting in South Georgia.

The *Salta* and *San Luis*, however, successfully approached the British task forces's ASW screen on 4 May and claimed to have attacked British ships. If they actually did attack, their torpedoes evidently malfunctioned, although the submarines may have been detected and attacked by British Sea King helicopters using Stingray-guided torpedos before they were properly positioned to attack. This highlights the threat that similar coastal submarines can present to even a modern task force equipped with advanced ASW ships and sensors. The Argentine submarines might also have posed a significantly greater threat if they had been committed during the British landings. The frequent British false alarms and heavy British expenditure of ASW munitions long after the Argentine submarines left the area also suggest that even unused conventional submarines can provide at least a great deal of harrassment value against a modern fleet.[137] Argentina has ordered six modern West German submarines. This may be an important lesson for the future. Advanced conventional submarines are slowly proliferating into the Third World, and even the very existence of such ships in enemy forces may affect the security and operations of U.S. and other Western naval task forces.

Sea-Based Air and Missile Defenses

Manufacturers' claims since the war have tended to create pointless controversy about the effectiveness of the missile defenses on British ships. As has been stressed earlier, the British task force suffered from problems that made many of these issues somewhat moot:

- It had no real AEW capability.
- Ship, air, and missile defenses could not be integrated.
- The bulk of British ships with such defenses were cost engineered and lacked adequate sensor and fire control integration, adequate ESM and passive countermeasures, and an adequate mix of long- and short-range defense.
- Accurate data on the number of engaging aircraft, the conditions for missile firing, and hit to engagement and kill ratios evidently were not kept by the task force.
- The bulk of the systems deployed were not state of the art.

Nevertheless, the broad pattern of missile combat is of interest. The major British systems used in the Falklands are shown in Table 3.18. The two sea-based systems in Table 3.18 which played a major role in defending the British fleet against air attack were the Sea Dart surface-to-air missile and the Sea Wolf point defense system. It is important to note that both systems had an important limitation: both

TABLE 3.18 Sea-Based Missiles and Guns

Missile/Gun (Manufacturer)	Range	Function
Sea Dart (British Aerospace)	24	Surface-to-Air (SAM)
Sea Cat (Short Brothers)	3	SAM
Sea Slug (British Aerospace)	28	SAM, Surface-to-Surface
Sea Wolf (British Aerospace)	1/2 mile plus	Close-range SAM and interception of conventional shells

SOURCE: *Aviator Recognition Manual*, FM1-402 (Washington, D.C.: Department of the Army, 1984).

the Type 42 destroyers (Sea Dart) and Type 22 frigates (Sea Wolf) have only two guidance channels and must devote each channel to a given target throughout engagement. This meant their missile defenses were saturated the moment more than two aircraft attacked. The standard British air search radar, the Type 965, also proved relatively ineffective against low-flying aircraft.

The Sea Dart is a long-range system which grew out of the design concepts of the late 1950s. It is better suited to bombers flying at medium altitude than fighters flying at low altitudes. It is, however, a Mach 3 plus system and has a maximum range of up to 24 miles (38.6 km). The Sea Dart has the advantage of being able to kill an aircraft at a considerable distance from the ship. It is mounted on a twin handling and launch system and operates in conjunction with a Marconi tracking radar and the ship's surveillance radar.[138] It has its own semiactive radar. These systems are not fully integrated, however, and have a relatively low data rate.

The Sea Dart is credited with eight kills throughout the war. The Sea Dart was also in service on Argentine ships, and knowledge of this system helped force the Argentines to attack at low level. This tactic severely reduced the effectiveness of the Mirage fighters and helped cause the fusing and delivery problems in the bombs dropped by Argentine planes.

The problems in the Sea Dart, however, were substantial. It relied on radar that was not associated with the system itself. It did not have its own IFF and had to depend on manual decisions to decide if a target was hostile and to fire. The Sea Dart normally cannot hit a target which flies below 2,000 feet at long ranges and below 15 meters at close range. Its illumination radar has limited coverage, and the system takes two minutes to align its Gyros. It cannot maintain a ready state. Even when its Type 909 guidance radars tracked a target, it sometimes could not respond in time to prevent an air strike.[139] These weaknesses were also known to the Argentines. Their tactics of low-level attacks were therefore dictated by their understanding of the limitations of the Sea Dart and by their knowledge of the fact that only two British frigates within the task force were equipped with Sea Wolf missiles for defense against these tactics.[140]

The Sea Wolf GWS-25 point defense system has a 5.6-kilometer range and speeds over Mach 2. It is the weapon system associated with the Type 22 destroyers and with the *Andromeda*, which is a converted *Leander* class frigate that was part of the Falkland Islands task force. The Sea Wolf system is fully automatic and was originally designed to neutralize Soviet missiles in combat in the North Atlantic. It was also fast and accurate in its sea trials. It proved capable of destroying a 4.5-inch shell in flight. As a point defense system, however, Sea Wolf is designed only for ship self-defense. Its guidance computer automatically detects, identifies, and fires missiles at an enemy aircraft, but its fire control cannot be linked to the defense of another ship. The Sea Wolf also lacks the ability to properly engage two targets simultaneously and to engage in prolonged rapid fire. It is deployed in two six-round launches which must be manually reloaded.[141]

The Sea Wolf did perform effectively in providing short-range protection against single fighters, but it did not have a chance to down any missiles. It was used only against low-flying fighter aircraft. The Sea Wolf is credited with the destruction of five Argentine aircraft by the British White Paper, but this figure is somewhat uncertain.

The British also used the Sea Cat during the war. The Sea Cat is a short-range air-to-surface or surface-to-air missile with a maximum range of 2.95 miles (4.95 km). The Sea Cat deployed in the Falklands was largely the obsolescent radio command version, but it still has been credited by the British White Paper with responsibility for eight confirmed kills and two probable kills. This information has, however, been strongly contested by other sources who claim the figures are inflated and the effectiveness of the Sea Cat has been exaggerated. Whatever kills the Sea Cat achieved, it did result in high expenditures of missiles and provided an interesting lesson regarding the trade-off between high-cost technology and expenditure of missiles.

The Sea Slug missile system is an obsolescent long-range air defense system with ranges up to 36 miles (58 km). It achieved no kills throughout the war. It may, however, have been used for shore bombardment. The fact that it was still present on British ships reflected cost constraints and not the state of British technology.

It is tempting to bog down in debates over the performance of these individual missiles and ship defense mixes, but the main lesson of the Falklands seems to be that no ship can afford major economies in one aspect of its mix of armor, defense, electronics, and damage control, even in Third World conflicts. Modern ships must be able to provide both long-range and terminal defense and have good multiple engagement capability against low-flying fighters and missiles. A second lesson is the need to develop far more effective models of fleet defense and counterthreat operations and to adopt more effective test and evaluation procedures. The French and U.S. navies have also provided disturbing indications that they test individual weapons systems and ships rather than operational defense capabilities. The Falklands shows the need for far more rigorous testing on a fleet basis.[142]

The electronic warfare aspects of British ship defense are also interesting, but the details remain obscure. The *Sheffield* seems to have suffered from a lack of compatible satellite communications and radar/ESM gear; its Abbey Hill (UAA-1) electronic support measures system was switched off to allow the ship to transmit when it was hit by an Exocet. If the gear had been on, it might have used chaff or the Sea Dart. The satellite communications gear may have been American, however, and it is unclear what lessons should be drawn about electronics compatibility. The British seem to have used chaff successfully to shield the *Hermes* on 25 May, when the *Atlantic Conveyor* was hit by an Exocet, but the broad value of chaff is unclear. British ability to detect the radar on the Super Etendards forced the Argentines to rely on the radars of a Neptune fly to the rear and/or the TPS-43 on the Falklands. They could survive using their own radars only if they launched at near maximum range, which may have presented as many problems as the British use of chaff.[143]

The problems imposed by British treatment of the Exocet as a friendly weapon in some of their ship defense programming is very unclear. So is the extent to which British naval jammers affected the "home on the jammer" technology of the Exocet.[144]

Amphibious Lessons

Neither the Argentine landings nor most of the smaller British landings provide any clear lessons regarding amphibious operations. Both sides could have benefited from a well-armed, well-armored, light amphibious vehicle capable of operating in rough seas, but this is almost axiomatic. Neither side had modern amphibious ships or craft, and even the newer British ships relied on World War II technology. The Argentine landings at South Georgia and Port Stanley took place against little more than token opposition. The British landing at South Georgia involved a small helicopter operation supported by naval gunfire. The only consistent pattern in all three landings is that the landing force underestimated the size of the enemy and could have benefited from better real-time intelligence capability or recce assets.

The San Carlos landing was more an object lesson in air vulnerability than one in conducting amphibious operations against an aggressive shore force. It did, however, demonstrate the value of speed and of mixing heavy lift helicopters with fast landing craft. The British clearly increased the vulnerability of their ships and suffered tactical delays and problems whenever they had to rely on loading craft because they could not load and off-load quickly enough and were tied to shore deployment. In addition, they were vulnerable to sea conditions and greatly increased fatigue. The British also suffered from a lack of deck space and fast loading capability from their larger ships, along with problems in launching their landing craft.

The need for adequate air defense and naval gunfire capability can scarcely be viewed as new lessons, but the Falklands experience did reinforce these lessons. It also provides a useful caution about the need to be prepared for "forced entry" under totally unpredictable conditions. This point has long been stressed by the U.S. Marine Corps, but the British lacked the firepower and special equipment to properly deal with such a situation. If the Argentine army and aircraft in the Falklands had fought more aggressively, if the Argentines had had more shore-based artillery or Exocets, or if the Argentine air strikes had produced more bomb explosions per hit, the British might have had serious problems. Good as British improvisation was, its ships were not really armed to support "forced entry." Further, the long underfunding of the Royal Marines and British amphibious equipment clearly eroded Britain's ability to properly support its forces. As for the special forces aspects of the conflict, the weather and sea conditions were so severe that it is unfair to draw any lessons from the failure of some of the more demanding helicopter and small boat operations described in the chronology. It is equally unfair to question the judgement used in committing such forces. The point is often forgotten that elite forces like the SAS and SBS are designed to be expendable and take high risks when the objective merits such risks. The objective seems to have been valid in every case, but inexperience with the weather conditions may well have been a factor in the mission in the heights of South Georgia. In general, small special forces elements often succeeded in sabotage, raiding, and scouting missions where much larger regular forces would otherwise have been required to do the same job or no alternative force or technology was available.

Chemical/Biological Weapons

No chemical or biological weapons were used throughout the Falklands War. The British do claim, however, to have found Argentine 81-mm mortar shells filled with a toxic chemical at Port Stanley. This chemical was chloro-sulphonomine, an agent which kills through asphyxiation.[145]

Nuclear Weapons

Nuclear weapons were not used in the Falklands War, and it seems virtually inconceivable that they would have been used, despite press reports that this was discussed by British Prime Minister Thatcher and her advisors. The British were trying to limit the war to fighting between the militants of Argentina and Britain. They, therefore, made it a policy that there would be no strikes against the Argentine civilian population. A controversial corollary to this policy involved the prime minister's announcement that the Argentine mainland (including its military bases) would not be bombed. The policies of limiting the war to certain very definable limits ruled out the use of not only large-yield nuclear weapons, but also such things as nuclear artillery shells, depth charges, and torpedoes. Although such weapons would be used only to strike at military assets and personnel, they would, nevertheless, appear escalatory and project a level of controversy which Britain did not want associated with its war effort in the Falklands. In this regard, even the sinking of the *General Belgrano* was considered unnecessary and therefore controversial to some members of the British opposition.

The Key Lessons of the Falklands

Tragic as the Falklands conflict was for many of the participants, it was a "neat little war" in a military sense. An unusual amount of what happened can be documented precisely, and its "lessons" are far more measurable than those of most other conflicts. At the same time, the importance of these lessons is easy to exaggerate and must be kept in careful perspective. The Falklands conflict was fought on a limited scale and under unique conditions, and it was a war that neither side was prepared to fight.

The conflict also was one in which each side's ability to innovate was ultimately more important than its prewar plans and capabilities. With a little luck, and a little more innovation on the part of Argentina, it also could have had a very different ending, in spite of the fact that Argentina never used its sea power and was forced to rely on pilots who had never trained for naval attack missions and fighters over two decades old which were restricted to the use of aging "iron bombs."

The Argentine air force came remarkably close to defeating the British task force. Minor shifts in technology, training, and fusing might have allowed it to sink one of the British carriers and force the British to withdraw. Ten British ships were hit with bombs that failed to explode, and if a few more ships had sunk, the British might have been forced to withdraw. The British lost all of their heavy lift helicopters on the *Atlantic Conveyer*. Much of the British success in the land war was dependent on the 42nd Commando's ability to march unopposed for fifty-five miles across the tundra in near-arctic weather conditions with sixty-pound packs. More aggressive patrolling and counter-operations by the Argentine ground troops might have halted this British advance or held it long enough for winter to set in and force the British task force to withdraw.

In contrast, Britain consistently showed ability to innovate and improvise and do so on a combined arms basis while the Argentine air force had to fight alone. In fact, the key lesson of the Falklands conflict is not one of tactics or technology, it is the importance of both military professionalism and institutionalizing that professionalism on a combined arms basis. Shifts in tactics or technology *might* have altered the outcome, but Britain's superior training, readiness, and leadership *did* decide the outcome. This is a critical lesson to bear in mind in assessing low-intensity conflicts and the nature of any conflict fought under unique or improvised conditions. Regardless of force numbers and weapons, professionalism and innovation will often be the decisive "force multiplier."

Another lesson of the conflict is that the British reinforced their professionalism with a unified command and with a heavy emphasis on joint operations and interservice cooperation. The value of such an approach to managing modern war has been a key lesson of every conflict since the beginning of World War II. Virtually any command barrier or problem in creating an effective command and capability for joint operations leads to major military problems, whether the barrier is an interservice barrier or one within a given service. Similarly, the

Falklands conflict again demonstrates that although central management of the basic policy decisions affecting a conflict can occur from a capital or remote central command, a command cannot actually "fight" a war which is physically separated from the actual area of operations.

The best indication of the validity of these lessons is the fact that Argentina has partially recognized the need for such professionalism in reorganizing its army. It is also interesting to note that Argentina has taken several major steps to improve its war-fighting capability and professionalism. These steps include:

- Restructuring its command system to emphasize both civilian control and combined operations capabilities and to improve its joint planning and command and control capabilities.
- Refitting its Mirage and Dagger fighters with refueling probes to extend their range and endurance (critical problems during the Falklands fighting). It is interesting to note that Iraq also found refueling to be a critical problem in the Iran-Iraq War, that Israel has steadily improved the fuel-carrying and refueling capability of its fighters, and that the USSR changed its fighter mix throughout the Afghan conflict to increase the range payload of its attack aircraft. This need for added fighter range and endurance is a consistent lesson of modern war.
- The Argentine air force has purchased improved versions of the Exocet and Israeli Gabriel III anti-ship missiles and has reorganized to fight a war at sea. At the same time, the Argentine navy is trying to improve its missile capabilities and make its carrier fully effective as a means of operating its Super Etendard aircraft. It is clear that air and missile power are essential aspects of naval operations in the Third World and that any system that is bought and maintained largely for its "glitter factor" or value as a status symbol can rapidly turn into a critical weakness in military capability.
- The Argentine air force has purchased the French Durandel anti-runway bomb and has organized and trained for air field suppression. This reflects a broad trend in the Third World to move away from reliance on air-to-air or surface-to-air combat and to develop a capability to attack the air bases and facilities that are essential to conduct air operations.
- The Argentine air force and navy are expending their maritime reconnaissance and submarine warfare capabilities. Argentina is improving the radar and ESM sensor equipment on both its ships and aircraft and seems to be slowly upgrading its surface sensors and munitions to deal with British submarine threat.

- Argentina is seeking to purchase or construct six German Type 1700 submarines to present a threat to surface forces. This also reflects a common pattern in Third World countries. A number of nations such as Iran, Israel, and Syria, are also purchasing modern submarines in an effort to pose at least a limited threat to Western or Soviet surface vessels.

There are few indications at this point that Argentina has any serious interest in renewing the Falklands conflict. Its near economic and political collapse under President Raul Alfonsín has forced the government to sharply cut real defense spending after 1983. The annual conscript intake also dropped from a peak of 77,000 in 1980 to 64,000 in 1984, and then to only 28,000 in 1987. Alfonsín proved to be too weak politically to fully reform the officer corps that had fought what he called the "dirty war." In addition, he was not strong enough to cut officer strength as he cut total forces, and the officer-to-soldier ratio grew from 1:10 in 1982 to 1:5 in 1987. In early 1989, half of the army had an operational capability of only 40–50 percent, and half of the army's helicopters and 30 percent of the drive trains of its armor were not operational. The navy's surface ships were training at less than 50 percent of the required level, 40 percent of the fleet air arm was not operational, air force training was at less than 60 percent of the desired level, and 30–40 percent of the air force's aircraft were out of service because they lacked adequate spare parts.

It is clear, however, that Argentina has tried to act on some of the key lessons of the fighting. Further, many of Argentina's purchases are similar to those of other Third World nations—an indication that Western power projection forces will encounter steadily growing limits on their freedom of action and steadily more lethal threats in fighting low-intensity conflicts.

Notes

1. This chronology draws heavily on *The Falklands Campaign: The Lessons*, Cmnd.8758 (London: HMSO, December 1982); and Lawrence S. Germain, "A Diary of the Falklands Conflict," in Bruce W. Watson and Peter M. Dunn, *Military Lessons of the Falklands War* (Boulder, Colo.: Westview Press, 1984). Germain's work gives an excellent summary of diplomatic exchanges and British command decisions which are not relevant to this work. The chronology has had informal Argentine review and also draws on work by Robert Fox, Brian Hanrahan, and Bryan Perrett; and by Jesus Romero Briasco and Salvador Mafe Huertas, *Falklands: Witness of Battles* (Valencia, Spain: Frederico Domenech/S.A. Gremis, 1985).

2. For a good summary description of the U.S. role in the Falklands, see "America's Falklands War," *The Economist* (March 3, 1984), pp. 29–31; James

Brown and William P. Snyder, *The Regionalization of Warfare* (New Brunswick: Transaction Books, 1985), pp. 195–219; and the *Baltimore Sun* (March 16, 1984), p. 7.

3. See H. A. Klepak, "Continuity and Change in the Argentine Army Since the Falklands War," *Armed Forces*, Vol. 4, No. 8 (August, 1985), pp. 293–296; and "Argentine Forces Lacked Cooperation in the Falklands," *Jane's Defence Weekly* (November 30, 1985), p. 1174.

4. Major Jonathan Bailey, "Training for War: The Falklands 1982," *Military Review* (September 1983), p. 60.

5. Watson and Dunn, op. cit., pp. 64, 125.

6. *Jane's Defence Weekly* (November 1985), p. 1174.

7. These studies have never been released, but their broad content can be surmised from such sources as Phil Williams, "Miscalculation, Crisis Management and the Falklands Conflict," *World Today* (April 1983); *The Falklands Campaign: A Digest of Debates in the House of Commons, April to June, 1982* (London: HMSO, 1982); Peter J. Beck, "Britain's Antarctic Dimension," and Guillermo A. Makin, "Argentine Approaches to the Falklands/Malvinas: Was the Resort to Violence Foreseeable?" both in *International Affairs*, Vol. 59, No. 3 (Summer 1983), pp. 391–452. An excellent chronology of many of the details is provided in Max Hastings and Simon Jenkins, *The Battle for the Falklands* (New York: W.W. Norton, 1983), pp. 1–61.

8. *The Economist* (June 19–25, 1982), pp. 36–38, and (March 12, 1984), pp. 26–27. Also see Gerald W. Hopple, "Intelligence and Warning Lessons," in Watson and Dunn, op. cit., pp. 97–125.

9. The task force commander, Sir John Woodward, supports this point in his 20 October 1982 speech, "The Falklands Experience," to the Royal United Services Institute.

10. U.S. Arms Control and Disarmament Agency, *World Military Expenditures and Arms Transfers, 1972–1982* (Washington, D.C.: GPO, 1984), p. 97.

11. *The Economist* (March 3, 1984), pp. 26–27; *New York News* (March 3, 1984), p. 6; *Baltimore Sun* (March 16, 1984), p. 15.

12. Bryan Perret, *Weapons of the Falklands Conflict* (Dorset: Blandford Press, 1982), pp. 134–140. Also see the chronology of Soviet satellite launchings and Argentine actions in Watson and Dunn, op. cit., pp. 135–170.

13. *The Economist* (March 3, 1984), pp. 26–27.

14. Major Ralph Brunck, "Soviet Military Science and the Falklands Conflict, Part III," *Proceedings* (December 1985), p. 148.

15. Major Ralph Brunck, "Soviet Military Science and the Falklands Conflict, Part II," *Proceedings* (December, 1985), pp. 145–147.

16. For more details of the technical strengths and weaknesses of the sensors on British ships, see Norman Friedman, "Surface Combat Lessons," in Watson and Dunn, op. cit., pp. 21–66; *Weyser's Warships of the World, 1984/85* (Annapolis, MD: Nautical and Aviation Publishing Company, 1983); and *Jane's Fighting Ships, 1985/86* (London, 1986).

17. Brown and Snyder, op. cit., pp. 64–65; Friedman, op. cit., pp. 28–29; *The Falklands Campaign: The Lessons*, p. 19. The Blue Fox began development in

1973 and was a Ferranti derivative of the frequency-agile Sea Spray radar in the Lynx helicopter. It can support both air-to-air and air-to-ground missions but has no look-down or BVR missile capability. It is being replaced with the Blue Vixen radar as part of the modernization of the Sea Harrier from FR8-1 to FR8-2 standard. The new radar will be able to fire AMRAAM and have a limited look-down and multiple engagement capability.

18. *Canada's Maritime Defence Report of the Sub-committee on National Defence of the Standing Senate Committee on Foreign Affairs* (Ottawa, May 1983).

19. The Sea King helicopter is the primary ASW weapon in the British fleet air arm (FAA). Six airborne early warning (AEW) variants were equipped with Searchwater radars after the fighting in the Falklands ended. The emergency fit had only mediocre success, and a new version of the radar is being fitted to six new versions of the Sea King designed for the mission. Two will be assigned to each of Britain's three VSTOL carriers. The ASW version of the Sea King has a crew of four, and it is a comparatively large helicopter with room for a full AEW console. It can carry 6,000 lbs. of cargo, but it is range limited. Its cruising speed is 208 km/h and its range is 1,230 km (664 nm). Its limit is 975 to 1,575 meters (3,200 to 5,000 feet), and its endurance in AEW missions is 4 to 6 hours. Look-down capability is poor, multiple track capability is moderate, and its size and ceiling limit radar range. This seems to be an inherent limitation in heliborne AEW systems.

20. Briasco and Huertas, op. cit., pp. 57–58.

21. Jeffrey Ethell and Alfred Price, *Air War: South Atlantic* (New York: Macmillan, 1984), p. 132.

22. *Journal of Electronic Defense* (May 1985), p. 16.

23. Ibid.

24. *The Economist* (March 3, 1984), pp. 26–27.

25. *The Falklands Campaign: The Lessons*, p. 18; Robert Fox, *Eyewitness: Falklands* (London: Methuen, 1982), p. 7.

26. Vojtech Mastny, "The Soviet Union and the Falklands War," *Naval War College Review* (May–June 1983), p. 48.

27. *The Falklands Campaign: The Lessons.*

28. Ibid., p. 16.

29. *Armed Forces Journal* (August 1986), p. 24.

30. *Jane's Defence Weekly* (November 30, 1985), p. 1174. The British tried and failed to hit the TPS-43 above Port Stanley with Vulcan bombers. The British then tried to use Shrike anti-radiation missiles. This attack seems to have failed either because the Argentines operated the radars intermittantly or because they homed in on the fire control radars of Argentine AA batteries.

31. For typical reporting on these problems, see "Argentine Forces Lacked Cooperation in Falklands, Claims Air Force Chief," *Jane's Defence Weekly* (November 30, 1985), p. 1174.

32. Watson and Dunn, op. cit., p. xii.

33. *The Falklands Campaign: The Lessons*, p. 298.

34. See Klepak, op. cit.; Gary L. Guertner, "The 74-Day War: New Technology and Old Tactics," *Military Review* (November 1982), pp. 65–72;

Adrian J. English, "Drastic Argentine Army Reorganization," *Jane's Defence Weekly* (April 12, 1984); "Argentina Better Set for War in Falklands," *Defense Week* (January 21, 1985), p. 11; and "Argentine Forces Lacked Cooperation in Falklands," p. 1138.

35. *The Falklands Campaign: The Lessons*, p. 23; Perret, op. cit., pp. 100–123. See also Harry G. Summers, "Ground Warfare Lessons," in Watson and Dunn, op. cit., pp. 67–81.

36. Geoffrey Manners, "Falklands Soldier's Best Friend Was His Milan," *Jane's Defence Weekly* (April 7, 1984), p. 525.

37. Ibid.; Perret, op. cit., p. 121.

38. *The Falklands Campaign: The Lessons*, p. 17. Also see Watson and Dunn, op. cit., p. 168; and Perret, op. cit., pp. 55, 105, 112, and 117. The British used at least 30 105-mm weapons in some engagements.

39. Also see Watson and Dunn, op. cit., p. 88.

40. Cited in Geoffrey Manners, "Mines Still Prevent Return to Normality in Falklands," *Jane's Defence Weekly* (February 25, 1984), p. 276; and "British Abandon Mine Research in the Falklands," *Jane's Defence Weekly* (June 21, 1986), p. 1141.

41. Manners, "Mines Still Prevent Return to Normality," p. 276.

42. *The Falklands Campaign: The Lessons*, p. 23.

43. Sunday Times Insight Team, *War in the Falklands* (New York: Harper & Row, 1982), p. 255.

44. The British credit Harriers with cluster bombs with some AA gun kills, but these claims do not seem to be correct. See Hastings and Jenkins, op. cit., pp. 247–248; and Briasco and Huertas, op. cit., pp. 157–161.

45. For a good summary of Rapier capabilities, organization, and tactics at the time of the Falklands, see P. J. Birtles, "BA Dynamics Rapier Low Level Air Defense System," *Armed Forces* (August 1982), pp. 253–257.

46. William J. Ruhe, "Smart Weapons," in Watson and Dunn, op. cit., p. 90.

47. Hastings and Jenkins, op. cit., p. 205; Watson and Dunn, op. cit., pp. 91–92.

48. It is unclear whether this was for security or sales reasons. The British magazine. *The Economist* implies that references to the Stinger were censored for sales reasons: (March 3, 1984), p. 26.

49. Neville Trotter, "The Falklands Campaign: Command and Logistics," *Armed Forces Journal International* (June 1983), p. 40.

50. Mastny, op. cit., p. 51.

51. It is not clear which missile should get credit for the GR3 kill. Bryan Perret attributes the downing to a Blowpipe; see Perret, op. cit., p. 96. However, the pilot, Lt. Jeff Glover, believes the cause was three hits from a 20-mm cannon; see Ethell and Price, op. cit., p. 107. Virtually every source claiming original figures differs slightly from the others.

52. "Falklands War Pressured British EW Development," *Defense Electronics* (January 1985), pp. 56–62; *The Economist* (March 3, 1984), pp. 27–29; Alfred Price, *Harrier and Sea Harrier at War* (London: Ian Allan Ltd., 1985); *Journal of Electronics and Defense* (May 1985), p. 16.

53. Watson and Dunn, op. cit.

54. Ibid., pp. 166–167; Ethell and Price, op. cit., p. 20; Brown and Snyder, op. cit., pp. 64–65.

55. Quoted in Jacques Closterman, "The Argentine Air Force Today," *International Defense Review* (September 1988), pp. 1099–1100.

56. Chris Chant (ed.), *The World's Air Forces* (London, 1977), p. 179.

57. The Blue Fox radar was a noncoherent air-intercept and air-to-surface search and strike radar with radar sector scan, ranging, and tailchase tracking capability. It was designed to allow the Sea Harrier to intercept Boar and Badger bombers at medium and high altitudes. It could also detect small surface ships at high sea states and under adverse weather conditions. It was designed only for visual intercepts using IR missiles. The Blue Vixen, which will replace the Blue Fox, is a coherent multi-mode pulse doppler radar designed for full look-down–shoot-down capability and the ability to use the Hughes Aim-129 AMRAAM beyond visual range (BVR) missile. Blue Vixen also has ground mapping and sea surface search capability and 15536 data burst capability. Its installation in the Harrier marks a major advance in giving it full "force structure" fighter capabilities.

58. Chant, op. cit., p. 179; *Journal of Electronic Defense* (May 1985), p. 16.

59. *Janes's Defence Weekly* (October 1, 1988), p. 767.

60. Bill Gunston, *An Illustrated Guide to the Israeli Air Force* (New York: St. Martin's Press, 1980), p. 134.

61. Chant, op. cit., p. 15.

62. Information was provided by the British Aerospace Dynamics Group.

63. Hastings and Jenkins, op. cit., p. 152.

64. Ibid., p. 207. The second British source is Ethell and Price, op. cit.

65. The Sidewinder proved to be about 82 percent effective, although at least one missile did not home properly. See Hastings and Jenkins, op. cit., p. 207. See also Ethell and Price, op. cit., p. 215.

66. See "International Report," *Defense Electronics* (October 1982), p. 16.

67. Ibid.

68. Ethell and Price, op. cit., p. 127.

69. See, for example, comments on viffing in Hastings and Jenkins, op. cit., p. 207. See also Ethell and Price, op. cit., pp. 21 (for the technical/tactical reasons for not employing viffing), 214.

70. Lt. Benito Rotolo of the Zud Escuadrilla, quoted in Ethell and Price, op. cit., p. 128.

71. On the continuing efficacy of the A-4 Skyhawk, see Gunston, op. cit., pp. 101–104.

72. Anthony H. Cordesman, "The Falklands Crisis: Emerging Lessons," *Armed Forces Journal International* (September 1982), p. 37.

73. It is also important to note that the Sea Harrier is now being modified extensively. The Sea Harrier FSR-2 adds an all-weather, look-down, shoot-down capability with BVR missile capability. It incorporates a modern radar warning system, JTIDS, modern data display, added external fuel capacity, and improved autopilot and control facilities. CAP capability is extended to 1.5 hours at 100 nm. with two missiles and two 30-mm cannon. The intercept ranges are 116 nm. against a Mach 0.9 target and 95 nm. against a Mach 1.3

target. Its nominal hi-lo-hi radius is 200 nm. with two Sea Eagle missiles. Its recce radius is 525 nm. with two 30-mm cannon (a flight endurance of 1.75 hours). These ranges assume 300- to 450-foot deck runs and a 12° ski jump. A straight VTOL operation would reduce range and/or endurance by at least a third.

74. Cordesman, op. cit., p. 132.

75. Hastings and Jenkins, op. cit., p. 145.

76. See Sunday Times Insight Team, op. cit., p. 196.

77. See Hastings and Jenkins, op. cit., p. 207.

78. Closterman, op. cit.

79. The Argentines never bought adequate parts and spares, and President Jimmy Carter had embargoed military items, including aircraft parts, in 1978. While Israel sold some parts, the Argentines still had shortages. Some planes had to be flown without explosive cannisters for their ejection seats.

80. Cordesman, op. cit.

81. Major General Ken Perkins, British Aerospace Dynamics Group, "Air Defence In and Around the Falklands 1982, Lessons of the South Atlantic War," *Conference on the Lessons of the South Atlantic War*, September 2 and 3, 1982 (London: Royal Aeronautical Society, 1982), p. 75.

82. Watson and Dunn, op. cit., pp. 40 and 170.

83. *The Falklands Campaign: The Lessons*, p. 24.

84. The C-130 could still operate. Opinion differs over whether the Mirage or A-4 could operate with greatly reduced fuel and payload. Most experts feel the runway was too short even without cratering.

85. Ethell and Price, op. cit., pp. 44–52.

86. Ibid., pp. 155, 173–174, 180–182, 205, 218–219.

87. Perkins, op. cit., p. 78.

88. Ibid., p. 83. This figure is higher than that quoted by British writer John Fozard, who asserts that the Argentines shot down only three GR3s flying attack missions out of a total of fifteen sorties, for a mission loss rate of 2 percent and no casualties. The discrepancy in figures seems to be definitional: Fozard's sortie count refers only to the close air support mission; Perkins refers to the total number of missions flown by Harriers.

89. Perkins, op. cit., p. 83.

90. Ethell and Price, op. cit., p. 217.

91. Ibid., p. 165.

92. David A. Brown, "Countermeasures Aided British," *Aviation Week and Space Technology* (July 19, 1982), p. 136.

93. Perret, op. cit., p. 87.

94. See "Falklands Spawns New PAPI Unit," *Jane's Defence Weekly* (July 26, 1986), p. 138.

95. Brown, op. cit., p. 162. See Briasco and Huertas, op. cit., pp. 133–137, for descriptions of typical Pucara missions.

96. A good discussion of the Exocet fusing problem is provided in Perret, op. cit., p. 93. The author ascribes the fault to poor tactics by Argentine pilots who failed to loft their bombs from a sufficient height to allow fusing.

97. Perret, op. cit., p. 46. For a slightly different perspective, a net

assessment of the Exocet against HMS *Sheffield*, see David M. Russell, "How Exocet Sank the HMS *Sheffield*," *Defense Electronics* (July 1982), pp. 38–47.

98. Perret, op. cit., p. 83; and Watson and Dunn, op. cit., pp. 85–87. For a good discussion of the technical side of the Exocet–Super Etendard weapon system, see "Inside the Exocet: Flight of a Sea Skimmer," *Defense Electronics* (August 1982), pp. 46–48.

99. On the importance of chaff to the Royal Navy's air defense system in the conflict, see Brown, op. cit., pp. 18–19. According to this article, the British used the Corvis rocket launcher system to provide a chaff barrage, probably supplemented by an active ECM which caused the Exocet to veer off the carrier HMS *Invincible*. Other British sources claim chaff decoyed attacks on the *Hermes* and *Invincible* on 25 May 1982. The British claim they sent up "clouds" of chaff to the *Atlantic Conveyor*. The Argentines claim they simply fired at the first large blip they detected, and the missile homed on this target; Watson and Dunn, op. cit., pp. 86–88.

100. *The Falklands Campaign: The Lessons*, p. 21.

101. Watson and Dunn, op. cit., pp. 84–86; Ethell and Price, op. cit., pp. 40, 77, and 252; and Perret, op. cit., pp. 11, 124–125, and 128.

102. Perret, op. cit., pp. 47–48, 68–69, 125–126.

103. John Godden, *Harrier: Ski-jump to Victory* (Oxford: Brassey, 1983), p. 17.

104. For a general discussion of the need for airborne early warning (along with a discussion of large versus small carriers), see Adm. Thomas H. Moorer and Alvin J. Cottrell, "ECM in the Falklands War Proves Its Point the Hard Way," *Military Electronics/Countermeasures* (November 1982), pp. 48–49. The authors, one a large-carrier admiral and one a noted naval analyst, contend that only the big carrier is capable of the kinds and quantities of AEW and attack aircraft capable of detecting and downing an attack aircraft/sea skimmer like the Super Etendard/Exocet.

105. *The Falklands Campaign: The Lessons*, p. 24.

106. See the remarks by Lieutenant David Smith, RN, on the frustrations of flying combat air patrol in Godden, op. cit., p. 104.

107. Ethell and Price, op. cit., pp. 14–16, 154.

108. On the use of the Blue Fox radar in the Falklands crisis, see ibid., pp. 14–16, 154.

109. "New Approach to Blue Vixen Software," *Jane's Defence Weekly* (August 16, 1986), p. 243.

110. Ibid., pp. 34, 46, 93. The first reconnaissance missions were flown by Victor aircraft on 20 April 1982 and covered 7,000 miles—the longest operational aerial reconnaissance flight in history. Later flights by Nimrod aircraft concentrated on naval bases and forces along the Argentine coast. These covered 8,300 miles and established yet another reconnaissance record. The Nimrod used the Searchwater radar, which was sensitive to electronic emissions from warships or aircraft in the area.

111. "New Approach to Blue Vixen Software," p. 219.

112. Ibid., p. 252.

113. Lt. Col. David W. A. Swane, "British Light Helicopter Operations

During the Falkland Islands Campaign," *U.S. Army Aviation Digest* (November 1983), p. 12.

114. Watson and Dunn, op. cit., p. 169.

115. Hastings and Jenkins, op. cit., p. 127.

116. Ibid., p. 203.

117. Swane, op. cit., p. 12.

118. Hastings and Jenkins, *The Battle for the Falklands,* op. cit., p. 242.

119. Major General Sir Jeremy Moore and Rear Admiral Sir John Woodward, "The Falklands Experience," RUSI (March 1983), p. 29.

120. *Jane's Defence Weekly* (October 22, 1988).

121. The Crespo report was published in full in various editions of the *Buenos Aires Herald.* For a summary, see "Argentine Forces Lacked Cooperation in Falklands, Claims Air Force Chief," *Jane's Defence Weekly* (November 30, 1985), p. 1174.

122. "America and the Falklands," *The Economist* (November 12, 1983), p. 34.

123. *The Falklands Campaign: The Lessons,* pp. 25–26.

124. Major Ralph Brunck, "Soviet Military Science and the Falklands Conflict," Part III, *Proceedings* (December 1985), pp. 142–148. Also see Valerie Adams, "Logistic Support for the Falklands Campaign," *RUSI Journal* (Spring 1983), pp. 43–49.

125. Commander P. G. Hore, RN, "Ascension Island April 1982," *Armed Forces,* Vol. 3, No. 7 (July 1984), p. 274.

126. For an interesting discussion of the tactical details of the Royal Marine Commando Logistic Regiment, see John Reed's series in *Armed Forces* (May 1983), pp. 180–183, and (June 1983), pp. 212–216.

127. For a good description of the problems in Argentine airlift and helicopter lift see Briasco and Huertas, op. cit., pp. 133–137 and 175–249.

128. A number of sources present such data, but the disagreements between them are so sharp that no meaningful extrapolation is possible.

129. Aluminum melts at 700°C compared to 1,500°C for steel.

130. *The Falklands Campaign: The Lessons,* p. 19.

131. See Watson and Dunn, op. cit., pp. 88–89; Perret, op. cit., pp. 24–26; and Ethell and Price, op. cit., pp. 88–91 and 145–151.

132. Rear Admiral E. F. Gueritz, "The Falklands: Joint Warfare Justified," *RUSI Journal* (September 1982), p. 48.

133. *The Falklands Campaign: The Lessons,* p. 19.

134. Ibid., p. 17.

135. Watson and Dunn, op. cit., pp. 24–25; Ethell and Price, op. cit., p. 76; Perret, op. cit., pp. 36, 43, 46, 85–88.

136. Robert King, "Will Tigerfish End UK Torpedo Problems?" *Armed Forces Journal* (August 1986), p. 23.

137. Norman Friedman, "The Falklands War: Lessons Learned and Mislearned," *Orbis* (Winter 1983), p. 914; and George C. Wilson, "Argentina Is Said to Have Penetrated British Sub-Defense," *Washington Post* (September 13, 1982), p. 1.

138. Perret, op. cit., p. 128; Watson and Dunn, op. cit., pp. 25–27 and 88–90.

139. Sunday Times Insight Team, op. cit., p. 161.

140. Air Vice-Marshall Stewart W. Menaul, "The Falklands Campaign: A War of Yesterday," *Strategic Review* (Fall 1982), p. 87.

141. See Hastings and Jenkins, op. cit., p. 225.

142. For overviews of British progress, see Anthony Preston, "Air Defense at Sea: A Vital Choice," *Jane's Defence Weekly* (August 31, 1985), pp. 405–408; and "New Anti-Missile Weapons for the Royal Navy," *International Defense Review*, Vol. 15, No. 9 (1982), pp. 1152–53.

143. Major Ralph A. Bruner, "Soviet Military Science and the Falklands Conflict," *Proceedings* (January 1986), pp. 140–142.

144. Ibid.

145. Perret, op. cit., pp. 111–112.

4

ANALYSIS OF THE LESSONS OF LIMITED ARMED CONFLICTS

Certain lessons of war seem to be constants and emerge regardless of changes in tactics and technical progress. These include the importance of setting meaningful political and strategic objectives, the value of proper tactics, the significance of leadership and training, the importance of logistics and support capability, and the need for proper basing and strategic mobility. It is almost a cliche to reiterate the fact that these lessons emerge from all the wars under study. Unfortunately, these same wars make it clear that the most obvious and proven lessons of war seem hardest to learn.

The wars under study—the October War of 1973, the Israeli invasion of Lebanon in 1982, the Iran-Iraq War, the Falklands conflict, and the Soviet invasion of Afghanistan—also provide a number of more detailed insights and "lessons." All five wars provide valuable insights into the impact of advanced technology on low-level wars. In several cases, they are the only conflicts involving a new tactic or technology. In others, they provide an important update regarding a given weapons system or military capability. In many cases, the wars were fought with weapons developed for high-technology forces to fight high-intensity wars which were then called upon to perform different tasks under radically different conditions. High-technology weapons were sometimes more effective than they are likely to be in high-level wars, but in many cases high-technology weapons systems proved unsuitable for low-level wars. These lessons are particularly important because Western forces cannot afford technical suprises of this kind. They cannot afford to enter low-level conflicts with the "right" equipment for the "wrong" war.

The major military systems and technologies that have been discussed in the analysis of each conflict are noted in Table 4.1. These systems are listed in rough order according to their marginal utility in

TABLE 4.1 Marginal Utility of Expensive and Complex Military Systems

---

HIGH
- — Sophisticated SHORADS
- — Advanced multiple rocket launchers—RPVs
- — SAM suppression
- — Targeting aids
- — Missile defense
- — AEW and AC&W systems

MODERATE
- — Helicopter
- — PHOTINT and SIGINT
- — Anti-tank guided missiles
- — Conventional artillery
- — Tanks

LOW
- — Air-to-ground fixed wing
- — Medium and heavy surface-to-air missiles
- — Chemical warfare

---

all five limited wars. The reasons for this ranking, and the impact of each technology, are analyzed in this chapter.

Threat Assessment Technologies

One of the most dramatic lessons of recent limited wars is that Western threat assessment technologies have a number of shortcomings when they are used against unsophisticated opponents. Most Western threat assessment technologies are designed to be used against technologically advanced forces, such as those of the Soviet Union and Eastern Europe, and many have limited value in dealing with low-level wars.

There are a number of reasons for this situation:

- Infantry and guerrilla forces do not follow patterns or have movements that can be characterized easily by modern sensors and intelligence systems.
- Natural cover, artificial barriers, bunkers, urban and built-up areas, and other types of concealment and fortifications provide much better cover for the forces in low-level wars. They often allow extensive movement without detection and characterization by both tactical reconnaissance systems and national technical means.

- Third World and popular or revolutionary forces often lack a tightly organized, formal logistics system and place heavy emphasis on small-unit or night movement and the use of improvised logistics and civil systems.
- The high degree of politicization of every aspect of Third World and popular or revolutionary forces, plus the exceptional impact of personalities, ethnic and religious factors, tribalism, and so on, on military actions and decision making, makes intentions and human factors far more important than force numbers, deployment, technology, and order of battle. Further, major command decisions are often highly personalized at the top leadership level and rarely involve extensive communications. The actual communications net may be little more than a web of half-truths and outright lies, and even the electronic order of battle may involve units with such radically different proficiencies that normal ELINT has little value. This politicization problem is compounded by the tendency for new major "actors" to emerge during the course of prolonged conflicts and by the inability to predict or characterize the emergence of new political, ethnic, religious, and revolutionary groups.
- Reconnaissance and intelligence technology cannot be applied to forces with unknown tactical and military behavior patterns, target structures, efficiency, and effectiveness. Every unit and unit element has unique levels of proficiency. Unless good prewar HUMINT is available, normal intelligence indicators may have little value.
- The success of technology transfers to developing states can be fully characterized only in war. Further, many combat conditions and interactions are unique and have no precedent. There is no basis of historical experience for accurate assessment.

One of the most obvious examples of the problems the West may face is the limited effectiveness of signals intelligence (SIGINT) assets against some Third World targets. Western assets are tailored to intercept communications intelligence (COMINT) and electronic intelligence (ELINT). Yet the volume and importance of both types of emitters have been relatively low in several of the conflicts under examination. Afghanistan is the most obvious example, since the Afghan Mujahideen have almost no equipment that can leave an electronic signature. The PLO in Lebanon and the Iranians in the Gulf War were also forces that produced far less SIGINT than is expected of modern forces, although the PLO still produced enough SIGINT to allow the Israelis to exploit a significant amount of information, and

Syria produced enough SIGINT, COMINT, and ELINT to provide Israel with major help in planning and executing air defense suppression and air-to-air combat.

Britain and the U.S. did obtain significant SIGINT and ELINT during the Falklands conflict, although the British lacked adequate forward collection assets and could not use such data to adequately estimate the size, activity, and probable capability of the Argentine forces on the island. Neither side made effective use of SIGINT or ELINT during the Iran-Iraq War, but it is clear that Iran's loss of much of its Western equipment led to a steady decline in reliable SIGINT. At the same time, various Gulf sources indicate that both Iran and Iraq had very poor ELINT discipline, making it possible to monitor the location, character, and approximate readiness of many of the systems on both sides.

These "mixed signals" regarding the value of SIGINT imply that SIGINT continues to be valuable in higher-level conflicts. This may, however, be misleading. The use of pulse code modulation, one-time pads, low probability of intercept (burst or spread spectrum) radios, and land lines is becoming far more common, and some of these techniques are now routine for forces such as the rebels in El Salvador. It seems highly likely that SIGINT collection will grow steadily more difficult even in higher-level conflicts in the Third World in the future. Coupled with the almost inevitable problems of language and often erratic "political communications" patterns, meaningful SIGINT analysis may be difficult or even impossible.

ELINT should be different. Few Third World states exhibit much sign of ELINT discipline or much consciousness of electronic warfare in general, although Syria has sharply improved its efforts since 1982. The problem may be to combine ELINT collection with sufficient understanding of local conditions to weigh properly the effectiveness of the forces involved. Targeting is unlikely to be a major problem, although the basic techniques of reducing detection and vulnerability have attracted far more Third World attention since 1982. The key issue will often be estimating the effectiveness of individual units and of the related $C^3I/BM/AC\&W/EW$ systems. Special analytic techniques and support equipment may be needed to estimate just how well a given force can use what it has. To assume that most Third World states can use properly most of their electronic order of battle (EOB) could be extremely misleading.

Photo intelligence (PHOTINT) targeted against unsophisticated forces can sometimes be more valuable than SIGINT, but it also has shortcomings in dealing with less sophisticated forces. PHOTINT is capable of detecting large formations of troops regardless of the degree of sophistication that characterizes the C^3 of their equipment. PHOTINT is much less effective, however, in conflicts against irregular forces such as those in Afghanistan, in conflicts that involve critical night small infantry movements as Iran, or in conflicts that involve extensive infantry and low-level activity in mountains and built-up areas as in Lebanon. Formations of troops and logistic units are usually too fluid and ephemeral for PHOTINT to be effective. Once forces are locked in place—as in the Iran-Iraq War or along the Suez in 1973—PHOTINT cannot predict intentions or the moment and place of attack.

Satellite collection is too limited in swath coverage, has poor resolution against such targets, has only limited "time windows" for coverage, and usually takes too long to process and interpret. Photo reconnaissance also generally lacks loiter or time-over-target capability and often takes too long to process, correlate, and interpret. Electro-optical systems can provide near–real-time collection and processing capability, but most collection platforms now do not provide such processing capability and lack the ability to reliably detect low-level infantry movements even in daytime. Weather and night can make certain types of PHOTINT difficult to impossible.

The analysis of all the conflicts under study shows that time is a critical problem in all aspects of SIGINT, ELINT, and PHOTINT. Collection platforms need time to collect and characterize the scattered patterns of movement, action, and communications. "Snapshot" use of sensors will often fail to provide a clear basis of understanding or to detect key activities. Platforms that can endure or "loiter" in the area and use "stand-off" assets like SAR, SLAR, FLIR, and electro-optics to maintain surveillance over an extended period of time can be great value. Useful as fighter aircraft and RPVs may be, every war under study indicates the value of heavier aircraft with more endurance and range, a wider mix of sensors, at least some on-board analysis capability that can directly support field commanders, and near–real-time allocations of aircraft and helicopters. Similarly, there is a need for suitable sensor and communication satellites tailored to supporting Western forces in low-level wars.

All five wars also reveal the potential value of dedicated theater assets that could respond to commanders in near real time. All of the commanders involved, for example, would have benefited from better AC&W and AEW assets. All would have benefited from a small airborne platform that could combine SAR, SLAR, all-weather electro-optical capability with a computerized correlation capability, ESSM, and COMINT capability. All would have benefited from improved airborne targeting systems. Britain and Israel had some elements of such systems, but no power on any side had access to a wide range of modern tactical threat assessment technology in a rapidly deployable form with near–real-time readout and analysis capability.

Useful as satellite systems may be under some circumstances, they are not a substitute for dedicated theater assets that are constantly in place and directly responsive to theater needs. At the same time, none of the conventional reconnaissance aircraft or RPVs on any side had a sufficient range of technical and data processing and analytic needs. Israel's E-2Cs and RPVs and reconnaissance aircraft came closest during Israel's 1982 invasion of Lebanon; but the E-2C lacked the capability to support land combat, the Israeli Defense Forces (IDF) RPVs had limited area coverage and sensor packages, and the IDF's recce aircraft lacked the mix of sensors and loiter capability to fully support the IDF's needs and deal with guerrilla, mountain, and built-up area targets. Further, the IDF often could not process and distribute air reconnaissance data in time to meet the needs of land combat commanders.

These lessons tend to validate the conceptual proposals which many aerospace firms are putting forward for advanced theater collection platforms tailored to low-level wars, but it also raises major issues about what mix of sensors, processing, and "fusion" techniques is most desirable. Most of today's advanced collection systems have severe limits in urban and mountain warfare and against infantry. Photography, the highest resolution system now available, is too slow in terms of processing and interpretation. The technical challenge of creating an effective theater collection platform is far more serious than most current proposals and demonstration aircraft indicate.

All five wars were characterized by basic failures in HUMINT on every side and in each conflict. This was particularly true of each side's ability to analyze the probable course and outcome of a conflict and the behavior of opposing leaderships and commanders, but it was also true of warning, the ability to predict the behavior of potential regional allies and enemies, and a host of other factors. In most cases, these failures occured in spite of considerable SIGINT and PHOTINT indicators that might have been highly useful if the proper HUMINT had been available. These failures stemmed from: (a) inadequate policy-level guidance and lack of interest in intelligence that disagreed with existing policy and preconceptions, (b) a lack of adequate analytic resources and objectivity, and (c) a failure to allocate adequate resources to HUMINT and particularly to obtaining a wide range of view and inputs. It is striking to note that the most serious intelligence failures in all five wars occurred in HUMINT and that most failures were at least as much the result of policy-level action as of action by intelligence elements. Helpful as improved intelligence technology might have been, no key strategic intelligence failure would have been overcome by such assets. The intelligence failures with strategic importance all occurred because of problems in HUMINT, interpretation of HUMINT, and policy guidance that limited the objectivity and depth of intelligence analysis.

These issues indicate the potential value of friendly states, forces, and political movements in supporting joint action in defense of regional security and in providing warning. Friendly local forces can use Western reconnaissance and warning technology to characterize the situation and the individual behavior patterns of potential and actual threats. Local forces can support Western forces in HUMINT and provide the linguistic and other specialized resources that Western forces lack. Egypt, Israel, Jordan, and Saudi Arabia provide examples of such forces in the Near East, and nations as diverse as Honduras, Pakistan, and South Korea are examples in other parts of the world.

This mix of lessons indicates the need for a new kind of "fusion" in threat assessment technology and activity. The Saudi purchase of the U.S. E-3A AWACS, for example, is a good example of a technology transfer to key friendly states in strategic areas that might be of massive value to the West in creating in-theater assets long before a need arises for Western intervention. The sale of E-2C aircraft to Israel and Egypt could have a similar impact. French and British sales to the other Gulf states like the United Arab Emirates and Kuwait will have a similar impact in building up the infrastructure for cooperation and joint action without affecting local sovereignty.

The practical problem for the U.S. and the West will be to create the kind of technology transfer that (a) is suitable for developing states, (b) supports effective regional cooperation and security, and (c) will allow joint action with Western forces like USCENTCOM. The ideal structure would be one in which rapid "fusion" can take place between local and Western forces. This is as true of secure and effective C^3I as it is of threat assessment technologies and applies to joint action between Western forces as well as to action between local and Western units. The Falklands conflict demonstrated that U.S. and British cooperation could be of critical value in threat assessment, and U.S., British, and/or French cooperation might be as essential in future low-level wars as in NATO.

Secure and Effective C^3I

All five conflicts demonstrated the importance of a strong and effective command system backed by excellent secure communications at all levels. Britain and the USSR, however, were the only powers to introduce a fully effective command system, and Britain was the only nation to combine a clear hierarchy of command with suitable flexibility and initiative at every major level of operations. The Soviet system was more rigid and less flexible, although it adapted to local conditions during the course of the Afghan conflict. The Israeli C^3 system improved strikingly between 1973 and 1982, but it was crippled during much of the 1982 war because the Israeli Defense Minister and Chief of Staff had to improvise a command responsive to their private goals rather than to pre-war planning and cabinet direction. Iraq, Iran, the PLO, Syria, and the Afghan freedom fighters all lacked an effective C^3 system, although Iraq, Iran, and Syria had most of the necessary equipment and technical assets. Argentina had a good national C^3 system but did not establish a particularly effective system in the Falklands.

The air and naval C^3 capabilities on all sides generally proved more effective than land and air-land C^3. Only Israeli and the UK had access to a modern land communications system, and even Britain and IDF had considerable trouble in handling communications in mountain and built-up areas. There was only limited fusion between C^3I and the targeting and reconnaissance systems in every war under study. Only the British fleet and the British and Israeli national command seem to have had anything approaching an effective fusion center. As will be discussed shortly, all sides tended to experience serious C^3 problems in combined arms and in allocating and controlling air support.

Many of the more detailed lessons to be drawn regarding C^3 methods and technology are discussed later in this chapter, but there is no question that many of the failures and tactical problems during each conflict occurred for three reasons. First, the failure of most nations to create suitable fusion centers was compounded by a lack of interservice and intercommand fusion centers and by compartmentation of intelligence away from command and control activities. Second, communications and control systems were inadequate to link together small combat units, particularly in urban and mountain warfare. Most nations placed far more emphasis on middle- and high-command communications and control than on detailed battle management and information at the small unit level—where wars are lost and won. Finally, no nation was ready to fully integrate targeting, C^3/BM, and execution at the near–real-time speeds required, although Britain was better prepared than the rest. The IDF was crippled more by internal politics than technology, and the Soviets steadily evolved an improved C^3/BM system for fighting in Afghanistan.

Several of the conflicts, however, indicate that C^3 problems will sharply increase the vulnerability of Third World forces even if they deny the West easy SIGINT collection. Third World nations generally have stressed weapons numbers and firepower and made C^3 systems and electronics a secondary or peripheral concern. This means their C^3 equipment may be relatively easy to intercept and disrupt in cases where the electromagnetic spectrum is involved. Land-line communication or communication with messengers is not subject to interception or disruption with modern CW and ECM equipment, but these systems have a variety of shortcomings that are exploitable by air or other attacks.

Many Third World states also fail to apply the principle of redundancy and protection which is always important with C^3 systems. This means that Third World army and air units can be isolated from each other and lose their ability to reinforce or conduct flanking movements on the battlefield. Western forces may be able to concentrate overwhelming combat power against isolated units that connot receive assistance readily from other maneuver units. These hostile units will be acutely vulnerable because of the lack of a survivable, releasable, and flexible C^3 system utilizing redundancy of assets. This will occur, however, only if the West is willing and able to exploit this weakness.

At the same time, it is dangerous to become too confident about Western ability to exploit superior C^3I. There are many indications that some Third World countries are beginning to integrate complex C^3 systems into their command structures. Iraq and Syria, for example, are learning from past mistakes and have made substantial efforts to obtain modern C^3 equipment. Most other Near Eastern states are making a major investment in C^3I, and many have access to tactical technology roughly equivalent to that of the West.

Combined Arms

All of the conflicts under study involved both combined arms (the interaction between various land force elements) and combined operations (interservice operations). The distinction between these two categories was blurred in all five conflicts because of the growing role of army and navy air units included in all land operations, but certain lessons do have importance for combined arms:

- *Infantry*: The role and importance of infantry was critical in all of the conflicts under study. In every case but the October 1973 conflict, infantry combat and infantry weaponry, C^3, equipment, and logistics dominated the course of combat. Three of the countries involved were not fully prepared for this reality. The

USSR in Afghanistan, Israel in Lebanon, and Iraq in Iran all put too much initial emphasis on armor and artillery. Argentina failed to use its infantry effectively, but this was more a failure of leadership than a failure of combined arms. One of the most critical lessons of all five wars is the need to give infantry tactics and technology a critical priority in combined arms.

Urban and Mountain Warfare: This priority for infantry is reinforced by the fact that none of the forces involved was fully prepared to fight combined arms combat in urban and built-up areas or in mountain warfare. No force had a clear doctrine, or special equipment, for using its artillery and armor in urban and mountain conflict. Targeting, C^3I, and battle management technology were designed for other kinds of combat; tanks had major visibility and gun elevation problems; artillery lethality and targeting ability was limited; and the other fighting vehicles available were generally unsuitable. Most advanced military technology could not be used effectively in this kind of fighting, and it failed to give the more sophisticated power a decisive advantage.

As was described earlier, the USSR took several years to adapt to the problems of mountain warfare against a primitive and badly equipped opponent, and then it equired major local troop superiority plus the use of helicopters, area bombing, AA guns, and light AFVs. The UK improvised successfully in conducting mountain warfare but exploited its superior infantry training and tactics against an inflexible enemy. It is unclear how well British forces would have performed in mountain combat against trained mountain infantry.

Neither Israel nor Iraq was prepared for urban or built-up area warfare. Israel failed to fight successfully in its limited urban engagements on the West Bank in 1973, was badly delayed at several points during its northern advance in 1982, and avoided high-intensity combat in Beirut. Iraqi armor was defeated in Abadan, and Iraqi infantry and artillery succeeded temporarily in Abadan only through sheer mass—and were later thrown back. This again illustrates the need for urban warfare training and equipment for suitable infantry forces.

The critical deficiencies which emerged in the tactical technology available for combined operations in mountain and urban warfare were targeting and battle management systems, specialized munitions for artillery and AFVs, specially configured AFVs, highly portable heavy weaponry with low signatures that was fireable in contained areas (e.g., in buildings), body armor and night vision aids, and surveillance systems specially designed for urban and mountain warfare.

- *Time on Target*: The most critical difficulty in combined arms encounters was the classic problem of bringing all arms to bear at the proper time and in the proper mix. The key shifts in the wars in question were the need to rapidly alter the mix between armor and infantry and the "time on target" problem in firepower.

  It is difficult to generalize about the problem of rapidly altering the mix between armor and infantry because of the different conditions involved in the conflict under study, but several common threads emerge: (a) infantry and armor C^3 must be good enough to allow rapid cross-support; (b) infantry mobility must match that of armor in speed and cross-country capability; (c) infantry must be able to rapidly dismount from APCs and AFVs with heavy weapons and C^3; (d) MICVs must have suitable armor and firepower to directly support tanks; and (e) at least some AFVs must be available that are specially configured for urban, mountain, and low-level war.

  The "time on target" problem is essentially the problem of bringing a suitable mix of combined arms firepower to bear with the near–real-time response needed to support forward combat elements or rapidly moving targets at the precise moment required. No force under examination succeeded in using modern technology effectively in this mission, although the problem was not relevant to the British experience in the Falklands, and Israel's failure to properly improve its performance between 1973 and 1982 was as much a function of political interference at the command level as of defects in its organization and technology. There is a critical need for the targeting, C^3I, and battle management systems necessary to solve the problem.

- *Artillery and Combined Arms*: Artillery consistently presented the most critical "time on target" problem. No force on any side in any of the five wars under examination had the mix of C^3I, targeting, battle management, and firepower capabilities necessary to immediately respond with artillery firepower within the few minutes generally available, correct immediately on the basis of forward observation, and exploit the fact that only the initial rounds of fire have major tactical effect.

  Every force engaged, except the UK, at least occasionally made the mistake of relying on barrage or mass fire as a substitute for precisely targeted initial fire. In case after case, such fire proved dismally ineffective—often delaying the maneuver capability of the firing side in ways that degraded its overall tactical position. This confirms a pattern of military behavior, and a requirement for tactical technology, that emerged at least as early as World War I but which seems extraordinarily difficult for modern armies to react to.

Infantry

In all five conflicts, infantry played a critical role in dealing with enemy forces in both conventional and unconventional warfare settings. While technology and combined arms have consistently improved the effectiveness of other arms, none can substitute for infantry combat. The importance of infantry is underscored by the fact that at least once combatants in all five conflicts suffered tactical setbacks because of an excessive reliance on armor or an unwillingness to have mechanized troops dismount from their APCs. The key combatants who suffered the most serious setbacks were Iraq, Israel, and the Soviet Union.

Infantry troops who tried to fight from APCs, rather than by dismounting, experienced serious problems in most of the fighting under study. An APC loaded with troops who fight from within the vehicle must try to perform the function of a small tank and act as an armored ground-gaining system. The APC is inherently inferior to the tank in performing this function, as it has thinner armor and is vulnerable to a variety of weapons that would do less harm (if any) to a tank. Most APCs (including the M113 and the BMP) do not have enough armor to prevent a heavy machine gun (50 calibre) from shooting through their sides and killing the troops within. The effectiveness of the APC as a system, and the need for improved light armored vehicles, will be examined shortly, but the key lesson for infantry is that most of today's APCs and MICVs simply are too vulnerable to be committed against defended positions.

At the same time, infantry benefits from every possible improvement in combined arms support. The Falklands are a good case in point. Without naval gunfire and artillery support, it is doubtful that British troops could have broken up Argentine defenses around Port Stanley. This is because the British had only a limited number of troops. The Israelis made sporadic use of combined arms teams in many of their battles. When they did use combined arms teams, they were usually successful, although never to the degree called for in Israeli plans. When they relied too much on armor, they usually experienced serious problems. Israeli attempts to repeat their experience in the 1967 war—when friendly infantry was generally unnecessary to protect their armor from surprised and disorganized Arab troops—have failed consistently ever since.

In considering the operations that characterize warfare in the Gulf, it is significant that Iran has adopted infantry strategies and tactics that exploit both (1) a superiority in manpower and (2) its willingness to accept high casualties as a substitute for tanks and AFVs. Iranian troops have been able to partially compensate for a lack of combined arms effectiveness by sheer manpower and a willingness to accept high casualties. It is true that many of Iran's tactical failures were caused by a lack of armored mobility and firepower and the logistics equipment necessary to exploit their initial successes with infantry and "human wave" attacks. Many of Iran's infantry failures, however, have been the result of poor command and tactics rather than the lack of combined arms, and virtually all Iranian infantry attacks have inflicted serious casualties on their far better armed Iraqi opponents.

Dismounted or unsupported infantry has been particularly effective in the wars under study in the defense of good terrain and urban areas. This is hardly a new phenomenon, but one fairly interesting insight can be drawn: troops with rather mediocre training and simple weapons have consistently been seen to perform effective defensive infantry roles against far better equipped and more sophisticated opponents. This occurred in Iran, Lebanon, and Afghanistan.

Tanks

It is interesting to note that there was some doubt as to the future of the tank in the immediate aftermath of the 1973 war. Subsequent conflicts, however, have shown that the tank remains an important and useful element of combat power in a variety of circumstances. The IDF's problem with tanks in 1973 owed more to the misuse of armor and the lack of adequate combined arms support than to any basic change in tank vulnerability.

One of the key lessons of the four wars in which tanks were employed is that proper C^3/BM, tactics, support, recovery, and repair capabilities were generally more important than the technical differences in tank types and performance. Differences in tank armor, mobility, and firepower do not seem to have influenced the outcome of a single major battle or conflict. All of the battles involving main battle tanks—whether Chieftain, Merkava, M-48, M-60, T-62, and/or T-72—were fought under conditions in which each side's tactical skill was more important than technical performance.

Recovery and repair capability were probably as important a technical capability as mobility and firepower. The IDF vastly increased its effective tank strength in 1973 through its ability to rapidly recover and repair its tanks and exhibited similar skills in

1982. In contrast, Iran, Iraq, and Syria rarely repaired or recovered tanks, and some reports indicate that as many Iraqi and Iranian tanks were lost to abandonment after minor hits, breakdowns, and fuel and ammunition supply problems as to true tank kills.

It is also clear that the continued effectiveness of the tanks on the modern battlefield does depend upon the three classic factors shaping armor development: maneuverability, firepower, and protection. Significant improvements in all these factors have occurred since 1973, and these have generally offset the increases in the effectiveness of anti-tank weaponry. The Soviet-made T-72 and the Israeli Merkava have had the most significant advances in tank protection, and the cumulative experience in recent fighting has indicated that this protection did increase their survivability over competing tanks.

Indeed, some Soviet tanks now have so much protective armor that serious concern has arisen about the ability of American weapons to penetrate that armor. This question was partially answered in Lebanon, where the Merkava tanks proved that a shell fired from the standard NATO 105-mm tank gun could penetrate the frontal armor of a T-72 tank. This is a significant lesson, although the reactive armor that has since been added to the T-64 and T-72, plus new Soviet developments such as the T-80 and other future Soviet tanks, seem to have changed this equation. Like NATO, the Soviet bloc may adopt composite armor (sometimes called Chobham armor after the area where it was developed in the United Kingdom). This armor involves laminates of armor separated by ceramics, aluminum, plastics, or carbon fibre. It at least doubles the resistance of a vehicle to a high-explosive anti-tank (HEAT) charge, as compared to an equal weight of steel. The armor can be used for the entire tank or for its more vulnerable areas. As composite armor improves, the current anti-tank weapons in Third World inventories will become less useful. In any case, the classic elements of tank performance continue to be important, along with the added elements of training, maintainability, recoverability, and repairability.

Some other useful lessons regarding the role of armor within limited armed conflicts relate to mountain and urban warfare. In Lebanon and Afghanistan, tanks were forced to fight in mountains with mixed results. It is clear that tanks can operate in such an environment, but they have proved to be much more vulnerable, and they need guns capable of high elevations, specialized anti-personnel rounds, and improved visibility and target acquisition capability. Without these characteristics, tanks are unsuited for mountain warfare.

Further, even when tanks can be used in the mountains, other systems may perform similar tasks more effectively. Several problems seem to consistently emerge during armored warfare in mountain areas. For example, there are many places in mountainous areas where tanks cannot go because of their bulk and structure. Even when tanks are able to operate, they are often vulnerable and channelized. Using tanks in mountainous areas can be a costly and wasteful enterprise. This vulnerability offers the West an important defensive option, but it also indicates that small Western forces could rapidly lose the comparatively small number of tanks they could deploy if they were attacked by local forces equipped with anti-tank weapons.

The problem of urban warfare is equally severe. Iraq could not employ its armor in Iranian cities and was forced to pull it back from Khorramshar and send in mechanized infantry. Israel could not employ tanks successfully in the Egyptian cities across the Suez in 1973 and did not risk intensive tank combat in Beirut. Israel lost significant numbers of tanks and other AFVs during its push through other built-up areas.

The critical technical problems in armor proved to be vulnerability imposed by the inability to maneuver and take advantage of the range of the main gun, problems in gun elevation and the limited effective lethality of the tank's main armament against scattered well-hidden infantry with anti-tank weapons, and the lack of visibility and target acquisition capability. These problems do not prohibit tank combat in built-up areas. Indeed, for all the real and potential losses in recent wars, the tank often represented the least vulnerable way of delivering direct firepower, particularly when screened by suitable amounts of infantry. They did, however, greatly reduce the value of tanks, particularly when nations like Iraq and Israel could not afford the political consequences of large-scale casualties.

These problems highlight the potential value of finding substitutes for tanks in mountain and urban warfare. The Soviet experience in Afghanistan illustrated that rapid-fire anti-aircraft systems can be used quite effectively against guerrilla forces operating in the field. AA guns have often been used by the Soviets as effective substitutes for tanks. Israel also seems to have made effective use of its Vulcan AA guns under somewhat similar circumstances. This may be a worthwhile example for Western defense planners to consider, since the key requirement has been sheer volume of suppressive direct fire and not accurate anti-armor capability.

The questions remain (a) what technical advances can best provide tanks with suitable munitions, fire control, elevation, and target visibility and target acquisition capability for mountain and urban warfare? and (b) how can a lower-cost easy-to-transport substitute for these missions be found? There are no easy answers to these questions—which can be dealt with only through extensive operations research and field trials—although improved vertical visibility, gun elevation, wider angle sights, and specialized urban and mountain anti-personnel munitions are obvious potential solutions.

The potential value of such research cannot be overemphasized. Mountain and urban warfare have proved to be as historically important as the classic tank battles of the Sinai, and such battles are far more likely to characterize Western combat in the northern Gulf, Levant, the Yemens, and most Red Sea contingencies than desert warfare. There is a good case for a dedicated high-technology combat vehicle for such missions. Such a vehicle would have to be suitable for combat at relatively short ranges, have excellent visibility and advanced targeting aids, use some form of advanced armor, combine area anti-infantry and point-fire anti-barrier capability, and allow for rapid evacuation and easy recovery. It might well be a classic light tank and/or AFV.

Other Armored Vehicles

Armored personnel carriers were also of critical importance in most of the conflicts under study, particularly because each of these conflicts was shaped as much by infantry as by any other combat arm. The importance of the infantry fighting vehicle is underscored by the fact that it was a key means of providing transportation and direct firepower support for infantry in four of these five wars.

At the same time, two key problems appeared on a recurring basis in all of the APCs and MICVs that participated in the conflicts under examination. These problems were an unacceptably high level of vulnerability and ineffective or insufficient firepower.

The American-built M-113 APC is a good example. The M-113 proved particularly vulnerable. While it proved to be far better in terms of armor, horsepower, maintenance, and overhead protection than the World War II vintage half-tracks used in 1973, the 1982 fighting in Lebanon showed the M-113 had too little armor, too high a profile, and too little firepower. The 0.5-inch Browning heavy machine gun occasionally mounted on these systems proved particularly inadequate. The use of this relatively low-powered weapon required one crew member to expose himself out of the vehicle. Modern combat requires a turret, longer ranges, and either more penetrating capability or much higher volumes of suppressive fire.

Israel originally adopted the M-113 nickname of "armored taxi" but changed it to "armored coffin" after 1982 because of the vehicle's vulnerability to anti-tank systems. One clear lesson of the limited armed conflicts under consideration is the need to phase the M-113 and similar systems out of the inventory of battlefield maneuver units and rapidly replace them with a more survivable and combat-effective system.

The performance of the M-113 has, however, been overcriticized because of the use of aluminum alloy in its armor. This armor is also being applied to the new Bradley M-2 and M-3 infantry fighting vehicles, although the M-2 and M-3 have been designed to be resistant to .50 caliber machine guns, blast mines, and 155-mm airbursts. There is no question that such armor can increase casualties because of its tendency to spall, but it does not really "burn" when penetrated by HEAT rounds.

This raises the issue of whether or not special coatings, additional armor, and other protective and modification technology can be developed that can modify the M-113 and similar vehicles. Israel has developed a composite armor add-on for the M-113 that it used with some success in 1982 and is now fitting to additional vehicles. In addition, Israel may now be adding reactive armor. This cannot correct for the high profile and firepower, visibility, and evacuability defects of the M-113, but it might be of major value in making the M-113 a more survivable battle taxi and off-road vehicle away from the forward combat area. Even more advanced add-on armor might, however, allow Western forces to upgrade better designed APC/MICVs and eliminate the extremely high cost of procuring new systems to meet each advance in anti-armored warfare. In fact, a vehicle with modular improvement in protection, firepower, C^3, and targeting capability may ultimately be the only way to allow the APC/MICV to compete cost-effectively with improvements in ATGMs and other battlefield weapons and adapt quickly to different combat conditions and climates.

Although the Soviet BTR-60 and BTR-70 have not proved to be more effective than the M-113, the Soviet-made BMPs and BMDs, which have seen action in Afghanistan and the Middle East, do seem to have been more effective systems than the M-113 or similar APCs. They still, however, have serious deficiencies. They have experienced significant problems with maintenance, and breakdowns tended to be frequent in such areas as the mountains of Afghanistan. Other problems relating to the BMP involve the system's extensive firepower. While this firepower makes it a drastic improvement over American APCs, its defenses are by no means flawless. The design of the vehicle requires the driver to fire the SAGGER system and renders the system much less effective when the vehicle is on the move. Furthermore, firing ports which enable troops to fire from within the vehicle do not alter the fact that most modern anti-armor systems have longer ranges than infantry assault rifles.

Another problem with the BMP and BMD may owe as much to tactics and psychology as to its technical characteristics. This involves the reluctance of troops to leave the vehicle and fight in a dismounted mode. By structuring the system with firing ports and encouraging their use, the Soviets have created an environment in which tactical situations that require dismounted action lead to a "war wagon" mentality and behavior that degrades effectiveness and increases casualties. In addition, the firing ports are so small in all but the most recent Soviet vehicles that it is almost impossible to aim a rifle accurately, and the additional firepower provided by these firing ports results in little more than random fire for effect. This does not mean that the U.S. should take comfort in the fact that Soviet APCs have firing ports or that the U.S. should not stress the need for these assets in conjunction with its own systems in the future. What this does mean is that the firing ports have been used in situations in which such use was not appropriate. No aspect of a weapons system will work well if it is misused.

The IDF's experience with the Merkava and M-113 has also shown that rapid evacuability is critical in any armored vehicle. At the same time, none of the APC/MICVs used in the five wars under study could provide the surge firepower needed in close combat (and sometimes available from AA guns), a fully effective anti-tank weapon for situations involving meeting engagements, and a suitable mix of visibility and ability to fight infantry from within the vehicle. These improvements do not involve complicated technical problems and need to be solved in some of the West's new APVs. A brief examination of new Western vehicles indicates, however, that they lack such advances and raises continuing questions regarding their suitability in the face of the urban and mountain warfare issues discussed earlier.

Anti-Armor and Surface-to-Surface PGMs

One of the more interesting lessons that has emerged with regard to anti-armor weapons involved in the conflicts under study is that low-cost, easy-to-operate rocket launchers can often be as effective as an equal investment in fewer high-cost, difficult-to-operate PGMs. The large number of infantry available, the short engagement ranges common in mountain and built-up area warfare, and the effectiveness of Soviet rocket launchers have combined to make such light anti-tank weapons a key threat. In fact, the impact of RPGs may be even greater than most forces estimate, since many APC and tank commanders trained to expect attack by PGMs assumed that this was what happened when they were hit by RPGs or other similar weapons.

Accordingly, the West cannot write off the modest RPG too quickly in favor of the more elaborate anti-armor PGMs. RPGs are simple, portable, and inexpensive and have sufficient range, accuracy, and armor penetration to make them a real threat to a wide variety of tactical vehicles, including some tanks. They can also be used at short range, unlike many PGMs that have missiles that are stabilized only after they have been in flight over a significant amount of territory. In fact, on the basis of tanks and APVs killed, RPG technology has proved to be as important as that of tanks and ATGMs.

Additionally, RPGs are weapons that the United States can expect to see on future Third World battlefields. They are affordable and relatively easy to copy and repair. Iranian defense officials, for example, claim that they have established facilities to repair the RPG-7, which has played an important role in the Iran-Iraq War.[1] It is therefore vital not to dismiss these weapons as obsolete or ineffective when compared to anti-armor PGMs.

The utility of RPGs and light anti-tank weapons does not, however, mean that anti-armor PGMs do not play a critical role on low-intensity and Third World battlefields. RPGs have very marginal effectiveness against well-armored main battle tanks. Every force equipped with ATGMs has been able to exploit their added range and accuracy as well as use them against many other forms of hard targets. This use of ATGMs was, in fact, so important that it highlights the need to design ATGMs to kill all hardpoint targets and not just armor. Nations such as Egypt, Syria, and Iran were also able to use ATGMs as a substitute for tanks as long as they fought defensively in terrain with suitable cover and could not be outflanked or suppressed by artillery fire.

More generally, the interviews and writings of the forces engaged strongly indicate that ease of training and operation, low firing signatories, and crew cover of some kind are more important in ATGM design than range, night vision, and sighting. In fact, many complaints have emerged about the inability to use most ATGMs at ranges of less than 100 meters while virtually none have emerged about the difficulties of achieving kills over 1,500 meters. Ease of proliferation of large numbers of systems seems to be the dominant demand growing out of the wars under study, although considerable comment has emerged regarding the desire for an anti-personnel round and more capability in killing bunkers and other hard targets. This desire for proliferation will present problems, however, if tanks with advanced armor such as the M-1 and the improved T-72 are deployed to the

Third World. Existing ATGMs cannot penetrate the frontal armor of these tanks and will have to be replaced with more sophisticated or higher-cost replacements.

Tube Artillery and Multiple Rocket Launchers

Several key insights relating to artillery have been discussed under combined arms, but a review of a wide range of the artillery engagements in the wars under study validates the need for systems such as the MRLs, which can provide large amounts of surge firepower with great accuracy. They also validate the need for smart submunitions and minelets which would increase initial kills and paralyze or cripple rapid dispersal and the search for cover.

Recent conflicts confirm previous indicators that artillery fire has most of its effect in the first one to three minutes of engagement. Follow-up fire by tube weapons firing ordinary ammunition often had little killing effect and rarely had significant tactical effect, although it should be noted that little use was made of "rolling barrage" techniques to exploit mass tube artillery fire in direct support of advancing maneuver units—a technique that is probably beyond the C^3I/BM capabilities of Third World nations and that Israel and the USSR lacked the target mix to employ.

The multiple rocket launcher was the most effective area weapon in the limited conflicts under examination. The range, firepower, and coverage of the multiple rocket launcher make it an ideal weapon for attacking large numbers of moving troops. It has the same lethality in this mode as large numbers of artillery pieces which usually have much shorter range. It should be understood, however, that in most of the instances where MRLs were used, they were used to batter hostile forces in dug-in, built-up, or rough terrain positions. They were effective in this role, but MRLs were rarely used to bring down fire on top of enemy troops in the field seeking quick and expedient ways to slow down enemy offensives.

Turning to counterbattery fire, it is interesting to note that there are remarkably few instances in which any force on any side observed that it suffered significantly from counterbattery fire. The only major exception was Israeli forces in the Sinai in 1973, where Israel lacked mobile support with cross-terrain capability for its artillery and Egypt captured maps showing Israel's preplanned artillery locations. Even then, the effects of Egyptian fire were more suppressive than lethal. In the other conflicts under study, artillery was either so well dug-in or so mobile that counterartillery fire had only a marginal suppressive effect. Reports of successful counterbattery kills by the firing artillery unit were almost invariably incorrect. Even most accounts of successful suppression seem false and are not reflected in the reports of the forces being attacked. The artillery units in question moved or halted fire for other tactical reasons.

This failure of counterbattery fire reflects long-standing problems in lethality, targeting, rates of fire, and the lack of technical sophistication in many of the forces involved. It is interesting to note, however, that there is little indication that Israel, which had very sophisticated counterbattery radars and RPVs, made effective use of such systems, and Iraq came to regard its Soviet-supplied equipment as virtually useless. It is not clear whether this was the result of operational failing or, as seems likely, a tendency to overestimate both retargeting capability and lethality against well-positioned or dug-in artillery.

Surface-to-Surface Rockets and Missiles

Surface-to-surface rockets and missiles armed with conventional warheads were used in only two of the conflicts under study. In both conflicts, they did not inflict damage significant enough to make a strategic impact on the military situation. The chief utility of such weapons was to:

1. build up domestic morale by striking at the enemy in a very visible way (Iraqi missile launches were, for example, televised);
2. inflict terror on local populations, although the real-world result was invariably to solidify opposition to the adversary attempting to use rockets and missiles in this way; and
3. signal an intention to escalate a conflict by using a weapons system that can also be used with chemical or nuclear warheads.

No surface-to-surface rocket or missile was used to effectively disorganize army staging areas or strike rear-area troops in accordance with the designated purpose of these weapons. The targeting and C^3I/BM technology was not available to any of the forces in question, except possibly Israel, for such operations. Israel, however, seems to have concentrated on using its MRLs/C^3/BM systems to hit at SAM sites or support its units in combat.

Mines and Barriers

The use of land mines in the limited armed conflicts had mixed results. Mines and barriers did inflict casualties and slowed down various advances. Mines also proved hard to remove. In some cases, such as in Afghanistan or the Falklands, nonmetalic mines presented serious detection problems. Minefields never, however, proved impassable, and they normally could be overcome within hours by a relatively determined force. If by no other means, they could be cleared by the use of artillery or saturation attacks by infantry. Mines represented a barrier but provided only minor delay and harrassment. They could not halt a major attack unless combined with other, and far more dominant, forms of defense; and they never succeeded in being a prolonged barrier to infiltration and infantry assault.

The lack of Western countermine warfare technology may, however, present problems for U.S. forces in general and USCENTCOM in particular. This technology has traditionally been a low priority for the United States, as shown by the Army's continued lack of interest in procuring new systems for either detecting or neutralizing enemy mines.[2]

Another important lesson that emerges from recent limited armed conflicts is the importance of engineering barriers in inhibiting enemy movement and in channeling attacking troops. Such barriers were particularly important during the Iran-Iraq War, where a mix of fortified barriers, rapid road construction, deliberate flooding, and other uses of barriers proved extremely effective on both sides. In general, "passive" barriers and effective use of combat and civil engineering resources proved to be far more effective than mines. They will almost certainly be a major factor in future low-level wars.

All-Weather and Night Target Acquisition Systems

Night combat occurred in all of the conflicts under examination. Night vision and night targeting devices were useful or would have been useful in most of the combat operations considered. In fact, it is interesting that in several conflicts, the less sophisticated combatant had some of the most sophisticated weaponry. In 1973, Egypt and Syria had more sophisticated night vision devices than Israel. In 1982, the Argentines had more modern night vision devices than the British. Both Israel and Britain managed to overcome these disadvantages through various combinations of luck and planning. For example, the Israelis were particularly lucky in 1973 when the death of a Syrian general on the Golan Heights delayed a major night attack for which the Israelis were not prepared and caused it to take place the following morning.

It is also interesting to note that the USSR made extensive use of search lights rather than night vision systems in Afghanistan and that Iraq still lacked adequate advanced night vision systems in the sixth year of the war and in spite of extensive problems with Iranian night attacks.[3] It is unclear why this Iraqi failure occurred. The Soviet troops in Afghanistan seemed to lack a night surveillance and detection system as distinquished from individual night vision devices, IR searchlights, and other night vision aids for its tanks. In general, wide area night coverage which was immune to flare or flash blinding and allowed prolonged coverage was needed and lacking in all of the conflicts under study.

The potential value of the proper mix of night vision devices has, therefore, been indicated as much by the effects of its absence as by its presence. This is particularly true of the absence of some integrated night surveillance system with extensive area coverage. It is still clear, however, that the outcome of future combat could be decisively affected by the quantity and quality of night vision devices.

Anti-Aircraft Artillery

A wide variety of SHORADS, including anti-aircraft guns and shoulderfired missiles, perfomed well in the conflicts under study. While precise figures are lacking, it seems likely that about half the ground kills of aircraft and helicopters in the wars under study have come from unsophisticated anti-aircraft machine guns or other unguided automatic weapons used in "curtain fire" or area fire modes. This fact was disguised in the 1973 war by a tendency to credit gun kills or damage to IDF aircraft to the ZSU-23-4. Actually, these guns were present only in small numbers and later proved not to have been deployed in the area involved. In later conflicts, it is clear that the proliferation of large numbers of low-cost, unguided AA guns and automatic weapons have dominated hits/kills and combined with the deployment of large numbers of low-cost systems like the SA-7 to degrade the effectiveness of low-altitude sorties.

The use of rapid-fire anti-aircraft guns in dual-purpose roles is of particular significance. Their effectiveness in ground combat in mountain urban areas was also noteworthy, and this effectiveness has clear implications for the West. In particular, MICVs armed with anti-aircraft guns have considerable potential for Western forces that might be forced into fighting in mountain and built-up areas. There is a clear need for a cheap, unguided AA cannon that can be used for both air defense and rapid and effective neutralization of centers of resistance within urban areas.

This suggests a need for more and better dual-purpose anti-aircraft guns which are organic to Western military units at a variety of levels.

It is important that guns be stressed to an even greater extent than other forms of SHORADS because of the dual-purpose nature of these weapons. These weapons have proven themselves to be useful in all of the conflicts under study. Furthermore, they have proven especially effective in urban areas (see the chapter on Lebanon in Volume 1) and mountainous areas (see the chapter on Afghanistan in this volume), where they have compensated for the deficiencies of other systems, including tanks.

This is a particular problem for the U.S. in that there are only 379 towed and 221 self-propelled Vulcan systems in the U.S. Army inventory. These numbers are far too low and reflect the high cost of the Vulcan weapons system.[4] Furthermore, the Sergeant York DIVAD vehicles which are replacing the Vulcans are much larger and less transportable than their predecessors.[5] It is unclear whether other Western forces are much better equipped, and this may pose a serious problem for NATO out-of-area operations.

Another interesting point about the dual-purpose anti-aircraft gun relates to the increasing importance of helicopters. As helicopters come into a more decisive role on the battlefield, it will be important to maintain effective countermeasures for dealing with these systems. The presence of more dual-purpose guns within Western and friendly forces could help to address this threat and prepare those same forces for operations in built-up areas or mountainous terrain. The possibility of better preparing U.S. and other friendly forces for operations in urban environments is of course especially significant, as this type of combat generally produces extremely high casualties.

Surface-to-Air Missiles

Some precision guided anti-aircraft weapons also performed well in the conflicts under examination, although none came close to their theoretical kill probability. These surface-to-air missiles had three basic types of impact on the combat in which they were involved: (1) shooting down hostile aircraft, (2) damaging hostile aircraft to the point that they could not perform assigned missions, and (3) interrupting an aircraft's attack pattern by causing it to take evasive action. The importance of these latter two functions is often overlooked because of the tendency to focus on kills rather than overall combat effects.

It is significant that light and relatively low performance systems like the SA-7 and SA-7B, Blowpipe, and Rapier were often employed effectively against modern aircraft flown by well-trained pilots. Soviet, Israeli, British, and Israeli-trained Argentine pilots were all tested against anti-aircraft PGMs in the limited armed conflicts under examination. Many American-trained Iranian pilots also had to deal with ground-launched PGMs. Only the Israelis in 1982 were able to use maneuver countermeasures such as flares and active suppression to provide a high degree of operational immunity to attack. After the Soviets withdrew from Afghanistan in 1989, both they and the Republic of Afghanistan greatly improved their countermeasures.

Heavier SAMs were far less effective than most experts predicted after the 1973 war. This seems to have been as much a human factors problem as a problem in technology. In all cases except the Falklands war, the forces engaged either lacked the training and C³I assets to properly use their SAMs or did not have the most modern systems available. Iran and Iraq, for example, achieved remarkably poor hit rates with their Hawks, SA-2s, SA-3s, SA-6s, and Rolands. Egypt and Syria did achieve considerable success in 1973, but Syria lost virtually all its major systems in 1982. The weapons utilized were not the most modern available. Line-of-sight weapons, or weapons with infrared guidance such as the Blowpipe, SA-7, Grail, and the U.S. Redeye, were the most important systems on the battlefields of the four most recent wars. Newer weapons such as the Stinger were associated only with the Falklands and Afghan conflicts. Israel, which has such systems, did not need to use them in the 1982 war in Lebanon, although they could have been helpful against attacking helicopters.

Suppression of Ground- and Sea-Based
Air Defenses

Every conflict under study involved a major struggle between air forces and ground- and sea-based air defenses, although the various conflicts had very different results. In 1973, Israeli ground forces had to open up gaps in the main Egyptian SAM belt before air suppression became effective. In Afghanistan, the Soviets had to deal with a relatively minor threat from guns and SA-7s. Iran and Iraq were not able to use their massive medium and heavy SAM defenses effectively, and their aircraft had to deal largely with AA guns and SA-7 variants. In 1982, Israel fought the most successful SAM suppression battle in modern history in Operation Peace for Galilee. Britain and Argentina fought the first battle between an air force and modern shipborne air and cruise missile defenses. Each case illustrates how delicate the balance can be between the dominance of air power and that of ground- or sea-based defenses as well as the critical impact of different levels of tactics, C³I, technology, and training.

Several lessons emerge from this complex mix of efforts at SAM suppression. The first such lesson is that improvements in air defense technology have shifted the priorities attached to counter–air defense or SAM suppression efforts. This shift grew out of Israel's experience in the October 1973 war, and the shift to an Israeli emphasis on SAM suppression was validated by the Lebanon 1982 conflict. Israel's success in 1982 has given the suppression of SAM systems further priority, especially against Third World countries that have acquired air defense missile systems.

The second lesson is that anti-radar missiles and electronic countermeasures will probably not be enough against a moderately well trained opponent. The Israeli tactics employed in destroying all of the SAM sites in Lebanon in 1982 strongly suggest that a high-technology combined arms approach may be the most cost-effective and reliable approach to this mission. This needs much more examination given the Western tendency to concentrate on anti-radiation missiles and ECM.

Air-to-Air Combat

The Soviet invasion of Afghanistan is the only conflict that did not involve air-to-air combat. The others revealed the critical importance of advanced air-to-air missiles, avionics, C^3I, tactics, and training. Each of the other four conflicts showed that the outcome of aerial combat is increasingly a function of advanced, sophisticated computer technology incorporated in radar, guidance, computer interface, C^3, and EW assets.

This suggests that air combat mission effectiveness will increasingly move away from the traditional visual dogfight and that the effectiveness of fighters will steadily become a function of the proper use of (a) advanced air-to-air missiles, (b) the associated avionics for on-board and weapon tracking and guidance, and (c) the supporting $BM/C^3I/EW$ system. The intensive technical training of pilots and ground personnel that are required to fly, command, control, and communicate with sophisticated aircraft in a hostile, multiple-threat environment will be equally important.

A steady shift toward technology-dominated air combat seems to have occurred between the 1973 Arab-Israeli conflict and the 1982 Lebanon and Falklands conflicts, where air-to-air missiles and associated avionics made decisive contributions. These experiences suggest that close air combat will play a steadily diminishing role in future aerial conflicts. Although the cannon scored a significant number of hits/kills in the October 1973 and 1982 Lebanon wars, the trend has clearly favored the air-to-air missile.

This trend also contradicts the American experience in Vietnam, where the F-4 was refitted with the Vulcan cannon after the unsuccessful use of air-to-air missiles, i.e., early versions of the Falcon and the Sidewinder. In fairness to these weapons systems, however, it should be noted that mass air combat was not a major part of the Vietnam War. Aerial encounters were relatively rare, and Vietnam conducted a selective "slash and run" approach to combat. More importantly, the rapid leaps in computer technology have since had a counterpart in advances in missile systems and avionics. Today's weapons have far more sophistication and capability.

Close Air Support

All five conflicts involved extensive close air support (CAS) activity. In each case, however, CAS activity had far less impact on the ground battle than either the participants or the outside observers anticipated. This was partly the result of inadequate target acquisiton, C^3I, training, and munitions lethality. It also, however, was the result of the almost universal failure to insist on ruthlessly realistic operations research and combined arms exercises, testing, and evaluation before combat. Air forces seem almost congenitally incapable of honestly assessing and improving their capabilities in these areas.

It is particularly notable that the Israelis continued to have problems in coordinating and executing concentrated air support attacks in the 1982 campaign in Lebanon in spite of years of effort to correct the weaknesses exposed in 1973. This performance was partly a function of the ad hoc nature of attack required by close air support (targets tend to vary widely over terrain and battle circumstances and according to differing requirements of weapons and logistics commitments, pilot performance, and C^3 coordination).

Ironically, the key lesson as to how the West might counter these problems is probably the Israeli suppression of the SAM systems in Lebanon in 1982. Although this operation was not a close air support mission, it indicates that the technology for effective close air support missions now exists if sufficient assets are brought to bear. This is evidenced in the extensive and successful use of C^3 support systems, sophisticated new computers, and tracking systems, including radars and PRVs providing near–real-time data to command centers. These systems facilitated the necessary coordination between various and disparate support elements in a complex system in a period of intense crisis.

On the other hand, the SAM suppression mission has the distinct advantage of allowing a tailored planning effort for air strikes against specific targets. In addition, training exercises can be designed to meet specific battle needs, such as the detailed attributes of the target environment, special timing requirements, and coordination between C^3 assets. New and dedicated technologies will probably be needed to deal with most other ground force targets. The mix of emerging technologies now under examination in NATO, which combines advanced real-time targeting with smart area munitions, may be the answer. These technologies must be coupled, however, to dedicated C^3I systems and adequate planning, training, and organization.

Interdiction and Long-Range Air Attack

Each of the five conflicts have revealed slightly different lessons about air interdiction and long-range bombing attacks. All, however, reveal some common targeting, munitions lethality, damage assessment, and tactical problems. In general, long-range bombing rarely had anything approaching the anticipated effectiveness. In fact, interdiction and long-range air attacks played a prominent or decisive role in only two conflicts. The first was in 1973, when the Israeli Air Force was compelled to launch desperate long-range bombing efforts to force Syria to halt its armored advance on the Golan Heights. It seems doubtful from Syrian comments since the war that it had any such effect. More recently in Afghanistan, the Soviet Union utilized long-range bombers to deny the guerrillas an economic and social base in the villages. This "terrorist" campaign had the effect of displacing hundreds of thousands of Afghans who either became foreign refugees (e.g., in Pakistan or Iran) or fled to the cities, which were under Republic of Afghanistan control.

The technology employed in the interdiction or long-range bombing role has improved since the October 1973 war. This is especially the case in terms of navigation, C^3 apparatus, on-board radar and threat assessment instruments. However, it is clear that even more accurate and effective targeting systems and weapons need to be developed and deployed for "low-level wars" as well as for NATO. Examples of the problems to be solved are evident in every war: The British were barely able to hit the runway at Port Stanley once during their attacks with Vulcan bombers. The Soviets did not prove particularly adept at accurate bombing in the carpet bombing campaign in Afganistan. Neither Iraq nor Iran showed much competence in interdiction and long-range bombing, although the Iraqis did destroy some factories early in the war. Certainly, the Iraq campaign against Iranian shipping and Kharg Island was far less successful than most experts predicted. More recently, the USAF and U.S. Navy must acknowledge considerable margins of error in their bombing efforts in Grenada, Lebanon, and Libya.

It is particularly clear that much more effort needs to be expended in developing improved versions of such air-to-ground weapons as Shrike and anti-runway weapons such as the new French Durandel. In addition, it is clear that deploying such weapons does little good if air crews are not trained to use them in realistic exercises. This lack of training may help explain the British failure to use the Shrike effectively in the Falklands. On the other hand, an effective anti-radar missile that can home adequately after the radar transmission has been shut off has yet to be developed.

A further dimension of interdiction and long-range bombing missions involves the need for improved planning, targeting, and C^3I/BM. Many missions in low-level wars will involve strikes at fixed targets that can be targeted far in advance of a conflict. The Israeli air force is particularly adept in such advanced target analysis, and a key component of consistently smooth execution of missions is thoroughness of intelligence, planning, and training. This capability was demonstrated in 1982 in Lebanon in suppression of the SAM sites. Unfortunately, targets will not always be in fixed sites and, as in the case of the Egyptian airbases in 1973, they will not always be vulnerable to attack tactics used in the "last" war.

The most effective use of interdiction attacks in the wars under study has been against naval targets. The sinking of the HMS *Sheffield* and the HMS *Atlantic Conveyor* in the Falklands War are reiterated in the lesson provided by the sinking of the Israeli destroyer *Eilat* in 1970: Large surface ships are extremely vulnerable to attacks by anti-ship tactical missiles. The defensive lesson is that surface ships and other targets, i.e., airbases, need as much active air defense and passive protection, i.e., ECM, as necessary.

Air Reconnaissance, C^3, IFF, and AC&W

Many of the issues regarding reconnaissance, C^3I, IFF, and AC&W have been discussed in the previous operational categories. At the same time, each conflict reinforces the need for integrated C^3I/AC&W/IFF. Further, each of the five wars shows that a mix of highly advanced reconnaissance, C^3I, IFF, and AC&W technology is well worth its high cost. In one case, the Falklands War, the lack of a British capability in one single area—continuous airborne early warning—was nearly decisive in determining the outcome of the war. As it happened, the British had no effective means to detect a low-level attack on their fleet. They had to rely on "close in" air defense, and luck played a critical role in limiting ship losses.

In Afghanistan, Soviet aerial reconnaissance seems to have failed from a lack of adequate sensors. Reconnaissance could not be expected to be effective in locating the guerrilla enemy. Individuals and groups could only occasionally be glimpsed in exposed positions, and most trail networks and caravans are visible from the air only during the day in fair weather. In the Iran-Iraq War, the lack of adequate reconnaissance was commensurate with the low level of technical prowess shown by both sides. The Iranians were especially hindered by a lack of aerial platforms from which to conduct reconnaissance. Although in the early stages of the war the F-14 was utilized in a "Mini-AWACS" role, the Iranians did not appear to have a reliable, ongoing reconnaissance or an airborne early warning capability. Although Iraqi capabilities were better in this regard, their lack of planning and intelligence in the early stages of the war also suggests a lack of appreciation of the role of reconnaissance and certain technical gaps.

In contrast, the 1982 Lebanon war marks a high-water mark in the successful use of sophisticated reconnaissance and C^3I, IFF, and AC&W systems throughout the war. Israel showed it can be critical to employ the newest technical developments in each area. The Israeli experience also suggests that a second- or third-level power could conceivably develop some very sophisticated, world-class technology with the help of the United States.

Helicopters

Every conflict made extensive use of combat and support helicopters. Each war also indicates, however, that the impact of the helicopter is highly dependent on tactics, the availability of advanced helicopter technology and munitions, and the availability of modern air defense weapons to the opposing side. The race between helicopter effectiveness and countermeasures is, and has been, a close one.

The combat helicopter is clearly becoming more important, but its effectiveness in the wars under study was affected by several different factors. The first is the need for air superiority on the part of the force utilizing the helicopter. In the 1973 war, for example, the Israeli air force shot down fourteen helicopters loaded with Egyptian commandos during the opening stage of the conflict. This upset efforts to use special troops to disrupt Israeli reinforcement operations. A second major factor shaping the success of helicopter operations was the absence of a high density of SHORADS within the enemy order of battle. SHORADS can be very effective against combat helicopters, although this can be alleviated through the use of pop-up tactics. Helicopters that linger over the battlefield place themselves in extreme danger.

More generally, the helicopter usually proved superior to fixed-wing aircraft in striking at dispersed and infantry ground targets and in providing close air support for ground forces. This seems to have been as much the result of a more responsive chain of command and the ability to directly assign and target sorties as anything else. The helicopters were generally under much tighter army control and much more responsive to combat commanders, although their loiter capability, slow speeds, and ability to fly nap-of-the-earth tactics give helicopters a natural advantage. Bringing fighter aircraft into a target at precisely the right time, designating targets, and killing while they are still exposed poses a problem that the IDF, USSR, and the Third World forces under study have not solved either in terms of C^3I/BM or munitions lethality.

The helicopter offers a partial solution to this problem without highly expensive and complex C^3I/BM systems, although every side using combat helicopters would have benefited from an effective forward-area helicopter air control system at the brigade or division level.

The steady increase in direct-fire weaponry and loiter time for helicopters has also steadily improved the killing capability of such forces. Further, the helicopter offered many of the forces involved in the wars under study an effective means of bypassing built-up areas and barriers, countering terrain, and maneuvering where armor was forced into positional warfare, although Iran and Iraq scarcely exploited the full potential of helicopters in this regard. All sides would also have benefited greatly from the improved troop life and combat support helicopters now coming into service in the U.S. and Soviet forces.

At the same time, it seems clear from the experience of the forces engaged that every possible measure needs to be taken to improve the protection and survivability of such helicopters, that improved armament has second priority, and that improved avionics has third priority. Although it is difficult to project the experience of the conflicts to all future conflicts (Britain clearly needed sophisticated C^3 and navigation systems in the Falklands), survivability and numbers generally were more important than such matters as firepower and night and poor weather warfare capability.

In at least two of the wars, Afghanistan and the Falklands, the nature and structure of warfare would have been decidedly different without the helicopter. The Soviet experience in Afghanistan parallels that of the U.S. in Vietnam in that it indicates that the helicopter can provide the firepower, mobility, and versatility to counter a guerrilla opponent. Without the attack helicopter and the Mi-8 Hip and other helicopters used to transport airmobile troops and cargo, the Soviets would have been in a much more untenable position in Afghanistan during the first stages of the conflict. As the subsequent deployment of Stinger missiles demonstrated, however, heliborne mobility is itself extremely vulnerable to ground forces equipped with sophisticated air-to-ground missiles.

The helicopters in the Falklands proved vital in providing overall mobility and especially in ship-to-shore operations. The war in the Falklands could probably not have been fought and certainly could not have been easily won by the British unless they had had helicopters to ferry men and equipment from ship to ship, ship to shore, and in land operations all the way to Port Stanley. The potential utility and importance of the heavy transport helicopter was also demonstrated after the loss of three (of four) Chinook helicopters on the *Atlantic Conveyor*. The single surviving Chinook was utilized to carry an incredible variety and number of loads of men and equipment, several times surpassing the aircraft's recommended limits.

On the negative side, helicopters in the Falklands demonstrated another general lesson: Light helicopters are extremely vulnerable to enemy fighters and SAMs. This reputation for vulnerability is the main reason why the Israelis have not, heretofore, invested in a serious attack helicopter. There is no doubt, however, that the trend of future weapons development will be in the direction of tougher attack helicopters in the vein of the Mi-24 Hind and the AH-64 Apache.

Combined Operations

None of the forces under study made full use of the potential synergy of combined or land-air-naval operations. In one case—the British use of combined operations in the Falklands—these shortfalls were dictated by the terrain and by the logistic and range problems imposed on aircraft and combat helicopter operations: having to fight (a) at the far end of Britain's power projection capability, (b) in an area that did not permit mechanized warfare, and (c) under conditions that limited air power to small numbers of relatively unsophisticated Harriers. British performance otherwise reflected good combined arms operations, effective training, and high military professionalism. Although Britain was forced to improvise heavily and did not have all the elements of a modern tactical C^3I system, it was able to forge effective links between its various services. It is important to note, however, that Britain was greatly aided by the fact that Argentina's army and navy lacked the professionalism and drive of its air force. The course of fighting might have been very different if the Argentine army had fought with the same flexibility, skill, and commitment as the air force.

Israel exhibited far better combined operations capability in 1982 than in 1973, particularly in suppressing Syrian SAM defenses. It failed, however, to solve the most critical single problem in modern combined operations: creating an effective interface between offensive air artillery and maneuver units in support of the air-land battle. This was partly the result of political problems, and of the fact the Israeli defense minister was fighting a private war in a manner that deprived the IDF of effective command cohesion; it was also the result of the fact that the IDF (a) could not properly target artillery and close air support, (b) could not ensure that aircraft or artillery could strike with the proper munitions and precision, (c) experienced serious coordination and delay problems, and (d) could not always cope with the special conditions imposed by rough terrain and mountain and urban warfare. In spite of years of effort, Israel lacked both the C^3I/BM resources and combination of targeting, lethality, and munitions delivery capability necessary to implement its ambitious tactics and plans.

The IDF's key failures seem to have been that it had an exaggerated view of the lethality of current air and artillery munitions, did not fully realize the stress war puts on C^3I/BM systems, exaggerated operational accuracy in the absence of terminal homing and target designator systems, failed to consider just how much target conditions could alter from coastal plain to mountain to built-up area, and simply failed to realize how critical immediate delivery following target acquisition was to effectiveness. Air and artillery lethality was a particular problem. Syrian and PLO forces again demonstrated how quickly forces can "dig in" or disperse after the first air strike or artillery round, emphasizing the critical importance of massive initial area lethality over single precision strikes. This tends to validate the present NATO emphasis on improved C^3I/BM and smart area weapons and the experience of past wars that air force and artillery officers greatly exaggerate the effectiveness of their weapons in peacetime and underestimate the need for constant training and practice.

As for the other nations involved, all failed to adequately develop an effective mix of combined operations doctrine, C^3I/BM, and weapons technology. Syria fought a brief air-to-air struggle in 1982 and at best provided limited helicopter support to its ground forces. Its performance was worse than that of Egyptian and Syrian forces in 1973, when both Arab states at least generated significant numbers of attack sorties, albeit with negligible military effect.

The Iranian revolution so disrupted Iranian forces that Iran's combined operations capability was never really tested. Iraq did make major improvements in the performance of its air force between 1980 and 1988. Even when the war ended in 1988, however, Iraq still failed to use its air force effectively in supporting its ground troops. Its sortie rate remained low, it lacked adequate target acquisition and precision strike capability, its air force still reacted too slowly to meet ground force needs, and it was often forced to rely on compat helicopters to perform the role of attack aircraft. These problems were partly the result of continuing politicization of the army and air force command, but also reflected inadequate C^3I/BM, avionics, and munitions lethality.

The USSR improved its combined operations in Afghanistan, particularly in providing combined helicopter and close air support for its ground units, but it clearly lacked effective targeting and munitions to deal with the scattered forces of the Mujahideen. It also was forced to rely on "brute force" area attacks of small towns, hamlets, and individual farms. This may be partially successful in destroying the ability of guerrillas to operate among a friendly populace but is scarcely an effective use of combined operations.

In summary, recent experience with combined operations reflects both a warning and an opportunity. The warning is that even a highly professional and sophisticated force like the IDF continues to fail to fully master combined operations and the air-artillery-maneuver unit interface. The opportunities are twofold: First, Britain has shown just how much of an edge military professionalism and adequate training may give a Western or Western-supported nation in combined operations; second, the lessons of recent wars generally validate the West's search for sophisticated air and MRL area munitions and more effective C^3I/BM systems. The only alternative seems to be to proliferate dedicated MRL, helicopter, and air support in direct support of brigade- or regiment-sized maneuver units, a solution no Western nation can really afford.

Logistical Systems

All five conflicts confirmed the importance of adequate logistics and support. While the basic lessons that emerged are not new, they do seem worth reiterating:

- *Logistics and support are a substitute for mass*: Iraq used its massive logistics stocks to help reinforce its superior weapons numbers and compensate for Iran's superior manpower. Israel's ability to rapidly repair, service, and rearm its tanks and aircraft gave it a far greater edge over Syria and Egypt than its weapons numbers imply. The West should find its superior logistics and support to be similarly important force multipliers against most Third World forces, most of which buy major combat equipment numbers far in excess of their logistics and support capabilities. Similarly, improvements in logistics and support technology can be used as a substitute for weapons numbers and maneuver forces.

- *Expenditure rates generally exceed prewar predictions*: Every force engaged expended munitions, weapons stocks, and war reserves more rapidly than planned, with the exception of the Afghan Mujahideen, who lacked supply depots to draw on and often had to quit combat early because of lack of supply. These "overdraws" on planned consumption rates included such disparate firepower systems as ARGMs, SAMs, and artillery munitions. Much of this expenditure resulted, however, from a tendency to try to use the rate of firepower to substitute for adequate tactics, C^3I, maneuver, or other arms. The practical problem is that no Western force is likely to be less vulnerable to such problems in fighting in an unfamiliar area or under unpredictable conditions. Improved lethality per round may substitute for numbers, but demand is always likely to exceed planned supply. This should be considered in Western and USCENTCOM planning.

- *Logistics vulnerability*: No indigenous force proved particularly vulnerable to attack on its logistics, but Britain had high potential vulnerability in the Falklands because of its dependence on comparatively few ships with specialized cargoes. No Western force can assume that its sea, land, or air logistics and support facilities will be sanctuaries in a future war.

- *Speed of deployment and regional contingency facilities*: Speed of concentration of military force is a basic axiom of military science, and all of the wars under study confirm the importance of the ability to rapidly deploy or "surge" maneuver, logistics, and support capabilities into the forward area or to be able to draw on existing logistics and support facilities and capabilities. This confirms USCENTCOM's emphasis on regional facilities and the more general need for regional friends that can provide inter-operable stocks, bases, and support facilities. Such regional facilities are critical force multipliers. The overall course of the five wars also emphasizes the importance of being able to rapidly deploy logistics and support stocks and capabilities as close as possible to the user facility or the forward edge of the battle area. One of the most critical factors in each conflict was the presence or absence of sufficent local and intra-theatre air, helicopter, and all-terrain vehicle assets to move critical stocks directly to the user with minimum delay. Britain succeeded in solving this problem in the Falklands, Israel generally solved it in 1982, and Iraq solved it through sheer mass in the Iran-Iraq War. In each case, it was essential that combat needs could cut through any bureaucratic or organizational problems and that forward deployed stocks or immediate lift were available.

- *Simplicity versus complexity*: More speculatively, there is considerable evidence that overly complex, demand "pull," and "supplier-managed" systems are less effective, and ultimately more costly, than pushing a steady stream of "oversupply" forward to the front, maintaining large numbers of forward deployed stocks and relying on "user-managed" systems. The C^3I/BM problem is complex enough without trying to layer complex logistics and management support systems over the conduct of more critical phases of war.
- *Terrain and weather*: Finally, the failure of many munitions and systems to operate in a mix of desert, marsh, and mountain conditions not only reduced weapons lethality; it vastly increased consumption. For example, adequate fusing and/or temperature tolerance would have sharply reduced the need for artillery in the 1973, Afghan, and Iran-Iraq wars. The logistic implications of terrain and weather need careful consideration.

It is also vital that Western and friendly local forces should not underestimate the capabilities of a potential enemy that has to rely on "primitive" logistical systems. Iran and the Afghan freedom fighters did very well indeed with such systems, as the North Vietnamese did in invading South Vietnam.

By the same token, it is equally vital not to ascribe characteristics to primitive logistics that can honestly be associated only with more advanced systems. An advanced high-technology logistics system can provide the tactical commander with the ability to freely expend his material resources without fear of resupply problems. Yet it is clear that in some Third World conflicts, various forces with primitive logistics simply make do with limited supplies of resources and weaponry. This has been seen to be the case, particularly in Afghanistan where supplies were slow to reach guerrilla fighters and every bullet was precious.

The Afghans and Iranians also substituted a willingness to accept high casualties for adequate logistics to preserve precious resources. They were willing to take risks rather than expend resources. Anti-tank and anti-aircraft weapons were hoarded despite the numerous occasions when they would have useful. Often these weapons are utilized only when their use appeared inevitable, as it was not known when they would be replaced. However heroic these actions might be when engaged in by a traditional society struggling against a superpower, they hardly represent a model that the U.S. can emulate.

The logistics role of the helicopter was also important in all the conflicts under study, as was the value of reliable off-road supply capability by vehicle and the existence of a system that rapidly responded to forward small combat unit demand as distinquished from one that fed forward echelons according to some central system. Iraq, the IDF, the British, and the USSR all learned that rapid "oversupply" and "overreaction" in supporting forward combat units according to their evolving or changing needs is critical to success.

Naval Systems

Several lessons regarding naval systems have been discussed during the analysis of the Falklands fighting and Iran-Iraq War. It is worth noting, however, that sea power could have had a substantially greater impact on the 1973 Arab-Israeli conflict and the Iran-Iraq conflict if the U.S. Navy had not acted as a tacit guarantee against Russian naval pressure on Israeli and Iranian efforts to create a major naval or air threat to tanker and other maritime traffic in the Gulf. The "over-the-horizon" impact of U.S. sea power played a significant role in both conflicts, just as it was decisive in enabling the U.S. to intervene in Lebanon in 1982–1983 and in Western ability to secure the Gulf in 1987–1988.

Chemical and Biological Weapons

Chemical and biological weapons do not seem to have been particularly effective in the two limited armed conflicts in which they were used. They seem to have been used initially as terror weapons in Afghanistan and the Gulf. Their purpose in Afghanistan was probably to deter prospective sympathizers from supporting the Mujahideen. An additional reason might have been a desire on the part of the Soviets to test their CBW munitions under actual combat conditions. In the Gulf War, Iraq seems to have used CW in order to panic Iranian troops and hint at possible escalations in the conflict.

The Iraqi's use of CBW was initially limited but later expanded in attempts to use it as a mass area weapon. This escalation seems to repeat a political pattern that has been characteristic of some other Third World conflicts, such as the 1963–1967 war in Yemen. This pattern involves one side's use of small amounts of a CB agent in order to test the reaction of the world public opinion to such a move. If the world (and most notably the allies of the offending nation) remain unconcerned, this can be seen as a green light for expanded operation. If world reaction (and allied reaction) is strong, then the nation in question might choose to discontinue operations. In this regard, Iraq would be particularly concerned with the reaction of France, which is a key arms supplier state. Iran appears to have realized this and reacted by sending troops wounded by the CW agent to Europe for treatment.[6]

Iraq has also set an important precedent that has almost certainly been compounded by the Indian tragedy in Bopal. It has shown that chemical warfare materials are readily available to Third World nations. This has already led Iran to begin importing the ingredients and materials for chemical warfare, and India has developed contingency plans for using nerve gas against Pakistan's evolving nuclear capabilities. It is also uncertain whether or not Iraq halted its use of chemical warfare because of Iranian protests or because of problems in fusing, delivery accuracy, dispersal, and weather prediction. There is a high probability that chemical warfare capability will proliferate widely in the Third World and hence make its use more acceptable.

The political considerations restraining the use of gas warfare might also be disregarded by a Third World nation under attack by Western forces. Under such circumstances, a Third World nation might respond with any and all systems that could inflict harm on Western forces. This would naturally include CBW weapons if stocks were available and retribution in kind was not feared because of different political pressures on the West. Western retribution in kind would be unlikely, as it would have severe domestic and international repercussions, even if these repercussions reflected a "double standard."

Nuclear Weapons

Nuclear weapons were not used in any of the five conflicts under study. The USSR did make tacit nuclear threats during the Arab-Israeli conflict in 1973, and there is a possibility that the Israeli government gave the order to assemble nuclear weapons during the height of Egyptian and Syrian success. Still, no serious threat of nuclear use seems to have occurred. Britain has denied that it made any nuclear contingency plans for the Falklands, although it may have given such plans some preliminary study.

Nuclear weapons would, however, have been decisive in virtually all the conflicts under study. Israel, Egypt, and Syria could not sustain combat after a strike on their largest cities. A single ground burst on such a city would almost certainly create a new political regime in Egypt and Syria and threaten Israel's national existence. A limited number of lesser strikes against airbases and key C³I facilities would be equally decisive, although it is important to note that Israel won the air battle decisively in 1973 and 1982 by relying on superior conventional technology.

Iraq is similarly vulnerable to a strike on Baghdad and its critical military facilities. Iran is more resilient. It has much more territory, more population centers, and less political centralization. Nevertheless, it is very vulnerable to a combination of strikes on Tehran and Kharg Island. At the same time, Iraq and Iran both have large, well-dispersed military forces. It would be difficult to use nuclear forces to defeat them in detail, and the end result might well be lasting regional hatreds and a guerrilla war at least as serious as the recent conflict.

The Falklands War would have been ended by a nuclear strike against either the British fleet or the airport at Port Stanley. Its unique logistics and deployment conditions made both forces particularly vulnerable to a single strike. The Afghan conflict could have been affected by nuclear strikes on a key Russian site, Kabul, or a rebel-held city, but such scenarios either involve forces that do not exist or suggest such catastrophic and unpredictable actions as to be completely unrealistic. This war was essentially a war of attrition between a modern military power that can occupy any given center, but not the countryside, and a dispersed guerrilla force that used the countryside and population to deny the USSR the ability to use its superior technology against a large-scale target. This is not a climate in which nuclear weapons could be used as anything more than terror weapons.

Several other insights can be drawn regarding the use of nuclear weapons. First, no Western government could survive the use of nuclear weapons in any of the conflicts under study; the internal political consequences would inevitably be far worse than the military benefits. Second, the major, purely military, nuclear targets in the Third World nations under study include airbases, key logistics facilities, and command facilities. Striking these facilities would cripple their abilities to conduct modern military operations but not end their abilities to conduct extensive land or guerrilla combat operations and, in every case but the Falklands, would probably unite the target nation against the attacker. Third, the regional and/or global political consequences of using nuclear weapons would be equally negative. Even had they resulted in a local military victory, they would probably have resulted in a regional strategic and political defeat.

Notes

1. Tehran Ettela'at, "Interview with Mohammad Salimi, Minister of Defense," *JPRS Near East/South Asia Report* (December 1983), p. 97.

2. Deborah G. Meyer, "Deadly Game of Hide and Seek Using World War II Technology?" *Armed Forces Journal International* (March 1982), pp. 22–24.

3. "BTR-70 in Afghanistan," *Jane's Defence Weekly* (June 16, 1984), pp. 956–958.

4. Figures cited in Edward C. Ezell, "U.S. Lightweight Air Defense Systems," *International Defense Review* (February 1984), pp. 198–199.

5. Kathleen Day, "Sgt. York Gun System Misses Mark; Delivery Slow and Tests Poorly," *Los Angeles Times* (February 29, 1984), Pt. IV, p. 1.

6. Cited in "Tests on Iranian Soldiers Show Use of Gas, Doctor Says," *Los Angeles Times* (March 11, 1984), Part I, p. 11.

5

A STRATEGIC TECHNOLOGY STRATEGY FOR LIMITED FORCE ENGAGEMENTS

The technological implications of each conflict under study have been examined in detail, but it is critical that the West transform these lessons into a suitable strategy for technological development and determine how these lessons should influence Western technology and force-structure needs. The projection of Western power into Third World areas is of particular importance, but so is the need to deal with the strengths and weaknesses of friendly and hostile regional forces.

Although there are many ways in which such a "technology strategy" can be developed, the best approach seems to be to consider how the lessons of the conflicts under study relate to a contingency use of U.S. Central Command (USCENTCOM) forces. Although France, Britain, Turkey, and Italy also have important power projection capabilities, USCENTCOM is the key Western power projection force that would be involved in the defense of the Gulf and the West's oil supplies. Lessons which apply to USCENTCOM will often be equally important for other uses of other Western out-of-area forces.

Force Structure and Contingency Requirements

USCENTCOM forces are currently composed of a variety of units from all four U.S. military services (see Table 5.1). The units in Table 5.1 are not exclusively assigned to USCENTCOM, but they perform USCENTCOM missions in the event that forces are needed in the area. This means that the technology and equipment assigned to USCENTCOM forces must be able to perform in other combat environments and theaters of war.

USCENTCOM's area of responsibility includes nineteen nations that

TABLE 5.1 USCENTCOM Forces in 1988

U.S. Central Command Headquarters (augmented)	1,100
U.S. Army Forces Central Command	131,000

Headquarters U.S. Army Central Command (Third U.S. Army)
XVIII Airborne Corps Headquarters
82nd Airborne Division
101st Airborne Division (Air Assault)
24th Infantry Division (Mechanized)
6th Cavalry Brigade (Air Combat)
1st Corps Support Command

U.S. Naval Forces Central Command

Headquarters U.S. Naval Forces Central Command	123,000

   3 Aircraft Carrier Battle Groups[a]
   1 Surface Action Group
   3 Amphibious Groups
   5 Maritime Patrol Squadrons
   U.S. Middle East Force (Bahrain)

U.S. Marine Corps Forces	70,000

   1 1/3 Marine Amphibious Force, including
   1 Marine Division (reinforced)
   1 Marine Aircraft Wing[b]
   1 Force Service Action Group
   1 Marine Amphibious Brigade, including
   1 Marine Regiment (reinforced)
   1 Marine Air Group (composite)
   1 Brigade Service Support Group

U.S. Air Force Forces Central Command	33,000

Headquarters, Central Command Air Forces (9th Air Force)
   7 Tactical Fighter Wings[c]
   3 1/3 Tactical Fighter Wings (available as attrition fillers)
   2 Strategic Bomber Squadrons[d]
   1 Airborne Warning and Control Wing
   1 Tactical Reconnaissance Group
   1 Electronic Combat Group
   1 Special Operations Wing

Unconventional Warfare and Special Operations Forces	3,500
TOTAL	361,600

(continues)

TABLE 5.1 (*continued*)

---

[a]A typical active Navy carrier wing consists of nine squadrons (approximately 86 aircraft): two fighter squadrons; two "light" attack squadrons; one "medium" attack squadron; plus supporting elements for airborne early warning, anti-submarine and electronic warfare, reconnaissance, and aerial refueling operations.

[b]An active Marine Corps air wing typically consists of 23 to 25 squadrons (339 to 370 aircraft in all): four fighter/attack squadrons; two or three "light" attack squadrons; one or two "medium" attack squadrons; plus supporting elements for electronic warfare, reconnaissance, aerial refueling, transport, airborne assault, observation, and tactical air control.

[c]Each Air Force wing typically contains three squadrons of 24 aircraft each. Combat support units, such as those composed of EF-111 electronic warfare aircraft, are generally organized into squadrons of 18 to 24 aircraft. By the end of FY 1989, the U.S. will have the equivalent of 40 tactical fighter wings, 27 active and 13 ANG and reserve.

[d]These bombers and associated reconnaissance, command and control, and refueling aircraft make up the Air Force's Strategic Projection Force.

SOURCES: Data furnished by USCENTCOM in 1988, and Department of Defense, *Annual Report, FY 1986* (Washington, D.C.: GPO, 1986), p. 212.

stretch over an expanse of 7,000 to 12,000 miles from the continental United States. It extends from Pakistan in the east, moving westward through Afghanistan, Iran, and Iraq, to Jordan in the north and the entire Arabian Peninsula, and southward to the African continent into Egypt, Sudan, Ethiopia, and Djibouti, Somalia, and Kenya, including the Horn of Africa. USCENTCOM's most critical responsibility, however, is to be ready to help secure the West's sources of imported oil and to ensure the security and independence of friendly states in the Near East and southwest Asia.

In most contingencies, USCENTCOM forces must have access to friendly bases and the support of friendly forces. In order to gain this access, USCENTCOM has developed an extensive list of military facilities and contingency bases. This list is shown in Table 5.2. It is important to note that most of the bases shown in Table 5.2 are either (a) "way stations" that can help in deploying U.S. forces or in prepositioning U.S. equipment but cannot support forward combat operations in the most likely operating areas, or (b) bases in friendly or allied states to which USCENTCOM is not guaranteed access and that are not equipped to fully support U.S. forces. These bases are also limited in number and coverage.

There is, therefore, a high probability that USCENTCOM forces may have to rapidly convert friendly bases or civil facilities for USCENTCOM use or fight their way onto hostile bases. Further, USCENTCOM will almost certainly have to fight in alliance with

TABLE 5.2 U.S. Military Contingency Facilities in the Near East

Base	Status
NORTH AFRICA AND STAGING POINTS	
Morocco	
Slimane	Agreement signed in May 1983. A former B-47 base closed in 1963, which is now being modernized to support C-141 and C-5 operations.
Navasseur	This base or Rabat may be given similar modernization later.
Liberia	
Monrovia	Agreement signed in February 1983 to allow U.S. to make contingency use of international airport to stage air operations. U.S. will fund expansion of airport to allow use of C-5s, C-17s, and C-141s.
Portugal	
Lajes	Negotiations were completed in 1983–1984 to keep Lajes as a major air staging point for U.S. air movements. The fuel, runway, and other facilities at this base in the Azores are being upgraded.
EASTERN MEDITERRANEAN AND RED SEA AREA	
Egypt	
Suez Canal	U.S. has been granted tacit permission to move warships through the canal.
Cairo West	The U.S. shares an unnamed air base with Egypt and normally deploys about 100 men on the base. It has been used for joint F-15 and E-3A AWACS operations.
Ras Banas	Still under negotiation. Ras Banas could provide basing capabilities for C-5 aircraft and for unloading and transit of SL-7 and other fast sealift ships.
Djibouti	Access agreement and arrangements with French allow port calls and access to maritime patrol aircraft.
Turkey	
Mus Batman Erzurum	The U.S. has informal arrangements to use three Turkish air bases near the Soviet border, Iran, and Iraq. These bases are NATO bases and are being funded to allow the deployment of U.S. heavy lift aircraft and fighters.

(continues)

TABLE 5.2 *(continued)*

GULF AND RED SEA

Diego Garcia	Used through a long-term lease with the UK signed in the mid-1960s. The base provides 12,000-foot runways and facilities suitable for B-52 and heavy airlift facilities and is where seven U.S. prepositioning ships in the Gulf are now deployed.
Seychelles	Satellite tracking and communications base with NASA and Air Force personnel.

Kenya

Mombassa Moi Airport Kenya Naval	Provides a potential staging point, maintenance facilities, and port call. Access agreement signed in mid-1970s. Facility expansion program completed in 1983.

Somalia

Mogadishu Airport Berbera	Staging facilities for U.S. air and sea movements. Limited repair capability. Expansion completed in 1983.

Oman

Al Khasab	Small air base in the Musandem Peninsula near Goat Island and Straits of Hormuz. Limited contingency capability. Largely suited for small maritime patrol aircraft.
Masira	Island being expanded to a major $170 million air base, air and naval staging point, deployment of prepositioning ships, and possibly army prepositioning in 1986–1987.
Thumrait & patrol Seeb Air bases	Contingency air base facilities. Now used by U.S. maritime aircraft.
Saudi Arabia	No formal basing agreements, but the U.S. has deployed F-15s and E-3As to Saudi air bases in emergencies and operates E-3As from Dhahran. All Saudi air bases have the sheltering and facilities to accept extensive U.S. air reinforcements and/or support U.S. deployment of heavy lift aircraft.
Bahrain	U.S. Middle East Force deploys in Bahrain, although formal agreement has lapsed. A 65-man U.S. support unit is present.

SOURCES: Adapted from material provided by USCENTCOM and from Barry Blechman and Edward Luttwak, *International Security Yearbook, 1983/84* (Washington, D.C.: CSIS, 1984), pp. 154–159.

local forces, a condition which is now likely to affect most Western use of force in the Third World.

This establishes several key thrusts for a technology strategy:

- Designing equipment for forces where reliability, minimum support requirements, ease of repair, and minimum consumption rates are given equal or higher priority than other performance characteristics.
- Emphasizing advanced technology systems for critical mission needs that minimize the need for weapons and equipment numbers.
- Developing C^3I/BM and rapidly deployable basing and support technology that can minimize the strain and delay inherent in creating or converting new basing facilities.
- Facilitating arms transfers, which will encourage friendly local states to create bases using U.S. equipment or directly compatible with U.S. equipment.

The lack of dedicated forward bases will present many of the problems that the British experienced in the Falklands. The West, and the U.S. in particular, normally tends to underestimate the value of improving technology in terms of reliability, repairability, and ease of support. It should be clear from the analysis of previous conflicts, however, that this aspect of advanced technology will be critical to any power that must fight at long distances from its sources of supply. It will be equally critical to the other Western out-of-area forces shown in Table 5.3. Even small Western forces can play powerful roles as political symbols. Belgium, Italy, and the Netherlands proved this in 1988 by sending limited naval forces to help defend the right of navigation in the Persian/Arabian Gulf. However, serious fighting imposes different requirements.

Britain and France are the only Western states likely to play a major out-of-area role, and both have the same need to minimize the need for basing and support facilities. Britain has no major active bases east of Suez, although it leases its facilities in Diego Garcia to the U.S. France has only one major forward base at Djibouti. Both the UK and France have naval forces in the Indian Ocean and play critical roles in supplying advisors, arms, and military technology to states throughout the USCENTCOM area, but neither can support significant operations from carrier forces or the existing facilities on most friendly bases.

These support problems will be compounded when Western forces need to support local forces in a coalition strategy. In spite of the

TABLE 5.3 Maximum Probable European Amphibious and Ground Forces for Low- to Medium-Level Contingencies in Southwest Asia and Africa[a]

Country	Amphibious Forces		Air Transportation Forces			UN Forces	Garrisons
	Commando[a]	Marine	Airborne	Air-Portable	Specialist		
Belgium			1 regt				
Canada	1 ranger regt		1 regt			UNICYP, UNDOF, & UNTSO	
Denmark			—[b]			UNFICYP	
France	1 bn[c]	1 div[d]	1 div[e]		1 lt arm arm bde[f]	UNIFIL	Djibouti/ Indian Ocean (g 8000) Africa (g 4500)
Fed. Rep. Germany			3 bdes[g]				
Greece[h]	1 regt 3 bns	1 regt	1 regt				
Italy		3 bns[i]	1 bde			UNIFIL/ SINAI/ MFO[j]	
Netherlands		2 cbt gps		2 bns		UNIFIL	
Norway						UNIFIL[k]	
Portugal	1 regt	3 bn[l]		4 bns	1 regt		
Spain	2 coys	2 co.	1 bde	1 bde	1 regt[m]		Africa/ Canaries (4 regts)
Turkey	1 bde1	1 bde	1 bde				Cyprus (17,000)[n]
United Kingdom	3 gps	1 bd[o] 1 boat sqd., 2 raiding sqn.	2 bns	1 bn	1 regt (SAS)	UNFICYP	Sovereign Base Areas, Cyprus (2 bns, 1 recce sgn) Gibraltar (1 bn)

(continues)

TABLE 5.3 *(continued)*

---

[a]Elements of paramilitary forces with antiterrorist and other relevant expertise are not included, nor are reinforcement forces for Allied Command Europe (ACE) which could, in principle, be committed outside the boundaries of ACE.
[b]One battalion.
[c]Marine commandos—590 men in 4 assault units.
[d]Seven regiments.
[e]13,700 men in 10 regiments and one battalion.
[f]2,700 men with one motorized rifle and one infantry division.
[g]Fully assigned to defense of Central Region.
[h]All units organized into one para-commando division.
[i]Amphibious battalions in army.
[j]Sinai MFO has 90 men and 3 minesweepers; UNIFIL has 2,038 men including 1 Mech Inf., 1 Paratroop, and 1 Logistic battalion, plus a Marine detachment and counter sabotage company.
[k]839 men with 1 battalion, 1 service, and 1 medical company.
[l]2,687 men, 2 infantry, and 1 police battalion.
[m]Foreign Legion. Does not include 5 light regiments (1 Cadre) in Canary and Baleric Islands.
[n]1 corps of 2 infantry divisions with 150 M-47/48, M-113 APCs, 212 105-mm, 155-mm, and 203-mm artillery weapons and 40-mm AA guns.
[o]Royal Marines have 7,754 men, including 1 commando brigade, 1 Special Boat, and 2 Raiding Squadrons with 18 105-mm, light guns, 318 81-mm mortars, MILAN ATGM, Blowpipe SAM, 19 Rigid Rider and 10 Gemini assault boats, and 15 Gazelle AW-1 and 5 Lynx AH-1 helicopters.

SOURCES: IISS, *The Military Balance 1983–1984* (London, Autumn 1983); Peter Foot, *Beyond the North Atlantic: The European Contribution*, Aberdeen Studies in Defense Economics (November 21, Spring 1982), p. 33.

expansion of USCENTCOM forces and steady increases in the speed with which USCENTCOM can deploy, the U.S. cannot afford the domestic political costs of the kind of sustained infantry combat and casualties that characterize several of the wars under study. It must mix the ability to cooperate with local land and air forces with the kind of advanced tactical technology that reacts to the lessons of past conflicts.

Further, it is clear that a technology strategy for power projector forces must deal with unique problems in terms of terrain, climate, and political conditions. The most difficult of these conditions may well be political. Some of the special conditions imposed in recent limited armed conflicts are summarized in Table 5.4, along with possible technology responses. Responding to the interaction between local political problems and the special constraints imposed by terrain,

TABLE 5.4 The Political/Terrain/Weather Challenge

Challenges	Technology Response
o Mixture of desert, wetland, mountain, and urban terrain.	o Advanced technology, LAVs, and combat helicopters. Man- or crew-portable weapons tailored to MOBA and mountain combat with the range needed for desert warfare.
o Widely different weather conditions from snow-covered mountains to semi-tropical to arid desert.	o Equipment with minimum support, logistic, and repair requirements.
o Uncertain availability of U.S. contingency bases.	o "All weather" design of all critical equipment.
o Lack of threat assessment major targets and easily identifiable military targets.	o Creation of high technology C^3I/BM and rapid basing equipment.
o Need to operate with friendly local forces.	o Long-range fighter and combat helicopters. Land vehicles with extended operating ranges.
o Need to minimize U.S. casualties and losses.	o Emphasis on HUMINT, specially tailored theater collection platforms, advanced targeting aids for land forces, and supporting C^3I/BM technology.
o Need to maximize shock or surge impact of Western forces. Overcome superior threat numbers and willingness to take losses.	o Specially tailored C^3I/BM systems allowing easy netting with allied forces while preserving the security and autonomy of the U.S. system.
o Potentially hostile local forces and political movements.	o High technology weapons coupled with advanced intelligence and surveillance systems tailored to MOBA, mountain, and infantry-dominated warfare.
	o Deployment of "emerging technology" systems designed to rapidly suppress threat air bases, use of weapons like the MRLs to deliver mass artillery fire, area munitions, and bombs with smart submunitions. High technology targeting.
	o Arms and technology transfer strategy design to maximize pre-conflict cooperation and interoperability with local forces, allow joint operations, and minimize the need for U.S. or other Western presence.

weather, and other local conditions will be especially important because indigenous enemies will be completely familiar with the terrain.

These problems will be especially severe in North Africa, the Middle East, and southwest Asia. The rise of Islamic fundamentalism, Islamic operations, and U.S. ties to Israel create another challenge for technology: fighting in a hostile region where the alignment of friend and foe is unstable. Any unilateral intervention by USCENTCOM forces could meet with widespread anti-American feeling among significant elements of the Middle Eastern societies. The U.S. has already had a taste of such problems in Lebanon. Future situations in which USCENTCOM faces large numbers of forces, or entire local populations, motivated by an equally hostile ideology would pose far greater problems. The Soviet experience in Afghanistan and the U.S. experience in Vietnam provide equally grim warning of these risks.

The very act of Western intervention will be offensive to some elements within any Islamic society unless Western states fight in direct cooperation with, and in direct support of, local forces and national movements. The issue of foreign domination is an extremely sensitive political problem throughout the Third World. Forces hostile to the West could thus have a distinct advantage in terms of political will and a willingness to incur casualties.

Even friendly local forces could divide into hostile factions, or support the opponents of the West, unless any Western power using force in the region clearly supports a coalition strategy. Western forces cannot hope to conduct successful operations in a situation in which they are unable to distinguish their friends from their enemies.

All of these factors argue that an appropriate technology strategy for the West must include a substrategy for arms sales and technology transfer to friendly local states which will allow those states to fight effectively with Western forces and deter and defend in low-level crises with only limited or indirect Western aid.

In the event that larger crises or conflicts do make Western intervention inevitable, it will be equally critical that the West have a technology strategy that will allow it to compensate for a lack of superior force numbers and minimize Western and friendly losses by mixing superior technology with a careful tailoring of military assets to power projection and low-intensity combat missions. This will include operations against poorly armed and organized guerrilla, radical, or insurgent forces. Under no circumstances can any sustained USCENTCOM or other Western operation treat such opponents as inconsequential.

Technology Requirements and Thrusts

The following specific recommendations in implementing a technology strategy grow out of the lessons set forth in the previous chapters. They necessarily generalize on past experience, but they reflect recommendations that have broad future application in shaping the technology of Western and friendly local forces in future low-level conflicts.

Threat Assessment and Intelligence

Threat assessment and intelligence are not only powerful force multipliers; they are the key to avoiding the use of force. As has been noted throughout this analysis, the initiation and escalation of combat in all five wars occurred as much through the failure to rapidly process, integrate, and objectively analyze the available intelligence indicators as from any other cause. The reasons for these failures were generally more political than technical. The policy level and high command users created a climate in which warning and objective intelligence simply were not desired and failed to heed the indicators that were provided and properly respond to them.

At the same time, it is clear that a far less politicized threat assessment system like that of the U.S. could also face critical problems. The U.S. is heavily oriented toward photo intelligence of a kind that would generally provide only limited warning or information in many Third World or low-level conflicts of the kind under study. Its emphasis on centralized satellite and aircraft systems also leads to limited coverage, although most low-level conflicts require surveillance and intelligence platforms with long endurance over the target area.

Neither the U.S. nor any other Western power can count on reliable SIGINT information, particularly in dealing with infantry, guerrilla, and insurgent forces. Currently available collection capabilities are likely to decline steadily during the next five to ten years. ELINT may provide a more enduring source of data, but it is not a source of political infomation, and extensive pattern analysis and HUMINT may be necessary to interpret the meaning of Third World ELINT data. Intelligence should be structured to provide maximum fusion of HUMINT, PHOTINT, ELINT, and SIGINT to support politically constrained warfare and deal with less sophisticated forces.

It has already been seen that types of Western intelligence systems designed for NATO can fail to obtain vital information due to the absence of certain key indicators and order-of-battle characteristics from the structures of unsophisticated forces. This problem does not, however, result from a situation in which there is no intelligence data to collect, process, and disseminate. It results from a situation in which a large amount of relatively low-quality PHOTINT, SIGINT, and ELINT information must be processed quickly and combined with extensive amounts of HUMINT in order to obtain useful intelligence. In Lebanon, the Falklands, and even in Grenada near–real-time fusion of intelligence data presented a very significant problem which was compounded by a lack of prior and current HUMINT. The intelligence process bogged down, the analytic skills and time were lacking to provide adequate policy-level warning and threat assessment, and intelligence often was not disseminated to tactical commanders in time for them to utilize this information when making tactical decisions.

This creates the requirement for sophisticated "fusion" technology that can blend all sources of intelligence in near real time even in the period before a crisis turns into conflict. It makes the availability of such technology essential in dealing with conflict initiation and escalation. Such fusion, however, will require greatly improved HUMINT processing as well as the technology to correlate large volumes of often below-grade SIGINT and HUMINT data. It will also require a data base and the analytic capability to integrate both news media and policy and command level communications from the State Department and U.S. military command system. Past experience has shown that much of the key data available may not be classified or may not come from intelligence sources. At the same time, decoupling intelligence analysis from an understanding of policy and command developments can be equally disastrous. The need for this kind of "fusion" has been discussed for at least a decade but has never been transformed into practical hardware and software.

At the same time, any technology strategy for Western power projection forces must provide for similar fusion of intelligence at the theater command level and be able to transmit and receive suitable threat assessment and intelligence data at every major level of operational command. The hierarchy of a fusion system must be structured to support operations in every way possible.

Western power projection forces must act as a highly mobile force that is able to strike at ephemeral targets of opportunity. It therefore becomes vital that Western commanders "see the battlefield" at all times. This is of course impossible if intelligence is not tailored to near continuous coverage, is over-oriented toward policy-level and high-command users, or becomes bogged down in the processing stage.

Near–Real-Time Targeting

The West will also need to improve theater and battlefield near–real-time threat assessment, targeting, and reconnaissance assets. Improvements of theater and battlefield near–real-time targeting and reconnaissance assets will be particularly important. This reflects the underlying reality that Western power projection forces cannot routinely expect to match Third World opponents in terms of numbers of equipment and must compensate with superior intelligence, targeting, C^3I/BM, and other combat technologies to make better use of such equipment. This must be accomplished through the use of "force multipliers" in the hope that each piece of equipment in Western forces can be utilized to its maximum possible effectiveness.

Improved targeting, C^3I, and BM assets will, therefore, be critical factors in any technology strategy. They can bind together Western and friendly local forces, and they can help compensate for overwhelming numbers of enemy firepower assets which may have inadequate target acquisition systems. This may well indicate the need for the kind of specially tailored airborne sensor program discussed in the previous chapter, both for targeting and threat assessment purposes. Sensors like SLAR, SAR, EO, FLIR, and real-time photo processing, combined with suitable on-board processing, could be of immense value to both theater and combat unit commanders.

The massive use of artillery "area fire" in the Gulf War is a warning that many unsophisticated opponents will rely on massed firepower to compensate for a lack of targeting assets. While this tends to be an extremely wasteful approach to artillery, it may, nonetheless, be effective for Third World enemies seeking to inflict casualties on U.S. forces. The U.S. could, however, counter this type of unguided artillery fire through the use of well-targeted counterfire. Systems such as improved countermortar and counterbattery radars coupled to multiple rocket launchers with smart submunitions could be exceptionally helpful.

Another targeting system that should be included in an overall technology strategy is the use of low-cost, remotely piloted vehicles (RPVs) that can be used in large numbers without complex support, recovery, or downlinks. The performance of these systems in the Middle East is known to have been outstanding. In this regard, it might be recalled that Israeli RPVs played a major role in the destruction of the Syrian missile batteries in the Bekaa Valley. While RPVs were not used in the other limited armed conflicts examined, it is clear that RPVs have great potential capabilities.

In many cases, reconnaissance assets are the same systems that are used for targeting. Their reconnaissance function will be equally important since local forces hostile to a Western presence will have a significant advantage in terms of familiarization with the terrain and knowledge of the best defensive positions, ambush sites, and so on. The net result can be to both solve the "time on target" problem in combined arms and operations and deny the enemy much of the advantage of his superior knowledge of terrain.

Urban Combat

Western forces will also need to emphasize technology for "MOBA" (military operations in built-up areas). The risk and significance of military operations in built-up areas emerged in four of the limited armed conflicts examined and played a critical role in two. MOBA operations halted Saddam Hussein's 1980–1981 advances into Iran. They caused significant Israeli casualties in the Suez in 1973 and helped prevent the Israelis from blocking the PLO retreat and seizing Beirut in 1982. They were also significant for the Soviets, who were forced to fight in a number of Afghan cities after the December 1979 invasion. The Falklands War was the only conflict in which MOBA operations did not take place.

The battle of Beirut is probably the most important example of the dangers Western forces may face in urban combat. One of the most modern military machines in the world was pitted against a poorly organized opposition whose weaponry was largely confined to hand-held technologies, a limited amount of medium artillery, and a few obsolete tanks. Nevertheless, these elements first forced Israel to halt its advance, and then, even though all PLO elements had been evacuated, small radical ethnic movements forced U.S. and European peacekeeping forces to withdraw.

A number of factors will be important in developing ways to deal with potential MOBA problems. Not all of these factors are technological. One nontechnological factor that is crucially important is training. Yet at the present time MOBA training is receiving only limited attention within U.S. forces. This shortcoming is particularly significant since this type of warfare would also come into play in a European-based scenario.

A technology strategy for MOBA is equally important, however, and a number of aspects of urban warfare must be considered. Technology is needed that can deal with such problems as:

- the inability to distinguish friend, foe, and noncombatant;
- the inability to use most sensors and intelligence systems;
- the difficulty, if not impossibility, of adequately targeting air power and artillery (and Western inability to use such systems against civilians and noncombatants);
- the need to fight in confined areas;

- the excessive channelization of advancing personnel and vehicles, which results in a total absence of maneuver warfare;
- the difficulty of reconnaissance;
- the wide array of defensive structures available to urban defenders and snipers;
- the increased possibility of close quarters and hand-to-hand combat;
- the slow rate of advance in such environments;
- the increased effectiveness of barriers;
- the decreased effectiveness and increased vulnerability of armor;
- the reduction of urban areas to rubble, which often presents as many problems as intact urban structures and can be even worse in terms of movement of vehicles; and
- limitations on the range of fire and on the time available to employ anti-tank weapons, machine guns, and other small arms.

These problems are by no means easy to solve, but there are some relatively simple ways that Western and friendly local forces may be able to deal with them. These involve emphasizing weapons systems that can be used in both urban and non-urban environments. For example, the following problems exist in present U.S. weapons systems:

- No current U.S. Army anti-tank weapon is designed to be fired from an enclosed room. In some cases this means that the backblast could seriously injure an operator. U.S. systems should be replaced with improved U.S. designs or European systems at the earliest possible date.
- Existing high-profile vehicles were designed without consideration of the visibility and firepower needs of urban warfare.
- The wire-guided TOW, as well as many of its foreign counterparts, fire anti-tank missiles that do not stabilize in flight until they reach ranges too long for most urban actions to occur.

Western nations have discussed the need for such improved MOBA systems for years. The West now needs to initiate a far more significant effort to develop weapons systems and doctrine for dealing with urban environments. This means a greater stress on advanced technology versions of close-combat weapons such as manportable PGMs; light mortars firing improved area ordnance; and improved rocket launchers, grenade launchers, and anti-tank grenades.

The effectiveness of the Vulcan anti-aircraft guns in the urban areas of Lebanon suggests that similar weapons could be very useful in future Western MOBA operations, although lower-cost systems are needed. Crews need to be trained in the urban use of such assets, however, and combat commanders must be trained to think of these systems as assets for future urban combat. Future anti-aircraft gun designs should be designed for secondary anti-ground operations in both urban and mountain environments.

Improved technology is needed to improve the effectiveness of heavier weapons and munitions in urban environments. Some anti-armor weapons have been designed exclusively for long-distance targets and thus have been untested at close distances. In some cases, older weapons are known to be more effective than modern ones simply because there has been no attempt made to incorporate effective MOBA characteristics from one generation of weapons systems to the next. World War II bazookas, for example, were reported to be more effective than the much more modern M79 light anti-tank weapons in shooting through walls during the 1968 Battle of Hue.

Specially designed ATGMs, tank rounds, and artillery rounds may be required. There also seems to be a requirement for ground-designated bombs designed for urban warfare and suitable armament for heli-copters. The key challenge will be to bring carefully controlled amounts of firepower to bear precisely against urban targets in direct support of infantry with minimum damage to civilians or friendly forces.

There also is a need for improved C^3I, including communications systems designed for MOBA operations and improved intelligence and reconnaissance systems such as expendable squad-level RPVs and suitable night vision and surveillance systems.

Mountain Warfare and Rough Terrain

Western and friendly local forces must be similarly equipped and trained to fight in mountain environments as well as deserts. Environments such as those found in the Zagros mountains of Iran are key potential battle sites for U.S. forces, and similar areas exist in many other areas where the West or its allies might use military force. Such efforts will need specially tailored technology to fight in these areas.

One of the main lessons of the Afghan war, for example, has been the usefulness of specially configured light armored vehicles and, in some instances, light tanks. The performance of the BMDs in Afghanistan and the limited performances of the British light tanks (Scorpians and Scimitars) in the Gulf and Falklands wars indicate that high-technology LAVs designed for mountain warfare have great potential value. Other important lessons relate to a variety of special problems associated with mountain warfare. There is a need for improved tactical systems to:

- Increase munitions lethality in mountain areas, shooting uphill and downhill.
- Provide suitable vision and targeting aids.
- Provide adequate helicopter lift and armament.
- Allow rapid resupply of artillery shells and other supplies that have to be carried in a mountain environment.
- Improve all-terrain mobility.
- Improve visibility and fields of fire of weapons such as artillery, tank guns, and MRLs so that they can engage enemy troops on the crests of hills.

Advanced training technology, as well as weapons technology, may also be required. Maneuvers, range firing, and live firing practice in mountain environments can do a great deal to acquaint forces with the special problems and advantages of fighting in the mountains. If one side has the training technology to exploit these advantages and the other does not, there could be a significant difference in the outcome of the fighting. A technology strategy should stress advanced simulation and training in mountain environments so that the effectiveness of standard military equipment could be increased through an understanding of how this equipment operates in mountain environments. This would allow Western forces to increase the mix of useful weapons for mountain warfare prior to a deployment to mountainous regions. Some specific examples of this might be to provide infantry units with more PGMs as well as light and heavy mortars. These are systems that troops can be taught to use quickly.

In other instances, it may be necessary to draw elements from active military forces not involved in the conflict or to mobilize selected reserve units. This is an ad hoc and incomplete solution, but it unfortunately may be the best solution possible since U.S. forces must be able to fight in a variety of circumstances and therefore cannot be restructured to depend less on weapons that will serve them well in nonmountain environments.

Improving the elevation of certain weapons systems can be accomplished either by redesigning the system or by stressing the use of different types of weapons for mountain warfare. Improved light armored vehicles may be more useful in mountain warfare than redesigned tanks, as the tank has not proved an effective system for mountain warfare. Likewise, an attempt to redesign self-propelled tube artillery for mountain warfare may be an expensive and time-consuming process that produces fewer benefits than specially designed mountain artillery and MRLs.

One area that clearly merits high-technology development is that of creating a specially tailored mixture of targeting, C^3/BM, and munitions for mountain warfare. Key problems that have emerged in most recent mountain warfare are the lack of specially tailored targeting and surveillance assets, the inability to reliably and securely communicate and "feed" a suitable battle management system, and the fact that many munitions have unsuitable fusing and kill characteristics for use in such terrain. It is unclear just how much advanced C^3I/BM and munitions technology can do against scattered infantry, infiltrating forces, and "dug-in" or sheltered units, but there is a clear need to find out.

There is also a need for improved targeting and air control for helicopter operations and testing new killing mechanisms in mountain environments. Well-armed and protected helicopters have emerged as the dominant high-technology weapon in recent mountain combat. Their use and effectiveness have never been fully exploited because of their (a) lack of specially tailored sensor systems; (b) relatively poor C^3I/BM interface with infantry and artillery; and (c) lack of an overall BM system that will support and exploit helicopter forces to solve the "time on target" problem in mountain and urban warfare, minimize helicopter vulnerability, and allow effective near–real-time allocation of helicopter forces.

The issue of improved munitions is more complex. Direct-fire automatic weapons seem to vary in effectiveness according to volume of fire, ricochet, and penetrating capability. The effectiveness of artillery and mortar rounds is more uncertain. Iraq and the USSR have experienced considerable problems, but neither seems to have used any form of improved conventional munitions (ICM). This is a key area for operational testing and the development of suitable advanced technology munitions, as is the testing of suitable air ordnance for helicopters and aircraft. The performance of fuel air explosives (FAE), smart submunitions, scatterable mines, improved cluster weapons, and other ordnance all need high-technology evaluation and refinement for use in mountain warfare.

Manportable Anti-Infantry Weapons

Mechanized and nonmechanized infantry are likely to play a major role in any Western ground-based action in the Third World. Western forces need to achieve major advantages in manportable weaponry with an emphasis on surge anti-infantry kill capacity. Since hostile infantry forces are likely to have the advantage in manpower,

Western forces must be able to neutralize this advantage with superior weapons technology. This includes improved area weapons and targeting technology. Another important potential advantage, however, lies in improved manportable anti-personnel weapons such as advanced-technology rifles, grenade launchers, machine guns, Claymore-type mines, small mortars, or even anti-tank weapons equipped to fire canister rounds. American weapons must also equal or surpass comparable enemy systems in terms of range.

One weapons system that could be particularly important in defeating enemy infantry is an advanced rapid-fire grenade launcher. This system, if used in conjunction with friendly machine gun fire, could have a devastating effect on advancing enemy infantry since these infantry would then be faced with large volumes of direct and indirect fire. Another useful weapon, presently under evaluation for possible use by U.S. forces, is the 40-mm M-19 automatic grenade launcher. This weapon can deliver either anti-personnel or anti-armor 40-mm grenades at a rate of 350 to 400 rounds per minute. With projectiles this deadly and a rate of fire this rapid, the M-19 is a devastating anti-infantry weapon. It is significant that the M-19's less effective Soviet counterpart, the AGS-17, is helicopter-mountable. The effectiveness of helicopters has already been reviewed in an earlier portion of this report. Thus, if one could combine the high mobility of American helicopters with the more rapid firepower of the M-19 grenade launchers, an even more effective weapons system would result.

In the long run, however, the West needs to find advanced technology solutions to every aspect of manportable weapons technology. Many Western systems are now inferior to Soviet systems in this regard, and this is particularly true of U.S. weapons. These systems need far higher force improvement priorities.

Light Armored Vehicles

An advanced technology high-firepower, low-profile light armored vehicle or LAV is needed for a wide variety of environments including both mountain terrain and urban warfare. This LAV must deal with the disadvantages of present light armored vehicles. The first of these disadvantages is the "thin skin" of the vehicle. The LAVs can be destroyed by a variety of weapons that have only moderate armor-piercing capabilities. This would include RPGs, heavy machine guns, anti-vehicle mines, and recoilless rifles. To make matters worse, the newer RPG-16 and RPG-18 have longer ranges and more armor-penetration capability than the still widely utilized RPG-7. This means that in the future LAVs will face a much more formidable light anti-armor weapon threat.

Future LAVs must, therefore, use high-technology protection and firepower. Even the most well-armed and well-designed LAV will, however, be vulnerable to a variety of enemy weapons. It is not a tank and cannot be used as such. While the LAV should have a great deal of firepower, it should not usually be used as a vehicle for sheltering troops during combat. Troops would be expected to dismount and fight apart from the vehicle during many types of combat.

The U.S. so far has done more to debate an advanced LAV than build one, although other Western nations have more advanced designs. By recognizing and refining the lessons of previous conflicts, the West can avoid recurring mistakes that the Soviets have made in calling upon their vehicles to perform in situations where these same vehicles are more vulnerable than dismounted troops. The characteristics that recent wars indicate are important for such a vehicle are:

- low silhouette and profile;
- good external visibility with special attention to upper areas;
- high firepower with high rates of area fire capability in addition to a weapon suited to killing tank, MOBA, and urban targets;
- speed equal to that of main battle tanks;
- room for a squad of troops and firing ports for these troops to fire on the move if necessary;
- rapid evacuation capability; and
- good helicopter and intratheater air transportability.

There also may be political value in relying on such LAVs rather than tanks or APCs. British Major General Rowley Mans has suggested, "Whether we like it or not, the early appearance of heavy tanks excites world opinion, whereas lighter vehicles are accepted without too much comment" in certain scenarios.[1] While General Mans's point is somewhat speculative, it seems clear that an advanced technology LAV could be particularly useful in meeting Western needs in low-level conflicts.

Long-Range Strike Capability

Another key priority for a technology strategy is the creation of long-range strike capability to decisively destroy or interdict key air bases and facilities with minimal losses. One of the most important features of the 1982 war in Lebanon was the way in which the Israelis quickly eliminated the Syrian air defense system and much of the Syrian air force. The elimination of such significant assets at the outset of any conflict creates a psychological and material advantage that can shape the future course of the war. In similar situations it will be equally important for Western forces to quickly and methodically eliminate major enemy assets so that decisive combat power can be brought to bear upon enemy formations of ground forces.

The British use of Vulcan bombers to attack the Falkland Islands is instructive. It suggests the need to use strategic assets (in the U.S. case, B-52s or possibly European-based or tanker-supported FB-111s) to strike at enemy theater assets outside the range of U.S. fighters.

Long-range strike capabilities can also be improved through the use of some technologies that make "deep strike" attacks feasible for tactical aircraft in the NATO theater. Two especially important forms of technology for this purpose are stand-off air-to-ground guided dispensers like LOADs and improved MRLs systems with ranges of up to 70 kilometers. These can use munitions like PGMs, modular glide bombs, dispensers of "smart submunitions" runway and hard target killers, and a host of other "emerging technologies." They allow an aircraft to extend its striking range and reduce its vulnerability to at least some forms of air defense, and they allow multiple rocket launchers to substitute for close support aircraft. This can increase the amount of destruction inflicted on the enemy while reducing Western aircraft losses.

Surge Firepower

The West needs to emphasize surge firepower from air, artillery, and helicopters to provide area kills of infantry in rough terrain and tailor "deep strike," "modular" glide bomb, MRL technology to the needs of low-intensity wars.

The ability of potentially hostile forces to field large numbers of troops and accept significant numbers of casualties is particularly well illustrated by the losses incurred by the combatants in the Iran-Iraq War. Iran's actions also indicate the possibility that "human wave" tactics could be used against Western forces. Khomeini's militias, occasionally described as the "Army of Twenty Million," were originally formed to fight any possible U.S. intervention force. There is no reason to assume that Khomeini would be any more conservative about preserving Iranian lives if he were fighting the Western forces rather than Iraq.

Manportable weapons systems to be used against infantry in the field have already been discussed. Heavy ordnance will, of course, be equally important both for close support and for use against targets some distance behind the forward edge of battle area (FEBA). It is, therefore, vital that advanced area weapons systems like the MRL and improved submunitions be included in Western inventories in sufficient numbers to be able to break up hostile formations in their assembly areas, since it is not enough to inflict losses on enemy troops only when they come into the range of direct-fire weapons.

This type of surge firepower should be able to devastate large numbers of enemy troops in as short a time as possible. With these types of systems, it should be possible to break up enemy formations with huge volumes of fire over a short period of time. This will be a marked improvement over conventional artillery barrages, which usually give the enemy an opportunity to react by moving into defensive positions.

Several types of weapons systems are capable of such surge firepower, including fuel air explosives, improved cluster bombs, improved napalm, and artillery shells utilizing flechettes. The multiple rocket launcher, however, seems to be the key near-term option, and it is more than possible that Western powers need more than the planned one battery per division planned for USCENTCOM units. Modern battlefields present numerous opportunities for the use of area fire. Conventional artillery usually is utilized only in a massed firepower mode after several shots have been fired as part of an initial effort to pinpoint the exact direction and distance of the target from the gun. These initial shots warn an enemy to take cover or move or otherwise react. An advanced multiple rocket launcher can saturate a target without the need for initial registration shots or prolonged fire.

Short-Range Air Defense

Light missiles and AA guns have had a major impact on the survival, and lethality, of aircraft in all of the wars under study. Even relatively primitive shoulder-fired infrared missile systems, such as the Redeye or the Grail, performed relatively well in the conflicts being examined. In the Gulf war, they were particularly effective against hostile aircraft, in contrast to larger SAM systems.

These weapons, however, are now in a technology race. Their level of technology is rapidly being overtaken by new SHORAD systems. At the same time, relatively simple and effective countermeasures have been developed. For older systems these include flares and thermal balloons, which distract such missiles from their targets. Since current SHORAD systems are limited in range, speed, and acceleration and are usually heat seeking, they are usually only effective after a low-flying enemy plane has made a pass over a target and made itself vulnerable to a "tail shot." The rear portion of a jet plane is usually the only area hot enough to attract the missile. Finally, current systems require continuing training and simulator use. Unlike RPGs, they cannot be rapidly disseminated to under-trained troops.

Western and friendly forces will need the most advanced substitutes available. This now is the Stinger POST, which has an IFF system and advanced seeker technology. In the future, however, consideration should be given to a more sophisticated "high-low" technology mix which could include:

- An advanced man- or light crew-portable system that makes use of emerging hypersonic missile technology and advanced technology that has both its own sighting and IFF system as well as the option of data links or low-cost networking to external sensors and C^{3}I systems.
- A cheap manportable system that can be proliferated in large numbers, has an IFF capability, and is as much oriented toward degrading attack sorties as actual kills.
- A next-generation system that can combine anti-aircraft and anti-armor capabilities.
- A cheap, high-rate-of-fire AA gun designed for dual use in "curtain fire" air defense and in area fire against land targets. Such a system might come in vehicle and turret form. The experience in recent wars raises serious questions about the value of either IFF or guidance for such systems. The trade-off in terms of increased numbers versus a more sophisticated guidance and IFF package would seem to favor numbers in the case of comparatively short-range guns—although this would not be true of a light SAM.

At the same time, the West will need the most effective SHORAD countermeasures possible for its own aircraft and those of friendly states. There is a basic asymmetry in the position of Western- and Soviet-supplied air forces. Western aircraft are far more expensive in real terms, Western-supplied air forces generally play a more important role in the overall mix of land and air forces, and Western and Western-supplied air forces face more political constraints in taking casualties.

This again argues for a technology strategy emphasizing standoff munitions and low-vulnerability attack profiles using the advanced avionics and area and smart submunitions discussed earlier. These should be used with suitable targeting and C^3 systems, standoff delivery systems, and "single pass" munitions dispensers to minimize exposure of the aircraft to enemy SHORADS. This will not eliminate the need for advanced SHORAD countermeasures on the aircraft, but it seems unlikely that such countermeasures can solve the growing problem SHORADS create.

The steady improvement of enemy SHORADS also creates further reservations about the value of current air-to-ground PGMs versus area munitions. PGMs now force exposure of attack profiles or multiple passes. This situation is virtually certain to worsen as threat SHORADS increase in number and capability. Finally, as Israel demonstrated in 1982, it is critical to be able to locate SHORADS both for air defense suppression and for avoidance. Israel is the only state so far to dedicate key sensor assets to this mission, such as RPVs, forward observer aircraft, recce fighters, and E-2C/E-707s. In the future, USCENTCOM and possibly friendly air forces will need more advanced platforms.

The High-Technology Content of Low-Level Wars

No improvement to Western forces will be enough to substitute for an effective strategy for technology transfer to friendly forces. This is a global problem that affects every major Western nation transferring arms and military technology to the Third World, and it is particularly critical for the Gulf states and Western operations in this region. Table 5.5 shows the mix of friendly and unfriendly forces in the region. The key to the Western position in the Gulf lies in improving the technology both in Western power projection forces and in pivotal friendly states such as Saudi Arabia and Oman and states outside the region such as Egypt, Israel, and Jordan.

Table 5.6 provides an even clearer illustration of the problems involved. It shows the pattern of technology transfer already moving into the region from Western and Soviet bloc sources, and it provides a clear indication that future low-level wars will demand even higher levels of technical proficiency than the conflicts analyzed in this study. Low-level war is obviously becoming something of a misnomer for conflicts in the Third World, and it is clear from the data in Tables 5.5 and 5.6 that a technology strategy for the Third World must put the West firmly in the lead in supporting friendly states with advanced technology if it is to reduce its own commitments, improve Western and Third World security, and deny the Soviet bloc the opportunity to exploit its own arms transfers to hostile states and movements.

Western forces must have the C^3I/BM technology and assets to help overcome the difficulties in operating with local forces, which often will have a different language, tactics, and weapons systems. The sheer diversity of such systems is illustrated by the mix of air C^3I and weapons systems that Western forces may have to use in the Gulf. These forces are shown in Table 5.7. The West cannot simply tailor its assets to its own needs. Western C^3I/BM technology and tactics must

TABLE 5.5 The Critical Impact of Indigenous Gulf Forces on Western Operations

	Manpower	Tanks	Other AFVs	Artillery	Combat Aircraft	Heli- copters	Paramilitary Forces	Reserves
SOVIET- ORIENTED EQUIPPED								
Ethiopia[a]	227,000[b]	1,020	835+	700+	145	56	169,000	20,000
South Yemen	27,500	470	400+	350	113[c]	45	45,000	45,000
Total	254,500	1,490	1,235+	1,050+	258	101	214,000	65,000
WESTERN- ORIENTED EQUIPPED								
Egypt[d]	445,000	2,250	4,430	2,112	442[e]	242	439,000	604,000
Kuwait	12,000	240	435	42+	80	40	18,000	—
Oman	21,500	75	27	93	52	34	5,085	1,000
Qatar	6,000	24	209	14	23	22	some	—
Saudi Arabia	67,500	450	1,310+	481+	216	80	25,000	—
UAE	43,000	196	516+	88	43	52	some	—
Total	595,000	3,235	6,927+	2,830+	857	470	487,085+	605,000
UNCERTAIN								
Iran[a]	704,500	1,050+	1,360+	600+	68+	76+	70,000	350,000
Iraq[a]	845,000	4,500+	4,000	5,500+	500	397	31,800	654,800
North Yemen	36,550	659	440+	295+	95[f]	33	25,000+	40,000
Total[a]	1,586,050	6,209+	5,800+	6,395+	663+	506+	126,800+	1,044,800

[a]Excluding expatriate personnel.
[b]Some 1,400 Soviet, 500 Cuban, and 300 East German technicians are engaged in Ethiopia, operating aircraft and heavy equipment.
[c]Some believed in storage; some flown by Soviet and Cuban crews.
[d]Egypt was previously equipped with Soviet armaments.
[e]Most Soviet equipment is now in reserve, although some has been rebuilt using Western, Chinese, and domestically produced components.
[f]Some aircraft in storage.

SOURCES: IISS, *The Military Balance, 1986–1987* (London, 1986); Anthony H. Cordesman, *The Gulf and the Search for Strategic Stability* (Boulder, Colo.: Westview Press, 1984), p. 855.

take account of the need for translators and even the need to disperse systems or small units to local forces to "net" them into a common command and control system. This problem will be less severe with the more sophisticated Third World states but could be critical in other contingencies.

TABLE 5.6 Probable Shifts in Force Quality in the Near East by 1990–1995

Weapon/Technology	Impact
Challenger, AMX-40 M-1, T-80, Merkava II	Advanced tanks with 3rd- and 4th-generation fire control systems, spaced and other advanced armor, and advanced 120-mm guns. Will be matched by advanced types of other armored fighting vehicles.
ITOW, HOT, AT-6, AT-7, AT-8, Hell-fire	Advanced anti-tank missiles with full automatic tracking or fire-and-forget capability.
MRL, BM-24, BM-25, ASTRO	Western and Soviet multiple rocket launchers capable of firing advanced submunitions and "smart" minelets at ranges beyond 30 km.
Night vision devices	Widespread use of night vision devices. "24-hour" infantry, helicopter, and armored combat.
Secure, switched, advanced tactical communications	Conversion to advanced secure communications with auto-mated message traffic and battle management capabilities.
SA-10, Patriot, Improved Hawk, SA-6 Mod	Advanced surface-to-air missiles that cannot easily be suppressed with current weapons and electronic warfare means. Many will be netted with advanced sensor and battle management systems and linked to advanced short-range systems.
SHORADS: SA-14, Stinger-POST, etc.	Next generation short-range crew- and manportable surface-to-air missiles and radar-guided AA guns with far better tracking and kill capability and greater ranges. Many will be "netted" into an integrated battlefield and point defense system.
E-3A (Imp), E-2C (I), IL-76 SUAWACs	Airborne warning and control aircraft capable of manag-ing large-scale air wars using radar and electronic support measures (ESM) equivalent to NATO-level capabilities.
F-15E, MiG-29, Su-27, Lavi, F-16C, F-20A, Mirage 2000, Tornado, Lavi	Next-generation air combat and attack fighters with far more accuracy and up to twice the range payload of existing fighters.
Aim 9L/M, Phoenix, Mica, AA-8, AA-X10, AA-X-P2, Super 530, Python III	Advanced short- and long-range, multi-aspect, air-to-air missiles which greatly improve the air-to-air combat capability of all modern fighters.

(continues)

TABLE 5.6 *(continued)*

Weapon/Technology	Impact
Durandal, Paveway, ERAM, ACM, SUU-65, WASP, JP-233	Advanced air-to-surface munitions including runway suppression, anti-armor, anti-personnel, and other PGMs, smart submunitions, earth penetrators, minelets, etc.
RPVs, IMohawk, MiG-25 (I)	Improved airborne sensor and reconnaissance platforms that can provide advanced targeting, intelligence, and battle management data.
PAH-2, AH-64, Mi-24	Next-generation attack helicopters with much longer ranges, improved protection, third- or fourth-generation anti-tank guided missiles, and Aim-9L level air defenses. Will be supported by steadily improved troop lift helicopters with improved protection and firepower.
Peace Shield, Project Lambda, Lion's Dawn capabilities	Air sensor and battle management systems equivalent to NATO NADGE level systems for integrating fighter and SAM defenses. Many with advanced attack mission control.
Maritime Patrol Aircraft	More advanced versions of E-2C type aircraft armed with ASW weapons and air-to-surface missiles.
FAC(M), Missile Frigates: Saar 5, Lupo, F-2000, etc.	Next-generation missile patrol boats and corvettes with Improved Harpoon and other moderate-range advanced ship-to-ship missiles.
Sea Skua, Harpoon II, Exocet II, Gabriel III/IV, AS-4, AS-6, AS-7	Advanced ship-, shore-, and air-launched anti-ship missiles with advanced sensors and electronics and far more lethal payloads. Can kill warships and tankers far more effectively than today.
Coastal submarines	Advanced diesel submarines with excellent silencing, moderate cruise ranges, and smart torpedoes.
SS-22/SS-23	Advanced surface-to-surface missiles with ranges up to 900 miles.
Nerve gas	Widespread stocking of single or binary nerve gas agents and limited CBW defense capabilities.

TABLE 5.7 Progress in Creating an Effective Air Defense System in the Southern Gulf States

Country	Air Defense System Type	Air Defense System Supplier	Aircraft Type	Aircraft Supplier	SAM Missiles Type	SAM Missiles Supplier
Kuwait	Radars[a]	Thomson CSF	19 Mirage F-1 (24 F-1C in delivery)[b]	Dassault (France)	1 IHawk Bn.	Raytheon (US)
	AN/TSQ-73[a]	Litton, ITT (US)	30 A-4KU	US	SA-7 Missiles	USSR
	C[3] System[b]	($8.2M) Gifilian, Northrup (US)			SA-8 Missiles	USSR
Saudi Arabia	5 E-3A AWACS and Air, Ground C[3] ($5.8B)	Boeing (US) (Mitre, USG)	40 F-15E or Tornado[b]	US or Europe	2 Shahine Btes.	Thomson CSF (France)
	C[3] System ($1.6B)	Litton Data Command (US)	62 F-15A/8 Aim-9L	MacD (US)	16 IHawk Btes. ($270M)	Raytheon (US)
	Peace Shield C[3] ($3.9B)	Boeing	65 F-5E	Northrup (US)	400 Stinger ($30M)	CD (US)
	17 Seek Igloo Radars ($330M)	General Electric (US)	40 F-5B/F	Northrup (US)	AMX-30SA 30mm SP AA Guns	France
	5 Underground Centers ($184M)	CRS-Sirrien, Metcalf & Eddy (US)	15 Lightning	UK	12 Shahine Btes. and Crotale point and naval defense	
	Al Theqib System with 100 radars ($4B)	Thomson CSF (France)				
Bahrain	Teleprinter Data Link to Saudi Arabia		12 F-5F with Aim-9Ps[b]	Northrup (US)	6 RSB-70 Btes. IHawk[c]	Sweden Raytheon (US)
Qatar	Negotiations on C[3]I System	France, US	13 Mirage F-1	Dassault (France)	Rapiers	British
			14 Mirage F-1c		5 Tigercat	Aerospace (UK)
			8 Alphajet	FRG		
			2 Hunter	BA (UK)		

(continues)

TABLE 5.7 (continued)

Country	Air Defense System		Aircraft		SAM Missiles	
	Type	Supplier	Type	Supplier	Type	Supplier
UAE	Project Lambda[c] Air Defense C3I and Electronic Warfare with C-130s	Lockheed, HRB Singer (US), Consultant USCENTCOM	18 Mirage 2000 18 Mirage 2000[a] ($422M)	Dassault (France)	Rapiers Crotale	BA (UK) Thomson CSF (France)
	Skyguard 35mm Radar Guns	Contraves (Italy-Swiss)	30 Mirage 5 6 Alphajet	Dassault (France) FRG	24-42 IHawk RSB-70	Raytheon (US) Saab (Sweden)
Oman	28 Blindfire Radars	Racal (UK)	8 Tornado ($280M)[c] 24 Jaguar 16 Hunter 12 BAC-167	Europe BA (UK) BA (UK) BA (UK)	28 Rapiers	BA (UK)

a Ordered.
b Planned.
c Discussion only.

SOURCES: IISS, *The Middle East and the International System*, Parts I and II, Adelphi Papers Nos. 114 and 115 (London, 1975); SIPRI, *Defense and Foreign Affairs*, various editions.

Further, the West must be prepared to accept the bulk of its HUMINT from local forces and create "fusion" centers that can combine this data with PHOTINT and COMINT/ELINT and then pass relevant data back to local forces. The problems of threat assessment, C³I/BM, and targeting must be solved in a way that can support joint operations. This is particularly true because these are areas where even the most sophisticated friendly Third World states find technology transfer most difficult and where outside aid can be most effective in helping local forces.

The West also needs to give consideration to using limited amounts of high-technology forces to strengthen local forces rather than deploying full-scale intervention forces. The West should also consider deploying small high-technology firepower assets to support local forces in joint operations. The deployment of land- and sea-based air assets is a good example of high technology forces that can be deployed alone in support of local forces. Advanced sensor platforms like the E-3A or E-2C have already sufficed in some minor confrontations; similarly, small U.S. multiple rocket launcher units could provide field artillery support to fairly large units of the local army. A local army could also be supported with small SHORAD units or similar high-technology packages. The reduced size of any such Western unit would also help solve interface problems.

Well-armed attack helicopters and fixed-wing aircraft could also play a major role in augmenting local forces. Even in those cases where these systems are already in the possession of local forces, Western augmentation could be useful. This is because the loss of any significant portion of the local air force, due to inexperience on the part of the pilots, could take years to recover from. Furthermore, the destruction of a fledgling air force could have a devastating effect on the morale of the remaining local pilots and the ground forces.

Restructuring Technological Priorities to Minimize Casualties and Collateral Damage

Military planners in radical and authoritarian states often have the luxury of being able to accept high casualties in their planning. Western planners do not, however, have this luxury. Western planners must develop plans and forces that not only win a war, but win it with a minimum number of casualties. High casualties severely strain the resolve of democratic nations, and most interventions will be subject to intense domestic debate. There is little point in intervening in an area where public and legislative action will force a premature withdrawal. In fact, premature withdrawal is generally worse than refusing to intervene at the start of a crisis. For these reasons, minimizing casualties is not only a humanitarian requirement, it is also a military requirement.

Battles that may not destroy the fighting capacity of an army can, nevertheless, destroy the resolve of the nation. Such losses also need not be higher than those of the local enemy forces. The anti-Israeli forces in Lebanon, for example, suffered massive casualties, yet it was the Israelis with their smaller but significant losses who were forced to halt and withdraw. An earlier example of this same phenomenon can be seen in the 1973 war when Egypt's General Ismail repeatedly told his staff, "Loss of personnel is more painful to Israel than loss of territory or combat material."[2]

It is significant that many of the potential opponents of the West consider casualties in a different manner from the West. Iran may be the most extreme example in accepting hundreds of thousands of war dead in the struggle against Iraq. This acceptance came out of the fervor of an Islamic revolution, but secular revolutionaries can display similar types of devotion. The now-deceased revolutionary theorist Franz Fannon, for example, spoke of the need for "revolutionary violence" to restore "dignity" to Third World peoples. He considered a person not involved in the process of violence to maintain the mentality of a "slave." Similar logic, or the lack of it, has shaped the views of many extremists in the Third World. In a situation where violence is seen as the only answer, casualties seldom become much of an issue.

These factors help resolve the debate of high-technology versus low-technology forces in favor of high technology. Mass is always at least a partial response to the lessons of this report. Mass, however, implies a willingness to absorb casualties, which neither Western nor friendly local states share. Moderate and conservative Third World states are just as unwilling to expend their people's lives as those of the West.

Finally, these factors raise the challenge of creating a technology strategy that will minimize casualties and is concerned with the prevention of casualties and the rapid treatment of wounded. With regard to the first problem, this involves technologies that should be able to help American forces in taking advantage of good defensive terrain and, if possible, compensate for the disadvantages of less than optimal terrain. It is not really possible or even desirable to go into every technology that can limit casualties, as these technologies relate to all aspects of combat power.

Notes

1. Major General Rowley S. N. Mans, CBE, "Light Armor in the Rapid Deployment Force," *Armed Forces Journal International* (July 1981), pp. 49–50.

2. Cited in Colonel Trevor N. Duprey, *Elusive Victory: The Arab Israeli Wars 1947–1974* (New York: Harper & Row, 1978), p. 389.

SOURCES AND METHODS

No effort to describe a process as complex as war can ever hope to be complete. This is particularly true when much of the material on the conflicts under study is still classified and so many of the sources available on the war are in conflict. It should also be obvious to the reader that this study is affected by the inevitable limitations of dealing with unclassified material, which both increases the uncertainty in much of the analysis and forces it to focus on those areas where the most information is available.

The Afghan Conflict

It was possible to interview some of the journalists and scholars who have traveled to Afghanistan and a few Mujahideen who had served in the conflict, but it was not possible to talk to serving Soviet military. The vast majority of the sources used for the analysis of the Afghan war include translations of radio broadcasts and news materials, articles, books, and similar materials.

Most of this literature is Western and is biased toward the Mujahideen. There were, however, a considerable number of translations of Soviet military writings available in working form. These often cannot be referenced by name, but they provided useful background. So did other material provided informally by Pakistani officials.

The analysis of the the events and lessons of the Afghan War has also presented the inevitable problems of trying to analyze history in "real time." Although the use of computer data bases allows the rapid cross-correlation and checking of media reporting, it became obvious that on-the-scene observers often drew totally opposite conclusions about the performance of Soviet forces and the Muajhideen. This was particularly true of the performance of Soviet elite infantry forces.

The Falklands War

The analysis of the Falklands War is based on both British and Argentine sources and has been reviewed by officers serving on both sides. A limited number of interviews took place, but the primary sources are wartime press and radio reports from both sides as well as post-war writings.

Far better access was available to British sources than to Argentine sources. The same is true of access to the literature. The British have written far more serious material on the military details of the war than the Argentines have, although some excellent Argentine articles and interviews have appeared, plus a number of working papers that were made available for use in this study on an informal basis.

The exact tactical rationale of the senior officers of the Argentine navy and army for many of their actions is particularly unclear. The Argentine air force has been much more forthcoming and convincing in explaining its conduct in the conflict than the other services. The history of the command decisions the Argentine commanders in the Malvinas made during the fighting was not apparent from the limited post-war reporting available to the authors. The material that was available was clearly self-serving propaganda for the officers involved.

The reader should also be aware that significant conflicts emerged in various British sources available on the war. Most seem to stem from the different times at which given sources were written and the different amounts of data that had been released at the time. Nevertheless, minor conflicts emerged even in materials provided by the British government, and it was difficult to resolve many of the differences between the accounts actually written on the scene.

General Problems in Sources and Methods

Many of the data on both the Afghan and Falklands conflicts disagree in detail. In some cases figures and data had to be adjusted on a "best guess" basis. In others, the original data provided by a given source have been used without adjustment, even though this leads to some conflicts in dates, place names, force strengths, and so on within the material presented. The authors felt the reader would benefit more in these cases from being able to directly trace the data to a given source than from an effort to standardize all figures, names, and similar material.

Judgments had to be made throughout this book as to which report was right; many of these judgments were based on private interviews. It became all too clear, however, that if truth is the first casualty of war, then history is the first casualty of peace. No one outside the actual commands involved can be certain which interpretation of many issues is right.

The reader should also be warned that one of the lessons that has emerged from this project is how impressionistic most lessons learned in combat really are. Participants in war are scarcely objective observers of the details of tactics and technology. They operate on the basis of limited and constantly changing knowledge, and their priorities are combat and command, not recording keeping and analysis. While some data can be reconstituted after the fact, much cannot. Once again, this forces any analyst into making judgments and informed guesses on the basis of inadequate data and sharply conflicting viewpoints.

Another problem that is apparent in many of the written sources used in this work is the tendency of post-war analysts to focus on their area of interest and to exclude the importance of other factors in the conflict. Much, if not most, of the specialized technical literature on given types of weapons and operations is filled with special pleading, arguments for given weapons and technologies, or analysis which focuses solely on the area of tactics and technology under study. Many writers add a strong service or national bias to this problem.

The authors of this book fully recognize these limitations, as they do similar problems in previous volumes. The "fog of peace" is just as much a problem in understanding conflict as the "fog of war" and is just as unavoidable. In practice, therefore, the reader should be aware that any given lesson in this book requires careful analysis of other sources before it should be taken for granted. At the same time, we believe that the mix of interviews, data bases, and written sources upon which this book is based represent a valid starting point for what is ultimately an impossible process—understanding the overall nature of modern conflicts.

BIBLIOGRAPHY

The Afghan Conflict

Adams, James, "Afghanistan Becomes War Laboratory for the Soviets," *Los Angeles Times*, January 4, 1987.

Adelman, Jonathan R., "The Soviet Uses of Force: Four Cases in Soviet Crisis Decision Making," *Crossroads*, No. 16 (1985), pp. 47–81.

Alexiev, Alex R., "Soviet Strategy and the Mujahideen," *Orbis*, Vol. 29, No. 1 (Spring 1985), pp. 15–20.

———, *Inside the Soviet Army in Afghanistan*, R 3627-A, Santa Monica, Rand, 1988.

Amnesty International, *Afghanistan: Torture of Political Prisoners*, New York, Amnesty International, 1986.

Amphibious Warfare School Conference Group on Afghanistan, "Battle Study: The Soviet War in Afghanistan," *Marine Corps Gazette*, July 1986, pp. 58–70.

Amstutz, J. *Afghanistan: The First Five Years of Soviet Occupation*, Washington, D.C., National Defense University Press, 1986.

ARCO Series of Illustrated Guides, New York, Salamander Books, ARCO.

———, *Military Helicopters*.

———, *Modern Soviet Air Force*, 1982.

———, *The Modern Soviet Air Force*.

———, *The Modern Soviet Navy*.

———, *The Modern U.S. Air Force*.

———, *The Modern U.S. Navy*.

———, *Weapons of the Modern Soviet Ground Forces*.

Arnold, Anthony, "The Stony Path to Afghan Socialism," *Orbis*, Vol. 29, No. 1 (Spring 1985), pp. 40–71.

———, *Afghanistan: The Soviet Invasion in Perspective*, Stanford, Stanford University Press, 1981.

———, *Afghanistan's Two Party System*, Stanford, Hoover Institution, 1983.

Aviation Week and Space Technology, various editions.

Banuazizi, Ali, and Myron Weiner, *The State, Religion, and Ethnic Politics*, Washington, D.C., Joint Commitee on Near and Middle East, 1986.

Baylis, John, and Gerald Segal, eds., *Soviet Strategy*, Totowa, N.J., Allanheld, Osmun & Co., 1981.

Baxter, William P., "New Soviet Airborne Artillery," *Jane's Intelligence Review*, September 1988, pp. 18–20.

Bertram, Cristoph, ed., *Third World Conflict and International Security*, London, Macmillan, 1982.

Betts, Richard K., *Surprise Attack*, Washington, D.C., Brookings Institution, 1982.

Blechman, Barry M., and Stephan S. Kaplan, *Force Without War*, Washington, D.C., Brookings Institution, 1978.

Bodansky Yossef, "New Weapons in Afghanistan," *Jane's Defence Weekly*, March 9, 1985, p. 412.

———, "Learning Afghanistan's Lessons," *Jane's Defence Weekly*, February 20, 1988, pp. 310–311.

———, "Most Feared Soviet Aircraft in Afghanistan," *Jane's Defence Weekly*, May 19, 1984.

———, "General of the Army D.T. Yazov: Victor in Afghanistan," *Jane's Defence Weekly*, March 31, 1984.

Bonner, Arthur, *Among the Afghans*, Durham, N.C., Duke University Press, 1987.

Bonosky, Phillip, *Washington's Secret War Against Afghanistan*, New York, International Publishers, 1984.

Bpoullada, Leon, "The Failure of American Diplomacy in Afghanistan," *World Affairs*, Winter 1982–83.

Bradsher, Henry S., *Afghanistan and the Soviet Union*, Durham, N.C., Duke University Press, 1983.

Brassey's Defense Yearbook (later *RUSI and Brassey's Defense Yearbook*), London, various years.

Bussert, James C., "Signal Troops Central to Soviet Afghanistan Invasion," *Defense Electronics*, June 1983, pp. 104–111.

———, "Soviet Military Maintenance Looks to ATE for Solutions," *Defence Electronics*, March 1983.

———, "Can the USSR Build and Support High Technology Fighters?" *Defense Electronics*, April, 1985.

Canfield, Robert L., "Islamic Sources of Resistance," *Orbis*, Vol. 29, No. 1 (Spring 1985), pp. 40–71.

Cardoza, Capt. Anthony A., "Soviet Aviation in Afghanistan," *Proceedings*, February 1987, pp. 85–88.

Carrington, Tim, "CIA Resisted Proposal to Give Afghan Rebels U.S. Stinger Missiles," *Wall Street Journal*, February 16, 1988, p. 1.

Carver, Michael, *War Since 1945*, London, Weidenfeld and Nicholson, 1980.

Central Intelligence Agency, *Afghanistan: Major Insurgent Groups*, Washington, D.C., CIA, 1983.

Chalian, Gerald, *Guerrilla Strategies*, Berkeley, University of California Press, 1982.

Chicago Tribune, various editions.

Christian Science Monitor, various editions.

CIA, *Handbook of Economic Statistics, 1985*, Washington, D.C., Government Printing Office, various years.

CIA, *World Factbook*, Washington, D.C., Government Printing Office, various years.

Clemens, Walter C., Jr., *The U.S.S.R. and Global Interdependence*,

Washington, D.C., American Enterprise Institute Studies in Foreign Policy, 1978.

Collins, Joseph J., *The Soviet Invasion of Afghanistan*, Lexington, Mass., Lexington Books, 1986.

———, "Afghanistan: The Empire Strikes Out," *Parameters* 12(1), 1982.

Congressional Presentation for Security Assistance Programs, various editions.

Congressional Research Service, Library of Congress, *Soviet Policy and the United States Response in the Third World*, Washington, D.C., Government Printing Office, 1981.

Cordesman, Anthony H., *The Gulf and the Search for Strategic Stability*, Boulder, Westview, 1984.

Cronin, Richard P., and Francis T. Miko, "Afghanistan: Status, U.S. Role, and Implications of Soviet Withdrawal," Congressional Research Service document IB88049, Washington, D.C., Government Printing Office, January 1989.

Curren, James B., and Phillip Karber, "Afghanistan's Ordeal," *Armed Forces Journal*, March 1985.

Davis, Jacquelyn K., and Robert L. Pfaltzgraff, *Power Projection and the Long Range Combat Aircraft,* Cambridge, Mass., Institute for Foreign Policy Analysis, 1981.

de Ponfilly, Cristophe, *Le Clandestin*, Paris, Editions Robert Lafont, 1985.

Defense News, various editions.

Defense Update, various editions.

Dupree, Louis, *Afghanistan*, Princeton, Princeton University Press, 1980.

Eaton, William J., "Key Afghan Rebel Reportedly Eludes Capture," Part I, *Los Angeles Times*, May 2, 1984, p. 10.

Economist Publications, London and New York.

The Economist, various editions.

Elliot, Theodore L., "Afghanistan After the 1978 Revolution," *Strategic Review*, Spring 1979.

Farr, Grant M., and John G. Merriam, *Afghan Resistance: The Politics of Survival*, Boulder, Colo., Westview, 1987.

Financial Times, London and Frankfurt, various editions.

Freistetter, Colonel Franz, "The Battle in Afghanistan: A View from Europe," *Strategic Review*, Winter 1981, pp. 41–53.

Frith, Captain Steven A., "Soviet Attack Helicopters: Rethinking the Threat," *Military Review*, March 1981, pp. 55–69.

Fullerton, John, *The Soviet Occupation of Afghanistan*, Hong Kong, 1982.

Galeotti, Mark, "Afghan Army Elite Forces," *Armed Forces*, September 1988, pp. 424–427.

Ghaus, Abdul Samad, *The Fall of Afghanistan: An Insider's Account*, Washington, D.C., Pergamon-Brassey, 1988.

Girardet, Edward, "Afghans Lament Lack of Guns," *Christian Science Monitor*, May 13, 1980, p. 3.

———, *Afghanistan: Occupation and Resistance*, London, Croom Helm, 1985.

Godwin, Jan, *Caught in the Crossfire*, New York, E. P. Dutton, 1987.

Gopalakrishnan, R. *The Geography of Afghanistan*, New Dehli, Concept,

1982.

Gorley, Scott, "The Soviet Army—Air Defense and Aviation," *Defense Electronics*, March 1989, pp. 100–103.

Griffiths, John Charles, *Afghanistan: Key to a Continent*, Boulder, Colo., Westview, 1981.

Grimmett, Richard F., *Trends in Conventional Arms Transfers to the Third World by Major Suppliers*, Washington, D.C., Congressional Research Service Report, various editions.

Grinter, Lawrence E., "The Soviet Invasion of Afghanistan: Its Inevitability and Its Consequences," *Parameters* 12(4), 1982.

Gunston, Bill, *Modern Airborne Missiles*, New York, ARCO, 1983.

Gunston, John, "Afghanistan USSR Terror Attacks," *Jane's Defence Weekly*, March 31, 1984, pp. 481–484.

Gyllenhall, Lars, "Soviet Tanks in Afghanistan," *Armed Forces*, February 1987, p. 88.

Hammond, Thomas T., *Red Flag Over Afghanistan*, Boulder, Colo., Westview, 1984.

Hansen, James H., "Afghanistan: The Soviet Experience," *Jane's Defence Review*, 1984.

Hardt, John, and Kates Tomlinson, *An Assessment of the Afghanistan Sanctions: Implications for Trade and Diplomacy in the 1980s*, Washington, D.C., Government Printing Office, 1981.

Harrison, Selig S., "Dateline Afghanistan: Exit Through Finland," *Foreign Policy*, No. 41 (Winter 1980–81), p. 170.

———, *Washington Post*, December 20, 1985.

Hart, Douglas M., "Low-Intensity Conflict in Afghanistan: The Soviet View," *Survival*, Vol. 24, No. 2 (March/April 1982), p. 62.

"Helicopter Protection from IR Missiles," *Jane's Defence Weekly*, October 5, 1983.

Helmsley, John, *Soviet Troop Control: The Role of Command Technology in the Soviet Military System*, New York, Brassey's, 1982.

Hill, John, "Afghanistan in 1988: Year of the Mujahideen," *Armed Forces Journal*, March 1989, pp. 72–79.

Hosmer, Stephen T., and Thomas W. Wolfe, *Soviet Policy and Practice Toward Third World Conflicts*, Lexington, Mass., Lexington Books, 1983.

Hutcheson, Major John M., "Scorched-Earth Policy: Soviets in Afghanistan," *Military Review*, April 1982, pp. 36–47.

Hyman, Anthony, *Afghanistan Under Soviet Domination, 1964–1981*, New York, St. Martin's Press, 1984.

International Defense Review, Special Series, various editions.

International Defense Review, various editions.

International Institute for Strategic Studies, *The Military Balance*, London, various years.

Isby, David C., "Afghanistan 1982: The War Continues," *International Defense Review*, Vol. 15, No. 11 (November 1982), p. 1524.

———, "Jihad in Afghanistan," *Soldiers of Freedom*, Vol. 3, Issue 1, February 1987, pp. 16–24.

————, "Soviet Tactics in the War in Afghanistan," *Jane's Defence Review*, Vol. 4, No. 7 (1984).

————, *Weapons and Tactics of the Soviet Army, Fully Revised Edition*, London, Jane's, 1988.

————, "New Non-Contact Mines from Afghanistan," *Jane's Intelligence Review*, September 1988, pp. 21–25.

Jacobs, G., "Afghanistan Forces: How Many Are There?" *Jane's Defence Weekly*, June 22, 1985.

Jane's Naval Review, London, various years.

Jane's All the World's Aircraft, London, various years.

Jane's Armour and Artillery, London, various years.

Jane's Aviation Annual, London, various years.

Jane's Combat Support Equipment, London, various years.

Jane's Defence Review, London, various years.

Jane's Defence Weekly, London, various years.

Jane's Fighting Ships, London, various years.

Jane's Infantry Weapons, London, various years.

Jane's Military Annual, London, various years.

Jane's Military Communications, London, various years.

Jane's Weapons Systems, London, various years.

Jeffries, Ron, "Freedom Fighter's Medcap," *Solider of Fortune*, December 1985.

Kaplan, Stephen S., *Diplomacy of Power*, Washington, D.C., Brookings Institution, 1981.

Karp, Aaron, "Blowpipes and Stingers in Afghanistan: One Year Later," *Armed Forces Journal International*, September 1987, pp. 36–40.

Karp, Craig, "Afghan Resistance and Soviet Occupation: A Five Year Summary," U.S. State Department Special Report, Washington, State Department, April 1984.

————, "Afghanistan: Eight Years of Soviet Occupation," *Department of State Bulletin*, Vol. 88, No. 2132 (March 1988), pp. 1–24.

————, "The War in Afghanistan," *Foreign Affairs*, Summer 1986.

Karsh, Efraim, *The Cautious Bear*, Boulder, Colo., Westview, 1985.

Keegan, John, *World Armies*, New York, Facts on File, 1979.

————, *World Armies*, 2nd ed., London, Macmillan, 1983.

————, "The Ordeal in Afghanistan," *Atlantic Monthly*, November 1985.

Kemp, Ian, "Abdul Haq: Soviet Mistakes in Afghanistan," *Jane's Defence Weekly*, March 5, 1988, pp. 380–381.

Khrobrykh, Col. A., "One Mountain Pass After Another—From the Afghan Notebook," *Aviatsiya I Kosmonautika*, No. 10 (Trans-Soviet Press), March 1981, p. 73.

Klass, Rosanne, "The Accords," *Foreign Affairs*, Vol. 66, No. 5 (Summer 1988), pp. 922–945.

Korb, Edward L., ed., *The World's Missile Systems*, 7th ed., Pamona, Calif., General Dynamics, Pamona Division, 1982.

Kurian, George, *Atlas of the Third World*, New York, Facts on File, 1983.

Lambeth, Benjamin S., *Moscow's Lessons from the 1982 Lebanon Air War*, Santa Monica, Rand Corporation, 1984.

Leites, Nathan, *Soviet Style in War*, New York, Crane, Russak & Co., 1982.

Leltenberg, Milton, and Gabriel Sheffer, eds., *Great Power Intervention in the Middle East*, New York, Pergamon Press, 1979.

Macksey, Kenneth, *Tank Facts and Feats*, New York, Two Continents Publishing Group, 1974.

Magnus, Ralph H., "The Afghan Stalemate," *Parameters* 15(2), 1985.

Magnus, Ralph H., *Afghanistan: Marx, Mullah, and Mujahid*, Boulder, Colo., Westview, 1985.

Malhuret, Claude, "Report from Afghanistan," *Foreign Affairs*, Winter 1983/84.

Martin, Mike, *Afghanistan, Inside a Rebel Stronghold*, New York, Blandford, 1984.

McCormick, Lt. Kip, "The Evolution of Soviet Military Doctrine," *Military Review*, July 1987, pp. 52–72.

MERIP *Reports*, various editions.

Meyer, Deborah G., "What's in the Soviet Arsenal?" *Armed Forces Journal International*, May 1982, p. 42.

Middle East Economic Digest, London.

Middle East Insight, various editions.

Middle East Journal, Washington, D.C., Middle East Institute, various editions.

Middleton, Drew, "In Afghan War, Soviets Learn from Guerrillas," *New York Times*, January 23, 1983, p. 6.

Monks, Alfred L., *The Soviet Intervention in Afghanistan*, Washington, D.C., AEI, 1981.

Moorcraft, Paul L., "Bloody Standoff in Afghanistan," *Army*, April 1985.

Natkiel, Richard, *Atlas of the 20th Century*, New York, Facts on File, 1982.

Nearby Observer, "The Afghan-Soviet War: Stalemate or Evolution?" *The Middle East Journal*, Spring 1982.

New York Times, various editions.

Newell, Nancy Peabody, and Richard Newell, *The Struggle for Afghanistan*, Ithaca, Cornell University Press, 1981.

O'Ballance, Edgar, "Soviet Tactics in Afghanistan," *Military Review*, August 1980.

Parker, Brig. Gen. Ellis D., "Soviets Stress Helicopter in Anti-armor Role," *Aviation Week and Space Technology*, January 16, 1984, p. 92.

Pierre, Andrew J., *The Global Politics of Arms Sales*, Princeton, N.J., Princeton University Press, 1982.

Ra'anan, Uri, *The USSR Arms the Third World*, Cambridge, Mass., M.I.T. Press, 1969.

Rawles, James W., "Stinger: Requiem for the Combat Helicopter," *Defense Electronics*, November 1988, pp. 30–33.

Rees, David, *Afghanistan's Role in Soviet Strategy*, Conflict Studies No. 118, London, Institute for the Study of Conflict, May 1980, p. 1.

Roy, Oliver, "Afghanistan: Four Years of Soviet Occupation," *Swiss Review of World Affairs*, Vol. 32, No. 12 (March 1984), p. 11.

————, *Islam and Resistance in Afghanistan*, Cambridge, Cambridge University Press, 1986.

Royal United Services Institute/Brassey's, *International Weapons Development*, 4th ed., London, Brassey's, 1981.

Sena, Cearnakya, *Afghanistan*, Boulder, Colo., L. Rienner, 1986.

Schmid, Alex P., *Soviet Military Interventions Since 1945*, New Brunswick, N.J., Transaction, Inc., 1985.

Schrage, Daniel P., "Air Warfare: Helicopters and the Battlefield," *Journal of Defense and Diplomacy*, Vol. 3, No. 5, pp. 17–20.

Sella, Amon, *Soviet Political and Military Conduct in the Middle East*, London, Macmillan, 1981.

Shavrov, I. Ye., General of the Army, *Lokal'nye Voiny: Istoriya i Souremenost* (Local Wars: History and Present Day), Voenizdat, 1981, pp. 79–84.

SIPRI, *World Armaments and Disarmaments: SIPRI Yearbook*, London, Taylor & Francis, various editions.

"Soviet Air Force in Afghanistan," *Jane's Defence Weekly*, July 7, 1984, pp. 1104–1105.

Stahel, Albert A., and Paul Burcherer, *Afghanistan: Five Years of Resistance and Guerrilla Warfare*, Washington, D.C., Freedom Policy Foundation, 1986, pp. 8 and 11.

Studenkin, Major P., "From an Afghan Notebook: In the Land of Mountains and Hopes," *Pravda*, April 14, 1981; translated in *Strategic Review*, Summer 1981, pp. 80–81.

Suvorov, Victor, *Inside Soviet Military Intelligence*, London, 1984.

Sweetman, Bill, "New Soviet Combat Aircraft," *International Defense Review*, January 1984, pp. 35–38.

Tapper, Richard, *The Conflict of Tribe and State in Iran and Afghanistan*, London, Croom Helm, 1983.

Taylor, John W. R., "Gallery of Soviet Aerospace Weapons," *Air Force Magazine*, March 1984, p. 118.

Turbiville, Jr., Graham H., "Ambush! The Road War in Afghanistan," *Army*, January 1988, pp. 32–42.

U.S. Arms Control and Disarmament Agency, *World Military Expenditures and Arms Transfers*, Washington, D.C., various editions.

U.S. Army Armor Center, Threat Branch, *Organization and Equipment of the Soviet Army*, Fort Knox, Kentucky, January 1981.

U.S. Army, *Weapon Systems*, Washington, D.C., Government Printing Office, various editions.

U.S. Army, *Soviet Army Operations*, IAG-13-U-78, Washington, D.C., Government, Printing Office, April 1978.

U.S. Army, *The Soviet Army: Specialized Warfare and Rear Area Support*, FM 100-2-2, Washington, D.C., Department of the Army, 1984.

U.S. Central Intelligence Agency, *Handbook of Economic Statistics*, various editions.

U.S. Defense Security Assistance Agency, *Foreign Military Sales, Foreign*

Military Construction Sales and Military Assistance Facts, Washington, D.C., Government Printing Office, various years.

U.S. Department of Defense, *Soviet Military Power*, Washington, D.C., Government Printing Office, various years.

———, *Afghanistan: A Year of Occupation*, Special Report 79, Washington, D.C., Government Printing Office, February 1981.

———, *Afghanistan: 18 Months of Occupation*, Special Report 86, Washington, D.C., Government Printing Office, August 1981.

———, *Chemical Warfare in Southeast Asia and Afghanistan: An Update*, Washington, D.C., Bureau of Public Affairs, November 1982.

———, *Afghanistan: Four Years of Occupation*, Special Report 112, Washington, D.C., Government Printing Office, 1985.

———, *Chemical Weapons Use in Southeast Asia and Afghanistan*, Document 553, Washington, D.C., Bureau of Public Affairs, February 21, 1984.

———, *Afghan Refugees in Pakistan*, Washington, D.C., Bureau of Public Affairs, July, 1985.

———, *Afghanistan: Eight Years of Occupation*, Special Report 175, Washington, D.C., Government Printing Office, 1987.

U.S. News and World Report, various editions.

Urban, Mark L., "Soviet Forces in Afghanistan," *Jane's Defence Weekly*, January 12, 1985.

———, "A More Competent Afghan Army," *Jane's Defence Weekly*, November 23, 1985, pp. 1147–1151.

———, "Afghanistan: A New Horizon for the Soviets," *Jane's Defence Weekly*, February 8, 1986, pp. 209–210.

———, "Russia's Costly Bargain in Afghanistan," *The Economist*, November 20, 1985.

———, *War in Afghanistan*, London, St. Martin's Press, 1988.

Valenta, Jiri, "The Soviet Invasion of Afghanistan: The Difficulty of Knowing When to Stop," *Orbis*, Summer 1980.

Victor, Jean Christofe, *La Cité des Murmures*, Paris, Editions J. C. Lattes, 1983.

von Senger, F. M., and Etterlin, *Tanks of the World 1983*, Annapolis, Md., Nautical & Aviation Publishing Co., 1983.

War Data, special editions of the *Born in Battle* series, Jerusalem, Eshel-Dramit.

Warhurst, Geoffrey, "Afghanistan—A Dissenting Appraisal," *RUSI Journal*, September 1980, pp. 26–36.

Washington Post, various editions.

Washington Times, various editions.

Wheeler, Capt. Charles G., "The Forces in Conflict, Perspectives on Afghanistan," *Military Review*, July 1987, pp. 52–72.

White, B. T., *Wheeled Armoured Fighting Vehicles in Service*, Poole/Dorset, Blandford Press, 1983.

Williams, E. S., "Only Two Mistakes: Mine Warfare in Afghanistan," *Armed Forces*, October 1988, pp. 451–452.

Willis, Guy, "Hind Weapons and Countermeasures Fit," *International Defense Review*, February 1989, p. 136.

Wimbush, S. Enders, and Alex Alexiev, "Soviet Central Asian Soliders in Afghanistan," N-1634/1, Santa Monica, Rand, 1981.

The Falklands War

Aerospace Daily, various editions.

Air Force Magazine, various editions.

Albrecht, Gerhard, *Weyer's Warships of the World 1984/85*, 57th ed., Annapolis, Md., Nautical & Aviation Publishing Co., 1984.

ARCO Series of Illustrated Guides, New York, Salamander Books, ARCO.

————, *Weapons of the Modern Soviet Ground Forces.*

————, *Military Helicopters.*

————, *Soviet Army Operations*, April 1978.

————, *The Israeli Air Force.*

————, *The Modern Soviet Air Force.*

————, *The Modern Soviet Navy.*

————, *The Modern U.S. Air Force.*

————, *The Modern U.S. Navy.*

Argentine Ministry of Defense, various working papers.

"Argentine Ship Update Now Under Way," *Jane's Defence Weekly*, October 22, 1988, p. 999.

Aviation Week, various editions.

Bailey, Major Jonathan, "Training for War: The Falklands 1982," *Military Review*, Vol. 63, No. 9 (September 1983).

Baker, A. D. III, ed., *Combat Fleets of the World*, Annapolis, Md., Naval Institute Press, various editions.

Bass, Gail, and Bonnie Jean Cordes, *Actions Against Non-Nuclear Energy Facilities: September 1981–September 1982*, Santa Monica, Calif., Rand Corporation, April 1983.

Baylis, John, and Segal, Gerald, eds., *Soviet Strategy*, Totowa, N.J., Allanheld, Osmun & Co., 1981.

Beaver, Paul, *Encyclopedia of the Modern Royal Navy*, Annapolis, Md., Naval Institute Press, 1982.

Bertram, Cristoph, ed., *Third World Conflict and International Security*, London, Macmillan, 1982.

Betts, Richard K., *Surprise Attack*, Washington, D.C., Brookings Institution, 1982.

Birtles, P. J., "BA Dynamics Rapier Low Level Air Defense System," *Armed Forces*, August, 1982.

Blechman, Barry M., and Stephan S. Kaplan, *Force Without War*, Washington, D.C., Brookings Institution, 1978.

Brassey's Defense Yearbook (later *RUSI and Brassey's Defense Yearbook*), London, various years.

Braybrook, Roy M., *Battle for the Falklands (3): Air Forces*, Men-at-Arms Series #153, London, Osprey Publishing Ltd., 1982.

————, "Is It Goodbye to Ground Attack?" *Air International*, Vol. 10, No. 5 (May 1976).

Briasco, Jesus R., and Salvador M. Huertas, *Falklands: Witness of Battle*, Spain, 1985.

British Army Review Board, *The British Army in the Falklands, 1982*, London, Her Majesty's Stationery Office, 1983.

British Governmental Review Committee, *Falklands Islands Review: Report of a Committee of Privy Counselors*, London, Her Majesty's Stationery Office, 1983.

British Ministry of Defense, *The Falklands Campaign: The Lessons*, London, Her Majesty's Stationery Office, 1982.

Brown, David A., "Countermeasures Aided British," *Aviation Week and Space Technology*, July 19, 1982.

Brown, James, and William P. Snyder, *The Regionalization of Warfare*, New Brunswick, Transaction Books, 1985.

Brunck, Major Ralph, "Soviet Military Science and the Falklands Conflict," Parts I, II, & III, *Proceedings*, October, November, and December 1985.

Bussert, Jim, "Can the USSR Build and Support High Technology Fighters?" *Defense Electronics*, April 1985, pp. 121–130.

Calvert, Peter, *The Falklands Crisis: The Rights and the Wrongs*, New York, St. Martin's Press, 1982.

Carver, Michael, *War Since 1945*, London, Weidenfeld and Nicholson, 1980.

Chalian, Gerald, *Guerrilla Strategies*, Berkeley, University of California Press, 1982.

Chant, Chris, *A Concise Guide to the Military Aircraft of the World*, London, Temple Press, 1984.

————, *The World's Air Forces*, London, Chartwell Books, 1979.

Chicago Tribune, various editions.

Christian Science Monitor, various editions.

CIA, *Handbook of Economic Statistics, 1985*, CPAS-85-10001, Washington, D.C., Government Printing Office, September 1985.

Clemens, Walter C., Jr., *The U.S.S.R. and Global Interdependence*, Washington, D.C., American Enterprise Institute Studies in Foreign Policy, 1978.

Conference on the Lessons of the South Atlantic War, London, Royal Aeronautical Society, September 2–3, 1982.

Congressional Presentation for Security Assistance Programs, Vols. 1 and 2, Washington, D.C., Department of State, Fiscal Year 1987.

Congressional Research Service, Library of Congress, *Soviet Policy and the United States Response in the Third World*, Washington, D.C., Government Printing Office, 1981.

Conway's All the World's Fighting Ships 1947–1982, London, Conway Maritime Press, 1983.

Davis, Jacquelyn K., and Robert L. Pfaltzgraff, *Power Projection and the Long Range Combat Aircraft*, Cambridge, Mass., Institute for Foreign Policy Analysis, June 1981.

Day, Kathleen, "Sergeant York Gun System Misses Mark, Delivery Slow and Tests Poorly," *Los Angeles Times*, February 29, 1984, Section IV.

Defense and Foreign Affairs, various editions.

Defense Electronics, various editions.

Defense Marketing Services, computer data base.

Defense News, various editions.

Dicker, R.J.L., "RDF Sealift Program," *International Defense Review*, Vol. 16, No. 7 (July 1983).

"Drastic Argentine Army Reorganization," *Jane's Defence Weekly*, April 12, 1984.

"ECM in the Falklands War Proves Its Point the Hard Way," *Military Electronics/Countermeasures*, November 1982.

Economist Publications, London and New York.

The Economist, various editions.

Eddy, Paul, ed., *War in the Falklands: The Full Story*, New York, Harper and Row, 1982.

English, Adrian, and Anthony Watts, *Battle for the Falklands (2): Naval Forces*, Men-at-Arms Series #134, London, Osprey Publishing Ltd., 1982.

Ethell, Jeffery, and Alfred Price, *Air War: South Atlantic*, New York, Macmillan, 1984.

Financial Times, London and Frankfurt.

Fowler, William, *Battle for the Falklands (1): Land Forces*, Men-at-Arms Series #133, London, Osprey Publishing Ltd., 1982.

Fox, Robert, *Eyewitness: Falklands*, London, Methuen, 1982.

Friedman, Norman, "The Falklands War: Lessons Learned and Mislearned," *Orbis*, Winter 1983.

Frith, Capt. Steven A., "Soviet Attack Helicopters: Rethinking the Threat," *Military Review*, March 1981.

George, Bruce (MP) and Michael Coughlin, "British Defense Policy After the Falklands," *Survival*, September–October 1982.

Godden, John, *Harrier: Ski-Jump to Victory*, Oxford, Brassey's, 1983.

Goldblat, Jozef, and Victor Millan, *The Falklands/Malvinas Conflict: A Spur to Arms Build-Ups*, London, Taylor & Francis, 1983.

Grimmett, Richard F., *Trends in Conventional Arms Transfers to the Third World by Major Supplier, 1978–1985*, Congressional Research Service Report 86-99F, Washington, D.C., May 9, 1986.

Gueritz, Rear Admiral E. F., "The Falklands: Joint Warfare Justified," *Journal of the Royal United Institute for Defense Studies*, September 1982.

Guertner, Gary L., "The 74 Day War: New Technology and Old Tactics," *Military Review*, November 1982.

Gunston, Bill, *Modern Airborne Missiles*, New York, ARCO, 1983.

———, *Modern Soviet Air Force*, New York, ARCO, 1982.

Hanrahan, Brian, and Robert Fox, *"I Counted Them All Out and I Counted Them All Back,"* London, British Broadcasting Corp., 1982.

Hastings, Max, and Simon Jenkins, *The Battle for the Falklands*, New York, W. W. Norton, 1983.

"Helicopter Special," Number 60, *Defense Update*, March 1985.

Hemsley, John, *Soviet Troop Control*, New York, Brassey's, 1982.

Hope, Adrian F. J., "Sovereignty and Decolonization of the Malvinas (Falkland Islands)," *Boston College International and Comparative Law Review*, Vol. 6, No. 2, 1983.

International Defense Review, Special Series, various editions.

International Defense Review, various editions.

International Institute for Strategic Studies, *The Middle East and the International System*, Parts I and II, Adelphi Papers Nos. 114 and 115, London, 1975.

————, *The Military Balance*, London, various years.

International Journal of Middle East Studies, various editions.

Jacques Clostermann, "The Argentine Air Force Today," *International Defense Review*, September 1988, pp. 1099–1100.

Jane's All the World's Aircraft, London, various years.

Jane's Armour and Artillery, London, various years.

Jane's Aviation Annual, London, various years.

Jane's Combat Support Equipment, London, various years.

Jane's Defence Review, London, various years.

Jane's Defence Weekly, various years.

Jane's Fighting Ships, London, various years.

Jane's Infantry Weapons, London, various years.

Jane's Military Annual, London, various years.

Jane's Military Communications, London, various years.

Jane's Naval Annual, London, various years.

Jane's Naval Review, London, various years.

Jane's Weapons Systems, London, various years.

Jenkins, Brian Michael, et al., "Nuclear Terrorism and Its Consequences," *Society*, 17, No. 5 (July–August 1980), pp. 5–25.

Jones, Rodney W., *Small Nuclear Forces and U.S. Security Policy*, Lexington, Mass., Lexington Books, 1984.

Jordan, John, *Modern Naval Aviation and Aircraft Carriers*, New York, ARCO, 1983.

Kaplan, Stephen S., *Diplomacy of Power*, Washington, D.C., Brookings Institution, 1981.

Karsh, Efraim, *The Cautious Bear*, Boulder, Colo., Westview, 1985.

Keegan, John, *World Armies*, New York, Facts on File, 1979.

————, *World Armies*, 2nd ed., London, Macmillan, 1983.

King, Robert, "Will Tigerfish End UK Torpedo Problems?" *Armed Forces Journal*, August, 1986.

Kingston, Lt. Gen. Robert C., "From the RDF to Centcom," *Journal of the Royal United Institute for Defense Studies*, Vol. 129, No. 1 (March 1984).

Klare, Michael T., *American Arms Supermarket*, Austin, University of Texas Press, 1984.

Klepak, H. A., "Continuity and Change in the Argentine Army Since the Falklands War," *Armed Forces*, Vol. 4, No. 8 (August 1985).

Koburger, Charles W., Jr., *Seapower in the Falklands*, New York, Praeger, 1983.

Korb, Edward L., ed., *The World's Missile Systems*, 7th ed., Pamona, Calif., General Dynamics, Pamona Division, 1982.

Kurian, George, *Atlas of the Third World*, New York, Facts on File, 1983.

Laffin, John, *Fight for the Falklands*, New York, St. Martin's Press, 1982.

Leites, Nathan, *Soviet Style in War*, New York, Crane, Russak & Co., 1982.

London Sunday Times, various editions.

London Telegraph, various editions.

London Times, various editions.

Macksey, Kenneth, *Tank Facts and Feats*, New York, Two Continents Publishing Group, 1974.

Manners, Geoffery, "Falklands Solider's Best Friend Was His Milan," *Jane's Defence Weekly*, April 7, 1984.

Mans, Maj. Gen. Rowley S. N., "Light Armor in the Rapid Deployment Force," *Armed Forces Journal*, July 1981.

Marcella, Gabriel, *The Malvinas/Falklands War of 1982: Lessons for the United States and Latin America*, Carlisle Barrack, U.S. Army War College, Penn., 1983.

Mastny, Vojtech, "The Soviet Union and the Falklands War," *Naval War College Review*, May–June 1983.

Menaul, Air Vice Marshall Stewart W., "The Falklands Campaign: A War of Yesterday?" *Strategic Review*, Fall 1982.

"Mines Still Prevent Return to Normality in the Falklands," *Jane's Defence Weekly*, June 21, 1986.

Moore, Maj. Gen. Sir Jeremy, and Rear Adm. Sir John Woodward, "The Falklands Experience," *Journal of the Royal United Services Institute for Defense Studies*, March 1983.

Moorer, Adm. Thomas H., and Alvin J. Cottrell, "In the Wake of the Falklands Battle," *Strategic Review*, Summer 1982.

Natkiel, Richard, *Atlas of the 20th Century*, New York, Facts on File, 1982.

Neuman, Stephanie, *Defense Planning in Less-Industrialized States*, Lexington, Mass., Lexington Books, 1984.

New York Times, various editions.

Newhouse, John, "The Diplomatic Round, Politics and Weapons Sales," *New Yorker*, June 9, 1986, pp. 46–69.

NEXIS, computer data base.

Nott, John, "The Falklands Campaign," *Proceedings*, Vol. 109, No. 5 (1983).

O'Ballance, Edgar, "The Other Falklands Campaign," *Military Review*, Vol. 63, No. 1 (January 1983).

Perret, Bryan, *Weapons of the Falklands Conflict*, Poole/Dorset, Blandford Press, 1982.

Petrow, Richard, "The Smart Weapons Debate," *Electronic Engineering Times*, September 10, 1984.

Pierre, Andrew J., *The Global Politics of Arms Sales*, Princeton, N.J., Princeton University Press, 1982.

Preston, Anthony, *Sea Combat Off the Falklands*, London, Willow Books, 1982.

———, "Air Defense at Sea, A Vital Choice," *Jane's Defence Weekly*, August 31, 1985.

Price, Alfred, *Harrier and Sea Harrier at War*, London, Ian Allen, Ltd., 1985.

Proceedings of the U.S. Naval Institute, various editions.

Ra'anan, Uri, *The USSR Arms the Third World*, Cambridge, Mass., M.I.T. Press, 1969.

Reed, John, "Military Sealift Command," *Armed Forces*, November 1982.

Royal Navy Today and Tomorrow (The), Surrey, England, Ian Allen Ltd., 1981.

Royal United Services Institute, various working papers.

Royal United Services Institute/Brassey's, *International Weapons Development*, 4th ed., London, Brassey's, 1981.

Ryan, J. W., *Guns, Mortars, and Rockets*, New York, Brassey's, 1982.

Sanders, John, "How Rapid? How Deployable?" *Defense and Foreign Affairs*, Vol. 9, No. 1 (January 1981).

Scheina, Dr. Robert L., "The Malvinas Campaign," *Proceedings*, Vol. 109, No. 5 (1983).

Schmid, Alex P., *Soviet Military Interventions Since 1945*, New Brunswick, N.J., Transaction, Inc., 1985.

Schrage, Daniel P., "Air Warfare: Helicopters and the Battlefield," *Journal of Defense and Diplomacy*, Vol. 3, No. 5, pp. 17–20.

Schultz, James B., "New Strategies and Soviet Threats Spark EW Responses," *Defense Electronics*, February 1985, pp. 17–21.

Snyder, Jed C., Samuel F. Wells, Jr., eds., *Limiting Nuclear Proliferation*, Cambridge, Mass., Ballinger Publishing Co., 1985.

Standing Committe on Foreign Affairs, *Canada's Maritime Defense*, Ottawa, Canadian Government, May 1983.

Stockholm International Peace Research Institute, *Tactical Nuclear Weapons: European Perspectives*, New York, Crane, Russak & Co., 1978.

Stockholm International Peace Research Institute, *World Armaments and Disarmament: SIPRI Yearbook*, London, Taylor & Francis, Ltd., various years (computer printout for 1982).

Sunday Times Insight Team, *War in the Falklands: The Full Story*, New York, Harper and Row, 1982.

Swane, Lt. Col. David W. A., "British Light Helicopter Operations During the Falklands Islands Campaign," *U.S. Army Aviation Digest*, November 1983.

Sweetman, Bill, "New Soviet Combat Aircraft," *International Defense Review*, January 1984, pp. 35–38.

Trotter, Neville, "The Falklands Campaign: Command and Logistics," *Armed Forces Journal*, June 1981.

U.S. Arms Control and Disarmament Agency, *World Military Expenditures and Arms Transfers*, Washington, D.C., various editions.

U.S. Army, *Weapon Systems*, Washington, D.C., Government Printing Office, various editions.

U.S. Central Intelligence Agency, *Handbook of Economic Statistics*, Washington, D.C., Government Printing Office, various editions.

———, *World Factbook*, Washington, D.C., Government Printing Office, various years.

U.S. Congress, House of Representatives, Committee on Foreign Affairs,

Proposed Arms Sales for Countries in the Middle East, 96th Cong., 1st Sess., 1979.

U.S. Defense Security Assistance Agency, *Foreign Military Sales, Foreign Military Construction Sales and Military Assistance Facts*, Washington, D.C., Government Printing Office, various years.

U.S. Department of Defense, *Foreign Military Sales, Foreign Military Construction Sales and Military Assistance Facts*, September 1984.

U.S. Department of Defense, *Soviet Military Power*, Washington, D.C., Government Printing Office, various years.

U.S. Department of the Navy Study Group, *Lessons of the Falklands: Summary Report*, Washington, Department of the Navy, 1983.

U.S. Navy, Office of the Chief of Naval Operations, *Understanding Soviet Naval Developments*, Washington, D.C., Government Printing Office, April 1985.

U.S. News and World Report, various editions.

von Senger, F. M., and Etterlin, *Tanks of the World 1983*, Annapolis, Md., Nautical & Aviation Publishing Co., 1983.

Wall Street Journal, various editions.

Washington Post, various editions.

Washington Times, various editions.

Watson, Bruce W., and Peter M. Dunn, *Military Lessons of the Falklands War*, Boulder, Colo., Westview, 1984.

White, B. T., *Wheeled Armoured Fighting Vehicles in Service*, Poole/Dorset, Blandford Press, 1983.

Index

AA. *See* Anti-aircraft guns
Abadan, 371
Achakzai Militia Brigade, 86
Aeroflot, 88, 90
Aerospacio, 299
AES. *See* Soviet Aviation Engineering
    Service
AEW. *See* Airborne early warning
Afghan Airlines, 56
Afghan Communist Party, 64
Afghan Interests Protection
    Association (AGSA), 13, 15, 24, 26,
    29, 30, 32
Afghanistan, 23–24, 221–222(n34)
    agricultural infrastructure, 127, 206
    Air Force, 11, 13, 14–15, 30, 59, 73,
        98, 133, 177, 178, 180, 193,
        221(n22). *See also* Aircraft,
        Soviet/Afghan
    area of, 99, 108
    armor use, 154
    arms imports, 17
    Army, 11, 12–13, 14, 39, 43, 66, 98,
        220(n9), 226(n107)
    blood feuds in, 12
    border areas, 53, 56, 99, 130
    bride prices, 29
    captured officers, 144
    casualties/losses, 57, 133. *See also*
        Refugees
    cities, 102(fig.)
    civil service defections, 34
    civil war, 77
    Commandos, 193
    communist party in, 12
    conscription laws, 39, 40
    creation of DRA, 24
    creation of RA, 75

C^3, 122–123
defense expenditures, 16–17
Department of Tribal Affairs, 110
desertions/defections, 12, 25, 26, 30,
    35, 55, 66, 74, 86, 93, 143, 155, 165
economy, 104
elite units, 143
equipment holdings, 12–13, 14–15,
    81
equipment maintenance, 209
ethnic estimates, 221(n34)
executions, 221(n22)
food prices, 51
helicopters, 178, 193, 194, 204
infantry, 143–144
intelligence agencies, 21. *See also*
    Khedemati-e-Dolati
literacy campaign, 29
manpower, 98, 220(n9), 221(n20)
media, 104
military areas, northeast, 104(fig.)
Ministry for Nationalities, 110
Ministry of Defense, 49, 122
Ministry of State Security, 11, 60, 98
Ministry of the Interior, 15, 16, 42,
    60
missiles, 163, 164
mutinies, 39, 73, 116, 143
paramilitary forces, 8(table), 13, 15–
    16
parliament, 81
population, 108, 221(34)
power struggles in, 22
regular forces, 7–8(table), 11–15
SA-7 missiles, 155
secret police. *See* Afghan Interests
    Protection Association;
    Khedemati-e-Dolati

Soviet aid/arms to, 17, 30, 77–78,
97–98
and Soviet CARBs, 143
state of emergency, 94
tanks, 208
terrain/weather, 99, 100(fig.), 101,
144, 145, 148, 149
training of military personnel, 13,
59, 128
transportation infrastructure, 101,
103, 106–107, 133
and United States, 25
USSR creation of zones, 39
weapons from evacuating Soviet
forces, 98
youth corps, 59
See also Afghanistan War;
Mujahideen; Soviet Union forces
in Afghanistan
Afghanistan War, 96(fig.), 365
casualties/losses, 10(table). *See
also* Afghanistan,
casualties/losses; Aircraft,
Soviet/Afghan, losses;
Mujahideen, casualties/losses;
Soviet Union forces in
Afghanistan, casualties/losses
chemical weapons use, 30, 37, 47,
67, 90, 398
chronology of, 22–99
compared to Vietnam War, 1, 2, 95,
96(fig.), 108, 129–130, 131, 134, 143,
214
cost of, 16–17
countryside in, 76, 95, 125, 128, 132,
176, 188
highway war, 211–213
infantry in, 135. *See also individual
forces*
innovation and change in, 3, 136–
137
invasion routes, 32–33
lessons of, 95, 417–418
lines of communication, 101,
102(fig.)
political prisoners, 53
political warfare in, 130

Soviet initial invasion forces, 4
strategic background to, 23–26
See also Afghanistan; Mujahideen;
Soviet Union forces in
Afghanistan
Afridi tribe, 61
AGSA. *See* Afghan Interests
Protection Association
Ahmadzai, Najib(ullah), 64
Airborne early warning (AEW), 277,
307, 321, 323–324, 336, 341,
355(n19), 359(n104), 366, 390–
391
Airborne Warning and Air Control
System (AWACS), 67–68, 307,
324, 341, 368, 391, 431
Aircraft, Falklands War
A-4 Skyhawk, 250, 254, 256, 274, 295,
301–302, 308, 309, 310–311, 318,
329, 358(n84)
Alouette helicopters, 242, 329
Boeing 707, 245, 278, 279
Canberra bombers, 247, 301–302,
313, 315, 318
Chinook helicopters, 254, 287, 327,
332–333, 393
C-130 Hercules, 240, 241, 250, 274,
303, 334, 358(n84)
Dagger, 247, 301–302, 308–309, 311,
312, 313, 318–319, 352
Fokker F-27, 241
FSR-2 (Sea Harrier), 307–308, 357–
358(n73)
Gazelle helicopters, 253, 257, 325
Harrier, 245, 247, 249, 250, 251, 257,
263, 269, 274, 277, 294, 299, 300,
302, 303, 305, 307–308, 309–310,
311, 315–317, 323, 324, 325, 330,
341
Hercules, 330
HS-125, 279
Huey helicopters, 327
KC-130 tankers, 313, 320
Lynx helicopters, 246, 248, 254, 322,
325, 327
Macchi MB-326/329, 301–302
Mirage, 274, 289, 295, 301–302, 308–

309, 311, 312–313, 318–319, 346,
    352, 358(n84)
Nimrod, 277–278, 303, 322, 324, 330,
    359(n110)
Phantoms, 313
Pucara, 253, 289, 294, 298–299, 301–
    302, 313, 318
Puma helicopters, 242, 250
refueling of, 303, 313, 314, 319, 320,
    329, 330, 331, 352
Scout helicopters, 325
Sea King helicopters, 241, 250, 251,
    253, 274, 277, 326, 329, 345,
    355(n19)
Skyhawk. *See* Aircraft, Falklands
    War, A-4 Skyhawk
S-2E/SP-24, 325, 329
Super Etendard, 243, 245, 249, 254,
    256, 275, 301–302, 309, 313, 319,
    320, 329, 335, 348, 352
VC-10, 303
Victor, 247, 314, 324, 330, 359(n110)
Vulcan bombers, 243, 247, 249, 251,
    256, 257, 274, 294, 299, 300, 302,
    314–315, 323–324, 330, 355(n30),
    422
Wasp helicopters, 246
Wessex helicopters, 245, 246, 254,
    326, 327, 332–333
Aircraft, Soviet/Afghan, 178, 179(fig.),
    180, 352
AN-12/22, 33, 44, 65, 81, 98, 175, 177,
    181, 184, 213
AN-26, 72, 79, 175
AN-30 Clark, 108
Backfire bombers, 87–88, 89, 163,
    185, 190–191
bombers, 180
close support, 180–191
combat, 9, 11, 35, 51, 126, 127, 178,
    192
fighter-bombers, 180
helicopters. *See* Helicopters,
    Soviet/Afghan
Il-28, 180, 215
IL-76, 97
losses, 44, 49, 70, 133, 175, 176, 192,

194, 197, 231(n209), 232(n212)
L-39, 180
MiG-17, 180
MiG-21, 11, 35, 38, 44, 63, 127, 178,
    180, 181, 182–183, 207, 210
MiG-23/B/G, 11, 35, 38, 63, 127, 178,
    180, 181, 182–183, 184, 186, 205,
    210, 233(n240)
MiG-24, 183
MiG-25/B/D, 178, 210
MiG-27, 87, 88, 89, 127, 178, 185–
    186
MiG-29, 210
MiG-31, 38
repair facilities, 210–211
Su-7, 180
Su-17/25, 11, 35, 38, 44, 45, 48, 54, 60,
    63, 80, 108, 118, 127, 178, 180, 181,
    182–184, 186, 188, 205, 207, 210,
    233(nn 228, 233)
Su-22, 63, 180
Su-24, 88, 127, 163, 183, 185, 187, 188–
    189, 190(table), 211
Tu-16 Badgers, 50, 127, 180, 183, 187,
    188(table), 190, 211, 234(n242)
Tu-22, 187–188, 189(table)
Yak-28, 35
Aircraft carriers, 341
Air-to-air combat, 387–388
Air transportation forces (European),
    408–409(table)
Ajax Bay, 252
Alexiev, Alexander, 227(n117)
Alfonsín, Raul, 353
Alliance for the Liberation of
    Afghanistan, 35
Aluminum, 338–339
Ambushes, 139, 140, 145, 146, 149, 153,
    175, 195, 210, 213
Amin, Hafizullah, 12, 13, 25, 26, 28, 29,
    30, 31, 32, 33
Amnesty International, 68
Amphibious forces (European), 408–
    409
Andropov, Yuri, 47
Anti-aircraft (AA) guns, 62, 67, 127,
    147, 169–171, 205, 213, 225(n98),

294–295, 376, 384–385, 416–417, 423, 424

Anti-submarine warfare (ASW), 345, 355(n19). *See also* Submarines

APCs. *See* Armored personnel carriers

Arab-Israeli wars. *See* Lebanon; 1973 Arab-Israeli War; Six-Day War

Argentina, 1, 2
  aircraft, 300–302, 324. *See also* Aircraft, Falklands War
  aircraft losses, 250, 251, 253, 256, 295, 302, 303, 304(table), 305–306, 318, 328, 347
  Air Force, 282, 293, 303, 305, 311–313, 329, 351, 352, 353, 394
  air sorties, 302, 303, 309, 318–319, 334
  anti-aircraft guns, 294–295
  Army, 264, 265, 281–282, 283, 285–286, 328, 329, 352, 394
  artillery, 291
  bunkers/trenches, 284, 285
  casualties/losses, 242, 254, 258, 259, 266, 267(table), 288, 336(table). *See also* Argentina, aircraft losses
  and Chile, 263, 264
  combined arms, 283
  combined operations, 328–329
  commandos, 241, 263, 285
  conscripts, 264, 265, 285, 286, 353
  Crespo report. *See* Crespo, Ernesto
  C³I, 265, 281–282, 285, 369
  dirty war, 265, 353
  economy, 264
  electronic support measures, 279, 280, 352
  forces/assets available, 240–241, 261–262(table)
  helicopters, 327. *See also* Aircraft, Falklands War
  infantry, 283, 285
  intelligence, 329
  land forces, 264
  landing vehicles, 288
  logistical problems, 334

  military buildup, 264, 265(table)
  military improvements, 352–353
  mines, 291–292
  Naval Infantry Corps troops (Marines), 263, 283
  Navy, 243, 282, 328, 329, 334, 335, 341–342, 353, 394. *See also* Falkland Islands War, naval vessels
  night vision equipment, 293–294, 383
  officers, 265, 282, 285, 286, 334, 353
  politicized military, 281, 286, 334, 341
  radar, 278, 279, 294, 300, 308–309, 348, 352, 355(n30)
  rifles vs. British machine guns, 283
  ships lost or damaged, 336(table)
  submarines, 335, 343–345, 344(table), 353
  surrender of, 259–260
  threat assessment, 278–279
  training of military personnel, 264, 265, 266, 285, 353

Ariana Afghan Airlines, 88

Armored personnel carriers (APCs), 32, 124, 373
  M-113, 377–378, 379
  See also Armored vehicles

Armored vehicles
  BMD, 39, 124, 125, 139, 150, 151, 154, 171, 378–379, 417
  BMP/-1/2, 35, 124, 125, 150–151, 151–152, 154, 373, 378–379
  Bradley M-2/3, 378
  BRDM, 139
  BTR-60, 37, 150, 152–153, 154, 378
  BTR-70/80, 124, 139, 150, 153–154, 168, 378
  BTR-152, 154
  Panhard 90, 288
  See also Armored personnel carriers

ARMs. *See* Missiles, anti-radar

Army of the Republic of Vietnam (ARVN), 108

Army of Twenty Million, 422

Artillery, 372, 418–419, 423. *See also under individual combatants*
ARVN. *See* Army of the Republic of Vietnam
Ascension Island, 238, 247, 251, 262, 266, 278, 300, 324, 330, 331–332
Ashkhabad, 120
Assassinations, 40, 97, 130, 140
Assault rifles. *See* Rifles
ASW. *See* Anti-submarine warfare
ATGMs. *See* Missiles, anti-tank guided
Austria, 91
AWACS. *See* Airborne Warning and Air Control System

Badakshan, 64
Bagram Air Base, 11, 26, 30, 32, 33, 35, 42, 44, 72, 92, 181, 193, 210
Baklanov (CPSU Central Committee secretary), 90
Balar Hisar fort, 35
Barriers, 165, 291, 382, 383. *See also* Mines
Battle management (BM), 414, 419. *See also* Command, control, communications, and intelligence
Bazookas, 417
Beagle Channel, 264
Beheshti, Said Ali, 19
Beirut, 371, 376, 415
Bekaa Valley, 414
Belgium, 407
Belknap, 339
Bell, Roderick, 259
Berkeley Sound, 332
Bessmertnykh, Alexander, 89, 91
Black Buck missions, 247, 249, 250–251, 256, 257, 258, 314, 315
Blockades, 334. *See also* Falkland Islands War, maritime exclusion zone
Blue X, 216
Bluff Cove, 257, 258, 265, 333
BM. *See* Battle management
Boca Hill, 255

Bodansky, Yossef, 196
Bombs/bombing attacks, 218
  accuracy of, 184
  air burst, 216, 266
  anti-runway, 316–317, 390
  carpet, 131, 187, 189, 389
  cluster, 45, 181, 182, 183, 184, 207, 215, 216, 255, 315, 316, 323, 327
  combination, 184–185
  conventional iron, 276, 323
  Durandel, 315, 352, 390
  failures to explode, 254, 256, 317, 319, 323, 340, 351
  high-altitude, 50, 176, 177, 187, 192
  incendiary, 184, 185
  interdiction, 389–390
  laser-guided, 185, 323
  long-range, 187–191, 389–390
  retarded, 45, 316
  saturation, 276
  terror bombings in Pakistan, 65, 83
  truck bomb in Kabul, 79
Booby traps, 165, 166, 291. *See also* Mines
Bopal, India, 399
Bovin, Aleksander, 105, 219
Brazil, 257
Brezhnev, Leonid, 31, 47
Bribery, 130, 135
British Antarctic Survey team, 239, 245
Bulganin, Nikolai, 28
Bulgaria, 136
Bulletproof vests, 142
Buralamin Palace, 34
Bush administration, 93
Busser, Carlos, 241

Cambodia, 215
CARBs. *See* Combined arms reinforced battalions
Carter, Jimmy, 358(n79)
CAS. *See* Close air support
Casualties, 431–432. *See also under individual combatants*
Cease-fires, 47, 71, 73, 83, 88, 90

Central Intelligence Agency (CIA), 20, 25, 46, 65, 174
Chaff use, 256, 299, 300, 318, 321, 348, 359(n99)
Chamkani, Mohammed, 68–69
Chemical warfare, 30, 37, 47, 90, 126, 164, 183, 214–218, 217(table), 350, 398–399
Chesmibulbul, 218
Chile, 263, 264
Chloro-sulphonomine, 350
Chobham armor, 375
Chrag Sari, 161
CIA. *See* Central Intelligence Agency
Civilian(s), 382
    casualties, 36, 53, 68, 75, 80, 84, 89, 92, 164, 218
    homes/villages, 39, 46, 50, 58, 59, 68, 111, 123, 126–127, 129, 135, 139, 156–157, 185, 189, 190, 206, 215, 389, 395
    See also Refugees
Clingfilm, 269
Close air support (CAS), 180–191, 388–389
Combined arms, 117, 123–135, 282–283, 351, 370–373, 393
    basic principles of Soviet, 131
Combined arms reinforced battalions (CARBs), 124, 226(n107)
Combined operations, 206–208, 327–329, 370, 393–395
COMINT. *See* Communications intelligence
Command, control, and communications (C³), 112–123, 369–370, 372, 388, 389
Command, control, communications, and intelligence (C³I), 121, 122, 123, 280–282, 368–370, 372, 394, 397, 414, 419, 425
Communications intelligence (COMINT), 364–365, 366, 431
Comodor Revadaria, 263
Condor air base, 294
Cordovez, Diego, 44, 47, 50, 54, 68, 83
Cosmos satellite/spacecraft

launchings, 241, 243, 245, 246, 249, 255, 256, 257. *See also* Satellite reconnaissance
Counterbattery fire, 381–382, 414
Crespo, Ernesto, 302–303, 312, 328–330
C³. *See* Command, control, and communications
C³I. *See* Command, control, communications, and intelligence
Cuba, 132, 216
Czechoslovakia, 17, 26, 33, 138

Daoud, Mohammed, 24, 28
Darwin/Darwin Hill, 255, 289
Davidoff, Constantino Sergio, 239
Decoys, 300. *See also* Flares
Democratic Republic of Afghanistan (DRA), 3, 74, 75, 220(n12). *See also* Afghanistan
Desant forces. *See* Soviet Union forces in Afghanistan, elite units
Diego Garcia, 332, 407
Djibouti, 407
Dogs, 168, 213
Douglas settlement, 257
DRA. *See* Democratic Republic of Afghanistan
Draft dodgers, 43
Dragunskiy, D. A., 225(n92)
Drogue chutes, 207
DShB. *See* Soviet Union forces in Afghanistan, landing assault brigades
Dubs, Adolph, 25, 29

Economist, The, 356(n48)
Egypt, 43, 147, 172, 368, 380, 382, 383, 386, 391, 394–395, 396, 425
Eilat, 390
Electronic intelligence (ELINT), 109, 364–365, 412–413, 431
Electronic order of battle (EOB), 365
Electronic support measures (ESM), 275, 276, 279, 280, 299, 321, 325, 348, 352, 359(n99)
ELINT. *See* Electronic intelligence

El Salvador, 123, 365
EOB. *See* Electronic order of battle
Ermacora, Felix, 53, 68
ESM. *See* Electronic support
    measures
E-2C aircraft, 367, 368, 425, 431
E-3A aircraft. *See* Airborne Warning
    and Air Control System

FA. *See* Soviet Union forces in
    Afghanistan, Frontal Aviation
    forces
FACs. *See* Forward air controllers
FAE. *See* Fuel air explosives
Falkland Islands, 268(fig.). *See also*
    Falkland Islands War
Falkland Islands War, 1–2, 176, 238–
    239
    aircraft losses, 304–305(tables). *See
    also under individual countries*
    air-to-air combat, 306, 308, 310
    air war in, 300–323
    amphibious landings in, 266–267,
        333, 348–350
    Argentine assets available, 261–
        262(table)
    artillery in, 266, 289–291
    aviation fuel in, 262
    British Task Force, 244(table), 261–
        262(table)
    casualties/losses, 266, 267(table).
        *See also under individual
        countries*
    chronology, 239–260
    combined arms in, 373
    differences in combatants, 264,
        265–266
    heliborne lifts, 253
    infantry in, 283–286. *See also under
        indivdual countries*
    innovation in, 351
    intelligence fusion in, 413
    lessons of, 276–277, 286, 308, 317,
        321, 322, 327, 330–331, 335, 338,
        348, 350–353
    maritime exclusion zone, 242, 243,
        246, 247, 249, 260, 342

mines in, 284, 285, 291–293
naval systems in, 334–350. *See also*
    Falkland Islands War, naval
    vessels
and nuclear weapons, 400
prisoners taken, 246, 256, 259, 260
satellite intelligence in. *See*
    Satellite reconnaissance
submarines in, 341–345, 344(table)
surprise in, 269
tanks in, 259, 287, 288(table)
terrain/weather in, 266–267, 269,
    287, 300, 317, 349–350
threat assessment technologies in,
    269–279
Falkland Islands War, naval vessels,
    252(table)
    aircraft carriers, 341
    Alacrity, 250
    Alferez Sobral, 322, 325
    Almirante Irizar, 241
    Andromeda, 347
    Antelope, 253–254, 338, 339
    Antrim, 243, 245, 246, 253, 255, 319
    Ardent, 253, 276, 319, 338, 339
    Argonaut, 253, 318, 319
    Arrow, 247, 327
    Atlantic Causeway, 248, 250
    Atlantic Conveyor, 243, 248, 250,
        251, 254, 256, 287, 319, 326, 327,
        331, 333, 348, 351, 359(n99), 390,
        393
    Avenger, 256, 258, 323
    Bahia Buen Suceso, 239
    Bahia Paraiso, 240, 242
    Baltic Ferry, 248
    Brilliant, 246, 251, 253, 254
    Broadsword, 240, 254, 319
    Bulwark, 248–249
    Cabo de los Estados, 250
    Canberra, 242, 243, 245, 253, 260, 331
    Cardiff, 257
    Comodoro Somellera, 322, 325
    Conquerer, 248, 263, 341, 342, 343
    Coventry, 248, 254, 276, 325, 340
    Drummond, 241
    Elk, 242

Endurance, 239, 243, 245, 260, 263
Exeter, 256
Fearless, 243, 246, 251, 257, 281
Fort Austin, 240
General Belgrano, 243, 246, 248, 263, 305, 329, 334, 335, 341, 342, 350
Glamorgan, 259, 319, 338
Glasgow, 250, 319, 325, 340
Granville, 241
Guerrico, 242
Hercules, 241
Hermes, 241, 242, 249, 250, 251, 260, 263, 316, 348, 359(n99)
Hipolito Bouchard, 248
Intrepid, 243, 246, 257
Invincible, 241, 242, 251, 256, 257, 260, 263, 316, 359(n99)
John Biscoe, 240
Narwal, 250
Nordic Ferry, 248
Norland, 251, 260
Pearleaf, 242
Piedra Buena, 248
Plymouth, 246, 258, 319
Queen Elizabeth 2, 248, 250, 331
Salta, 344, 345
San Luis, 247, 250, 345
Santa Fe, 246, 322, 329, 344–345
Santissima Trinidad, 241, 266
Sheffield, 249, 250, 254, 274–275, 319–322, 339, 340, 348, 390
Sir Galahad, 254, 258, 260, 333, 343
Sir Geraint, 241
Sir Lancelot, 254
Sir Tristram, 258, 333
Spartan, 240
Splendid, 240
Tidespring, 243, 245
Type 42 destroyers, 340, 346
Type 21 frigates, 339–340, 346
Veinticinco de Mayo, 240, 243, 245, 329, 335
Wye, 256
Yarmouth, 240, 259
See also Falkland Islands War, naval systems in
Fannon, Franz, 432

Feldhouse, Sir John, 330
Ferranti, 324, 355(n17)
F-14 aircraft, 391
Fire control, 276, 277, 307, 321, 340–341
Fitzroy, 257, 265
Flares, 60, 84, 92, 172, 175, 176, 184, 196, 200, 205, 236(n282), 386, 423
Flechette munitions, 199
Fortuna Glacier, 245
Forward air controllers (FACs), 191, 196
Fox Bay, 251
Fozard, John, 358(n88)
France, 243, 299, 348, 368, 399, 402, 407
Fuel air explosives (FAE), 51, 184, 218, 419
Fusion centers/technology, 367, 369, 413

Gailani, Pri Said, 18
Galtieri, Leopoldo, 242
Gas warfare, 217(table). *See also* Chemical warfare
GAZ-66 communications vans, 152, 153
Geneva peace talks/accords, 45, 48, 52, 56, 58, 64, 66, 71, 74, 78, 83, 85, 86
Glover, Jeff, 356(n51)
Goat Ridge, 259
Golan Heights, 383, 389
Goose Green, 247, 251, 254, 255, 278, 283, 284, 294, 295, 306, 316, 327
Gorbachev, Mikhail, 60–61, 66, 77, 90
Great Britain, 1, 23, 62, 176, 402, 407
  air base/air defense facilities, 301(table)
  aircraft losses, 249, 253, 254, 300, 305(table), 306, 315, 325–326, 327, 332–333, 351
  airborne early warning, 323–324. *See also* Airborne early warning
  air reconnaissance, 324–325
  air sorties, 300, 302, 303, 315
  all-terrain vehicles, 333
  and Argentine arms imports, 270
  Army Air Corps, 306

artillery, 289–291, 290(table)
casualties/losses, 242, 249, 253, 254, 256, 258, 259, 266, 267(table), 283, 300, 335, 337–338(tables). *See also* Great Britain, aircraft losses
combined arms, 282–283, 373, 393
combined operations, 280, 327–328, 393–394
commandos, 286, 326
communication discipline, 282
C³I, 275, 280, 368–369, 393
elite reconnaissance troops, 278, 298
Falklands Task Force, 244(table), 261–262(table)
helicopters, 325–327, 332–333, 334. *See also* Aircraft, Falklands War
infantry, 283, 285, 286, 290
intelligence, 255, 263, 269, 270, 349, 365
land forces, 264
logistics and support, 330–334
mine detection, 292–293
Ministry of Defence, 300
missiles/guns, sea-based, 346(table). *See also* Missiles
Naval Air Command, 326
naval logistics, 332(table)
and night vision devices, 383
and nuclear weapons, 399–400
officer-troop relations, 265–266
operations and maintenance (O&M), 333
paratroops, 283, 284, 286, 316
radar, 274–277, 322, 324, 346, 347, 354–355(n17)
requisitioned ships, 331, 332(table)
Royal Air Force (RAF), 242, 300, 306
Royal Army, 333
Royal Fleet Auxiliary, 331, 332(table)
Royal Marines, 278, 306, 333, 349
Royal Navy, 289, 300, 334–335, 338, 339. *See also* Falkland Islands War, naval vessels
ships damaged/lost, 335, 337–338(tables)

ship vulnerability, 338–339, 349
Special Air Service (SAS), 240, 247, 251, 278, 281, 285, 289, 298, 305, 326, 328, 349
Special Boat Squadron (SBS), 240, 245, 247, 278, 285, 349
submachine guns vs. Argentine rifles, 283
submarines, 341–345, 344(table)
tanks, 283, 287, 288(table)
targeting, 284
task force problems, 345
threat assessment, 270, 274–278. *See also* Satellite reconnaissance
torpedos, 342–343, 345
training of military personnel, 266, 287, 371, 390
and U.S. assistance, 247, 260, 262–263, 263(table), 270, 280–281, 331–332, 368
and U.S. satellites, 263, 270, 280–281. *See also* Satellite reconnaissance
Welsh Guards, 287–288
White Paper on the Falklands War, 280–281, 283, 284, 290, 293, 314, 322, 324, 330–331, 339, 340–341, 342, 347
Greece, 232(n212)
Grenada, 390, 413
Grenade launchers, 156(table), 285
AGS-17, 125, 126, 127(table), 141, 153, 420
M-19, 420
RPG-7/16, 142, 155, 380, 420
RPG-18, 141, 143, 155–156, 420
RPG-22, 141–142, 156
RPO/-A, 142
Grimov, Boris, 81, 84, 85, 92, 93
Ground forces (European), 408–409(table)
Ground surveillance radar (GSR), 109
Grytviken, 239, 246
GSR. *See* Ground surveillance radar
GTVD. *See* Southern Strategic Theater
Gulabzoi, Mohammed, 16, 75

Gulf, Alef, 165
Gulf states, 23, 425, 426(table), 429–430(table)

Haq, Abdul, 82, 93, 122, 225(n94)
Hazara resistance front, 35
Hekmatyr, Gulbuddin, 82, 94
Helicopters, 391–393, 398, 419. *See also* Aircraft, Falklands War; Helicopters, Soviet/Afghan
Helicopters, Soviet/Afghan, 40, 47, 51, 62, 118, 119, 133, 182, 192–205, 207, 392–393
  AH-1/64, 200, 393
  deployments, 192, 193
  Havoc. *See* Helicopters, Soviet/Afghan, Mi-28
  Hind. *See* Helicopters, Soviet/Afghan, Mi-24
  Hip. *See* Helicopters, Soviet/Afghan, Mi-8; Mi-17
  Hook. *See* Helicopters, Soviet/Afghan, Mi-6
  Hound. *See* Helicopters, Soviet/Afghan, Mi-4
  Ka-136, 202, 203
  losses, 175, 176, 192, 197, 232(n212)
  Mi-2, 11
  Mi-4, 181, 194, 196, 204
  Mi-5, 38
  Mi-6, 11, 53, 124, 204–205
  Mi-8, 11, 127, 195, 197, 202, 203, 204, 216, 393
  Mi-17, 197, 203–204
  Mi-24, 11, 29, 30, 31, 33, 38, 47, 54, 60, 127, 131, 169, 170, 171, 172, 181, 194, 195, 196, 197, 199–202, 205, 206, 215, 393
  Mi-26, 139, 191
  Mi-27, 201–202
  Mi-28, 196, 202–203
  Mil-6/8/12, 45, 192, 204
  repairs, 211
  resupply use, 213
  specifications of Soviet, 198(table)
  tactics, 194–197, 205, 217
  training, 194, 235(n262)

Herat, 25, 43, 50, 55, 60, 65, 66, 72, 74, 117, 210, 223(n59)
Hestesletten, 246
Hezb-i-Islami, 17–18, 29, 78, 81
Hezbollah, 19
Himalaya Mountains, 99
Hindu Kush Mountains, 99
Hmong refugees, 215
Honduras, 368
Hue, Battle of, 417
Human intelligence (HUMINT), 105, 107, 109, 110, 128, 364, 367–368, 412–413, 431
Human Rights Commission, 68
HUMINT. *See* Human intelligence
Hunt, Rex, 241, 260
Hussein, Saddam, 415

Identification of friend or foe (IFF), 296, 297, 318, 347, 415, 424
IDF. *See* Israeli Defense Forces
IFF. *See* Identification of friend or foe
IFVs. *See* Infantry fighting vehicles
IISS. *See* International Institute for Strategic Studies
Illumination devices, 293
India, 399
Indian Ocean, 407
Infantry, 370–371, 372, 373–374, 418, 419–420, 422. *See also under individual combatants*
Infantry fighting vehicles (IFVs), 124. *See also* Armored vehicles
Inflatable tents, 210
International Institute for Strategic Studies (IISS), 12
Iran, 19, 20, 21, 22, 43, 44, 45, 51, 55, 66, 69, 72, 74, 78, 147, 218, 353, 364, 365, 369, 374, 375, 380, 395, 397–398, 400, 422. *See also* Iran-Iraq War
Iran-Iraq War, 218, 352, 364, 365, 366, 374, 376, 383, 384, 389, 391, 392, 398–399, 414, 422, 423. *See also* Iran; Iraq
Iraq, 315, 317, 352, 365, 369, 370, 371,

373, 375, 382, 396, 400. *See also* Iran-Iraq War
Isby, David C., 219(n6), 227(n117)
Islamic Alliance of the Afghan Mujahideen, 18–19
Islamic fundamentalism, 411
Islamic Movement, 19
Islamic Party, 17–18, 82, 94
Islamic Revolution Movement, 18
Islamic Society, 18
Islamic Unity for the Liberation of Afghanistan, 18–19
Islamic Unity of Afghan Mujahideen, 55
Ismail, General, 432
Israel, 214, 309, 317, 323, 328, 353, 358(n79), 364–365, 368, 371, 373, 381, 382, 388, 425. *See also* Israeli Defense Forces; Lebanon; 1973 Arab-Israeli War
Israeli Defense Forces (IDF), 367, 369, 374, 379, 394, 396
Italy, 402, 407
Izvestiya, 92, 219

Jaji Valley, 77, 79–80, 81
Jalalabad, 59, 67, 81, 93, 97, 117, 134, 164, 197, 208, 210, 211
Jammers/jamming, 176, 200–201, 205, 225(n95), 280, 294, 300, 315, 348
Jeeps, 167
Jones, Herbert ("H"), 255
Jordan, 368, 425

Kabul, 8, 35, 36, 70, 103(fig.), 117, 128, 134, 164
    defense/security, 40–41, 47, 59, 61, 79, 98, 158
    economic strain in, 37
    farewell parade in, 80
    food shortages, 88, 91, 92, 94
    fuel storage, 84
    Palace Guard, 92
    rocket/mortar attacks on, 52, 54, 55, 66, 71, 74, 80, 83, 85, 86, 90, 94
    Soviet airlifts, 93
    and Soviet withdrawal, 78

Special Guards Corps, 98
    surrounding provinces, 103(fig.)
    truck bomb in, 79
    vehicle repair in, 210
Kabul Airport, 33, 36
Kabul-Jalalabad highway, 73, 86, 90
KAM secret police, 32
Kandahar, 66, 69, 70, 71, 72, 79, 82, 84, 86, 88, 93, 134, 208, 211
Karmal, Babrak, 12, 24, 28, 39, 57, 59, 61, 63, 64, 68
KAVKAZ-76 exercise, 192, 207
Kerala, 30
KGB, 15, 28, 32, 33, 48, 58–59, 110, 121, 137, 206
KHAD. *See* Khedemati-e-Dolati
Khalilil, Masoud, 189
Khalis, Yunis, 74, 94
Khan, Ismail, 72, 82
Khan, Mohibullah, 223(n66)
Kharg Island, 389
Khedemati-e-Dolati (KHAD/WAD), 11, 34, 39, 43, 48, 49, 55, 60, 62, 63, 83, 110, 128, 130, 131, 185, 196, 206
Khorramshar, 376
Khost, 48, 55, 56, 75, 77, 81, 84, 86
Khrushchev, Nikita, 28
Khyyber, Mir Akber, 28
Kilikov, Marshall, 219
Kishtman, Sultan Ali, 94
Korean War, 283
Kunar Valley, 14, 26, 36–37, 53, 54, 207
Kunduz, 84–85, 88
Kushka, 120, 212
Kuwait, 368, 429(table)

Lafonia Plains, 325
Lakanwal, Abdul Ghaffer, 75, 89
Larijani (Iranian Deputy Foreign Minister), 91
LAVs. *See* Light armored vehicles
LAW. *See* Light anti-tank weapon
LCSFA. *See* Limited Contingent of Soviet Forces in Afghanistan
Lebanon, 309, 323, 328, 364, 366, 367, 374, 375, 386, 387, 388, 390, 391, 413, 421

Leith Harbor, 239, 246
Libya, 299, 390
Light anti-tank weapon (LAW), 155, 417
Light armored vehicles (LAVs), 417, 418, 420–421. *See also* Armored vehicles
Limited Contingent of Soviet Forces in Afghanistan (LCSFA), 37, 93, 115–116
Limited warfare. *See* Low-intensity conflict
Lines of communication (LOC), 101, 103, 106–107(table), 124, 150
Lizichev, Alexei, 225–226(n104)
LOC. *See* Lines of communication
Logar province, 56–57, 207, 216
Logistics, 395–398. *See also under individual combatants*
Low-intensity conflict, 2, 122, 284, 342, 343, 351, 363–364, 389, 410(table), 412, 425. *See also* Third World
Loyah Jirgah, 37, 54, 56

Machine guns, 36, 125, 141, 147, 153, 170–171, 255, 283, 284
  anti-aircraft, 170, 171, 192
Magometov, S., 35
Maidan Valley, 54
Maksimov, Yuri, 56
Malyshev, Nikolai I., 235(n262)
Mangal, Sawar Habib, 89–90
Mans, Rowley, 421
Masirah, 332
Massoud, Ahmad Shah, 37, 46, 47, 48, 49, 50, 66, 73, 75, 87, 110, 145, 164
Matlock, John, Jr., 91
Mayorov, Alexander, 35, 42
Mazar-i-Shariff, 59
Megaleconomou, Michael, 232(n212)
Menendez, Mario, 256, 259, 265
Mikhailov, V. M., 37
Military operations in built-up areas (MOBA), 415, 417
Mines, 42, 45, 59, 61, 67, 68, 83, 92, 98, 126, 131, 158, 161, 164–168, 213, 218, 284, 285, 291–293, 382–383

Missiles
  Aim-9L, 245, 262, 278, 303, 306, 307, 309–310, 318, 388
  air-to-air, 387–388
  air-to-ship, 322
  air-to-surface, 186, 188, 199, 201, 249
  AMRAAM, 307, 355(n17), 357(n57)
  anti-radar (ARMs), 278
  anti-tank guided (ATGMs), 147, 154–155, 199, 289, 380–381, 417
  AS-7/10/12/14, 186, 188, 246, 322, 335
  AT-6 Spiral, 199, 201, 205
  Blowpipe, 62, 67, 69, 70, 72, 134, 147, 174, 175, 176, 185, 205, 253, 255, 295, 297–298, 299, 305, 318, 385, 386
  Dragon, 148
  Exocet, 243, 249, 254, 256, 259, 275, 279, 307, 319–321, 322–323, 338, 339, 348, 352, 359(n99)
  Falcon, 388
  FROG 3/7, 68, 88, 162–163, 164
  Gabriel III, 352
  Grail, 386, 423
  Harpoon, 278, 322
  Hawk, 386
  Matra R.530, 309
  Maverick, 323
  Milan, 255, 259, 289
  Rapier, 176, 253, 295–297, 385
  Redeye, 174, 175, 297, 423
  Roland, 249, 299, 306, 315, 386
  Sagger, 151, 154
  SA-2/3/4/8/13, 171, 386
  SA-7, 44, 60, 128, 146, 155, 171, 172, 174, 195, 201, 230–231(n199), 294, 299, 384, 385, 386
  SA-14/16, 201
  Scud, 68, 88, 97, 134, 162, 163–164, 231(n199), 232(n212)
  Sea Cat, 259, 276, 295, 305, 339, 347
  Sea Dart, 259, 276, 295, 305, 311, 345, 346–347, 348
  Sea Skua, 248, 322, 325, 335
  Sea Slug, 348

Sea Wolf, 250, 254, 276, 295, 305, 319, 345, 347
Shrike, 256, 257, 262, 278, 300, 315, 390
Sidewinder. *See* Missiles, Aim-9L
SS-11, 325
Stinger, 56, 62, 67, 69, 70, 71, 72, 74, 79, 84, 97, 133, 134, 144, 147, 148, 157, 171, 174–177, 185, 205, 232(nn 212, 215), 263, 295, 298, 305, 424
Strela 2/M, 172, 230–231(nn 199, 200)
surface-to-air (SAMs), 44, 171–178, 173(table), 295–300, 385–387, 388
surface-to-surface, 162–164, 382
Swatter, 199, 203
TOW, 78, 148, 416
MOBA. *See* Military operations in built-up areas
Mohammed, Mohammed Nabi, 18, 94
Mohtat, Abdul Hamid, 91
Mojadedi, Sibgatullah, 94
Moody Brook, 241
Moore, Jeremy, 260
Mortars, 125, 151, 157, 160–162
Motorized Rifle (Tank) Battalion in Combat (Dragunskiy), 225(n92)
Mountain guns, 158, 159(table)
Mountain warfare, 45, 68, 101, 117, 120, 124–125, 140, 141, 144, 148, 149, 150, 158, 161, 269, 296, 369, 371, 375–376, 377, 384–385, 394, 417–419
Mount Challenger, 257, 285
Mount Harriet, 258, 259, 269
Mount Kent, 257, 265, 269, 285
Mount Longdon, 258, 269, 285, 293
Mount Williams, 259
Mozhdunaradnaya Zbizn, 17
MRDs. *See* Soviet Union forces in Afghanistan, motorized rifle divisions/brigades
MRLs. *See* Multiple rocket launchers
Mujadidi, Sibghatullah, 18
Mujahideen, 3–4, 22–23, 119
    administrative system, 145

advantages of, 144
aid to, 20, 57, 58, 59, 61, 65, 76, 78, 81, 97
air defense, 119, 132, 147, 170–171. *See also* Mujahideen, surface-to-air missiles
alliance of, 74, 88, 93, 94
arms/equipment, 20, 21, 40, 43, 52, 61, 78, 85, 144, 146–148
artillery, 148, 158–159, 162
casualties/losses, 36, 43, 45, 46, 63, 164, 196
combined arms, 131
command structure, 21
control of countryside, 76, 125
C³, 123, 369
disadvantages faced, 21–22
factions, 17–19
food supplies, 59, 61, 129, 189
forces, 8, 17–22, 93, 108
grenade launchers, 147
homemade weapons, 147–148
infantry, 144–148
and medical care, 214
and mines, 59, 165, 166–168
mortars, 161
and mountain warfare, 144. *See also* Mountain warfare
multiple rocket launchers, 85, 160
and Pakistan, 20, 21, 22, 25
and political legitimacy, 21–22, 59, 64, 69
and PRC, 25
radios/transceivers, 109, 111, 123
rifles/machine guns, 36, 146, 147
rockets, 88, 146, 161
and Soviet convoys, 212
Soviet prisoners of war, 88
spies in, 59
supplies/supply lines, 60, 63, 83, 95, 118, 140, 165, 213, 397–398
surface-to-air missiles, 44, 59, 128, 134, 144, 145, 146, 147, 148, 172, 174–177
surrender option to Afghan troops, 143–144
tanks, 154

training, 145, 162, 175
unity/disunity among, 19–20, 21, 37,
   59, 64, 69, 72–73, 74
and U.S. advisors, 175
and withdrawing Soviet troops, 88,
   89, 164
See also Massoud, Ahmad Shah
Mullett Creek, 241
Multiple rocket launchers (MRLs), 85,
   157, 159–160, 286, 381, 382, 395,
   421, 422. *See also*
   Rockets/launchers
Mushini, Sheikh, 19
Muslim clergy, 23
MVD. *See* Soviet Union, Ministry of
   Interior

Najib. *See* Najibullah, Mohammed
Najibullah, Mohammed, 15, 16, 34, 43,
   49, 55, 56, 59, 64, 73, 75, 79, 81, 86,
   88, 91, 93, 94, 222–223(n53)
Napalm, 36, 54, 183, 199, 255
Nasr, 19
National Islamic Front of
   Afghanistan, 18
Nationalist Revolution Council, 29
National Liberation Front, 18
National Reconciliation Commission,
   86
NATO. *See* North Atlantic Treaty
   Organization
Nazian border district, 218
Near East, 427–428(table)
Nerve agents, 47, 214. *See also*
   Chemical warfare
Netherlands, 407
Night combat, 139, 140, 141, 169,
   195, 258, 266–267, 283, 293, 383–
   384
Night vision aids, 168–169, 195, 258–
   259, 286, 293–294, 317, 383–384
1973 Arab-Israeli War, 371, 374, 376,
   382, 383, 384, 386, 387, 389, 390,
   391, 394, 398, 399, 415
North Atlantic Treaty Organization
   (NATO), 323, 331, 375, 389, 394,
   412

North Vietnamese Army (NVA), 108,
   111
Nuclear weapons, 218–219, 315, 350,
   399–401
NVA. *See* North Vietnamese Army

OAFVs. *See* Soviet Union forces in
   Afghanistan, other armored
   fighting vehicles
O&M. *See* Great Britain, operations
   and maintenance
Oerlikon AA guns, 62, 147, 294
Oerlikon Italiana, 62, 170
Oil, 402, 404. *See also*
   Persian/Arabian Gulf
Oman, 425, 430(table)
Operation Corporate, 243
Operation Peace for Galilee, 386. *See
   also* Lebanon
Operation Rosanio, 240–241
Oxus River, 37

Pacification, 111. *See also* Civilian(s)
Paghman, 44, 218
Pakistan, 23, 68, 79, 368
   airspace violations, 53–54, 89
   casualties, 71(table), 92–93
   C^3 facilities, 225(n95)
   DRA talks with, 62
   and Mujahideen, 20, 21, 22, 25, 66,
      69, 97
   and Mujahideen weapons, 147
   nuclear capabilities, 399
   PRC advisors in, 57
   Soviet/DRA attacks in, 42, 51, 60,
      70, 71(table), 75, 93
   Soviet relations, 51, 83, 130, 147
   and Stinger missiles, 174
   terror bombings in, 65, 71(table), 83,
      93
   and United States, 24
Paktia area, 32, 51–52, 54, 63, 70, 132,
   204
Palestine Liberation Organization
   (PLO), 364, 369, 394, 415
Panjshir offensives, 39, 40, 41, 44,
   46, 50, 52, 55, 117, 125, 138, 145–

146, 161, 184, 187, 195, 197, 209
Panjshir Valley, 47, 48, 207. *See also*
    Panjshir offensives
Party of God. *See* Hezbollah
Pavlovsky, Ivan, 27
PDPA. *See* People's Democratic
    Party of Afghanistan
Pebble Island, 251, 299, 305, 313, 328
People's Democratic Party of
    Afghanistan (PDPA), 15, 45, 86–
    87, 98
    Central Committee, 37
    creation of, 24, 28
    Khalq faction, 12, 15, 16, 24, 25, 29,
    87
    and Ministry of Defense, 49
    Parcham faction, 12, 15, 16, 24, 25,
    29, 43, 86
People's Republic of China (PRC), 25,
    52, 57, 62, 68, 147, 192
Perez de Cuellar, Javier, 44
Perrett, Bryan, 317, 356(n51)
Persian/Arabian Gulf, 74, 402, 407
Peru, 299
Peshghowr, 55
PGMs. *See* Precision-guided
    munitions
PHOTINT. *See* Photo intelligence
Photo intelligence (PHOTINT), 107,
    274, 367, 412–413, 431. *See also*
    Satellite reconnaissance
Pleasant Bay, 258
PLO. *See* Palestine Liberation
    Organization
Poison bullets, 140
Pol-e-Khomri Logistic Facility,
    212
Port Louis, 251
Port San Carlos, 252–253
Port Stanley, 247, 249, 250, 257, 258,
    259, 260, 265, 266, 269, 274, 279,
    281, 285, 287, 288, 291, 292, 293,
    303, 313, 314, 316, 323, 332, 334,
    349, 350, 373, 389
Pravda, 75, 85, 91, 93
PRC. *See* People's Republic of
    China

Precision-guided munitions (PGMs),
    154–156, 289, 319–323, 379–381,
    415, 425. *See also* Missiles;
    Rockets/launchers
Primakov, Yevgeny, 95
Puerto Belgrano, 242
Pushtuns, 17, 18, 20, 23
Puzanov, Alexander, 26, 31

Qadar, Abdul, 44
Qalat, 82

RA. *See* Republic of Afghanistan
Rabbani, Burhanuddin, 18
Radar, 109, 274–278, 294, 300, 307, 308–
    309, 320, 322, 324, 346, 347, 348,
    354–355(n17), 355(n30), 357(n57),
    359(n110), 382
Radios, 109, 111, 118
RAF. *See* Great Britain, Royal Air
    Force
Raphael, Arnold, 85
Rawalpundi, 79
Reagan, Ronald, 54, 89, 223(n57), 262.
    See also Reagan administration
Reagan administration, 61. *See also*
    Reagan, Ronald
Reconnaissance, air, 191–192, 324–
    325, 359(n110), 390–391. *See also*
    Satellite reconnaissance
Refueling. *See* Aircraft, Falklands
    War, refueling of
Refugees, 20, 40, 46, 47, 51, 52, 57, 68,
    73, 78, 92, 111, 129, 187, 215, 389
Remotely piloted vehicles (RPVs),
    366, 367, 414
Republic of Afghanistan (RA), 75,
    220(n12). *See also* Afghanistan
Revolutionary Guards, 19
Revolutionary Military Council, 24
Rezaj, Mohsen, 19
Rifles, 142–143, 283–284, 286
    AK-47, 36, 140
    AK-74, 125, 140–141
    AKMS/AKSU, 141
Rockets/launchers, 52, 379
    anti-tank, 255

BM-14/21, 159–160
BM-27, 54
Corvis, 359(n99)
FROG-7, 54
PRC-made, 52
RPG-7, 142, 380
smoke/phosphorus, 196
See also Grenade launchers;
Multiple rocket launchers
Ross, Michael, 259
Rozentak, Eduard, 80
RPVs. *See* Remotely piloted vehicles
Ruhe, William J., 296
Russia, 23
Ryabinin, Vyacheslav, 93

Saif, Abdul Rabbur Rasul, 18, 94
Salang highway, 88, 92, 134
Salang Pass area, 34, 47, 49, 117, 161,
171, 208
Salang Tunnel, 33, 64, 208, 212, 213
SAMs. *See* Missiles, surface-to-air
San Carlos, 267, 269, 274, 280, 292, 296,
311, 317, 318, 324, 332, 349
Sapper Hill, 259, 269
Sarandoy, 13, 15, 16, 25, 26, 30, 40, 43,
51, 55, 60, 78, 128, 130, 131
Sarandoy Academy, 16
SARIN nerve agent, 47
SAS. *See* Great Britain, Special Air
Service
Satellite reconnaissance, 270, 271–
273(figs.), 272, 274, 366, 367, 412.
See also Cosmos spacecraft/
satellite launchings
Saudi Arabia, 43, 46, 62, 147, 368, 425,
429(table)
Sawari, Assadullah, 40, 65
SBS. *See* Great Britain, Special Boat
Squadron
Scorched-earth tactics, 45–46, 58, 61,
131
Serebrov, Lev B., 90
Shah, Ahmad, 82, 94
Shah, Mohammed Zahir, 87, 91
Sharq, Mohammed Hassan, 87, 88, 89,
94

Shevardnadze, Eduard, 86, 92
Shi'ites, 19, 21, 43, 55, 66, 76
Shindand, 211, 215
SHORADS. *See* Short-range air
defense system
Short-range air defense system
(SHORADS), 315, 384–385, 391,
423–425. *See also* Anti-aircraft
guns; Missiles
Shura, 19, 94
SIGINT. *See* Signals intelligence
Signals intelligence (SIGINT), 65, 107,
109, 111, 270, 272, 274, 364–365,
367, 412–413
Six-Day War, 373
Sleeping death, 216
Sokolov, Sergei, 27, 34
SOMAN nerve agent, 47
Sorokin, M., 42
Southern Strategic Theater (GTVD),
8, 11
South Georgia Island, 239, 241–242,
246, 266–267, 326, 349, 350
South Korea, 368
Soviet-Afghan Friendship Treaty, 25,
29
Soviet Aviation Engineering Service
(AES), 210
Soviet Operations Main Directorate,
27, 31, 115
Soviet Southern TVD high command,
115
Soviet Union
and Afghani elite, 24
aid/equipment to DRA, 17, 26, 58,
97–98
aircraft vs. Western, 424
attacks/airspace violations in
Pakistan, 41, 53–54, 67, 70
conscription system, 135
cost of war to, 17, 49, 58, 76, 129–130
decision to invade Afghanistan,
222(n43)
lessons of Afghan War, 95
Ministry of Defense, 87
Ministry of Interior (MVD), 8
Pakistan relations, 51, 83, 130, 147

pre-invasion involvement in
  Afghanistan, 26–32
satellite reconnaissance, 270, 271–
  273(figs.). *See also* Cosmos
  satellite/spacecraft launchings
television war coverage, 49, 55, 57,
  77
Turkestan military district, 116,
  179(fig.)
war objectives, 22
See also Soviet Union forces in
  Afghanistan
Soviet Union forces in Afghanistan, 4,
  5–8(tables), 8–9, 69–70, 96(fig.)
advisors, 26, 31, 59, 62, 80, 93, 123,
  208
air assault forces (VDV), 47, 50, 121,
  126, 129, 137, 139, 191, 226(n107)
air attack model, 181–182
air buildup, 178, 179(fig.), 180
aircraft. *See* Aircraft,
  Soviet/Afghan
air support, 59
and Amin's death, 28
anti-aircraft guns, 171, 376
APCs, 9, 10, 32, 35, 136, 149
artillery, 10, 124, 132, 134, 156–158,
  185, 208
bases, 178
basic problem of, 119
casualties/losses, 44, 49, 70, 81, 84,
  129, 130, 132, 133, 140, 169, 175,
  176, 192, 197, 223(n66), 231(n209),
  232(n212)
chemical weapons, 37, 47, 67, 90
close air support, 180–191
combat aircraft, 179(fig.)
combat unit deployments, 105(fig.)
combined arms, 117, 123–135,
  226(n107)
combined operations, 206–208,
  395
commandos, 54, 169
command structure, 114(fig.), 115–
  122
communication system/
  equipment, 113(fig.), 115(table),

122, 209. *See also* Soviet Union
  forces in Afghanistan, C^3
conscripts, 135
control of countryside, 128, 132, 176,
  188. *See also* Mujahideen,
  control of countryside
convoys, 212–213
C^3, 112–122, 369
C^{3}I, 121, 122
desertion/mutiny, 9, 68, 225(n91)
and DRA Army training, 13
drug/alchohol abuse, 9, 57, 58, 70,
  135, 224–225(n91)
elite units, 27, 28, 59, 61, 67, 120, 121,
  133, 137, 181, 226(n107)
executions, 60
force mix, 179(fig.)
40th Army, 4, 27, 32, 34–35, 37, 38, 42,
  84, 116, 210
Frontal Aviation (FA) forces, 178,
  180
GRU troops. *See* Soviet Union
  forces in Afghanistan, Spetsnaz
helicopters, 9, 11, 29, 33, 35, 37, 38,
  45, 49, 59, 62, 118, 119, 124, 126,
  127, 129, 132, 133, 138, 179(fig.),
  192–205, 207. *See also*
  Helicopters, Soviet/Afghan
homosexuality in, 225(n91)
infantry, 119, 124, 126, 135–143, 150,
  207–208, 373
intelligence, 21, 48, 64, 65, 128, 185,
  206
KGB. *See* KGB
landing assault brigades (DShB),
  129, 137, 139, 226(n107)
LCSFA, 37, 93, 115–116, 120, 121
logistics and support, 208–214
manpower, 8, 9, 35, 44, 48, 58, 68, 70,
  83, 85, 108, 120, 127, 132, 226(n104)
marksmanship, 140, 142
missiles/launchers, 10, 134
mistreatment of new troops, 120
mortars, 160–161
motorized rifle divisions
  (MRDs)/brigades, 8, 34, 37, 38,
  42–43, 68, 116, 117, 124, 126, 209

mountain warfare, 124–125, 130, 136, 148, 149, 161, 371. *See also* Mountain warfare
multiple rocket launchers, 157
MVD, 48
noncommissioned officers, 121, 136, 211
new weapons developments, 46
and night vision systems, 383, 384
NVD, 59, 206
officers/commanders, 121, 136, 206–207
103rd/105th Guards Air Assault divisions, 27, 33, 38, 42, 116, 138
order of battle, 116, 219–220(n6)
other armored fighting vehicles (OAFVs), 10, 149, 150–154. *See also* Armored vehicles
and political control, 59
radios, 118, 209
raider troops, 140
reconnaissance forces, 137, 140, 206
repair and maintenance, 209–211
restructuring of, 37–42
rotations, 120, 121, 210, 211, 225(n104)
small unit actions, 126
sniper/anti-sniper operations, 142–143
Spetsnaz, 33, 49, 52, 57, 58, 61, 62, 63, 118, 120, 133, 137, 138, 140, 176, 185, 227(n117)
tanks, 9, 32, 35, 37, 124, 145, 148–150
training, 9, 46, 120, 121–122, 136, 137, 142, 150, 194
units returned in 1980, 38, 116
valley warfare, 125–126
White Russian troops, 9, 120
withdrawals, 62, 66, 71, 73, 76–94, 134, 164, 177
See also Afghanistan War; Soviet Union
Spin Boldak, 82, 86
Stromness Bay, 245

Submarines, 335, 341–345, 344(table), 353
Suez Canal, 366
Sunnis, 17, 18, 20, 21
Surge firepower, 422–423
Sussex Mountain, 251
Switzerland, 91
Syria, 353, 365, 369, 370, 375, 380, 383, 386, 389, 394–395, 396, 400, 421

Tanks, 9, 124, 148–150, 374–377
composite armor in, 375
IT-1 tank destroyers, 168
Merkava, 374, 375, 379
M-1, 68, 380
M-1987/1/2, 168
and mountainous terrain, 148, 149
PT-76, 35
repairs/maintenance, 148, 374, 396
roles of, 149, 375
Scimitars/Scorpions, 259, 283, 287, 288(table), 417
T-54/62/64, 32, 145, 148, 149, 208, 374, 375
T-55, 37, 148, 168
T-72, 35, 149, 154, 374, 375, 380
T-80, 375
Taraki, Nur Mohammed, 12, 24, 25, 26, 28, 29, 31, 32
Targeting, 365, 366, 372, 390, 413–415, 419. *See also under individual combatants*
Tass, 88, 91
Teal Inlet, 257
Technology, 269–279, 362, 363(table), 368, 371, 407, 409, 410(table), 411, 415–416, 418, 425, 431–432
Termez, 4, 8, 27, 117, 120, 212
Termez River, 37
Terrain/weather, 397, 410(table), 417–419. *See also under individual conflicts*
Teyurmi, Arbab Ghani, 74
Thatcher, Margaret, 242, 350
Third World, 109, 123, 276, 308, 315, 319, 323, 345, 353, 364, 365, 369–370, 399, 400, 411, 432

Threat assessment, 104–112, 269–279, 363–368, 412–413. *See also under individual combatants*
Thule Island, 260
Time on target, 372, 415
Torkham, 89, 90
Training technology, 418
Tricothecene toxin, 47, 214, 216
Trucks, 171, 209, 212, 213
Tumbledown Mountain, 259, 269
Turkestan Plains, 99
Turkey, 402
Turkic minorities, 23
Two Sisters, 258, 269

UAE. *See* United Arab Emirates
United Arab Emirates, 368, 430(table)
United Nations, 57, 58, 68, 75, 242
United States
    A-18 aircraft, 184
    aid to Mujahideen, 20, 43, 57, 61, 65, 76, 78, 81, 97, 223(n57)
    Air Force, 389–390
    anti-tank weapons, 416
    area defense concept of Aegis class vessels, 276
    assistance to Britain, 247, 260, 262–263, 263(table), 270, 280–281, 331–332, 368
    AV-8 aircraft, 324
    bases in Near East, 405–406(table)
    bombing raid errors of, 389–390
    and DRA, 25
    F-4 aircraft, 388
    helicopter losses in Vietnam, 192. *See also* Vietnam War
    Marines, 311, 324, 349
    and mines, 383
    MOBA training, 415
    National Security Agency, 263
    National Security Council, 260, 262
    Navy, 331, 348, 389–390, 398
    and Pakistan, 24, 78
    and Persian/Arabian Gulf, 398
    and photo intelligence, 412
    satellite reconnaissance for Falklands War, 263, 270, 271–272(figs.)
    State Department, 174, 413
    and Stinger missiles, 174, 175, 177, 263. *See also* Missiles, Stinger
    and UN peace agreement (Afghanistan War), 58
    See also United States Central Command; Vietnam War
United States Agency for International Development (USAID), 20
United States Central Command (USCENTCOM), 332, 368, 383, 396, 402, 403–404(table), 404, 405–406(table), 409, 411, 423
Urban warfare, 369, 371, 375, 376, 377, 384–385, 394, 415–417
Urgun, 48, 49
USAID. *See* United States Agency for International Development
USCENTCOM. *See* United States Central Command
USS *Guam*, 263

Varenniknov, Valentin Ivanovick, 87
VDV. *See* Soviet Union forces in Afghanistan, air assault forces
Velayati, Ali Akbar, 91
Viet Cong, 108, 111, 214, 397
Vietnam War, 1, 2, 95, 96(fig.), 108, 111, 128, 129–130, 131, 134, 142, 143, 192, 214, 231(n199), 283, 323, 387–388
Vorontsov, Yuli, 87, 90, 91–92
Vosper Thorneycroft, 339

WAD, 15. *See also* Khedemati-e-Dolati
Wakhan Corridor, 68, 99
Wakil, Abdul, 91
Warning, 367, 368. *See also* Airborne early warning

Warsaw Pact, 308, 323
Weather. *See* Terrain/weather
Weinberger, Caspar, 262, 332
Welsh Falcon training exercise, 248
West Bank, 371
Wideawake airfield, 247, 251, 263, 278, 331
Wireless Ridge, 259
Woodward, Sir John F., 242, 280, 328
Worden, 339
World War II, 277, 283

Yaquibi, Ghulam Faruq, 15, 60, 65
Yazov, Dimitri, 92
Yellow rain, 47, 216
Yemen, 399
Yepishev, Alexi, 25

Zagros mountains, 417
Zahir Shah, King, 28
Zaytsev, Mikhail, 56
Zia ul-Haq, Mohammed, 47, 77, 83, 85
Zini, Ruben, 310
Zwawar, 63, 167